ON THE EDGE

On the Edge: The Incredible Story of the 188th Armored Brigade and the Greatest Tank Battle Ever Waged

AVIRAM BARKAI

Producer & International Distributor
eBookPro Publishing
www.ebook-pro.com

ON THE EDGE

AVIRAM BARKAI

Translation: Ram Chopra
Editing: David Olesker

Contact: atirn105@gmail.com

ISBN 9798882941535

*"He stretcheth out the north over chaos,
he suspends the earth on nothing"*

(Job 26:7)

DEDICATION

This book is dedicated to all the soldiers of the 188th Armored Brigade who, on October 6, 1973, were sent, on behalf of the State of Israel and the Israel Defense Forces, to defend the country's borders. They went with hearts filled with trust, believing that Israel's leaders had done everything they could before sending them on this mission.

This book is dedicated to all these betrayed soldiers who sped to their prepared firing positions, with determination and complete faith. When they arrived, slightly before 14:00 that day, they discovered that their world, built on values that they held so strongly, had exploded in their faces.

This book is dedicated to the fallen soldiers that yearned so much to live.

This book is dedicated to the bereaved families who lost their loved ones – sons, husbands and fathers – and were never able to mend their wounds.

Contents

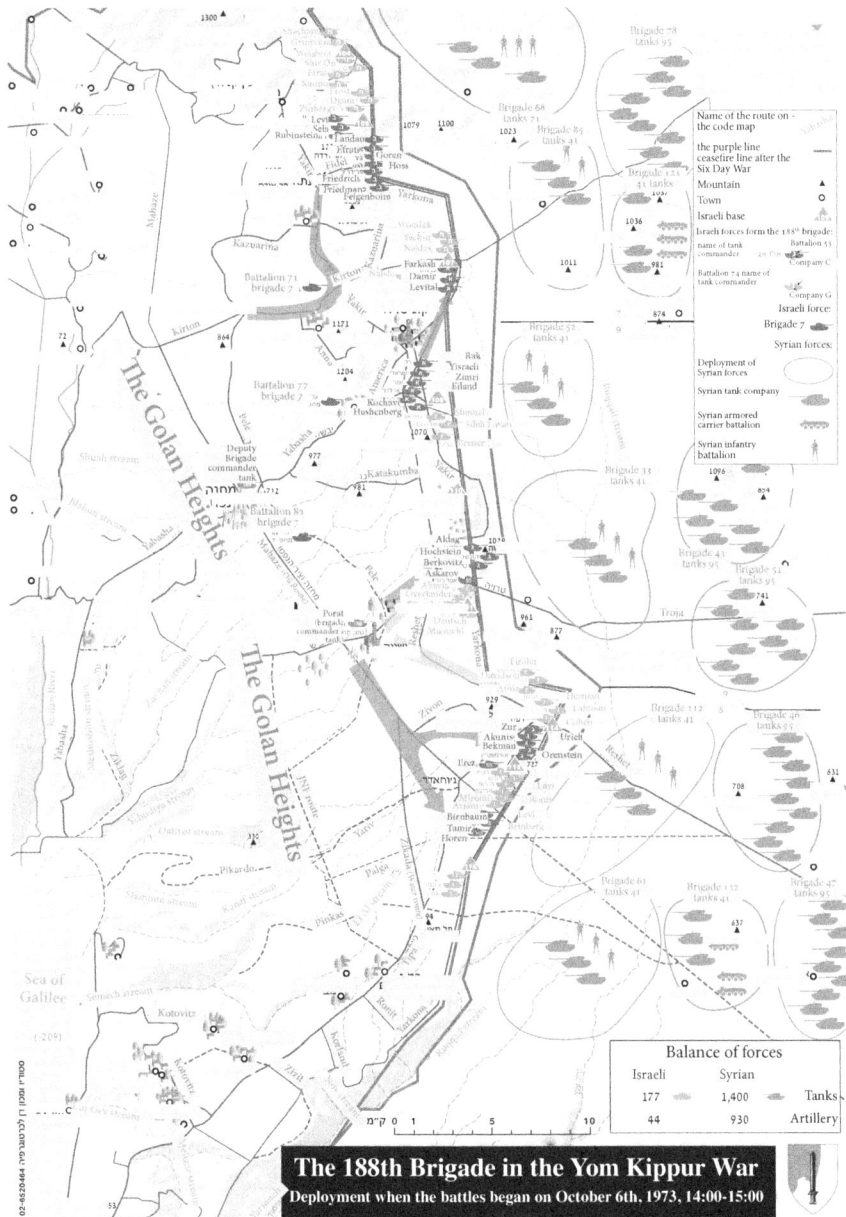

OGILA IIGCII LI /C/LCIFL GLI F99202-9-6-20

The Golan Heights

The 188th Brigade in the Yom Kippur War
Deployment when the battles began on October 6th, 1973, 14:00-15:00

Legend:

Name of the route on the code map

the purple line ceasefire line after the Six Day War

Mountain ▲

Town ○

Israeli base

Israeli forces form the 188th brigade:
name of tank commander — Battalion 53
— Company C

Battalion 74 name of tank commander
— Company G

Israeli force:

Brigade 7

Syrian forces:

Deployment of Syrian forces

Syrian tank company

Syrian armored carrier battalion

Syrian infantry battalion

Balance of forces

	Israeli	Syrian	
	177	1,400	Tanks
	44	930	Artillery

km 0 1 5 10

Sea of Galilee

(-209)

Brigade 78 tanks 95

Brigade 68 tanks 71

Brigade 85 tanks 41

Brigade 132 tanks 41

Brigade 52 tanks 41

Brigade 33 tanks 41

Brigade 43 tanks 95

Brigade 51 tanks 95

Brigade 112 tanks 41

Brigade 63 tanks 41

Brigade 132 tanks 41

Brigade 47 tanks 95

Battalion 71 brigade 7

Battalion 77 brigade 7

Battalion 82 brigade

Deputy Brigade commander tank

Porat brigade commander reserve tank

Troja

9

Author's Note

First, thank you.

From the bottom of my heart I thank Lt. Col. Zvi Ofer, the man who conducted the only study of the Barak 188th Armored Brigade's role in the Yom Kippur War for the IDF history division. He is a wise, open-minded and open-hearted man, who shared all the material he discovered with me. He dedicated many hours to me in his office at Glilot military base, spending days and nights helping me answer difficult questions and avoid invisible mines.

I also would like to thank military history researchers, Col. Yehuda Wagman and Col. Moshe Givati, who helped me in clarifying important questions regarding the battles of Nafah and Tel A-Saki.

My highest appreciation goes to each of the 230 interviewees who were willing to share their wartime experiences with me. For some it was a cathartic and purifying process, for others a real trauma.

* * *

Dozens of books have been written on the Yom Kippur War, hundreds of thousands of words about how the military and political leadership had suffered from arrogance and indifference, how they had adhered to the mistaken "concept" that so dramatically collapsed; how the revelation of these failings shook the fighting army and spread throughout the whole population. I am thankful for the right I had to study the details of the central facts of those dark days in 1973, to ask and review, to study and examine and to search for the truth.

This truth was not easy to digest. The knowledge that things could have been done differently. The difficult questions regarding the performance of the high-ranking Foreword in the military and government. The twinge of pain felt when re-living the angel of death effortlessly snatching away the lives of many young soldiers, some of whom, no doubt, could still be with us today.

When I decided to take on the task of writing this book, I had no idea how many Pandora's boxes I would be opening and the intense anger, fury, insult, frustration and bitterness that still accompany the warriors of the 188th Armored Brigade to this day. Some of these boxes revealed heroic stories I could not have imagined; in others, I found shudders of fear. Some of those who were young soldiers in 1973 did not want to look back on this time. I also, unintentionally, opened a few of my own boxes. The contents showed me and my family – who supported me with devotion and love throughout this sacred task – just how emotionally explosive my stand was toward the testimonies of my brothers-in-arms. Many sleepless nights will testify to this.

* * *

I took on the role of a *shaliach mitzvah*, a man on a sacred mission. This was the feeling that accompanied me in this task. I was to be the sho-far (the ram's horn we blow like a trumpet on the Jewish New Year) sounding the cry, telling the story of the heroism, the fear and sacrifice, "for every Hebrew mother to know."

I pray that this book will help improve the decision-making process of the future leaders of Israel. I pray that it will remain in the hearts and souls of the fathers, mothers. Most of all, I pray that it will live in the heart of young Israelis, who are to become soldiers soon enough, in memory of an armored brigade of unique and outstanding quality.

May the candles lit in memory of the soldiers of the 188th Brigade that died and the pain carried by those who remain, chase away the lingering vapors of complacency that remain in this land. In the words of Col. Yitzchak Ben Shoham, the Commander of the 188th Armored Brigade in the Yom Kippur War – "Let our hearts not become haughty."

Never. Towards anyone.

Aviram Barkai
August 2009

FOREWORD

Writing the Story of the Soldiers
of the 188th Armored Brigade

by David Eiland

Two weeks after the start of the Yom Kippur War, I came home for the
first time. It was a short visit, just for a few hours. After a long journey,
with many stops, I got off a bus full of soldiers that came from the
enclave we had created in Syria. I got off at the Country Club junction.
A big American car with three friendly older couples stopped and
offered me a ride. They crowded together to make room for me. I must
have looked strange to them. I had not shaved for two weeks. My hair
was long and wild, and over my stained tank overall I was wearing a
faded brown leather jacket with a scarf that was once white.

When they asked me how I was doing, I excitedly told them about
Syrian tanks and a pilot taken hostage. The family spoke Iraqi Arabic
between themselves, and I felt from their tone that they thought I
sounded smug. Even though it was out of their way, they insisted on
taking me to the door of my house. It was late at night, around 1:30 a.m.,
when I finally arrived. The house was completely dark. I knocked and
waited. There was no answer. I knocked again. "Who's there?" It was
my father's scared voice. A sudden knock at your door in these days
and at such an hour could only be bad news. "It's me," I said. My father
opened the door quickly. "David!" He cried, unbelievingly, and hugged
me hard. I noticed my mother behind him. She was lying on the sofa
in the dark, her head back. When she heard the knock at the door, she
had fainted. To maintain her sanity, from the first day of the war, my
mother had been taking many tranquilizers. Most of the time she was in
a state of apathy. The news from the Golan Heights battlefield was very

bad. The Syrians had conquered part of the Golan. There were bloody battles between tanks and an entire Israeli armored brigade had been destroyed. Rumors were that it was the 188th Brigade, my brigade. My mother slowly regained consciousness. "Esti," my father called to her, "look who is here. Dudu is here, Dudu!" My mother was in a complete blur. She still did not recognize me, her beloved son, the most precious person to her in the world. She continued to lie there with her eyes closed mumbling my name. The feeling of euphoria I had had until that moment, disappeared. All at once, I felt the pain of the anxiety and terror my parents were experiencing during those terrible days. I broke down and cried, weeping bitterly. A long and continuous weeping, letting out all the stress, tension and fear. The sound of the gunfire and explosions was in my ears and the sights of burning tanks in my head. I had managed to return home, safe and sound (at least that was what I thought at the time). I continued to weep, thinking of the parents of all the soldiers I knew who would never see their sons again.

After I calmed down, I sat down in the kitchen with my father and showed him the pistol of the pilot I had taken prisoner and told him about the sixteen Syrian tanks I destroyed.

"Unbelievable," my father said, when I finished. "I am proud of you, son. We will open a bottle of champagne after this war ends."

Over the years, when the matter of the war came up, I was asked many times by people I met or one of my clients: "Where were you in the war?"

"In the armored corps, in the Golan Heights," I would answer.

"Oh, you were with... in Brigade..."

"No," I would stop them, "I was in the 188th Brigade."

"188th? What is it? Never heard of it."

"It is the armored brigade that has the task of defending the Golan Heights in time of war. It still exists, by the way," I would reply. If I happened to be impatient that day, I would add, "It is the brigade that is the reason you do not have a Syrian tank in your backyard, like the one in Kibbutz Deganya Aleph."

A few years ago, I was driving home with my two sons, Ilan and Oren. "You know, it is unbelievable," I said.

"What is?" Ilan asked.

"In any other army," I answered, "people like me and my friends who stopped and destroyed hundreds of Syrian tanks would have received a chest full of citations. Here we did not hear a word of appreciation or encouragement, not even a pat on the back. We were completely ignored. My friends and I were sent home hurting and insulted, our actions taken for granted. As if nothing had happened. People in Israel think that 188 is a number between 187 and 189."

My sons were silent; they had heard me say this many times before.

"What did you think, Dudu?" Efi, my gunner, said over the telephone, quoting Schiller, "'The Moor has done his work, the Moor may go.' That is the way it is."

This time, despite the years that have passed, the Moor did not want to go.

It took thirty years for us to be able to talk to each other, to be able to stand up and act. We never discussed the war between us, even though it was a shadow hovering over us. It was a taboo, not to be talked about, too painful, too traumatic.

Two events broke this taboo.

The first event was the commemoration ceremony for the 188th Brigade on the Golan Heights, marking thirty years since the war. For the first time, in addition to the bereaved families, the soldiers who had fought in the Yom Kippur War were also invited to the annual ceremony. Prior to the general assembly, there were separate gatherings of each company with the soldiers and their families in the battle areas. Many of the people were returning to these sites for the first time since the war and people were very emotional. The encounter with the bereaved families was especially moving. We were surprised to find that every small detail we could relate to them regarding their loved ones and their part in the battles, filled their hearts with pride and joy.

The second event was less heart-warming but was very significant. This commemoration took place at Latrun, at the Armored Corps Memorial Site. Its topic was the first days of the regular army fighting on the Golan Heights during the Yom Kippur War. All of the senior officers at the time were invited. We soldiers, who were in the front line during the war, who could relate to the story firsthand, were not invited. We snuck into the event and watched the old military establishment attempting to rewrite history and clear itself of any blame. The only figure who received the blame was not present because he could not be there. It was our brigade commander, killed in the battle at Nafah and resting in the Kiryat Shaul military cemetery since the war.

"Dudu, this cannot be," Oded later said to me. The former commander of the 54th Battalion continued, "They are trying to erase us. We need to take the initiative to present the story of our brigade. At the very least, we owe it to the soldiers and the bereaved families."

"You are absolutely right," I said. To myself I wondered how to even approach such a task? How do you collect all the data and turn it into a written story that will both be of interest and demand justice? Where do you come up with the money for such a project? It would not be easy. On the other hand, we cannot just become a faint memory in the history books.

After a year and a half of continuous talks between Oded and myself, our salvation came from an unexpected source. The phone rang at my place of work one afternoon. It was a call from Dror. We had been soldiers together. He was a tank commander in Oded's Company.

Dror said that his cousin was insisting that we should join forces with a writer and publish a book telling the story of the 188th Brigade in the Yom Kippur War and that we have to meet him.

"Who is this cousin?" I asked.

"His name is Rafi Negler," was his response.

"Who is he? How old?"

"He is a 45-year- old oral and maxillofacial surgeon."

"He is not our age and was not even in the war," I said. "What does he have to do with this?"

"He claims that it is important for the Israeli people that such a book is written; he sees it as a mission."

Dear God, I thought to myself, who is this eccentric?

"It is a waste of time Dror," I answered. "Such a project requires a lot of time and money that we do not have." Dror insisted, and in the end I agreed to meet him and Rafi.

The rest is history.

The first meeting took place around five years ago, during 2004. It did not take long for Oded and I to be convinced that the time had come.

From the members of the Association of veterans of the 188th Brigade, we put together a task force that was mainly made up of the platoon leaders that survived the war. There also was one company commander and four tank commanders. This team, of about a dozen people, located and contacted soldiers from the brigade, organized company meetings and – led by Oded – returned to view the battle sites. The basic theoretic structure of the story began to materialize. An administrative team was also established.

The process was long and tedious. The first writer was replaced by another who started to recount the detailed story of our brigade. We took endless testimonies from soldiers and commanders. We examined the routes of battle and the combat posts. We researched and carefully verified the exact forces that took part in each battle.

Once again, as in the war, the leading force of this operation was the platoon and tank commanders.

Three people from outside the brigade joined this force of ex-188th Brigade soldiers.

The first we have already mentioned, is Dr. (later professor) Rafi Negler.

I have never encountered such absolute and fanatic devotion toward a cause. Rafi believes with all his heart that the story of the brigade had to be told at any cost. Not only because its troops are worthy of praise and honor but also because it has to serve as a lesson to all of Israel of how arrogance and detachment by the government and military leaders can lead an entire state to the verge of disaster. It is as simple as that.

With time, I understood that he had an additional motive. His childhood and high school heroes in Haifa, where he grew up, included soldiers killed in the battles on the Golan Heights and others who carry the horrors of this war to this day. He saw this book as redeeming all of these figures by doing justice to them.

More than once, when things were bogged down due to disagreements or clashes of ego, it was he who, with endless energy, pushed things back on track. Not a single day went by without him repeating his Zionist beliefs, in endless phone calls and emails, often encountering bitter responses but never relenting. I often wondered where his amazing strength came from.

The second person is Ofer Glusman. A man our age who commanded a tank platoon in a different brigade during the war. I remember the conversation we had when I asked for his advice. Ofer was glad to share the information with me and was invited to join the board of trustees of the veterans association. His vast experience, his calm and level-headed nature are what made him the actual project manager and the man who navigated the project through troubled waters, despite being extremely busy with other matters.

He once asked me to stop mentioning this. "I choose what I want to do," he said.

The third is a childhood and army friend of mine, Aviram Barkai. Aviram, a tour guide, off-road-vehicle trip leader and writer, offered us his services to continue the writing of the book, after we had almost given up. Aviram took it from the slow progress it was making to successful completion.

With great integrity and amazing self-discipline, he carried out an independent inquiry. He conducted hundreds of interviews that uncovered not only the impossible demands made of the 188th Brigade during the war but also its relations with the other units fighting on the Golan Heights. This required an extremely complex process of cross-checking testimonies and information to portray the most precise picture of the Golan front.

Only when I was personally invited to an interview in his house did I realize how involved he had become in this matter. When I came for my interview, the door was opened by an unshaved and exhausted man who did not waste time on small-talk. He led me straight to his room to hear my personal story of the war and only my story. After five hours of questions and listening to me, accompanied by the quick typing on his keyboard, he sent me home. This interview was repeated twice and also involved tens of telephone calls at all hours of the day, asking me to clarify details and to help clear up contradictions.

This process, which he led many others through, revealed to him the full story. He was filled within himself with such anger and outrage for the injustice caused to our wonderful brigade, that he came to feel that he was one of us.

His uncompromising nature, devotion, diligence and unflagging pursuit of the truth, left us all in awe.

Many others outside the brigade joined these three and the team of soldiers. They generously contributed funds or knowledge to make it possible for this story to reach the reader.

This large group feel that their work has been completed. We hope that this story will raise readers' interest and will bring honor and justice to all the soldiers who are no longer with us and to those who are here physically, but whose spirits were lost that month of October 1973. Any profits generated from sales of this book will go to the veterans' association for the welfare of its members.

David Eiland
August 2009

WAR DIARY

"Crew, we are moving up to an observation post. Driver, forward slowly."

Sharabi, the tank commander, was no longer shaking. "It's true that you get used to any situation," he reminds himself, thinking fondly of his three crew members below him.

Edri drives the tank slowly forward, tack link by track link, at just the correct pace, just as he always did in training.

"Driver, stop."

Sharabi is pleased. Edri brings the tank to a smooth stop, just like in training. He is now confident that his tank, the one and only 1B, did not send up any dust or black smoke, perfectly sliding into its observation position.

"A real pro," he says in the internal crew radio and everyone in the tank knows that Sharabi, the best commander in the battalion, the division and the entire world, is referring to Edri the driver, who smiles proudly behind the steering handle in the tight steel cell. He replies cynically into the VRC[1] microphone, "Commander, a sergeant rank would look good on me."

"It sure would," laughs Sharabi as a Yemenite smile smears over his face.

"Observation time," Sharabi tells himself, scanning the hills opposite him with the 8x30 binoculars. There is no need for binoculars; the plain beneath them is covered with enemy tanks.

"Schwartz, do you read me?"

"I hear you," a likable redheaded boy from Holon answers calmly, bent over below in the gunner seat, his eye in the periscope's telescopic viewfinder.

---

1. Vehicular Radio Communications.

"Listen, in the valley beneath us, less than 1,000 meters away, there are about twenty tanks and they are all heading toward our hill. We will have to move up higher into a 'hull up position.'[2] We will be much more exposed than we usually are. The speed at which you identify the target will determine how long we will be exposed. We'll move up, I'll point you toward the target, you confirm and start taking them out from left to right, as fast as you can. Do you understand?"

There is a moment of silence and Schwartz almost whispers an answer, "I understand, sir."

"Buchbut, do you hear me?"

"I hear you," the calm and imperturbable loader from Migdal Haemek answers nonchalantly from his position on the bottom left of the turret.

"Prepare ten armor piercing rounds. Make sure they are of the same series. Do it quickly. They are getting close."

A few seconds pass and just like in training, Buchbut calmly says "Everything is ready, sir."

Sharabi's legs shake again on the commander's footrest; he hopes the team doesn't notice. "Damn it," he thinks to himself, "this is very bad."

"Cannon, combat range, tank target."

"Unidentified," answers Schwartz, with a slight tremble in his voice.

"Driver, forward."

Edri edges the tank forward and Sharabi lowers the cannon and shouts to Schwartz, "Come on, come on."

Suddenly the usually indifferent Buchbut speaks on the radio, "Come on Schwartz, open your eyes."

They continue to rise higher and higher and Schwartz does not identify the target. Sharabi knows they are completely exposed and he knows that the crew knows it and Schwartz still doesn't see.

"What is going on Schwartz?" Sharabi shouts, losing the fondness in his voice. Now it just has a sense of urgency.

"Schwartz," Edri also shouts from the driver's seat, usually a gentle

2. Tanks can present three different profiles;
- Concealed: the entire vehicle is hidden behind a rise or mound and invisible to the enemy.
- Hull down: only the turret is exposed, meaning that the main body of the tank (the hull) is better protected. Although visible, it is not obvious to the enemy.
- Hull up: the entire vehicle is exposed and vulnerable.

and calm boy. "Are you blind? I can see them in my periscope." Then Schwartz shouts, "On target!"

"Fire!" shouts Sharabi as loud as he can and the first APDS[3] round leaves the muzzle, just as the rightmost tank burst into flames.

"Target, my hero," sings Sharabi on the radio. He immediately pulls himself together and says, "Do not repeat fire, move on, from right to left. Quick, quick."

Buchbut loads the next APDS round into the gun and the second target is already ablaze.

Over the intercom, it is Edri who suddenly sounds as if he has lost his nerve and in a tiny weak voice he whimpers, "Sharabi, when are we leaving this position?"

"A little longer," answers Sharabi, not so sure of himself.

Buchbut is loading as he has never loaded before and Schwartz hits the targets from right to left as he has never hit targets before.

"Only two more rounds left," Buchbut shouted from his seat, a big lump of indifference who suddenly sounds emotional.

"Two last ones and we will drive down to refill," Sharabi encouraged.

"Sharabi," shouts Schwartz, "they spotted us, I see their guns pointing toward us."

"Ok, Schwartz," says Sharabi, urgency in his voice, "two last rounds. Fire."

As Sharabi is shouting the command, a reinforced steel projectile penetrates the turret of the Sho't Kal[4] tank, beheading Schwartz, ripping open Sharabi's stomach and groin and the turret is filled with human tissue and blood.

"Mom, Mom," Edri hears the cries of Buchbut who was never affected by anything.

"What happened?" shouts Edri from the driver's cabin.

"Mom, Mom," he hears Buchbut again.

He throws the gear into reverse. It is too late, a HEAT[5] round penetrates the soft steel of the driver's cabin, turning Edri's dream of

---

3. Armor-Piercing Discarding Sabot.
4. Israeli modification of the British manufactured Centurian tank.
5. High Explosive Anti-Tank.

becoming a sergeant into a bloody mush on the driver's seat. The jet of fire from the HEAT's shaped charge continues toward the turret frying Buchbut's big body. Just before his last breath he says "Mom, Mom" again and this is the end.

THE TANK-MEN

Until June 1967, the Armored Corps was seen as an unworthy and undesirable place to serve. Any self-respecting soldier, not wanting to ruin his fingernails and destroy his lungs, would keep away from it.

Soldiers in the elite units, paratroopers and even regular infantry soldiers, not to mention the air force and navy, looked down at these poor figures trapped in these metal boxes, burning in the sun and freezing on the cold winter nights, living in an impossible blend of mud, grease, oil and water. They were shocked seeing the horror show of "armor all-nighters" watching them in their stained coveralls, working endlessly through the hours of darkness. It seemed that they never slept. These dazed shadows, moving around in circles, falling and getting back up, apologizing in their troubled voices. "We still have not finished repairing the rejects." The sun would rise and there they were again, on their tanks, in an endless loop of routine maintenance.

"Routine maintenance" was what they called this torture. On the tanks, day and night, slaves to millions of metal screws and bolts, demanding their regular tightening, greasing, oiling and painting.

They did have some compensation at least. They did not have to run through the fields, beaches and sands dunes. They did not dig pits in the tough earth, shaking in terror at the shrapnel, bullets and basalt rocks flying around them. Inside the steel tanks, they were detached from the infantry routine.

Yet still, until the beginning of June 1967, despite the remains of the euphoria of the Sinai Operation in 1956 and despite their better chances of surviving, motivation to join the armored corps was low. Despite it being so much easier on the muscles, despite the aura of blood and fire and pillars of smoke, despite some of them having their pictures published in the *Bamachane* army magazine, dust covered, sunburned faces and with their special dust glasses, the reluctance persisted. Despite all of this, in June 1967, the image of the tank crews remained that of being little more than mechanics, slaves to the machine.

Image is everything, as everyone knows, especially when we are dealing with young men's hormones.

As a result, until June 1967, with hardly any exception, "the best" youth stayed away from the armored corps, aiming to become pilots, to join the commandos, one of the elite units or the paratroopers.

Then the Six-Day War broke out and things changed.

All at once, the soldiers "exposed in the turrets" became the new stars. Tanks thundering across the vast Sinai desert became the symbol of Israeli strength and a loud compensation for the trauma of the pre-war anxiety. The image of the armor crews in their tanks moved to the front of the stage, a status symbol. Suddenly the endless work they had to engage in was worth it.

Shabtai Teveth's book "The Tanks of Tammuz," was the last step in the creation of the armored corps positive image. The tales of the battles of the 7th Armored Brigade, commanded by Col. Gorodish in Sinai, swept the imaginations of thousands. The elite youth still joined the clandestine Sayeret Matkal reconnaissance unit, the pilot's course, and the Shayetet 13 naval commando unit, but the glamor of the brigades that lead the battle – the Golani and the Paratroopers – was replaced by the allure of the armored brigades. Every recruitment cycle saw hundreds of volunteers joining, easily taking the bait that "the armored corps makes history."

The growing stream of new recruits joining the armored corps was now joined by the children of the Tel Aviv suburb of Neve Magen. Along with the neighborhoods of Neve Rom and Tzahala it formed the "khaki triangle," the home of Israel's military aristocracy.

The sons of Neve Magen did not debate whether to be in combat or not, the only question for them was how deep in combat they would be.

Of the high school graduates of 1970, there were already six Armored Corps officers, paving the way for even more. On June 13, 1973, at the end of the Armored Corps Officer course, in the Sho't Kal tanks specialization, twenty-four new officers marched across the parade ground, eight of them from the Neve Magen neighborhood.

After the Six-Day War, two additional dominant groups joined the ranks of the armored corps officers. One was the kibbutz youth, for them the transition from the tractors to the tanks was almost natural. The war stories and heroism of the classes above them influenced their choice when joining the IDF. The second group was graduates of the military high schools academies. In Tel Aviv, fourteen of the twenty-seven graduates of the class of 1971 joined the armored corps and became officers.

Yisrael Tal and the "New Armored Corps"

Gen. Yisrael Tal, "Talik," was the founding father of "The New Armored Corps." A Division Commander in the Six-Day War, Armored Division Commander in the 70s and the Deputy Chief of Staff in 1973. Who was going to stand in his way?

The principle that Gen. Tal taught the new armored corps soldiers, during the heady period after Israel's victory in 1967's the Six-Day War, was simple – "What happened before, will happen again." In other words, stop the victory parades; it is time to get back to work.

This is exactly what happened. "The new armored corps soldiers," many of whom joined the corps due to the aura of the victory of the Six-Day War, did not enjoy the prestige they expected. They were too busy filling the endless grease nipples and cleaning spotlessly inside the turret. In less time than it takes a projectile to reach its target, they were disillusioned, finding themselves facing a grinding and painful reality. The life of the armored corps crew member continued to be a blend of oil, grease and tedious labor from dawn to the point of exhaustion.

In every army, especially in units where the soldiers are dependent on and actually parts of the machines, detail orientation and continuous grinding Sisyphean work is the essence of the system. Of all the IDF units, the armored corps, certainly after the Six-Day War, was the most demanding and rigid corps. In the air force and the navy, the machines require excellence in maintenance but in the armored corps the rules of the game are tougher due to the massive number of machines and soldiers and the variability of the human resources.

"Variability of the human resources" is a nice way of saying that in the armored corps, there was a mixture of law abiders and law breakers serving together. Those who believe in discipline and those who despise it, working together. There were soldiers from privileged areas of the country and others from poor neighborhoods. Some from Zionist melting-pot families and others from families that did not live by the Zionist ethos.

Eiland from Neve Magen and Tzion from the Yemenite quarter in Tel Aviv. Nir from Kibbutz Afikim and Nissim from the development town of Netivot. Eyal from the privileged neighborhood of Tzahala and Eli from the underprivileged town of Dimona. Bed next to bed, shoulder to shoulder. Young men from all parts of society, all layers, all forms of communities and all levels of motivation, found themselves in the tough, relentless melting pot.

The commanders constantly stressed that only attention to detail – even apparently insignificant detail – would ensure the best gunner's performance and the highest level of maintenance of the tank. "Make sure that all the tips of the needles in the sewing kit are in the same direction" was drummed into the soldiers. They explained the logic behind this mental torture, "In order for this machine to function properly, there has to be a regular routine of tasks, and everything the crew member does must be on a schedule. If the soldier makes sure that the sewing kit needles are all always aligned and in the same direction, he will also make sure that the endless routine tank maintenance is done. In this manner, when the time comes, the gun will fire on demand and the tracks will roll."

The new armored corps soldiers learned that 99 percent is not good enough. They complained and held back tears and kept their needles pointing the same way. Gradually, without noticing it, they internalized the procedure. They waited, in the high-quality British steel they had been given, for the day the order would come.

After being trained to maintain order, discipline and cleanliness, they next had to learn to apply standard procedures. To react, automatically, in a standardized and structured way. In the armored corps terminology, these pre-set responses are called "drills." These were meant to turn them into semi-robots, programmed for perfect operation under pressure.

"In this manner we will get rid of the need to improvise; we will provide a mechanical, automatic response that will not let fear take over when the days are dark, and the next hell breaks out."

But who foresaw the next hell was coming?

Strange things happened to the young men who joined tank crews. One was the way they started to speak of their tank. As if it never caused them trouble or was the source of their pain and endless work. As if they never cursed and hated the tank, with their strength running out, forgetting the days and nights they became its slaves.

When they were on leave, just a few hours after the final greasing, things changed and the charm of the British steel would affect them. They forgot the suffering and their great love came bursting out.

"There is nothing like a Sho't Kal tank," they would say with loving eyes, to anyone willing to listen. To them it was obvious that the Sho't Kal, the British Centurion, from the '50s, improved by the Israeli ordnance corps, was better than the "Magach" (battering-ram), the designation for the American Patton tank, the other tank used by the regular brigades.

The 188th Armored Brigade was founded in the distant days of the War of Independence.

It all started with the Carmeli Infantry Brigade that had a key part in the battles conquering the Western Galilee and the cities of Acre and Haifa. After the battles ended, the name of the brigade was changed to 18.

The 18th Brigade did not take part in the Sinai Operation and that may be the reason that led to an additional dramatic change. The 18th Infantry Brigade became the 45th Armored Reserve Brigade, with two infantry battalions, the 25th and 74th, and the 39th Battalion, which was equipped with Sherman tanks.

Under the command of Col. Moshe Bar-Kochba (Brill), the 45th Brigade fought in the Six-Day War, taking part in one of the most difficult and bloodiest battles in this war, the battle of the Dotan valley near Jenin. Toward the end of the war, the brigade was called to join the forces on the Golan Heights, and its old Sherman tanks helped to breach the Syrian defense lines and stabilize the ceasefire line.

In August 1967, two months after the war, the 7th Armored Brigade, acclaimed in the book *Tanks of Tammuz*, parted from its two Patton battalions and remained with the veteran 82nd Centurion Battalion, reestablished the 63rd Centurion Battalion, changed its name to the 53rd and headed for the Golan Heights.

Col. Shmuel Gonen (Gorodish), the brigade commander, Lt. Col.

Avraham Rotem, commander of the 82nd Battalion and Lt. Col. Yitzchak Ben Shoham, commander of the 53rd Battalion, took responsibility over the Golan front.

Unlike the regular 7th Armored Brigade, the officers of the 45th Reserve Brigade, did not consider the Six-Day War to be a cause for celebration. The old Sherman tanks were proven to be inferior to enemy armor. Therefore, in the days of euphoria after the victory, the IDF decided to dismantle the tank battalion, and the infantry battalions were sent on security missions in the Galilee and the Golan.

No one seemed to take Moshe Brill into account. The decorated hero from the tank battles in the Sinai Operation refused to accept this decision. Out of sight of the decision makers, with patience, deviousness and determination, he started gathering Centurion (Sho't) tanks to the brigade base in Manzura near Elyakim in the Galilee, obtaining them in various ways.

It started with one company. Within a year, Brill already had enough tanks to establish a battalion. Another month passed and another tank was added and gradually Brill divided the battalion into two. This was the renewed 45th Brigade.

The 45th Brigade was no longer part of the order of battle of the IDF but was still alive. Since this brigade had somehow acquired Centurions tanks, capable of facing enemy armor, the Head of the Northern Command, Maj. Gen. David Elazar (Dado), a man who appreciated a sophisticated horse theft, decided to go along with the stubborn Brill. Despite the opposition of many of the officers at the General Staff, Dado fought for the right of the phoenix-like 45th brigade to receive recognition, and so it did.

At the beginning of 1969 there was a significant development. The 7th Armored Brigade was ordered from the Golan, to move down to the Suez Canal front and join the armored defense force in the War of Attrition.[6] The 45th Armored Brigade, created seemingly out of thin air, became a regular armored brigade overnight. The brigade was given the mission of being the armored force defending the Golan Heights.

---

6. A long drawn-out series of clashes between Israel and the forces of Egypt, Jordan, Syria, the Palestine Liberation Organization (PLO) and their allies, that lasted from 1967 to 1970. It consisted of large-scale shelling along the Suez Canal, extensive aerial warfare and commando raids.

The 53rd Battalion, commanded by Lt. Col. Yehuda Bachar, was ordered to become part of the new brigade, joining the 74th, the battalion Brill had collected from unknown sources.

The brigade headquarters was set up at Filon camp near the small town of Rosh Pina. Its two battalions were positioned along a line extending from the Bnot Yaakov Bridge through Nafah to Quneitra. At the end of 1969, this new creation managed to establish a third battalion, a reserve battalion maintaining its historic number of 39.

Someone decided that it was time to give the new armored brigade, responsible for the Golan Heights, a new name, and the 188th "Barak" Armored Brigade was born.

On June 24, 1970, the seed that had been planted sprouted into what became the glory of the 188th Brigade. On that very day, with the IDF clashing with the Egyptian army in the War of Attrition in Sinai and fighting against the Palestinians in the Gaza Strip and in the Arava, the Syrians surprised Israel with an armored raid attempting to conquer two IDF bases on the Golan.

Until then, incidents with the Syrians had caused only minor disruption to the daily lives of the residents of the Golan. But the IDF refused to remain silent after this last attack. The Head of the Northern Command at the time, Gen David Elazar, "Dado," demanded and received the approval of the Defense Minister, Moshe Dayan, for the IDF to carry out a proper retaliation action.

"Ok," said Dayan, "let them have it."

Two days later, the two regular battalions of the 188th Brigade launched a major raid into Syrian territory. Operation "Kiton 10" was accompanied with heavy artillery fire. The air force bombed five camps deep within Syria. Within two hours, six Syrian bases were occupied, fifty bunkers were blown up, twenty cannons destroyed, thirty-six tanks turned into fireballs, four MiG planes were shot down, tens of Syrian soldiers were killed or injured and thirty-eight were taken prisoner. The IDF suffered one fatality, one injured, three tanks were hit and damaged (and towed back to Israeli territory) and one Phantom plane was shot down and its pilot was taken prisoner.

Operation Kiton 10 marked the great change in the status of the 188th Brigade, the beginning of the establishment of its hegemony as the only fighting armored brigade in the armored corps.

On August 7, 1970, the process was completed. On this day, a ceasefire was declared in the Suez Canal and the War of Attrition between Israel and Egypt ended. From this moment, all the activity of the IDF armored brigades stopped, except for that of the 188th Brigade. At a stroke, this newborn creature became the spearhead of the armored corps.

Most of the live fire incidents in the Northern Command were limited "combat days," with a set and known course of action. In the morning, the Syrians would initiate an artillery attack on a wide area. In addition, when the sun blinded the Israeli tanks, the Syrian tanks in the front line left their dug out positions and fired at the Israeli tanks who were waiting for them in their own posts.

Before the sun set, the gunfire ended and the forces separated with a result known in advance. Beaten, licking their wounds, with their guns between their tracks, the Syrians withdrew, while on the other side of the cease-fire line, the soldiers of the 188th Brigade stood proudly, celebrating their superiority in victory ceremonies and opening bottles of champagne.

Then there were the armored raids on the terrorist strongholds in "Fatah Land"[7] in South Lebanon. Once again, it was the professionals of the 188th Brigade who sped forward, crushing and destroying the enemy forces.

The continuous, proven superiority of the Israeli Sho't Kal tanks and their Israeli crews, over the inferior Syrian tanks, enabled Fedale (Col. Aharon Peled), the Commander of the 188th Brigade at the time, to declare that "if a war breaks out, we will be in Damascus within twenty-four hours."

By the end of 1972, the soldiers of the 188th Brigade, with its two regular battalions, were very proud of their unit, a pride unprecedented in the armored corps. They had every reason to be proud. While the 188th Brigade continued to accumulate days of combat and raids into Lebanon, the 7th Armored Brigade, the first in such unit in the IDF, the roots of the 188th, became a "representative" brigade focusing on courses, drills and parades. The 7th Armored Brigade settled for the occasional "leftovers," when it was on the Golan Heights as backup. They

---

7. Fatah was the largest of the Palestinian Arab terrorist organizations and was synonymous, for most Israelis, with the PLO as a whole.

were on call in case something went wrong with the 188th Brigade but nothing ever went wrong.

* * *

In January 1973, another combat day ended on the Golan. It was to be the last combat day before the great conspiracy – plotted behind closed doors in Damascus and Cairo – was set in motion. The plan that would trap the over-proud 188th Brigade in the jaws of a huge war machine.

Immediately after the Six-Day War, Israel began to fortify her border on the Golan Heights. Relying on natural obstacles, in the form of ravines or high mountains, the IDF built infantry outposts on strategic high points, close to the ceasefire line from the end of the war. Anti-tank ditches were dug, some in front of the outposts, some behind, intended to act as a man-made obstacle that would delay any attack by Syrian tanks in the west.

Following the Syrian attack in June 1970, the Northern Command carried out extensive preparations based on lessons learned. Throughout the Golan Heights, anti-tank ditches were extended and deepened. This project was completed between 1972 and 1973. (The final additions and completions were carried out, mainly at stronghold 116 in the southern part of the Heights, during the "Blue and White" Alert in April 1973.) This period coincided with the tenure of Maj. Gen. Yitzchak Hofi (Haka) as Head of Northern Command.

In October 1973, the anti-tank ditches were in place all around the border-fence, except for where the topography created natural obstacles, for example, at the Ruqqad Canyon between A-Saki mound and to the south. There also was a continuous obstacle from stronghold 104, east of Mas'ade, to stronghold 116, a few kilometers north of Ramat Magshimim in the southern part of the Golan.

On higher ground, near the infantry strongholds or the anti-tank ditches, firing ramps were built for the 188th Brigade to use, whenever tension rose. The ramps would allow Israeli tanks to dominate Syrian territory with their fire.

When Fedale was appointed brigade commander, he found that these ramps were not sufficient for the brigade's needs. Without delay, in his uncompromising manner, he improved the existing ramps and personally marked new locations for additional ramps.

He would ask to be notified as soon as each ramp was completed. He would then take a tank himself, or if he was in a good mood, have the battalion commander drive up the ramp, look around and make sure everything was satisfactory.

Construction contractors, who thought they had seen everything, were horrified when they had to work on ramps in the Golan within range of Syrian guns. Fedale would repeatedly instruct them to improve the ramp until he was certain the firing ramp was perfect.

Within 5–10 minutes' drive of each infantry stronghold, contractors removed rocks and leveled out hilly areas, creating a forward tank depot. The tank crews' task, when the order came, would be to rush forward, to get to the ramps near the infantry strongholds and secure them against the Syrian army across the border.

Every tank commander in the 188th Brigade, not only those in the forward tank depots, knew which ramp he was to take up position on when the time came, the shortest route to it and which targets he was to fire on when he arrived. All the commanders and gunners memorized this information, including the range to every target from their ramps, and were expected to have the information at their fingertips when called to action in the middle of the night.

Infantry and armored corps soldiers operated together in routine security measures on the Golan (the Purple Line). Usually, there were two infantry battalions, one of Golani, the other of the Paratroopers, manning all the strongholds from Mount Hermon to El Hama in the south. Behind them, in the forward tank depots, was the armor of one of the 188th Brigade battalions. They alternated in securing the Purple Line between themselves every three months.

In the summer, all three companies of the battalion manned the forward tank depots and toward the winter, when the Syrians had fewer forces on the front, only two companies remained. The third company was back in base doing what armored corps soldiers do – cleaning, training, or improving the tank equipment. They enjoyed one week of "civil bliss" – an education course or relaxation in one of the Education Corps facilities.

The IDF's policy was that the forward tank depots of the 188th

Brigade would be the type of position that enabled routine life, even if not as comfortably as on the major bases.

In every forward tank depot, there were up to fifteen youths in olive-green, making up three tank crews and supplemented by a medic and a technician, sometimes two. They lived in a closed triangular area of 100 x 100 meters, protected on three sides with embankments of rocks and with a barbed wire barricade at the entrance. A little slice of nowhere converted into a small regular army base and some sort of home for the tank platoon soldiers.

The middle of each site housed a large, prefabricated structure. Made of asbestos (at the time, no one was aware of the danger of cancer the material posed) it was divided into three rooms. One room was the soldier's barracks, the second held a kitchen, dining room and platoon club. The third room served as the platoon office, with a small table in its corner for the platoon commander. In addition to its function as an office, the room was the residence of the three tank commanders and included a significant perk. While the two sergeants shared a bunkbed, like the rest of the soldiers, the platoon commander had an individual bed all to himself, a real luxury!

In the middle of the depot stood a flagpole, with the rocks surrounding its base painted white. The battalion commanders put up enlarged aerial photographs of the enemy targets in the club, so that every crew member knew why he was stuck in this back-of-beyond. The three tanks were parked behind the three embankments with their guns facing outward, and they seldom moved. "Do not waste engine hours," was the mantra.

So with the exception of days of combat, there were times when soldiers spent their entire three months on the front line without moving their tanks... unless Lt. Col. Yossi Ben Hanan (the 53rd Battalion commander until August 1973) came to visit with American "tourists." "Eiland, activate Pitchfork" he would order the 2nd platoon commander, using the code word to take position facing the Syrians, and Eiland would lead his tanks to their firing positions... hoping he would not order them to open fire!

At night, everyone took turns on guard duty. Crew members and commanders stood in their turrets, listening to the radio communication. As night passed into day, soldiers from the two infantry battalions patrolled the border in armored vehicles, making sure no Syrian entered Israeli territory.

The overnight guard duty was the prelude for the daily "Dawn Alert" drill when the tanks were started, their engines warmed up, all equipment checked and the cannons and machine guns cleaned. Every day, all along the Syrian border, in all the forward tank depots, these same activities took place. The tank crews, ready for action in their overalls, manned their tanks and the crews waited inside for an hour or two until the patrols completed their rounds and the regional brigade reported that the area was clear. Free at last from this task, the next mission was, of course, the morning inspection. In the armored corps, there is no rest.

Operating such a forward tank depot was like running a business. For this purpose, the armored corps came up with the tank depots' instruction manual. They called it 'the bible.' The bible had 100 pages. The operational parts of the book were the core, with chapters on command responsibilities, ammunition, intelligence, recreation and training. Every type of activity, even the least significant, was discussed in the book.

Every platoon commander had to sign dozens of forms, confirming that he carried out the procedures properly. So this manual contained the signature of the different platoon commanders, verifying that they had received cartons of tomatoes, trays of eggs, films, toilet paper, along with their confirmation that they carried out the daily maintenance of the tanks.

Despite the idyllic life, there was not a moments' rest. Hovering over them was the constant fear of a surprise inspection, especially by Brigade Commander Fedale. When a platoon received prior notification of his arrival, they would stay up all night preparing and sleeping only on the floor, so their beds remained in perfect order.

Fedale would sit in the dining room and make sure that the soldier appointed to cook did not forget to place eggs, cottage cheese, bread, vegetables, Halva and chocolate spread on the table, in the right order.

"When was the last time you changed your underwear?" he would suddenly ask the loader of one of the tanks, directing his lie detector gaze at him. "Two days ago." That was the wrong answer, dead wrong. "You are confined to the base for two weeks."

"Get me the depot manual," he would order the platoon commander toward the end of the visit. The commander was suddenly overcome with exhaustion, seeing, with certainty, his weekend leave evaporating.

The brigade commander was like God: he had a Plymouth Valiant car, a logistics jeep, a Command Post Carrier and, when he needed one, a combat tank. The battalion Commanders were his angelic deputies. Instead of the Valiant, they had an Israeli Carmel car and of course the jeep and the tank. The company commanders had the logistics jeep, the best equipped tank in the company and the best crew.

The platoon leaders took pride in their units and dreamed of moving up the ranks to receive a jeep, moving up the ranks to be able to speak freely with God and his deputies. Of course, they also aspired to save the country – and win the heart of the brigade commander's female soldier secretary along the way. Not always in that order of priorities.

Moshe Bar-Kochba (Brill)

Col. Brill, the founder of the 188th Brigade and its first commander, had started his career as a boy in the Irgun Tzvai Leumi (one of the resistance movements against British rule during the Palestine Mandate). He was a company commander in the 1956 Sinai Operation, receiving the Medal of Valor (Israel's highest decoration for heroism) for leading his company in the Battle of the El-Rawafaa Dam (a heroic and bloody battle, now taught in armored corps academies around the world). He commanded an armored battalion in the regular army, served as a reserve brigade commander and, in 1969, he became the commander of the new 188th Brigade, which he had created himself.

During Brill's term as brigade commander, Lebanon began to sink into turmoil.[8] He led the brigade during Operation Kiton 10 (a daring raid into Syrian territory during the War of Attrition on June 26, 1970) and he was credited with the improved ability of the new brigade. This led to the 188th becoming the armored brigade for IDF operations on the northern front.

---

8. Palestinian refugees in Lebanon formed about 12 percent of the population in 1960s. They were mainly located in refugee camps, which, after the Cairo Accords of 1969, became almost a state within a state, being run by the PLO and virtually exempt from Lebanese control. The balkanization of Lebanese society accelerated after the expulsion of the PLO forces from Jordan in 1970, with many of their fighters moving to Lebanon.

Col. Brill was the theoretical successor to GEN Chaim Laskov, the man who built the armored corps in his own image. Laskov had served in the British army, where he had assimilated the attitude of a tough British officer. With a hard face, with one eye searching for a random speck of dust and the other for the wrongdoer responsible for it, Brill walked around the brigade bases scaring the terrified soldiers and commanders, who were afraid to be caught in the brigade commander's gaze.

He was an extremely professional and courageous officer. Yet still what his soldiers and officers remembered the most about him were his violent inspection rounds, which made Moshe "War" Brill an unpopular man. He was seen as "the northern Gorodish" (the ex-commander of the 7th Brigade was known for his extreme attitude toward discipline and professionalism).

Avraham Baram

In the winter of 1970, Col. Avraham Baram replaced Brill. It was a smooth replacement. Baram too was an Irgun Tzvai Leumi youth member (three years younger than Brill, as a boy of fourteen he was already taking part in Irgun operations during the War of Independence). Like Brill, he too was a hero. He received a medal for leading a battalion of Sherman tanks in Sinai during the Six-Day War.

Unlike Brill, Baram had started his military service as an infantry soldier, moving up through the ranks to become a company commander in the Golani Brigade. In the early 1960s, Gen. David Elazar (Dado), the commander of the Armored Corps, called on leading infantry officers to transfer to the armored corps. There they would both improve the quality of the officer corps and imbue the units with a stronger Zionist spirit. Baram started from the bottom, as a tank crew member. From there he followed the regular track, from a company commander of Sherman tanks, commander of the armored corps officer course, commander of the 7th Armored Brigade and then of the 188th Brigade.

Baram brought a more relaxed approach than his predecessor. Nonetheless, the achievements of the brigade did not falter. During the summer of 1972, after further improving the abilities of the brigade, both in training and in combat, he handed over command to Col. Aharon Peled, who shared a similar military background as him: Nahal and Givati infantry brigades, release from the army to return home to Kibbutz Hulata, spending a few years as a civilian and then returning to the IDF as an infantry officer in the Givati reserve brigade. In the 1960s, when Dado had called for officers to join the armored corps, Peled also had responded and was appointed commander of a Sherman company. When the Six-Day War broke out he was serving as a commander of a reserve battalion with Centurion tanks, where he would serve with distinction.

Aharon Peled (Fedale)

No one knew him by his name, Aharon Peled. Everyone called him Fedale. His soldiers called him "Sir," usually saying "Yes, Sir." He was known to be the most professional and strictest commander in the armored corps, adding another chapter to the legacies of Brill and Gorodish.

Every Sunday Fedale returned from his home at Hulata and visited the forward tank depots from south to north. He would stick his finger, or nose, into everything, leaving behind memories of his displeasure.

"Your bathroom is a mess!" he barked at Lt. Roni Friedrich, platoon commander in the forward depot of B Company, 5th Battalion. Friedrich, who was acquainted with Fedale's weekly route and his approach, was confident that his bathroom, a bull's eye hole in the concrete floor, was clean enough to eat off. There was even a subtle scent of perfume sprayed in the air in the sparkling clean bathroom and he mumbled a few words of surprise.

"The bathroom protocol mandates that the toilet paper required on the shelf should be set in a pyramid of five rolls!" barked Fedale. He had only found four.

During June 1973, the office of the commander of the 188th Armored Brigade moved from the Filon Base, near Rosh Pina, to the Aleika Base near 53rd Battalion. The brigade commander hardly had the chance to sit in his new chair before he was forced to resign, against his will. In mid-June, during a conference of the officers of the 188th Brigade in the cinema hall in Aleika, Fedale had announced before everyone there,

"I would rather that we carry out one hundred Qibya operations[9] and never find ourselves in the opposite situation."

It was Fedale's bad luck that one of the officers present, a deputy company commander in a reserve battalion, was from Kibbutz Gan Shmuel, the stronghold of the left in the Kibbutz Movement in the '70s. He conveyed the statement to the left-wing Mapam who were angered by it. They demanded that Prime Minister Golda Meir do something dramatic and she responded. The successful career of COL Aharon Peled, Fedale, came to an end at Kibbutz Gan Shmuel.

On July 1, 1973 a change of command ceremony was held. Fedale, against his will, vacated his position as brigade commander to make way for Col. Yitzchak Ben Shoham.

On the same day, the deputy brigade commander was also replaced. Lieutenant Col. David Yisraeli replaced Lt. Col. Yossi Peled. A new chain of command was established in the 188th Brigade.

Yitzchak Ben Shoham

Col. Ben Shoham was an outsider. He had immigrated to Israel when he was thirteen with a group of youth from Turkey. He was absorbed by the Tirat Zvi religious kibbutz but left to help his parents who made aliyah after him, living in the Bucharim neighborhood in Jerusalem. During the day, he worked in a carpentry workshop, and in the evenings he made up his high school studies to take the matriculation exams. He joined the armored corps because that was where he was sent by the manpower department. As he moved up in the ranks of the IDF – as battalion commander, division operations officer, reserve brigade commander – he became part of a system that gave him a sense of belonging, pride and a future.

---

9. On October 12, 1953, as part of a series of cross-border raids against Israeli civilians, PLO terrorists infiltrated from the Jordanian controlled West Bank into the village of Yehud, close to Tel Aviv. The terrorists murdered a Jewish woman, Suzanne Kinyas, and her two young children, an act that shocked Israeli public opinion. Israel sent 130 troops under the command of Ariel Sharon to carry out reprisal attacks. These included an attack on the village of Qibya where IDF troops killed at least sixty-nine Palestinian villagers, two-thirds of them women and children. Forty-five houses, a school, and a mosque were also destroyed. The action lead to widespread international condemnation, including from the United States. As the facts became clearer, many Israelis condemned the attack as well. However, there were some who thought the action a regrettable but justifiable necessity.

When Ben Shoham took his position in the brigade commander's seat, everyone, especially the office clerks and the brigade staff, breathed a sigh of relief. The first time that Ben Shoham met with his officers, he said to them , "Start smiling." After a short while he organized a social event for his staff and their families and another one in his home, for the battalion commanders and their families. In contrast to the fearful atmosphere when Fedale was commander, Ben Shoham exercised his office in a relaxed and peaceful style. The constant tension evaporated, officers became friendly with each other and a new form of collaboration developed. Even the deputy brigade commander, David Yisraeli, a very strict officer, was affected and managed to encounter a soldier or a commander without leaving too terrifying an impression.

"Sir, come by for an omelet," Lt. Col. Yair Nafshi, commander of the 74th Battalion would call to invite Ben Shoham and he would come. Nafshi admired Fedale for his professionalism but he would never have dared to invite him for a meal.

When he returned from a weekend leave, Ben Shoham would leave his home in Tel Aviv and get on a flight at Sde Dov, landing at the airfield in Mahanayim. There, a car and driver waited for him, bringing him to the brigade commander's office. One Sunday, when no transport had been there to meet him on landing he walked into the office, and with his usual expression, said to the office clerks, "Very nice girls, an armored brigade commander has to hitchhike?" and that was the end of the matter. A sharp contrast to what would have been the likely response of Fedale.

Yossi Ben Hanan

The 53rd Battalion, Sufa, was located near the remains of the deserted Syrian village of Aleika, two kilometers west of the 74th. Its first commander was Lt. Col. Yehuda Bachar, followed by Lt. Col. Danny Vardi and then the colorful commander whose character and conduct made the battalion legendary in the brigade and outside it – Lt. Col. Yossi Ben Hanan, one of the veteran officers in the 7th Brigade who became commander of the 53rd Battalion.

There was no dispute regarding the professional skills of Ben Hanan, who started out in the military academy high school in Haifa. He was one of the best. Regarding his character, well that depended who you asked. Ben Hanan was an eccentric and energetic man who left the battalion a very vibrant tradition.

Oded Erez

On August 15, 1973, Maj. Oded Erez replaced Lt. Col. Yossi Ben Hanan as the 53rd Battalion commander. Oded, who looked young for his age, was considered to be just as talented as Ben Hanan in the professional aspects. Like Ben Hanan, he was a graduate of the military high school academy. As platoon commander, he had been sent to explore the feasibility of acquiring the British Chieftain tank for use in the IDF. He was a platoon commander in the Six-Day War and a company commander in Itzik Shoham's 53rd Battalion, in the 7th Brigade. That is also where he met Zippi, the battalion commander's secretary, his future wife. At the age of twenty-four, he was appointed by Gorodish to be deputy commander of the 82nd Battalion of the 7th Armored Brigade, commanded by Lt. Col. Ori Or. The path was then paved for him to become the commander of the brigade scouting unit, and in August 1973, before he turned twenty-eight – a meteor in the armored corps – he left his position as the head of the gunner's division in the armored corps school and was appointed commander of the 54th Battalion, under the command of his friend Col. Itzik Ben Shoham, the brigade commander. By nature, Erez was the opposite of Ben Hanan, "a good and quiet guy who did not cause trouble." Together now with his brother, the military correspondent and journalist Yaakov Erez, Ben Shoham's personal friend, he felt at home.

Yair Nafshi

And this was exactly what Lt. Col. Yair Nafshi, the 74th Battalion commander, could not stand.

The 74th Battalion (Saar), was positioned in Nafah, alongside the regional brigade headquarters, the divisional maintenance center and the headquarters of the new 36th Division. The close proximity to the main headquarters ensured that the offices of the 74th were always more presentable, with white painted stones and endless trees, shining black shoes and uniform pants perfectly creased. The soldiers and commanders of the 53rd said that the location of the base reflected the nature of the officers of the 74th, a group of nerds with no wild or rebellious side (as much as the armored corps enabled these traits to be shown at all).

The first battalion commander was Lt. Col. Uri Berez, a veteran officer. The second was Lt. Col. Bentzy Carmeli, who was later replaced by Lt. Col. Aharon Tal who transferred the command to Lt. Col. Yair Nafshi in June 1972.

Lt. Col. Nafshi was no kid. He was three years older than Lt. Col. Oded Erez and was in the army longer. He had seniority and had filled more positions. He was a company commander in the Six-Day War, commanded bridging and engineering tank units, and commanded the 7th Brigade's "Sayeret" (the reconnaissance company). He was the first deputy of the 77th Battalion and operations officer in the 188th Brigade during brigade commanders Baram and Fedale term. Now he was the 74th Battalion commander.

The special treatment that Erez received from Ben Shoham annoyed Nafshi. He preferred to compete with Lt. Col. Ben Hanan, the veteran, professional, adrenalin-packed, wild officer, not with the half-baked kid who just took command of the 53rd and was a close friend of the brigade commander.

For Nafshi, as for all the battalion commanders in the armored corps – and for him perhaps even more so – the competition between the battalions was the foundation on which they wanted to build a pyramid of excellence. It was the preparations for the competition that made the difference. The results were supposed to prove which unit was the best, and the winner had to be the 74th of course.

On Passover 1973, the 74th Battalion had the honor of hosting the army Seder meal, following its achievements in the last Days of Battle and winning first place in the "armored corps fitness competition."

Yair Nafshi was very proud. His soldiers walked around like proud peacocks, eyeing their rival soldiers from the "Philistines" of 53rd Battalion with professional contempt.

Intimations of War

Before Friday, the Eve of Yom Kippur

Egyptian President, Gamal Abdel Nasser, had died of a heart attack a month after the Six-Day War ended. Following the end of the War of Attrition, on August 7, 1970, intelligence was received by Israel's decision makers suggesting that Nasser's successor, Anwar Sadat, was not willing to give up on any of the land taken by Israel in 1967. Furthermore, he was preparing his army for a major conflict.

On December 10, 1972, the IDF Intelligence directorate received concrete information that "Sadat's decision to go to war still stands." Two days later, American intelligence reports confirmed this and determined that "there are concrete preparations in Egypt for war in December."

The warnings regarding war in December of course reached the Chief of Staff, Lt. Gen. David Elazar (Dado). This came in the midst of a heated public debate on the matter of shortening the mandatory service in the military, reducing the military budget and converting several regular army brigades into reserve brigades. The 188th Brigade was one of the candidates to become a reserve brigade, since no war was expected in the near future and "our situation has never been better..."

Dado was strongly opposed to the shortening of service and was pleased to have this intelligence to help prevent it. He now had the reason he needed to postpone the proposed budget cut and leave the regular force as it was.

In late 1972, the decision makers in Israel received intelligence assessments that Syria was well aware of its military weakness and would not join Egypt in its impending war against Israel. However, the Northern Command Intelligence began receiving reports that Syria was digging positions for heavy 180 mm artillery guns with a range that covered all of the Golan, including Rosh Pina.

December passed and all remained quiet along the Suez Canal. In March 1973 though, without any clear reason or explanation, the Syrians suddenly changed their behavior and thinned out their forces on the border, sending their brigades from the front lines to training. Had someone become confused in the Syrian General Staff?

The Northern Command Intelligence had become well acquainted with the Syrian military doctrine and conduct in the years after the Six-Day War. The armed forces on the other side of the Purple Line had several routines. One of these was thinning out the forces on the front lines before the winter (starting in September-October) and returning them to the front before spring (March-April). The entire intelligence community, particularly Northern Command intelligence, were constantly searching for any sign that would ring alarm bells. In spring 1973, Lt. Col. Shia Bar Masada, the Northern Command Chief Intelligence Officer, had two such indications: the digging of new artillery emplacements on the front and the change in the "behavior pattern" – the sudden thinning of the forces.

During the early months of 1973, as these signs appeared in the north, the IDF intelligence division received information from several reliable sources, according to which Egypt was planning to launch a war in May.

In light of these serious warnings about war, "Golda's kitchen cabinet" convened to discuss the matter. Maj. Gen. Eli Zeira, the Head of Intelligence, was also summoned. The meeting took place in Prime Minister Meir's home in Jerusalem. Attending were ministers Moshe Dayan, Yigal Alon, Yisrael Galili, Yaakov Shimshon Shapira, IDF Chief of Staff Lt. Gen. David Elazar and the Director of the Mossad, Zvi Zamir.

Zeira, the Head of Military Intelligence since October 1972, was given the opportunity to present his position. In his usual decisive manner, he said, "Any logical analysis of the situation shows that the Egyptians know they would be making a mistake by going to war, and if we accept this logic, there is no point in holding this meeting. However, the Intelligence Department accepts that Sadat's logic may be different, and therefore we are examining all signs on the ground to see whether there are preparations for war." Zeira also spoke of the northern front:, "The Syrian President knows that if our air force wants to, it can destroy his air force in two hours."

Zeira, the Head of Intelligence who had just seven months of experience, delivered his assessment, which was met with, "Noted," from Chief of Staff David Elazar, Defense Minister Moshe Dayan and Prime Minister Golda Meir.

They disregarded his assessment and unanimously supported the position of Zvi Zamir, the Mossad Director, who unlike Zeira believed there was a possibility of war.

On the following day, after the government meeting, the Defense Minister declared the "Blue and White" alert. This included wide IDF preparations for war, including a partial mobilization of reserve units.

May and June passed and then July came and there was no war.

Was it the Israeli preparations that deterred Egyptians? Maybe it was a general rehearsal for October? Or perhaps, an intentional deception meant to reduce the enemy's alertness?

Either way, the Blue and White alert that was wasted improved the status of the Intelligence Directorate and of Eli Zeira and his research division. The assessment of the research department became akin to receiving the "Torah from Mount Sinai," the decisive analysis.

Back to the Northern Command. During the Blue and White alert, a new Syrian ability was discovered: they could move large numbers of forces, in a single night, from their regular bases to the front, all the while maintaining radio silence. The commanders in the Northern Command became concerned, suddenly realizing that the amount of time they will have from when the Syrian units switched from regular deployment to war would be very limited.

In July 1973, the Syrians started to dig new emplacements. Analysis of aerial photographs showed that these sites were intended to house surface-to-air missiles (SAMs). In addition, the Syrians were thinning their missiles around Damascus, moving them forward along a new line, between Damascus and the Golan. Another indication of aggressive intentions was added to Bar Masada's list.

In the same month, an air force report was released, discussing the implications of the new deployment of the SAMs. In clear and unequivocal words, the report described the severe limitations they would place on the freedom of the Israel Air Force to operate in Syrian air space. Furthermore, the report stated that the deployment of the missiles toward the Purple Line would even seriously limit the air force's freedom to maneuver in significant parts of the Golan Heights, as well as reducing its ability to provide close air support to the ground forces.

Wednesday, August 1

On August 1, 1973, after only thirty days as brigade commander, unaware of the threatening air force report, Col. Itzik Ben Shoham, for the first time since taking his position, was required to demonstrate his command skills.

In a two-day brigade exercise, with participation of all three battalions: the 53rd, commanded by Lt. Col. Yossi Ben Hanan, the 74th commanded by Lt. Col. Yair Nafshi and the 39th, the reserve battalion, commanded by Lt. Col. (res.) Yoav Vespi, Ben Shoham justified the credit he had been given.

The brigade units convened in the assembling areas south of the Mahanayim–Bnot Yaakov Bridge road. Their mission was to push back the hypothetical Syrian forces that had supposedly taken control of large parts of the Golan, with their forward units already at the top of the final basalt step, poised to descend to the Jordan River and the Kinneret.

The 188th Brigade forces began the exercise by crossing the Jordan River in the shallows with their tank tracks crushing the river stones. In areas where the water was deep, they crossed using bridging equipment. After crossing the river, the brigade was divided in three battalion columns, and they all started climbing up to the Golan while firing ammunition at prepositioned targets acting as the enemy.

After two exhausting days, the three battalions, now deployed as a full brigade, launched their attack from the Kazabia-Hushnia area toward Nafah in the north and arrived at the finish line, proud and victorious.

Friday, August 3

On August 3, the day after the exercise ended, there was a review meeting and debriefing of all the brigade commanders. Efi Matityahu, a young lieutenant from the combat engineers bridging unit, stood up and questioned the maneuver. "Brigade commander, the training was very impressive but let me just say something about its assumptions. They seem unrealistic. Small-scale limited attack by the Syrian army is one thing, but how can you build an exercise on a scenario in which the Syrians attack and conquer most of the Golan Heights and reach its slopes?"

A murmur of agreement swept through the officer ranks.

Ben Shoham looked at the young lieutenant, heard the agreement and answered, "I agree that the scenario seems unlikely, but we still need to prepare for any situation and we should not become complacent."

Wednesday, August 15

August 15, 1973 was a festive day in the Northern Command. The veteran intelligence officer, Lt. Col. Shia Bar Masada, was being replaced by Lt. Col. Hagai Mann. At the hand over, their conversation focused on the three indications that something was happening on the ground. Added to these objective facts was the secret resource of every intelligence officer, Bar Masada's "gut feeling"

Hagai had hardly settled into his position and things began to deteriorate before his eyes.

It started when the concern regarding the new SAM sites materialized. From mid-August 1973, thirty surface-to-air missile batteries, half of them mobile SA6 missiles, had already been positioned in these sites.

It continued with the discovery of the first stages of digging emplacements intended for 240 mm mortars in the assembly areas of the front-line divisions. Hagai knew that according to the Russian military doctrine, 240 mm mortars were used to crush infantry strongholds and for the initial preparations for breaking through the lines of armored brigades.

The final indication raising the hackles of the new intelligence officer was the repeated anomalies in the behavior patterns of the Syrian front-line divisions. During August and the beginning of September, when the Syrians were supposed to start thinning out their forces, they suddenly started bolstering them. A large number of tanks and artillery, much larger than was expected, were deployed along the front line.

In early September, following on from the activity of the previous month, there were repeated warning signs that made the Northern

Command intelligence officer very concerned. He transferred the material, with the serious questions he was asking, to the high-ranking intelligence research officers.

The research department, soon to become the research division, was the focal point where all the intelligence material was gathered from all the sources – Military Intelligence, the Shin Bet (Internal security service) and the Mossad. The material consisted of signals intelligence from the enemy's phone and radio communication systems; information gathered by observers and analysis of aerial photography; reports from various agents as well as information from Arab media – newspapers, television and radio.

The research department was indifferent to all of this data. In response to Hagai Mann's request for an explanation of these indications, Lt. Col. Aviezer (Avi) Yaari, Head of the Syrian Front in the Intelligence Division (branch 5) replied, "The Syrians are moving into defensive positions, as they fear we will attack them."

Fearing an attack from Israel? At this point in early September 1973, the forward Syrian forces included 450 tanks, 600 artillery pieces and 10,000 soldiers. The Israeli force facing them was 72 tanks of the 188th Brigade, 12 artillery pieces and 2 infantry battalions. The IDF units were located, as always, in the platoon and company forward tank depots that the Syrians were well acquainted with. What attack indications did the Syrians see?

Thursday, September 13

Thursday, September 13, 1973 saw a major aerial incident in which thirteen Syrian MiG 21 planes were shot down. The Israeli air force lost one Mirage plane and its pilot was rescued from the sea.

From that moment on, in some sort of amnesia that had them ignoring the increased Syrian forces, the moving of the missiles and the newly place artillery batteries during the month prior to the aerial incident, the Intelligence Division explained every Syrian action as a preparation for a combat day, a response to the aerial incident.

With amazing timing, on the very day the Syrian MiGs were shot down, an announcement was made, on behalf of the IDF, regarding a plan to shorten the mandatory military service of new recruits.

The shooting down of the MiGs and shortening the military service should have been very good news for the 53rd Battalion soldiers, but on Thursday, September 13, 1973, the glory of the Israeli air force and the discussions of the general staff forum did not interest them. The soldiers of the 53rd were busy with something much more important to them. It was the last day of their battalion's recreation week in Acre. It was the day of the big game, the soccer final between C and A companies. Oded Bekman, a platoon commander in C Company, received a perfect pass from Daniel Yishai, the gunner-striker, and in a spectacular volley kick eluded Efraim Yosef, the gunner-goalkeeper of company A, and scored.

In 1963 Esther and Yaakov Bekman had left the Yad Eliyahu neighborhood in Tel Aviv and moved to the regular military neighborhood of Neve Magen, in Ramat Hasharon near Tel Aviv. The couple, who had fought in the highly controversial Lehi organization[10] suddenly found themselves in the heart of the military families neighborhood, mostly populated by Mapai[11] supporters who had grown up in the ranks of the Haganah and Palmach organizations.[12]

Despite this, their oldest son Oded became one of the pillars of the closed, unified children's group. What bought him such acclaim with his unique talent for soccer, the likes of which were never seen before on the fields of Neve Magen. Later on, in 11th grade, he was one of the leaders of the adolescent rebellion in the neighborhood, leaving high school and continuing his studies as an external student. Working during vacations and earning money, he bought the first motorbike in the neighborhood, discovered the pleasures of the big city and was the object of admiration for many of the youth who followed him when he starred in the local youth soccer team.

In the middle of the celebration of the spectacular goal and the victory celebrations, someone from the battalions' operations department contacted the company commanders and ordered them to return immediately to the Golan Heights and prepare the tanks. While they

---

10. *Fighters for the Freedom of Israel* – a militia movement against British rule identified with the political right.
11. *Workers' Party of the Land of Israel* – the dominant center left party in Israel at the time and the dominant force in Israeli politics since independence.
12. The militias that had been identified with the political left and who had been at odds with the right-wing militias in the pre-state period.

waited for the buses that came to take them back to the Golan, the new battalion commander, Lt. Col. Oded Erez, came up to Uzi Urieli, the acting commander of C company, and told him his appointment as company commander has been approved.

Uzi had already been an acting company commander for two months, but as someone who had started out as a tank driver in the brigade, he treated his formal appointment as company commander very seriously.

When he first came to the military induction center, Urieli had set a goal for himself: to become an officer in the armored corps. He was drafted in May 1970 and had been automatically marked as a tank crew member, just like Itzik Arnon and Shimon Akab, the rest of his crew in the company commander tank. They too were crew members for their entire service and happy to serve in that role.

Urieli made his way up to become a commander through all the courses along the way, shattering the glass ceiling for a crew member. After almost five years among the basalt rocks, the Golan was his home. His foundations were set in C Company, 53rd Battalion, the 188th Brigade and the Golan Heights. There was never a more prepared, happier commander in the IDF. "If the Syrians so much as make a muscle, C Company will show them," he told himself on September 13.

Immediately after September 13, the Syrians went into full emergency preparedness.

Hagai Mann, the Northern Command intelligence officer, was on full alert. "These are clear signs of an attack," he continued to warn his commanders in the Intelligence corps. "They continue to add forces in numbers greater than ever, and it is all being carried out, as you remember, in reverse timing that we have no other explanation for."

Friday, September 14

On the following day, Friday, September 14, the 53rd Battalion crews prepared for "scouting procedures." Lt. Col. Oded Erez, the commander of the 53rd, decided that the commanders needed to be reminded of the "taste of the firing ramps." He issued an order to take six command cars, with the commanders of one company in each pair of them, and drive to the front line. He told them not to skip any of the ramps, not one path or trail, to thoroughly scan the entire front, from Mount Hermon to Kibbutz Ramat Magshimim.

Each company was joined by Lt. Yuval Shachar, the battalion intelligence officer. He had been in the unit for half a year, in theory, but in practice much less. Three months earlier, in front of an assembly of the soldiers of the 53rd, the previous battalion commander, Lt. Col. Ben Hanan, proved the stories about his nature to be correct. "Intelligence officer, you are dismissed!" he shouted at the stunned Yuval, who excelled in the intelligence officer's course, after the 1:20,000 map he was supposed to use to give his intelligence briefing had disappeared and he was forced to improvise with a 1:50,000 map instead.

Yuval notified Moshe Zurich, the 188th Brigade intelligence officer and his commander, who spoke with Ben Shoham, the new brigade commander, who enabled Yuval to maintain his position in a creative compromise. He was to remain "outside the jurisdiction of the battalion."

Yuval continued to serve as the intelligence officer of the 53rd and his office was transferred to the brigade headquarters. When Lt. Col. Oded Erez took command, he was pardoned. He did not have much of a chance to enjoy the battalion's base before the ramp patrols began. He marked the access routes to them with green and black painted barrels.

On that same day, an angry letter was sent from the office of Lt. Col. David Yisraeli, the deputy brigade commander, putting all the frontline platoons on their toes: "We have discovered recent incidents of girl soldiers being in the forward tank depots, in violation of the regulations. Once again I stress that it is strictly forbidden for women to stay in these locations."

The battalion commanders conveyed the message to the company commanders who passed it on to the platoon commanders, who were forced to end the "womanly presence" of the girls who would occasionally visit them in the forward depots, mainly on the endless weekends when they stayed at the bases.

Monday, September 17

Monday, September 17, proved that even the level of alert condition had its limits, especially on the Golan, where everyone was so used to this situation. The soldiers of B Company, commanded by Avner Landau, were released from the reconnaissance patrol and were sent to complete a different duty, a company sports series in Kibbutz Ein Gev. Three days of soccer, basketball, tug-of-war but mainly time away from the uniforms and close to the kibbutz girls. The girls preferred pilots or commandos from the elite Sayeret Matkal unit, but when they were not around, were generous toward the most charming among them.

Tuesday, September 18

Tuesday, September 18, was another regular day of field trips for Tzachki Sarig, commander of the 2nd platoon of A Company. (This junior officer was the son of Nahum Sarig, the legendary commander of the Negev Brigade during the War of Independence.) They woke up while it was still dark outside, sipped tasteless army coffee, and slightly after 05:00 they were on the move, toward another front sector. They headed south toward Ramat Magshimim and half an hour later were approaching the notorious Juhader Junction road curve. Yisrael Maman, a young driver, sped into the curve. The command car was thrown off the road and rolled over. The commanders, not wearing seat belts, helmets not properly secured, were violently thrown clear.

Lying there, bleeding on the basalt stones, the countdown for the lives of Rafi Gal, the platoon sergeant, and Tzachki Sarig began. Less seriously injured were Yossi Gvili, commander of the 3rd platoon, who broke his pelvis, Avi Rotem, 2nd platoon sergeant, breaking both his elbows, and 1st platoon commander, Lt. Haim Damir.

Rafi Gal, Tzachki Sarig, Yossi Gvili, Avi Roten and Haim Damir were evacuated in a helicopter to Rambam Hospital. Damir had a few bruises and was released after two days. He returned to the Golan to resume command of his platoon. The others remained in the hospital, each dealing with his own injury (Gal's injury would prove fatal). They were unaware of the clouds of war approaching their comrades who remained on the Golan.

On the same day of the accident, Avner Landau, B Company commander, called 1st Lt. David Eiland, to inform him of the accident and tell him that he would be joining A Company as a platoon commander.

Not everyone was fond of the new boy who had just joined the 9th grade at the Hasharon high school in Nave Magen in 1968. There was something too prince-like in his manner, too put together and not wild enough. He dressed in a way that was different from the other boys in the neighborhood, smelling of cologne, and worst of all he was 1.82 meters tall, not the standard 1.75 like the other boys. As time passed, they became intrigued by the fresh spirit of the new boy from Jerusalem. The charisma of David Eiland, the son of Miki and Esther, made it possible for him to become part of the closed group of neighborhood youth.

In August 1971, he was drafted and volunteered to join the pilot training course. He was forced to drop out of the program for medical reasons, and in November 1971, he ended up, along with most of his classmates, in the armored corps basic training in Rafah.

David moved smoothly through the ranks to the officer's course. This proved very difficult for him. He barely made it through the course, graduating with the lowest grades of the cohort. In June 1973, immediately following his commissioning, David Eiland was posted to the 53rd Battalion on the Golan Heights.

When he arrived at the battalion, the commander, Lt. Col. Yossi Ben Hanan, received him with suspicion. How did this soft-spoken, artistic boy become an armored corps officer? "I don't think you chose the right position," Ben Hanan told him, holding back a bored yawn.

Eiland then found himself as a replacement platoon commander for two months in Avner Landau's B Company, waiting for the moment when he could become the permanent platoon commander. After the accident, that day had finally come.

In the days after the accident, the 188th Brigade's battalions resumed routine activities. The 74th Battalion continued to hold the front line, as in the previous month and a half. The 53rd Battalion recovered from the accident, bringing in new commanders to replace those that had been injured. They updated the safety instructions for vehicle travel and got back to work.

Since an armored soldier never says no to any activity that would get him away from his base, especially if it involves a tour and a trip, the commanders of the 53rd continued to comb every part of the Golan Heights, taking pride in becoming acquainted with every basalt rock.

Tuesday, September 24

On September 24, Maj. Gen. Yitzchak Hofi (Haka), the Head of the Northern Command, warned the General Staff that the statement that "the regular army will block the enemy forces until the reserve forces arrive" might no longer hold true, given the developments on the northern front. The Syrians had completed their emergency deployment of their divisions to the first line of defense, and their army was ready to open fire at any moment.

"How will we stop the huge mass of forces?" he asked.

"If you cannot do it on your own, the air force will assist you," someone answered.

"The air force?" Haka questioned. "The air force is saying it is almost paralyzed, unable to help, due to the SAM missile batteries deployed toward the border, turning the entire Golan into a hot missile-defended area."

As a result of Haka's questions and due to Dayan's concern that the Syrians may carry out a surprise strike destroying several settlements – "A catastrophe," as he put it – the Defense Minister called for another special meeting on September 26, the eve of Rosh Hashanah.[13]

On the following day, September 25, King Hussein secretly came to Israel to meet with Golda Meir. In the next room, undetected, Zusia Kaniajar (Zizi) listened into the meeting and recorded it. He was the head of Branch 2 in the Intelligence Research Division (Jordan front). He heard Hussein tell Golda that the Syrian army was in a "pre-jumping position." She asked him whether they would go to war without Egypt and he replied, "No, they will go together. They are coordinated."

Zizi called Brigadier General Arieh Shalev, the Head of the Research Division, notified him of what he heard, and then decided to tell Avi Yaari, the head of the Syrian front in the intelligence division.

Golda notified Dayan of the meeting and he checked with the Intelligence Division and told her that "the Intelligence Division is aware of this information and do not consider it to be of importance. Attend your meeting with Bruno Kreisky[14] in peace."

---

13. The Jewish New Year. Usually in September on the Gregorian calendar.
14. The Austrian Chancellor.

Dayan, with his sharp senses, noticed that the "woman of steel" was not at ease and added, "Tomorrow, when you are away, I will hold a meeting concerning the situation."

Why wasn't Zusia Kaniajar (Zizi), the veteran intelligence research officer, called in to present what he had heard before the head of the research department, or perhaps before the head of the Intelligence Directorate himself? How was it possible that such sensitive information – the Syrian army is prepared for war against Israel (in jump positions) and is coordinated with Egypt – conveyed to Arieh Shalev, the Head of the Research Department? How did this information not have all of the intelligence branch on their feet?

It seems that the Intelligence Directorate did not believe the meeting between Golda and Hussein to be significant. Such secret meetings with King Hussein had become routine. The Research Division and especially Branch 6, Egypt, considered Hussein's information regarding the collaboration between Syria and Egypt to be baseless.

The Intelligence Research Division, unlike the Northern Command intelligence, continued to interpret the growing Syrian forces as defensive preparations. They were certain of two things: Syria would never dare to go to war on its own against Israel, and Egypt was not going to war, period.

In the Northern Command, things continued as always. The command intelligence officer had continued to ask for clarifications regarding the indicative signs but was not even informed about the information received in the Golda-Hussein meeting.

On the night of 25/26 of September, the Northern Command observation posts identified Syrian convoys heading from within Syrian territory to the front line of the bases, with only minimal "cat eyes" lighting.

Wednesday, September 26

September 26, the morning of the eve of Rosh Hashanah. In the Northern Command, efforts were made to locate the forces that had moved during the night. Long-range observations and air force flyovers did not provide satisfactory answers. The veil of mystery remained. Hagai Mann was tense. Was it possible that the force that moved at night was a logistical addition to the forces already in position, or was it an attempt to get the Israeli side used to movement at night?

September 26, the eve of Rosh Hashanah. Following the Golda-Hussein meeting the previous day, which had not been reported to Gen. Hofi, a special General Staff meeting was held in Hakiryah[15] in Tel Aviv early that morning. The meeting was attended by the Defense Minister and his assistant (Zvi Zur), the Chief of Staff and his deputy (Gen. Yisrael Tal), the Head of the Military Intelligence Directorate and the Northern Command CO. At the end of a long and exhausting discussion, the conclusion was that the intelligence assessment was not to be altered, Syria would not attack alone and there was no indication that they would act together with Egypt. However, it was agreed that a local Syrian action, artillery shelling or even a mechanized attack toward an Israeli town, was possible.

In this meeting, Haka succeeded in convincing the Chief of Staff to increase the order of battle on the Golan Heights. Dado ordered the 7th Armored Brigade to send two tank battalions to the Golan and in addition he ordered another artillery battery to reinforce the front.

At the end of the discussion, the Defense Minister decided to go to the Golan, to visit the bases and Kibbutz Ein Zivan. He began his visit at the division headquarters at Nafah, where he was briefed on the enemy forces by the commanding general. Haka told him that in the latest aerial photos, the long-range artillery and Frog ground-to-ground missile launchers had not been pinpointed, and he added that "the Command cannot be surprised during the day, we see to a great distance..."

In the early afternoon, Gen. Elazar joined Defense Minister Dayan and together they met with representatives of Kibbutz Ein Zivan. After the meeting, the Minister met with the press and updated them on the reinforcements that would be joining the forces on Rosh Hashanah and expressed his concern regarding the Syrian activity on the Golan. "On the Golan there are [Israeli] civilian settlements on one side and a nation [Syria] and military notorious for their extremism on the other side, with hundreds of tanks and artillery in effective range."

---

15. The headquarters of the IDF, shared with certain civilian offices. A cross between the Pentagon and "Whitehall."

56

Toward the end of the visit to the Golan, the military leaders decided to meet with the "cannon fodder," the soldiers, to feel the atmosphere among the ones who, come what may, would guarantee victory in battle.

In the Juhader tank assembly area, in the Southern Golan, twenty tank crews of the 188th Brigade were waiting on tense alert for the high brass.

"Attention!"

"Be seated."

After talking for half an hour, Dayan and Dado, charged with the self-confidence they required, got on their helicopter and flew off in a whirl of yellow dust.

What were the two thinking when they looked down through the helicopter windows at the twenty tank crews in Juhader becoming small dots in the Southern Golan?

Was it possible that Dayan, the legendary father of the Israeli security conception, the man responsible for the concept, "They better not start with us, or we will reach their capitals," was not concerned at all seeing the comparative forces in the Southern Golan Heights?

It was Wednesday, September 26, in the office of Col. Ben Shoham, commander of the 188th Brigade. Consistent with his two main character traits, Ben Shoham remained calm and serious and notified the brigade staff and the two battalion commanders of the decision to raise the alert level on the Golan. While giving his orders, Ben Shoham announced a change in the deployment on the front.

"The second tank battalion of the brigade, the 53rd, will leave its regular base and move forward to the front," he determined, and added, "the division of the responsibility for the fronts between the two battalions, is parallel to that employed by the two infantry battalions deployed to the border area."

In order to maintain the deployment of the 74th, already on the front line, Ben Shoham decided to divide the companies of the 53rd. A Company, commanded by Zvika Rak, was sent to the front in the northern outskirts of the town of Quneitra, where its role was to seal off the Quneitra gap. B Company, commanded by Avner Landau, was sent to the Wasset junction, as a reserve force on the northern front. C Company, commanded by Uzi Urieli, was sent to Hushnia, as a reserve force for the southern front sector.

For the first time since the Golan Heights were conquered, as a result of the Rosh Hashanah alert condition, the Golan front was split in two between the two regular battalions. The southern Golan and part of the center, up to forward tank depot 110, became the responsibility of Lt. Col. Oded Erez, commanding officer of the 53rd. The area from the Hazeka Ridge to the northern Golan front became the responsibility of Lt. Col. Yair Nafshi, the commanding officer of the 74th.

No one knew what was going to happen. The Northern Command senior officers, including Ben Shoham, the brigade commander, did not expect there to be an incident that would develop beyond limited artillery fire. The common belief was that, at most, the Syrians might attempt an attack on Quneitra or Mount Fares. Therefore, everyone preferred to keep the platoons of the 74th that were holding the front area in their positions and not to move them to the north, to Nafshi's front.

As a result, an anomaly was created. Each battalion commander had one of his own companies on the front, along with two companies from the other battalion under his command. In addition, G Company, the front line company of the central sector, was divided between the two battalion commanders. Two platoons, with the company HQ, were reporting to Lt. Col. Oded Erez in the 53rd Battalion. Meanwhile, the northern platoon of the central front sector, located in the infantry HQ in Quneitra, was under the command of Lt. Col. Yair Nafshi, the commander of the 74th.

Toward the end of the meeting, Ben Shoham clarified with the commanders that activating the reserve companies would be done only with his approval. He recommended that they divide the front sector in two, one commanded by the battalion commander and the other by his second in command.

A recommendation from the brigade commander is actually an order, and right after the meeting the two battalion commanders deployed accordingly. Yair Nafshi notified Maj. Yossi Nissim, the deputy commander, that the northern front sector was now divided between the two of them. Nissim was to be in charge of the area farthest north, from the Druze village of Buqata to forward tank depot 104. Nafshi was responsible for the area from Buqata to depot 110.

Oded Erez did the same and notified Maj. Shmulik Askarov, the deputy commander, that the area was to be divided between them. Askarov was to be responsible for the northern part of the southern front, from Troja route/Kudna to the Rafid route/stronghold 113. Erez would be responsible for the area from forward tank depot 114 (Rafid) to the south.

On the afternoon of the eve of Rosh Hashanah, the commanders and crewmembers of A Company sat back in their seats on the bus, feeling sorry for the soldiers of the other companies and happy to be so lucky. They had just returned from recreation in Acre and from sports activities in Ein Gev and now they were being sent home for a four-day leave. They were well aware of the unstable level of alert condition of the 188th Brigade and stared out the bus windows, waiting to hear the engine start and moving away from the parking lot and from the envious faces of the soldiers remaining behind, before anything changed.

"Everyone off the bus," someone shouted. "All leave is canceled."

At around noon on September 26, the last day of the Hebrew month of Elul, the three companies of the 53rd Battalion were sent to take up their new positions as part of the two-headed defense plan of the Golan Heights, involving the two battalions.

A Company had the shortest distance to travel. They got in their tanks and sped forward to the Hahazit building, a large police station on the main road, one kilometer northwest of Quneitra.

At the same time, 1st Lt. Yossi Zimri joined A Company. He had been an instructor in the armored corps officer course and happened to be the personal instructor of Tzachki Sarig, the commander of the 2nd platoon who was lying unconscious in the hospital. He also was part of the instructor team of David Eiland, Sarig's replacement.

The plan was for Oded Yisraeli, the deputy company commander, to join the company commander's course and Zamri was supposed to replace him. In the meantime, they all headed toward the Hahazit building, staying close to Yisraeli. He started on the job training "in battle conditions" and had a hard time understanding what was going on in the chaos.

B and C Companies had to move further forward and continued to the Wasset junction and Hushnia accordingly.

As a result of the decision of the General Staff that morning to add forces in the Golan front, the first two companies of the 7th Brigade prepared to join the force on the Golan in addition to the internal reinforcement of the 188th Brigade.

The 7th Armored Brigade's commander, Col. Avigdor Ben Gal, or Yanush as everyone called him, did not limit himself to the orders of the general staff. As a man who always did things his own way, he decided that he would not send less than an entire battalion to the Golan and he ordered Lt. Col. Haim Barak, the 82nd Battalion commander, to send one of his operational companies to the Golan, in addition to the two companies of the 77th, Lt. Col. Avigdor Kahalani's battalion.

Thursday, September 27

On Rosh Hashanah in the afternoon, Kahalani and Ben Shoham set to meet "on the way," near the emergency warehouses unit, which was supposed to supply the 77th Battalion.

"How is Dalia?" Ben Shoham asked, getting out of the jeep to shake Kahalani's hand and to ask after his wife's welfare.

"Fine, thank you. How is Eti?" the smiling Yemenite officer asked in response.

Then they got to business. Ben Shoham notified Kahalani that he was putting the entire emergency supplies crew under his command. He also asked him to try to maintain the sandstone path, keeping the tanks off it. "Don't get me wrong, Kahalani. The pavement, the sandstone, all the money put into it is ridiculous if war breaks out, but we both know how these things end and it is a shame to ruin it."

They continued to discuss the situation on the front and Ben Shoham spoke of the Syrians' intentions, saying that he believed there would be heavy artillery fire along the front, perhaps an attempt to conquer one of the forward tank depots.

"Meanwhile stay here near the war reserve storage base with the battalion," Ben Shoham smiled. "Later on, I will probably move you to Nafah, to act as an independent force for counterattacks."

Then they parted. Ben Shoham returning to his office and Kahalani driving his jeep to the war reserve storage base, to wait for his battalion. On Rosh Hashanah, September 27, Yanush, the commander of the 7th Brigade, came to the Golan with his staff.

Why did Col. Avigdor Ben Gal, commander of the 7th Brigade, need to be on the Golan with his staff, when the majority of the brigade was in the distant south? How did he have the courage to upgrade the Chief of Staff's order and send another company to the Golan?

The answer has to do with the personality of Ben Gal. He was a veteran warhorse. A warfighter who had proven himself, full of confidence, always doing what he thought was right, regardless of what anyone thought and even if it meant disregarding guidelines or even an order.

Yanush knew that the companies on the Golan were to be under the command of Ben Shoham. This did not prevent him, a soldier always ready for battle, from sending the brigade headquarters to the Golan. He saw the sights, heard the sounds and he thought to himself that the 7th Brigade had been sitting around doing nothing for 3 years. There is a high risk of war on the Golan. Why miss such an opportunity?

On Rosh Hashanah, 1973, H Company of the 74th Battalion spread out on the northern most sector. Lt. Eyal Shaham, the company commander, and Lt. Avraham Kaimovitz (Kaimo), his deputy, settled in the company headquarters at Mas'ade, trying to pass the time somehow before touring the tank front camps areas.

Kaimo looked at Eyal and noticed his tense expression. Something changed in him, he thought to himself. "Something here doesn't make sense," Eyal said. "There are huge forces facing us and on our side everything is routine."

Kaimo agreed with him but what was the point of all this talk? The commanders above them know what had to be done. "Let it go Eyal," he said, "let me get some rest."

"Ok, I will spare you my insights," said Eyal. He ended the conversation and told Kaimo he was going to spend a couple of hours with his parents who were visiting family at Kibbutz Hagoshrim.

Rosh Hashanah night. The Shaham family had already finished their holiday meal. There was a knock at the door. It was Eyal; in his tank overall, with red sleepless eyes, loud army communications heard from his Jeep. Happy to see him, they brought him endless amounts of food, all the special dishes made for the holiday.

Eyal sat with his father Zonik and told him about the Syrian force build-up on the border. "The war has already begun," said Eyal passionately, "even though the first gunshot has not been fired yet." Eyal continued to lecture to his father, "The Syrians may surprise us and things will be very bad. For every tank of ours, there are fifteen of theirs."

His father Zonik, who had fought in Israel's wars, laid a calm hand on his son's shoulder. "We have seen these situations before. You will see that everything will be OK."

After midnight, Eyal returned to the base. "How was it?" asked Kaimo.

"I told my parents that a war will start within two weeks. My father said everything would be OK."

Just like a large number of the junior commanders of the 188th Brigade, who came from the "khaki triangle," the kibbutzim, and the military schools, Eyal also came from a family with a proud fighting heritage. His father was Col. Zonik Shaham, a senior reserve officer, one of the acclaimed fighters in the War of Independence and one of the founders of the IDF.

Eyal went through a lot before he was finally given command of the company. He was drafted in November 1968, completed the officer's course in 1970, and as a young officer was posted to the middle of nowhere in Sinai. He trained lazy reserve duty soldiers on primitive T-tanks taken from the enemy. He was far from the real action that the 188th Brigade was involved in.

Eyal's first meeting with the company, arriving from Sinai in early 1973, was traumatic. In his first talk with the company he gave them a comprehensive and impressive Zionist speech about our right to the land of Israel, adding a few procedural matters. "In the IDF we respect our officers," he told them. "There are armies where every morning the soldiers shine the officer's boots. It is a good thing this is not the case in the IDF but there are basic elements we all need to respect."

This was not the best way to start off with an operational company in the Golan. The chubby officer, with glasses, giving this speech, did not make a very good impression.

In April 1973, H Company completed its company training. At the end of the training, there was a skills test that had to do with grease, sweating, concentration, professional abilities and speed in carrying out drills, according to the armored corps manual and Fedale specifically.

At the end of the drill and the test, there was an inspection of the tanks. The company soldiers, standing in attention, awaited the ruling of the most terrifying and professional brigade commander in the armored corps. A moment of tense silence and finally, Fedale said, "I have nothing to say." He waited a few more seconds and added,, "Even the tank commanders stood with just their shoulders outside the tank."

Eyal stood tall with pride, his eyes looking straight ahead. "I think," added Fedale, "this company gave you the best wedding gift you could have imagined."

From that day on no one in the company remembered the speech he had given.

On the evening of the last day of Rosh Hashanah, another meeting of combat officers took place in Col. Ben Shoham's offices. Lt. Col. Avigdor Kahalani, commanding the reserve force, also joined. Maj. Benny Katzin, the operations officer (S3) of the 188th Brigade, described the deployment of the brigade and then Ben Shoham presented three possible courses of action the Syrians might take. One was a possible local attack, the second an artillery strike and the third an attempt to conquer the entire Golan Heights.

"I think the second option is the most plausible," he said, focusing his attention on Kahalani and Captain Ilan Sahar, the intelligence officer of the 7th Brigade. "I know Yanush thinks that Syria is going to launch a full war in the Golan but I disagree."

Intelligence officer Moshe Zurich then presented the state of the enemy forces to the forum, specifically to the commander of the 77th Battalion that had just joined the brigade. It was very late, and all the officers, knowledgeable and confident in their small but powerful Sho't Kal tanks, returned to their units.

Friday, September 28

On September 28, the Intelligence Directorate received information regarding the movement of Syria's 47th Armored Brigade from Homs, facing the southern Golan front. Joining the brigade in the front were bridging tanks and equipment. Aerial photos taken on that day showed some of the bridging tanks, extremely close to the front lines. Alongside them were tank platoons that were there to cover them when they would cross the anti-tank ditches.

Thirty years later, Hagai Mann, the Northern Command intelligence officer, was one of the participants in a seminar at the Ramat Efal education center. He was amazed to hear Brig. Gen. Amos Gilboa, the former Head of Research in the Intelligence branch, tell the following story. In June 1972, during an operation of Sayeret Matkal aimed at returning Israeli pilots and navigators from Syrian prison, five senior Syrian officers had been captured. When they arrived in Israel, the officers were interrogated on the order of battle of Syrian forces and on the indicative signs Hagai Mann was so keen on collecting.

"Tell us everything you know about the 47th Brigade," they were asked in interrogation.

In response, they said that "the brigade had been established less than a year earlier and positioned at Homs, where there was a revolt against Assad that was crushed viciously. The task of the brigade is to act as a force loyal to the President in case of any future revolt in the Homs area. They are 'Assad's whip.' Also, if this brigade ever headed toward the Golan, it could only mean that the army was heading toward war."

On September 28, a message was intercepted. The 47th Brigade asked not to send any more bread to Homs but to a new location in the southern Golan Heights, in the area of Nava, opposite Rafid-Kudna.

No one bothered to notify Hagai Mann of the information obtained from the interrogation of the Syrian officers, over a year earlier, even though he was the person responsible for warning the command! Without this information, it was just another hundred tanks. Hagai Mann was not satisfied with the addition of forces but he did not consider it to be the final nail in the coffin of the intelligence branch and the senior officers. This nail was only given to him now, thirty years later, by chance.

Saturday, September 29

The CIA apparently received the information Hussein gave Golda and passed it on to Israel. The Intelligence Directorate disregarded it again. "It's all just drills."

Sunday, September 30

The week begins with a terrible haze. With the basalt rocks of the Golan burning up in the heat, the decision was made to send the tanks of the 53rd Battalion back to their base. On the same day at the Filon base, there was a mobilization drill of the 96th Battalion of the 179th

Brigade, the rapid mobilization reserve brigade of the Northern Command. The drill, prepared for a long time, was intended to examine the actual ability of the brigade to complete its mobilization within eighteen hours. It went well and Maj. Gen. Haka and Col. Ran Sarig, the commander of the reserve brigade, were pleased. The reserve soldiers showed maturity, seriousness and responsibility and according to the speed in which they reported to the base in Filon, it would seem that when they were called to go to battle, it would take a lot less than the eighteen hours target time.

In the evening, the Syrian convoys moved toward the border once again, but this time in larger numbers and spread out along the routes. Hagai Mann was very troubled and called in two teams of the Long Range Observation Unit, sending them to several bases. During the night, he requested an aerial reconnaissance for the following morning and had a light plane placed on standby.

A special meeting was called for 6 p.m. in the office of the Chief of Staff in Tel Aviv, to evaluate the situation on the Syrian front.

Gen. Zeira presented his update on the situation, "The data collected by the Intelligence Directorate shows that the entire Syrian army is in its emergency disposition. According to the Soviet doctrine, this order of battle enables the army to go into attack mode without any further preparations."

While the data Zeira presented indicated a serious threat on the northern border, the interpretation that he and Arieh Shalev, the Head of Research, gave to this information, made it harmless. "Syria will not go to war without Egypt," Zeira stated clearly. "Even if Egypt goes to war, there is no certainty that Syria will join immediately, but only after they see that the Egyptian attack succeeded. Since Egypt has nothing pushing it toward war, it has no intention of going to war, and therefore, the preparations in Syria are not for war."

After presenting the data and their analysis of it, Zeira and Shalev's conclusion was that "the probability of the Syrians taking limited action is low."

Head of Northern Command, Haka, asserted that there was a need for immediate changes on the ground. Gen. Yisrael Tal (Talik), the Deputy Chief of Staff, vehemently agreed. Haka did not dispute the Intelligence Directorate's assessment but restated the problem of the lack of tactical warning on the front and demanded, as a solution, "positioning an additional brigade of tanks on the Golan." He also asked the Chief of Staff to extend the reserve duty order of the 96th Battalion, at least until after Yom Kippur.

Gen. Yisrael Tal stated that the IDF needed to prepare for war on the Golan. "The problem is not revenge for the thirteen downed planes... the problem is the danger of an attack on the Golan." Like Haka, he also recommended immediately sending another brigade of tanks and an artillery battalion to the Golan.

At the end of the meeting, mostly due to the "whining" of the two, the Chief of Staff ordered additional forces to the Golan, sending the last two companies of the 77th Battalion of the 7th Brigade and an additional artillery battalion (the three batteries of 405th Battalion, commanded by Maj. Arieh Mizrachi). Dado also ordered the 82nd Battalion of the 7th Armored Brigade to be on stand-by to join the forces on the Golan and also ordered the 33 tanks of the 96th Battalion, intended for the mobilization drill, to remain in the Filon base, fully armed and ready.

These actions were in accordance with what was accepted in the IDF when things heated up, refraining from mobilizing reserve soldiers and transferring small forces from front to front. It was called "pulling the blanket."

Why didn't they keep the Sho't Kal tank crews of the 96th Battalion of the 179th Brigade on active duty? Also, why didn't they send the entire 7th Brigade to the Golan that same day, as Gen. Tal recommended?

Monday, October 1

Hagai Mann was already at work before dawn, as he was every day that week. "It will be first light soon," he informed the intelligence officer of the 820th Regional Brigade and his deputy. "Make sure all lookouts on the front are alert."

"Hagai, General Staff wants to talk to you urgently," said his secretary.

On the line was Avi Yaari. "We have received information from a very reliable source that this morning, with the first light, Egypt will start a war and Syria will be joining them. Get the Northern Command on its feet."

In the commotion of the reserve duty mobilization drill at the Filon base, Haka was called to the phone urgently. "War today," was the message Mann conveyed to his commander.

"What are you planning to do?" Haka asked him.

"I am on my way to the Northern Command. I will try to get more information," he said.

Within a short while he arrived at the Northern Command headquarters and attempted to find out the status of Lt. Col. Gedalia, his counterpart in the Southern Command, who would be facing the Egyptian attack.

"Intelligence, what can I do for you?" was the tired response he received.

"Get me Gedalia please."

"He's asleep," was the response.

"Where is the deputy intelligence officer?

"Also asleep."

"What is going on over there?" Hagai was amazed.

"Nothing special."

Confused by this, he called Yaari back. "What about the information you gave me?"

"It is just as I told you," he confirmed and as they spoke, the information appeared on the tele printer.

"The hell with the mystery in the south," he thought to himself. "I am in charge of the north and here I have cross-checked information that war is here. Let's get to work."

Within a few minutes, all of the IDF units in the Golan received the warning of war. Haka took advantage of the surprise mobilization drill of 179th Brigade and issued orders not to release the reserve battalion. The regional brigade made preparations to evacuate civilians and the entire Golan became frantic.

Half an hour after he started getting the forces on their feet, he received a call. It was Lt. Col. Uri Simchoni on the line, the operations officer of the Northern Command. "Hagai, what is the deal with the information you gave us? We wanted to keep the 96th Battalion activated but the Operations Division is opposed."

07:00, the phone rings again. It is Brig. Gen. Arieh Shalev, the head of the Research Division on the line. "Hagai, why are you spreading panic over there? Didn't you get the information that it is just a drill?"

"No one told me that."

"Come to my office in Tel Aviv tomorrow, for an inquiry."

Monday, October 1. The Chief of Staff's order of the previous night became an order to add forces. The two companies of the 77th Battalion of the 7th Brigade boarded a flight at Refidim in Sinai and landed at Mahanayim. They were driven to the Filon base, prepared the tanks of the 96th Battalion of 179th Brigade and, after an exhausting day, were ready on the Golan.

In command of a big battalion with forty-four tanks, Avigdor Kahalani was told to leave the Yarden base and reposition at the Hashiryon junction, in the remains of the deserted village of Nafah, a kilometer east of the Nafah base.

The tanks of the 77th Battalion took position in their new "base," reporting directly to the 188th Brigade.

Tuesday, October 2

On the morning of October 2, there were 113 Sho't Kal tanks on the Golan Heights facing 650 Syrian tanks. On the artillery front, there were eight artillery batteries and heavy mortars (thirty-two artillery pieces in total), facing 600 Syrian guns.

While tanks of the 77th Battalion prepared to move to Hashiryon junction, the soldiers of the 53rd Battalion were relaxing on the old chairs in the battalion club, watching the heroic efforts of Israel's national basketball team playing against Russia, on a black and white television.

During halftime, they finished off the snacks and sodas they had in the canteen and even the joyful meeting of Bekman and Eiland was drowned out by the cheers of the soldiers, since the Russians were only two points ahead and seemed to be close to losing in the second half.

After a few moments of hope, it turned out that their celebration was premature, as the Russians won by 32 points in the end. Yossi Zimri, a new soldier in the unit, said cynically to a group of disappointed soldiers, "It's a good thing that the Russian tanks can't crush us the way the Russian players did."

Hagai Mann is at the office of Brigadier General Arieh Shalev in

Hakiryah in Tel Aviv, awaiting his reprimand, not understanding what he did wrong.

Shalev, "What is all the panic?"

Mann, "I received information from Avi Yaari and acted accordingly."

Shalev, "It was just a drill. 'Tachrir 41,' the large Egyptian drill that was already planned. There are no indications that Syria is heading toward war."

Mann, "I am all out of indications."

Reprimanded, on his way back to the Northern Command, Mann did not change his mind.

Even without the clues that had not been shared with him – the significance of the moving of the Syrian 47th Brigade as well as the warnings received from the CIA and King Hussein – the situation was clear to him: Syria was heading toward war. What other explanation was there for the hundreds of tanks and artillery pieces, along with the bridging and engineering equipment? Not to mention the convoys moving at night and the heavy concentration of enemy forces on the front lines, at a time when the line is usually thinner. What about the Syrian air force squadrons that left their distant bases and were positioned close to the Purple Line? What other meaning could there be to the intercepted messages and other data showing that the Syrians were collecting blood donations and food and clearing hospitals of patients that did not need urgent treatment? There were even tracks of reconnaissance foot patrols inside Israeli territory.

What more has to happen for the senior commanders in the Intelligence Directorate to realize that this is not an illusion and there was a very high probability of war? The writing was on the wall, and it could not be any clearer.

Upon arrival at the Northern Command, he was notified that in the latest aerial photographs taken by the air force, the command photo analysts saw that the tanks of the Syrian 1st and 3rd Divisions had left their bases and were not deployed for defense in the second layer. This was in contrast to the position of the Intelligence Directorate analysts.

Hagai notified Haka of this and he made an angry call to Arieh Shalev, "What is with you? You got the analysis wrong! The Divisions are apparently on their way to the front assembly areas, not to a second layer of defense. This is a clear movement toward an attack."

The Syrian defense deployment was based on two "layers." The first layer of defense was near the Purple Line with three mechanized infantry divisions, with their infantry brigades in strongholds, followed by the armored brigades in the rear. In the area east of the first defense layer the division artillery units were deployed.

The second layer of defense had the mission of defending Damascus. If this was the deployment, it would indicate clear defensive intentions. However, this second layer was not manned, and this implied that the Syrian army was not preparing for defense. So what was the Syrian army preparing for?

On April 27, 1973, the IDF Military Intelligence Directorate had distributed a report. The document estimated that "the Syrian attack is expected to come from three mechanized Divisions simultaneously (5th, 7th and 9th) along the front lines. The main attack route will be from Tel Fares toward Bnot Yaakov Bridge."

Now, in October, the Northern Command received a document originating in the 5th Syrian Division. Based on Jordanian intelligence transferred by the CIA, the document specified the Syrian attack plan in the Golan, exactly as predicted by the Intelligence Directorate report from April 27. A small addendum had been added. There would be two routes of attack instead of one. The main route would be from Tel Fares to Bnot Yaakov Bridge, with a secondary route in the Quneitra gap.

The intelligence branch prediction had stated that the Rafid gap would be the main area from which the attack would be launched to the west. Based on this estimate, the Northern Command had prepared the defense deployment.

In September, Hagai Mann had presented Northern Command's intelligence estimate of the matter.

> *The southern gap (Rafid-Kudna) is a better choice than the northern gap (Quneitra) for the Syrian main breaching effort.*
>
> *Firstly, because of the topography. Right after the southern gap, the topography enables the deployment of large, armored forces to the south, west and north.*
>
> *Secondly, the strength of the enemy forces. From the end of September 1973 there were 450 tanks in the southern front and 200 in the north.*

The Head of Northern Command read the intelligence assessment, and in spite of the warning signs over the southern front, determined that the more dangerous option for Israel was the northern one, fifteen kilometers north of the Rafid gap. He was supported by Northern Command Intelligence. There were two reasons for this. The Northern Command believed that the Syrian attack would be stopped at the first stage, and therefore the position of the main attack seemed less relevant. Second, the topography of the region enabled two options for a main attack, but the possibility of the Syrian army succeeding in an attack on the Quneitra gap would lead them to the Bnot Yaakov Bridge and would pose an immediate threat on the Galilee. This was unacceptable to the Israeli narrative.

Whether it was one route or two, the Northern Command did not take the threat seriously, since it was accompanied with the estimate of the Intelligence Directorate that "in Syrian eyes, it is still not the time for their attack plan."

Wednesday, October 3

More than 400 T-62 tanks of the 1st and 3rd Syrian Armored Divisions were moving around extensively and no one had managed to pinpoint their position. The estimate of the Northern Command Intelligence, supported by Maj. Gen. Haka, was that the tanks were on their way to the forward assembly areas, and due to the October clouds the aerial photos did not show them.

The Intelligence Research Division disagreed. They admitted to having misread the photos and that the divisions had, indeed, left their bases in Kiswa and Katna and were not deployed in the second layer of defense. Nonetheless, they still evaluated the general posture of the Syrian deployment as defensive.

On Wednesday morning, Maj. Oded Erez, commander of the 53rd, summoned all the staff officers for an urgent meeting in his office. "As a result of intelligence received regarding an escalation on the Syrian side, we have been ordered to return to reinforce the company forward tank depots. My wish for all of us is that we meet again in the battalion soon."

An hour later, the tanks of the 53rd were already on the move to the company front camps that they had left less than ninety-six hours earlier. Within a few hours three full tank battalions were deployed on the Golan. The 74th was positioned along the line in the platoon forward tank depots, the 53rd in company camps and the 77th Battalion from the 7th Brigade stood by as the brigade reserve force near Nafah. All the crews were in the tanks or close by, waiting to see what would happen.

Avner Landau, the commander of B Company of the 53rd, drove to the brigade headquarters to pick up an intelligence update. If he had to work on his own, he could at least get his soldiers the latest news.

A young corporal made a serious face at him and said, "Avner, there is going to be a war."

The armored corps company commander had heard the Chief of Staff promise that everything was under control. He wondered where this young girl had gotten such important classified information.

"In the intelligence course I was taught that if there are 250 tanks on the border, another 500 behind them and at their side there is artillery and missiles, these are indications of war," she said confidently.

Landau responded with a macho smirk, took the update, and disappeared with his jeep in a cloud of dust.

All the way to Hushnia, the tanks of C Company were raising heavy clouds of dust. The crews took up position in the ruins, on the western outskirts of the abandoned village. A kilometer to the east, in the "official" tank forward parking area of Hushnia, G Company of the 74th Battalion took position. They were close but apart – every company with its own issues and pride.

For Oded Bekman, the commander of the 2nd platoon, C Company, there was never a dull moment. A guitar borrowed from the injured Tzachki Sarig ended up in his hands and he played a medley of Beatles songs praising Liverpool and Hushnia.

Bekman had been drafted into the IDF in August 1971. After a failed attempt to join the elite Sayeret Matkal unit, his inability to become a pilot due to his glasses, and a possible torn groin muscle that prevented him from joining the Haruv reconnaissance unit, he almost made it to combat engineering. As all the new recruits marched in threes toward the truck that was to take them to their postings, Bekman ran away to the office of one of the fathers from Neve Magen, who served as a senior officer at the Induction Base. He was spared a disciplinary action and was sent to the armored corps. A few hours later, he was entering the basic training base in Rafah.

Like all his friends from Neve Magen, he sped through the training courses and became an officer. In February 1973, at the end of the officer's course, he was asked to list his preferences of where to be posted. "The 188th Brigade is my first choice and my second and my third," he said to Col. Yaakov Lapidot, the course commander.

"You got it," smiled Lapidot, impressed by the determination of the young officer. He joined the 188th Brigade, 53rd Battalion, C Company, as the commander of 2nd platoon. It was exactly the place he had dreamed of serving as an officer. Yet he was still not lucky. His first day of action, which he eagerly anticipated, did not seem to be coming anytime soon. "Is it possible that I will complete my service on the Golan without a single combat day?"

Welcome to Wasset

Something told the experienced commanders of B Company that this time they were going to stay longer than usual. Lt. Asaf Sela, the deputy company commander, called in someone from the construction unit to repair the windows. There also was a guest speaker who managed to keep them awake with a lecture on nature and distant worlds.

The soldiers of B Company asked themselves what they were doing in this forgotten junction, far from all the action. Avner Landau, a company commander with good instincts, knew that they could not relax and he demanded that they continue in their routine of drills and maintenance of the tanks. He reminded everyone that despite their location, far from the front line, they too might see some action when the combat day came. He said it but had a hard time believing it himself.

Right after he completed his Zionist speech, Lt. Col. Yair Nafshi, the tall commander of the 74th, appeared at Wasset with an update that "there are serious warnings that the Syrians are planning a brigade attack in the area of strongholds 104–105. This seems to be the most reasonable scenario right now. Don't worry guys, you will have work to do," he added.

Avner Landau, from Kibbutz Yagur, joined the 188th Brigade after fighting in the Six-Day War as a deputy company commander. After he was discharged, he was appointed a reserve company commander in the Harel Brigade of Sherman tanks. The unit was commanded by Col. Uri Ben Ari, the brigade commander, and Fedale, the deputy brigade commander. After a year as a civilian, he had decided to rejoin the military. He wanted to do something in education. He signed on as an officer in the Gadna (pre-military youth movement) and thought he had found his calling until Fedale, now the commander of the 188th Brigade, called to inform him, "Avner, you are coming with me, I need a company commander."

In December 1972, at the age of twenty-seven, older than all the other officers except for the battalion commander, he was assigned to be the company commander of B Company with young, professional commanders.

As in every group, especially a closed and young one like the commanders of the brigade, everyone had a role set by the members of the group. Landau, seven years older than his platoon commanders, was considered to be "the old man." They did not understand his past in the Gadna youth movement.

In A Company, things were very calm. The short distance from the battalion to the Hahazit building enabled them to take it easy and take a well-paved route.

The company was very happy, not because of the impending battles, but because of the good relations that developed between the new commanders after the difficulties and mistrust at the start. The new commanders that replaced those injured in the accident were accepted and things were going well.

Company commander Lt. Zvika Rak leaned on the wall of his office and watched the integration taking place in front of his eyes. David Eiland was warmly welcomed by the crew of Tzachki Sarig, the injured commander of 2nd Platoon. Nimrod Kochavi was also warmly accepted by the crew of Yossi Gvili, the injured commander of 3rd Platoon. He wondered to himself how well this integration would work when battle came.

Zvika Rak (as he would say when he arrived, "It is just Zvika") was twenty-six and a half years old, from the Magach[16] tanks. He had fought in the Six-Day War while still partaking in the tank commanders

---

16. Literally "battering ram," the Israeli designation for any version of the US Patton tank.

course. In early 1972, tired of the distance he had to travel from Sinai, "his place of work," to his home in Haifa, he asked to be transferred to the Northern Command.

Immediately upon joining the brigade, without any knowledge or experience of Sho't Kal tanks, he was appointed commander of A Company. With a little help from his friends, mostly officers of his company, he made the transition successfully and amazed everyone in his ability to teach himself.

This, however, was not good enough for Lt. Col. Yossi Ben Hanan, the battalion commander. In January 1973, he decided to dismiss him from the battalion. On the last day of the brigade's fighting that took place that month, just days before he was to be dismissed, Zvika fought alongside Yair Nafshi, the commanding officer of the 74th, who was very impressed by him.

"Don't let him go," Nafshi told Ben Hanan, "he is excellent."

Ben Hanan agreed but still, unsure of his decision, he passed on this sense of dissatisfaction to Oded Erez, the new commander, who did not fight to keep Zvika in the battalion.

Zvika had no intention of staying where he was not wanted and in September 1973 he acquiesced to leaving. He was offered the position of operations officer in the reserve brigade. Once again it was Nafshi who intervened on his behalf. "Don't let him go," he said again and praised him unstintingly, this time to Ben Shoham, the brigade commander.

"Stay on as a company commander and you will get the newest jeep in the brigade," Ben Shoham tried to convince Rak in his interview in his office.

"I'll take it," agreed Zvika straight away.

It was more than the jeep that kept Rak in the brigade. It was also the feeling that something big was about to happen. If you are an officer in the standing army, looking ahead at a military career, there is no way you will pass up putting combat experience into your personal file and getting some blood on your black army boots.

Thursday, October 4

The Intelligence Directorate Research Division received information regarding Soviet transport planes landing in Syria and later, that same day, in Egypt. In both countries, there was a quick, unexplained evacuation of the families of the Soviet advisors.

Haim Yaabetz, the head of the Superpower Branch in the Research Division (branch 3) determined that the quick evacuation had two possible explanations. The first alternative, judged to be more likely, was that there was a crisis in relations between the Soviet Union, Egypt and Syria. The second option, with lower probability, was that hostilities were to be launched and that is why the civilians are being evacuated.

Hagai Mann received the information of the evacuation of the Soviet advisors' families and immediately told Haka, "We are close to war." Haka took the information seriously. He sent combat engineering troops to mine the more problematic gaps. Between 08:00 and 23:00, mine fields were laid to the north and south of strongholds 105, 104, and 110 and east of the Petroleum Road.

On that same day, Hagai received additional intelligence, according to which the villagers in the area of the Syrians southern 5th Division received clear instructions from the Syrian military, "From Friday, October 5, you are not to move near the border, including agricultural work and grazing animals."

Hagai Mann passed this news on to Haka and added his own analysis, "This is the first crystal clear indication of the intention of the 5th Division to attack. We have a problematic front. We also have an indication of the time frame; starting Friday. It is also possible that the source that gave us this information is quicker than his counterparts on other fronts (if there are any) and this may be the plan for the entire front."

That night, Zvi Zamir, the Director of the Mossad, was called urgently to London. The urgent trip came as a result of an agreed code used by "Babylon," the most important agent the Foreign Intelligence agency had. The code had only one meaning – a warning that there was going to be war. Zamir notified Gen. Eli Zeira, the Head of the Intelligence Directorate, of his trip. In return, Zeira informed him of the evacuation of the families of the Soviet advisors.

In the Hahazit building, North of Quneitra, Eiland was extremely happy. Tzachki Sarig's platoon accepted him warmly and he had finally won back his lost place in the armored corps. Once again he was full of enthusiasm.

On Thursday, October 4, he was allowed to take a short leave at home. He had an amazing crew, outstanding soldiers, but there still was no place like home.

In the evening, as Eiland was on his way home for Yom Kippur, a new order was sent out in the 188th Brigade, "Tank crew members can take leave, providing the necessary measures are taken to ensure their quick return to their units, if necessary." Before homesick tank crews started going home, a new announcement came, "This is just a tentative permission," the important people in Operations determined, "the final approval, perhaps a cancellation, will come in the morning."

While the soldiers awaited the verdict on their leave, the senior officers were in Ben Shoham's office, smiling and confident. Ben Shoham conducted a brigade-level briefing, informing the battalion commanders of the distribution of fronts and the internal organization between the battalion commanders and their deputy commanders.

Toward the end of the meeting, the artillery assistance plan was presented and it was stated once again that the 77th is a reserve force for attacks in the area. "Guys," Ben Shoham said in summary, "Be prepared for battle. At the most it will be an attempt to carry out a small attack," and he sent off his elite team of commanders.

INDICATIONS OF WAR

Friday, October 5, the Eve of Yom Kippur

04:10

the Operations Branch declares a "Lock Down;" all planned leaves are about to be cancelled. The final decision would be made by 10:00.

05:00

with the darkness of night slowly ebbing away and the sky in the east turning red with the first rays of light tentatively illuminating the basalt hills of the Golan, Friday morning began.

In the tank camps scattered throughout the Golan, the officers and men began their tired routine of "Dawn Alert." This morning, however, things were a bit tenser, since the assessment of the higher ranks was that a combat day was expected soon, maybe even a Syrian attempt to launch a small attack.

The main concern of the soldiers, however, on that Friday of October 5, 1973, was still whether they would be released to spend the weekend at home or not.

08:25

A meeting took place in the office of the Chief of General Staff, with Dado himself, his deputy, Gen. Yisrael Tal, Gen. Eli Zeira, Head of the Intelligence Directorate, and Gen. Benny Peled, Air Force Commander.

Dado received the reports regarding the evacuation of the families of the Soviet advisors and he immediately approved the "Lock Down" already declared by the Operations Division. The Chief of General Staff did not leave it at that and added further orders:

- The air force is to go on full alert and all leave is cancelled.

- All tank crewmembers who were on leave are to report back to their bases immediately.
- Immediate reinforcements from the regular armored forces will be sent to the fronts in the north and the south.
- For the first time since the Six-Day War, the "State of Alert C" will be declared – activating the mechanism to mobilize all of the reserve forces.[17]

09:00

The entire forum that was in the meeting in the office of the Chief of General Staff moved to the office of the Defense Minister, where they convened for their weekly meeting. In addition to Dayan and the military personnel, there were also a number of civilians attending the meeting. These were officials from the Ministry of Defense: directors, assistants and advisors.

Dado started the meeting with a report of the discussion just held in his office and the decisions made. Zeira then gave them an update, saying that the only thing that had changed on the ground was the evacuation of the families of the Soviet advisors. He said he did not know the exact reason they left but he continued to state his position that the probability of war was low, "even lower than low."

In spite of all the indications of war, there was still a state of euphoria from the Six-Day War. The entrenched position of the political and military leaders was a result of the feeling that "no one can beat us." During this discussion, Dayan presented his position, "Normally we would have let the Arabs attack in order to teach them a lesson."

Even as late as Friday morning, the mass Egyptian and Syrian forces prepared for battle within spitting distance of the borders with Israel did not shake any of Dayan's confidence. Why would it? The army officials kept repeating to the decision makers how important the tanks in the field were. They called their fondness for the armored vehicle "the totality of the tank." "Give me twenty-four hours and I will conquer Damascus," said Fedale, and this became a mantra in the offices of the

---

17. To this day, almost every soldier who has served in the IDF is theoretically liable for regular and emergency reserve duty up to the age of forty.

country's leaders, strongly affecting the decisions made on the eve of Yom Kippur 1973.

09:00

Zvika Rak, A company commanding officer in battalion 53 who had just gotten married, decided to make a short visit back home. It was a short trip to nearby Tzfat (Safed). On his way out, he passed through the headquarters of the battalion in Aleika and discovered that his commander, Oded Erez, was in a meeting at the brigade offices. "There is a state of alert," Erez notified him, leaving the meeting for a minute to update him. "We need to bring back all the crew members that are on Yom Kippur leave."

The door of the Shaham family in Zahala opens and in walks Eyal and his wife Miki. "This is just a short visit, I have to get back to the company," he said. They sit down and talk, and Eyal's mother Gila had the feeling that he was hiding something. Suddenly she noticed he had a new rank on his shoulders, Captain.

"Don't let him move, I am coming," begged his father Zonik upon receiving the news. He entered, examining his boy from head to toe, gave him a manly slap on the back and invited him to a drink.

"I can't Dad," Eyal was forced to apologize, "I have to get back to the company. Next time."

Gila walked him to the jeep. "Take care of yourself," she urged him, referring – of course – to the drive north.

It was a regular Friday in Ben Shoham's office, just as it was for the soldiers in the field. The brigade commander knew nothing of the clear intelligence warnings of war. They did receive an order from the Northern Command to cancel any leave from 11:00 a.m. but this was not an unusual order on the Golan, especially since there had been talk of a combat day for over a week and the forces were waiting in a state of alert and anticipation.

10:30

The forum that had attended the meeting in the Defense Minister's office now moved to the Prime Minister's office. They had not made any significant decisions in the meeting. The only operational decision was Dayan's decision to recommend to Prime Minister Meir that she convey a message to the Soviet Union, through the Americans. They were to be told that, on the one hand, Israel does not intend to attack the Arabs, and on the other, is aware of the preparations Egypt and Syria are taking.

Zeira started the meeting by explaining the current situation, sticking with the interpretation the Intelligence Directorate presented all along: Egypt and Syria are afraid we are going to attack. Why? Because they are always afraid, and also due to the Paratroopers exercise and the partial mobilization drill on the Golan, along with statements made by decision makers in various public forums.

His summary was that "an Egyptian-Syrian attack is very unlikely. However, perhaps the Russians think that they are about to attack because they do not know the Arabs well."

In his book *The Watchman Fell Asleep*, Dr. Uri Bar Joseph analyzes this statement of the Head of the Intelligence Directorate:

> *If there is one statement that sums it all up, on the verge of the volcano's eruption – the intellectual arrogance, the over-exaggerated self-confidence and the disregard of the opinions of others – this is it. What did Zeira actually say to the Prime Minister, the Defense Minister and the Chief of Staff? It is true that the Soviets have a large deployment of military advisors and training in Syria and Egypt, and that there are Soviet military officials in the control and command centers and throughout the military industry, especially in Syria. For years, Moscow has been supplying these two countries with all their arms. In times of trouble, they turned and will turn to the Soviets to send forces to help them. There is an alliance and collaboration agreement between the countries, with a clause that calls for them to consult each other in times when their security is in danger. It is elementary that the two states will notify their patron of their intention of going to war, since they know they will need its assistance and may even ask for the support of its forces. But, in spite of all of this, there is no cause for concern. Because we [the intelligence branch] have better intelligence and we know they [the Russians] are wrong to think that Syria and Egypt are heading to war.*

At the end of the meeting, Dayan asked Golda for her approval to call an emergency government meeting an hour later. "We will conduct the meeting with the ministers that are available," he suggested.

11:00

At the Filon base near Rosh Pina: The senior commanders of the 188th Brigade – brigade commander Ben Shoham, Yisraeli the deputy brigade commander, Nafshi the commanding officer the 74th, Erez, the commanding officer of the 53rd – sat back on the plastic chairs in the office of their boss, the commander of the 36th Division, Gen. Rafael Eitan (Raful).

The commanders were honored to be sitting in this meeting with their legendary divisional commander, listening to the battle stories he told them. They then discussed the current situation and did not hear any statement that would lead to battle cries all across the front. What they heard was of the option of a short round of fighting in a comfortable – even deluxe – war. They did not see any need to discuss defense in place, a second line of defense, flexible defense, or containing battles and other professional jargon terms from commanders' courses.

On Friday afternoon the commanders of the 188th Brigade, along with the senior commanders of the IDF, believed that the moment the war would start, if it started, they would block the attack immediately and turn it around into a counterattack, chasing the enemy forces and crushing them. Therefore, the only plan relevant to them was this, "In no case do we retreat from the Purple Line and we strike the Syrian forces until our reserve forces arrive."

11:30

The government ministers that were available and in the Tel Aviv area, convened for an emergency meeting in the Prime Minister's office. Joining Golda and Dayan were ministers Bar Lev,[18] Hillel,[19] Hazani,[20]

---

18. Chaim Bar Lev, Minister of Trade and Industry.
19. Shlomo Hillel, Minister of Police.
20. Michael Hazani, Minister of Welfare.

Peres[21] and Galili.[22] Seventeen ministers could not be located or could not make it at such short notice.

Dayan opened the meeting in a minor key, explaining why they had not notified them of the incidents of the last few days and why things had changed. "Last night we received information that has changed our negative assessment of the previous information (that Egypt and Syria are preparing to renew the war on both fronts)."

What Dayan was actually saying was, until now we have not updated you in order not to bother you with all the details. There are increasing enemy forces on Israel's borders. Leave it to us, the security experts. We will take care of it. When there is a reason to update you, we will, just as we are doing now.

What Dayan forgot was that the government of Israel was not a group of marionettes. The 15th government had intelligent, independent, thinking people, no less knowledgeable than the "security experts." Had this government been notified when it should have been, in a forum of all the ministers, they may have been able to sweep aside the veil of arrogance, to remove the blindfold over the eyes of the experts and point the army in the right direction.

After Dayan completed his briefing, Eli Zeira presented a detailed intelligence report that ended with him saying, "We still consider the Syrian and Egyptian state of alert to be a result of their fear of an attack by us and it is less probable that they intend to carry out a limited attack."

Yisrael Galili, a former head of staff for the Haganah, a political Hawk, led a discussion on the mobilization of reserve forces and asked to authorize the Prime Minister and/or the Defense Minister to carry out such a mobilization during Yom Kippur, should there be an urgent need, without it being possible to convene the government.

The ministers present agreed and Galili added to the protocol, "On May 15, 1967 all the prophets and experts said that we would have two years without war and war broke out in June..."

The ministers attending the meeting did not receive the Intelligence Directorate report regarding the state of alert and the military action of

---

21. Shimon Peres, Minister of Transportation.
22. Yisrael Galili, minister without portfolio.

the Egyptian and Syrian armies as of 10:00 a.m. that morning. The report stated, among other things, that "the Syrian officers and soldiers believe there is going to be large-scale combat." The Chief of Staff was aware of Dayan's objection to mobilizing reserve troops on the eve of Yom Kippur and did not propose it. Since Dayan did not see any reason for it and relied on Eli Zeira's intelligence report, according to which "the probability of combat was low," the government meeting ended slightly after noon without the decision to mobilize the reserves, even partially.

12:00

Maj. Aharon Vardi, Operations Officer of the Northern Command, issued an order called "Ashur-2," defining the protocol for the armored corps and artillery reinforcements moving to the Golan. This included their deployment on the ground, the location of the headquarters and the medical team. The protocol presented the responsibility of the two armored brigades, the 188th and the 7th:

> *The 188th Brigade is on alert for local attacks, according to the Barak code map.*
> *The 7th Brigade is on alert for major attacks, according to the following priorities:*
>
> *1. The Quneitra gap*
> *2. The Rafid gap*
> *3. The Petroleum Road*
> *4. The areas of strongholds 104–105 and 105–107*

12:15

The Chief of General Staff decided to take an irregular action. Gen. Benny Peled, the Air Force Commander, was asked to present the number of reserve troops needed to bring the air force to full alert. Peled gave the number of several thousand. Without receiving the approval of the Defense Minister, Dado approved their mobilization.

12:30

A meeting of the General Staff in Tel Aviv. Gen. Zeira notified the forum of the developments with the families of the Soviet advisors. He said there are more questions than there had been twenty-four hours earlier and "the probability of war initiated by Egypt and Syria is still very low... in summary, there is no reason to think we are heading toward war."

14:30
The Northern Command, Nazareth. Haka was very troubled by the evacuation of the families in Syria and affected by the seriousness of the action taken by the General Staff in sending reinforcements to the Golan. He arrived at his office and ordered his staff to prepare to head to the operational command post in Nafah in the Golan Heights.

15:00
The Northern Command tactical command officers left Nazareth and headed toward the command post bunker at Nafah. Yitzchak Hofi (Haka), the commander of the Northern Command; Uri Simchoni, the operations officer; Hagai Mann, the intelligence officer; Avraham Bar David, the command's artillery officer; and Avraham Kayam, the communications officer, all got into their vehicles with their own concerns regarding what was about to happen and headed up the winding road between the Bnot Yaakov Bridge and Nafah.

While the officers made their way to the headquarters, Ben Shoham, who had just returned from the division headquarters, issued a series of commands to the battalion commanders and all the staff officers of the two armored brigades on the Golan. The situation evaluation was still the same – "a combat day, a small attack at the most."

During the afternoon, information was received at the Intelligence Research Division that "the evacuation of the families of the Soviet advisors from Egypt and Syria took place because war was about to break out between Israel, Egypt and Syria." This information was not transferred to the Northern Command intelligence officer who was on his way to the Nafah headquarters at the time.

On Friday, in response to the Ashur-2 command, sixty additional tank crews were sent toward the Golan. The first to arrive at the Filon war reserve storage base near Rosh Pina, were the last three companies of the 82nd Battalion. They began preparing the tanks of the 179th Reserve Brigade. In the evening, the tank crews of the 71st Battalion also arrived at Filon, completing the sixty tank crews sent as reinforcements.

The 71st Battalion was officially part of the armored corps training school but only formally. This was a Corps reserve battalion, staffed mainly by the soldiers in the armored corps officer training course and the staff of the training school and Facility 500 (the training base for reserve units at Ze'elim). Lt. Col. Meshulam Ratess, commander of the company commander's course, would be commander of the "Virtual Battalion," if it was ever activated.

Along with the armored corps soldiers, three additional artillery batteries also made their way to the Golan. These were from the artillery training school battalion, commanded by Lt. Col. Ben Ami Cohen.

Friday night, the Filon base

While the tanks were being prepared and equipped, Yanush arrived at the war reserve storage base and notified Haim Barak, the commander of the 82nd Battalion, "Once the preparations are completed, deploy the battalion at the Sindiyana training area, to the east of Nafah. Once you are there, get ready to continue training the companies."

Yanush continued, "I am staying with Zamir (the commander of the fourth company of the 82nd who was sent to the Golan a week earlier) as a brigade reserve force. You will only be commanding these three companies."

Friday night, 74th Battalion

The lights were on in the office of the battalion commander. "Tomorrow we are expecting a combat day," said Nafshi. He saw that this did not make an impact, so he added, "It may be a more significant combat day than usual. Maybe even an attempt to grab some ground."

Zvika Rak was still pumped up with adrenalin from the command group meeting. He assembled his officers in the company assembly area in Quneitra. Attending were his deputy, Oded Yisraeli; 1st Platoon leader Haim Damir, who had survived the car accident; Nimrod Kochavi, who had replaced Yossi Gvili as 3rd Platoon leader; Yossi Zamri, who was about to replace Oded Yisraeli the following week; and David Eiland, replacing Tzachki Sarig as 2nd platoon leader, just returning from a short leave at home.

Earlier, after buying himself the latest Pink Floyd and Deep Purple records that afternoon, David Eiland had parked his mother Esther's "White Princess" outside his home (a slow, 2-cylinder, white NSU Prinz car with a maximum speed of 80 km/h). He heard her speaking on the phone in an uncharacteristic soprano voice, "I'll tell him when he comes."

"The army called," she told him. "They want you to come back immediately. There is an alert."

"Bullshit," he answered in anger. "That is a load of crap."

In the evening, he took the white Prinz and set out on his way. The car climbed up the hills, groaning and moaning and eventually reached the Golan. When he arrived at Aleika, he was taken by jeep to Quneitra, to the Hahazit building where A company was assembling .

Six young officers sat there. In civilian terms, they were just boys.

"Tomorrow we are expecting a combat day," Zvika told the five commanders in the room he called his office. His room had an unmade field bed, an armored corps soldier's combat vest hanging on a nail in the wall, a map of the area and a clean, ironed overall. "The Syrians are going to try to carry out a ground operation. We will stop them and respond with our own maneuver on the ground," he said with confidence.

None of the boys in uniform responded with any drama beyond the accepted mumble. After going over what was required in this situation, perhaps due to the holiday spirit, they remained seated in the room, enjoying the comradery developing in the Hahazit building.

First Lt. David Eiland, who considered himself to be someone who knew about music, proudly took out the records he had brought from home. He was very surprised at the knowledge Nimrod Kochavi displayed regarding music. It was one thing that Kochavi was a blond heart-breaker with the girls, a perfect professional, with the most knowledge in the brigade; now he has to be the expert on contemporary music as well? Even in this field, he has to outdo me?

That Friday night there was a consensus at Nafah that there would be a routine combat day the following day. Haka heard warning bells ringing in his ears and was agitated and restless. A few minutes later, he sent out an order, "Simchoni, have the Golan combat engineering battalion spend the night laying out chains of anti-tank mines along the Quneitra gap."

Around 23:00, with the combat engineers on their way and Haka regaining his calm, the Northern Command staff officers made their way to the guest house in Ayelet Hashachar, getting ready to catch some sleep.

Saturday, October 6, Yom Kippur

02:40

On the night between Friday and Saturday, Zvi Zamir, the Mossad Director, sent out a sign of life. Almost twenty hours after he had left the country, his office received notification that his source "Babylon," Israel's most important agent in history, had informed him, "Today (Saturday) at 18:00 Syria and Egypt will launch an all-out war against Israel."

03:40

The information reached the Prime Minister's military secretary, who sent it out to the defense forces.

As if a warning of war had not just been issued, the Intelligence Directorate released a report saying that "all the activity on the Syrian front is for defensive purposes only."

Manifestations of War

04:30

The information from "Babylon" finally reached the Chief of Staff at his home in Zahala. Dado jumped out of bed, rushing through his morning activities. For the first time he began to realize that as hard as it was to grasp, the Intelligence Directorate had been mistaken all along.

It no longer matters what Zeira and his team of fools say, Dado thought to himself. Now was the time to run, without stopping for anything. He had to get the country and the army ready for war, within this impossible timeframe.

Early Morning

At the forward tank depot areas of the 74th Battalion of the 188th Brigade, the on-call tank crews got into the tanks, in a dawn alert drill longer than usual. Everyone was waiting for the moment they could take their boots off, airing out the stench after having had them on all night.

Sleeping with your boots on becomes second nature for soldiers on the front. The order to sleep with their boots on came often. At the end of the day, it is pretty annoying to sleep with your boots on.

In this reality, in order to help them to rest and remain calm, or just to be prepared for any surprises – perhaps a surprise inspection from the restless "brass" – the armored corps soldiers came up with the idea of the zipper on the side of the army boot. That way it was possible to keep the laces tied and in place, and with hardly any notice the soldier was ready with his boots on, the rubber band on his ankle. Commanders lacked X-ray vision to see if the soldier was wearing socks or not.

05:10

By now, Dado is wide awake. He leans forward on his simple chair in his office. With him is his deputy, Gen. Tal, and they are in war mode. They discuss the option of a preemptive strike by the air force, mobilizing the reserves, preparations on the front lines and evacuating part of the civilian population from the Golan.

05:30

Dado summons a meeting of a limited number of the General Staff. He authorizes Benny Peled to prepare to mobilize all the reserve units and he gives the order to carry out all preparations for a general mobilization, so that it can be carried out as soon as there is approval from the government.

Haka's executive officer calls Hagai Mann to the general's room in the guest house. "Remember the information you received on the 1st that turned out to be a drill? Zvika Zamir received the same information from his source in Europe. According to the source, this time it is definitely war."

***

The first rays of sun appear on the Golan. The soldiers of the reserve companies of the 188th Brigade, scattered throughout the Golan, wake lazily to a long and slow morning. There is no activity on the tanks, the crews just relax, read the paper and pass the time.

Not only there. Hundreds of kilometers south of there, the soldiers of the 68th Brigade, the Jerusalem reserve brigade responsible for the defense of the Bar-Lev line, on the banks of the Suez Canal, awake to a regular day only slightly more tense than usual. "Be alert, there may be shooting. The air force is taking photos and the Egyptians may respond with fire." At 11:30, the alert was lifted. "Back to routine." The reserve soldiers came out to enjoy the warm sun. Some of them join the regular morning prayers in the improvised synagogues on the bases.

05:45

Hagai Mann calls the Command in Nazareth and speaks to his deputy, Maj. Shlomo Tagner. Nothing. They have not received any information from intelligence about the war. Not on the phone, not on the teleprinter, nothing.

05:50

Haka prepares to fly to Hakiryah in Tel Aviv. The Command team prepares to head to Nafah.

* * *

In Yair Nafshi's 74th Battalion there is no information about war. Even so, Nafshi decides to go into the field and see for himself if all the forward positions are alert and ready. Joined by Danny Avni, the operations officer, they drive south, planning to begin with the two companies of the 74th Battalion under the command of the 53rd Battalion, led by Oded Erez.

05:55

Avner Landau, the Commander of B Company, takes Asaf Sela, his deputy, along as he sets out to check how prepared their company is at the Manzura junction (code named "Yakir-Carton"), "just in case should something happen." They tour the area, reach Bukata, and head east on the road leading to the border road, making sure everything is still in place, as they remembered it from the last time they were there.

06:00

In the office of the Defense Minister in Hakiryah, the Chief of General Staff brings up the matter of the preemptive strike by the air force. Such a strike, he says, is more crucial now than ever, because IDF ground forces are not prepared for war. In response, Dayan fixes his one eye on him and without hesitation rejects the suggestion. Dado, with one of his hands just tied behind his back, decides to see where the response of the Defense Minister to his second request will lead, before he fights for the first request.

"I want to mobilize 200,000 soldiers,"[23] Dado continues.

Dayan looks at him with amusement, not believing his ears. "Twenty to thirty thousand only," he declares.

06:30

Avner Landau leaves the border fence area and heads back toward Bukata, in a rush to get Asaf Sela back to the company and return to forward tank depot 104 before 08:00, when there is to be a meeting of all the company commanders with Hofi, the Northern Command commanding officer.

* * *

Nafshi, the battalion commander, and Avni, the operations officer, arrive at forward tank depot 116, the most southerly tank depot on the Golan. There they find the platoon of Yoav Yakir, of F Company, 74th Battalion. Nafshi gets the impression that they are all ready and he encourages the soldiers to break the Yom Kippur fast. "You need to have energy for the combat day that is about to start." Just before leaving, he approaches Nir Atir, the veteran sergeant, and says in his ear, "It looks like you are going to mark another combat day on your gun. Let's see what you get us this time." Then he gets into his jeep and speeds off to the north.

07:15

A meeting of the General Staff in Hakiryah. The Head of the Intelligence Directorate gives an update on the latest information from the source in London. He speaks of the rushed evacuation of the Soviets, says he does not know the reason for it and sums it up by saying that he sees no need to change in the basic assessment; despite the concrete warning, he does not think that the Syrians and Egyptians are attacking. Even so,

---

23. This would be almost the entire reserve.

he agrees, since there is some doubt, the precautionary measures taken are justified.

07:30

Avner Landau is back at the Manzura junction again and together with Zvika Rak, commander of A Company, they head toward the Druze village of Mas'ade to pick up Eyal Shaham, commander of H Company. Three company commanders, full of combat spirit, are heading toward forward tank depot 104 .

08:00

In the 3rd Platoon, the tank platoon farthest south on the Syrian front, the commanders implement the approval to break the fast. The table in the dining room of forward tank depot area 116 is filled with a mixture of IDF combat meals alongside the gourmet food the kibbutz soldiers had received from home. The soldiers eat with hearty appetites. Atir, the platoon sergeant, is there with everyone, but he is staring blankly, not focused.

It was easy for the members of Kibbutz Afikim to notice the change in Nir Atir, the emotional turmoil, how he was lost in thought, when he arrived on short leave, in the middle of the state of alert in late September. After they left him alone, still concerned about what caused this change, he started to talk.

In a long and emotional monologue, unlike the manner of the tough guys of the Jordan Valley, he explained the change to Efrat, his girlfriend from Kibbutz Deganya Bet. He told her:

> *The day before yesterday, Brigade Commander Ben Shoham and Prof. Zvi Yaavetz, the head of the history faculty at the Tel Aviv University, arrived without notifying us in advance.*
>
> *It turns out that Ben Shoham was a student and a fan of Prof. Yaavetz. He asked him to come to the Golan and give a lecture to the soldiers. He asked him to evaluate the mental state of the soldiers, to what extent values like Zionism, the homeland, sacrifice, were part of their DNA.*

Before leaving, the professor toured the tanks of the platoon and I heard him ask Ben Shoham how many tanks the Syrian enemy had on the front. Ben Shoham answered that in the entire region they had about 700, 500 of them here in the southern-Golan front. He then added with a smile that all the Syrians need to do is start their engines and drive.

Then the professor asked Yoav Yakir, the platoon leader, if his three tanks could face this mass. Yoav said with full confidence that they would stand until the reserves came.

Yaavetz did not leave it at that and turned to Andrei Sakal, a new immigrant from Hungary, asking him what the platoon's mission was. "We are here on the front to stop enemy forces until the reserves arrive."

"When will the reserve force arrive?" Yaavetz asked him. "Within twenty-four hours," Sakal replied. We would always repeat this whenever another nag came along and tested us.

Yaavetz continued, "But how will you do that?"

"We know the battalion commander on the other side," Andrei said calmly. "We know what they know, and we have ranges to each target, but mainly, we are better than them."

Yaavetz was not satisfied with this. He may have been a history professor, but he saw the simple math of the relationship between the forces and the short two to three kilometer distance separating them, and he asked the big question. The question no one had ever asked us before.

"There are only three of your tanks, facing 500 Syrian tanks. Even if you somehow hit and destroy every target with your first shot, a simple calculation of 72 shells per tank with three tanks, does not add up here."

Sakal responded calmly, "Don't worry, we will stand until the reserves arrive." He saw that the professor was uneasy, and in order to reassure him he added, "It will not be easy, professor, but we are good enough. We will manage to deal with it."

Nir stopped and leaned back. This was the first time since they were together that Efrat saw her wild boyfriend in distress. He then seemed to relax and they did what young men and women do when they need each other.

In the morning, still in bed, postponing his return to the base, Nir was in distress again and said, "We are very good but I am not sure we will be able to stop this huge mass. I thought about what the professor said, and he is right. If we are not reinforced now, before it all starts, it is very likely that if it develops into something more serious than a combat day, we will not be able to block them. We have no chance. After they finish us off, the path to Deganya and Afikim will be open to them. It will be like in the War of Independence. You will have to prepare Molotov cocktails again."

Efrat looked at her boyfriend with the same affection women have always had for a hesitant man in uniform, caressed his head and, as Andrei Sakal and Yoav Yakir said, whispered in his ear, "You are good enough, you'll see, everything will be fine."

08:05

The first meeting of the day in the Prime Minister's office. Present were Yisrael Galili, Haim Bar Lev, Dado, Zeira and, of course, Golda. Dayan began his briefing with the policy in the West Bank... he then remembered that the Syrian army was ready to act on the border in the Golan and recommended that civilians be evacuated from the area. "There are thirty children on the Golan. This afternoon or evening we will suggest sending the children on a trip, to get them away from there."

Then they came to the meat of the meeting, the need for Golda to make urgent decisions in matters relating to Israel's existence. The defense minister on one side and the chief of staff on the other presented their arguments in favor and against a preemptive strike and mobilization of the reserves.

Based on the intelligence we have, Dayan said, and the assessment of the Military Intelligence Directorate sent to the Americans, according to which Syria and Egypt do not intend to attack, we cannot fire first. Regarding the mobilization of the reserves, my position is that we should only mobilize the forces we need for defense. There is no need for more than 50,000 soldiers.

In response, Dado said that the warning received that morning has changed the possibility of war into a certainty. Therefore, the effects on world opinion, of whether the mobilization is limited or full, are irrelevant. Either way, they will characterize any Israeli mobilization as aggression.

Golda listened to both of them intently and decided that in the matter of the preemptive strike they have no choice but to accept Dayan's recommendation. She was then unsure whether to approve a full or partial mobilization. Twenty minutes later, Dayan surprisingly withdrew and said that "he would not lie down on the road if there was a larger mobilization." Golda approved calling up as many as 120,000 reserves.

08:30

On that Yom Kippur of 1973, as in every year throughout the generations, the State of Israel was engaged in the regular process in which the Jewish people – with different levels of faith – repented for their sins.

That weekend, thousands of ultra-Orthodox Jews had demonstrated to demand the preservation of ancient Jewish graves found beneath the parking lot of the Panorama Hotel in Tiberias. The less ultra-Orthodox and traditional Jews agreed with the words of Rabbi Isser Frankel in the *Haaretz* paper, "This [festival of] Yom Kippur gives us back our mental balance."

Public debate focused, not on the Syrian and Egyptian fronts, but on the Palestinian threat and the Lebanese border that was slowly bleeding. The secular population in Israel and many of the soldiers of the 188th Brigade were much more interested in the big soccer game between Hapoel Tel Aviv and Hapoel Petach Tikvah.

＊＊＊

On the outskirts of the Manfucha hills, at forward tank depot 104, the farthest north in the Golan, routine activity continued. David Amsalem, the loader, and Shlomo Yifrach, the driver, the religiously traditional soldiers in Platoon 2, were trying to blow the shofar they had received for the holidays. They did not blow it very well. No one bothered to warn them about the fire-spitting dragon that was about to attack them.

* * *

Maj. Yossi Nissim, deputy commanding officer of the 74th Battalion, made the rounds of the platoons on the northern sector of the northern front. He was very impressed by the attempts of Yifrach and Amsalem to blow the shofar. He continued to the platoon of Lt. Muli Dgani, 1st platoon leader in forward tank depot 105, and tried his best to sound serious. It was important to him that the young crews understand the seriousness of the situation. He too did not mention war, however, since no one had told him.

* * *

In the offices of the 188th Brigade at Aleika, Hadassah Weiss, the office secretary, sees off brigade commander Ben Shoham, his deputy David Yisraeli and the intelligence officer Moshe Zurich, who are going to visit the tank companies on the front.

09:00

The three company commanders of the northern front are notified that the general is not going to make it to the meeting. They take the opportunity to stop in at stronghold 104, the infantry base, to take a look at the Syrian forces. All they see is Syrian farmers and pastoral views. Yom Kippur never seemed so peaceful.

09:15

Haka had been updated by the Deputy Chief of General Staff, Gen. Yisrael Tal, that mobilization of reserves has been approved. Haka then called Lt. Col. Uri Simchoni, the Northern Command operations officer, and notified him that he is about to head back to Nafah. He instructs him to send out the call to prepare for an immediate mobilization of the Northern Command reserves and to issue an immediate call to evacuate the women and children from the Golan settlements. "I will be in the forward command group at about 10," he tells Simchoni. "Make sure that Raful and all the brigade commanders are there to receive orders." A few minutes later, the 36th Division receive the "Prepare for Basalt" order (the code name for the emergency mobilization of reserve forces).

09:30

At the building at Quneitra, there is a last-minute change. Yossi Zamri refuses to be left without a tank. He takes the tank from Eiland and his crew and becomes their commander.

Two sergeants had been removed from platoon 2, Avi Rotem due to an injury and Itzik Hamo due to the decision of deputy battalion commander Maj. Askarov to take him as his gunner. This meant that two tanks in the company were without commanders. Eiland considered Zamri's veteran status and his position as an instructor in the officer's course and accepted the request. The platoon now had two officers; Zamri got the tactical designation and call sign 2 and Eiland 2A.

On Saturday morning, the young officer, David Eiland, took command of a crew of three veteran soldiers who had been together for a year and a half, and had experience of fighting battles in Lebanon.

The crew (who were of course, themselves, just boys) examined the skinny, distant and shy character and, surprisingly, accepted him with open hearts.

Dror Sofer and the command APC (armored personnel carrier) of the 188th Brigade arrive at Nafah.

Two hours earlier David Yisraeli, the deputy brigade commander, had ordered Uzi Arieli, the commander of Company C, to take the technical crews' new armored personnel carrier and send it to Nafah immediately, without its equipment. It was to be prepared to be the brigade commander's vehicle. Dror Sofer, a tank commander waiting to be assigned, was detailed to drive it.

Dror didn't know if there was going to be a combat day or not, but he knows he needs to fulfill his duties as commander of the APC. He and the crew ran to the armory and took a 0.5 machine gun and two 0.3 Browning machine guns. Dror went to the food warehouse and filled the APC with combat rations. "The brigade commander needs to have enough food to command the battle and remain alert and well fed until dinner, when we all return to base," he thought.

As Dror debated what he was going to do with the communication equipment already in the carrier, Maj. Hanan Schwartz, the brigade communications officer, arrived and his team assembled all kinds of additional equipment in the APC.

10:00

The first thing Haka did when he returned from Tel Aviv was to notify Hagai Mann. "Dado and Benny Peled suggested carrying out a preemptive strike by the air force. I think they are still in a meeting with the Prime Minister on this. If the decision is approved, I will stay here. If not, the Chief of General Staff will summon me to present plans."

He then convened a command group. Present were Brigadier Gen. Raful Eitan, the division commander; Col. Itzik Ben Shoham, the 188th Brigade commander; Col. Yanush Ben Gal, commander of the 7th Brigade; Zvi Bar, commander of the 820th Brigade; Brigadier General Uri Brown, Head of the Northern Command staff; Lt. Col. Uri Simchoni, the operations officer; Lt. Col. Hagai Mann, the Command Intelligence officer; and Lt. Col. Avraham Bar David, the artillery commander.

"Dear Friends," he began. "According to confirmed information we have received, this evening at 18:00, general war is going to break out between Israel, Egypt and Syria." (This is the version as told by Gen. Hofi. There are other, contradictory versions, as we will see later.)

Hagai Mann detailed the status of the Syrian enemy, including its possible courses of action. He stated that, according to the evaluation he conducted with the general, the most dangerous possibility is an attack in the Quneitra region in the northern Golan. The danger is not due to the size of the force – the force in the south is bigger – but rather due to the topography that enables widespread and rapid tank movement. In addition, there was only a short distance from Quneitra to the Bnot Yaakov Bridge and the Jordan Valley. As a result of the evaluation of the situation, with every option still open, Yanush received an order to keep the 7th Brigade in its position as a reserve armored force for the command.

10:30

In Nafah the orders are still being given. The eight tanks of the deputy battalion commander Askarov formed one force. The three tanks of deputy company commander Davidson form the other. They are deployed outside the forward tank depot area in Hushnia, in the open space between there and Tel Fazra, facing East.

* * *

G Company 74th Battalion was the unit responsible for the central sector of the Golan front. Each of its platoons had its own forward tank depot and defense sector. To the north was H Company and to the south F Company.

In Company F the platoons were organized differently. The 2nd platoon, commanded by 2nd Lt. Doron Sadeh Lavan, was located in the forward tank depot area in the deployment camp inside Quneitra. There it was tasked to provide operational response around infantry stronghold 109. This area was part of the northern front, under the command of Yair Nafshi, commanding the 74th Battalion.

The other two platoons of G Company – 1st platoon, commanded by Danny Overlander, and 3rd platoon, commanded by Moty Amir – were with their company commander, Uri Akavia, and his deputy Lt. Yoni Davidson, in the Hushnia forward tank depot area.

On that Shabbat Yom Kippur, they were not alone. A kilometer west of them, the tanks of C Company of the 53rd Battalion had been deployed since Wednesday. Zeev Hochstein, the redheaded platoon commander of C Company was temporary assigned to G Company to be part of the Askarov force deployed outside the forward tank depot.

A kilometer to the west were the tanks of C Company, commanded by Uzi Arieli. Accompanying them were the artillery fire coordination officer's tank, the battalion commander's tank and the tank of the brigade commander. They all moved west, a few hundred meters out of the base. They spread out in a semicircle facing south, covered the tanks with camouflage nets and waited.

F Company is the force manning the southern front and its soldiers spent the holiday without any excitement or special preparations. The company was responsible for the area between stronghold 114 opposite the Rafid gap, behind Tel (mount) Fares, to 116, the stronghold farthest south in the Golan.

The tanks of platoon leader Avi Lachman were deployed in the forward tank depot behind stronghold 114. Outside stronghold 116, Yoav Yakir's platoon was in place at the forward tank depot. In the Juhader forward tank depot area, Nati Levi's platoon was deployed, along with the two tanks of the company commander Ronis and his deputy, 1st Lt. Netanel (Tani) Aharon, who was on leave at home, as well as an additional tank intended for the fire coordination officer.

At 10:30, the radio on the Juhader parking area comes to life with an order to tie on panels (panels that identify the tanks as "friendlies" for Israeli air force planes). The crews get them out and tie them on – a routine drill. No one is affected by this and most of the soldiers return to the rooms, dress, and doze off with their boots on. All of this is routine alert behavior for them.

2nd Lt. Yoni Maidovnik – the Golani brigade officer commanding infantry stronghold 104 in the northern Golan – suddenly notices that Syrian forces in his sector are removing their covers and camouflage nets. He reports this to Aviv Shir-On, commander of the 2nd Tank Platoon, who is with him in 104 forward tank depot area and to his direct commanders in Golani. Aviv passes on the report to Eyal Shaham, commander of H Company.

10:40

In the course of the meeting at Nafah, Haka verifies that the mobilization of the reserves has begun. He instructs Raful, commander of the 36th Division, to head to Filon base after the meeting and to personally supervise the mobilization of his brigades. He instructs Zvi Bar, the commander of the 820th Regional Brigade, to reinforce each of the infantry strongholds on the front with three to five additional soldiers and to start the evacuation of women and children from the civilian communities on the Golan.

10:45

Lt. Col. Finya Kuperman, deputy commander of the regional brigades, issues an alert to 1st Lt. Efraim Sarid, one of the two brigade operations officers. This directive confirms the order of the general regarding reinforcement of the bases (by redeploying all the troops from the reconnaissance units). Later, at 12:00, he will order the evacuation of the women and children. A platoon of soldiers from Golani is to be positioned in each settlement with the remaining civilians and that all troops not necessary for combat – the civilian coordination unit, women soldiers, and the coordination with the UN unit – be transferred beyond the Rosh Pina line. He also orders the Military Police to be ready to close off the Golan.

11:00

The Chief of Staff arrives at the office of the Defense Minister to update him. During their meeting, the following conversation took place (quoted from Hanoch Bartov's book):

> **Dayan:** *If the Arabs do not open fire, when will the reserves be released?*
>
> **Dado:** *If this matter is not but canceled completely, but postponed by a day or two, we will send the reserves home.*
>
> **Dayan:** *What happens if by the end of Yom Kippur, at midnight, it turns out there is no war?*
>
> **Dado:** *The reserves will not be released for at least 48 hours.*
>
> **Dayan:** *100,000 people will be wandering around for an entire day before they are sent home?*
>
> **Dado:** *They will not be "wandering around;" they will be going to the front. If it turns out there is no war, we will release them after 48 hours.*

This discussion is additional evidence of what we already know. Dayan, like the senior intelligence officers, still does not think war is certain at 11:00. Hours after receiving the data from "Babylon" he is still fighting against the mobilization of the reserves.

Yair Nafshi completes his tour of the front lines and arrives at the northern front sector. On the way, he passes through the tanks in forward tank depot 104. He picks up Aviv Shir-On and they enter infantry stronghold 104, to check on the reports themselves.

Nafshi takes a look in the 20x120 binoculars. He thinks he sees villagers heading out for their final grape harvesting. He then sees what Maidovnik was referring to – anti-tank missiles, tanks and armored personnel carriers out in the open.

"So what?" he thinks to himself. "It is not Yom Kippur for them, they are allowed."

Despite this initial response, he does not want to take a chance and orders all the company commanders to order their crews to be on their tanks and be alert. In addition, he orders the soldiers to break the fast in the company parking areas.

***

Avner Landau is on his way back to the company when he receives Nafshi's order and conveys it to Asaf Sela, who is with the company at the Wasset junction.

The soldiers and commanders reacted to Nafshi's order indifferently. Someone said war? It is just a combat day and we have already shown which side always wins such confrontations.

11:10

The senior officers of the Golan front come out of the meeting at Nafah with their orders. Raful gets in his vehicle and speeds down to Filon to speed up the preparation of his division and the mobilizations of the 9th, 679th and 179th Brigades.

Ben Shoham turns to the corner of the command operations room and calmly updates his battalion commanders – Nafshi in the north and Erez in the south. He speaks of a "day of expanded battle." He also says, "We are expecting something. We do not know what. Raise your level of alert regarding anti-aircraft. Be ready. Everyone should be in coveralls."

Yanush takes Ben Shoham aside, places a large hand on his shoulder and says, "Ben Shoham, please take the 82nd Battalion and give me back the 77th."

The Ashur-2 Operational Order that had been sent the previous night to the headquarters of the three regular brigades stated clearly, "The 77th Battalion will be under the command of the 7th Brigade, from Saturday at 06:00." Yanush does not have to apologize to anyone for his request, including Ben Shoham. The 77th Battalion is his. It is stated clearly in the order.

On Saturday morning, no one in the Northern Command knew how things would develop. How intense will the Syrian fire be? Where will they focus their effort? Will there be a number of attempts to break through in different areas? Will it be necessary to activate the 7th Brigade, or will the tanks of the 188th be enough to stop the attack? If the 7th Brigade is activated, will the Command send them out as an armored fist? In which direction – north or south? What if the Command decides to split up the battalions in different areas? Yanush, with experience of war, assumes that the Syrian attack will be across the entire front. He knows that his forces are closer to the northern front and that his brigade has already trained according to an existing Israeli counterattack plan. He therefore understands, that there is high probability that at some point in the combat, he will have to divide his battalions. If this is the situation, Yanush decides, the best is to have 77th Battalion with him.

He had three good reasons to want this:

First of all, it is led by Lt. Col. Avigdor Kahalani, the most experienced and admired battalion commander in the brigade. He has seen what Kahalani could do in the battles of the Six-Day War. In contrast, the commander of the 82nd, Maj. Haim Barak, was newly appointed.

Second, it is made up of soldiers who have just completed their training and were extremely professional. In contrast, although the 82nd Battalion has two operational companies, its other two companies are inexperienced and barely managed to pass the tank gunnery training course.

The third reason was that Kahalani and his men had already been on the Golan for ten days. Their familiarity with the front gave them a clear advantage over the 82nd. As the brigade commander, it was natural and logical for him to keep the best with him.

Ben Shoham agreed without hesitation.

11:30

Yanush comes to Sindiyana to update Haim Barak. "War today," he informs him. Since Barak's acquaintance with the Golan was limited to the main roads, he gladly agreed to join the brigade commander on a comprehensive tour of the region.

"One more thing, Haim," Yanush gives the young battalion commander a grave look, "make sure you are on time for the command group at 14:00 – in the Saar base (the regular base of the 74th, near division headquarters)."

Yanush is, once again, demonstrating how much control he likes, how hard it is for him as the brigade commander to "let his fledgling fly away." According to the agreement with Ben Shoham, the 82nd Battalion is supposed to be under the command of the 188th Brigade. Why isn't Yanush informing Barak, in their meeting in Sindiyana, of this agreement? Why is he summoning a meeting of the battalion commanders of the 7th Brigade in his office?

***

Haka is summoned to the General Staff in Tel Aviv again. The picture becomes clear to them. The air force cannot carry out a preemptive strike. A ground war is about to start.

Before leaving, Haka instructs operations officer Simchoni to notify Ben Shoham that from that moment until he returns from Tel Aviv, Ben Shoham is in command of the Golan front. He adds that from 14:00, the operational headquarters at Nafah shall be manned by the 188th Brigade commanders.

Why did Haka choose Ben Shoham to act in his place? Although Yanush was a more senior brigade commander, Ben Shoham was "his" brigade commander. Ben Shoham was the commander of the regular army brigade in the Northern Command, living the daily tensions of the front and the readiness of his forces. They understood each other and he preferred him to someone who had just joined the front, regardless of his seniority.

11:45

Maj. Benny Katzin, operations officer of the 188th Brigade, no longer wore the skullcap of an Orthodox Jew, but he was keeping Yom Kippur, according to all the Torah's laws. The urgency of the situation dawned on him, the knowledge that the 188th Brigade was responsible for the Golan, until the general's return. He immediately started transferring the headquarters of the 188th Brigade from Aleika to the bunker at Nafah.

* * *

Landau returns to the Wasset junction and is very impressed by the efforts of his deputy. He moved all the tank crews into place and had taken the initiative to position them outside the base, spread out facing east.

12:00

The government convenes for an emergency meeting. Fifteen of the twenty-one ministers are informed for the first time of what has been happening in the last few days. At this moment they were being asked to make one of the most important decisions in Israeli history with only partial information from Defense Minister Dayan regarding the events of the previous ten days and only just now hearing about the possibility that Egypt and Syria were going to start a war. Golda presented her reasons for not carrying out a preemptive strike and started a discussion on whether to attack Syria, even if only Egypt strikes.

Fourteen of the ministers were in complete shock. One minister, Finance Minister Pinchas Sapir, was furious. He was horrified and angry at the Prime Minister and Defense Minister for hiding the matter of war from the ministers, and now suddenly they want them to make a decision on such a crucial matter, with so little time?

* * *

Baluza in the Sinai; 300 kilometers from where the government is convened, 500 kilometers south of the tanks of the 188th Brigade and twenty-eight kilometers from the Suez Canal, headquarters of the Northern Tank Brigade, Sinai Division. At high noon on Shabbat, the brigade command group convenes. In attendance: Lt. Col. Amir Reuveni, commander of the 68th Reserve Infantry Battalion; Lt. Col. Yom Tov Tamir, commanding officer of the 9th Armored Battalion; Col. Pinchas Noy (Alush), commander of the 275th Regional Brigade, in charge of the northern front sector.

Alush had just returned from a briefing by the division commander, Maj. Gen. Avraham (Albert) Mendler. He tells the group:

> *The large Egyptian military drill continues. It may end at 18:00 with an opening of hostilities. Therefore, all units are to be deployed according to the "Shovach Yonim" command (defense positions on the waterline against firing from the Egyptian side), starting at 17:00. Move into positions along the canal no earlier than 16:00.*

Lt. Col. Yom Tov Tamir asked why they should not move into position immediately. Alush responded, "Immediate movement may cause an escalation when opening of hostilities is not certain." The battalion commander insisted on hearing the position of the division commander on this and got the same answer.

* * *

Yair Nafshi drops Aviv Shir-On at the forward tank depot and continues toward the Hermon base. It is from here that the reports of Syrian forces removing camouflage covers are originating. Shir-On notifies his platoon, "The Syrians have removed their nets. According to Nafshi's orders, we need to increase the level of alert."

Shir-On feels very confident. As far as he is concerned, he has the best platoon in the best company, in the best battalion, in the best brigade, in the best army in the world...

In the internal competition between the platoons on the front, Shir-On's had proven to be the finest. They were first by almost every measure. Not only did they get the best results in inspections, arms and even cleanliness of their posts, more importantly, they were the first to take up positions on the firing ramps. The 2nd Platoon was not only the best in their results, their forward tank depot was a happy place. Aviv was a much less intense and more relaxed platoon commander than the others. In spite of the usual tension of the armored corps and Fedale's heritage, in the 2nd there was a more relaxed atmosphere. Perhaps it was due to the veteran 1st Sgt., Koby Greenbaum, who knew how to keep things in proportion. Or the young commander, Sgt. Yossi Weissbart, an artist and musician, who had painted the walls of their post with graffiti, writing things like "The Order of the Nipple Knights" (named after the hill that was one of their firing positions).

Shir-On, however, had a dilemma. The forward tank depot protocol clearly stated that one of the crews should be on alert 24 hours a day, with coveralls and boots on at all times. The second crew would have the joy of sleeping without boots but wearing coveralls and the third crew would be allowed to wear "normal," i.e. civilian clothes. Now the question was what they were supposed to do, given the order to increase the level of alert?

Aviv decided to be original and ordered them to take their mattresses outside and to lay down next to the tanks in coveralls and boots. The soldiers took the mattresses, assessing where they would have shade, and settled down.

12:30

The operational officers of the 188th Brigade – Moshe Zurich, the intelligence officer; Benny Katzin, the acting operations officer; and Hanan Schwartz, the communications officer, took up position in the command pit at Nafah. Shraga Ibler, the usual brigade operations officer, was absent from the pit. At that moment, he had been called to read from the Torah in his neighborhood synagogue, in honor of his wedding with Hani that was to take place the following day, Sunday.

***

Yair Nafshi comes to the Hermon base to make sure that this is not a case of someone crying wolf. It was the real deal. In front of him, all over the horizon, the Syrian army was removing its camouflage covers.

12:45

Maj. Moshe Zurich, the intelligence officer of the 188th Brigade, calls his friend Maj. Kuty Mor, in the Syrian branch of the research division in the Intelligence Directorate.

"What's happening, Kuty?" he asks.

"This is not a 'combat day,'" Mor replies. "There is going to be a big war."

13:00

Moshe Zurich gets hold of Yair Nafshi and Danny Avni, the battalion's operations officer, leaving the base. "Hurry, you do not have long to live," he says.

13:20

Ben Shoham arrives at the command center at Nafah. Zurich updates him that he is in command of the entire front until the general returns.

13:25

As Ben Shoham gets organized with the new position he was given, he receives a call from Aharon Peled, or Fedale, as he is called by most. The previous commander of the 188th Brigade is currently commander of a reserve brigade of Sherman tanks based in the Sinai.

"Don't carry out the 'Capital' command," he advises Ben Shoham. "Go with the other plan, ask the veterans."

The defense plan of the Golan, as updated in July 1973, included four statuses. Each one was supposed to deal with a different scenario.

Routine security – responding to a local incident, using the force routinely in position and/or with the assistance of regular army units that are positioned farther back.

1. **"Sea Sand"** (enhanced routine security) – following an escalation in regular security such as extended artillery incidents, aerial attacks within our territory, cross-border raids, attempts to take

control of limited territory. In such situations, the IDF will respond by reinforcing the order of battle on the Golan. The troops in place will be joined by a tank battalion and seven artillery batteries.

2. **"Limestone"** (enhanced Sea Sand) – the regular force will be reinforced with four tank battalions and twelve artillery batteries. The Golan will be divided into two brigades, each consisting of one tank brigade and one infantry battalion. This plan requires twelve hours' notice.

3. **"Rock"** – the IDF defense plan when there is a warning of a general war. It is an enhanced version of Limestone but with an additional two reserves divisions. Requires thirty-six hours' notice.

4. **"Capital"** – a code name for the "Days of Battle" of the Northern Command and the 188th Brigade. A combat day did not fit into any of the frameworks mentioned above. It fell somewhere between defense and offense. Usually the Syrians initiated and the Israeli units responded. This was usually done with the forces in position and occasionally with minor reinforcements from the company forward depots or even further in the rear. This is the plan that Fedale mentioned to Ben Shoham.

In January 1973, Fedale conducted a brigade exercise for "a more serious incident." Not exactly Capital but a scenario in which the infantry bases become observation points and behind them companies of tanks.

This is the root of one of the main problems in the preparations of the force and the perception of the battle: the absence of discipline in defense. Many studies carried out in this field after the Yom Kippur War clearly showed that IDF training failed to instill discipline in defensive battles.

The IDF was successful in the Six-Day War and the Kadesh Operation in Sinai in offensive combat. The IDF victories brought honor and prestige to the senior commanders. This led the Army to focus on attack strategies and neglect developing its defense doctrine. The commanders were not interested in studying defense strategies. Over time this failure to focus on and practice defense harmed the professional skills of commanders at all levels and led them to improvise under pressure and come up with all kinds of ideas that were often unsuccessful.

Emanuel Wald, The Curse of the Broken Vessels

This is the reason that Fedale was forced to come up with a new method, "the second method." No one had bothered to tell him that the Northern Command had a contingency plan for defense and there was no need to improvise.

13:30

Yair Nafshi returned to the Hahazit building, the parking area of Company A. "Well baked" with understanding what he had just seen at stronghold 104 and the reports from the Hermon base in mind, he said to Ben Shoham, "Itzik, the Syrians have taken off their camouflage nets. Requesting permission to deploy the tanks outside their forward tank depots. It is obvious that the area is going to be shelled."

Ben Shoham, closer to the decision makers, knew he was not authorized to send up clouds of dust without approval. "Negative, wait."

* * *

"Zamir, stop." Haim Barak, commanding officer of the 82nd Battalion, was on a tour of the front with Meir Zamir, Tiger company leader. Barak, acquainted with the area from his previous activity here, decided that, if they were going to be back on time, their time was up. "We need to get back to Nafah," Barak instructed him. They turned around and headed back to the brigade command group at 14:00.

* * *

In the command bunker at Nafah, Hagai Mann receives reports from all fronts that the Syrians are taking off their nets and he notifies Simchoni.

13:35

Nafshi nags Ben Shoham who finally agrees. "Ok, send them out, but stay five minutes' drive from the parking area, no more. Do not mount the firing ramps."

Nafshi meets with company commander Zvika Rak and gives him the order to leave the building and move into an open area. "Guys," Nafshi says to the soldiers of Zvika Rak's company, improvising something to convince the religious soldiers as well, "we have approval from the rabbi to break the fast."

The tanks move out and take position 500 meters from the building, on both sides of the route heading northeast, toward the Booster Ridge.

13:50

Yair Nafshi also mounts his tank and heads out into the open area. He looks around at the Golan and feels a tense silence. Is anything going to happen today?

* * *

Zvika Rak is sitting on the turret of his tank and having a snack. He opens some canned grapefruit and enjoys the sweetness of it.

On the road near the tanks, Yitzchak Ben Shushan drives the company jeep with lunch for the soldiers. "Each tank send a soldier to me to get food," he shouts out the order in his parade ground roar.

Zeev Tuashi, the "sniper" gunner of Oded Yisraeli, the deputy company commander, comes down and Ben Shushan piles up a combat meal, two challahs, a bag of oranges and a bag of vegetables.

13:55

Tuashi has his nose in the vegetables and is making his way to the tank with difficulty when he suddenly hears a loud roar, increasing into a thunder. Directly above, four Sukhoi jets dive toward Mt. Avital and fire at the antennas and satellite dishes on the top of the mountain.

It is not the terror but the huge loud roar of the diving planes that causes Tuashi to throw the food in the air and run to the tank for shelter. He climbs in only to discover that this is not his tank. It is the tank of Sgt. Shuki Hashenberg.

From the nearby tank, he hears Yisraeli, always ready for battle, shouting, "Come on Zeevik, get inside, it is starting!"

Capital! Capital!

At 13:55 on Saturday, Yom Kippur, October 6, 1973, without any previous knowledge, or notification, the "Yom Kippur War" began, with a coordinated surprise attack by the Syrian and Egyptian armies against Israel.

At 13:55, the Syrian hell opens its mouth and lashes out the evil fire it had been gathering since September.

In a barrage that lasted just five minutes, 800 Syrian cannons fired over 25,000 shells at the tens of Sho't Kal tanks and the ten infantry strongholds. With deafening explosions, the Golan basalt turned into crushed gravel. Fields of dry vegetation and thorns went up in flames and the clouds of smoke covered the blue October skies from horizon to horizon.

In these five minutes, enemy planes appeared from over the hills, where secret intelligence bases lay; endless fires were lit and the sky filled with black smoke.

The Syrian military wanted to start the war early in the morning, with the sun rising and blinding the Israeli infantry and armored corps soldiers facing east. For Egypt, however, this would not work, since at this hour the sun would blind their soldiers. A compromise was reached: 14:00 would be the time.

When they opened fire, the Syrians had three mechanized divisions ready on the front lines, two armored divisions, two independent armored brigades, an independent mechanized brigade, an elite armored brigade (the Rafat Assad force) and seven commando battalions. In numbers, the force included 185,000 soldiers, 1,500 tanks and 1,200 artillery pieces.

Leaving behind only a small force for defense, the majority of the Syrian army was deployed in attack positions, at ranges of five to fifteen kilometers from the border.

The three mechanized divisions – the 7th in the north, the 9th in the center and the 5th in the south – were the spearhead of the Syrian attack plan. Their forward forces – six infantry brigades, two in each mechanized division, and 276 tanks – were located just a few kilometers from the Israeli firing ramps.

At 13:55, six Syrian infantry brigades were given the order to move toward the border with Israel. Like a tight spring, they were released in an amazingly coordinated movement, heading out to destroy the infantry strongholds and the small number of tanks of the 188th Brigade. A few kilometers back, behind the infantry brigades, 657 additional tanks awaited orders to join the combat.

13:55

The First Moment

Lt. Col. Yair Nafshi, commander of the northern front sector and the 74th Battalion is on the phone with Moshe Zurich, the intelligence officer of the 188th Brigade. Suddenly fighter jets pass above him heading west, with the markings of the Syrian air force painted on them. Before Nafshi could grasp what he was seeing, the ground is shaken from falling artillery shells.

"Get me the brigade commander!" he demands, adrenalin levels rising. When Ben Shoham comes on the line Nafshi reports, "It is starting."

"Good luck," Ben Shoham responds in a calm voice.

From the buildings of the destroyed village of Hushnia, Maj. Oded Erez – commanding officer of the 53rd Battalion and in charge of the southern sector of the front – looks up to the sky. He sees two planes flying low over Tel Hazeka, where stronghold 110 is located. "Look at how those Phantoms are provoking the Syrians," he said with pride in the IDF power. Before he completed the sentence, these "Phantoms" fill the hills with smoke and fire.

74th Battalion HQ at Aleika. The planes and artillery explosions take Maj. Yossi Nissim, the deputy commanding officer of the 74th Battalion, by surprise. He had been at the brigade headquarters to finalize logistics for his battalion. He runs to his jeep and orders the terrified driver to speed as fast as possible to the northern forward sector.

Lieutenant Colonels Haim Barak, commander of the 82nd Battalion, and Avigdor Kahalani, commander of the 77th, have just parked their vehicles outside the office of the commander of the 74th battalion, where they have gone to receive commands from Yanush. Everything explodes around them.

"Get back to your battalions," Yanush shouts, and jumps into his jeep on his way to the command post at Nafah.

Maj. Hanan Schwartz, the communications officer of the 188th Brigade, had just came out of the bunker to get some fresh air, away from the war room that smells of male sweat and smoke. Before he could enjoy a breath of air, he hears an unbearably loud sound. He looks up and sees six Sukhoi planes diving toward him. The fetid chamber suddenly seems like a warm and cozy place to be and he runs wildly back toward it, trying to save himself from the bombs heading his way.

Outside there is chaos. Tens of soldiers shoot out of their offices, running for their lives. Beneath them, the Nafah base is turned into a live fire exercise for the Syrians.

Within two minutes, the command bunker is full of tens of soldiers and officers. Most of them are not supposed to be there, having fled their posts, but the instinct to save their life sent this terrified, shocked group looking for shelter from the Syrian bombing.

13:57

From the dark command bunker, full of soldiers who had fled the bombing, Ben Shoham sent a first command to Nafshi. His voice is steady, conveying calmly on the radio, "10 of Peleg, this is 20 of Tofi. Send the 'Beitza' unit (B Company) forward, take observations throughout the front."

He immediately continued with a command to Oded Erez, commanding the 53rd Battalion and commander of the southern front sector, "10 of Fleece, this is 20 of Tofi, take observations throughout the front."

Yair Nafshi, tall and strong, shouts in the battalion radio, "Capital, Capital." He roars to his driver Shpitzer, "Go, go." He races past the tanks of A Company, crushing the pots and containers holding their putative lunch, heading toward the controlling Booster Ridge he was designated to take as the battalion command post.

Oded Erez, short and well built, jumps into his tank, quickly connecting to the battalion radio and shouting the order, "Capital,

Capital, copy." He waits for the tanks of C Company to start moving with him toward their designated position.

Immediately after receiving the "Capital" order from the battalion's commanders, the tanks of the 188th Brigade begin to move into their positions. As planned, the tanks of the 7th Brigade remain where they are, as a reserve force.

Six companies of the 188th Brigade – 69 tanks, 276 soldiers – roar off, sending up clouds of dust, adding to the turmoil of battle and the loud radios. All of them – Eiland, Friedrich, Atir and Bekman, Yakir and Shir-On – are happy to move away from the artillery death dance, waiting for the moment they will be on their firing ramps, where as in previous Days of Battle, they will repay those who dared to take them by surprise with such intense fire.

While Eyal Shaham, Avner Landau, Zvika Rak, Uri Akavia, Uzi Arieli and Avi Ronis – the six company commanders of the 188th Brigade – jump into their tanks, the Syrian artillery continues to pound the bases and forward tank depots. Six Syrian infantry brigades move forward together, with 276 tanks and 10,000 soldiers. Some are walking on foot, others mounted on trucks or armored personnel carriers.

In the first five minutes of the Yom Kippur War, the entire Golan had been plunged into flame. Syrian MiG planes controlled the skies over the Golan and the six Syrian brigades were heading toward their prey. In the first five minutes, before the tanks of the 188th Brigade took up position on their ramps, 150 Golani and Nahal infantry soldiers, deployed in nine strongholds, were facing this hell on their own. They are reporting what they saw. "The entire Syrian army is on us."

14:00

Nafah Headquarters

The headquarters at Nafah is in darkness. In the chaos, someone produces flashlights and lighters, and the blackness is overcome.

Lt. Col. Uri Simchoni, the Northern Command operations officer, goes outside to see the situation with his own eyes. He nimbly jumps out of the bunker and takes a radio, a map and a communications NCO with him. As far as he can see, from the Hermon to the Ruqqad, there is a wall of thick black smoke arises from the remains of the camp –

crushed asphalt, ruined buildings, green and black trees and garbage cans, some still with slogans printed on them "The man is the steel" and "Soldier, keep the base clean."

14:00
Tel Aviv, the Prime Minister's Office
Wailing sirens come in through the windows of the Prime Minister's office in Hakiryah in Tel Aviv.

"What is that?" Golda Meir asks Mitka, the legendary stenographer.

"It seems like the war has started," she answers.

Golda looks at the government ministers she had convened for an emergency meeting two hours earlier. Her eyes look into Dayan's single eye. Just a few hours earlier, he had said confidently that there is no apparent reason for a preemptive strike and for mobilizing the reserves. She mumbled in Yiddish, "*Nar das felt mir*" (just what I needed...).

14:05
Simchoni returns to the bunker. The situation is still unclear but the wall of smoke and the bombing of Nafah make it very clear that this is not just another combat day. "Where will the main force come from?" he asks himself, sitting behind the radio, next to Ben Shoham.

The commander of the 7th Brigade, Col. Avigdor Ben Gal, Yanush, is at the entrance to the bunker, his head almost touching the doorpost. He looks around in the dark, in the space of about 100 square meters; there is a sea of people shouting at each other through the radio.

Yanush immediately sees that things are a mess. An impatient man who is quick to get angry, he realizes it will take at least another ten minutes for someone to be able to talk to him. "To hell with it," he says, and leaves in his jeep, heading toward 77th Battalion, located at the nearby Hashiryon (armor) junction, among the destroyed buildings of Nafah village.

A few minutes after 14:00, Maj. Haim Barak, commander of the 82nd Battalion, completes the drive to the battalion assembly area in Sindiyana, three kilometers from Nafah. He is glad to see that Maj. Danny

Pesach, his deputy, has already deployed the tanks, and the crews have folded their camouflage nets and stowed them away.

The 82nd Battalion was now under the command of the 188th Brigade, as had been agreed between Itzik Ben Shoham and Yanush that morning at 10:00, but Barak did not know about this. He knows that he is supposed to be a reserve force in the sector. Since there is a clear chain of command in the army and a battalion commander only does what "his" brigade commander tells him to, and since his commander just called him to deliver his orders and what he said was "Get to your tanks immediately," Barak remained in position, with his three companies, away from the front line, waiting for orders from Yanush.

H Company, 74th Battalion

Syrian planes pass over forward camp 104. They are returning from attacks on the Hermon. The sound of missiles fired is everywhere, and 1st Lt. Aviv Shir-On leads his platoon down to lower ground, in an attempt to hide from the planes. A minute later, realizing that the danger has passed, he speeds toward his ramps. He has good reason to be in a hurry, the reason is Yoni.

Two minutes earlier, he was called by 2nd Lt. Yoni Meidovnik, the commander of stronghold 104 from Kfar Vitkin and the Golani brigade. Yoni was usually in full control of his emotions but on the radio he reported that "three 'heavies' are heading toward me on the Zin route (a route from Khader in Syria into Israeli territory, right near the base)."

Yoni Meidovnik was not the only one in trouble. The only hope of the infantry soldiers in the front line strongholds, in the face of the endless mass of Syrian tanks heading toward them, was the tank platoons of the 188th Brigade.

After six minutes that felt like a lifetime, Aviv, along with Sgt. Yossi Weisbrott, took up position on the southern ramp of stronghold 104. The platoon sergeant, 1st Sgt. Koby Greenbaum, had been sent, as planned, to the Shechita hill, a few hundred meters north of Aviv's ramp. There he took up position at the bottom of it, awaiting the tanks of the company command.

The 1st Platoon, commanded by 2nd Lt. Muli Dgani, leaves the forward tank depot behind stronghold 105, on the northern outskirts of

Mt. Varda, northeast of Bukata. They head down the hill toward the anti-tank ditch and the border. Five minutes later, Dgani is positioned in the center of the firing ramp, above the anti-tank ditch, Gitai Zinberg is to his right and Avraham Frost, the sergeant, to his left.

The 3rd Platoon, commanded by 1st Lt. Shmulik Yachin, leaves forward tank depot 107, the southern post of H company, a few hundred meters west of Booster Ridge. The Syrians, a nation of hard-working farmers, had established a number of waterworks on the Golan to improve their agriculture, including the water line buried in the ground. Along this line, a number of booster pumps had been installed, one of them on the top of the hill where Yachin's tanks were positioned.

On the way to his firing ramps, Yachin received a distress call from Lt. Elimelech Avraham (Miley), commander of infantry stronghold 107, reporting large numbers of Syrian forces heading toward junction 107. Yachin reported to his company CO, Eyal Shaham, that he is initiating the Axe procedure – joining the infantry base – and within five minutes he is at stronghold 107. Yachin takes up position on the ramp south of the base, positions Yoni Vodak to his right, Yossi Nades, the sergeant, to his left. In 3rd Platoon, they all know they are located east of the main defense obstacle of the Golan, and they are confident that they have the power to stop the Syrians, even without the help of the anti-tank ditch.

From the fortified base at the entrance of the Druze village Mas'ade, three tanks emerge. Company commander Eyal Shaham, his deputy Kaimo, and Yoni Efrat, the artillery liaison tank commander (17C). They leave the company command post and head to their designated firing positions.

Eyal calls the three platoon leaders and makes sure they are on their way to their designated posts. Calmed by the reports, seeing that the platoon commanders are operating exactly according to protocol, Eyal reports to his commander, to deputy battalion commander Yossi Nissim. He adds that he is on his way to his post in 104.

Nissim, still in his jeep, smiles to himself in satisfaction. The company is performing in the most professional manner. He is a deputy battalion commander, appointed to command this region of the northern front, but at heart, he is a disciplined armored corps officer. He reports to Nafshi and he knows that things are in good hands.

A Company

A few minutes before 14:00, with the shells and planes coming down on the tanks of the company spread outside the Hahazit building near Quneitra, David Eiland holds on to a box of grapes and a fresh challah that he received from Ben Shushan and refuses to put them down. "Throw down the food and get over here," his veteran crew, which he just received that morning, shout to him, but he refuses.

There are explosions all over and black smoke mushrooms rises from the hills above. The planes are back again, flying lower than the soldiers ever imagined a fighter plane could fly. Eiland, still holding the food in his hands, sees the symbol of the Syrian air force on the blue wings.

His legs are operating automatically and take him to the tank. He climbs up, hands the package of food to Borko the loader, puts on his VRC helmet and hears company commander Zvika Rak ordering the tanks to move out, take up position and open fire.

The ten tanks of A Company, commanded by Zvika Rak, advance slightly and seven of them improvise positions in the extended Booster Ridge, facing southeast. Five officers and two sergeants lift their binoculars, scan the area and wait for the Syrians to arrive.

The 1st Platoon leader, 2nd Lt. Haim Damir, and the three tanks of his platoon do not join the company and are sent, as determined in advance, to Nafshi the battalion commander, to join him on the ramp below and east of Booster Ridge.

On the route leading to Booster Ridge there is one tank in movement, that of the CO of the 74th. Standing tall in the turret, his head above the cupola is Lt. Col. Yair Nafshi, commander of the northern front. To his left, on the loader's seat is Lt. Danny Avni, the operations officer. Nafshi looks at him with affection. He had arrived just a few months earlier from the staff of the tank commander's course and Nafshi learned to appreciate the management skills of the short blond officer. A good choice, he thought to himself, recalling Uri Akavia, the previous operations officer, who had just returned from the company commander's course and was far from him in the southern Golan, commanding G company. While continuing eastward, he wondered how Uri was doing. They would be at the ramps within minutes.

On the intercom radio, Nafshi checks on the loader, Yossi Marder from Kibbutz Hulda and the gunner, Yaakov Veidenfeld, who everyone calls Videy, from Kibbutz Ayelet Hashachar. Videy usually acts as the tank commander, taking care of the battalion commander's tank, but this morning, when his tank came from Mas'ade, he was assigned to serve as the gunner.

Nafshi is relaxed. He knows that the company commanders are doing exactly what they have been trained for. Even the Syrian planes flying into Israeli territory, the first such attack since he was appointed battalion commander in the Golan, do not fracture his peace. He tells Avigdor Shpitzer, the driver, "Step on it!."

Five hundred meters east of the Booster Ridge, they reach their position. Nafshi raises his binoculars and... it looks like the entire Syrian army is moving in front of him. Alone in his post in the front, with Yachin east of him, Nafshi asks Zvika Rak, "Where is Damir? Why isn't he coming?"

2nd Platoon

As the tanks of A and H Companies are moving into position, the platoon of 2nd Lt. Doron Sadeh Lavan, of G Company, speed out of Quneitra deployment camp. Fifteen minutes later, they are positioned on their firing ramps, south of stronghold 109.

Doron leads his three tanks to observation positions, making sure they lower their antennas, to make it harder for the Syrians to spot them. He looks around with his binoculars but there is nothing to see, it is completely silent.

B Company

Gidi Lefver, a young artillery corps officer, had just been appointed the forward observation officer and joined Avner Landau's B Company. He finds himself in the company bathroom, were privacy is provided by tarpaulins on all sides. While doing his business in there, he hears sounds, looks up to the open sky and sees swept wing planes. "MiGs!" he says to himself. He rushes to get out of the bathroom and hears tanks starting their engines. He is eager to finally experience battle, but realizes that none of the tanks are going to wait for an artillery officer that they do not even know. He is about to run toward the tanks when he sees that the zipper of his coverall won't close.

In a surreal striptease act, he drags himself and his coverall to the tank of Asaf Sela, joins as a fifth crewman and experiences the concentrated firepower of all of the company's machine guns aimed at the Syrian aircraft. The MiGs are not impressed.

Company commander Landau calls them to move out. "Move in order. I lead, deputy closes, move out, over."

Eleven drivers get into their compartments, close the hatches, start the engines and steer to the right or the left according to the instructions of the commander, with endless artillery ordinance falling around them. They put their 750 horsepower Continental engine into action and move out.

G Company

"It's starting," Capt. Shmulik Askarov, deputy CO of the 53rd Battalion, thinks to himself. It's true that the artillery is surprisingly intense and that a number of enemy planes just flew over but none of that will dampen his enthusiasm.

"Move out!" he shouts in the radio, sending out the Askarov force to the combat day they had been waiting for.

Like many boys from the kibbutzim in the '70s, the young Askarov, from Kibbutz Kiryat Anavim, had fought to become a combat soldier. Despite his asthma, he demanded to join the armored corps and was accepted. He trained in the 7th Brigade and six months before the war, he was posted to the 188th Brigade. Here he was appointed deputy commander of one of its two most acclaimed battalions – the 53rd. Just a month and a half earlier, Lt. Col. Oded Erez had been appointed the new battalion commander, and Askarov enjoyed his position as the deputy to the new commander who relied on him, being an important part of this efficient machine.

Askarov's eight-tank force sped eastward toward their positions on the Shaf-A-Sindiyan hills (outpost 111) and Tel Abas. In less than fifteen minutes five of them were in position, with an anti-tank ditch below them and the Kudna route (the Troy route) to the left.

A few days earlier, to the north of where these tanks are now, a fence had been erected as part of the preparations for taking position in the ramps. Now Zeev Hochstein's platoon, along with the other three tanks, rolls over the fence without getting tangled in barbed wire. They climb up to their natural positions in the steep Tel Abas hill, and three minutes after the first five, they too are in position, three tanks grouped close together, facing east.

At the same time the Askarov force was in motion, so were the three tanks of the Davidson force – G Company. They left Hushnia, staying off the asphalt roads and sticking to the dirt paths. The first in line was 1st Lt. Yoni Davidson, deputy commander G Company, followed by 2nd Lt. Moty Amir, leader of 3rd Platoon and, finally, 1st Sgt. Dan Tiroler in the last tank. They head toward Tel Mahir (daytime observation position/ unmanned outpost 113), east of Tel Fares, on the purple border line.

C Company

Uzi Urieli, C Company CO, jumps into his tank as the roar of the planes echoes in the ears of the company's crewmen positioned at Hushnia. He is followed by his gunner, Itzik Arnon, an accurate and fast shooter, and Mordi Erez, the loader, who had to be both acrobatic and fast in order for the tank to fire quickly. Finally, the driver Yossi Avramovitz joins them.

The choreography of the rush to the tank is the same drill they practice every day, in what to them appeared to be another combat day.

Oded Bekman, commander of the 2nd platoon, gave the order to mount the tanks and is already running with his crew, remembering to take Tzachki Sarig's guitar and placing it with the sleeping bags. "So this is what a combat day looks like," Bekman says to himself, while helping Eli Rachamim, the gunner, into his seat. He takes his place and suddenly his body shakes uncontrollably. He tells himself to wait a few seconds before giving the orders, what they think of you is affected by the way you sound.

What the hell is the meaning of this intense bombing? wonders Ilan Orenstein, Bekman's sergeant. An experienced battle veteran, he nonetheless feels the blood draining from his face when confronted with this new, unfamiliar form of action. He has a bad "gut feeling" about it.

Uzi, the commander of C Company, thinks to himself that no matter how much artillery there is, the Syrians are making a mistake. He has just been appointed company commander and he knows this is the right time and place to be. He will show the arrogant enemy that dared to start this dirty battle what an error they have made.

The camouflage nets are quickly folded and stowed, the crew members are in place, connected to the intercom. Uzi starts moving, leading the seven tanks of C Company and the two tanks of the battalion command (the tanks of the battalion commander and of the artillery coordination officer). Nine roaring steel chariots, guiding themselves toward the Petroleum Road, cutting diagonally through the field (the Yeshiva route).

Several hours earlier, in the middle of the night, two artillery officers from the 334th Artillery Battalion had arrived at Hushnia. Second Lt. Ariel Kovlanz had joined the Askarov force, located in the Hushnia forward tank depot, and 2nd Lt. Yaron Shapira, who had arrived at the headquarters of the southern forward battalion, western Hushnia, joined Uzi Urieli's C Company. "Get organized to be a fifth crew member in Birnboim's tank," Uzi ordered.

In the morning, all the tanks of the company spread out and Shapira was with them. After an hour he had had enough. What did he need this tank nonsense for? Why not head back to the camp? And so he did.

A few minutes before 14:00, he was sitting in the battalion HQ offices talking to Oded Erez, the battalion commander. They were outside his improvised office with his private steel chariot next to it.

When the ground started shaking, Yaron Shapira ran the 500 meters to the tanks as if his life depended on it. He was too late. Following the armored corps maxim that when given the order "Move out," you move at all costs (with the artillery officer or without him), 1st Sgt. Yaakov Birnboim had started advancing with the other tanks of C Company. He left behind – disappearing in a cloud of dust – an out-of-breath and helpless artillery officer, in the middle of a burning field of thorns, waving his arms desperately at the tank convoy.

The tank of 2nd Platoon commander Oded Bekman is delayed. "Wellman!" Bekman shouted as loud as he could. Wellman didn't respond. Bekman, seeing the explosions getting closer to them, shouts even louder, "Wellman, start the engine!."

Wellman does not. He is enclosed in his compartment, not connected to the radio and is detached from the chaos outside. As an observant

Jew, he knew – and explained to the crew – that nothing bad could happen on the holiest day of the Jewish year. Since God is responsible for everything, Wellman is not troubled by his own detachment, because God will take care of everything. As Bekman climbs into the tank, putting on his helmet and connecting the radio, with everyone around him rushing to move out, Wellman did exhibit the same sense of urgency.

As Wellman is waiting for God's salvation, Bekman watches the fire heading toward him with terror. He sees all the tanks of the company rushing to their positions.

Bekman carried out the procedure for the driver who is not functioning; he rotates the cannon to 5 o'clock and shouts to the loader, "Mark!" Once he has his attention, he continues, "Eylenberg, wake Wellman up, quick!"

Above Mark Eylenberg's head there is a spare antenna, wrapped in nylon and grease, ready for any inspection. Like in every other situation, also here there is a drill. After rotating the cannon, the loader can stab the driver in the shoulder.

Mark Eylenberg, the new immigrant, does exactly what Bekman tells him to do. He moves the shells, stabs Wellman hard, waking him from his afternoon rest. Wellman hears and starts the engine and they are on their way. Bekman looks back and sees a shell crater where they had just been standing.

As the tanks of C Company make their way from the assembly area to the front, soldiers of the battalion operations section, the medical platoon and the technical support teams are left behind in Hushnia, exposed to the terror of the falling artillery. A shard from one of the shells hits 1st Sgt. Nachshon Hermoni in the head. Hermoni was an intelligence NCO from Kibbutz Sarid who always seemed to have a smile on his face. The 53rd Battalion's doctor, 1st Lt. Dr. Danny Englehard, who is not only the battalion's doctor but also the commander of the medical unit of the southern front, carries out his first attempt at resuscitation in his medical career. Working with four medics, they try to keep Hermoni alive.

Between the shells and the resuscitation efforts, the soldiers remaining at Hushnia split into two survival groups. Dr. Englehard, in the medical team's armored personnel carrier, head west and take up position at the Mashta junction (two kilometers west of Hushnia). Second Lt. Yuval Shachar, intelligence officer of the 52nd and the senior officer in the group, tries to organize all the soldiers remaining at Hushnia and makes an effort, ridiculous under the circumstances, to gather communication equipment, poster boards and maps that are scattered all around. They load all the equipment on the APC and a passenger van left by the deputy battalion commander. The driver starts the engine and Yuval remembers the technical team of C Company.

"The company's teams know we are at Hushnia. We are staying here. Don't worry, we'll manage," Sgt. Mishali Menachem smiles as he notifies him.

Yuval says goodbye, heads toward the helicopter landing-pad at Tel Fares and takes position at the bottom of Tel Farej, the location chosen in early planning as the location for the battalion communications center.

Bekman is shaking again in the commander's seat. Aware of the trembling, he tries to sound tough. "Glufa commander, this is 2, in movement," he reports to Uzi using the code name for the company commander. The words are that of the armored corps but the voice sounds frail.

"This is Glufa commander, increase speed." Uzi's voice is the model voice for commanders, the voice familiar from training.

A few hundred meters from him, between the buildings at Hushnia, Yaron Shapira, who was in officer's course with Bekman, gets in the technical unit APC and succeeds in contacting Uzi, the company commander.

"Stay where you are," Uzi orders. "Don't worry; it will be over soon, there is no reason to bother."

"Relax, relax," Bekman tells himself.

He manages to calm himself and his voice is steady, just like that of Uzi. Now he is the confident platoon leader again, just like in training. He is waiting expectantly for the tank battles about to begin, for his platoon to show the Syrians who has the upper hand. He quickly closes the distance to the company convoy and the Petroleum Road.

F Company

A Syrian MiG plane dives over the forward tank depot in Juhader, releases a load of bombs with the whistle of a sword cut, and disappears. Six tank commanders – Avi Ronis, Yoram Miromi, Avi Lavi, Nati Levi,

Moty Aviam and Asher Brinberg – and their eighteen crew members understand immediately that time has come.

Ptachya Azarya, the gunner of Ronis the CO, is lying on his bed in the barracks, focusing on Yom Kippur and its prayers. The shells exploding around him send him outside.

On his way to the tank, he passes the technical unit APC and sees that the company commander's tank is already in motion. What is Ronis going to do to me? He drags himself, terrified, to the tank and sees the company commander leaning down to him. He gives him a hand and pulls him up to the tank. Ptachya climbs into the gunner seat and feels at home, with the tank shaking him and the periscope hitting him in the forehead.

Ronis organizes the three tanks of the company command and 2nd Lt. Levi organizes the three tanks of his platoon. They all fly into position, like a spring being released.

First Lt. Avi Ronis is not someone you want to disobey. A city boy, the son of two Holocaust survivors who separated when he was young, he found himself at the age of sixteen joining the agricultural school at Kibbutz Hefziba as an external student. After completing his studies, he stayed on at the kibbutz, and in the months before he was drafted he became an admired counselor in the Olim Camps youth movement. In February 1970, he joined the army. He completed the officer's course and stayed on for a few months as a course instructor. He insisted on joining the 188th Brigade and got what he wanted. He was appointed deputy company commander in Company F of the 74th battalion, where he took part in two days of combat.

In February 1973, three years after being drafted, he was promoted to company commander. The position turned the always-smiling kibbutznik into a miniature Gorodish, strict and tough. His relentless demand to be consistent with the notorious "armored corps values" – your cannon is not sparkling clean? You are confined to the base for twenty-one days – caused his soldiers to tremble every time they had to report to his office.

Still, they worshipped the ground he walked on. In the September 1973 alert, Avi Ronis was seen by his troops as the perfect company commander. Not only was he tall, handsome and professional, but most importantly, he was the most experienced company commander in the battalion. A few weeks before the war he married Zohar, from Kibbutz Hefziba. The state of alert ruined their plans for a honeymoon. "We will find the time for it," he promised his new wife, before disappearing into the company tanks.

Fifteen minutes after departing their base, Ronis, Miromi and Lavi reach the big tank ramps near outpost 115.

Second Lt. Nati Levi, leader of the 2nd Platoon, turns right and then left and is on the Petroleum Road, ordering his platoon to cover the three kilometer distance to their ramps as fast as possible.

"The most important thing is to get out of this artillery shelling and plane bombing safely," Moty Aviam, commander of tank 2A says to himself. They are distancing themselves from Juhader and no one is after them and Aviam has a different thought,, "The most important thing is to get to the ramps already and start doing what Nati and Avi taught us."

Nati is wondering how he will cope with his first combat day. He looks back, sees Moty and Asher standing in their commander's cupolas proud and determined, and he knows it will be okay. The swimming pool the Syrian officers have set up is behind them, the large eucalyptus forest is on their left and they are almost at their ramps. Nati, like all the platoon commanders of the 188th Brigade, sends his tanks to observation positions.

In the Juhader parking area, the technical unit of Company F take cover from the Syrian shelling. The company sergeant, Rachamim Yitzchak, and the medic, Sgt. Menahem Minjersky, take cover as the ground shakes from the falling shells. The air is full of the smoke of explosives and Minjersky digs in, trying to disappear into the landscape and prays that he will not have to give medical care to anyone.

Second Lt. Avi Lahman, 1st platoon commander in forward tank depot 114, is on the forward edge of the area Company F occupies. He does not wait for the "Capital! – move out" order from Ronis. The entire front facing the 1st platoon leader is a chaos of dust, fire and pillars of smoke. He starts his tank, shouts the order to Shmuel Herman and Shimon Cohen to follow his tank.

They stay off the road, following the brigade rules not to damage the asphalt. Three minutes later, chased by continuous artillery fire, Lahman is positioned at the ramps.

Second Lt. Yoav Yakir, commander of the 3rd Platoon, leaves parking area 116, on route to outpost 116, one kilometer west of the depot. The plan he received from the senior officers – who surely knew what they were doing – decreed taking the shortest route to the ramps, which would involve traveling to the north of the stronghold. Instead, he leads Yair Waxman and Nir Atir, with their tanks, southward. They speed in their steel chariots toward their ramps, far south of the outpost, four kilometers from the forward tank depot.

"The fifteen-minute drive passed quickly," Nir Atir thinks to himself, as they take up an observation position on the ramps. "I wonder what the point of this is?"

When the first shells hit forward tank depot 116 tank, Mordechai Ukavi the medic finds himself resting peacefully on a tank, passing the fast while listening to the communication radio.

"Tell me if anyone calls me," Yakir instructs him.

When the first bombs crush the parking area, Ukavi runs for his life, reaches his bed, puts on his medic's vest, reports to the "safe room," a tiny room, and hears the tanks heading off to the ramps.

"Fire!"

During the first twenty minutes of the Yom Kippur War on the Golan, by 14:15, forty-two Sho't Kal tanks of the sixty-nine tanks of the 188th Brigade completed the distance from their parking areas to their assigned ramp posts.

On the northern front, under the command of Yair Nafshi, twenty-two tanks start to exchange long-range fire with the enemy. They are attempting to stop 153 enemy tanks and 5,000 infantry soldiers, some of them in armored personnel carriers. They focus on the immediate threat – breaching units approaching the anti-tank ditch.

On the southern front, under the command of Maj. Oded Erez, the remaining twenty tanks of the 188th Brigade are doing their best to prevent 123 enemy tanks and another 5,000 soldiers, led by special breaching teams, from reaching the anti-tank ditches.

In the commander's compartments in these tanks, forty-two surprised commanders try to organize their thoughts. Only their heads, necks and shoulders protrude above the steel frame of the tank. Their feet are rattling on the commander's footstool. Those who have already experienced "Days of Battle" are amazed: Why have the Syrian forces advanced? What is this massive force? Did someone forget to notify the Syrians that a "combat day" is just artillery fire and tanks firing from fixed positions?

The others, who did not have experience in combat, were used to hearing the stories of the brigade history and are just as confused: Has something gone wrong in the "combat day" routine? Or did the veteran soldiers fail to tell them the truth?

The Syrian command for war, "Mashroa 110," which their General Staff had issued, specified their army's objectives:

- Starting from October 6
- Conquer the Golan
- Destroy the IDF forces on it
- Lay down a defense line along the Jordan with three mechanized divisions (5, 7 and 9) and two additional armored divisions in reserve (1 and 3),
- Ending by October 7 at 7:00 a.m.

Forty-two tank crews, 168 soldiers – they are the best trained crews in the world, but they know nothing about Mashroa 110. Yet still, all of them – Aviv Shir-On, Shmulik Yachin, Moty Aviam, Asher Brinberg, Nir Atir, Yoav Yakir, Zeev Hochstein and Danny Berkovitz – understand that they have reached the moment when they will be tested, a test such as they have never faced before. They are confused, upset, they do not understand what exactly has hit them. But then they look around them and see their friends standing with them, tall and determined in their Sho't Kal tanks, the best tanks in the world.

Northern Sector – 104

The first thing that Aviv Shir-On identifies when he takes position is the "three heavies" that Yoni, the commander of the infantry stronghold, had reported. An enemy tank platoon driving confidently on the Khader–Mas'ade road, headed for the Purple Line. From a distance of 700 meters, it seems that the tank commanders who are driving with their hatches closed are unaware of his platoon aiming their cannons at them.

"2A, combat range," Aviv orders Yossi Weissbart next to him. "You take the last one, I will take the first."

"Fire!" Aviv shouts to his gunner Eli Kopilevitz.

"Fire!" shouts Weissbart to his gunner Eitan Frish.

Two flashes of light mark the armor-piercing projectiles hitting the Russian steel. Another minute passes and the two manned steel vehicles become pillars of fire. The middle tank, seeing the fate of his friends, panics and drives back. He chooses the wrong place to turn and overturns on a bridge. The tank threat to outpost 104 is temporarily lifted.

"Champagne!" Kopilevitz shouts and Yossi Gershoni the loader and Uri Yona the driver compliment him.

"Champagne!" Eitan Frish shouts from his compartment, and in their tank, too, there are celebrations, congratulations and compliments.

Aware that one enemy platoon means that the entire company is on its way, Aviv Shir-On does not relax and scans the area in front of him.

To the southeast of him, in the valley below the Manfucha hills and outposts 104 and 105, he sees ten different vehicles – trucks, APCs and a bridging tank – heading toward the fence. They lay at ranges from 750 to 1,500 meters.

"2A, division of targets," Aviv calmly commands his platoon. "I will take the bridging tank, you start with the APCs and then choose whoever you want."

Then it is Kopilevitz who registers his second champagne, taking out the bridging tank. Yossi Weissbart joins the festival too and Eitan Frish shows that he too knows a thing or two about shooting.

The valley fills with flames and smoke and burned soldiers fleeing.

Northern Sector – 105

South of sector 104, 2nd Lt. Muli Dgani, commander of 1st Platoon, H Company, is facing toward the anti-tank ditch below him when he identifies enemy forces heading openly toward the fence.

Dgani's platoon tries to fire at the targets in the valley but discovers a problem. The three gunners are having trouble depressing their cannon enough. They never imagined they would have to fire at such close ranges. The ramp had been intended to deal with distant targets, not local problems, right in front of them, close to the anti-tank ditch.

Muli responds and moves his tank and the tanks of Zinberg and Frost to an alternative higher ramp with a better angle .

Not far from Dgani's tanks, the sector commander arrives. Maj. Yossi

Nissim instructs his driver to turn off the jeep engine and walks up on foot with his binoculars. He identifies the attempts by the Syrian forces to reach the anti-tank ditch.

In the Syrian war doctrine, in preparing for the war that would regain their honor, together with the Golan Heights, great emphasis had been placed on the artificial ground obstacles they faced – anti-tank ditches and minefields. They had a detailed plan for breaching them. They had worked out access routes, prepared special teams to cross them and a methodology of operation.

Syrian intelligence had located the best spots to bridge the ditches. These were locations that were less visible to the Israeli infantry outposts and/or the tank ramps, thus enabling wide deployment, as close as possible to main routes. The doctrine continued with the exact timing of how long the breaching operation would take. This would determine the speed of progress for each brigade. This had all been prepared in advance, along with the detailed operational commands the six infantry brigade commanders delivered on D-Day.

The combined attack of the Syrian and Egyptian forces started a few minutes before 14:00 but the official time in the brigade commands that the Syrian General Staff planned was 15:00. This was not the time the attack started but the time the anti-tank ditch would be crossed, the start of the major attack onto Israeli territory.

With the beginning of the artillery fire, sixty minutes before zero hour, the command specified that designated breaching forces – including combat engineers, infantry, counter-mines flail tanks, bridging tanks and bulldozers – would, under the veil of the artillery fire, move forward to the anti-tank ditch.

The Syrian Tiran tanks (Russian T tanks) that joined their 68th Brigade – those that attacked in the sector under the command of 74th Battalion deputy CO Yossi Nissim – were supposed to leave their waiting position at sixty minutes before zero hour, and drive at a speed of 15–20 km/h. According to the Syrian calculations, this would bring them into position right behind the infantry forces at fifty-four minutes before zero hour. From there, in joint forces, they would continue toward the anti-tank ditch.

In the first stage, the tanks were to move in behind the infantry forces, thus securing the activity of the breaching force first. At thirty-five minutes to zero hour, the force would take up position, fifty meters from the ditch, with the tanks slightly to the east of it.

Five minutes before zero hour, the breaching force would complete the bridging of the anti-tank ditch. At the head of each team, a mine plowing tank would clear the mines in front of the ditch. If it completed its mission, the combat engineers would improve and mark its point of passage. Once this was done, the infantry force would be free cross the ditch – on foot or with ladders – and secure the attacking force. Then it will be the turn of the bridging tank to place the bridge across the ditch. If successful, a plowing tank and a flail tank would cross the bridge and clear the minefield on the other side of the ditch.

At 15:00, zero hour, tanks of the six brigades – 276 tanks in their initial order of battle – would cross via the paths already cleared for them. Once the first tanks would cross the canal and take position to the west of it, the bulldozers would cave in the edges of the ditch to prepare as many additional crossings as possible. This would increase the chances of the divisional force behind them, 150 to 250 tanks per division, to make it across the obstacle quickly and elegantly.

All this careful planning is met with the three tanks of Dgani's platoon. They start doing what they do best, hitting enemy tanks: Nissim Benuzio, Zinberg's gunner; Avraham Berger, Frost's gunner; and Natan Nager, the best gunner in the platoon, taking out two tanks for every tank his friends hit. The crews are elated. "We are beating them, like we always do."

Northern Front – 107

Shmulik Yachin's platoon was positioned south of 105, on the ramp south of stronghold 107. Yachin raised his binoculars and immediately saw tanks, APCs and trucks heading his way. They had already crossed a quarter of the distance from the Syrian "Ten Houses" outpost.

Shmulik places the tank approximately on target and issues the order that will allow the gunner to make the final adjustment. "Cannon, armor piercing, 1,500 meters, tank on, fire."

Vodak and Naides earn their bottles of champagne first. The immediate danger passes and Yachin is now free to deal with the report from Elimelech, the commander of stronghold 107. He says that a Syrian infantry company is heading toward the outpost, while firing machine guns and anti-tank rockets.

Elimelech's report also reaches the regional brigade, which orders one of the artillery cannons to open fire on their position, to lift the threat from the outpost.

Before the artillery commanders can grasp the meaning of this strange order (Syrians in our territory?), Yachin's platoon has located the infantry soldiers, aimed their parallel machine guns at them and hit most of them. There are a few minutes of calm and then there is another attack, and again the Syrian wave is broken by the platoon's fire.

The area is still full of enemy vehicles: APCs, trucks, bridging tanks and combat tanks protecting them. This large force is spread out and moving forward. Some are coming from the Ten Houses outpost and others from Khan Ureinve (the America route). They are all headed for the Roman Arches bridge (Ahmadia), a crucial crossing point on the Ruqqad channel, 400 meters from Shmulik's ramp.

"Come and get it," Shmulik says to himself, aware of his platoon abilities and counting on the mines on both the Israeli and the Syrian sides awaiting any fool that would attempt to cross.

"Forget the range," shouts Moshe Ben Chaim, Yoni Vodak's gunner. He looks in the peri-telescope and pulls the trigger. "I am shooting whatever I see."

It is the dream of every armored soldier – endless targets, right there in front of them. After a few minutes of free firing, Yachin pulls himself together. Issuing a professional, armored corps order, he succeeds in turning down the flame.

"Sigalit stations, this is commander," calls Yachin on the platoon communication. "Hold your fire. Hold your fire." He divides the targets between the tanks, so they do not waste ammunition. They cannot have two tanks firing at the same target. Who knows how much longer they will be there.

In the two months prior to the war, Shmulik Yachin had come to stronghold 107, commanded by Elimelech Avraham (Miley), every two weeks. They met, memorized the range card, studied the location of the targets and created a common terminology. Now, with Shmulik's ramp near the outpost, this effort has paid off. Slightly to the rear,

Elimelech, impressed by the work the tanks were doing, tries to help them correct their fire. "Shmulik, short," "Shmulik, long." Shmulik accepts the corrections, adjusts and hits his targets.

The Yachin family was also from Neve Magen, a few streets from the home of Oded Bekman. Shmulik, the oldest child of Sarah and Yitzchak Tzalalichin (Yachin), like Bekman, was raised by veterans of the "Irgun" (one of the resistance organizations against the British mandate), unwelcomed in the neighborhood of the Mapayniks, veterans of the Haganah and the Palmach.

A year older than Bekman, Shmulik was what teachers and parents call "a model child." He was quiet, polite, mainstream, not the type to lead motorbike rides through South Tel Aviv. He sat at home and worked on his studies. He spent his childhood years making his parents and teachers proud. He was one of the leading students at school, the teacher's favorite. He spent his time out of school at the Scouts and the Aviation Club, as both a participant and an instructor.

Northern Sector – The Booster Ridge

Four kilometers from his company's tanks, two kilometers beyond the anti-tank ditch, still in Syrian territory, Zvika Rak, A company CO, sees a wall of dust with two bridging tanks leading it.

Zvika was pleased. This was exactly the job of his company, to defend outpost 109 and the Quneitra area. The range is long, almost too far for tanks to fire effectively. The dust did not make it any easier but this was no excuse.

"Ace stations, this is Ace," Zvika announced festively to his company. "Here are your targets. I will fire a phosphorus shell. To the right of it, deputy, 2, 2A and 17. To its left, me, 3 and 3A. Confirm. Over."

They all confirm. The phosphorous shell is fired and marks the center of the targets area. The seven tanks of Ace company open fire. Efraim Yosef, Eiland's gunner, fired his first round and another and the first bridging tank had his name written on it. Other gunners in the company also tried to take credit for the first hit but to Eiland and Burko (Moshe Baram) the loader, as well as Yehuda Shani the driver, it is clear that Efraim called "target" and is the one who hit it.

For Oded Yisraeli, the deputy commander, it is easier to determine. A moment earlier, as they had been taking up position, Yisraeli had aimed the cannon at the second bridging tank and ordered Zeev Tuashi the gunner, "Zeevik, straight in front of you, a range of over 3,000!" Tuashi had identified the bridging tank at a distance of 3,500 meters. He had fired and missed. He had waited for Reuven Goldsheft to load another round, corrected his aim a little, and, with the second shot, he had hit the target. "Great shot!" Oded exclaimed.

Zvika watches the company's fire performance, announces champagne to the winners and knows he has a fine unit.

Southern Sector – 111

Captain Shmulik Askarov, the deputy battalion commander; 1st Lt. Uri Akavia, commander of G company; and 2nd Lt. Danny Overlander, leader of 1st Platoon, G company, take position in the ramps near outpost 111, on the northern side.

At a distance of two to four kilometers from them, they identify a vast number of tanks and soft-skinned vehicles, coming from the Kudna Gap, heading straight toward them. At the front of the force are five bridging tanks, and behind them, a number of bright yellow bulldozers.

Uri Akavia, the company commander, had not had a combat day on the Golan yet and shares his amazement with his crew at the nerve the Syrians have. The gunner Asher Peretz is also amazed. Before his eyes, his peri-telescope quickly fills up with numerous Syrian vehicles heading straight at him. The threat they pose still does not register in his mind; they still are at a distance and some of their guns are aimed in the opposite direction.

The three commanders open fire, aiming for the bulldozers and bridging tanks first, as they had been trained to do. The targets start to explode in front of them. Peretz gets down to business and lights up two tanks on the main route. He continues to fire non-stop. Whatever shell the loader loads, he fires and hits. Three bridging tanks are already in flames, but the Syrians, displaying admirable determination, continue to advance.

At the bottom of the ramp, there are two additional tanks, the rest of Overlander's platoon. Yair Deutsch and Zvi Mizrachi, their commanders, are without any work. "Why doesn't Shmulik send us to the southern side of the outpost?" Deutsch wonders.

Shmulik Askarov was not keeping them where they were on a

whim. The Syrian 33rd Brigade with its three infantry battalions and its armored battalion, were moving in an endless column on the Troy route, just as the IDF expected. Why "waste" tanks on the south of the base, when every tank was crucial in stopping the force traveling on the road and around it? It made sense for Askarov to concentrate the five tanks on the northern ramp, facing the main route, a steel fist against the endless stream of forces. When two tanks drove down to replenish ammunition, Deutsch and Mizrachi would come up to take their places.

On the steep slope of the Tel Abas hill, above the north side of the Kudna Gap, the platoon of the redhead Hochstein is under heavy fire.

Hochstein, the platoon commander, Chaim Aldag and Danny Berkovitz, see the same picture as the platoon on the ramp near outpost 111. In a cloud of dust, large forces of tanks, infantry soldiers and BTR armored personnel carriers are heading toward the anti-tank ditch.

"Fire!" the three of them shout.

Fifteen minutes after arriving at the northern ramp, as the Syrian mass of forces continue to make progress, the commanders need to replenish their ammunition. While they start to move their tanks into waiting positions, Zvi Mizrachi and Yair Deutsch get their chance.

Deutsch takes up position and spots muzzle flashes from behind a burned Syrian bridging tank. He places Shmuel Rosenblau, the gunner, on target and he identifies a Syrian tank hiding and appearing from behind it. He fires and hits the target on his first shot and the flashes vanish.

Now they are all on the ramp, they have no choice; they cannot let the enemy through. The five IDF tanks are positioned close to one another, doing their best to fire on the Syrians.

Askarov, the tall deputy battalion commander, runs the battle confidently. In spite of the large force heading toward him, he is calm. The force he is in command of is, as always, operating professionally, just like in training. In his own tank, things are under control. He just has to direct Itzik Hamo, the gunner, to the target area, and he will do the rest from there.

In August 1973, the brigade conducted an exercise on the Golan. For the exercise, Askarov borrowed a tank from A Company, telling Itzik Hamo, the tank commander, that "this just the way things are." Hamo, not one to give in easily, decided that if he cannot be a commander, he at least should be a gunner. With his eye glued to the peri-telescope for two days, Itzik proved that a good tank commander can also be an excellent gunner. Askarov was very impressed by the performance of the commander/gunner. Knowing a combat day was coming up, Askarov borrowed Hamo and his tank again. "Ok, show us what you can do from the gunner's position."

Southern Sector – 114

From his ramp, 2nd Lt. Avi Lahman faced east. Nothing. Someone in the Syrian army decided to leave 1st Platoon out of it. Enemy forces? Not in front of 114. Despite the chaos throughout the southern sector, the twelve soldiers of Lahman's platoon enjoyed the landscape in the east in what seemed like a serene nature film. And all the while, the roar of artillery fire could be heard in the background.

Southern Sector – 115

Avi Ronis, with tank commanders Lavi and Miromi, hears Asher Brinberg cheering from his ramp on the Petroleum Road, "Champagne, champagne!"

Ronis calms everyone down. From his elevated position, which is under heavy fire, he sees what Brinberg can't see: a huge convoy heading toward the Petroleum Road, directly opposite Brinberg's post. Between the artillery shells falling around him, and being careful not to have his head outside the tank too much, he notifies Erez the battalion commander of their approach. Meanwhile, the artillery hits the firing ramp.

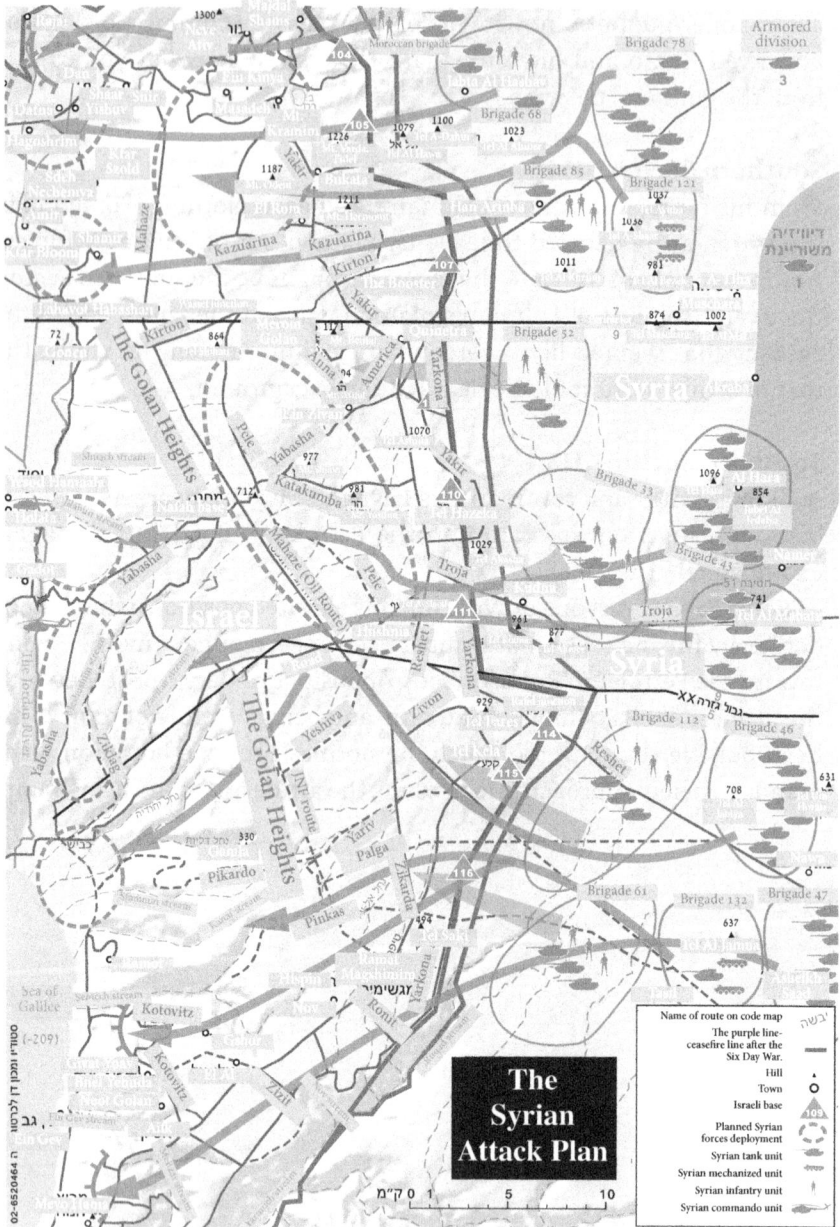

The Syrian
Attack Plan

Armored
division
3

Brigade 78
Brigade 68
Brigade 85
Brigade 121
Brigade 52
Brigade 33
Brigade 43
Brigade 112
Brigade 46
Brigade 61
Brigade 132
Brigade 47

Moroccan brigade

The Golan Heights
The Golan Heights
The Jordan River
Sea of Galilee

Israel
Syria

Name of route on code map
The purple line-
ceasefire line after the
Six Day War.
Hill
Town
Israeli base
Planned Syrian
forces deployment
Syrian tank unit
Syrian mechanized unit
Syrian infantry unit
Syrian commando unit

קמ 0 1   5   10

140

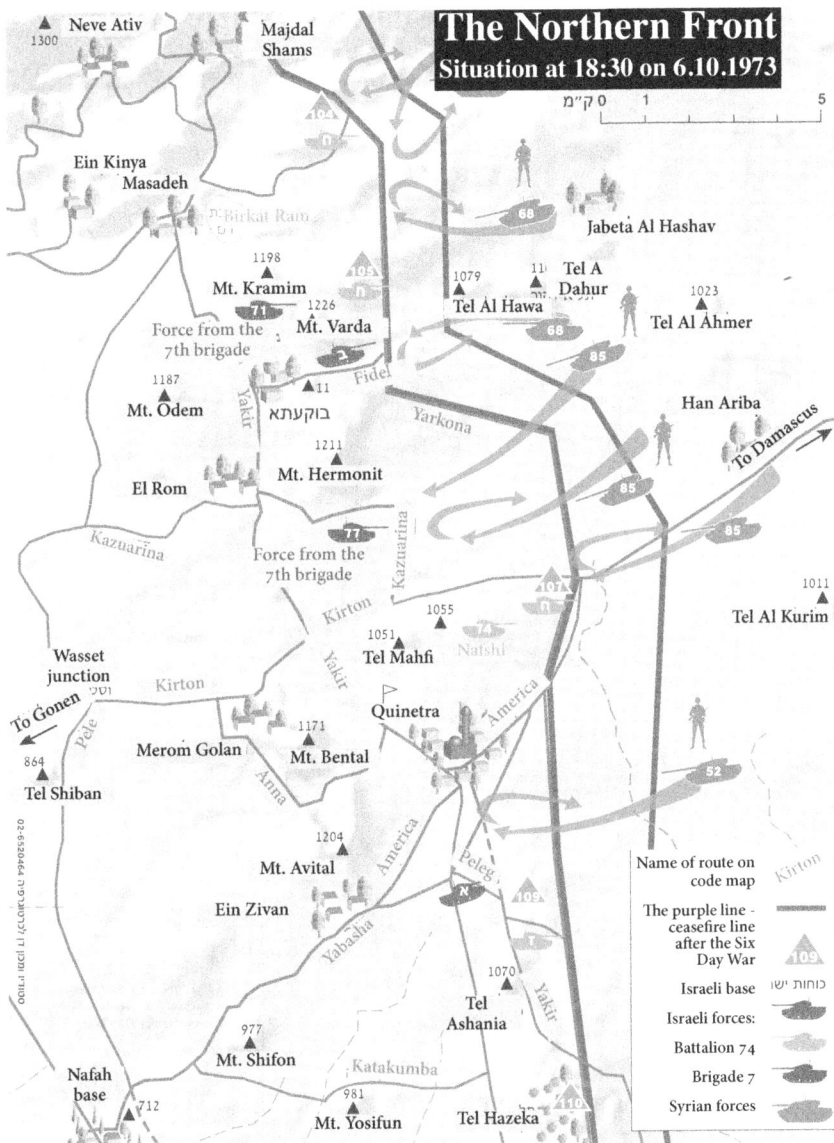

The Northern Front
Situation at 18:30 on 6.10.1973

Neve Ativ
1300

Majdal Shams

Ein Kinya
Masadeh

Birkat Ram

Jabeta Al Hashav

1198
Mt. Kramim
1226
Force from the 7th brigade
Mt. Varda

1079
Tel Al Hawa

Tel A Dahur

1023
Tel Al Ahmer

1187
Mt. Odem

בוקעתא
11

Fidel

Yakir

Yarkona

Han Ariba

To Damascus

1211
Mt. Hermonit

El Rom

Kazuarina

Force from the 7th brigade

Kazuarina

1055

Tel Al Kurim
1011

Kirton

1051
Tel Mahfi

Natshi

Yakir

Wasset junction

To Gonen

Kirton

Pele

Quinetra

America

864
Tel Shiban

1171
Merom Golan
Mt. Bental

Anna

52

1204
Mt. Avital

America

Peleg

Ein Zivan

Yabasha

1070

Tel Ashania

Name of route on code map — Kirton

The purple line - ceasefire line after the Six Day War

Israeli base — כוחות יש

Israeli forces:

Battalion 74

Brigade 7

Syrian forces

977
Mt. Shifon

Katakumba

Nafah base
712

981
Mt. Yosifun

Tel Hazeka

141

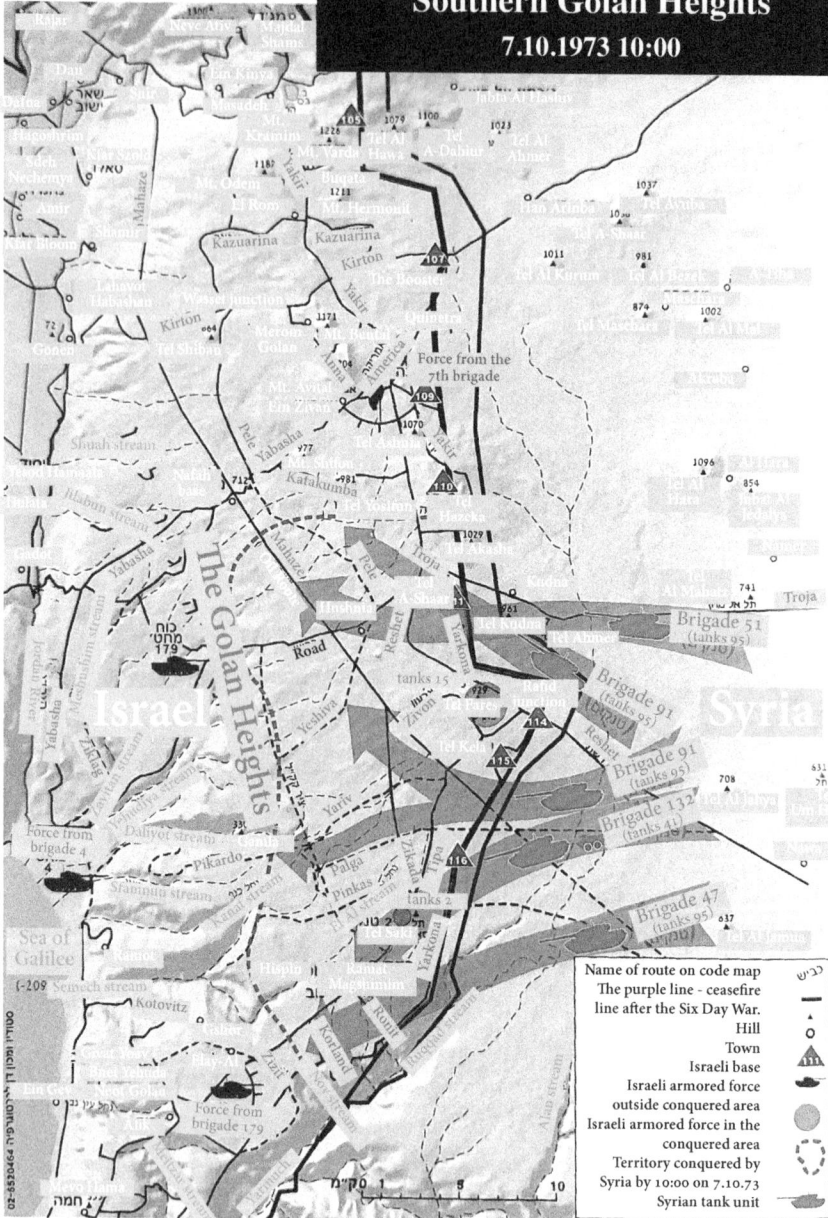

The Syrian infiltration in the Southern Golan Heights
7.10.1973 10:00

Name of route on code map
The purple line - ceasefire line after the Six Day War.
Hill
Town
Israeli base
Israeli armored force outside conquered area
Israeli armored force in the conquered area
Territory conquered by Syria by 10:00 on 7.10.73
Syrian tank unit

The Battle at Nafah
7.10.1973, 13:00

Name of route on code map	Pele
The purple line - ceasefire line after the Six Day War	
Israeli base	
Israeli forces	
Syrian forces	

1171

Yakir

Anna

America

Yarkona

1204

Yabasha

Peleg

679
679

2 פלוגות
מגד' 82

Yabasha

A force from brigade 679
(13 tanks) commanded
by Moshe Harel and
Uri Or returned from
Quinetra and surprised
the Syrian 91st brigade

1070

977

Katakumba

679
679
כוח מחט'

Pele

981

Mechanized anti-
tank battalion

679 (4
tanks)

188
188
188

armored brigade 91
((100 tanks

Troja

188 Brigade
commander/
deputy brigade
commander force
(15 tanks)

51st armored
(brigade (80 tanks

873

Syrian
armored
Division
headquarters

Ziklag

Pele

Reshet

Zavitan stream

179
brigade
force

179

JNF route

ק"מ 0   1   5

Southern Sector – The Petroleum Road

On the Petroleum Road ramp Nati Levi, Moty Aviam and Asher Brinberg are dug in at their posts at Um Lucas Syrian outpost and around it. They are operating according to the "combat day" procedure – firing at ranges of 2,000–2,500 meters at Syrian tanks. It is just what they repeatedly trained for. For Nati and Moty this was their first combat day and they were elated. Brinberg, the veteran sergeant, with the other veteran crewmembers from 2nd Platoon, were unimpressed.

Levi calls orders and the crew respond just as they have drilled many times. Brinberg fires and corrects his hits, Aviam spots anti-tank missiles and he himself also fires. In front of them a mushroom of black smoke rises and the platoon celebrates, "Well done 2, the first champagne of the platoon."

They had arrived at the northern ramp fifteen minutes earlier. Having scanned the horizon, the tank commanders of the 2nd Platoon had put down their binoculars. They are amazed to see the head of an endless convoy of armored vehicles, only 1.5–2 kilometers away, moving up and down on the Petroleum Road, all headed to the ramps of Moty, Asher and Nati the platoon commander.

* * *

In the late 1940s, the American Tapline company had received authorization to lay a huge oil pipeline that started out at Ras Tanura on the shore of the Persian Gulf, continued through Saudi Arabia, Jordan and Syria, and ended at the refineries in Sidon, Lebanon. Beside the pipeline, a service road was built – the Petroleum Road.

The pipe entered the Golan Heights between outposts 115 and 116, passed the slopes of Juhader, Hushnia, Tel Fares and Nafah, then continued to the north. The width of the Petroleum Road was slightly wider than a tank. In its route in Syria and in Israel, it crossed numerous low hills and streams and driving on the route was like riding a roller coaster, with endless ups and downs.

* * *

Nati acknowledges the new information from Ronis and instructs Brinberg to join him in firing. He orders Aviam to retain his role as missile observer. The wave of Syrian forces continue to approach them. Nati decides to stray from protocol and have Aviam join in firing on the forces. Three Sho't Kal tanks alone on a ramp, facing an endless stream of forces moving forward, seemingly unaffected by their losses. The commanders of the Syrian 112th front-line brigade send their forty-one tanks and 1,500 soldiers to take control of the anti-tank ditch and to destroy the three annoying tanks that continue to strike at them.

Southern Sector – C Company

Ten or fifteen minutes after 14:00, the nine tanks of the Urieli force reach the Petroleum Road. They turn to the southeast and speed toward their positions.

Bekman's driver Wallman had no respect for their location. For years, the fence along the Petroleum Road had stood in place, without being harmed, until Wallman arrived. He was driving too fast, turning too sharply and approaching too close. He uprooted the fence from its place. Unaware of the wire caught up in the tanks tracks, he continued, full speed ahead, following the other tanks of the company.

Wallman's driving gets to Bekman, who starts to lose it. The machine guns spin wildly, released from their locked position, with the bumpy ride. The ammunition belts of the 0.3 Browning machine gun slip out of reach, the maps, the flare gun and other equipment fly at Mark, the loader.

"2, this is 2B, is everything alright?" asks Ilan Orenstein, the sergeant driving behind Bekman, concerned to see the way the tank is driving, unable to hide his amused, mischievous tone.

Bekman raises his hands in the air helplessly, as if to say "What can I do? The driver has lost his mind." Fifty-five tons of steel, fuel and explosives, speeding into battle, totally out of control.

After dragging a few kilometers of the fence, sending up dust like a brigade of tanks, with the gas pedal pressed all the way down, Wallman hears a shout from his commander.

"Slow down!!! Slow down!! Wallman, slow down!" Bekman, out of breath, finally manages to regain control of the tank.

It is now or never, Bekman tells himself.

"Wallman, do you hear me?" speaking in his restrained instructor voice.

"I hear you," it is the hesitant reply from the driver.

"Listen, Wallman, the holiday is over. You have a canteen with water next to you. Did you find it? Good. Drink it now. That is an order."

"In the intercom radio they hear gurgling.

"Drink more!"

More gurgling.

"Are you listening, Wallman?"

"Yes."

"From this point, Wallman, pretend we are in training. Do you understand? Training, like in Sinai, like in the battalion. Life is good, Wallman, a bit of action and we will return to base in the evening. Ok, Wallman?"

"Ok."

"I say 'left,'" Bekman continues, sounding like a social worker, "and you pull the left lever gently. If I say hard left, you pull it hard. Is that clear?"

"Alright," again comes the laconic quiet answer on the radio. Bekman pictures Wallman enclosed in his metal cell, with bruises on his face, all his muscles tense. In front of him and to his left are the fuel tanks, to his left twenty-four shells. He holds on to the steering handles, like a child's bicycle handlebars, with red plastic handles, looking at the world from a height of a meter, through dusty periscopes, shaking his view. It is him and his God, against the world.

"Ok, Wallman?" he asks again.

"Ok."

"Is the gunner alright?"

"Alright," answers Eli Rachamim, the gunner from Beit Hashita.

"Is the loader alright?"

"What?" asks Mark Ilenberg.

Nafah

At 14:15 reports start coming in to the command bunker at Nafah that the tanks of the 188th Brigade have reached their positions, identified enemy forces on the move, have made contact and are exchanging fire.

"Conserve your ammunition," Ben Shoham implores the commanders on the brigade radio.

Southern Sector – The Petroleum Road

Someone in the Syrian 112th Brigade decides to show the enemy that they mean business. The artillery barrage, which has continuously accompanied the progress of the Syrian armored vehicles, hits directly on the ramp of the 2nd Platoon, crushing everything around it. A huge explosion blows Moty Aviam's bazooka defense plates all over the place.

Before they have the chance to absorb the fact that the artillery is now hitting them, Nati shouts, "Cannon, 1,500, tank target, fire!"

He searches to see where Michael Zibula, his gunner, hit and then... boom! He touches his forehead, it is damp; looking at his finger, he sees blood. He bends down and looks through the peri-telescope that has a small mirror and sees a scratch. It is nothing. He calls Aviam on the radio. There is no answer. Scanning the tank, he sees that the shell that hit the tank destroyed the commander's machine gun and cut the radio antennas.

The construction of the ramps, which began right after Operation Kiton 10 in July 1970, had been monitored by Syrian intelligence, across the border. Before the war, when the ramps were improved, Fedale kept explaining to the officers, "We do not need a ramp everywhere. Leave room for natural positions as well. It is obvious that the Syrians will locate the ramps and shell them with artillery fire." No one listened. Who bothered to place themselves in natural positions? Hardly anyone. Everyone else took position in the known, regular spots they had trained in and that were the easiest to fight from, the ramps.

Now, it was hell on the ramps. From 13:55 for an hour without break, the Syrians bombarded the ramps with heavy artillery that made it very hard for the tank platoons to function, and what was even worse, they hit some of the commanders, right at the start of the fighting.

In addition, after carrying out a thorough analysis of the area before the war, the Syrian intelligence officers knew the nature of every ramp: what angles each ramp was built at and how large an area they could control. The intelligence officers considered all this information and planned the attack route accordingly. Some of the forces were therefore able to pass through "blind spots" where the tanks could not see.

Aware of Nati's communication trouble and the more severe problem increasing in front of the platoon, Moty Aviam took the initiative and with a shaky voice called to Ronis, the company commander. His voice was not shaking because of the Syrians but because of Ronis, who did not like to be bothered with small matters. "Commander, this is 2A, requesting aerial assistance."

"There is no aerial assistance, out." The answer from Ronis burned in his ears.

Northern Sector – 104

At around 14:20 the three additional tanks of H Company command reached a fork in the road, in front of forward tank depot 104. Eyal, together with Yoni Efrat, continued to head north. Kaimo, the last in the convoy, looked to his right and could not believe his eyes.

"They promised me a combat day," Kaimo mumbled to himself, "but this is something completely different." Three enemy tanks in Israeli territory, descending from Tel Manfucha above the fork, were heading toward the anti-tank ditch. All this, not on the border but a kilometer west of it, inside Israeli territory.

Kaimo calms himself, directs his driver David Sabo into a good position for firing and gives the first command to open fire. He notes that Shmulik Shtiglitz, the loader, is doing well keeping up with the pace of Yehuda Markovitz, the gunner, who destroys the three threats.

14:20

The Hermonit Range

Since the morning, the 820th Regional Brigade has been located in an observation post on the Hermonit Range (Tel A-Shicha). Now, Asher Sadan, deputy intelligence officer of the brigade, spots a large Syrian force, led by seven bridging tanks, heading for the Quneitra gap. He immediately sends the report to the command center at Nafah.

The Syrian attack was in process across the entire front, but it was clear to the decision makers in the bunker that the Syrians were trying to locate the weak spot in the Israeli defense and to focus all their efforts on it.

The Syrian air force had already attacked all of the strategic posts of the IDF on the Golan and destroyed the communication antennas. Listening to Syrian radio frequencies in order to identify Syria's main effort was no longer an option. Do the reports from Sadan, the most senior lookout on this front, regarding mass forces heading toward the Purple Line, indicate where the main effort is directed?

Southern Sector – The Petroleum Road

A few minutes before 14:30, the breaching "storm group" of the Syrian 112th Brigade reaches the fence, located 500 meters from the ramp of the 2nd Platoon, and a "mine roller" anti-mine tank starts to blow up mines, clearing the way for the huge stream of forces.

Just a few days earlier Moty Aviam had been on this same ramp, guarding the combat engineering force. He had stood there, yawning and bored, watching the sappers that crossed the border and laid out endless lines of anti-tank mines in Syrian territory, on the Petroleum Road. No tank can get through these mines safely, someone from the force told him. They must know what they are talking about, he thought.

14:30

The mine roller tank knocks down the fence and the first battle tank appears behind it.

Aviam instruct Fachima the gunner, "Listen Fachima, fire the cannon like a machine gun. The second David shouts 'loaded,' you fire. Like a machine gun, ok?"

David Riv loads ammunition and Fachima shoots at everything moving, like a machine gun. Since the situation is very serious and the three commanders of the platoon tanks get the feeling that "it is us or them," they fire as fast as they can, lighting up the first company of tanks that tries to infiltrate the Petroleum Road. They continue with actual machine gun fire at the enemy crews that flee from the burning tanks.

Southern Sector – 116

The commanders of Yakir's platoon look through their binoculars and do not see anything.

"No chance for champagne today?" Nir Atir shares his frustration with his crew.

Yoav Yakir keeps them on their toes. He takes out a range card and instructs everyone to carry out the known target hitting procedure. They fire at the Zaida bunker, at a range of 2,000 meters with a squash-head shell.[24] Yakir and Atir fire and Waxman takes position slightly behind them and identifies their hits.

Twenty minutes pass. It is almost 14:30, and the Syrians give Atir what he wants. Twenty T55 tanks, accompanied by other armored vehicles, appear on the Roman road (Pinkas route), south of where they are, at ranges of 1,500–2,000 meters. They are all heading west toward Israeli territory.

Menachem Shmueli and Ami Moshe, the gunners of Yakir and Atir, prove they still are the best and justify the awards they received at brigade firing contests. Hallelujah. The 3rd Platoon has also earned some champagne.

Northern Sector – 104

A few minutes before 14:30, Eyal Shaham and Yoni Efrat arrive at their positions in forward sector 104.

At the same time, Eyal receives the report from his deputy, Kaimo, of the incident behind them. "Well done, deputy." His pride is even evident over the radio. He positions Yoni alongside Weisbrott and Shir-On in the southern ramp. He then continues northward, a lone tank, heading toward the Shechita hill, the farthest north tank post in the Golan. Sergeant Koby Greenbaum has been waiting for him for half an hour, frustrated and eager to join battle.

Eyal drives up to the Shechita hill and pulls Koby and his crew with him. He doesn't have to say a word to his driver, Moshe Nili. The repeated training brings the crew into position on the shortest and fastest route. The mountains and wadis are spread out beneath them. He knows every canyon he can hide in, every spot that can be used as a firing position. He has the best tanks in the Middle East and the best company in the battalion. All of the IDF and the country are behind

---

24. High explosive squash head (HESH) or high explosive plastic/plasticized (HEP) shells are filled with plastic explosive that "squashes" against the surface it is fired at before detonating. They differ from HEAT (high explosive anti-tank) projectiles, in that they do not break through a tank's armor, but produce a shock wave that sends lethal fragments (spall) shooting out from the inside of the armor.

him, it is time to prove to his crew – who share his pride – and to the rest of the company and the battalion, that H Company is the best.

Nafah

A few minutes before 14:30, Erez and Nafshi report to Ben Shoham in the bunker at Nafah. They tell him that the Syrian army is launching a widespread attack that includes bridging equipment. They also enumerate the tanks destroyed from their brigade. Nafshi updates him on the attempt to infiltrate in the Manfucha front. They both sound calm. There is a lot of fire and smoke but it is all under control.

Absorbing the data flowing in from the front, with the warning of the assistant intelligence officer regarding massive movement of Syrian forces opposite the Quneitra gap, and the Syrian progress made on the northern Manfucha hills, Ben Shoham decides to position the majority of his reserve force facing the northern sector. There, they wait tensely.

Yanush makes his way, with the 77th Battalion, to the Quneitra gap, since there is a war on and he does not want to miss it. While he is on his way, Ben Shoham sends out an order on the radio of the 7th Brigade, "20 of Mishbetzet, this is 20 of Tofi, assemble 71st and 77th battalions at the Wasset junction and send the 82nd to Hushnia."

The veins in Yanush's neck pop up. It is true that Ben Shoham's order fits in, at least partially, with his plans to use his forces to fight on the northern front, but still, how dare this young brigade commander give him an order? Yanush, never one to suppress even a shred of frustration, responds, "20 of Tofi, this is 20 of Mishbetzet, who are you to give me orders?"

Gaining Power

Until 14:30, just forty-five Sho't Kal tanks of the 188th Brigade faced 276 Syrian tanks. By 14:30, some of them already had been in full combat for thirty minutes. Others were taking up position, and they all noticed and reported that something much bigger than usual was happening.

While these tanks fought, twenty-four additional tanks continued to cross the routes on the Golan. These were tanks of B Company, the Davidson force from G Company and the majority of the tanks of C Company , including the commander of the Southern sector, Lt. Col. Oded Erez.

Erez, Urieli and Davidson realized, based on the magnitude of the artillery fire and the MiG planes flying over them, that this time it is big. As the commanders of the forces on their way to battle, they have no doubt that they were needed at the front, either to join the forces in combat or to take over a new sector. Twenty-four tanks, race horses in steel capes, led by jockeys in khaki. "Faster, faster," they said, "we do not want to miss the battle."

B Company

Shortly after 14:30. The tanks of B Company are forced to cross the road to the other side, on their way to the Manzura/Brown junction. "Beitza forces, this is commander," they hear Landau on the radio. "Just like in training, OK? Everyone crosses on tires."[25] After a few minutes, the tanks reach the junction and spread out. While shells fall close to them, Landau awaits orders.

Northern Sector – 105

Shortly after 14:30. Still in his jeep, ignoring the artillery falling all around him, Yossi Nissim, deputy CO of the 74th Battalion and commander of the northernmost sector, sees a puncture in one of his tires. He instructs his driver to change the tire, quickly, before the combat day gets away from them.

He looks through his binoculars again and sees that things are not getting away from him so quickly. This does not seem to be a regular combat day. The entire area beneath outpost 105 is full of enemy forces. Nissim contacts Ben Shoham directly and asks to send B Company, the reserve force, to his sector. Ben Shoham agrees and instructs Nafshi to call in the company from its assembly spot at the Manzura junction.

Nafshi receives the update from Yossi Nissim, starts to put together the general picture in his sector and decides it is time to change their method of operation. I do not need bodyguards, he decides, and he releases the platoon of Haim Damir to join Yachin on the 107 ramps. The remaining tanks of A Company are sent to outpost 109. The tanks of Landau's B Company are sent to Bukata and sector 105.

---

25. In order to avoid damaging the road surface, standard operating procedure in peacetime was to lay tires on the asphalt and drive the tanks across this protective layer.

3rd Platoon, led by deputy company commander Asaf Sela, are kept as a reserve force that will wait in place, at the Manzura junction (Yakir–Carton).

Nafah

Shortly after 14:30. Zurich, the brigade intelligence officer, is sitting next to Ben Shoham and hears the communication between the brigade commanders. He whispers to Ben Shoham, "Sir, ask Simchoni to deal with Yanush."

Ben Shoham takes his advice and tells Uri Simchoni about the exchange between him and Yanush and has him deal with the hot potato. Simchoni, although only ranked Lt. Col., holds the most senior position in the command center. He understands that Col. Yanush had not been informed that Col. Ben Shoham is in charge of the whole front and that he is partly to blame for that. As the operations officer, the highest ranking officer there, he was supposed to inform the two remaining brigade commanders (Yanush and Zvi Bar) of the order given by the Northern Command CO.

"20 of Mishbetzet, this is 82. Move out to where you were told before," Simchoni instructs Yanush. He continues, "Leave 82nd Battalion in its place, for the southern front."

There is silence on the line and then finally Yanush confirms and accepts.

Sindiyana

From his tank in Sindiyana, Haim Barak, commander of the 82nd Battalion, hears this strange conversation between the brigade commanders and Simchoni's order to Yanush and does not understand. "What is going on here?" he wonders in frustration. "Why isn't anyone giving me my orders?"

The Syrian artillery is in control of the ground, the MiG and Sukhoi planes control the airspace, his three tank companies are deployed and ready but no one is saying a word.

Southern Sector – C Company

A few minutes after 14:30, the Urieli force, including Bekman and Orenstein who – having cleared their tracks of the tangled remnants of the fence wire – had caught up with the rest of them, reach Juhader. To the north, a huge cloud of smoke rises above Tel Fares, and there are fields of thorns on fire, with an east wind blowing a mixture of dust and smoke all along the Golan. There is a strong smell of explosives, mixed with crushed basalt rocks and burnt thorns.

"This is it," Bekman says to himself, "the combat day begins."

At the Juhader junction, they split up. Six tanks of the Urieli force – led by Oded Erez – turn left toward the area near stronghold 115. Boaz Tamir, the deputy company commander, with Yaakov Birnboim's tank, continues straight along the Petroleum Road in order to join the 2nd Platoon of F Company that was fighting for its life.

Slightly behind them, without them being aware of it, the ninth tank – Shabtai Horen's – of the force was also in motion. It carried 1st Lt. Yigal Sapir, the artillery coordination officer. According to the battle plans, the artillery coordinator's tank was supposed to be with that of the battalion commander, but this time, it was not. Its position in the column was not behind the CO and it continued straight on the Petroleum Road instead of turning left with Oded Erez. Was this navigation error a result of the tank being manned by crew sent from B Company, which had not had the chance to integrate into C Company? Perhaps. Was it the unusual switch of position of Horen to the loader's seat? Perhaps. At first, Horen had taken the commander's seat but had withdrawn when Sapir – who outranked him – had demanded his place. This made it harder for Horen to see the way and to identify the tank of the battalion commander. Either way, it was one of those small things that determine people's fates.

Northern Sector – 107

Shmulik Yachin is so angry at Shalom Manan that he is about to explode. "What is going on, Maman?" he exclaims to the gunner. "Are you going to continue to screw up, the way you did in the last exercise?" Maman does not respond, and Shmulik does not know if the approach he took was very smart, but he does not have time to overthink it. There is a truckload of soldiers 800 meters from them, and Shmulik knows that every infantry soldier that crosses the bridge can fire an anti-tank rocket at them. Before he gives the order, Maman fires a shell at the Syrian infantry carrier, crushing it and strewing body parts everywhere.

More trucks arrive, full of Syrian soldiers waving their Kalashnikov rifles enthusiastically, as if they were in the middle of a march. They are unaware of the presence of Maman, who is now performing excellently, hitting every target.

Once again, the explosive squash-head shells (HESH) and hollow-charge shells (HEAT) were hitting the Syrian trucks, turning the bridge into a pile of flaming ruins and a cemetery for the Syrian soldiers.

Southern Sector – Yuval Shachar
The Syrian artillery is relentless at Tel Faraj. The ground is shaking, and the NCOs indicate to the enthusiastic intelligence officer that they might be better off finding a calmer spot for the communication command center.

Yuval agrees and leads the group to the south. They cross the Petroleum Road and settle at the top of Tel Danir. Just two kilometers separate the two hills but they are in different worlds. They see the sights, hear the sounds, but are at a safe distance. Yuval switches stations on the different radio frequencies trying to understand what is going on. He gradually begins to understand that something big is developing in front of the tanks on the front lines.

Southern Sector – Dr. Englehard
A military ambulance, called in from Nafah, hits the brakes at the Mashta junction that is currently under artillery fire. The 53rd Battalion's medical team , led by Dr. Englehard, place the bleeding intelligence NCO Nachshon Hermoni on the stretcher. He is still conscious, fighting for his life.

"Go as fast as you can," Dr. Englehard orders the driver, who speeds toward the Ziv Hospital in Tzfat.

Nachshon is now in the ambulance, between life and death. A young man from Kibbutz Sarid, with a love for meteorology, astronomy and graphology, who in a letter he wrote to his parents said, "I am waiting to be discharged, so that I can continue to contribute to the kibbutz again." At the entrance to the hospital in Tzfat, Nachshon breathes his last breath and someone closes his eyes. He is the first to fall from the 188th Brigade. He will not be able to contribute to the kibbutz anymore.

Booster Ridge – Nafshi

It is 14:45. Lt. Col. Yair Nafshi is, without Damir's platoon, alone on the ramp below the Booster. He decides that it is "artillery time." Without the presence of the artillery coordination officer, Nafshi, together with Danny Avni, the operations officer in the tank with him, direct the artillery pieces of the northern sector.

Nafshi's extraordinary knowledge of the Syrian territory is highly effective now. Who needs help directing the artillery when he has a list in his head of all the crossings on the Ruqqad? Nafshi measures ranges on the map, directing the fire, easily compensating for the absence of the artillery coordination officer.

Northern Sector – 104

At around 14:45, Aviv Shir-On, leader of the 2nd Platoon, H company, identifies a single tank moving on the western slopes of the Manfucha hills, in Israeli territory.

"Great," Shir-On thinks in satisfaction, "this is probably the first tank of the 71st Battalion that we were promised as back up." Another look at the shape of the tank reveals a low, flat façade and a cannon facing west, toward Israeli territory. A Syrian Tiran tank! He hardly has the chance to grasp what he is seeing when another four appear next to it.

Blind to their sad fate, moving across the slopes of Manfucha, the five Tiran tanks, the first of the Moroccan Battalion force, are peaceful and calm. They are unaware of the three tanks of the 2nd Platoon that improve their position by moving southwards, then open fire on them. This was the first action of the Moroccan force, who had arriving in the northern front in April 1973 as back up. They now face Shir-On, Kaimo and Shaham, the company commander.

Within seconds, three Tiran tanks are destroyed. Panicking at this miserable start, the two remaining tanks locate Shir-On's platoon, take up position and return fire.

Boom! Yoni Efrat, positioned next to Aviv, is hit in the cannon. The tank can no longer fire but is still fit to drive, and in an immediate decision, Aviv decides to turn it into a mobile ammunition supply vehicle for the five tanks of 104 sector.

14:40

Southern Sector – Davidson Force

The three tanks of the Davidson force complete their drive and in a rain of fire, with shells falling all around them, they take up position at Tel Mahir.

A company of Syrian tanks exposes itself by the fence, 2.5 kilometers from them, and an exchange of fire begins. "A big combat day," Moty Amir thinks to himself. "Just what we were trained for."

Southern Sector – 115

Oded Erez positions himself on the battalion commander's ramp, on the slopes of stronghold 115. He calls to the artillery coordination officer to come join him and does not understand where he has disappeared.

A minute or two later, Bekman and Orenstein take up position 500 meters north of the battalion commander. They are taking advantage of natural positions alongside the road to the north of stronghold 115 (Tel Al-Kela). From here, the Petroleum Road is out of view and all they see is the south of the Rafid Gap, where nothing is moving.

At about the same time, Company Commander Uzi Urieli takes position, with Hagai Zur, leader of the 1st Platoon, and Yehuda Akunis, his sergeant, in natural positions north of the Botmia swamp, 500 meters north of Bekman. They see no movement in front of them, and like Bekman and Orenstein, they do not have any action.

The Rafid Gap (the Reshet route) was considered to be one of the preferred locations for a possible Syrian attack. It is wide, enabling quick deployment of enemy tanks. In the afternoon of Saturday, four platoons shut off the gap – two platoons from F Company of the 74th, Davidson/Moty Amir in stronghold 113, Lahman in 114 – two platoons from C Company of the 53rd, Urieli/Zur near Botmia, Bekman in stronghold 115.

A few hundred meters south of Bekman, things are completely different.

Avi Ronis, commander of F Company and the tanks with him, are conducting long-range battles with Syrian forces. At the same time, artillery continues to fall on them. Unlike Bekman and Urieli, Ronis is in constant action. A huge mass of Syrian forces is moving south of his ramp toward the anti-tank ditch, between stronghold 115 and the Petroleum

Road. Ronis does not know that this is the armored battalion of the 112th Infantry Brigade, and it would make no difference to him if he did.

Southern Sector – The Petroleum Road

First Lt. Boaz Tamir and Sergeant Yaakov Barenboim arrive at "their" ramp, in the southern sector near the Petroleum Road. They immediately join the combat. On the northern ramp, tens of meters from them, Nati Levi's three tanks are in position and have already been in battle for forty-five minutes. Slightly behind, without them having noticed it, is the tank of the artillery coordination officer.

An officer, but at his foundation an artillery soldier, Yigal Sapir, the 53rd Battalion's artillery coordination officer, never imagined he would be in the commander's compartment in a Sho't Kal tank on a ramp on the front line of the Petroleum Road, fighting for his life.

His radio was not working, so Sapir was unaware of the repeated calls from Erez the battalion CO to come join him. What he did know was that in his current position, he was not effective in directing the artillery.

Southern Sector – 116

Yair Waxman, the "cub" (junior tank commander) of Yoav Yakir's platoon, joins the fun and gives his gunner, David Levi, quality time, and like many of his friends, he also marks a number of hits of enemy tanks.

Yoav watches his platoon perform. He hears the battle cries of his soldiers and his heart is full of pride.

Yoav, from Kibbutz Kfar Rupin in the Beit Shean valley – not far from Kibbutz Afikim, the kibbutz of his sergeant Nir Atir – was always the best at everything. He excelled in his studies, loved poetry and literature, was a natural entertainer (he wrote songs and music), an outstanding athlete, and a social activist; he was aware of the environment and had a deep love for the Land of Israel. What else could you ask for?

Yoav did not ask for much. He just wanted to be a combat soldier. He volunteered for the pilot training course, was dismissed after a year and was assigned to an aerial control unit but turned down the position. "I have to be a combat soldier," he insisted and begged. In the end, he ended up in the armored corps.

His friends in the armored corps told him he was crazy. "It was not that bad there, why didn't you stay? You'd be living the easy life. You would have completed your service healthier, fresher and cleaner."

With a profound smile, he dived deeper into the can of grease, helped others navigate in tank commander's course, learned to cope with sleepless nights and at the end got what he wanted, to be a tank platoon commander in the 188th Brigade.

14:45

Nafah

It is crowded in the command center at Nafah. The commanders sit shoulder-to-shoulder, among the incessantly chattering radios, information constantly streaming in and Ben Shoham trying to run the show.

Simchoni sees Ben Shoham sitting with earphones and five radios, talking to all his companies and platoons on the ground. "What incredible pressure," Simchoni thinks to himself. "Being a brigade commander during war is a full-time job; he can't deal with any other tasks."

He takes the initiative, sensing that time is running out and now is the moment to make command decisions. He is confident that when the commanding officer returns, he will support him.

Simchoni is of a lower rank than Ben Shoham, but in his senior position in the command, he is sure he has to take responsibility and that is what he does. Instead of keeping the 7th Brigade as a reserve force at the Wasset junction, as Ben Shoham suggested, he sends the brigade straight to the front.

Simchoni knows that the 7th Brigade is the only armored reserve force on the Golan, and will remain so for at least another twelve hours. He knows that Ben Shoham wants its two reserve battalions to act as an armored fist, immobile at this point, at the Wasset junction. He knows that this sort of decision is either praised or reprimanded, not to mention that he is acting out of the regular chain of command. Still he decides to follow through, without consulting anyone (neither Ben Shoham nor the Northern Command CO who is in a helicopter on his way back to the command center).

When Simchoni decides to move the 7th Brigade toward the Quneitra Gap – forty-five minutes after the war started – there are three tank companies in the northern front, under the command of the 74th Battalion commander. On the southern front, there are three tank companies, under the command of the 53rd Battalion. What caused Simchoni to send the only reserve force that the Northern Command had, to the front lines? Why maneuver seven additional tank companies – four of Kahalani, commander of the 77th Battalion, as well as three of Ratess, 71st Battalion CO – to the northern front, before things become clearer?

As General Haka's right-hand man, Simchoni spent days and nights around him, getting to know his approach, learning that the Quneitra gap will be the most attractive front for the Syrians and the most dangerous for IDF. In light of the reports he received from the forces, Simchoni was able to put together a picture that bore out the general's scenario. The Syrian forces were concentrating their main effort at the Quneitra gap. Haka's biggest fear had materialized. "If I do not close the opening immediately," Simchoni tells himself, "the Syrians will break through in the north and the IDF and the Israeli people will lose the Golan Heights."

Simchoni is sure of his ability to run this battle from the command bunker. A former Golani battalion commander, a former Egoz reconnaissance battalion commander and the current operations officer of the Northern Command, he feels that he has the experience and the expertise to command this front with judgment and confidence. Simchoni is as familiar with the Golan as his own backyard, knowing every route in the code maps by heart. He can get to any spot in the area, in the dark, whether it is a trail, a base, or the remains of a Circassian village. He feels confident that his perfect knowledge of the area will help him make the right decisions in maneuvering forces to crucial spots, as he just decided with the 7th Brigade.

"Yitzchak," Simchoni implores Ben Shoham after sending the 7th Brigade to Quneitra, "go join your brigade on the ground. Take the 82nd Battalion and go to battle with them. I am relieving yo u. Don't worry, I will run things from here."

Southern Sector – 115
From the control position near stronghold 115, Oded Erez the battalion commander, continues to call Yigal Sapir, the artillery coordination

officer. He does not understand why he is not responding and why he is not with him.

Yossi Sapir, the battalion operations officer, is with Erez, helping him run the battle. He too does not understand where the artillery officer disappeared to. According to the basic battle procedure, he is supposed to be with them and relieve them from the need to choose the targets and direct the artillery. He is not with them and is not answering.

Southern Sector – The Petroleum Road

On the Syrian side of the border fence on the Petroleum Road lies an endless stream of armored vehicles. Facing them, on two ramps, on both sides of the Petroleum Road, six Israeli tanks try to stop them.

Nir Elimelech, the gunner of the artillery officer tank, is ecstatic. He destroyed two enemy tanks, in combat range of course. He is all smiles and confident but then something starts to go wrong. From his position, slightly behind the tank of platoon sergeant Asher Brinberg, on the northern ramp, he sees a powerful flash between equipment cells 7 and 8 on the turret and things fly out of the tank.

"2 this is crew member 2B," the loader Avi Shachar reports to Levi, the platoon commander. "Commander is injured. I am evacuating him to Venus." With a fatal injury, gasping desperately for air, Brinberg is evacuated with his tank to Juhader tank camp.

Shells are still falling in the camp when the company medic Minjersky, hears the engine and tracks of a returning tank. He lifts up his head and sees Brinberg's tank 2B speeding wildly and Avi Shachar the loader shouting in a voice never heard before in Juhader, "Menachem, Menachem, hurry, hurry!" The tank comes to a sudden stop and the driver, Alex Perlstein, begs, "Menachem, save him. You have to. Do something. Asher, it is Asher, hurry. You have to."

"Let's get him down into the pit," Minjersky orders them, trying to remain calm. "It is better down there."

Booster Ridge – Nafshi

At 14:45 Yair Nafshi decides to activate the rest of his reserve force.

"Deputy Beitza, this is Peleg commander," Nafshi calls Asaf Sella. "Take your unit, move to the foot of the big hill (Hermonit). Contact the commander of Beitza and join him."

The deputy Commander of B Company, Asaf Sella, leaves the Manzura junction, accompanied by a tank platoon, takes the route the tanks of the company had taken half an hour earlier, and finds himself at the foot of the Hermonit.

From his post on the Booster, Nafshi hears a call from infantry stronghold 109. The commander, 1st Lt. Ehud Ben Gera, reports with a sense of urgency, "A force of twenty tanks and mechanized infantry soldiers are heading toward me."

In the regular inspections of the Northern Command, stronghold 109 had always met the required standards. There was a deep bunker, protected positions for a 20 mm cannon and a machine gun, thick fighting trenches, double fences, mines and twelve brave Golani soldiers, with their motto, "You better not mess with us."

For two weeks the soldiers at 109 had been reporting to their commanders that there was a mass of Syrian vehicles opposite them. "Thank you, we copy that," was the response they always received. Since nothing happened, they got used to it. Besides, why worry? They have the whole army there with them.

"Commander Ace, send a unit to 109," Nafshi commands Zvika Rak, commander of A Company .

*　*　*

Although his body is limp, his mouth is clamped tightly shut, hardly breathing and Minjersky sees a black hole in his helmet. He has a weak pulse. He forces an airway into his mouth, almost breaking his jaw. He tries to insert an IV but there is no discernable vein. Minjersky knows he has to lay Asher down in the right position but there is no room for the stretcher in the tiny pit they are all hiding in. "Everyone move, I need space," he shouts with an inhuman voice, and everyone crowds together in the corner, enabling Minjersky to bend over Asher. "We need a doctor," he shouts to Yitzchak Rachamim, the company sergeant. "He has to get to the medical center at the Rafid junction." Minjersky lifts Brinberg's limp body into the APC and climbs up after him. He takes a quick look at the Juhader camp. It is no longer the base he knew.

Nine days later, On October 15, Asher Brinberg's strength gives out and he passes away. He was from Ramat Gan, a happy, mischievous, optimistic young man, happy with his life. He was an outstanding student in sciences and dreamed of studying nuclear physics after completing his army service.

As Brinberg's tank is hit, Elimelech, the gunner of the artillery officer tank, realizes that the direction of the hit suggests there may be Syrian tanks in their flank area. He is right.

Diagonally to his right, 400–500 meters from their post, he identifies the black cannon of a Tiran tank aiming at them. Elimelech knows there is nothing he can do. Since the radio is not working, he turns his head back, opens his mouth to shout to Shabtai Horen, the tank commander, that they are in trouble. He sees Yigal Sapir, the artillery officer, working on the radio in the commander's seat. There is a terrible whistling sound, the tank shakes and Shabtai's shattered body falls into the loader's seat after a shaped charge shell hits him. He falls on Zvi Yahalomi, the loader, who starts shouting, "Mom, mom!"

With the tank commander dead, the loader in shock, in a tank that looks like hell and reeks of burnt flesh, without external radio communication, still in an exposed firing position, Yigal Sapir, the artillery officer, himself in pain, realizes it is time to take command.

"Driver, reverse," he orders Armin Shneir the driver; he tries to report that they were hit but the intercom is not working. "Yigal, get us out of here," he hears someone half begging, half instructing, on the internal radio. He does not know who it is talking but he knows it is his job to do exactly that. With a sense of responsibility and an instinct for survival, he finds the way to guide Shneir out of hell.

14:50

Boom! Now it is Nati Levi's tank that is struck, from the same direction Brinberg and Horen were hit from. The crew jumps out of the tank, runs and lies in the ditch on the side of the route. Moty Aviam rushes to them and they enter his tank. Nati connects to the radio and orders, "Drive to Juhader."

Within less than ten minutes their luck completely changes. Four tanks – of Brinberg, Horen, Levi and Aviam – leave the ramps of the Petroleum Road and head toward Juhader. Tamir, the deputy company commander, and Barenboim remain on their own on the Petroleum

Road, conducting a desperate battle to hold off the forces of the Syrian 112th Brigade with their bridging tanks.

Northern Sector – A-Kahtania

In a cloud of dust and with engines roaring, three tanks rush to help stronghold 109. Manning them are deputy company commander Oded Yisraeli, 3rd Platoon leader, 1st Lt. Nimrod Kochavi and sergeant Shuki Hashenberg.

They take the shortest route to the base, passing the ruins of the villas in east Quneitra. While enjoying the power of the tank and the route he had taken endless times before, Yisraeli notices unusual additions to the landscape. No more than 300 meters from him he identifies a company of Syrian tanks rolling along, hatches closed and exposed to the Israeli Sho't Kal tanks. Ten Syrian tanks, forty enemy soldiers, are in the sights of Yisraeli's tanks.

"Fire!" Yisraeli commands Zeevik Tuashi, the gunner.

"Fire!" Nimrod Kochavi commands Dubi Zolden, the gunner.

"Fire!" Shuki Hashenberg commands Zion Awad, the gunner.

Zeevik looks in his peri-telescope and instead of a tank, he sees an unidentified surface.

"Fire now!" Yisraeli screams.

What is this idiot aiming me at, Tuashi wonders, looking to the right and left, when he suddenly realizes this surface is a tank.

"Fire already, fire already!" Oded shouts and Tuashi fires and lights up the tank.

"What range should I use now?" Tuashi asks.

"Any combat range," Oded answers. "Anything will hit here, fire Zeevik, fire."

Yisraeli rotates the turret and Tuashi puts the crosshairs on target and fires and destroys the tank. He elbows Yisraeli's leg, signaling him to move to another target. "We will have the most champagne bottles in the company."

A number of Syrian soldiers jump out of one of the tanks that have been hit and take cover in the trench. Tuashi hesitates.

"Fire, before they come back in another tank!" Yaakov Moshe shouts from the driver's seat. Tuashi is easily convinced. He just needed an explanation, and he ends their short lives with a squash-head shell.

In the course of a few minutes, with the advantages of the element of surprise and professional gunning, the three tanks destroy the entire Syrian company. Oded Yisraeli is joyous on the company radio. "Guys, there's a party going on here, come see!"

Just when it seemed like their personal war was over, Nimrod Kochavi identifies a Syrian bridging tank and places Duby Zoldan on target. He hits the target on his first shot. Nimrod hears the crew celebrating, and the world seems pink and promising.

Southern Sector – 115

The Avi Ronis force fires at long ranges, hitting a small number of targets but unable to slow down the pace of the Syrian convoys heading toward the Petroleum Road. Next to Ronis, the festival of hitting targets ends for Avi Lavi's tank. A Syrian shell hits his tank and destroys the cannon rotation system.

"We need reinforcements," Ronis reports to Erez.

The battalion commander did not even get the chance to acknowledge the request from Ronis before Shmulik Askarov – his deputy commander – asks him for artillery fire at Kudna Gap, to help stop fifteen tanks approaching the anti-tank ditch.

Before he gets the chance to deal with this request, Askarov sends another urgent call, as he identifies another thirty vehicles a kilometer south of the Kudna village. As Erez completes Askarov request, he identifies the Syrian force Ronis reported moments before. "In urgent need of more tanks. They are breaking through the Petroleum Road," Erez notifies the brigade command at Nafah.

As he is waiting for reinforcements, the commander of the 53rd Battalion understands that he is going to have to win with what he has. He decides to redeploy his forces. He instructs the tanks of C Company, in the 115/Botmia area, to leave their posts and head quickly to the Petroleum Road and reinforce the force there.

Then he instructs Avi Ronis to send the platoon in area 114 to area 113.

"1, this is commander," Ronis says to his platoon commander at 114.

"This is 1, over," Avi Lahman answers, understanding that now things are going to change.

"This is commander, move to purple 351 on the Raia route (area 113) and join the force in place there" (the Davidson force).

"This is 1, roger."

Southern Sector – 111

Infantry base 111 identifies three columns of tanks heading its way and reports this to the regional brigade.

From his controlling position, Shmulik Askarov does not need the report from the outpost. He sees the endless clouds of dust clearly, with enemy tanks moving on the Troy route. Askarov orders his team to hold their fire, to conserve ammunition until the enemy is within combat range. The first Tiran tanks reach 1,000 meters from the ramps and all the tanks of the Askarov force, hungry for fire, open fire quickly. They then immediately go down, into waiting positions, reload and come back up and hit their targets, over and over.

On the Tel Abas front, on the other side of the Troy route, there are also festive hits. Danny Berkovitch's crew is hoarse from shouting "champagne" so many times. Kupstein, the best gunner in the company, and Berkovitch, its most experienced and admired commander, count the tanks destroyed and Kupstein is excited when they reach twenty.

Chaim Aldag, the 1st Lt. who recently joined the battalion after a long training at the Tze'elim base, feels like he is at shooting practice. The only difference is that there the targets didn't return fire.

Yet still, the Syrian force continues to move forward. In the wide valley beneath outpost 111, the vehicles that were hit are passed and the convoy continues forward, spreading to both sides of the Troy route, split into five combat spearheads all heading toward the anti-tank ditches beneath the outpost. The first soldiers are already crossing the ditch and tens of Syrian soldiers are moving toward the fences of the stronghold.

Northern Sector – 107

While Yachin's platoon is resupplying, a company of Syrian tanks passes to their south. Elimelech Avraham (Miley), commander of base 107, identifies the infiltration and reports it to Yachin, who rushes up to his position to join him. Yachin takes out his binoculars and takes a look. Miley was not exaggerating. Next to the UN base, 400 meters from his ramp, there are eight tanks. Luckily they are driving in a column with their hatches closed, not aware of the tank watching them. But not all of them.

In the leading tank, there is a Syrian company commander with his head out. Yachin sees him direct the cannon toward him, and Yachin, terrified, shouts into the tank, "Fire, fire!." Rachamim Cohen, the loader, does not load a shell. Instead, in a cold, quiet voice he reports, "There are no ready shells."

"Fire, fire!" shouts Yachin again, ignoring the report he just received, transferring the sense of urgency to Rachamim, who manages to load from the back and Shalom aims and fires. An anti-tank shell hits the Syrian tank in front of them, cleaving the body of the brave Syrian company commander, and Yachin starts breathing again.

Now they are in complete control. Another of Yachin's tanks is in position and the Syrian tank company are hit, one by one, without their managing to fire even one shell at Yachin's platoon.

Sindiyana

As Maj. Haim Barak is about to lose his mind to boredom and too many unanswered questions, Yanush, the commander of the 7th Brigade, finally contacts them on the radio of the 82nd Battalion. "10 of Neka, this is 20 of Mishbetzet." There is a moment of silence and Barak wonders where he is going to be sent. "Move at full speed on the Pele route, until it meets the Kvish route on line 57 (Hushnia) and await my orders."

Filled with a combat spirit, having one operational company (Eli Geva's A Company) and two young training companies (Yaakov Chessner's B Company and Danny Levin's D Company), the 82nd Battalion's CO sets out, leading thirty-two tanks in a long column along the rocky Pele route, connecting Sindiyana–Ramtaniyot–Hushnia.

"I wonder what Yanush was waiting for?" Barak wondered while sending out the first commands. The command he received just now is the same one Yanush received from Ben Shoham thirty minutes ago.

An hour after the start of the war, the commander of the 82nd Battalion is still unaware of the agreement between the two brigade commanders, according to which the 82nd will be under the command of the 188th Brigade. Yanush, the "biological father," was supposed to inform his "son" of the change but he didn't.

What about Ben Shoham? The commander of the 188th Brigade had received command of a new battalion from the 7th Brigade. Wouldn't it have been reasonable for him to contact the new battalion commander and verify he is joining him? He too failed to do so.

14:55

Southern Sector – The Petroleum Road

C Company has run out of luck. Without any warning, Barenboim's tank, on the southern ramp of the Petroleum Road, is hit. The angel of death is back, this time for a double visit.

The explosion that shook the tank threw Yehezkel Kelner, the driver, around in his compartment. His glasses flew off, leaving him confused, but his training pays off and he responds, puts the tank in reverse and drives to a safer spot.

"Akeb and Barenboim are dead, we are finished," Yishai Daniel, the gunner, shouts to him. He himself, hit by numerous shards of shrapnel, pulls himself out of the tank and starts running toward the deputy CO's tank, fighting for his life, unaware that death has already visited there.

Kelner, with steel shards in his back, opens his compartment hatches, crawls out of the tank, and automatically, with his mind blank, runs the fire-extinguishing drill, putting out the flames.

Boaz Tamir, preoccupied with staying alive, waves Yishai to move away. Yishai makes his way back to his own tank, already stinking of death, and meets Kelner, who had just finished fighting the fires. "What are we doing now?" he thinks, leaning on the cold steel that doesn't protect them anymore. Kelner, crushed from the sights and the smells, makes another attempt to get out of the lethal open air. On trembling legs he crosses the thirty meters to the deputy's tank, the only one still trying to stop the Syrians on the Petroleum Road. He waves his hand to Boaz Tamir that returns a short tempered wave as if saying "Are you crazy? Leave me and take care of yourself. Don't you see I'm left alone against the whole 112th Brigade?" Kelner actually understands. There is nothing to do here with a wounded tank on the basalt ramp. "I'm driving to Nafah," he shouts, returning to the driver's compartment and checks the systems. The engine, transmission and steering respond. Now, a routine drill; taking the damaged tank to the workshops. Kelner seats Yishai the gunner beside him on the front of the tank and they start zigzagging between the basalt terraces along the Petroleum Road in order to get away from the artillery. Inside the blackened turret, the crushed bodies of Akeb and Barenboim shake with every movement.

Boaz Tamir is alone, the last tank on the Petroleum Road. The force leading the 112th Brigade is not showing signs of generosity, not considering the unimaginable differences between the sides. It continues to push forward.

15:00

Oded Erez

It is almost 15:00. Oded Erez feels exposed in the battalion commander's post. The position is drawing fire and is starting to take endless artillery shells. He knows that if he does not act immediately, the sector will be left without a commander.

Yossi Shechter, the driver, drives in reverse. Yitzchak Keres, the gunner, and Rachamim Simchi, the loader, sigh in relief, and Oded Erez comes down from the ramp, heads back to the main route (Tapa) and takes up position on a hill, between Juhader and Tel Fares.

In a different position than he planned to be, partly cut off from the events due to communication problems, Oded Erez still does not know that the angel of death has started to take the lives of his soldiers and demand its pound of young flesh. He also does not know that someone on the Syrian side has studied and copied the drills of the 188th Brigade and carried out a quick firing drill at the northern ramp on the Petroleum Road, destroying it. He continues to call the artillery officer and receives no response.

Nafah

It is almost 15:00. Simchoni again turns to Ben Shoham. "Itzik, take the APC and go out to join your forces, they need you there."

With the chaos of reports on the radio and the uncertainty of what is going on, Col. Itzik Ben Shoham, the commander of the 188th Brigade, has just one principle left in his considerations on how to act, the order from Gen. Haka, putting him in command of the Golan front until he returns. Ben Shoham hears Simchoni's request; but Simchoni is also aware of Haka's order and Ben Shoham cannot understand the pressure the aggressive operations officer is putting on him.

15:00–15:56

In October 1973, the defense concept of the IDF on the Golan Heights was that of "Steadfast Defense"– not allowing the enemy to achieve any success on the ground, not even temporary. Therefore, for the soldiers of the 188th Brigade, the first infiltrations of the Syrian forces beyond the Purple Line – at Mafucha in the northern front and in Kahtania near Quneitra – were an outrageous insult. Kaimo could not believe he was seeing Tiran tanks heading down the slopes of Manfucha to the west, and Oded Yisraeli was particularly concerned about them infiltrating the village of Kahtania.

No one bothered to notify Kaimo and Yisraeli that there was an option of a rear line or an intermediate line or a stop line, according to the battle doctrine. There was no reason to notify them, since the Chief of General Staff and the Northern Command CO had decided that the stop line would remain, as always, the Purple Line. This was not to be crossed. Therefore, at 15:00 on Saturday of Yom Kippur, Kaimo, Yisraeli and all the tanks on the front failed in their mission. The Purple Line, the line determined after the Six-Day War, marking the 1,260 square kilometers of territory controlled by Israel on the Golan Heights, had been crossed.

At 15:00 the Syrian forces continued to attack all along the front. Some of the designated attack units, under the command of the infantry brigades, succeeded in carrying out their missions on schedule according to the "Mashroa 110" command. They were positioned on the anti-tank ditch or close to it, working on creating more passageways for the armored forces to enter the Golan.

By 15:00, the decision makers at the Nafah command center had seen the active participation of the Syrian Air Force and the intensity of its preliminary air strike. They had seen the massive numbers of forces moving forward. They had seen the determination with which the divisions were trying to cross the anti-tank ditch. They had also witnessed the infiltration of the first enemy forces into Israeli territory. It was clear to them that this was not another combat day. It was war.

Yet still, in spite of the surprise and the ratio of forces, despite the first casualties, the general feeling coming from the fighters on the front was "we are holding on."

Northern Sector – 107

On the southern 107 ramp, Damir's platoon joined Yachin's platoon and gets to fire on targets beneath them that are already raising black smoke.

With six tanks under his command, Yachin decides it is time to divide the area up. He leaves Damir's platoon on the southern ramp and moves with his platoon 300 meters north to the northern ramp.

To Damir's right, on the southern ramp, Avishai Levital takes up position. From here he sees the front in flames, with numerous enemy vehicles burning.

Together with Damir in the center and Moshe Farkash, the sergeant, on the left, Levital joins the platoon's fire. He scouts for enemy AT missiles while the other two shoot and correct each other. Suddenly the trauma of the road accident at the Juhader junction seems less significant. The endless artillery fire hitting the ramp and the enemy tanks continuing to flow toward him prove to him, this being his first combat, that reality is a series of jigsaw puzzle pieces.

For Yachin the war was already a routine. He fires and destroys. He pauses to discover that he is enjoying it. It is all working just like it is supposed to. "How wouldn't it?" he thinks to himself, seeing Yoni Vo-dak on his right and Yossi Naides on his left, fighting like fearless lions. He assumes this is exactly the test that Nafshi was talking about.

In November 1970, when he was drafted, Yachin, a young aviation instructor at the aero-club, had tried to get into pilot school. After the initial training he was sent back to the induction center with a strong sense of failure. He overcame it quickly, and like everyone else in his neighborhood, decided that if not a pilot, he would be in the armored corps.

He went directly into the corps' officers course. He graduated and was commissioned with the rank of 2nd Lt. From there he was posted to be an instructor for reserve soldiers at the Tze'elim training base. After a year, he asked to be transferred to serve with the regular forces of the 188th Brigade.

July 1973, and Yachin is posted to the adjutancy of the 188th Brigade. "I'm supposed to get my 1st Lt. rank today," he announces as he waves the form confirming his request in front of Maj. Ben Moshe, the brigade adjutancy officer.

"You are new in the brigade. We still don't know you. We can't give you the rank," was Ben Moshe's response, true to the tradition of excellence and restraint in the 188th Brigade. He wondered to himself who this young officer is – he has not even smelled the odor of a can of grease on the Golan and is already demanding a rank.

Outside the office of the adjutancy officer Shmulik Yachin proved that even good boys like him have their limits. In a short, surreal ceremony, he grants himself the rank, replacing the rank of 2nd Lt. with that of 1st Lt. and shaking his own hand. "Good luck," he wished himself and as a new first lieutenant, he walked over to the office of Yair Nafshi, the battalion commander.

"You are supposed to be a deputy company commander," they had promised him. Promises were not always kept. "The position of deputy company commander can wait," Nafshi said straight out at the start of their conversation. "For now, be a platoon commander. We are about to receive responsibility for the front, replacing the 53rd Battalion. It will be the best way for you to learn. Get experience, learn and see how things work. As I am sure you realize, being a platoon commander in an operational battalion is very different than what you have done until now. Complete the round of front employment in November and become a part of the brigade. Only then will you be able to become a deputy company commander."

Without objecting, as always, Yachin accepted the decision. This is how in August 1973, 1st Lt. Shmulik Yachin, leader of the 3rd platoon, H Company , was positioned at 107 tank front depot on the Booster Ridge, ready for an advanced course on operational tankmanship.

Northern Sector – Fidel Hadash
Avner Landau, together with the 1st Platoon commanded by Rani Friedrich and the 2nd Platoon commanded by Moshe Efrati (Kakun),

arrives at the Bukata route (Fidel Hadash route). He turns east and speeds forward toward the Border route and the ramps near it.

Five hundred meters before the anti-tank ditch, Avner divides the force. He sends Friedrich's platoon to natural positions 500 meters to the right of the road, on a hill overlooking the Quneitra gap. He himself, together with Efrati's platoon, continue to the east.

Friedrich leads his platoon to its post, when suddenly, right in front of him, on Israel's Border route, there is a Syrian truck. "Fire!"

At the same time, Landau and the Efrati platoon are 100 meters from the anti-tank ditch when they turn north. As he is sliding around a bend, 150 meters in front of him, not a range for tanks, moving west, inside Israeli territory, there is a convoy of Syrian vehicles, who must not have heard the assessment of the Intelligence Directorate.

Should he reverse, back onto the exposed slope? Avner has to decide quickly. He will be identified by the convoy. Should he stop and open fire from where he is? There are no alternative positions to move to and the Syrian force has an advantage. Then he makes his decision.

Together with Efrati's platoon, four Sho't Kal tanks dash down the slope, at full speed, cross the Syrian convoy, throwing grenades at the green tanks and hurrying to take cover behind a bend in the route, on their way to the northern ramp that controls this area.

After two terrifying minutes, on the controlling ramp, Landau sighs in relief. Now he will be calling the shots.

"Fire!" the four commanders on the ramp shout. The Syrian bridging tank is hit first. "You scum. Let's see you now," Landau thinks to himself, furious at the Syrian infiltration into our territory.

The skill of the 188th Brigade overcomes the advantage that the element of surprise had given to the Syrians, and within minutes the convoy is destroyed. Now they can focus on the new forces crossing the ditch.

On the Syrian side of the anti-tank ditch, an SU100 tank destroyer appears with its intimidating black cannon. "What is going on, Natan?" Landau complains to Natan Cohen, the outstanding gunner who does not identify the target. Avner realizes they have a problem with depressing the gun and cannot place Cohen on target. Boom! Dust rises up in front of them, where the Syrian shell hit. Avner sees he has only two choices; to expose himself further or to withdraw to a holding position. Or… to try a trick. He calls Friedrich to come to him immediately.

Friedrich heads his way, having received the location of the enemy tank destroyer. Avner returns to his position, encouraged by Friedrich's presence. Boom! The Sho't Kal is shaken. According to a Syrian or Russian drill – or just combat spirit of the Syrian force, not foreseen in Hakiryah in Tel Aviv – the old destroyer had fired a shell that hit Landau in his gun mount shield. The company commander's tank is now out of use and Benny Mauda, the loader, is lightly injured.

Avner jumps out of the tank and with his two crew members that were not injured, he runs to the tank next to him. He instructs Efra Goren, Efrati's tank "cub" commander, to leave the loader and to run with his crew to the company commanders' damaged tank. Landau connects to the radio in Efra's tank and wants revenge. It is too late.

Friedrich takes position and identifies the Syrian destroyer exposed to him. One accurate shell puts an end to the threat.

"You can return to your previous position," Landau instructs Friedrich. He returns and sees a Syrian soldier climbing out of a burning truck and running toward his tank. While debating whether to end his life with his machine gun, the terrified balding older man climbs on the tank and holds onto the commander's hatch, shaking.

Friedrich reports to Landau, who tells him clearly that "we do not have time to deal with prisoners." Friedrich, using humane and strategic discretion, grants the man his life, ties him to the tank and improves his position toward the anti-tank ditch.

Northern Sector – Sela Force

Guided by the order from Nafshi to join the other tanks of the company, Asaf Sela – deputy company commander B Company – advances on the Tarzan route, beneath the Hermonit hill. He identifies a trail heading right, toward the anti-tank ditch. Sela does not know exactly where the rest of the company tanks are but he knows there should be a ramp at the end of the trail, and most importantly, he knows this is a combat day and he needs to move forward. He turns right and forgets to maintain visual contact with Avshalom Levi's platoon, 200 meters behind him. They do not see him turn and they continue north on Tarzan.

Sela keeps going, one tank alone moving east. Sliding down a valley of vineyards, he climbs up and, directly in front of him, 1,000 meters away, he sees tanks. These are not his company's tanks.

On a series of low hills, still in Syrian territory, behind the fence and the anti-tank ditch, tens of Syrian tanks and armored vehicles are preparing to move west, into Israeli territory.

"Driver, stop." The tank stops. Asaf knows something went wrong with his plan. As he is deciding what would be the best thing to do, a mortar shell falls on his tank, and the loader hatch and the antennas collapse. In an omen of bad luck, smoke bomb no. 5 goes off.

Asaf takes the smoke bomb and insists on throwing it off the tank. In his rush he forgets to put on gloves and he burns his hands. Giving in to the smoke, he and his crew jump out of the tank and lie down beside the tank, waiting for the smoke to disperse.

"Gidi, fire artillery," Asaf says to the forward artillery observer accompanying him.

With shrapnel in his legs, ignoring the sharp pain, Gidi Lefever tries to make contact with Asaf, choking as the smoke enters his lungs. There is no response. "We are going to be taken prisoners," he thinks to himself. He wanted a combat day so badly.

A minute passes and another and the smoke drifts away. Asaf orders everyone back into the tank. Now is the time to get out of there, while firing at the enemy

There is just one problem. Like a bird with a broken wing, the gun cannot be elevated or depressed nor moved to the sides. To completely bring down their morale, the transmission system is also not working.

With curses and threats, the transmission finally agrees to intertwine but only in one direction, reverse. With a tank that can only move in reverse and cannon that will not move, the crew of the deputy company commander flee for their lives. Crushing rocks, terraces, beheading trees, driving in reverse with the engine at full RPM, praying for mercy.

Meanwhile, Avshalom Levi calls Asaf Sela. Nothing. Asaf Sela calls Avshalom Levi. Nothing.

After a few minutes, Avshalom's platoon arrives at Fidel Hadash route and there is no sign of Asaf. Where is he? Avshalom is concerned.

Part of the Syrian battle strategy had been based on jamming the radio communication of the Israeli forces throughout the front. This proved to be very efficient, harming the professional performance of the 188th Brigade, dividing forces and spreading uncertainty and at times even chaos.

Asaf ends the longest reverse drive of his life and finally meets Avshalom at the junction. He transfers to the tank of Avshalom's sergeant and sends his damaged tank to Bukata with his crew and the injured artillery forward observer. Together with Avshalom, they start to climb up toward stronghold 105, where a distress call had gone out a few minutes earlier from Nissim, the battalions' deputy CO.

Northern Sector – A-Kahtania

"Hey, why are you so quiet?" Oded Yisraeli does not understand the lack of cheers for the numerous hits he just carried out and adds, "I can be discharged this evening, I have taken out enough tanks."

As he attempts to increase the enthusiasm of the other tanks of A Company on the Booster Ridge ramp, the victory cheers are replaced with dread. From out of nowhere, a number of tank shells have been fired at him.

Another Syrian tank company has crossed the ditch, appearing from the area of the Yisraeli force, no more than 500 meters from them. Suddenly the hunters are now the hunted.

With urgency in his voice, Nimrod Kochavi instructs the gunner, Dov Zolden, "Dov, I am placing you on the first target, aim and fire with combat range. After you hit the first one, I will put you on the second. Hurry, we don't have much time."

Zoldan fires and hits the target.

Then boom! They are hit. A Russian shell slips on the British steel, disrupting the radio communication. "That was lucky," Zoldan thinks to himself, "statistics are on our side. Now they won't hit us again."

Yisraeli, Kochavi and Hashenberg maneuver to try to evade the enemy and in addition to the armor fight, they begin to feel the threat of the Syrian infantry soldiers that have crossed the ditch. They have taken up position close to the remnants of the first company that they had destroyed, among the terraces of the village of A-Kahtania. The infantry now start to hit them with anti-tank fire.

He is brave, determined and eager for battle, but Yisraeli understands that there are times when you need to concede your honor and call for help. Yisraeli's call for help reaches the Booster Ridge, and Zvika the company commander orders his tanks to start moving toward A-Kahtania, realizing that something is going wrong there.

At 15:30 Nimrod Kochavi, commander of the 3rd Platoon, hears on the radio, "Infantry on the hill, fire!" and he immediately moves out to find a good position from which to engage them. Syrian soldiers appear and disappear, running between the rocks and the pits. Kochavi fires his machine gun, guiding Dov Zoldan where to aim the cannon. Suddenly there is silence.

"Nimrod, Nimrod," Dov calls his commander.

As he is wondering what is going on up there, Nimrod folds into the commander's seat in slow motion, his beautiful eyes open but frozen and Dov notices a trickle of blood from his temple.

Zoldan pushes himself aside with great effort and finds himself facing the bloody face of Nimrod Kochavi his commander. Somehow he finds the strength to push him into the gunner's seat, takes his place in the commander's cupola, connects to the external radio, announces that the commander has been hit and asks to fall out.

"You can't now," someone, maybe Yisraeli, says.

In the commander's position, with his head and shoulders above the turret frame, Dov cannot believe his eyes. A mass of enemy soldiers is running all over the place, with green tanks heading toward him.

Zoldan comes to his senses and fights back. Without a commander, he fires the cannon with the emergency fire generator and fires the commander's machine gun. After a few minutes, maybe a few too many, he receives the approval to drive to the base and evacuate Nimrod, whose life is slipping away.

Southern Sector – 111

High above the Kudna gap, the redhead Hochstein has a problem. The closer the Syrian tanks get, the harder it is for the platoon gunners to draw a line of fire to the targets. They have no choice but to move up higher.

Hochstein edges the tank forward, one track link after another and the tank rises up, exposing itself to the enemy tanks and now Marko Avigdor the driver, in the lowest position in the tank sees the enemy tanks.

"Yossi, what is going on?" Hochstein shouts to Yossi Eliyahu the gunner, who still cannot get the cannon low enough to fire.

Boom! The tank is hit in the cannon, knocking the gun steering system out.

Hochstein jumps out of the tank and runs over to the tank of Chaim Aldag, who was starting to enjoy this combat day and now is disappointed to have to vacate his spot for the angry redhead.

Southern Sector – 115

Responding to Erez's command, the tanks of C Company withdraw from their posts and speed toward the Petroleum Road. Bekman's tank is hit just before he reaches the main road (the Tapa route), causing the sprocket to fall out of place and the bazooka shields to fly off. Bekman climbs onto Orenstein's tank and joins Urieli. Orenstein's is the only tank out there, unable to move, with a tank full of shells, an intact firing system, and a box of Time cigarettes that Bekman left behind along with a can of pineapple. Ilan Orenstein, 2nd platoon sergeant, is lost in thought. "The guys left, they left."

Southern Sector – The Petroleum Road

All alone facing the Syrian 112th Brigade, under accurate artillery fire, Boaz Tamir, the deputy commander of C Company makes the right decision. He leaves the ramp, moves back and takes position 1,500 meters west of it, near the Eucalyptus grove and the Syrian officer's pool next to it.

As he is moving back, three tanks from C Company arrive after leaving sector 115. They turn left and in front of them appear Sho't Kal tanks that have been hit. Itzik Arnon, Urieli's gunner, identifies Barenboim's 2A tank and is horrified to see a hole going into the turret in the area of the loader's compartment. The combination of tank 2A and the hole are enough to drive him mad. In the tiny spot that is the gunner's seat, he is full of anxiety thinking of the fate of Shimon Akeb, his best friend in the world.

Urieli does not let Arnon drown in self-pity. The war has just started

A few minutes after 15:00, Urieli, Zur and Akunis reach the Eucalyptus trees on the right side of the road, and identify the deputy company commander's tank. He joins them and they move forward together. They had hardly started moving, when to their right, at ranges of 500–1,000 meters, three round metal shadows appear with their guns aimed at Urieli's four-tank force.

"Fire!" the four commanders shout at the same time. Itzik Arnon does not understand what the huge lump he sees in his lens is, and Urieli takes control and fires with the emergency trigger.

At 15:15 Boaz Tamir is hit. His face and eyes fill with shrapnel and blood. It is painful but bearable. An examination of the damage to the tank shows that the shell has penetrated between the tank body and the turret, making it difficult to rotate the turret.

Tamir leaves the damaged tank and signals Yehuda Akunis to switch with him. Yehuda gets in the damaged tank and tries to rotate the turret. Nothing. He tries to fire at a random target and nothing happens. He reports to Uzi, the company commander who orders him to drive to Juhader.

A few minutes pass and Bekman joins the Urieli force, noticing Akunis evacuating Tamir's tank and he understands that there is action on the Petroleum Road. But not everyone is part of the action. The electricity system in the tank of the company commander starts to have trouble and then suddenly shuts down, leaving the crew unable to move the cannon. The commander of the 1st Platoon, Hagai Zur, receives an order from Urieli to switch tanks and crews.

Has his luck run out? Hagai guides the tank into the repair workshop in Nafah, frustrated to be missing out on the combat day.

Since everyone had been waiting for a combat day, and no more than a single day of battle, the logistical preparations were adapted for this and not for war. A damaged tank with the ability to drive? The commander is to take it to the workshop in Nafah, an hour's drive from the front. It is not a problem; things will be over by the evening. Just like every other combat day.

2nd Lt. Nati Levi is ready for war again, after half an hour of cleaning in the tank of Sgt. Brinberg. The veteran sergeant had been fatally injured, and the crew try to ignore the blood and tissue as Levi and Aviam drive out of the Juhader base and head back to the war, to "their" ramp on the Petroleum Road.

As Levi and his crew had been leaving, Hagai Zur had arrived, joining with the damaged tanks of Akunis and Shabtai Horen who had been killed. "What is going on here?" Hagai wonders to himself. "Just an hour and a half ago this insane artillery had started to fall; I only managed to fire one shell and there already are soldiers killed and injured and five tanks damaged." At 15:30, 2nd Lt. Hagai Zur drives quickly along the Petroleum Road, leading three tanks on their way to the brigade repair center at Nafah. He suddenly realizes that this is not just another combat day.

15:30

Levi and Aviam complete their short drive on the Petroleum Road and join Urieli's three tanks force. "Five tanks is half a company," the young company commander from Bat Yam thinks. In the last few minutes, they have not seen any Syrian tanks and in a spur of the moment decision, he decides to change their mission.

"Glufa stations, this is commander. Move forward, carefully. Out."

They hardly have the chance to start moving and a volley of Sager missiles flies in their direction. One thousand meters from the ramps they are forced to take cover in terrain, Bekman and Tamir to the left of the Petroleum Road, Levi, Aviam and Urieli to the right.

The entire area in front of them is full of smoke and dust and Syrian tanks emerge out of the haze. It is like they appear out of thin air. So this is what a combat day is like, Bekman tells himself. He continues to get Yossi Zuridiker to fire at anything that moves.

Waves of Syrian tanks disregard Bekman and Zuridiker, trying to get through the narrow passage between the ramps. Targets in firing range. Everything goes. The first tanks of the Syrian force are hit and the others try to push them away to continue.

"You want war? You sons of bitches, you got it," Bekman shouts, firing another shell at them. Another Syrian tank is destroyed, and another, but they do not withdraw.

"No doubt it is just a matter of time until things will return to normal," Moty Aviam thinks. "They cannot beat us."

Southern Sector – 116

Yoav Yakir proudly reports to Ronis, the company commander, what 3rd Platoon achieved in sector 116. He assumes the "party" is over and so is the combat day.

In early 1973, 2nd Lt. Yoav Yakir had joined the 74th Battalion and been given command over the 3rd Platoon.

A month before Yom Kippur, Yoav had been notified that the IDF ordnance inspection would arrive at forward tank depot 116. Being such a charismatic commander and a perfectionist, he had spoken to all his soldiers, including the religious ones, and convinced everyone that the inspection was something that was allowed on Shabbat. On Friday night, they had their regular Friday night tradition of songs, with Yoav singing all the words by heart and all the soldiers, on and off key, singing along lustily, forgetting the goulash that Andrei Sakal had cooked for them.

On Shabbat they went to work on the tanks. Their platoon commander, two years older than most of them – an eternity in military terms – cleaned the Browning machine guns, dried and oiled them, and completed the treatment with verifying target precision.

Southern Sector – Hushnia

The 82nd Battalion, commanded by Haim Barak, arrives at Hushnia. The houses of the second largest Circassian village in the Golan are severely damaged; the only thing standing untouched is the large mosque. The battalion tanks deploy southeast of the buildings and the main road and wait for orders.

Northern Sector – 105

The B company reinforcement force reaches the junction near forward tank depot 105. The Sela force locates Dgani's ramp and heads toward it to join the effort to stop the enemy troops. But there is a problem: the ramp is built for one platoon, not more. So the three tanks of the Sela force decide to move eastward, toward infantry outpost 105. Perhaps they will be able to take up positions there and supply assistance. They are positioned without a ramp, exposed on a frontal slope. Avshalom identifies a terrifying sight to their right, in the "large tub." Syrian tanks are attempting to cross the anti-tank ditch at every possible point. Although some of the bulldozers and bridging tanks have already been hit, others are in position.

A number of shells fall close to the Sela force, making it clear to them that the positions they have taken are not those they were trained to take. "There is no reason to kill ourselves here," Asaf thinks and moves back. He explains that the position is problematic and asks Yossi Nissim for a different job.

Still wondering where their next problem will come from, Avshalom

Levi looks to his right and sees Syrian tanks serenely gliding down the slopes of Tel Manfucha. For all the world as if they were in training, they appear entirely at home in Israeli territory. Without knowing he was part of a three-headed force, with Shir-On and Kaimo, each in his own area, Avshalom contributes his part in destroying the rest of the Moroccan company, and the argument begins as to who deserves the most champagne.

Still in position, at the junction near tank base 104, infuriated by the unbelievable Syrian nerve, deputy company commander Kaimo identifies two additional Moroccan tanks firing at Aviv's platoon. With the nonchalance of a professional, he flanks them and with quick fire, destroys them both.

In the meantime, deputy battalion commander Yossi Nissim decides that he is putting the three tanks of B Company at risk for no reason. He sends Asaf Sela back to the Fidel Hadash route and instructs him to join the battalion commander and take his orders from him.

The Sela force leaves sector 105, heading back toward the Fidel Hadash route, leaving Dgani's platoon with the job of stopping the Syrian 68th Brigade tanks.

As they start their journey back, the Syrian tanks continue trying to cross the ditch, in the "tub" beneath 105. Some of them are hit when they activate mines that had been quickly laid two days before. Some of the Syrian tanks are destroyed by Muli Dgani's platoon, an exhibition of professional gunners at work.

15:45

The first of H Company's soldiers is injured. Muli Dgani is hit by a rock or metal shard that makes a hole near his nose. His face fills with blood and he notifies Nissim of the injury and asks for evacuation.

Nissim, still not armored, is trying to survive among the shells falling, and from his position, he sees the Syrian stream of steel relentlessly trying to cross the anti-tank ditch.

"Commander 1, hold on a little longer." Muli does not argue and remains in the tank, bleeding.

Nafah

There is light again in the bunker at Nafah, but the reports they receive are darkening the atmosphere, especially those coming from the besieged Hermon stronghold that is under attack. At 14:00 the base had been bombed, and at around 15:00 four Syrian helicopters had landed near the outpost, with twenty commandos in each one. There were no tanks on the Hermon stronghold, but the base was part of the front, and it serves as the northern eyes for the army. Ben Shoham, the commander of the front until further notice, contacts the air force and asks to send planes to hit the attacking force.

At around 16:00, four Phantom planes, on their way to the Egyptian front, receive a change in their mission and are sent to the north to strike at the Hermon.

Northern Sector – Fidel Hadash

An artillery shell hits the cannon of the tank of Udi Friedman, part of Friedrich's platoon, and he suffers an injury to the head. Avner instructs the tank crew to drive back and evacuate the injured commander to the medical station.

15:45

Northern Sector – A-Kahtania

Tanks from A Company, led by Lt. Zvika Rak, pass the outskirts of the eastern villas neighborhood of Quneitra, on their way to join Yisraeli, who is under attack. David Eiland sees a tank heading toward the Ta'asuka (deployment) base, which he identifies as Nimrod's tank. The handsome, blue-eyed, knowledgeable commander of the 3rd Platoon , who has been hit by shrapnel in his brainstem. Gidi Hertz, the driver, speeds in a frenzy toward the bunker in Quneitra, which is also under continuous fire. Inside, there is a chaos of doctors and injured and dead soldiers.

On October 17, Nimrod kept his promise to his girlfriend Pitzy. A month before the shard hit his brain, he had written to her, "I have never loved anyone like I love you, and I think you will be the last one I will love this much. You will always be mine..." Indeed, she was the last love he had and this handsome and talented young man became a memory.

The company commander's tanks had not even joined up with the deputy company commander yet, but they had already experienced their share of war. They had been fired at from among the terraces and the ruins of A-Kahtania with the entire gamut of Syrian ordinance. Eli Sharoni, the company commander's gunner, has his eye in the peri-telescope when he suddenly hears an explosion; his field of view fills with blood and he cannot see anything. He turns to look behind him and sees Zuaretz, the loader, on the floor, beheaded. Blood is flowing all over the place, turning Zvika's coverall into a red rag. He orders Zimri and Eiland to continue driving toward Yisraeli. He stops the artillery officer's tank, the last in the company chain of command, and has the entire crew leave, including the artillery officer, leaving the loader inside. He instructs Sharoni the gunner and Haim Safda the driver to settle into their new home. He changes his coverall, and instructs the artillery officer's tank crew to take the damaged tank, with the body of Zuaretz, to the base at Quneitra and makes his way to the front.

A few minutes later, the tanks of Zimri and Eiland join Shuki and Oded. Hashenberg, who is without his commander Kochavi, joins Eiland's tank. Just like that, without saying a word on the radio. He takes position, according to the "imitation of the commander" drill, and from that moment he does everything Eiland does.

15:55

Southern Sector – Hushnia

"What is going on?" Haim Barak is wondering. He hears Ben Shoham instructing Yanush, on the 7th Brigade radio, to order the 82nd Battalion to send a company to Juhader.

When did the commander of the 188th Brigade start giving orders to Yanush? Five minutes pass and Yanush gives the order to send a company to Juhader.

Barak is confused, unaware of the new order agreed upon in a gentleman's handshake a few hours earlier between the two brigade commanders. He orders Yaakov Chessner, the CO of B Company, to move out southwards on the Petroleum Road and to join the southern front commander.

Chessner leads his company south on the Petroleum Road, wondering whether the 82nd will finally get to take part in the battles.

Southern Sector – 116

Yoav Yakir believes that the big combat day is about to end, but if the Syrians dare to attack again, they will surely do so on the Roman route (Pinkas), the direction in which his platoon had been firing until now. He decides to head toward this spot, leaving Atir in his position, covering them. Together with Waxman, they drive a kilometer south to their new ramp on the south side of the Roman route.

Waxman and Yakir take position on the new ramp. There is nothing in sight. Are the twenty tanks they have destroyed all there is in store for them today?

A few minutes pass and Yakir calls Atir to join them. Atir arrives and takes position between the platoon's tanks. They scan the area east of them and see no signs of enemy forces. They ask themselves, is that it? They are sure that, soon, they will be called to disarm the tanks and return to base.

In his control position in outpost 115, Avi Ronis, F Company CO, identifies Syrian forces heading toward outpost 116. "They are on me!" 2nd Lt. Yossi Gur, commander of 116 outpost, shouts on the radio, at the exact moment Ronis identifies the Syrian force.

Yossi Gur, from the moshav Kfar Vitkin, had been a platoon commander for half a year in A Company, 50th Battalion Nahal paratroopers. On the Thursday night before the war, he was asked to replace the reserve officer who served as the commander of outpost 116, so that he could take leave for the weekend.

Yossi arrived at the base, located on the northern peak of the Bachta spur, 100 meters east of the ceasefire line. He had a five-minute briefing and slipped into the day-to-day life of the outpost. There was nothing to worry about, except for how to pass the time in this hole in the ground.

After examining the forces he had in the stronghold, most of whom he did not know, he discovered that they were made up if soldiers from various units and a number of non-combat soldiers.

On Saturday morning, an order was sent out to reinforce the strongholds and three additional soldiers arrived, bringing the number of soldiers in the outpost to fifteen.

When the artillery shelling started, he had everyone come inside until he realized that the periscope view did not cover the area to the northeast of them, the turn in the anti-tank ditch. Every few minutes he forced himself to overcome his fear. He left the bunker to scan the area, running in the trench to the left, to the north, to the northeastern "porcupine" fire position.

Slightly before 16:00, while he was in the northern position, he was horrified to see two columns of armored vehicles coming from Um-Lu-kas heading directly toward the fifteen soldiers of stronghold 116.

* * *

Atir barely had the chance to say hello to the guys when he was already heading north, toward outpost 116.

"We are on our way," Yakir calmed Gur, urging the 3rd Platoon to cover the four-kilometer distance between them quickly.

Just a few hours earlier, at 10:30, with the Golan in a Yom Kippur daze, Yossi Gur had driven to the nearby forward tank depot, where he met 2nd Lt. Yoav Yakir. They had coordinated a possible linking of forces procedure, and Gur was amazed to learn that the basic battle plan for Yakir's platoon sent the tanks far south of the depot.

"Don't worry," Yakir told him, "if someone comes near you, let me know and I will join you immediately." Now this was happening.

Gur got his soldiers out of the bunker, assigned them to their battle stations and took position at the gate, where the best view of the north was.

He knew Yakir's tanks were coming but in the meantime, Syrian forces were heading his way, without opposition. They were going to have to delay them. He called Goldwasser, the deputy commander of the Mesayaat company of the Nahal Brigade in stronghold 115, and requested artillery fire support. A few minutes passes and he received a ranging shell. That was it.

Now he is alone. His mortar team fires the few explosive shells he has at the convoy, which continues moving forward, unaffected by it.

The shelling of forward tank depot 116 continues. The generator is hit and starts leaking oil, and Mordechai Ukavi, the platoon medic who had been left behind, is praying. When there is a break in the shelling, he sneaks out and discovers that the parking area is completely ruined and that there is no one there but him. He enters the shattered staff room, finds a radio, tunes in to the company frequency, returns to the generator room and hears Yoav Yakir's live reports of the battles.

16:00–16:59

At 16:00 a soldier from the 71st Battalion of the armored corps, confused by the artillery shells falling all over, unfocused and disoriented, tries to locate the only thing he knows for certain on the Golan.

"2 of Glufa," he called on the radio, waiting for the reply of Oded Bekman, his best friend. There is no answer.

"2 of Glufa, 2 of Glufa, do you read me?" he continues to disrupt the radio frequency and does not understand why Bekman is not answering.

Thirty kilometers from there, a thousand meters from the ramps of the Petroleum Road, Bekman is fighting for his life. Five Sho't Kal tanks are trying to stop hell breaking loose from the east and for the first time, Bekman realizes that something has gone wrong for the 188th Brigade and he is worried.

He is not the only one. Oded Erez, already counting his casualties, is also wondering what went wrong. Yair Nafshi, who is fighting at the Booster, is also having a hard time understanding what is happening. Efraim Yosef, firing from the gunner's seat in Eiland's tank is troubled and so is Itzik Ben Shoham who is running the Nafah command center.

The answer is nowhere to be found.

16:05

Nafah

Extremely concerned by the reports coming from the southern sector, Ben Shoham, who is at the command center at Nafah, issues instructions to his deputy David Yisraeli, commander of the brigade headquarters at Aleika. He is to prepare a convoy of fuel and ammunition and to locate meeting points in the southern Golan where the tanks that are in combat can stop to resupply.

A few minutes later, the air force reports good hits on the Hermon. Ben Shoham is not at ease. What is happening up there, in the tunnels of the "country's eyes?" What difference would the withdrawal of enemy forces from the Hermon make when the entire front is under attack at the same time? The six Syrian brigades are on the anti-tank ditches; some of the armored forces have already crossed into Israeli territory.

The faces of the commanders at Nafah are very serious, and Ben Shoham, commander of the Golan front, is still unaware that he is fighting the battle of his life.

Simchoni tries again. "Yitzchak, leave the bunker. I will manage. You have a brigade and a front to run."

Yitzchak, an officer and a gentleman, answers him, "I am staying here until the general returns," and he continues to run the war from the bunker.

Southern Sector – 111

"There are tanks to the south of me, right beneath the outpost."

The cry for help of the commander of outpost 111 is like a stab in the heart of Shmulik Askarov, deputy commander of the 53rd Battalion, who is commanding the armored forces in this sector.

Askarov, an experienced war horse, leaves the northern ramp and moves to the southern side of outpost 111. He takes up position at a commanding spot and sees the main reason for the cry of the infantry commander – the Syrian forces heading toward the UN base (point 958).

Not far from there, in the Tel Abas positions, Hochstein takes his second hit. This time it is in the commander's cupola. Pini Ben Yisrael, the gunner, feels something wet on his back. He turns around and sees it is Hochstein's blood. He stares at Efrati, the loader, who stares back at him, and they watch Hochstein collapse inside in slow motion.

Efrati takes off his helmet and reports that the platoon commander has been injured.

At the same time, Shmulik Askarov is running the battle around 111, from his controlling position near the infantry outpost in the south. His developed instincts tell him that trouble will be coming from the south. And he orders Hochstein to transfer his platoon to the southern front.

Hochstein does not answer. Askarov calls again.

"Commander has been injured," someone answers from his tank.

"Didn't anyone teach you that even if the commander is injured, you continue to fight?" Askarov asks angrily.

Hochstein's crew explains that the firing system is out of order, the gun had been hit and is now stuck.

"Drive the tank to outpost 111, position it at the entrance, so Syrian tanks cannot enter," Askarov instructs them. He calls Danny Berkovitz, the veteran sergeant, telling him to leave the Tel Abas sector and bring the three tanks to the outpost area.

Southern Sector – 116

Waxman and Atir locate a hill providing a firing position facing north. With their heads and shoulders above the cupola, they raise their binoculars and try to identify the enemy. They are shocked and horrified. The infantry officer was right. Right beyond the hill, a thousand meters from their position, in Israeli territory, there is the "tub" (the low area of Bachet al Juhader) and it is full of Syrian armored forces.

Atir knows there is not a single Israeli tank facing the Syrian force moving westward. Somewhere out there, there is a platoon commander, a company commander, a battalion commander, a brigade commander, a division commander, the Northern Command general, the Chief of General Staff, the Defense Minister and the Prime Minister and maybe even a God. But out here it is just him, Waxman. And Yakir, who will probably be arriving shortly.

Someone on the Syrian side did their homework, Atir thinks. Someone studied our movements and while we were busy with small matters, far from outpost 116, they managed to cross the ditch north of the base.

Atir decides that is enough with the self-pity, and he and Waxman open fire at the "tub."

A moment later, Yoav Yakir joins them, identifying the size of the Syrian force in the "tub" and the area east of it – still in Syrian territory – on its way to the three bridges laid over the anti-tank ditch. He reports to Ronis, who reports to Erez, who reports to Ben Shoham.

Southern Sector – Chessner

Yaakov Chessner is troubled. On his way out of Hushnia, he discovers that his communication protocol card is for training days and no one is answering. Finally, someone tunes into the frequency, understanding it is a bit difficult for Chessner, the commander of B Company of the 82nd Battalion, who does not know where the commander of the 53rd is. He cannot join him without contacting him. The helpful interlocutor gives him the frequency, openly, on the radio, of the 188th Brigade.

Now Chessner is no longer all alone. He can finally communicate, not on the battalion frequency but the brigade frequency is good enough. He calls and calls, and in the end, Oded Erez answers him.

Chessner's company arrives at the Juhader junction sometime after 16:00 and Erez sees it from his vantage point. Erez instructs them, according to what he knows about the weak spots on the front, to leave a platoon under the command of the deputy commander at Juhader to help the forces fighting on the Petroleum Road, and to proceed, with the rest of the force, toward the Kudna gap (point 56 on the Troy route).

Southern Sector – The Petroleum Road
Sometime after 16:00, the first three tanks of B Company of the 82nd Battalion try to join up with the forces on the Petroleum Road.

"Glufa commander, this is the deputy of Band of Neka, over," the deputy commander of B Company, 1st Lt. Jack Hillel, calls to 1st Lt. Uzi Urieli, a company commander in the 53rd Battalion.

"This is Glufa commander, what is your position? Over."

"This is deputy of Band, I am at the Tapa-Mahaze junction (Juhader). Over."

"This is Glufa commander, continue forward 1,000 meters and join me, out."

Two minutes later, commander Glufa and deputy Band discover who the faces behind the voices on the radio are and they are happy. They shared a room in officer's course together. Now one is the commander of the other. Uzi instructs Jack and the two tanks of Gidi Maklef's platoon to spread out along the route.

Eight Sho't Kal tanks stand in position and stop any Syrian attempt to improve their hold of the Petroleum Road and Israeli territory. "We are strong, we are professionals, we are the best," thinks Bekman. "Things will be back on track in no time."

Southern Sector – Hushnia

Uri Simchoni, speaking on the radio frequency of the 7th Brigade, instructs Yanush to take the commander of the 82nd Battalion, Haim Barak, and send out two additional companies. One of these is to go to the Petroleum Road and the other to the unmanned outpost 112. Simchoni calls Yanush repeatedly but Yanush does not answer.

Ten minutes pass and Simchoni contacts Haim Barak directly and instructs him to split his forces.

Barak answers, "Wait" and tries to contact Yanush. "Mishbetzet commander, this is 10 of Naka. I have received orders from 82, should I carry them out?" Yanush does not answer.

After the tenth attempt, Barak has still not decided. The 7th Brigade commander, Avigdor Ben Gal, is known for his wrath. What will he do if he operates without his authorization? Will he be charged with going over him? In the end he decides to take the risk and face the unknown. He announces that he is on his way, whatever happens.

D Company, 82nd Battalion, commanded by 1st Lt. Danny Levine, starts its journey on the Petroleum Road and right away saves someone. Not just anyone, but an airman named Yanki Yardeni, a Skyhawk pilot who had suffered a direct hit while trying to hit Syrian tanks on the Petroleum Road. He had ejected and landed in our territory, near the Petroleum Road. D Company, heading south, has the pilot join the tank of the deputy battalion commander.

Southern Sector – The Petroleum Road

Forty-five minutes before sunset, four armored corps officers on the Petroleum Road change the course of the battles on the Golan. Urieli leaves two tanks from the 74th Battalion and three tanks from the 82nd Battalion at their position to cover the other forces. He gets his friend Jack Hillel to join the three tanks of C Company, and the four tanks attack in order to take back control of the Petroleum Road ramps.

The Urieli force moves slightly down hill, climbing a fold on the other side, and 300 meters in front of them, they see that the ramps of the Petroleum Road are occupied by Syrian forces. There are Syrian soldiers everywhere. Twenty-five meters from the company commander's tank, completely ignoring the anti-tank ditch and the rules of tank war, a Syrian tank appears and starts to lay the gun toward him.

Uzi pulls the emergency trigger and Partosh the gunner asks, "What? Where? Where to?" and Uzi just shouts, "Pull the trigger!" and Partosh does, firing two more shells and completing the task.

A hundred meters to his left, unaware of the drama in the company commanders' tank, Bekman identifies soldiers with helmets whose design remind him of the helmets of the German Wehrmacht in the war films he saw in the neighborhood cinema. When a bullet whistles by his head he realizes this is not a film and he shouts, "Machine gun, 300, infantry on. Fire!"

Yosef Zuridiker and Shmuel Solomon, Bekman's turret crew, lone soldiers who made aliyah from India, are scared in this unfriendly situation they are suddenly in the middle of and they return to their mother tongue, shouting to each other in Indian English, and Bekman no longer knows if this is a war film or an Indian film.

The four officers' tanks fight with determination and fury against hundreds of soldiers that are small dots behind the anti-tank ditch. After getting rid of the tank that threatened him from close range, Urieli knows that moving forward is suicide. Following such an exposed path would allow the Syrian infantry – equipped with anti-tank weapons – to massacre them.

As he is considering what to do, the hundreds of soldiers are joined by the Syrian 112th Brigade tanks that appear between the ramps, demanding the attention of the four Israeli tanks.

As they join the fun, suddenly from within a thick cloud of smoke, four Russian-built, Syrian BTR armored personnel carriers appear. As they pass in front of the tanks and continue west into Israeli territory, Bekman thinks, "These sons of bitches are driving faster than we can rotate the turret!"

A few minutes pass and it is Bekman who, again, identifies a bridging tank 1,000 meters away, sneaking toward the anti-tank ditch. Again Bekman is amazed at how much it looks like a toy and he then sees two rows of soldiers who look just like toy soldiers.

He reminds himself that this is war. He allows the bridging tank to lay the pathway and only then hits it. "Let's see what the sons of bitches do now," he smiles to himself in satisfaction. "Let's see if they can withstand the temptation."

They can't. Three Syrian tanks start climbing the bridge; Bekman lets them get close together and then destroys them one by one. Two minutes later, another bridging tank tries to lay a span across the ditch. "We can't let these bastards sneak in on one bridge while we are busy with another," both Bekman and Urieli think. This time, they change their tactic and hit the bridging tank before it can lay its link.

While they are busy blocking Syrian progress on the Petroleum Road, another force from the 82nd Battalion joins in the discussion on the radio. D Company deputy company commander, 1st Lt. Gabi Refaeli, with Gigi Oren's platoon, has arrived at Juhader. Urieli guides them to move ahead slightly on the Petroleum Road and to take positions on the slopes of Tel Juhader. They take up position and start to fire to the southeast, as much as the landscape allows.

Nati Levi and Oded Bekman, the childhood friends from the 188th Brigade, have no idea that in the two tanks of the 7th Brigade, right next to them, there are another two of their friends from the neighborhood of Neve Magen. Gidi Maklef and Gigi Oren are there with them, trying to stop the Syrian forces from breaking through the Petroleum Road.

16:10

Northern Sector – 104

The two Moroccan companies that had tried to sneak up on Shir-On and Kaimo through the Manfucha hills have been destroyed.

Yair Nafshi, who had never thought that an enemy force would infiltrate from the Manfucha, is relieved when Eyal Shaham, H company CO, reports that the hills between 104 and 105 are clear of Syrian forces. The attempts of the Syrian 68th Infantry Brigade, using the Moroccan force, to take hold of Israeli territory had not succeeded. They had been thwarted by the shells fired by Shir-On's platoon, Deputy Company Commander Kaimo and the Sela force.

Northern Sector – 105

Further south, in the valley under outpost 105, the Syrian 68th Brigade is still attempting to break through. The brigade's tank battalion, its two infantry battalions and its engineering units are blocked. A joint effort by Muli Dgani, on ramps between the 105 outpost and the tank front camp, the tanks of B Company on the sides of the Bukata road, and the minefields have stopped them. On the night between Friday and Saturday, the combat engineers had been called in to lay mines throughout the Quneitra gap. With the short amount of time they had, some of the mines were laid on the ground and not dug in. Many of the enemy tanks hit in this area had been stopped by the determination of these soldiers.

Northern Sector – 107

The Syrian 337th Infantry Battalion and the attached tank company from the 169th Battalion have been defeated. Yachin's six tanks gave the Syrian forces the severest blow in the 85th Infantry Brigade's sector.

Slightly after 16:00 there is silence around 107. The tank battles and the Syrian artillery stop. Two hours of continuous fire leaves a ringing in the ears of the armored soldiers. Is it over? Yachin wonders.

Northern Sector – A-Kahtania

Not far from Kahtania, out across the rocky area, four tanks of A Company are fighting the battle of their lives. Syrian infantry companies are firing at them from the flank, from ranges of up to 300 meters, and they have already hit Nimrod. In addition, at ranges of up to 500 meters, they face a company of Tiran tanks opposite them.

"Zamri, infantry on your right," Yisraeli warns. "Hashenberg, watch out from the left," Zamri warns. In the middle of the battle, a soldier in khaki appears, walking determinedly toward Yisraeli's tank. At the end of a surreal walk, dodging bombs and gunfire, 1st Lt. Asher Diamond, the fire support officer who was taken out of the tank of Tzvika, the company commander, ends up with Oded Yisraeli, the deputy commander.

Yisraeli, in full battle mode, is not quite free to host visitors at the moment and orders Asher to sit in the back of the turret, to stay low and not to bother him. Without any alternative, Diamond slips into the tank; waiting for the moment he will be able to adopt a better posture.

The Northern Front – 109

In response to worrying reports from outpost 109, Yair Nafshi orders Doron Sadeh Lavan to leave the southern ramp and take his platoon to the northern ramp.

In the months before the war broke out, Syrian intelligence had collected, updated and analyzed data on the area. The results of their impressive work were apparent in sector 109. The designated assault groups of the Syrian 52nd Brigade progressed without being spotted by the Sadeh Lavan tanks. They crossed the anti-tank ditch slightly north of the southern ramp, at a spot where they could not be seen. The Syrian forward brigade had managed to deploy, beneath 109, a mechanized infantry battalion with two tank companies, all out of sight of Sadeh Lavan's platoon.

Doron passes the Peleg-Yakir junction, enters the opening between the Nanas Hill (point 1003) on the left and outpost 109 on the right, and turns right on the path leading to the ramp. The three tanks slide down the slope, exposed to the enemy, passing the UN post and the blue uniformed soldiers watching the war game played in front of them in amazement.

The Sadeh Lavan platoon takes position on the ramp that they find to be wide, large and overlooking the gap. They too join the "combat day" that they had almost missed out on.

Danny Barzilai is the first to identify targets at close range. Shraga Shmuel, his commander, lets him fire at whatever he wants to, and Danny fires. He gets the loader to work, self-corrects his misses and hits the targets. Sadeh Lavan's platoon also has its first champagne. No one is surprised by this. Several months earlier, the armored corps had a contest between the gunners. Danny Barzilai, the gunner of tank 2A, G Company, 74th Battalion, scored first place, destroying three targets in seven seconds.

Barzilai was not acting alone. Haviv Amario and Herzl Daniel, the two other platoon gunners also take part in destroying a mechanized infantry company. They hit the armored forces at the back of the convoy heading toward the village of Kahtania and manage to avoid Sagger missiles fired at them, thanks to Shraga Shmuel, who is on missile lookout.

But Sadeh Lavan's platoon has only the leftovers, the tail of the Syrian force, and 1,500 meters northwest of the northern ramp the real war is taking place. The tanks of the Syrian 52nd Brigade are in battle with the four tanks of A Company: Eiland, Zamri, Hashenberg and Yisraeli. Once again, Doron Sadeh Lavan cannot see the main battle.

16:30

Southern Sector – 113

The two platoons of Moty Amir and Avi Lahman, under the command of deputy company commander Yoni Davidson, fire at long-range targets. They are not under threat. They do not quite know what is going on, on the slopes of Kudna. The commanders of the six tanks want one thing, champagne. A lot of it and fast, before it all ends. They already had four bottles in their name and want more.

Shortly after 16:30, Moty Amir discovers that the Syrian forces are also after champagne. An armor-piercing shell hits his turret and luckily does not cause serious damage to the tank or the crew. A few minutes pass and Davidson receives a report on the radio and understands that it is not over yet. "Save your ammunition," he tells the other tanks, just as they identify a large Syrian force flanking outpost 111 from the south, as well as another force heading straight east from the Kudna hills. They are all at long ranges, appearing and disappearing in the distance.

Southern Sector – 116

The 3rd Platoon starts moving toward 116 when a technical problem halts the tank of the commander. Nir Atir and Yair Waxman continue on their own toward the opening Yossi Gur is reporting. "He was exaggerating," Nir Atir thinks to himself. "He must have seen a tank on the horizon and he hurried to call us in."

While 3rd platoon is on their way to join him, Yossi Gur identifies the bridging tanks of the Syrian 61st Infantry Brigade at the anti-tank ditch. He is horrified to see the bridges laid out at three different spots, the closest about 150 meters from the outpost's fence. The Syrian army is about to flow into Israel on these bridges and there is no one to stop them, he tells himself. One Tiran tank decides to check if the outpost is prepared and starts the climb up to it. Before the defenders can open fire on him, he is stopped short between the fences, damaged and spouting smoke, after a painful encounter with a mine.

In the meantime, at the 116 forward tank depot, Ukavi the medic is following the battle closely. He is not a tank crew member and not fighting on the ramps, but he does have his Uzi on his back, a helmet on his head and a portable radio in his hand, and he receives the live reports. "The guys seems to be doing pretty well," he thinks.

Southern Sector – Yuval Shachar

At around 16:30 the intelligence officer (S2) of the 53rd Battalion, 2nd Lt. Yuval Shachar, hears the nervous talk. He understands that there are casualties and has a hard time believing this is happening to them. The minutes pass, and he decides to get in the deputy battalion commander's pickup and head out north to the Mashta junction where the battalion medical center is located, taking Aharon (Henry) Vidal from the operations platoon with him.

With a short *"ahlan wa sahlan"* ("welcome" in the Arabic sometimes used in slang by Israelis) greeting, Yuval arrives at Mashta and offers his evacuation services to Dr. Englehard, the battalion doctor. Second Lt. Yuval Shachar is appointed the first IDF injured soldier's evacuation officer. "Start at sector 111," the doctor says. "I heard Askarov report the first injuries."

"Alright," Yuval answers and prepares to move out.

Southern Sector – 111

The three tanks of the Hochstein platoon leave their positions at Tel Abas, descend to the Kudna gap road and immediately ascend on the main route, toward outpost 111, with the injured Hochstein in the tank with shrapnel in his back.

At the entrance to the stronghold, they separate. Berkovitz leaves them and continues 100 meters south to join Askarov. Aldag follows Hochstein's tank into the outpost. He sees the redhead evacuated to the soldier's bunker and jumps back into his own tank, ready for battle.

Back with his original crew, he now joins Askarov and Berkovitz near the entrance to the outpost. They exchange fire with a Syrian force to the south, who is attempting to ascend at point 958.

The medic of stronghold 111 starts to treat Hochstein, who sees the shaking hands trying to get an IV in him. "Get lost," Hochstein shouted at him, still a hotheaded redhead.

Then it is the turn of the infantry platoon commander, who comes to see who this fuming redhead is and to get more information. "Do we have enough tanks outside? Can we be evacuated?"

"Call your commander," Hochstein suggests, but no one answers.

"Try the battalion," Hochstein continues but the infantry commander does not have the frequency. He takes out the list of frequencies from his pocket and hands it to him.

At the Nahal Battalion HQ they do not know what is going on. Hochstein thinks to himself that evacuating a stronghold under fire is a job for tanks, but all the tanks are busy fighting for their lives.

In light of the reports coming in to the headquarters at Nafah, it seems that the area south of outpost 111 is the spot the Syrian forces prefer for their main effort to break through, at least on the southern sector. The 82nd Battalion's A Company, led by Eli Geva and battalion commander Haim Barak, are sent there, to a position near outpost 112.

Haim Barak, the newly appointed battalion commander, looks around. He sees the operational company speeding forward, and he says to himself with pride and concern,, "This is it, time to prove ourselves."

Southern Sector – Chessner

Seven tanks of the Chessner force descend on the western slopes of Tel Fares, joining the main route (Reshet, point 61), and Chessner realizes this is not the "combat day" he was promised. In the horizon all he can see is Syrian forces, heading west from Kudna, the clouds of dust behind them hiding the blue October sky, long rays of sun coloring what remains of the sky in dark purple.

For the last two hours, below outpost 111 and on the Troy route (Jasam–Kudna–Hushnia), the Syrians' 33rd Brigade, 9th Infantry Division, has continued its efforts to cross the anti-tank ditch and infiltrate Israeli territory. The commanders of the attack are in a state of panic; they have less than half an hour left to position the spearheads of the division, and something has gone wrong. The tank crews facing them on the Shaf-A-Sindin hills and Tel Abas are very stubborn, rudely disrupting their battle plans. The 43rd Armored Brigade CO, who is part of their division, will not like delays. They are especially afraid of Walid Hamdon, commander of the 51st Independent Armored Force Brigade, attached to them a few days ago. From 17:00 Hamdon is supposed to head west, like his counterpart from the 43rd Brigade, on the crossings prepared by the assault teams. But things are far from satisfactory at this stage. They understand that they will need excuses, a lot of them.

Hamdon, a Syrian brigade commander, like Fedale and Gorodish, will not take no for an answer.

Southern Sector – 111

Aware of the threat of a breach from the south, Askarov decides to concentrate all the forces in his sector together.

The commander of G Company (Ze'evim), Uri Akavia, receives an order on the radio. He leaves Deutsch on the northern ramp and has Overlander, the platoon leader, and Mizrachi, the sergeant, join him, and they head toward Askarov. Before Akavia gets the chance to stop, he is sent farther south, to try to take up a natural position near hill 958.

Akavia is well acquainted with the area from reconnaissance he has conducted in the area and he understands how problematic his task is. Any movement toward hill 958 will leave him completely exposed, exactly what tanks try to avoid. He checks with Askarov to see if he can change the plan to give him a better chance of surviving.

"Move out immediately," Askarov orders him impatiently.

Despite his great distress, Akavia accepts his fate. The three tanks of G Company head toward the UN position, understanding that this is not going to be easy and that their task is to save outpost 111 from invasion and to block a stream of Syrian tanks that are heading there, marking Hushnia and perhaps the entire southern Golan Heights as their target.

Northern Sector – A-Kahtania

The four aces of the 53rd Battalion's A Company are positioned in an open area, not what is recommended in the armored corps combat doctrine. They complete the destruction of the second of the four Syrian Tiran companies that the Syrian 52nd Armored Brigade can muster.

The joy of destroying the enemy tanks is accompanied by a troubling reality. The Syrian artillery and infantry troops, positioned among the ruins of A-Kahtania, are continuing to fire at them. Oded Yisraeli announces that he is disengaging and improving his position. Together with Zamri, Eiland and Hashenberg, they leave the exposed position, moving south on the Yakir route. Zvika Rak, the company commander, joins them.

Five Sho't Kal tanks are in motion west of A-Kahtania when suddenly two Syrian tanks appear from a wadi that crosses the route. The determined "experienced warriors" are furious for the death of Zuaretz the loader and the injury of Kochavi, and they prove to the Syrians how mistaken they were to appear at that time. Yisraeli, the deputy company commander, is the fastest and fires at the two tanks at the head of the force, and the vanguard of the 3rd Company of the 52nd Syrian battalion turn into torches.

16:45

Northern Sector – Fidel Hadash

At 16:45, the tanks of the Sela force take position somewhere between Bukata (Fidel Hadash route) and the border, behind the other tanks of the company. From here they open fire on everything moving on the horizon.

Over three kilometers from them, a huge yellow bulldozer keeps sending them obscenities in the face of their attempts to hit it. Avshalom gets angry, "Kagan, self-correct your hit and take it out."

Kagan knows this is important; he fires, locates where his shell hit, corrects himself and fires again. There is a flash and a big explosion and the yellow bulldozer goes up in flames and black smoke.

* * *

For the first time since the fighting began, Yair Nafshi feels elated. All along the north sector, his tanks have stopped enemy forces much bigger than their own. He knows that their work is not done but he is confident in their ability to continue to stop them.

From his controlling position on the Booster Ridge he sees Yachin's tanks going up and down the ramps near outpost 107. "Yachin is operating according to procedure," he tells himself with satisfaction, "as if he were in training."

Not far away, Yachin is in the clouds. "In France, they have to start producing the amount of champagne battles the gunners deserve." He smiles to himself, looking ahead. He doesn't see another attack effort from Han Ureibe and Jaba and decides that this is it for today.

Southern Sector – 111

In a state of quiet tension and with cannons prepared, Uri Akavia, the commander of Ze'evim company of the 74th Battalion and his sergeant head toward 958, which sticks out alongside the UN base. "Let's get there already," Moshe Kahalani mumbles beneath his VRC helmet, feeling the tank sliding down a frontal slope, knowing this is not a good sign. As he thinks this, Uri Akavia, his company commander, identifies Syrian tanks, positioned exactly where they are heading.

"Fire," Akavia shouts, and Kahalani puts whatever he can lay his hands on into the cannon. A high explosive squash head (HESH) round, a shaped charge (heat) round, a phosphorous shell, anything will work. Peretz the gunner fires quickly. "Champagne," they shout while on the down slope, and again Kahalani in the loader's compartment thinks to himself that Uri Akavia is the best.

Uri Akavia had been drafted in August 1970. After graduating from the Reali school in Haifa he joined the armored corps. His family was very proud of him. He was an outstanding soldier in every course, continuing the family's tradition of excellence.

His father Avraham, a soldier who fought with Ord Wingate[26] during the 1936–1939 events in the Land of Israel, and had gone on to serve as his right-hand man in Ethiopia. There he won a citation from the British army and a medal of honor from the Ethiopian Emperor. The apple had not fallen far from the tree.

In 1972 Uri was appointed platoon commander in the 74th Battalion. The CO Nafshi saw his potential, and within a short while he appointed him his right-hand man, the battalion operations officer (S3).

Two weeks before Yom Kippur Uri Akavia completed the Company Commander's training program. He excelled, of course, and returned to the battalion, where he was appointed commander of G Company. He had hardly had time to settle when and the Rosh Hashanah alert was declared and the talk in the company was all about the repeated inspections – to the smallest detail – by the young company commander, working on his hold over the company.

---

26. Major General Orde Charles Wingate (DSO & Two Bars) was a British army officer, Christian Zionist and pioneer of unconventional warfare. In 1938, as an officer in the British Mandate of Palestine, he set up the Special Night Squads of Jewish volunteers. These units would have an enormous influence on the future IDF.

A few days before Yom Kippur, when the brigade started to dismantle companies and reassemble designated combat crews, the company was divided and the force he was part of was placed under the command of the deputy battalion commander. "You will get your chance," he reassured himself.

Nafah

At 16:30, two senior officers arrived at the HQ at Nafah. The commander of the Northern Command, Raful, was accompanied by the 36th Division CO and Maj. Gen. (res.) Moty Hod, the former air force commander, currently serving as the Command aerial support officer.

After the battles had begun, Haka had called Simchoni in Nafah, from the office of the Chief of General Staff, to ask him how things were going and if the helicopter landing could be used. Simchoni, who had just returned from a violent tour outside, hearing artillery shells fall all over the Golan, suggested that he land at Mahanayim and drive to the headquarters in an armored vehicle. Haka instructed the helicopter pilot to land at Mahanayim; they stopped in the Division HQ in Filon, where Raful joined him. Together the three experienced battle veterans made their way to the bombed and burning Golan Heights.

As Raful enters the bunker, Ben Shoham briefs him on the situation. The Hermon is under Syrian attack. The air force is reporting good hits and the battles are raging all along the front, concentrated around the front-line outposts. In general, Ben Shoham says with pride, with the exception of some small infiltrations that were stopping and the troubling matter on the Hermon, things are under control.

Southern Sector – 116

Not far from outpost 116, three tanks of the 3rd Platoon find improvised positions. Atir, the sergeant, remembered that just that morning Zurich, the intelligence officer, had told them calmly, "You are going to fight a combat day against static, known targets. There is no reason to fear the growing Syrian force facing you."

Yoav Yakir, Nir Atir and Yair Waxman look at the tanks surging before of them and wonder whether they are the static targets the intelligence officer was referring to. Three Sho't Kal tanks facing the forty-one tanks of the Syrian 61st Armored Line Brigade, accompanied by 1,500 infantry soldiers, some on foot and others in BTR armored personnel carriers. The flood of Syrian forces was not showing any sign of relenting. The endless Syrian forces continue to attempt to cross the anti-tank ditch on the three crossings already bridged for them.

The three tank commanders of the 3rd platoon set aside everything they learned about managing orderly fire. "Aim and fire as often as you can," that is the only existence they now know. "Faster," Atir rushes Nagarker, the loader. "Faster," he lightly kicks the back of Moshe Ami the gunner. Hurry, before they reach us, before they cross the Golan road and from there head straight to Efrat.

The Yakir platoon moves in closer, leapfrogging north and approaching the parking road (the Palga route). The enemy is already 300–600 meters away. The Israeli troops can pick out the crewmen In the Tiran tank's turrets and see infantry soldiers all around the enemy tanks.

Yakir's platoon is firing at a fast pace. Menachem Shmueli, Yakir's gunner, continuously fires and hits the targets. He knows it is just a matter of time before he hears Andrei the loader tells him they are out of shells.

Each tank commander is having trouble choosing which enemy to focus on, those trying to cross the bridges or those already in Israeli territory. "We have to stop them," Atir tells himself.

Yakir watches the two commanders next to him and they are fighting like lions. He is amazed at the endless stream of Syrian forces but is still proud to be part of this effort.

Right after Rosh Hashanah, at the end of September 1973, a letter had been received by the Yakir family in Kfar Rupin. "I hope you celebrated Rosh Hashanah properly and that you understand that in order for you to celebrate peacefully, someone has to be on the border maintaining this peace," Yoav wrote. "I am happy and proud that this time it is my privilege to be here."

Northern Sector – 109
Zvika Rak does the inventory. Everyone is with him. His soldiers are full of fighting spirit. He has five tanks fit to continue the defense efforts. It is time for orders.

Oded Yisraeli, an experienced fighter, is sent to the southern ramp to act as forward reconnaissance and to defend the flank. The other four tanks take position at the top of the southern hill of Kahtania, trying to eat something to give them strength for later on. They barely had the chance to eat a couple of crackers when the Syrian artillery gets them back into battle stations inside the tanks.

The sound of shells fired stops. "Refill," Zvika announces.

While everyone is busy taking out shells from beneath the turret floor, Eiland decides it is time to get some fresh air outside the tank. He sticks his head out of the commander's cupola, and out of the corner of his eye, he sees the tip of an antenna between the tree branches, on the hill on the right.

"Reverse," he orders Yehuda Shani the driver, calmly.

Eiland's tank enters the opening of the wadi, gingerly edging around the hill, moving along the wadi. Suddenly, eighty meters in front of them, he sees the black cannon of a Syrian tank aimed at them.

"Fire!" Eiland shouts, while slewing the cannon toward the Syrian tank. Efraim Yosef, the gunner, identifies the target, aims and pulls the trigger. Nothing happens. Burko, the loader, who is very quick, forgot to release the gun safety.

"Burko!" Eiland shouts and before he completes his order – or curse, or whatever he planned to say – Burko releases the safety and Efraim fires. The slow Syrian tank explodes in front of their eyes.

Eiland identifies another two tanks and aims at them. He shouts to Efraim, "Fire!" "Target hit," comes back the response. "Fire," Eiland shouts a third time, aiming at the tank behind it. "Target hit."

In those unforgettable seconds, it was Efraim who saved them. Or maybe it was Fedale. During drills, Fedale, the brigade commander, would watch the firing practice and a master gunner that did not hit three targets in reasonable time would be reprimanded by the company commander, then by the battalion commander, and sometimes, when the result was especially bad, he even got a nasty remark from the brigade commander himself.

In one of these occasions, after training, Fedale gave them one of his penetrating looks and said, "Listen carefully. In the next war you will be alone until the reserves come. Twenty to thirty Syrian tanks against each platoon of yours. You have to be fast as lightning. Fire quickly. Do you understand?"

In the moment of truth, it seems that they had understood.

Three enemy tanks are in flames in Efraim's peri-telescope and Syrian soldiers jump out of the smoking vehicles. Efraim aims at them, switches to machine gun fire but nothing happens. Despite the war going on, there is a malfunction in the bolt and the electric solenoid.

"Fire manually," Efraim instructs Burko and he does, according to the emergency drill. One aims, the other fires, together they kill without remorse, the memory of their fallen comrades fresh in their minds.

"Hold your fire," Eiland shouts. He has not forgotten Kochavi and Zuaretz but lacks enough rage to shoot fleeing soldiers in the back.

Southern Sector – 111

The tank of the platoon commander descends to a waiting position on the rocky ground and refills. Danny Overlander, a new officer in the company, full of adrenalin, rushes his crew. He wants to get back into position. Yehuda Raz, the loader, pulls out the shells from under the turret floor at record speed and they are quickly back in position.

"Krasenty, can you identify targets?" Meir Ben Ritan, the driver, hears Overlander asking Yehuda Krasenty, the gunner. Instead of a response, the tank shakes wildly from a hit and a hellish wave of heat spreads throughout the steel compartments.

Zion Sharabi, Sergeant Zvi Mizrachi's tank driver, sees the flash of the hit on Overlander's tank to the left of them. "Shit," he mumbles, "it is only a matter of time before all of us are hit on this damn frontal slope."

Meir Ben Ritan gets out of the driver's compartment in Overlander's tank. Stunned, he looks at what was the best tank in the world a moment ago and now is melted steel with Danny the platoon commander and the two Yehudas. With machine gun fire stitching the earth around him, he runs to the nearby tank of the company commander.

"What should I do?" he asks Akavia.

"Go back to the tank and see what the situation in the turret is. Then see if you can disengage driving back," Akavia instructs him.

Ben Ritan runs back, staying low. He climbs up and takes a look inside. There is a wave of heat and a thick cloud of yellow and red smoke and three still bodies. He jumps into the driver's seat and tries to start the engine. It is dead. He tries to move the gears. Nothing.

He runs back to Akavia and makes a universal sign to him. They are all dead.

"Go on foot to the outpost and wait there," Akavia shouts to him from the turret above.

Almost like on a hike, between the Golan basalt rocks, hidden from the enemy tanks, Ben Ritan walks toward outpost 111.

While Meir is hiking, Uri Akavia, the company commander, and Zvi Mizrachi, the 1st Platoon sergeant, continue to fight for their lives. Askarov had told them to move forward and stop, so they continue to move forward. Maybe they will get lucky and find a place with cover. At the moment they are totally exposed, and Zion, the driver, does not stop cursing. "Lunatics, idiots, this is hopeless, we are all going to die here."

A few seconds pass and through the periscopes, Zion, sees a black cannon aiming at them.

"Zion, left, left," he hears Zvi Mizrachi shout, standing exposed in the commander's seat. Zion turns left. "Where now, Zvi?" Mizrachi does not answer.

In the turret, there is chaos. Danny Mechani, the loader, finds himself in a situation he was never in before. The body of his commander is crushed in the turret and inside the tank a fire is cooking off the machine gun bullets and in a moment, everything is going to explode.

The radio is out, and Danny shouts to Zvi the gunner, "Let's get out of here!" hoping that Zion, the driver, will stop the tank. Boom! Another shell hits the tank. This time Zion feels something bad is happening in the turret and he stops.

"Zvi!" Danny shouts again and Zvi Mansbach, the gunner, does not answer. Danny climbs out and shouts to Zion, "Get out quickly, Mizrachi is dead. Mansbach is not answering me." He runs toward the infantry base at the top of the hill.

Zion opens the hatches, jumps in the air and before he lands, he sees the tank shaken by a third shell hitting it. He has to see what happened to the crew. He climbs up and sees the remains of Mizrachi's shattered body and he sees that Zvi, the gunner, is still alive and both his legs are broken.

With inhuman strength, he grabs the rescue strips on the gunner's coverall and manages to pull him up out of the tank. He drags him thirty meters and finds a small terrace and lies down behind it, with the bleeding gunner beside him.

Zion assesses the situation. He has 300 meters of an exposed climb up to the base. He sees two Sho't Kal tanks at the side of the base, firing on the Syrian forces. "It will be okay," he tells himself. "We will beat them soon."

Southern Sector – Danny Pesach force

The Danny Pesach force – the eight remaining tanks of Danny Levine's company, take positions in area 114, trying to identify enemy tanks in the east. They spot enemy forces over three kilometers from them and fire at them behind clouds of fire and smoke. They see immediately that there is no point in firing from this range. The eight tanks remain in position, with nothing to do, They are restless and await new orders.

The decision to leave a platoon at Juhader and continue with the rest of the force of D Company toward 114 seemed very strange. Oded Erez, 53rd Battalion CO, who is in charge of the whole southern sector, had sent the Pesach force to an area where there was no Syrian threat. That is exactly why Lahman's platoon was transferred from 114 to 113 and why Urieli, C Company CO with a number of tanks with him in the area, also left. So why did the commander of the 53rd Battalion give this order?

Analysis of the landscape and of the enemy's intentions sent to the field officers before the war by the brigade intelligence put emphasis on the Rafid-Kudna gap area and did not consider sector 116 to be of importance.

The brigade and command intelligence assessed that the Fares–Rafid-Kudna triangle, especially the Nawa–Rafid route and the ramps of area 114, may act as the main route for the Syrian attack, since it would allow the forces a wide deployment and quick movement to the west.

Even now, with the pressure at 116 clear, the commander of the 53rd Battalion still preferred to send most of the reinforcements to 114. After all, they had been told that they had to have a strong force at 114, to be ready before it was too late. The perception was that the rest of the forces were still holding on. On the Petroleum Road they withdrew and left the ramps, but they were sure that they would be able to regain control of it soon.

Southern Sector – 116

Yakir platoon reaches the "Parking Route." Suddenly, without warning, the incoming fire ends.

Nir pulls out the platoon radio from his tank. There are a few beeps and finally he hears the baritone voice of the newscaster notifying the twelve soldiers of 3rd Platoon that, since 14:00, Israel is at a general war with Egypt and Syria. Twelve boys in khaki, who thought they were on a combat day, look at each other in disbelief. They look around and see the tens of Syrian armored vehicles soaked with blood and spouting smoke, their own professional workmanship and they understand that the newscast was right.

Southern Sector – 115

Boom! Company commanders also get hit. Avi Ronis gets hit in the suspension and cannot steer the tank to the left or the right. So what? They can still move forward and backward, the cannon can still fire. Ronis stays in position and tells Gideon Aharoni the driver that they will have time to deal with the steering later. "Tomorrow, when we return to base."

Southern Sector – 111

While Mizrachi is getting hit, Danny is running and Zion is pulling the bleeding Mansbach, fighting for his life, Uri Akavia is trying to stand his ground in the inferior position he is in, between outpost 111 and the UN post.

"Driver, drive backward fast!" Akavia suddenly shouts.

"Why back?" Peretz does not understand. "Commander, I have more targets."

Akavia does not answer.

"What is going on?" Pozlantz, the driver, asks hesitantly.

Kahalani, the loader, looks over his side. Uri Akavia, the admired, smart commander of his company, the soldier's God, is sitting on his commander's seat, immobile, with binoculars on his neck and his head missing. His head is lying between his legs, his dead eyes still open.

Now it is Kahalani, the loader, and Peretz, the gunner, who understand that they have no time to scream and lose it. They need to get themselves out of there and quickly. Peretz removes the gunner's backrest and pushes Uri's body aside and takes the commander's position. He looks out and sees a Syrian tank right in front of him. For the first time in his life he pulls the emergency trigger, and Kahalani detaches himself from the sights and smells, loads another shell and Peretz fires it, as he shouts to Pozlantz the driver, "Reverse, now!"

Behind them, there is a minefield and while they move to the right and left, another explosion rocks the tank. They pull themselves together and try to continue movement and are hit by another shell. Now the tank is immobile.

Kahalani and Peretz climb out of the tank, take a last look at their commander's body, and they realize that Pozlantz is stuck in the driver's compartment: the gun lowered on top of his hatches will not let them open. Peretz climbs back up to the tank, slides into the gunner seat and ignores Uri Akavia lying next to him. He closes his heart to the shells and the terror, rotates the turret to the left and enables Pozlantz to climb out.

"What is going on?" Pozlantz asks. Peretz looks at him and does not understand how he doesn't understand that the company commander is gone, while he was the one giving him commands. He then realizes it is what they call repression and maybe it is the best way to deal with the situation.

"We got hit," Peretz answers.

"What about Uri Akavia?"

"He went to the infantry base," Peretz says, suddenly becoming the big brother and therapist to his fellow crew member, trying to spare him the news and the sight.

Southern Sector – Evacuating to Nafah

While Uri Akavia died defending outpost 111 and the 3rd Platoon was fighting the battle of its life defending outpost 116, a number of damaged tanks are driving on the Petroleum Road.

At 16:45 three Sho't Kal tanks arrive at the Mashta junction and continue toward Nafah. Yuval Shachar, the intelligence officer who was appointed injured soldiers' evacuation officer, does not understand what the skinny platoon commander in the turret is doing. What is he thinking? He is supposed to set an example.

"Hey!" he shouts toward him, sticking his hand out and turning it. "Have you lost your mind? Why are you driving the tanks on the road?"

From his position up on the tank, leading the three tanks with him, Hagai Zur does not bother to answer. He puts his hand down to the right, opens his palm in front of the amazed intelligence officer. The open hand eloquently states, "Get off of me, whoever you are," and he continues on his way to Nafah.

A few kilometers ahead of them tank 2A is on the Petroleum Road, carrying the bodies of Barenboim the commander and Akeb the loader. Kelner, a driver with balls of steel, had appointed himself tank commander. His knowledge of the routes of the Golan assures him he is on the right path. Continue straight and you will get there. Yishai Daniel, the gunner, is sitting next to him on the tank's wing. He could not ride with the dead bodies of his friends.

A kilometer and a half before Nafah, Kelner reaches a descent and has trouble with the tank's brakes. The shrapnel in his back makes it hard for him to lean on the seat backrest and press the brakes forcefully. In excruciating pain, biting his lips, he manages to stop exactly as a jeep and an ambulance approach him from Nafah.

In bloody coveralls, Kelner and Yishai limp out of the tank and split up between the two vehicles.

"What is going on over there?" demands Haim Arma, the driver of the company commander's jeep.

Yishai Daniel does not answer.

"What is going on, Yishai?" Arma persists.

"Everyone is dead," Yishai answers and buries his head in his hands.

From the ambulance, Hezi Kelner turns around and sees their tank, his pride, with a black hole in it and inside a picture he will never forget; the bodies of Barenboim and Akeb. The three damaged tanks approach Nafah, pass by tank 2A, abandoned on the side of the road. Itzik Arnon, the gunner, asks Hagai to stop.

"I have to see what the situation with Akeb is," he begs and his heart skips a beat.

"Leave it," Zur says. "You are better off not doing that, let it go."

Arnon lets it go and they continue driving; he looks back at the tank as they move away.

Southern Sector – Yuval Shachar

Hagai Zur, the platoon commander who Yuval Schar had pegged as insane, is gone and the preparations in the APCs for moving out are completed. Yehuda-Yehuda is driving. Inside are Aharon Vidal, a combat soldier, Udi Hevroni, the battalion medic, and the intelligence officer who has become the evacuation officer. As the APC passes by the mosque of Hushnia, an artillery shell lands near them, lifting them in the air like they were a toy, landing on the rocks of the Golan. They conduct a quick inspection to see that everyone is okay, but the left track is hit. With a damaged track but still able to move, Yuval continues.

Southern Sector – 113

Davidson's force of six tanks are not useful where they are and move to different positions.

The range is still too far, almost four kilometers. Armor-piercing ammunition is not efficient enough. Squash-head shells hardly peel off the paint of the enemy tanks. They occasionally get a hit but the Syrian force is not affected by it.

Southern Sector – 111

All the attempts of the Syrian forces to advance on the Troy route, the Kudna gap and their attempts to attack stronghold 111 in the south are blocked by the brigade's tanks, They have destroyed over forty Tiran tanks, five bridging tanks and a large number of BTR armored personnel carriers.

The joy over the massive destruction of the T tanks and the heroic blocking of the Syrian forces is bittersweet. The Askarov force that three hours ago had eight tanks, was left toward 17:00 with just four. Three commanders (a company commander, a platoon leader and a tank commander) and two crew members (a gunner and a loader) have been killed. The redheaded Hochstein has been lightly injured and is in the outposts' bunker. Zvi Mansbach, who told his friends that his favorite thing is being with his family, is bleeding and leaning on the knees of Zion, who continues to pray for him and does not know what to do.

Still, the remaining crewmen defending outpost 111 and Shmulik Askarov – just like the attack forces of the Syrian 33rd Brigade that has been stopped for now – are unaware of the real plan set into motion just two kilometers to the south of where they are fighting.

Walid Hamdon, Syrian 51st Armored Brigade CO, is not concerned by his forces being stopped. He knows the battle plan well and he knows that the attack force fighting against the defenders of 111 are the cannon fodder of the 33rd Brigade, since at the same time as they are failing here, a well-planned operation is succeeding south of this sector.

The main force of the 33rd Infantry Brigade is moving "head on" along one route – the Kudna (Troy) route. Here they are wisely engaging all of the tanks of sector 111 (the Askarov force). At the same time, a number of bridging tanks and armored forces sneak in further south. Without anyone noticing them they bridge the ditch, south of the Shaf-A-Sindin hill (where outpost 111 is located). They enter into an open area with hill 958 as its northern border, its center at hill 868 (the unmanned outpost 112) and its southern border a kilometer south of 112.

The southern flanking maneuver was not an improvisation. It was the original plan. The Zionist motto of "By way of deception you shall wage war"[27] had spread to Israel's neighbors as well. So in a well-planned deception, the Syrians focused their force on sector 111, on the Troy route, while south of there the real plan was in motion.

The deep flank maneuver south of outpost 111 enables the Syrian forces to bridge parts of the anti-tank ditch, far from the sight of the defenders of 111, to take control of land bridgeheads and await the arrival of the main force of their 51st Armored Brigade, intending to plunge deep into Israeli territory.

The Syrians are sure of their success. Front-line observers report that there are no Israeli tanks south of 111, in the area of outpost 112. It was just as they predicted. Without anyone watching and able to report the incursion, they infiltrate with full force.

It is almost 17:00. Askarov realizes that something bad is happening south of the outpost. "What about reinforcements? Ammunition? Fuel?" Askarov urges the brigade HQ in Nafah.

---

27. Proverbs 24:6.

17:00–17:59

The Syrian war plan for the war on the Golan, "Mashroa 110," consisted of three phases.

The first phase, from 14:00 to 17:00, was called the "Direct Mission." In these three hours the six forward infantry brigades, assisted by their tank battalions, were

to set up crossing points along the anti-tank ditch,

crush the infantry strongholds on the Purple Line,

destroy the front-line forces of the IDF, and

conquer a strip of land west of the Purple Line 6–8 kilometers wide.

At the end of the time set by the Syrian General Staff for the Direct Mission, the forward brigades had only managed to achieve part of what had been planned.

The northern infantry brigades (68th and 85th) had completely failed to achieve their objectives.

The central infantry brigades (33rd and 52nd) had achieved partial success. The 52nd Brigade had penetrated into A-Kahtania and had been stopped there. The 33rd Brigade had managed to infiltrate and reached a partial position on the Shaf-A-Sindiyan hills (111).

The southern brigades (61 and 112) had achieved reasonable success. The brigades had penetrated and taken control of a sector between 116 and the Petroleum Road.

In their attempt to complete the Direct Mission, the Syrian brigades had suffered a fatal blow. The estimate is that by 17:00, out of a total of 276 Syrian tanks taking part in the attack, 200 had been destroyed.

Was this a defeat for the Syrian army? A huge victory for Israel?

What if the Syrian forces had been forced into an ignominious withdrawal, such as they had suffered many times before, at the end of the Direct Mission phase? Then there is no doubt that the battles fought by the tanks of the 188th Brigade – side by side with A Company of the

82nd Battalion – would have gone down in the history of the armored forces as one of its greatest achievements. This time however, uncharacteristically, the Syrian forces did not withdraw. Without hesitation, they continued on to their next mission.

The second phase in the Syrian attack plan, from 17:00 to 20:00, was called the "Second Phase Mission." In this phase, the armored brigades of the mechanized divisions were to destroy all of the tactical reserves of the IDF on the Golan, expanding the conquered area to 12–15 kilometers from the Purple Line.

Southern Sector – Yuval Shachar

Peretz the gunner, Pozlantz the driver and Kahalani the loader see the Syrian forces between them and outpost 111 and know they cannot reach the base. There is only one direction for them to withdraw, to the west. Three young soldiers, forced to leave what had become their safe home of steel, had lost the pride of being the company commander's crew and had to leave the body of their commander sitting in the tank. They walk on foot, with the red sun setting in the western sky, confused and afraid.

A few minutes pass and they reach the main road ("Reshet") and from there it was a short distance to the road leading to Hushnia ("Kvish").

They walk and walk and opposite them, on the road, an armored personnel carrier appears.

With darkness falling, Yuval Shachar, 53rd Battalion's intelligence officer, sees three mirages walking on the road toward him. He wonders where they came from, and he stops by the soldiers in tank coveralls. They do not know each other. "What happened guys?" he asks them.

Something about this encounter, with the officer they do not know, gives them the sense that there is still hope. There is even an M113 moving confidently toward the front. They tell him everything they know and continue on their way.

"Don't the people know there is a war going on at the outpost?" They nod to each other and behind the M113 suddenly they see the jeep of Akavia, the company commander, with Avi Arbiv, the technical sergeant, driving it.

"Did you meet the technical crew?" Avi asks them.

215

No, they have no idea where the technical crew is.

"Get in, we'll go back to Hushnia."

The APC and the intelligence officer it carries continues on its way to outpost 111 and Akavia's jeep continues with the remains of his crew, driven by Arbiv, the technical sergeant who has been left without soldiers. They stop at Hushnia to pick up two pious Chabad volunteers. They had come to Hushnia on the eve of Yom Kippur to help the soldiers get through the holy day peacefully and then found themselves in the midst of a huge battle.

"Where are you?" Arbiv shouts to them. They rise up from the ground, their beards broken by big smiles of relief.

Black with smoke, smelly, terrified and most of all grateful, they drive north to Nafah, crowded in the jeep of the company commander, who is lying dead beneath outpost 111.

Nafah Gate

Shortly after 17:00, 2nd Lt. Hagai Zur arrives at the entrance gate of the division HQ at Nafah, leading a convoy of damaged tanks.

Exhausted but with genetically determined politeness, Hagai turns to the guard at the entrance and asks him to open the gate for the tanks heading toward the tank repair workshop.

"It is Saturday, the workshop is closed," the guard replies. "Come back in the morning."

Hagai smiles, he is sure this is a joke.

"Come on man, there is no time, open up."

"Don't you understand what I am saying? It is closed, come back tomorrow."

Hagai is no longer amused. His shouts cause the on-call sergeant to run over and ask Hagai if he has a repair order form. Hagai is about to explode. Three damaged and crushed tanks return from the valley of death and here these "royal guards" still do not understand that the situation has changed dramatically.

Hagai has a big heart and is good natured, and he does not have the energy for another fight. He instructs the three crews to get out of the tanks. He remains in the tank and calls out on the radio, hoping that someone will hear him and convince the guards to get out of his way. There is no response.

The war started over three hours ago, the Golan is under heavy fire, his friends on the Petroleum Road need help and the guard at the gate refuses to let him in.

His patience ends and he decides to set aside his good manners and break through the gate, but before he does, deputy commander of the 188th Brigade, Lt. Col. David Yisraeli, responds.

Within two minutes Yisraeli comes out toward him, accompanied by Shmulik Ben Moshe, his adjutant. The deputy brigade commander gets the guards to return to their senses, the gate opens and the three tanks enter the base.

Ben Moshe climbs up on Horen's tank, sees a terrible sight and calls the Northern Command and tells them to send a Rabbinate team urgently to clear out the remains of Shabtai's body.

"Drivey," "loady" and "gunny," that is what Gali Maimon, from Kibbutz Ein Harod, the gunner of the company commander crew, decided to call us, his fellow crew members. Shabtai Horen, the loader, was from Tel Aviv and I was the driver, Barkai from Neve Magen. We were very proud, since only the best became the crew of the company commander.

At the end of the tank basic training we continued to tank commander's course and then we went our separate ways. Shabtai became a tank commander on the Golan, Gali told me, when we were in officer's course. I wondered how he was doing without us. Now Shabtai, who wanted to study movie-making after he was discharged, would not get to do anything of what he planned. His crushed body lay lifeless on the tank's floor.

Yoav Barkai

Southern Sector – The Petroleum Road

At 17:00 Avi Ronis, commander of "Venus," F Company, 74th Battalion, orders Nati Levi, 2nd platoon leader, to leave his position on the Petroleum Road and rush to the assistance of Yoav Yakir, to join him in the defense of sector 116. Levi notified Urieli that he was leaving and left the two tanks of the 82nd Battalion in position to cover them.

Nafah

Shortly after 17:00, Oded Erez reports that Syrian tanks have penetrated his sector and that the opening in area 116 is widening. The main attention of the HQ at Nafah, however, is focused on the Hermon outpost, where the trapped soldiers are reporting that Syrian commandos are trying to break open the doors of the stronghold.

The fall of the Hermon outpost was an unacceptable scenario for the leaders of the country. There was a lot at stake here. On the base there was priceless intelligence equipment, top secret information in the heads of the Intelligence Directorate soldiers, losing the outstanding observation point of the entire northern front – "the country's eyes" – and most of all, a severe blow to morale.

The battle to keep the Hermon under Israeli control had everyone involved, from Moshe Dayan to Ben Shoham and Simchoni at the Nafah HQ, closely monitoring the situation there. As a result, the urgent distress calls from the southern Golan were ignored. They did not see what the big deal was over there. The 82nd Battalion is deployed there, and now that the general is back at Nafah, Ben Shoham will be sent to the southern Golan front, and they all expected Itzik to show leadership and stop the Syrian forces.

Oded Erez

Gigi Daniel, Boaz Tamir's gunner, and Ron Pearlman, Bekman's driver, have faith in their officers. Those, in turn, know that Uzi Urieli will get them out of any trouble. Uzi, a company commander for less than a month, knows that they are relying on him, and he too looks up, to Erez the battalion commander. Up there, at the top, bearing the heavy burden of responsibility, at the lonely top of the pyramid, Erez is on his own.

Himself barely more than a boy – not even twenty-eight years old yet – he is already responsible for the lives of so many boys. They are not much younger than him, scared, waiting for answers, looking to him with eyes full of uncertainty, like children looking to their father, who knows every answer.

All of the armored corps soldiers on the southern front believe that Erez knows something they don't and that this unplanned matter that was thrust on them will end because it is getting dark and the Arabs do not fight in the dark. The reserve forces must be on their way by now and a tank battalion commander, especially the acclaimed CO of the 53rd, surely knows a trick that will change things. That is exactly what he is there for.

From the start of the battles, Erez was in constant contact with Ben Shoham and Simchoni and could not see any reason to be optimistic. He kept imploring them to support him with artillery fire but this did not happen. When it finally comes, it is only a drizzle and off target.

The commander of the 53rd Battalion looks around him concerned and frustrated. How is he supposed to command the forces, encourage the soldiers and plan and carry out an operation to stop the unimaginable torrent of Syrians without air support or artillery?

His soldiers are unaware of the difficulty, are sure it will be okay. They believe someone higher up the chain of command will take care of everything.

Southern Sector – 111

While Akavia's crew was evacuating itself to Hushnia, Zion Sharabi is seeking cover behind a terrace. The driver of Zvi Mizrachi, the tank commander who was crushed to pieces, is racking his brain trying to remember how to place an arterial tourniquet to hold on to Zvi the gunner's life.

From the day that Yair Nafshi had come to the 74th Battalion, he had insisted that his soldiers be ready for any scenario. Combat days may escalate, he would say. Within a short period, he had required all the tank crews learn first aid.

In the cold night of the battle, Zion is going crazy in frustration. Zvi, lying next to him, continues to lose blood, his body is shaking and his thirst is driving him mad. Zion sees the life of his crew member drifting away.

Suddenly he has an idea. Running low, he guides himself between the basalt rocks, sliding like a cat into the turret and moves the body parts of Mizrachi. With a jerry can of water in one hand a half disintegrated coat in the other, he returns to Zvi, who is fading.

As he continues to wonder what to do in this situation, ten meters from him, an unarmed injured Syrian soldier passes him, heading east. They exchange gazes and Zion, his gun pointing at the soldier, takes his finger off the trigger and indicates to him to continue on his way.

Southern Sector – Haim Barak/Chessner

While they are on the move northward, the Chessner force receives a change in mission. "Move immediately to outpost 111," an urgent voice instructs him. "The outpost is under attack, in need of immediate help."

For Chessner, leaving the Zivon route with his seven tanks and getting on the main road (the Reshet route) heading west, it does not make much difference. It is the same direction, with a shorter distance.

After three kilometers, he swerves north, on the fork of the main road and... "What is that in front of us? Enemy tanks in our territory?" No. At the same time Chessner and his company had moved north, Haim Barak and the Eli Geva company were moving south. At the last moment, the commanders on both sides identify the Sho't Kal tanks, order their tense gunner's fingers off the electric triggers, preventing "friendly fire." They sigh in relief and wave to each other.

What is the cause of this unclear movement of each force to the other's sector, Haim Barak wonders, as he continues on the way to his mission. What was the logic behind the order to send Chessner's company on a twenty-five-kilometer drive, at the end of which it was to take position and block the Kudna Gap (the Troy route)? The distance from there to Hushnia, where Barak's forces had started their journey, was not even five kilometers.

The logic, or in retrospect, lack of logic, was another result of the unnecessary lack of communication between the forces.

In this situation, why doesn't Oded Erez decide to make the best of things? Why not have all of Chessner's force with him, on the Petroleum Road/116 front where the forces are in desperate need of assistance, and send Haim Barak who is still with Geva's company to the Troy route/ Kudna sector instead. Once again, the communication problems are to blame for this.

Barak is not tuned into the frequency of the 188th Brigade or to that of Erez's battalion. Why would he be? Barak, who is supposed to be under Erez's command according to the "Yanush–Ben Shoham agreement," does not receive any updates in this matter and is certain he is under the command of Yanush and therefore is only listening to the 7th Brigade radio. During the first few hours of battle, there had been no communication between the two battalion commanders!

Oded Erez knows nothing about Haim Barak being under his command and of him being located in Hushnia with his companies as a reserve force. So he works with what he has. Chessner, who suddenly appears, is what he has and who he can use to deal with the two weak spots on his front: the Petroleum Road 116 and, even more importantly, 111.

Once again, as a result of poor performance of the senior commanders – the Nafah HQ and the brigade commanders – the allocation of missions and deployment of the 82nd Battalion in the southern front is foolish, wasteful and unnecessary.

Nafah

At this point, partly detached from the actual occurrences on the ground, the commanders at the HQ in Nafah see the situation to be very reasonable. "16:59: All throughout the front, with the exception of the Hermon, the enemy is standing still, not attacking." This was the official record in the Command's log of events.

Southern Sector – 116

From his position, near 116, Yoav Yakir would gladly accept the content of the headquarters' log. In contrast to the optimism of the Northern Command, he reports to Ronis that they are running out of ammunition.

"Only air support will work," Ronis tells Erez.

"Only air support will work," Erez tells his brigade commander Yitzchak Ben Shoham, sitting in the bunker at Nafah as the commander of the Golan front.

"It is on its way," he tells him. "In the meantime, do whatever you can to hold on."

At around 17:00 two flights of four Skyhawk planes arrive and release bombs from long range in the Rafid-Tel Fares junction area. Six kilometers from there, Yakir does not have any help from the air force and is doing as he was told by Ben Shoham, trying to hold on. He is fighting for his life and the lives of his platoon and of all the Israeli people.

Southern Sector – On the way to 116

While Urieli is fighting on the ramps and Yakir is calling for help, the two tanks of Nati Levi's platoon come to Yakir's assistance. They make sure, as if they are not in the middle of a dramatic war, to stay off the asphalt paved road. Even though the war started four hours earlier, 2nd Lt. Nati Levi – 2nd platoon leader, Venus Company – is following the strict brigade procedures, still fearing the regulations even more than the Syrian tank fire.

The four kilometers until the turn to 116 and the rendezvous with Yakir's 3rd platoon are endless and Nati Levi decides to hurry and engage the enemy. Maybe they can help from a distance.

"We are cutting through," he announces, indicating to Moty Aviam to follow him. Together they look for good positions on one of the hills east of the road.

Southern Sector – The Petroleum Road

Toward sunset, things on the Petroleum Road seem to be under control. "The ramps are not held by us but they are controlled with our fire," Urieli calms himself.

At the same time there are continuous reports of repeated attempts to infiltrate through the undulating ground below 115. Erez, concerned by the reports from Ronis, who is located on 115, instructs Urieli to send reinforcements to the area. Uzi sends in Boaz Tamir.

17:10

Southern Sector- 112

A kilometer east of the fork on the Reshet route, near 112 – an unmanned daytime observation outpost – a volley of shells is suddenly fired at the tanks in front of Barak the battalion CO and Geva the company commander.

Barak gives the order to fall back and Geva instructs the last platoon still in the area to spread out. While moving up into firing positions, they see the Syrian tanks that fired at them. They are 1,500–2,000 meters away, heading west toward the main road.

The Geva company opens fire, the gunners start to register their first hits and the colorful, darkening sky at sunset fills with black smoke.

Southern Sector – 111

A new and fresh voice comes and joins the brigade frequency.

"Hi, Chess!" Askarov exclaims, recognizing the voice of his friend from their previous service together in very different times.

The chaos of battle is forgotten for a second with the wave of friendly warmth. Then Askarov realizes there is a war going on and he warns him, "Be careful when you move up, Chess. There are enemy tanks here; some of them may have passed the hill line already."

Nafah

Meanwhile at the Command HQ in Nafah, the feeling that everything is okay intensifies. "There are no more infiltrations of Syrian tanks," they write in the log. "Our forces are in control of the area."

17:15

Southern Sector – 111

Below outpost 111, Chess finds an unknown path he plans to take in order to climb up toward the east and join the Askarov force. As he starts climbing up the difficult path, enemy tanks appear and open fire on him. He falls back and cuts north toward a main route he knows, praying not to hit a mine.

Boom!

Chessner counts the first casualty of the company, leaving the damaged tank where it is hit. Chessner continues, his dark feeling matching the darkness outside.

"Hamo!" Askarov shouts to his gunner when he sees a Syrian tank aiming at them. It is too late. The Syrian shell hits the cannon and throws Askarov into the tank.

Berkovitch watches the tank being hit and reports it to Erez the battalion commander. Leaving the radio, he rushes over and finds Askarov's upper body bleeding. He gently wipes his neck, noticing a shard stuck in it and bandages the wound, with the shard still inside.

Knowing Berkovitch's amazing tank skills, Askarov appoints him sector commander, and Rosenzweig, Askarov's driver, rushes to evacuate him to the nearby outpost.

With the final rays of sun falling over the horizon, Yuval Shachar's evacuation APC starts its return journey to the battalion medical center. On the way, there is a report on the radio that the deputy battalion commander is injured.

"Move back," Yuval orders the APC driver, seeing the attempt to evacuate him as an impertinence. After fifteen minutes of arguing, during which Askarov insists that he is fit to continue fighting, medical sergeant Hevroni loses his patience, pointing to the shard still stuck in the neck of the deputy battalion commander, a danger to the artery and determines, "No way."

Surrendering to the medical authority, Askarov is transferred to the M113 APC that speeds in the dark toward the medical center.

17:20

In the twilight following sunset, the Syrian forces are no longer showing their teeth. Things on the Petroleum Road come to a stop, and Uzi decides this is the time to reinforce sector 115 with another tank. He asks Jack Hallel, who is near him, to send one of the two covering tanks behind them. 2nd Lt. Gidi Maklef leaves Rafi Simanovsky alone in covering position and starts heading toward sector 115.

The evening twilight above the 111 hills does not impress Berkovitch and Aldag, who take position near the base. They act like two gunslingers in a Western film, firing at the Syrian forces that continue to climb up to the UN position. They are unaware of the casualties that the tanks of the Ze'evim (G) Company have suffered, just 200 meters from them. And of Zion Sharabi, the driver of the dead Zvi Mizrachi, only 100 meters from them, who is still trying to stop the bleeding of Zvi Mansbach, his crew member.

In his lone position on the northern ramp, Deutsch sees a platoon of enemy tanks moving from north to south, on the path below the northern ramp. He brings the tank into position, calls out the range, realizes they are within combat range and gives the order to carry out quick fire from right to left, just like in training.

Itzik Ripstein, the loader, reports to Deutsch that they do not have a complete series of shape charge or armor piercing rounds and loads a squash head. Shmulik Rosenblau, the gunner, is unaffected by this information, aims, fires and destroys the three tanks with five squash shells.

The Syrians respond with a round of Sagger missiles. The Deutsch crew, alone in its post, without another tank calling the missiles fired, thank God and slap each other on the back in relief. On the surface behind the ramp they were just fighting from, they see a pile of thin, white guidance wires from the Sagger missiles.

A Question of Geography

In the first hours of the war, geography had led the Syrian force to direct their main effort to the southern sector, mainly to the areas of 111–112 and 116–A-Saki.

The ceasefire line on the Golan, which had been drawn after the Six-Day War, crossed a number of hills and ridges. These hills were to act as a topographical separation line, based on the commanding positions they offered. Along this line of hills, fortified outposts were built and, over the years, anti-tank ditches were dug beneath them.

The northern part of the Golan is easier to defend. It is more closed, hilly and rocky. Even the Quneitra gap, the bogeyman of the attack scenarios of the northern front, is under more control from the hills that flanked it. If attack forces tried to climb up to the outposts' line from any route other than the Quneitra gap, they would encounter a rocky landscape that offered limited maneuverability for armored vehicles and that made it harder for them to cross.

The southern region of the Golan Heights is a different story. From the southern slopes of the Shaf-A-Sindiyan hills (111) to Mevo Hama settlement, the landscape is characterized by open flat areas and friendlier paths, a combination allowing armored vehicles to pass freely.

What about the Ruqqad creek?

Deep and broken, the Ruqqad creek is a natural obstacle impossible to pass. Will the Ruqqad obstacle prevent any attack on this sector? Apparently not. Any Syrian force wishing to bypass the Ruqqad obstacle, can pass it from the north, starting from Tel Saki-116. Once they pass the Ruqqad line, the enemy forces are free to spread out and move forward quickly in all directions. The only thing to stop them would be a small number of platoons.

Now to the riddle – considering the landscape analysis and the gaps, if you were given the choice, as senior commanders in the Syrian army, to decide where to break through, in a position that would give you the advantage of superior numbers, where would you choose?

Exactly. That is what the Syrians chose.

Southern Front – 116

The sun has just set. The world is illuminated with deep shades of red, lighting ruby flares above the Tzaida hills. Yakir, in desperate need of shells, knows that with every minute that passes his situation is deteriorating. He also knows that the darkness will not protect him. As soon as the first stars come out, the Syrian tanks, equipped with night vision equipment, will continue to fight and at an increased pace.

"Requesting approval to disengage and carry out resupply," he asks Ronis.

"Negative. Stay where you are." Ronis waits a few seconds, checking to see how much further he can try Yakir's patience. In his characteristic tough nonchalance, he adds, "3, eight tanks of Domem (D Company), of Naka (82nd Battalion) are on their way to reinforce you."

At forward tank depot 116, Ukavi the medic hears Nir Atir asking Ronis, the company commander, "What about the medic who was left at the camp area?"

"I don't know," Ronis answers and Ukavi shouts into the radio, "I am here" but no one hears him. A minute passes and the sound of tank tracks brings him joy. The guys are back.

No, they aren't. A Syrian tank enters the camp and Ukavi is sure he hears Yoav Yakir saying, "Let's fire at the Syrian tank" and a shell is fired, maybe ours, maybe theirs. It hits somewhere nearby and a huge force throws the terrified medic into the ceiling and brings him down, unconscious, on the generator.

Southern Sector – On the way to 116

Nati Levi and Moty Aviam drive up into observation position, take out their binoculars and do not see anything.

Less than a kilometer from their position, to the east, there are tens of Syrian armored vehicles, moving in all directions. Some of them are hit, courtesy of 3rd Platoon; the others are alive and moving, waiting behind the undulations in the landscape, waiting for the right dark moment to continue moving. Nati takes another look at the "empty" area in front of him. "Let's move out," he says to Aviam, "we are not effective here."

17:25

Southern Sector – 116

As if they were listening to what the 3rd Platoon leader had said and wanted to resolve his distress, the Syrians slice through the darkness in a quick maneuver.

"Tanks ahead!" someone shouts on the radio. A few seconds pass and the three tank commanders identify the force moving, terribly near, in front of them.

Waxman, Atir and Yakir fire with what they have. The shortage of ammunition does not affect the performance of the gunners, until Nagarker notifies Atir that all they have left is three phosphorous shells. Firing phosphorous shells at human beings is prohibited, Atir knows this. Even if they are a determined and vicious Syrian enemy, it is not allowed. What are they supposed to do?

Atir is a kibbutz member from Afikim, with developed social and moral values, and since Yakir, his platoon commander from Kibbutz Kfar Rupin, is busy firing, he asks Ronis, his company commander from Kibbutz Hefziba directly.

"You are authorized," Ronis replies, knowing it is either the phosphorous shells or the platoon.

Ami Moshe pulls the trigger and again and one last time and hits three T55 tanks. The Tirans are just slightly damaged but the explosion and the "fireworks" that come with the phosphorous shells, have the Syrian tank crews flee out of their steel protection, becoming easy targets for the machine guns of the 3rd Platoon.

Not far from outpost 116, a slaughterhouse for Syrian tank crews is opened and Nir Atir, a man of high morality, does not feel the slightest bit of guilt.

Southern Sector – On the way to 116

Still in position, Aviam identifies a company of Syrian tanks preparing for an ambush on the southwestern edge of the area they call the "tub" (Bachet-al-Juhader). Levi and Aviam try to lay the aiming cross on them, but they are unable to depress their gun far enough. With their hearts beating fast, they are forced to slide down the hill to advance.

The first shell fired from Aviam's tank misses, someone in the Syrian company sees them and ten gun barrels start turning toward them.

Totally exposed, on a frontal slope, Nati decides that their platoon still needs them and so do their families. He sees no reason to become the Hero of Bachet-al-Juhader.

Having come down the main road (Tapa), Nati orders Aviam, "Move back – fast!" and together they hastily head back the way they came.

Nafah Gate

After getting past the obstacle of the gate guards, the crew waits for the Rabbinate soldiers to come and collect the body parts and for the mechanics to repair their tanks.

In the meantime, Itzik Arnon receives the final confirmation of the death of Akeb. There were just three months remaining until "David and Jonathan" were to be discharged. They were childhood friends whose friendship became even closer during the sleepless nights in khaki in the armored corps. They slept bed by bed, dream by dream, they were about to be discharged and continue into civilian life together. But that would not happen, Itzik Arnon grieves, his head in his hands.

17:30

Hagai Zur, officer and commander, realizes it is time to rise up. "Come on guys, snap out of your depression. They are waiting for us on the Petroleum Road." There is no reply.

Southern Sector – 53rd battalion Medical Center

At the Mashta junction, Askarov tries his luck again, this time with the doctor. "It is not a serious injury, I think I can continue. Let me go back to the tanks."

Dr. Englehard, a thin, calm, pedantic, sharp-gazed man, turns to the brave deputy battalion commander and explains to him in a dry medical tone that since he does not see an exit wound in his neck, there is a possibility that the shard will move around inside until it hits an artery, causing internal bleeding and sudden death. He completes his explanation and smiles widely, the way doctors encourage patients in their final moments.

The silence that follows leaves Askarov no choice, and the tough war horse surrenders to the hands of Yuval Shachar, who had taken it upon himself to evacuate the injured soldiers. He takes Askarov, with the other soldiers, to the Ziv Hospital in Tzfat.

Southern Sector – 116

It is 17:30 and it is still not over. A second wave of Syrian infantry is not giving up on Nir Atir and starts to head toward his tank, located slightly ahead and to the east of the tanks of Waxman and Yakir.

He is busy firing from the machine guns and suddenly he is horrified to see the battle situation change again. Two T55 tanks, leading a convoy with ten APCs, are on the Palga route. They will notice him in a minute – a tank without any heavy ammunition left. Atir is sure he no longer has any chance. Or maybe he does.

"What do we do?" he asks Yakir with panic in his voice, explaining the situation.

There is a moment of silence and then he hears Yakir's voice and it is stable and confident.

"3b, this is 3." He is still talking according to the regulations, even at difficult times.

"This is 3b, over," Atir answers quickly, praying for a magic solution.

"This is 3, stay where you are. I repeat, stay where you are. You will act as bait and we will hit them from the side." There is a moment of silence and then, aware of the sensitive circumstances, Yakir lets himself speak more intimately. "3b, it will be okay, don't worry."

Without ammunition, Atir cannot believe his ears. Standing openly exposed? As bait? But if that is what Yakir said, he must know what he is doing. Even though he is an atheist, he sends a prayer to the One up there. He moves the microphone from his mouth, so the crew do not hear his distress and mumbles to himself, "Yoav, don't let us down, Yoav don't let us down." Yoav does not let them down.

The Syrian force sees Atir, they start to aim at him and Yakir is waiting for them slightly behind, partly hidden by Atir's tank. He aims half right, northeast and gives the order to open fire in the radio net.

"Brilliant," Atir smiles to himself, as he shouts, "Danny, reverse, fast!" Danny Dather, a race driver, puts the 750 horsepower engine in motion. Atir and Ami Moshe fire with their machine guns and somehow the two Syrian tanks at the head of the convoy go up in flames.

At 17:30, from the Petroleum Road in the north, to Ramat Magshimim and the Jordan Valley in the south, there is no real armored force facing the Syrians, except for the 3rd Platoon.

Yoav Yakir, Nir Atir, Yair Waxman, Menachem Shmueli, Andrei Sakal, Brom, Yitzchak Nagarker, Moshe Ami, Danny Dather, David Levi, Danny Levinstein and Berkovitch Moshe. Nine crew members, three commanders, boys aged nineteen to twenty-two. In normal times, rebellious, but now obedient crew members waiting for their orders from the commanders Waxman and Atir, who look to Yakir for answers.

Yakir, an admired officer, is just a boy like them, not 22 yet, and he is silent. He has no answers.

Northern Sector – 105

Still positioned at the same junction where he encountered tanks sliding down from the Manfucha hills, Kaimo hears Nissim, the deputy battalion commander, calling on the radio for him to come to his area. He speeds forward, trying his best to look out for Syrian tanks, as it is getting completely dark. He does not want to be surprised again.

Nissim puts Kaimo in charge; he places the injured Dgani in a jeep that comes to evacuate him to the medical center at Quneitra and feels that things have calmed down. He has been notified that there was a problem with the logistics company commander and so heads, in his jeep, to Nafah to organize the logistics himself.

"The gate guard has been killed," Nissim is told by a number of shocked soldiers at the base.

"What about the logistics company commander?" Nissim asks.

"He is here," they exclaim. Yissachar Tal, the previous company commander, appears. Everyone calls him Jackson.

"What are you doing here?" Nissim asks, surprised.

"I heard there was a mess, so I came up," Jackson smiles in the dark.

"Listen," Nissim looks at the new-old company commander with affection, "I am returning to sector 105 and am not going to deal with logistics at all. Take Moshe Shpitzer, the battalion sergeant major, with you and get to work."

A short while earlier Jackson had left the battalion and joined the advanced logistics company commanders' course. As soon as the war started, he came to the Golan Heights, since this is his home. As the new company commander was not functioning, Jackson took over, and together with Shpitzer, they became a determined and brave logistics team.

Southern Sector – 115

Boaz Tamir takes up the battalion commander's position, a small ramp below outpost 115. He drives up to an observation post and begins sending a series of reports to Urieli and Erez. He identifies enemy forces on the move throughout the entire sector between him and the Petroleum Road. In addition, a Syrian force is now deployed on the conquered ramps on the Petroleum Road, the ones he fought on three hours earlier and the same ones he had tried to take back an hour ago.

As he is reporting, enemy tanks try to sneak up on him from the east, but the precise shooting of Gigi Daniel, the gunner, stops them.

Boom! A shell hits his other tank, ruining its ability to move. Tamir's glasses are shattered and blood is oozing from his eye sockets. Blinded and in the dark, he finds his way to the loader's seat and checks his chest. He is okay. He inspects his body again to make sure he is fit and discovers a metal shard in the binoculars on his chest. This shard takes him straight back to his childhood, to a story he heard from his father Haim.

Tamir, like the Neve Magen bunch, had grown up with stories of his father's battles. At the age of forty-six, his father, Haim Plechser, was the oldest tank company commander in the Six-Day War. In the battle at Bir Gafgafa he was injured and his leg was amputated. His father's injury was serious but could have been worse. One large shard cut his leg but another large shard, heading straight for his heart, hit the binoculars on his chest and did not go through.

With a face slashed with shards, smeared with black soot and clotted blood, with the remaining eyesight that was slipping away, Tamir smiled at his stunned crew. "I lost my eyes? That's okay as long as I have my balls. Can't a blind man screw?"

Zion the loader sees that if the deputy is talking about screwing, everything is okay and he continues to update him with what is going on. Now Boaz can make decisions without having to see what's going on. A few minutes pass and it turns out that the optimism was not misplaced – not only are his balls intact, his eyes are also still working. Another canteen of water and another and Boaz can see. It is a blur but better than nothing.

Southern Sector – 112

At 17:30 the Geva Company ends its battle on the Reshet route, leaving twenty-seven Syrian armored vehicles in flames. Their joy is mixed with sadness. They did have one tank destroyed by the Syrians. Eitan Ron, the tank commander, was killed and will never be joining the celebrations again.

They stand in place, darkness starts to surround them and they occasionally hear a Syrian vehicle that was not destroyed, trying to withdraw in the dark.

While the Askarov force was stopping the tanks of the Syrian 33rd Infantry Brigade, the Eli Geva Company encountered the spearhead battalion of the enemy's 51st Armored Brigade of the 9th Central Division.

The twenty-seven tanks they had destroyed at sector 112 were the opening shot for the second phase of the Syrian attack plan on the Golan, the phase of the Next Mission, planned to the last detail by Walid Hamdon, commander of the Syrian 51st Brigade.

"A Syrian-made Swiss watch," he proudly presented the plan. Hamdon determined the number of forces in each of the two parallel columns setting out 1,500 to 5,000 meters apart from each other. He determined where and when they would split into companies (Tel Azbach in the center of 111–112 sector), when and where the company would split into platoon attack formation (right after the anti-tank ditch that should be secured and bridged for them by then).

"Commanders," Hamdon declared before the brigade staff officers, commanders of the 451st, 452nd, 453rd tank battalions and the commander of the 454th Mechanized Infantry Battalion, "one hundred and thirty minutes after we start moving from the assembly areas east of Jasem, at exactly 16:40, with Allah's help, we will already be in the enemy's territory, ready for the final assault."

Nafah

Meanwhile, the report from Haim Barak – "Everything is fine, we are in control of the situation"– reaches command headquarters at Nafah and from there continues to the General Staff in Tel Aviv, leading to celebrations. "Our outstanding men have proven their superiority again and it will soon be over in the north."

17:40

Southern Sector – 111

Chessner continues to cut through the field, roughly in a straight line from west to east, hoping with all his heart to get to the end of this rocky path that he chose in order to remain out of sight of the enemy forces. A little more and the nightmare will end, a little longer and the road to the outpost will appear before him. He will turn right on the road and that will be it. Then he will meet with Askarov of course.

A short distance from the base, one of the tanks has its track break and is stuck in its position, unable to move. Five tanks continue to climb up in the dying light.

Southern Sector – On the way to 116

Nati Levi and Moty Aviam continue to head south, on the route beside the road, attempting to join Yakir, still not daring to cross the asphalt with their steel tracks.

Nati's radio communication is stuttering. Aviam realizes that Ronis notified them of the 82nd Battalion tanks that were sent to reinforce them and knows they have a problem. The Syrian company they disengaged themselves from half an hour ago, was preparing for a night ambush, right along the main road. He calls Ronis on the radio. There is no answer. Aviam decides to try again when they reach the road leading to outpost 116 (Palga route), a few hundred meters away.

The message is not received by Ronis and it is not sent to the Pesach force, marching blindfolded into the valley of death.

Southern Sector – 115

Second Lt. Gidi Maklef, a platoon commander in the 82nd Battalion, had been sent to help the forces, and he arrived at the battalion commander's ramp with the last light. Beneath the ramp, to its right, he sees the damaged tank of Boaz.

Hearing the reports regarding Syrian forces moving beneath outpost 115 and the injuring of the Golan Company deputy CO, the battalion commander decides to reinforce sector 115. Six tanks from the 82nd battalion, commanded by Jack Hallel, remain on the Petroleum Road, while Bekman and Urieli are sent on a mission to save the forces at sector 115.

Beneath the positions of outpost 115, in the southern Golan, every-thing is burning. Tanks, APC's, trucks, thorns, lizards and snakes. A thick mixture of smeared colors of the last light of the day covers the tanks on the large ramp, with fire, dust and smoke.

Boom! Avi Ronis suffers another hit on his tank. He jumps out and runs to sergeant Yoram Miromi's tank, instructing him to take his place in the damaged tank.

In the final remaining light, before darkness covers the Golan, Avi Ronis returns to his position, standing in cupola of Miromi's tank. Pta-chya Azaria, his original gunner, who remained in the damaged tank, happens to look to his left and just as it becomes dark, he is blinded by a bright flash that is an anti-tank shell hitting steel, and he sees Ronis fall.

Miromi's terrified crew runs for their lives, dragging Ovadia the gunner, who was injured by shrapnel in his back. They all find shelter in the original company commander's tank.

Then they come to their senses, return to the damaged tank, drive it down to a waiting position, they cover Avi's body with a blanket. It is cold and mangled, lying with the empty shells. The two crews crowd into one tank and try to report to everyone that Avi Ronis, their compa-ny commander who they took so much pride in, who they feared and admired, is lying dead behind them.

17:45

The Syrians' clever flanking of outpost 111 leaves the rest of the Israe-li force helpless. From all around them, from unexpected directions, Berkovitch and Aldag hear the sound of enemy tracks. They know they are surrounded by enemy tanks. In the dark, they try with all their might to see who is threatening them and where they will come from.

17:50

Maj. Benny Katzin, 188th Brigade's Operations Officer (G3), gets ahold of Danny Berkovitch on the radio and asks him to help locate the Chessner Company tanks. Apparently they are very close to the road near the outpost. In his quiet and efficient way, Berkovitch flashes the commander's searchlight in the direction where he is supposed to meet the 82nd Battalion tanks, then he slides down the road, meets the five tanks and leads them to stronghold 111.

Southern Sector – The Pesach force

Danny Levine is sick of waiting. "Where is my war?" he fumes into the intercom. He is in position, doing nothing in sector 114. Yoav Ben David nods in agreement in the driver's compartment. This is not what they brought us here for, all the way from Beer Sheva.

17:55

Finally! God hears their request. They receive an order on the radio, the Pesach force is to leave their position and move to sector 116, to quickly reinforce the 3rd Platoon as it fights for its life.

Southern Sector – On the way to 116

It is dark. Levi and Aviam turn onto the road leading to forward camp 116, on their way to join Yoav Yakir. Suddenly, on the left, in a low opening between the huge basalt rocks, Aviam spots a tank with a flattened turret and a gas releasing unit on the end of its cannon. A Tiran!

The Syrian tank is moving lazily, to the side of their direction of travel. On the turret, detached from the commotion of battle, the tank commander is smoking a cigarette. What big lungs, Aviam thinks to himself, seeing the small red flame burning bright.

Did Nati see it? Aviam does not see the platoon commander's tank turning its cannon toward it.

"Fachima, lower the cannon and fire a shell," Moty whispers, bending into the turret, hoping the Syrian soldier did not hear him.

"Maybe it is our tank?" Fachima hesitates.

"Fire now," Moty snaps out at him quietly.

As he pulls the trigger, he sees that the platoon commander is also alert. Both tanks fire at the same time toward the indifferent Syrian commander, who explodes in a huge fire with his crew.

A wave of heat washes over Aviam and he dives into the tank. The flame reveals additional tanks in the area. Without the ability to locate targets and to conduct night combat, the two blind Sho't Kal tanks move back, taking position behind a small hill, and Nati Levi makes a decision.

"3, this is 2," Nati calls to Yoav. "The route to your location is blocked."

"2, this is 3. Copy that," Yakir answers. "It is good to hear you. Move south until the Pinkas route (the Roman road north of Tel-A-Saki) and then ascend north on Yarkona (the border route). Meet us at the fork near the outpost."

Northern Sector – 104

In the most northerly part of the northern sector, no one in Eyal Shaham's company knows quite what is happening. All they have learned is that there were enemy tanks and infantry have had the nerve to try to infiltrate into the Golan. In their area it continues to remain quiet, so Eyal turns on the transistor radio and listens to the news to try and discover what is going on elsewhere. He immediately notifies the company, "We are in general war," he reports. "The Hermon has been conquered by Syrian forces and the shells are falling on us with terrible precision, since it seems they are targeting us from there."

Nafah

A few minutes before 18:00, with the Golan already in darkness, the initial euphoria in the headquarters at Nafah that followed the reports from the Barak force, is replaced with serious concern in light of news that enemy forces appear to have broken through on the southern sector.

The entry in the Command log reads:

17:53 The situation in the southern sector is severe. At Kudna a force is preparing to break through. The deputy battalion commander is injured. Command is being transferred to the 82nd battalion commander.

Following the reports, Ben Shoham instructs Oded Erez to take all the tanks that survived on the Petroleum Road and concentrate them at the Juhader junction in order to block the breach through the Petroleum Road. He appoints Haim Barak as commander of the northern sector of the Southern Golan, which includes area 111. He asks him to work with him on the Tofi brigade frequency and to make sure that Chessner is coordinated with him.

17:54

While Ben Shoham is trying to stabilize the front and prevent the breakthrough, Haka makes two important decisions.

He confirms Simchoni's order to divide the Golan between the two brigades. From outpost 110 to the north is the responsibility of the 7th Brigade, commanded by Yanush. From 110 to the south is the responsibility of the 188th Brigade, commanded by Ben Shoham.

After a minute, he asks Simchoni to instruct Yanush to send a battalion to the Hushnia area.

Yanush confirms that he received the order but instead of sending a battalion to the south, he settles for instructing Meir Zamir's company (Tiger), next to him, to move to sector 110. Not a battalion, not exactly the southern sector.

Once again, Yanush does whatever he wants. He is in uniform? He was given orders? So what?

Why doesn't the command learn its lesson and make sure that this time its order was carried out properly?

It is almost 18:00, Haka turns to Ben Shoham, placing a fatherly hand on his shoulder and instructs him to move out and join his forces on the southern sector.

"Ok," Ben Shoham says to Zurich, who is bent over the radio next to him, "we are leaving."

18:00–18:59

At 18:00 a purple moon appeared in the eastern sky, accompanied by the first stars of night.

Throughout the country, hundreds of thousands of men and women were sitting down to eat the meal breaking the Yom Kippur fast, listening with growing concern to the news reporting the announcements of the IDF spokesman. The reports were given in the special tone used for historic events. The Israeli public learns that, since 14:00, there have been fierce battles on the Golan and in the Sinai, in the air and on the ground.

The civilians eating their meals, obey the orders of the spokesman instructing them to observe a complete blackout. They continue eating and wonder if this inconvenience will be temporary, as it was in the Six-Day War, and whether it will end in another quick and easy victory.

Nafah Gate

Out of nowhere, a tall, dazzlingly blond first-lieutenant appears at the gate of Nafah. He is wearing a Class A uniform and, in a deep bass voice, asking the tank crews near the gate what is going on.

The soldiers cannot be bothered and ignore him. The blond officer, who is not used to soldiers disregarding him, is about to use the authoritative voice he has as a company commander, when Lt. Col. David Yisraeli, the deputy brigade commander, emerges from the command bunker. He sees 1st Lt. Zvika Gringold, points to the damaged tanks and says, "Organize a platoon and take them out to the war."

Just ten days before, on the eve of Rosh Hashanah, Zvika Gringold, the commander of the Golan (G) Company, 74th Battalion, had passed on command to Uri Akavia and had gone on leave for the weekend. Right after Yom Kippur he was scheduled to start the company commander's course. The war caught him at his kibbutz, Lochamei

238

Hagetaot. He hitchhiked to the base at Nafah, found Jackson, the logistics company commander, and realized that this time things were different. He then crossed the fence to the division headquarters, where he met Benny Katzin, Operations Officer (G3) of the 188th Brigade, who reported that all hell was breaking loose on the Golan and sent him to the gate.

Southern Sector – 116

Sector 116 is veiled in darkness mixed with numerous Syrian "fireflies." The headlights of these tanks cast occasional weak rays of light. On the northern point of the Bachta spur, a few hundred meters from stronghold 116, sit the crew members of the 3rd Platoon. They are commanded by Yoav Yakir, the wonder boy from the Beit Shean valley, and they accept the night that is falling on them with apprehension. They are in the dark, exhausted, hungry, almost out of ammunition and with the sense that they are fighting against an enemy much stronger than them.

"All around us there is a storm but our heads will not bow," Atir thinks in admiration of his "Palmachnik" platoon commander, who is not letting them fall into self-pity. Rather, he is contacting Yossi Gur in the outpost above them and asking him to illuminate the area for the tanks.

A few minutes later, an impressive collaboration between tanks and infantry takes place below outpost 116. The infantry mortar team get to work on the task and they fire illuminating flares. In the light, Yakir and Waxman continue to hit the Syrian tanks coming closer to the base trying to penetrate farther beyond the Purple Line.

With no heavy ammunition left, Atir watches them, correcting their hits and encouraging them. Every few minutes he uses the emergency radio to warn the Pesach force of Syrian vehicles threatening them, hoping someone is listening to him.

Nafah

In the bunker at Nafah they continue to receive reports of Syrian pressure on the southern front. As Ben Shoham prepares to leave and join the forces, he hears the sounds and the distress and realizes that something has gone wrong in the southern Golan.

Southern Sector – 115

In the darkness, Uzi Urieli climbs the narrow route that leads to the battalion commander's ramp. He leaves Bekman to cover them and joins Tamir and Maklef in the crowded position. The visibility is poor. It is hard to see how bad the breach is. There is one thing Uzi has no doubts about. The Syrian artillery is doing a terrific job. The ramp is completely crushed. It feels as if all the Syrian artillery forward observers joined forces to destroy it.

As he is wondering what they can do with this night, suddenly he hears distress calls on the radio. "I am being attacked!" It is Jack Hallel shouting and Urieli is trembling.

"Jack, this is Uzi," he calls to him. "Jack, this is Uzi," he calls again but there is no reply.

18:05

Urieli realizes how inefficient it is to stay on such a crowded ramp, in complete darkness, preventing them from fighting the enemy that is sneaking in. He notifies Boaz that he is leaving. He takes Bekman with him, and together they rush back to the Petroleum Road. This completed their second circuit since the start of the war; 115 to the Petroleum Road to 115 and the Petroleum Road again.

18:07

Nafah

Ben Shoham finishes updating Benny Katzin, the 188th Brigade S3, who will be his right-hand man in the forward command groups on the Golan. Right before they left, Haka had presented the new distribution of forces on the Golan front. "You are responsible for the area from outpost 111 and south. Get going. Join your forces. Good luck."

18:10

Jack Hallel finally answers and Uzi explodes in joy. He instructs him to return on the Mahaze route toward the junction and join him.

Southern Sector – The Petroleum Road

To the crews of the 82nd Battalion's tanks, fighting for their lives on the Petroleum Road, Uzi's order sounds like joyous bells. They have no idea what the situation is and have the feeling that something unfair has fallen on them here in the dark. They had barely completed their first firing practice in the basic training course, they are supposed to be fighting in Sinai and here they are, struggling with the basalt rocks of the Golan, in the dark on the Petroleum Road. The Syrian Tiran tanks are firing at them and they didn't even know that the Arabs fought at night.

Right after the Six-Day War, the Arab armies bordering with Israel had begun rebuilding themselves. Air and sea lifts started flowing in to Egypt and Syria, with the Soviet super-power committed to rebuilding its allies' ability to defend themselves and – when the time came – to go to war to regain their pride.

One of the things the Soviets had supplied to Egypt and Syria was advanced night-fighting equipment. The IDF had received indications of this development, but had chosen to disregard it, and also to ignore anyone who dared to suggest that it would be wise to purchase night-vision equipment for its own tanks as well. "It is too expensive," was the excuse.

The IDF did not understand that the cost of one Israeli tank destroyed is the same as purchasing hundreds of advanced night-vision systems. The common view, however, was that Israel was still an "empire" and its borders were as stable as ever. So the night-vision equipment was not purchased, leaving Jack Hallel on the Petroleum Road, along with all the other tank crews on the Golan and the Suez Canal, without the means to fight back. This would determine the fate of many of them.

Southern Sector – 111

Outside outpost 111 there is chaos, with tanks parked together in a hodgepodge of various units. Aldag and Berkovitch raid five of Chessner's tanks to get ammunition for theirs.

In a demonstration of wise leadership, Chessner got 1st Sgt. Berkovitch to help him. The non-com is in control of the front; he knows the area and the conditions of the battle better than anyone and is exceptionally calm. Chessner consults him regarding every action he is planning to take.

Aldag and Berkovitch are sent to take up a position right next to the outpost, with their cannons pointing south, toward hill 958 and the gap beside it. Chessner's five tanks move to the northern ramp, where they find Deutsch, "the camp guard." They huddle together and divide the sectors of fire.

At the same time, south of the Chessner force and outpost 111 – that the Syrian forces had left – the Syrian 51st Tank Brigade crosses the Purple Line, as if it is an open freeway.

In the big opening between 958 and outpost 112, Tiran tanks pass between the two companies – Chessner and Geva – of the 82nd Battalion. They struggle with the rocky path and head toward the ruins of Hushnia and the Mashta junction that is on the Petroleum Road.

Nafah

Ben Shoham steps out of the Nafah headquarters and heads toward the brigade command APC. "Notify my tank to prepare to meet us at a point we will specify later on," he instructs Maj. Hanan Schwartz, the communications officer who gets in the carrier with him.

The order Haka gave Ben Shoham was strange. Leaving the bunker at night to join his forces? That was something he should have done during the day, as Simchoni suggested, but then Ben Shoham was unable to leave the HQ following the general's instructions, appointing him as his replacement until he returns.

In the darkness, Ben Shoham and his warriors were half blind. The window of opportunity that was open during the day to improve the command of the brigade closed at night. He was not going to gain any added value in getting a better sense of the battle situation in the dark. Therefore, he did not have the ability to make better decisions.

Was his mere presence there worth going out at night? A commander who is on the battlefield with his forces gives the soldiers support and encouragement, but not at night. How could his troops see him in the dark? How would they be get inspiration from his invisible presence? In one of the interviews with Maj. Gen. Haim Laskov, he described this "commander's syndrome" in the IDF, "Commanders are supposed to be out there, at the front. The important thing is for them to be out there."

18:15

Nafah Gate

Gringold decides that Itzik Arnon will help him. In his deep bass voice, he tries to get through to him. "Tell me, can we organize a crew here?"

Arnon looks at him numb and shrugs his shoulders.

"I am Zvika," the blond officer continued. "Come help me. It's a shame to wait for the Rabbinate team to arrive. Let's take the body out of the tank and start getting it ready."

Arnon stares at him blankly. Who can think about war when Akeb is lying there crushed in the tank on the Petroleum Road? He is not willing. "Leave me alone," he says.

Southern Sector – The Pesach Force

The Pesach force arrives at the Juhader junction and continues south toward outpost 116. Before they get a chance to enjoy the beauty of the Khan Juhader ruins in the uncertain moonlight, Danny Levine, who does not remember where exactly to enter the outpost, receives instructions from Benny Katzin, the brigade operations officer at the Nafah headquarters.

"About four kilometers after Juhader, there is a left turn with a sign that says 116 on it. Turn left there and you will reach the outpost."

On the way to Juhader

Uzi Urieli, as calm and decisive as he always was in training, stops by Bekman's damaged tank and has Ilan Orenstein and the rest of the crew join his tank. He tells himself, "I will get to the junction, see how many tanks are left from the 82nd Battalion and then I will decide what to do." The Juhader camp area appears before him when he hears the order from Erez the battalion CO for all the tanks to convene at the tank depot.

There is no doubt that the order that came from Ben Shoham, was transferred to Erez and from him to Urieli, the company commander, was the right decision. It is dark, and the Syrian forces have the advantage in night fighting. Infantry forces, some with anti-tank weapons, had already been spotted on the Petroleum Road ramps two hours earlier. Moving the forces to fight at night on the Petroleum Road would be suicidal.

At the Juhader camp area, Uzi Urieli and Oded Bekman are waiting for the 82nd Battalion's tanks. Soon Jack and his group will be joining them, after fighting a battle blind.

Urieli counts eight functional tanks in his force. Him and Bekman, two of the 188th Brigade, and six of the 82nd. He deploys the force in a perimeter defense of the junction and the camp area, passes through the crews, makes sure they are alert, gives them a pat on the back, a word of encouragement, trying to keep up the spirits of the exhausted soldiers. He knows now is the time to organize the tanks for night parking. They will soon be fighting for their lives.

Nafah

In the meantime, at Nafah, Ben Shoham completes his preparations to set out to join the forces. Thirty minutes pass from Haka's order until he completes the preparations and is ready to set out in the carrier. These are long, exhausting, difficult minutes.

The final reports that accompany Ben Shoham on his way to the carrier contradict the feeling in the bunker that "everything is under control" until then.

The 18:23 entry in the command log states, "A tank force moving south encountered twenty enemy tanks at the Juhader junction. The tanks are currently engaged in armor battle." Ben Shoham understands the meaning of this. Inside Israeli territory, at the place he is heading to, there are at least twenty enemy tanks.

Southern Sector – The Pesach Force

Not exactly at the Juhader junction, as was written in the command log but two kilometers to the south, the Pesach force, led by Levine, arrives at the center of the Bachet Juhader swamp. In a surprising moment of light in the sky, Asher Goldman, 1st platoon leader, identifies what appears to be a mass of unidentified tanks to the left of the route. As he is wondering who these tanks are, all hell breaks loose.

Even though the tanks of 3rd platoon F company destroy an amazing number of tanks, many "live" Syrian tanks remain. These are the same tanks that Nir Atir and Moty Aviam are –unsuccessfully – trying to warn them about.

The remains of the tanks and carriers of the Syrian 61st Brigade, probably together with pioneers of the 46th Armored Division, take up position in the western outskirts of the Juhader swamp and wait in the dark for easy prey. The prey arrives.

The tank of Eran Avrutzky, leader of the 2nd platoon, is the first that is hit. The tank explodes and starts to burn. A few seconds later, the tank in front of it, of sergeant Ofer Tamir, is also hit and goes up in flames. A second later the tank behind them, 2B of Danny Biran, also goes up in flames.

The last in the line, Meir Lavi, commander of 2A sees the horror on the front, understands the magnitude of the catastrophe, shouts to the driver to turn around and withdraw north toward the Juhader camp area, fleeing as fast as he can.

"Fire!" Asher Goldman shouts on the external radio, kicking the gunner so he hurries up. They are hit by two shells in compartment 1 and the turret basket and they disengage with the platoon to the right, fifty meters off the road.

Goldman, a tough moshav man in regular times, tries to control the pressure cooker he is in but is unsuccessful.

"Domem, this is 1 over," he shouts over the radio to his company commander.

There is silence.

"Domem, this is 1. Your position," Goldman shouted again.

Still there is no response.

"Naka commander (82nd Battalion), this is 1 of Domem. Commander has been killed. We are under attack by hundreds of Syrian tanks," Goldman let out the pressure rising in him.

"We are busy, continue the task on your own," the battalion commander responds.

While this one is busy and that one is calling for help, Iser Sosnovsky, commander of tank 1A, is hit in the head and collapses into the tank, squirting blood all over.

18:29
Nafah
The five minutes between the time Itzik Ben Shoham left the command bunker, until he connects to the radios in the carrier, are the first quiet minutes he has since 14:00. They will also be the last.

18:34

Ben Shoham puts on his VRC helmet and connects to the radio. He immediately hears Erez in his ear, "20, this is 10. I need artillery at sector 116 and the Petroleum Road immediately."

Southern Sector – On the way to 116

Levi and Aviam turn east on the Roman path north of Tel Saki (the Pinkas route) and stop for Levi to switch tanks with Aviam and to be able to communicate again. That is when they identify, a few kilometers north, on the main road, three British steel vehicles in flames. Aviam has no doubt that this is the Pesach force, the 82nd Battalion reinforcement that was hit by the Syrian ambush they were trying to warn them about.

Ben Shoham Force

"Dror, drive!" Dror Sofer drives, or more accurately stands in the M113 commander's cupola and guides the driver out of the Nafah gate. He does not know any of the officers with the brigade commander in the carrier. Not Hanan Schwartz, the brigade communications officer, not Moshe Zurich, the intelligence officer, not Itzik Weiss, the brigade fire support officer, not Sefi Ben Yosef, the reconnaissance officer, not even Yossi Gavrieli and Avi Sak, the communications NCOs. He is annoyed that there is no one from his company there and wonders how they are all doing on the Petroleum Road.

While he is wondering about them, Ben Shoham sticks his head outside and sees three tanks near the gate and notifies Benny Katzin who stay at the headquarters, "Three of our tanks are near the gate, with technical problems. Check out their situation. When they are repaired, send them back to the Mahaze route (the Petroleum Road) southeast."

Southern Sector – 116

Once again Yakir tries to contact Ronis, the company commander, but there is no response. Now he tries to contact Oded Erez. Again there is no response. Not knowing what else to do, he tries "his" battalion commander Yair Nafshi, who is thirty kilometers north of him on the Booster Ridge, running the battle on the northern front.

"Peleg commander, this is 3 of Shadar, in your frequency."

"This is Peleg," Nafshi replies. He does not understand why the commander of the platoon farthest south on the Golan is calling him suddenly in the night.

"This is 3 of Shadar," Yakir continues, a bit hesitant. "I have eight 'candies' left and I identify twelve enemy tanks in front of me. What should I do?"

Nafshi does not know what to reply. He suddenly realizes that the battle in the north is nothing compared to what is going on in the south. Then, he answers the way commanders speak on the radio, even when things are bad. He uses the usual formula, "3 of Shadar, this is Peleg. Do everything to hold on. Good luck, over and out." He feels terrible inside.

Southern Sector – 111

In the darkness around him, Zion decides to take action.

"Zvi," he whispers to the gunner who is fading in front of him. "I am climbing up to the outpost. If it is still under our control, I will get help and take you there."

Zvi does not answer.

"Don't worry, Zvi," he tries again. "I promise you, I will go up and be right back."

With great fear, he climbs up to the outpost and stops. He listens to the voices. Hebrew. Not just any Hebrew, the unique Hebrew spoken by Marko Avigdor from Tiberias, the driver of the redheaded Hochstein, from the 53rd Battalion.

"We need help down there," he notified Marko and together they walk down with a stretcher. They put Zvi on the stretcher and carry him all the way up to the stronghold.

"It will be okay, Zvi," Zion whispers in his ear. "Don't worry, now everything will really be fine."

Southern Sector – On the way to 116

The two tanks of Nati Levi's platoon arrive at the border route (Yarkona) and start the slow drive north, toward Yakir's platoon.

"Out of the north the evil shall break forth upon all the inhabitants of the land,"[28] Aviam thinks to himself, seeing the war intensifying as he continues to the north. There is a thick veil of smoke coming from tens of Syrian tanks and carriers that have been hit and that are burning. There is a strong smell of gunpowder and gasoline and above all of this there is the threatening silhouette of outpost 116.

Without the evil-bearing tanks and the terrible smells, this could be a spectacular night trip, Aviam, a nature lover thinks, as he looks at the half-moon smiling in the center of the sky.

18:35

"1, this is Domem, over," suddenly it is the voice of Levine, the company commander.

"This is 1, continue," Goldman exclaims, joyous to have him back from the dead.

"This is Domem. Me and deputy of Naka (deputy battalion commander Danny Pesach) have moved forward," Levine notifies him.

Goldman understands, says he is on his way to join them, leading the injured Iser Sosnovsky in a wide right flank. Five minutes later, Goldman decides that he has had enough time away from hell and he returns to the main road and meets the tanks of the company commander and the deputy battalion CO. He takes up position behind them and together they head south on the road toward the ascent to Tel Saki.

Confused and upset, leaving behind their comrades in three burnt tanks and one whose fate is unknown, the four steel chariots climb up the path to the top of Tel Saki. Goldman is determined to figure out how to get out of this mess and start fighting back.

From the observation bunker at the top of the hill, scared by the sounds of the tracks, a number of soldiers approach the tanks of the 82nd Battalion.

"I am Menachem," 1st Lt. Menachem Ansbacher, commander of a bomb squad platoon, introduces himself. He tells them that he and four soldiers from the 50th Nahal Battalion, a driver and a BTR armored personnel carrier had been sent here, to the fortified observation point at the top of the hill, on Saturday afternoon. They were told that there was a need for eyes to watch the eastern side.

---

28. Jeremiah 1:14.

19:00–19:59

Toward 19:00, the Syrian forces assemble two concentrated steel fists, in an attempt to break through the defense wall the armor crewmen have established on the Golan. It is as if they read the Intelligence research division's document distributed just four days earlier.

With the darkness covering them, this northern Syrian fist provokes the tanks of the 188th Brigade, commanded by Yair Nafshi that until an hour ago had halted them on their own, shedding their blood and prevented them from carrying out their plan. Now things have changed.

The tanks of the 188th Brigade are blind in the dark, and the Syrian officers know that this is the time for a change. It will not be easy. The "second level forces" tanks of the 7th Infantry Brigade, the 78th Armored Brigade and the 121st Mechanized Brigade are supposed to carry out the Next Mission. However, they are unable to move forward. All of the bridges laid on the anti-tank ditch have been destroyed by the 74th Battalion's tanks. Some had been hit immediately, others after a few tanks of the Syrians' 85th Brigade had managed to cross.

Nonetheless, Brigadier General (Akid) Omar Abrash, commander of the 7th Brigade of Syria's 7th Division, is determined to continue. He orders the remaining tanks to move forward, into the undefended region between outposts 105 and 107.

Without unnecessary talk on the radio, with their lights off, with extraordinary determination and courage, unseen by Yachin, Damir and Landau, the Syrian Tiran tanks head toward the Hermonit hills. There the 7th Brigade will have their first chance to open fire efficiently and join the forces that are in combat.

While the remaining tanks of the Syrian 85th Brigade move forward toward the forces of the 7th Brigade that await them, alert and fresh beneath the Hermonit hill, in a second improvised line of defense, the situation in the southern Golan is apparently very bad.

Brigadier General Ali Aslan, commander of Syrian 5th Division and Brigadier General Hassan Turkmany, commander of the 9th Division, identify the weak spot in the southern Golan – the Tel Fares–Tel Saki area on Aslan's front and the Kudna gap on Turkmany's front. They break through with full force, crossing the Purple Line.

To the south of outpost 111, south of the Petroleum Road, all along the front between 116 and Tel Saki, a large Syrian steel fist spreads out. Its deadly fingers are seven hostile, fresh and motivated tank battalions, and they are thrusting straight toward the few tanks of the 188th Brigade.

Nafah Gate

A jeep arrives at the forward tank depot near the Nafah gate and out jumps Yaakov Hershkovitz, until recently, Zvika Gringold's tank driver. Hershkovitz was at home at his kibbutz of Kfar Szold in the Galilee on Shabbat and was called back in the afternoon. He got a ride to the company headquarters at Hushnia, where he discovered that his tank was manned by another driver. Just then the Golan started to explode all around him and the tanks sped to the ramps. He took cover in a pit and waited. After a while he found a jeep outside one of the buildings, started the engine and drove all the way to Nafah and Zvika Gringold.

Zvika hugs him and tries to understand what is going on in the field.

Hershko describes what he saw from the pit he was in, describing the shells and the Syrian MiG planes. Zvika hugs him again, kicking the stony ground, and asks him to help him clean the remains of the body from the tank.

"Are you crazy?" the scared driver askes. "I am not an undertaker, I wouldn't be able to take it."

In regular times Zvika would insist but in these terrible circumstances, he gives in and softly says to him, "Ok, Hershko, but after I am done cleaning, you are coming back to be my driver."

Hershko nods in agreement.

Gringold returns to the tank, pulls the body of Shabtai Horen out of the tank by himself and he feels it ripping in his hands. "Get me water jerrycans," he shouts and someone hands him one.

He pours water wildly and then more water and more. Then the Army Rabbinate burial service people arrive, sending Zvika to deal

with what a company tank commander is supposed to be dealing with. They continue cleaning the tank from the remains of blood and bones and tissue.

Southern Sector – Meeting at 116

Nati Levi suddenly disappears into the pillars of smoke around them, and Aviam, somewhat alone and scared, sees the shadow of a tank and aims the cannon at it. He places Fachima the gunner on target and at the last second sees that he is about to fire at a tank of the 3rd platoon.

Detached from Levi, with a one-way radio without reception, without the sounds of war in the background, Aviam decides it is time to take care of logistics.

"2, this is 2A, I am leaving to repair the radio."

He does not wait for an approval, which he wouldn't hear anyway. He hopes Nati heard him and moves back a thousand meters and stops in a hidden spur on the side of the route.

"Turn off the engine," he instructs Swisa the driver.

In the silence, a few hundred meters away, Aviam sees the flash of lights and hears voices.

"I have to get out and pee," David Riv the loader grunts.

"Absolutely not," Aviam warns him. "Take a canteen and piss in it."

The radio undergoes gentle cleaning, with a series of banging and cursing and magically it starts working again.

"2A, come help me," he suddenly hears Nati saying. "I hit a mine at the entrance to the outpost and threw a track."

Once again, Aviam is back on the route alone, no lights, trying to see through the dark. He tries to keep Swisa on track, looking to the right, to the lights he saw.

Night is no time for war, Aviam thinks, shaking in the commander's cupola, cursing the night vision equipment they left in the platoon parking area. He knows the enemy tanks have night vision.

He was right. A bright flash of light shoots out from the lights he saw, passing a few centimeters above the commander's cupola.

"Swisa, step on it," he says, trying to stay calm. Swisa, a psychologist of war, hears the urgency in his voice and obeys. He speeds up as fast as possible in the dark, keeping them from getting hit by the Syrians ambushing them.

When he reaches the junction of the Yarkona route with the outpost route (Palga), Nati Levi calls again. "2A, head east toward the base, I am on the side of the entrance path."

Aviam ascends the path to the base and the platoon commander's tank, his original tank, appears. This is the second time today that he is hosting Levi's crew, this time on Brinberg's tank, whose blood is still smeared on its turret walls.

One tank, the last of the 2nd Platoon, meets three tanks of the 3rd Platoon and the young armored corps soldiers sit on the tank, dirty, exhausted, exchanging stories of their experiences, giving each other hope.

Southern Sector – 115

Boaz Tamir, deputy company commander, continues to report that Syrian forces are trying to advance beneath outpost 115. Company Commander Uzi Urieli decides to send Bekman over. He takes the opportunity to switch tanks with him, since his tank is having communication problems again.

Bekman arrives at the battalion commander's ramp, finds Boaz and Gidi there, in ready positions at the bottom of the ramp, and Boaz indicates that he has a problem seeing. Bekman drives into an observation position on the ramp and identifies anti-collision reflectors and other flashes in the wide area beneath 115, the same area where he hit the bridging tanks two hours earlier.

Southern Sector – Juhader

The Urieli force, minus Maklef, Tamir and Bekman, are positioned at the abandoned Juhader base, a base that used to be a functioning army base, with all the army toys, but now all that remains are broken basalt buildings. They take position behind the south and eastern dirt ramparts.

Every few minutes, a brave Syrian tank attempts to take a short-cut and drive on the Petroleum Road but soon realizes its mistake. Urieli's tanks, using the moonlight, fire and destroy them. Between the tanks that go up in flames, they notice others that avoid the light and disappear into the dark.

Urieli promises himself that, as long as he is there and alive, no Syrian son of a bitch will pass Juhader toward the Petroleum Road. He does not know that to the south and north of him, in the darkness that is protecting them, the tanks of the Syrian 46th Brigade are crossing the anti-tank ditch beneath outposts 115 and 116, moving west toward the "big step," on the western slopes of the Golan Heights.

Ben Shoham Force

There is a light wind blowing in the commander's cupola in the carrier heading south. Dror Sofer, enjoying the fresh air, is sure that it is only a matter of time before everything will get back to normal. "We will get to Juhader, meet the guys and Ben Shoham will organize the situation," he tells himself.

While he is thinking optimistic thoughts, Oded Erez speaks on the radio and calls for urgent artillery support. The desperation in his voice gets Ben Shoham to immediately do what he asks. The man in the bunker activating the artillery is Simchoni, who was sitting next to him until recently, helping him command the battles. Now he hesitates to fulfill the request, since he has additional targets to hit.

"What exactly does Erez want and why?" Simchoni asks him.

Ben Shoham, uncharacteristically snaps, "Stop asking questions! Give him what he asked for. Out!"

Nafah

Side by side at the headquarters at Nafah are Raful, commander of the 36th Division; Haka, the Northern Command CO; and a group of operations staff officers. The 36th Division had just marked two years since it was established. Raful is a legend but without his staff, who has remained at Filon, Haka does not let him run the show.

In October 1973, the 36th Division was based on three reserve brigades: the 179th Armored Brigade, commanded by Col. Ran Sarig, with Sho't Kal tanks; the 679th Armored Brigade, commanded by Col. Ori Or, with Sho't-Meteor tanks; and the 9th Mechanized Brigade, commanded by Motke Ben Porat. It also possessed a reconnaissance battalion, artillery battalion and logistics battalion.

During the Blue and White alert (April 1973), Haka had wisely predicted the future, leading to the division moving closer to the Golan. Divisional Headquarters had been set up at Filon, near Rosh Pina, with the emergency supply depot of the 179th Brigade. The 679th Brigade's emergency supplies had been transferred to the Yiftach-Korazim base.

On Yom Kippur eve, all the commanders of the 36th Division had remained on base, as well as the commanders at the mobilization centers. On Saturday morning, when a general mobilization was announced, the division got straight to work.

The "Sela Order," which the Northern Command had issued following the state of alert, mandated that in a state of alert in which three brigades or more are positioned on the Golan, the 36th Division headquarters would take control of running the battles. Accordingly, as the final battalion of the 7th Brigade arrived on the Golan on Friday afternoon, the headquarters of the 36th Division were supposed to be positioned at Nafah. However, this did not happen.

Furthermore, the command section of the "Sela Order" instructed that the headquarters of the three brigades would be located as follows:

- The 820th Regional Brigade HQ at Nafah, alongside the divisional HQ.
- The Headquarters of the 188th Brigade at Nachal Geshor, with a tactical command group at Tel Fares.
- The Headquarters of the second tank brigade (in this case the 7th Brigade) at Kala, with a tactical command group at Tel Avital (Abu-Nida).

This did not happen either.

With the Northern Command running the entire show, mainly through Simchoni, the Divisional Operations Officer, Raful was given the immediate task "to rush and organize the reserve forces, as quickly as possible – even without complete units – to assist the effort of the regular army."

The first force of the fast mobilization 179th Brigade was already in Filon, and Raful urged Ran Sarig, the brigade commander, to hurry up and send out every company that was ready.

Ben Shoham Force
A lone armored personnel carrier continues southward on the Petroleum Road, fleeing from the artillery shells being fired at it, proving how easy it is to pinpoint a command vehicle by triangulating its position on the radio.

In the darkness, an intersection appears; it is the Mashta junction with an armored personnel carrier positioned at the cross roads. They greet each other warmly and they each go their separate ways. The brigade commander carrier heading south to Juhader and the technical team of the Golan Company toward Hushnia.

Nafah Gate

The Golan is on fire. A heavy stillness hangs over the forward tank depot at the Nafah gate. One of the crewman sitting there in silence is Doron Farkash, Boaz Tamir's gunner, who came with the tank that was hit on the Petroleum Road.

Zvika Gringold, who is still trying to put together a crew, approaches Farkash.

"No way," he answers. "I am only going with my own crew."

"Are you disobeying an order?" Zvika glares.

"Yes," Farkash says flatly, waiting to see the response of the tall company commander.

Suddenly there is a siren from Nafah and shouts, "Syrian commando." They all run to take cover in the bushes, waiting with their hearts pounding to see what will happen. When nothing happens, they get back to work.

Zvika continues with his conciliatory approach and lets Farkash off the hook. He finds Arnon again who is still sitting in the same position at the side and he turns to him with his bass voice.

Arnon has had enough of the sense of bereavement and he fills with a feeling of revenge, "Let's screw these bastards. For Akeb."

19:50

Ben Shoham Force

As if they are living in a bubble, the Northern Command has forgotten the order they gave Yanush two hours earlier and have not checked to see if it has been carried out. In a detached manner, they again instruct him to send tanks to reinforce the southern front.

Within a few minutes, the 71st Battalion leaves its position beneath Mt. Varda, north of the Hermonit hills and heads southward. Between the Manzura junction and the junction of the Hahazit building they stop. Someone from the 7th Brigade command center notifies Meshulam Ratess, commander of the 71st Battalion, that the Mishbetzet commander (Yanush) is waiting for them on the way.

Ben Shoham, who is unaware of Yanush's involvement, contacts Ratess.

"Are you on the move?"

"I am standing at Yakir 17."

"Copy that. I need you to let a few vehicles that do you not need through on the Yakir–Reshet route to the south because there is pressure here in the south."

Ben Shoham, still an officer and a gentleman, is considerate of Ratess and lets him send through the vehicles that "do not need to take any action." As long as he sends them already.

Nafah Gate

It is almost 20:00. Itzik Arnon and Mordi Arzi are looking for the driver who came with them after they were hit on the Petroleum Road. There he is.

"Let's get moving," Arnon says to him.

He ignores them, does not get up, his eyes on the ground.

Arnon and Mordi do not insist and decide to find a replacement.

"You are a driver in Golan Company, right?" Arnon asks someone thin who looks familiar in the shadows of the entrance light.

"Yes, my name is Philip Berkovitz," Boaz Tamir's new driver responds.

"Come with us" and he does.

Ben Shoham Force

The command APC continues to the south, heading toward Juhader, stopping near Tel Danir.

The Syrian artillery is closing in on them, and Ben Shoham realizes that if they stay where they are or continue toward Juhader, they will be blown to pieces.

The APC stops, turns around and takes up position two kilometers to the north, at the intersection of the Petroleum Road and the Water route. Ben Shoham instructs them to shut down the engine. They hear shells roaring around them but it is quiet where they are. For the first time in a while, the Syrian artillery give them a few moments of quiet.

While maintaining contact with Benny Katzin, his man at Nafah, Ben Shoham gives orders to the forces on the ground and waits for his tank and for the reinforcements from the 71st Battalion.

Southern Sector – Yuval Shachar

A few minutes before 20:00, 2nd Lt. Yuval Shachar returns to the Golan after transferring the injured soldiers from area 111, including deputy battalion commander Askarov, to the doctors at the hospital in Tzfat. The pick-up climbs on the Arik bridge, heading toward the Mashta junction, and all around them, the world they knew so well is disappearing. The Golan is in flames, lighting up the October night. The endless roar of the cannons dominates the background.

"Faster," Yuval motivates himself, feeling the rapid heartbeat in his chest. It is hard to give up the lighted, calm, safe city of Tzfat and return to the war zone. "They need me there."

20:00–20:59

At 20:00 the period set by the Syrian army to complete the Next Mission had come to an end. The mechanized and armored brigades, some of them organic parts of the infantry divisions and other independent, had planned to complete "destroying the tactical reserves of the IDF on the Golan and conquering the area, up to twelve to fifteen kilometers within the Purple Line."

The Syrian army did not achieve full success in its plan, but what it did accomplish was enough to put the entire Golan at risk.

At this time, the northern front awakened to a "calm" night battle against the remnants of the Syrian 85th Armored Brigade. Located in good defensive positions beneath the Hermonit hills, the tanks of the 75th Battalion of the 7th Brigade manage to destroy the enemy's remaining tanks, blocking their attempts to move forward.

Apart from these brief and not somewhat weak attacks, the northern front was calm. The tanks were in night positions, after halting every attempt by the Syrian tanks to break through the lines of the 188th Brigade. The only thing disrupting the snoring of the exhausted soldiers was the occasional round of artillery fire.

While the 188th Brigade's crewmen in the northern part of the Golan were recovering their strength and sharing the feeling that "We showed them and as always, we are on the winning side!" in the southern part of the Golan front, their brothers in arms were collapsing to an extent beyond imagination.

At the Northern Command forward HQ in Nafah, no one has realized the new situation. Even the majority of the armor fighters on the ramps were unaware of the catastrophe developing. Only the moon, high in the sky, sees and knows everything. The soldiers of the Syrian 51st Armored Brigade, commanded by Walid Hamdon, also know what is going on. The Syrian armored corps soldiers worshipped their commander, who since nightfall had ordered them to move without lights and in silence, just as they had spent months training to do long before the war. They continue moving until they see the buildings of the Hushnia area in the weak moonlight, within an arrow's flight in front of them.

The Syrian officers of the 46th Armored and the 132nd Mechanized Brigades continue to send in forces from both sides of the Petroleum Road, pushing forward continuously. They complete the bloody ambush of D Company and cross over to the other side of the Golan road (Tapa route). From here they begin their attack to the west, toward the cliff line and the routes rising from it. The slice the Southern Golan into isolated pockets of resistance, lacking a second line of defense.

Southern Sector – 116

A few minutes after 20:00, the silence surrounding Nir Atir was shattered by the roar of engines. One hundred meters from him, perhaps 200, a line of flat turret tanks appear, heading straight toward him. The 188th Brigade soldiers jump back into their vehicles and panicky orders to open fire are given over the radio.

A tank destroyer, a preposterous creature, leads the attacking force, and before the 188th Brigade's tanks can even manage to aim at it, it releases a shell at the only tank remaining of the 2nd Platoon, hitting compartment 6 (on the left wing), setting fire to its contents, with the evening breeze fanning the flames heading toward the turret. The two crews jump out of the burning tank, carry out the fire extinguishing drill and jump back into their steel home. Aviam is on the commander's seat, Nati Levi between his legs.

"Driver, drive back quickly," Nati orders, forgetting the anti-tank ditch behind them. The roar of the engine suddenly turns into a wail, there is a bang and then silence.

"We fell," Nati says, as if they didn't know.

While the 2nd Platoon was falling into the ditch, the tank destroyer continues to slay and opens fire from its machine guns at tank 3 just as Yakir rises up in the commander's cupola, ready to continue fighting.

Shmueli, the gunner, hears a thud above him and Yakir collapses onto his chair.

"3B, this is hunter (gunner) of 3, commander is down. I repeat, commander is down."

"What is his situation?" Nir Atir asks, trying to remain calm, hoping for the best.

"I am not sure," Shmueli answers with panic in his voice. "A Goryanov bullet, an RPG shard..."

"I repeat, what is his situation?" Atir asks again and feels the blood leaving his body.

"Commander is seriously injured," Shmueli reports. "Actually, I think he's dead."

There is silence and then Atir says quietly, "Hunter 3, listen carefully. Carry out the 'Forward Evacuation' drill. I repeat, 'Forward Evacuation' and move back immediately."

In the commander's cupola in tank 3B, Nir Atir from Kibbutz Afikim feels like the sky has fallen on him and he understands that now it is all up to him.

I promised to come a week ago and then I promised to come on Rosh Hashanah but unfortunately I didn't keep my promise and there is no need to explain that it is not up to me. I am sorry to say that I do not know the next time I will have leave. I might come soon, you may have to wait two or three weeks or more. As usual, send me rags to clean my tank, this may be the last time I will need them.

It was the last time. Yoav Yakir, loved by everyone, is lying dead in the tank, and the world continues to exist. The sky does not open up and neither does the ground. Only Sakal the loader, Shmueli the gunner and Brom the driver sob to themselves quietly.

The tank of the 2nd Platoon is on its backside in the ditch with its cannon pointing an accusing finger to the dark October sky. The two crews are wearing helmets, with their Uzi's on their chests, lying low in the ditch and looking for a way out.

They hear Arabic voices coming from the north. They are the crews of Syrian tanks that had also been hit, also hiding in the ditch. Nati decides to change direction and head south. The two crews run a short distance, locate a spot where they can climb up to reach the dark flat land above it.

They lie low and listen to the voices. The Arabic is gone and instead they now hear the sound of pulling and dragging and heavy breathing and they find themselves next to Yakir's tank just as his crew transfers the body of their admired commander to the back of the turret.

The two crewmen of the 2nd Platoon (Levi and Aviam) climb onto tank 3. Nati Levi takes command and forces himself not to look back. He realizes that this is it, there is no Yoav Yakir.

We are a tank platoon again, Atir tells himself, this time without Yakir. Things will never be the same. Three tanks, five crews, two unable to fire because they are out of ammunition. The third, Yakir's tank, is unable to fight because it has too many crewmen in the turret. What now? everyone is asking, and there is no responsible adult to answer.

Yoav Yakir was the twelfth casualty of the 188th Brigade on the southern Golan front. This was an overwhelming number for soldiers used to returning from combat days without any casualties and also in comparison to the northern front.

There is no reason to assume that the armored soldiers blocking the Syrian forces on the northern Golan were more skilled than their friends in the southern sector. They were all trained in the same melting pot, the battalions and brigades blended together. Zvika Rak in the north was not any better than Uri Akavia in the south. Eyal Shaham and Uzi Urieli were equally skilled and Avner Landau did not outperform Avi Ronis.

Nonetheless, slightly after 20:00 there was a dramatic difference between the situation on the northern and the southern Golan fronts, not only regarding territory conquered (in the south, not the north) but also in the number of casualties (soldiers and tanks).

The northern front was almost clear of enemy forces. Four tanks had been disabled, one soldier was killed and five injured.

On the southern front, the Syrian forces had conquered an area larger than the size of Tiberias, sixteen tanks were disabled, twelve soldiers killed and six injured.

What was the cause of the astounding difference in casualties between the two fronts? The ratio of forces and the landscape... Just as Hagai Mann, the Northern Command intelligence officer (J2), had been warning before the war started.

The northern front was easier to defend than the south due to the controlling landscape that was generously spread out over it. This was one side of the equation. The other was that the northern front was defended by three Sho't Kal tank battalions (10 companies) and the Syrian forces attacked alternately with four Tiran tank battalions (15 companies).

On the southern front, facing two Sho't Kal tank battalions (6 companies) were 10 Tiran tank battalions (33 companies)! It is simple math, a ratio of 1: 1.5 in the north and of 1: 5.3 in the south.

Southern Sector – Yuval Shachar

Slightly after 20:00, the 53rd Battalion intelligence officer arrived at the Mashta junction. The reports from outpost 111 were very bad. The Syrian force had passed south of the outpost and sneaked off somewhere to the west. There were injured soldiers at the stronghold, some in critical condition. Yuval looks Dr. Englehard in the eyes and trying his best to sound calm, he says, "Danny, I am going out to outpost 111."

When he manages to penetrate the veil of darkness and find the eyes of the officer and see the determination there, the doctor gives him the APC. He has Avi Grinfeld, the medic, join him, with Aharon Vidal, the operations sergeant, and with great misgivings he sends them on their way.

After driving two kilometers, they reach the outskirts of Hushnia and turn left to the north. From the base where they spent the morning, they hear the sound of tracks. Yuval thinks that the sound is different than those of the Sho't Kal tanks, but he is not certain of his musical skills when it comes to tank tracks.

To be on the safe side, he gets off the main road, continues on the path beside it and hoped for the best. The sound of tracks disappears in the night along with their fear and they arrive at the junction of the main road (Troy route).

"Driver, turn left," he instruct Yehuda, who is driving the APC. Again he hears the sound of strange tracks. A moment passes and in the moonlight he suddenly sees the flat shadows making this troubling sound. Tiran tanks! His blood freezes.

"Turn around!" he instructs Yehuda the driver, terrified, hoping that the soldiers do not hear his heart pounding. The medical carrier turns back south and Yuval prays that the Syrian tanks 100 meters behind the armored personnel carrier of the 53rd Battalion do not realize this was an IDF vehicle. A minute later he locates a trail that ascends to outpost 111 and they swerve onto it wildly.

Suddenly intense fire is opened at them, the machine gun bullets knocking on the carrier walls. Yuval is praying no shell hits them and blows them all away. Someone hears his prayer. Speeding insanely on the rocky hillside, they arrive directly at the entrance to the stronghold.

Southern Sector – 111

Very close to outpost 111, slightly to the south, Berkovitch and Aldag are in position. All around them is darkness, working against them. Anti-collision reflectors, like wandering stars, move to the west and they turn off their engines and listen in silence, trying to see where the evil will come from.

From somewhere, there is the shrill sound of the tracks of a Tiran, and it is getting closer.

"A Syrian tank," Berkovitch whispers to Kopstein, who sees nothing in his peri-telescope. "I will place you more or less on target."

Using the commander's joystick, Berkovitch rotates the cannon toward the source of the noise, and suddenly, 150 meters from them, moving like a huge bug, an armored shadow appears, right in front of them.

"Fire," Berkovitch says quietly and Kopstein fires and hits the bottom part of the tank. It is enough to stop it and light a small fire that marks its position, enabling Kopstein to correct himself and fire a second shell that causes the Tiran to explode in front of them.

The Tiran tanks had several disadvantages compared to the Sho't Kals, but at night, they had the clear advantage. The Tiran gunners had infrared sight, the Israeli tanks did not. In addition, a large part of the Syrian tank commanders had passive night vision equipment, without the need for infrared lighting.

The only night vision in the Sho't Kal tanks during the Yom Kippur War were active means: a *karnaf* (infrared searchlight) for the driver and a *shfanfan* (I. R. goggles) for the commander. The gunners did not have infrared equipment. In order for a commander or a gunner to identify an enemy heading toward them, they had to turn on the infrared lights at the front of the tank.

Turning on the infrared light put the crew at risk, since the Syrian gunner had infrared vision. If you turned on the infrared light, the

Syrian tank would locate you and you were most likely to get hit. In addition, turning the light on may enable the commander to identify the Syrian tank at close range but did not make the gunner's job any easier. He remained in the dark. The obvious conclusion was that it is better to pretend, hope for the best and demand illumination shells from time to time, knowing they would not come.

* * *

Deutsch was also busy. Chessner sends him to see what was going on with the tank stuck near the path up to the outpost and to stay and secure him there. Deutsch joins him, sees everything is alright and takes up position near the hill to the right, "behind the corner." He turns off his engine and waits in the dark for Syrian prey trying to head toward the outpost.

Logistics Convoy

1st Lt. Giora Goldberg had been the operations officer of the regional brigade for almost two years. In the weeks before Yom Kippur, most of the commanders of the brigade were replaced and he was almost the only one remaining, the anchor, expected to solve any problem.

At 20:15, Zvi Bar, the 820th Brigade commander turns to Giora, "I want you to go to Aleika and lead the logistics convoy toward Ben Shoham."

Goldberg immediately takes a jeep and heads out to Aleika. "I am here to lead the logistics convoy to the south," he says to Jackson, the commander of the logistics company.

Jackson recognized Giora and in accordance with his request, attaches two soldiers to each truck and makes sure they are fully prepared for combat, equipped with Uzis and wearing a bulletproof vest and a helmet.

Goldberg's jeep takes a lead position in the convoy of trucks (three with ammunition and two with fuel) and starts the drive to the Petroleum Road.

20:20

Ben Shoham Force

The minutes pass, the 71st Battalion is not arriving and Meshulam Ratess, the battalion commander, is not answering on the radio. "Zakik, this is 20 of Tofi," Ben Shoham calls to Ratess again. "You have to send a unit, whatever its size, southward on the Reshet route."

"I hear you unclear and weak" Ratess responds. "I have received new orders from 20 of Mishbetzet (Yanush). I have to move out to help him."

Ben Shoham, "Negative, you are joining me. You have to move on the Reshet route to Troy…"

Ratess, "20 of Mishbetzet just gave me an order. He is standing next to me and I have already started carrying it out."

Thirty-five years later, Benny Baratz, the operations officer of the 71st Battalion, recalled:

> *We got out of the tanks and joined Yanush's tactical command group. He told us that the order from the Northern Command is canceled and we are to remain there, since there is Syrian pressure and their tanks are advancing opposite Emmy Falant's company beneath the Hermonit hills. Obviously, we did what the brigade commander ordered us to do. Later we joined Emmy. We sat on the tanks and chatted, we did not fight. There was no need to reinforce them. The order was mistaken and unjustified.*

In order to back up his position, Yanush called the Command and explained the reason for Ratess's delay.

He made a few more sharp statements and clarifications, insisting that the situation on his front does not enable him to release the battalion. Haka is convinced by this and authorizes the 71st Battalion to stay there.

20:28

The Northern Command operations log reads, "The General gave an order not to send the battalion south. When the fighting there ends, he will send them to Ben Shoham."

Simchoni gets back to Ben Shoham and gives him the news.

"As soon as he is free," Simchoni promises Ben Shoham, "we will send him to you."

Ben Shoham knows that his line has been broken and his heart is breaking hearing the distress calls from Erez and he tries to get any reinforcement available in an attempt to save the southern front. He tries again, "This is 20, can you send me any part of Zakik (a company or platoon)?"

"I do not want to split them up," Simchoni answers, shattering Ben Shoham's hope.

"That is a shame," he answers and his sigh of disappointment from the frustration of the entire day is heard clearly on the radio.

The Agranat Commission of Inquiry that examined the conduct of the war asked Simchoni the exact same question. Why didn't he divide the forces in order to assist the southern front? His answer was, "I am sorry I did not concentrate all the forces in the south to assemble a brigade-strength assembly at Hushnia." That is right. According to all doctrines of activating forces, it is better to concentrate tanks into a steel fist and not divide them into small teams.

It is unclear why he and the commanding general determined the fate of the southern front to doom. Why was it more important to them to respond to the distress of Yanush in the north, that in retrospect turned out to be false, and not to that of Ben Shoham on the southern front, who had been sounding the emergency sirens for two hours and who needed the forces much more?

20:30

Nafah Gate

David Yisraeli, the deputy brigade commander, comes out of the bunker again and goes to the gate.

"What is the situation?" he asks Zvika.

"At the moment, I have only one tank that is operational. It will take a little longer and I will have another one," he apologizes.

"As fast as possible, Zvika. As fast as possible," Yisraeli repeats in his tone of urgency, hurrying back into the command bunker.

Southern Sector – Barak/Geva

At 20:30 Haim Barak receives an order from Ben Shoham to move north on the main road (Reshet) and to be prepared to block breaching attempts from east to west.

Barak leaves one platoon behind – its task is to prevent repeated penetration attempts from the open area – and together with Eli Geva and two additional platoons, he starts secured movement to the north. They spread out as much as the rocky landscape enables them to and move on both sides of the main road, keeping their eyes open wide trying to locate enemy tanks awaiting them in the dark.

Southern Sector – Tel Saki

Around 20:30 Danny Levine notifies Asher Goldman that he just received an order to join the three tanks of the 74th Battalion, still fighting a battle for their lives in sector 116. They are in desperate need of additional cannons or at least ammunition.

Anyone who could lend a hand on Tel Saki helped load additional ammunition on the tanks heading to sector 116. After ten minutes of fast loading, Goldman and Levine slide down the hill toward the main road and turn right, to the north.

The first three minutes of the drive are pleasant, as pleasant as driving a tank on the Golan can be, knowing that there are Syrian tanks in the area. Then, still far from outpost 116, they encounter a Syrian force in APCs right on the road. The two tanks speed right through them, running over soldiers, pushing carriers aside, with RPG and machine gunfire hitting the bazooka defense plates, but the gunshots also hit other places.

A sharp pain slices through Goldman's hand. It is a bullet wound.

Goldman bandages himself and reports to Levine. In Levine's tank, Yossi Ben Haim, his loader, is hit by a bullet and is killed.

"The area is full of enemy forces," Levine notifies someone in the command. "We will not be able to get to 116, we are returning."

They turn around, assuming the Syrians are waiting for them and speed through the Syrian APC platoon again. The surviving soldiers fire at them with every Guryanov gun they have and after what seems like an eternity, they reach the path to Tel Saki and climb up to the stronghold.

Goldman knows the area from his previous reconnaissance trips. He is injured but still functioning, and he warns Levine's tank,, "We are sitting ducks on the hilltop. Let's take position at the bottom of the spur, on the other side of the road."

Levine understands but still decides to check for himself and tries to descend through the rocks, on the southern side. With Ben Haim no longer alive, rattling around in the tank, they slide all the way down the hill and end up stuck and disabled. The crew flees on foot southward.

20:40

Southern Sector – Barak/Geva

Haim Barak, positioned below and to the west of outpost 111, receives an update from Chessner, who is at 111. He reports that Syrian tanks are apparently moving on the Troy route, heading west. Barak moves the company farther north. Every few minutes they stop and turn off their engine. They hear the sound of tracks to their left. Without any night vision, they guess that somewhere to the west of them there are Syrian tanks heading toward Hushnia.

20:45

Southern Sector – 115

At his observation position on the battalion commander's ramp, Bekman decides it is time to fight. Despite the dark night and the lack of night-vision equipment, he tries to direct Partosh the gunner onto the targets in the darkness beneath them. It does not work. After they both give up on identifying using the means they have (which is actually nothing), they jump out of the tank, lie behind the ramp and using their binoculars manage to locate targets. They return to their tanks and Bekman starts a tiring dialog asking the artillery to fire illumination ammunition to their sector.

Suddenly, without any warning, half an hour after he begged for light, the valley is lit up with a single illumination shell. It is too far off. Bekman contacts the artillery and corrects the firing. Another ten minutes pass and a second illumination shell is fired. It is not exactly where they want it but good enough for Partosh to make out the enemy tanks, aim and fire the first shell.

In the valley below, an enemy tank goes up in flames and three additional hollow charge rounds follow. Four targets, three tanks and an armored personnel carrier, are hit in the darkness beneath them.

There is one left. An armored vehicle carrying Sagger anti-tank missiles manages to fire one missile that misses the cowboy on the ramp. It immediately is hit with another round, and the fifth target is destroyed.

"It is cigarette time," Bekman says but then remembers that his cigarettes are in the tank that was hit and left behind. He comes down from the tank into the darkness, collects straw from the dry shrubs around the tank and rolls it in toilet paper. The smoke reaches his lungs and from there he sends out nearly perfect smoke rings into the air, which smells of gun powder.

Southern Sector – 116

Still with his original crew, Nir Atir takes command of what is left of the platoon. Next to him is Waxman. Nati Levi, leader of the 2nd Platoon, is in the third tank stuffed with three crews that neutralize any operational capability.

The night is lit by flashes and anti-collision reflectors around them. Atir calls the company commander on the radio, but he is not there. Finally someone from the brigade tactical command group answers and takes his report. Atir tells whoever it is that they are out of ammunition, that Yakir has been killed and that they are helpless near outpost 116.

"What do we do now?" Atir asks.

The unidentified voice instructs him to leave sector 116 and contact deputy of Domem (the 82nd Battalion's deputy commander, Maj. Danny Pesach), who is at Tel Saki.

"One more thing," the voice from the brigade continues, "deputy brigade commander David Yisraeli is supposed to be sending in the 188th Brigade's logistics with ammunition."

At the exact same time Ukavi, the company medic still hiding at the tank camp, hears on the radio that Syrian tanks are attacking the area he is in. Finding this hard to believe, he peeks out. A Syrian tank moves by like a huge grasshopper, his cannon moving from side to side like an antenna.

Ukavi cocks his Uzi, puts the Torah scroll in the safe generator room and waits where he is, alert.

20:50

Southern Front – Haim Barak

Ben Shoham gets on the radio and instructs Haim Barak to move on the Reshet route, to the north and to the east, according to developments.

Barak moves back and forth on the Reshet route from the Kudna junction to the Troy route and further north. There is not a soul in sight.

He receives a report from his ordnance officer of Syrian tanks moving in the Hushnia area. He conveys the message to Ben Shoham who estimates that these are not enemy tanks and it is probably his tank heading toward them.

How is it possible that the Geva Company, with Barak, the battalion commander, are patrolling back and forth on the Reshet route without seeing over 90 Tiran tanks of the Syrian 51st Brigade crossing the same route and arriving at Hushnia, at the same time? How did they not meet on the way?

Apparently, some of them crossed before the Barak force arrived and others after the Barak force passed. It seems that timing is everything.

In any case, from 20:30 onwards, Hushnia and the area near it started to fall into Syrian hands.

Logistics Convoy

Toward 21:00 a supplies convoy appears from the dark, led by Giora the operations officer. The convoy stops on the Petroleum Road, not far from the brigade commander's carrier, behind an opening in the fence.

Ben Shoham sees the convoy and instructs Oded Erez, the 53rd Battalion's CO, to send tanks over to resupply with fuel and ammunition.

"Negative," comes the tired response of the battalion commander. "We need every tank here."

"Alright," Ben Shoham encourages him. "I will take it with me and head your way.

Giora jumps out of the jeep, runs toward the carrier, climbs on the track, finds Ben Shoham and asks him where to position the convoy.

"Leave it where it is on the route, wait for my tank to arrive from Hushnia and then return to Nafah," the brigade commander answers.

Suddenly they hear tank tracks approaching. Ben Shoham assumes it is his tank coming from Hushnia and he asks Giora to go check. No, it is not the brigade commander's tank, and it is coming from Juhader.

As Giora is trying to understand this mystery, the tank stops in front of the supplies convoy that is blocking its path. He approaches it, sees the commander's cupola open and he hears Arabic inside.

As silent as a cat, with his heart beating fast, Giora leaves the tank, rushes to the convoy and whispers to all the soldiers, "Leave the vehicles immediately and lie in the ditch beside the road."

He runs back to his jeep, takes out a grenade, removes the safety and heads back toward the Tiran. As he is sneaking up to the tank, the commander's hatch closes and the Syrian steel chariot reverses and disappears.

Giora returns to the APC and excitedly tells the brigade commander what just happened.

They hurry to hide the five trucks behind the brigade commander's APC and for the first time since the war broke out, Ben Shoham sees what his soldiers have known for several hours. The Petroleum Road is no long sovereign Israeli territory.

21:00–21:59

At 21:00 the troops of the 188th Brigade, young boys in tank coveralls, find themselves in an undeclared ceasefire. From the northern part of the Golan Heights to the southern part, in what is a misleading wonder, the tank and artillery fire stops.

They still fear the night, the tremor of the darkness that has always been part of human nature. The natural instinct to keep ourselves and our loved ones close to us and away from the beasts that roam in search of prey at night. This primal fear spreads and sinks in, leaving exhausted commanders forcing themselves to stay awake in their tanks, looking out for Syrian infantry soldiers sneaking up to kill them. Trembling at the thought of the flat turrets of the Tiran tanks, with their night-vision equipment, finding and destroying them.

All the soldiers – Eiland on the northern 109 ramp, Bekman on the battalion commander ramp below 115, Urieli at Juhader, Shir-On at 104, Nafshi on the Booster, Yachin at 107, Atir on his way to Tel Saki and Kaimo on 105 – want just one thing: a responsible adult to come and tell them it is over and they can go home.

Southern Sector – The Mashta Junction
An hour has passed since the evacuation carrier was sent to sector 111. The angels in white of the 53rd Battalion are enveloped in a hostile silence. Dr. Englehard calls Yuval Shachar on the radio and there is no answer. He calls Oded Erez and, again, there is no reply.

They hear grinding tracks coming from Hushnia and Englehard understands the meaning, Hushnia has been occupied by Syrian forces. The doctor feels the helplessness creeping down his spine and for the first time since the battle started, it threatens to paralyze his practical approach. Only for a moment, however, and it passes.

"Get in the vehicle, we are moving out," he instructs the medics with him.

The sound of the tracks gets closer to them and the medical team heads north on the Petroleum Road, distancing itself from the enemy tanks.

Ben Shoham Force

Before they have a chance to recover from the arrival of the Tiran tank from the south, they hear another vehicle approaching, this time from the north. As they huddle in their vehicles, the radio brings them the voice of Shmuel (Shmil) Golan, the deputy battalion commander of the artillery corps training base, announcing that he will be reaching them in two minutes.

A few minutes pass and a pickup truck with two ammunition trucks behind it joins the convoy.

In the morning hours, five of the eleven artillery batteries allocated to the Northern Command were deployed in the southern Golan. Two batteries of 175mm guns of the 55th Battalion were spread out north of the KKL/Mapalim route. Despite their "southern" position, they served the entire front (they even fired toward the Hermon, forty kilometers away).

Two 155mm "Rochev" batteries of the 405th Battalion were deployed not far from Juhader. The fifth battery, from artillery training base 9, was made up of 155mm guns mounted on Sherman tank hulls, and was deployed beneath Tel Fares.

On Saturday morning, the commander of training base 9, Lt. Col. Ben Ami Cohen took up position at the top of Tel Fares. He acted as the fire support officer for the southern front. His deputy, Maj. Shmil Golan, was given the command of the three batteries of training base 9. During the day, Shmil brought ammunition to the two northern batteries (Ein Ziwan and Tel Mahfi). Now it was the turn of the southern battery.

They hug and update each other on the developments and then everyone looks to Ben Shoham. "What now?"

Before they get an answer, the world around them starts shaking. It seems that a Syrian artillery officer has located their position and has initiated the dance of death around them, crushing the basalt rocks along with their self-confidence.

Ben Shoham receives the update that Oded Erez is unable to send tanks from the forward area of operations to resupply with fuel and ammunition. This, along with his direct experience of the heavy artillery fire and seeing the Syrian Tiran that appeared from the south, leaves him in no doubt as to how serious the situation is. There is no way to join the forces in the south that are in such desperate need for fuel, ammunition and leadership.

Leading a fuel and ammunition convoy south without tanks to secure it, without night vision, would be suicide. The tank they saw may be waiting to ambush them in the darkness, and there may be others as well. Ben Shoham realizes that there is no point in keeping the convoy in its place, just sitting there waiting to be blown up.

"Return to Nafah," Ben Shoham instructs Giora the operations officer and Shmil the deputy battalion commander. "If things calm down, we will tell you where to go."

The Brigade Commander Tank

At 21:00 someone calls Yehuda Porat, the commander of the brigade commander's tank, on the radio and guides him to the meeting place with the tactical command group.

"Get there quickly," he hears the sense of urgency in the unidentified voice.

"It is about time," Yehuda thinks. "Soon there will not be anyone left to speak with."

On Friday afternoon, Yom Kippur eve, David Nurian, the sergeant of the Golan company of the 53rd Battalion, came to the door of Yehudit at Kibbutz Dafna.

"Is Yehuda Porat here?" he asks before taking the commander of tank 1A from his lover's arms.

"What happened, Nurian?" Porat rushed to the door, with a hostile look in his eyes.

"The level of alert has been raised. Uzi wants you back at Hushnia," Nurian answered.

On Saturday, Porat discovered that someone had mixed up all the tank crews. Without his original crew, he was not happy to receive his new position as the commander of the brigade commander's tank, with a young crew he does not even know.

"When the combat day begins, stay where you are. Do you understand?" someone instructed him. "When you are needed, you will be called."

When the ground shook, the MiGs fired their rockets and the tanks of Golan Company set out on their missions, only Yehuda Porat and his crew remained in Hushnia.

Slightly after 20:00, tank tracks were heard near the abandoned Circassian village but they were not the familiar sound of Sho't Kal tracks. Porat contacted the brigade and someone asked him if he is sure. He said yes.

"How many are there?"

"Maybe a battalion, maybe a brigade," Porat replied, yearning to get to a safer place.

Northern Sector – 105

In forward tank depot 105, Yossi Nissim, the deputy battalion commander, jumps out of the jeep and sends his driver back to the base that has been bombed. He takes command of the injured Muli Dgani's tank. He quickly introduces himself to the crew and they enter a secure night parking. Tomorrow is a new day.

Northern Sector – B Company

With the night progressing in his sector, Avner Landau has a chance to turn on the transistor radio to hear the news.

"Beitza stations, this is commander," he announces dramatically to all the company. "The people of Israel are at war. The Syrians are trying to conquer the Golan and, at this point, we are the only ones blocking their way."

A minute passes and he stresses the immediate meaning of this. "Tonight we will be sleeping out in the field."

Arieh Feigenbaum, commander of tank 1B, was an optimistic young man. He saw no reason for concern at 14:00. All the MiGs in the world were not going to prevent him from hanging his perfectly ironed class A uniform in the tank. According to his calculations, he should be going on leave right after the combat day ends and there was no way he was going home in his operational uniform.

When he hears Landau, it reminds him of the known military phrase, "Any plan is a basis for changes," and Feigenbaum realizes that his uniform will stay hanging in the turret tonight.

"There are threats of commando attacks all along the front," Landau continues.

"Commando Shomando," he says to Shuki Yisraeli the gunner.

"Goddamn, the leave I just missed!... and one more thing, Shuki," he says to his gunner, "tomorrow, after this is all over, someone will probably check the firing series we carried out." Feigenbaum does not have to say more than that. Shuki knows that they will be in trouble if there is a difference between the report they give and the shells left in the tank. They better get to work.

Ignoring the warning of the company commander, they get busy in reconstructing the series they have fired so far. They check, write it down and hope for the best. While they are doing that, Berliner, the loader, throws a dud shell out of the tank through the emergency opening and is sent outside to mark the shell with rocks.

Artillery fire falling on the 1st Platoon ends the ammunition inquiries in the platoon sergeants' tank, and Landau tries to see how close they fell. Feigenbaum puts down the notebook and answers, "Closer than close."

Northern Sector – 107

Yachin leaves the ramps at 107, transfers command to Damir and heads toward the "deployment base" at Quneitra to resupply the tank. The tanks of sectors 104 and 105 also head to the prepared ammunition dumps.

Although there are supply dumps throughout the southern front, the tanks are unable to leave the line of the ramps. The feeling in the south was that any tank leaving its post would be heading to its doom. Later on, they will be forced to fall back due to the Syrian attacks in what may be an opportunity to resupply but then they will find themselves surrounded, forming mere pockets of resistance and access to the supply points will be blocked.

A lone tank sits in the deadly darkness. Shmulik Yachin, enduring tremors and trembling which threaten to paralyze him, but, with a shell in the cannon, he is ready to fire. "What was I thinking?" he asks himself. "Why didn't I wait till morning?"

In the crowded steel vehicle the four crew members are in silence, each one in his own compartment, lost in thoughts. Feeling that this nightmare will never end, they finally make out the deployment base at Quneitra. Two damaged tanks are parked near the gate.

"Wake up," Yachin shakes the crew from its nightmares.

They wipe the dried blood from the shells taken from the turrets of the damaged tanks, transferring them to their tank till they get its belly full and combat ready.

The Zvika Force
Toward 21:30 the technicians of the 188th Brigade manage to repair another tank. Yisraeli, the deputy brigade commander, hears this and leaves the command bunker, heading toward the forward tank depot in front of the gate of Nafah. His face is very tense.

"Move on the Petroleum Road," he instructs Zvika. "Go into Hushnia, survey the area and make sure there are no Syrians there. Then move up and take position on the Kudna route near outpost 111. Join the forces left from Uri Akavia's Ze'evim Company and take over command."

Zvika climbs up to the tank. "What is my call sign?"

"Whatever you want," Yisraeli says, "just get going already."

Yisraeli's order to Zvika demonstrates how uncertain the command was of what was happening on the front. The fog of war was so thick that it even covered the command bunker in Nafah. Why send Zvika toward Hushnia and 111 and at this time of night?

Zvika gets inside the turret, puts on the VRC helmet and calls Hagai who is waiting in the tank next to him. "This is commander Zvika, follow me, out."

In the driver's seat, Hershko is trying to make out the path in the dark, listening carefully to Zvika's orders. Yehuda Akunis is standing in the loader's position, bracing himself for the bumpy ride. Nir Zvi, the gunner, cannot get the horrifying picture from the Petroleum Road out of his head. He keeps picturing Shabtai Horen, his commander, collapsing next to him.

"What a great crew," Hagai Zur thinks to himself as he joins Zvika. His crew includes two crewmen from the company commander's tank – Itzik Arnon the gunner, Mordi Erez the loader – and Phillip Berkovitch the driver of the deputy company commander. "Let's see what we can do together," Hagai ponders.

The tank still smells of burnt flesh and gunpowder, making it hard for them to breath and for Arnon and Arazi to remain sane. They start moving and Arazi reports to Hagai Zur that the gun breech block is broken.

"What is the matter with it?" Zur asks on the internal radio.

"I have no idea," Arazi answers.

Hagai bends down into the turret, looks to his left and in the weak overhead light he sees the remains of a severed hand that is blocking the breach.

Entering a tank that just had body parts, tissue and blood of your comrades washed from it, is something you can never be ready for. The gunner and the loader are the ones who suffer from it the most. The driver is in a separate isolated compartment, detached from the horrors and the commander can breathe fresh air with his head above the turret, regaining his sanity.

Zvika Gringold arrives at the Petroleum Road and notifies Ben Shoham that he is there. He does not report the number of tanks he has with him since the Syrians are listening. In Ben Shoham's command carrier, communication officer Hanan Schwartz sees how happy his commander is, convinced that he has another company joining him.

Hagai drives on the dirt path west of the Petroleum Road. Zvika is on the route itself. Zvika's cannon is facing ahead and to the right and Zur's is ahead and to the left. They both have a shell loaded and ready to fire, it is a matter of who shoots first.

Logistics Convoy

Near 22:00, the two logistics convoys turn around. Shmil is leading in a pick-up truck and Giora is in the rear, in a jeep.

A kilometer south of Mashta, Shmil announces that he has spotted tanks crossing the Petroleum Road. The convoy stops. There is definitely something fishy here. All the Israeli tanks are on the front line. Whoever is moving in the dark must be Syrian.

Terrified, they wait for the last of the Tiran tanks to cross the Petroleum Road to the west. They hurriedly move north to detach from them. Only after they cross the place where the Syrian tanks were, do they realize that they are now in Syrian-occupied territory.

The Mashta junction is behind them and another group of tanks cross the route. They stop, their hearts pounding. What is going to happen now? they wonder.

"82, this is Mavreg[29] Dror," Giora whispers into the radio, as if someone in the Syrian command were listening. "Everyone stay off the Mahaze route. I repeat, stay off the Mahaze route. There are Syrian tanks here."

Simchoni confirms he received the message and he tells him that there is someone on the Mahaze route. "Mavreg, straight in front of you is the Zvika force. Join them and update them."

21:30

Southern Sector – 116

"I am falling back," Nir Atir notifies Yossi Gur, commander of outpost 116.

Gur does not respond.

"I am going to refill and will be right back to protect you," Nir promises, trying to calm Gur.

"Roger," Gur answers.

Two young men look into the dark night, one from his tank and the other from his post in the infantry stronghold. They both see Syrian tanks and are very concerned.

"It will be okay Yossi, we will be back," Atir promises again and he is suddenly unsure. He does not expect an answer.

"Follow me," he commands, leading the three tanks south in the dark, toward Tel Saki.

"Hurry, hurry," Atir rushes himself. "We cannot waste time. We will get to Tel Saki, resupply with ammunition, join forces with the 82nd Battalion and return to Yossi with renewed energy. Then we'll show the Syrian tanks. It is true that Yoav's body is in Nati's tank but I cannot think of that now. Now the entire focus is on the mission, just as Yoav taught us."

The three tanks of the 3rd Platoon arrive at Roman route (Pinkas), they turn west and Moty Aviam recalls that just two and a half hours earlier they came from the opposite direction.

One hundred fifty meters before the main road (Tapa), right before crossing a small creek, they identify infantry forces on APCs on the main road. Enemy forces.

---

29. Operations officer.

Tank 3 is unfit to fight – it has eleven live crew members and one dead platoon commander. Atir suggests that Nati head toward Tel Saki while Waxman and he take care of the problem.

With three crews in it, tank 3 cuts through the fields alone, toward Tel Saki, whose silhouette they can barely make out in the darkness. A short distance from the main road something goes wrong. The tank shakes terribly and there is a loud thud beneath it. "We are sitting on a rock," Nati thinks, "more bad luck."

While they are stuck on a huge rock, with one track opened and on the ground, Waxman and Atir line up and open fire with their machine guns. They have barely had the chance to make any progress when Nati calls them to come help him out.

Nir decides they will disengage from the enemy. He sends Waxman to continue to Tel Saki and goes himself to evacuate the three crews stuck in the dead platoon commander's tank. Yoav's body is transferred to Atir's tank and with four crews in the tank, Danny Dathar the driver pushes the tank engine as hard as it can go, all the way up to Tel Saki.

After the tank platoon leaves them, the infantry fighters in outpost 116 are in a very bad mental state. Second Lt. Yossi Gur, the stronghold commander, knows the stories of the cruelty of the Syrian army toward its prisoners and he realizes that the only way to get out of this hopeless state is to fight. Now, right now.

Pleased with the opening created in the defense of outpost 116, the Syrian force sends five tanks to sneak up. The first tank breaks through the base gate and drives over the mines which do not explode. It continues to climb further into the base, until Arik, the bazooka operator, hits the tank from a few meters away, on his second shot. The tank crew jumps out of the steel vehicle and is shot down with precise gunfire. A second tank reaches the gate and Arik decides to do better, and this time aims and hits on the first shot. A cloud of white smoke bursts out of the tank and the crew flees. The others turn around and flee as well.

The Brigade Commander's Tank

South of the Mashta junction, Ben Shoham is waiting in his lone armored personnel carrier. "Where is my tank?" he asks the command group with him.

The brigade commander's tank is on its way, in a secured night drive, from Hushnia to the Mashta junction. The cannon is facing forward, a squash shell in it, ready to fire. Porat is taking his time. With an inexperienced crew like his, he has to be careful.

He constantly repeats his silent prayer, "Don't throw a track!" in the hope that someone is listening to him and will keep his young driver Menachem Ben Shoef from making a mistake.

The three crew members have just completed their basic training a month ago and, as always with new men, they were sent to take care of tank 20 Gimel (C), the brigade commander's tank.

Yehuda knows that this is the situation he has been given, and he has to win with this crew. He tries to see through the thick darkness, assisted by a thin moon smiling at him from the edge of the sky. They move forward slowly, aiming the cannon at the hidden shadows, which may be enemy tanks. He hopes the brigade commander will understand the delay in their arrival.

As they are about to reach the Petroleum Road, Fogelman, a loader with hawk eyes, identifies tanks parked on the road, with all their soldiers and vehicles silent in the dark.

"We found the brigade commander's force," Fogelman rejoices.

Porat, a veteran tank commander, with more experience, sees what the young loader does not. The tanks have flat shadows, meaning they can only belong to the Syrian army.

He distances the microphone from his mouth, not to make Ben Shoef nervous, and whispers in Fogelman's ear, "We are in the middle of a Syrian force."

Porat braces himself, chooses a random target, identifies a tank blocking their way. A Syrian tank commander has his head out of the tank and he shouts to him in the only Arabic he knows, "Yalla, Yalla."

The Syrian soldier does not hear him, or does not understand, or just doesn't feel like moving his tank because someone is shouting "Yalla, Yalla" to him in the night. Porat guides the tank in the narrow path left, heading out of the enemy tank park, with their cannon aimed behind them. He finds that both Fogelman and himself have tensed up, almost into the fetal position, waiting for a shell to hit them.

Southern Sector – Tel Saki

A few minutes before 22:00, two tanks of the 74th Battalion's Venus

Company reach the top of Tel Saki, where they find three tanks of the 82nd Battalion, five Nahal infantry soldiers, one BTR armored personnel carrier and a bunker.

Nafah

A few minutes before 22:00, while Ben Shoham and the command carrier are on the Petroleum Road waiting for the tank to arrive, a pale officer comes up to Hagai Mann, the Northern Command intelligence officer, and hands him a note. The intelligence unit have intercepted a report of the commander of the Syrian 51st Brigade announcing, "We have Hushnia."

"Uri!" Hagai Mann rushes over to Simchoni, the Operations Division officer.

Simchoni is beside himself.

"Where are you?" he asks Ben Shoham.

"Near Hushnia," he answers.

"My intelligence officer tells me that the Syrian forces are reporting that they have control of the Hushnia junction," Simchoni says with doubt.

"Negative," Ben Shoham responds. "They must have gotten the junction wrong, we are engaged with them at the Kudna (Troy–Reshet) route."

Reports of enemy forces trying to penetrate from sector 111 toward Hushnia had been flowing in since the early evening hours. Barak and Geva reported a destroyed Syrian battalion and that they had also heard sounds to their west. Ben Shoham knows all of this. He reports to Simchoni that they are engaged with the enemy at the Kudna junction, not far from Hushnia. An hour earlier, Barak reported to Ben Shoham that his technical unit had identified enemy forces on the main road and heard Arabic. In the Petroleum Road sector there is a massive breach and there are forces advancing on both sides of it, marking their path with green star shells.

Ben Shoham was not at Hushnia. The closest he come to it had been two hours earlier, when he passed through the Mashta junction, three kilometers west. So how did he make this statement with such certainty?

Here Ben Shoham, the calm professional and gentleman, fell into the trap of the false confidence that was a result of the Six-Day War. The Six-Day War led the officers to believe that Arab soldiers were worthless, confused and unreliable, leading the commanders to be overconfident.

22:00–22:59

Prior to the Yom Kippur War, every young platoon commander of the 188th Brigade on the Golan was considered to be extremely capable. So capable, in fact, that they were trusted with blocking any attempts of the Syrian army to launch a war against Israel.

Their reputation for effectiveness was hard won. They had demonstrated their skills in both day and night drills, ably running platoon sized front-line tank maneuvers. They turned three tanks, twelve crewmen and a logistic support team into a well-oiled machine. They demonstrated that they would not break under pressure. Only after this thorough preparation were they told to spread their wings and fly.

Fedale, the brigade commander who taught them to be so effective, knew that when the real test came they would be able to cope. Even if isolated and forced to work as independent units, their leaders would function as miniature generals.

It was approximately 22:00 on Saturday night when all of these preparations paid off. At the peak of the Syrian attack on the Southern Golan, they consisted of an injured deputy battalion commander, two company commanders and two platoon commanders – four tank commanders had been killed – with the forces more divided than ever before. They were unable to fight at night, cut off from logistic and operational aid. Yet the platoon commanders of the 188th Brigade maintained their professional standards. Despite being exhausted, confused, troubled and in pain, they stood firm and unbreakable.

They were no longer in control of the front, the natural state of circumstances had changed, but they still searched for the right way to stop the enemy, using their training as best as they could.

They remained focused, not complaining or asking why, and continuing to block the enemy, hoping that something would change and the endless lines of Syrian tanks, marking their paths in Israeli territory with flares, would disappear from the Golan.

22:00

Logistics Convoy

Zvika Gringold is still making slow progress on the Petroleum Road. He instructs Hershko to drive up to the hilltop; through his binoculars he combs the area for suspicious movement before heading out into the open. He sees a convoy moving in the darkness toward him. There is a moment of tense silence while they hide in cover, until Zvika identifies an IDF jeep leading a few trucks.

Giora Goldberg jumps out of the jeep and finds Zvika Gringold, who he has served with on numerous fronts. They hug and Giora gives him an update: "We set out to Juhader with a convoy of fuel and ammunition and here we are, without delivering our load. A Syrian tank stopped right next to us, at the Water route junction, and at least another twenty passed us on the Petroleum Road, both north and south of Mashta. Be careful!"

They part and go their separate ways. Giora continues north to Nafah and Zvika south toward the enemy. Giora looks back, watches the two tanks on the Petroleum Road and is very concerned.

Zvika Force

Syrian tanks on the Petroleum Road? How can it be? Zvika finds that hard to believe but Giora is a calm, level headed and reliable officer.

Who could have ever imagined such a scenario? Zvika recalls the brigade exercise they conducted just two months ago. All the officers had agreed with that lieutenant from engineering, who had told Ben Shoham that the scenario of the southern Golan being conquered was unrealistic. There was wide agreement at the time when that officer said that the exercise should be based on a different model. What was Ben Shoham's answer? That we shouldn't be overconfident. That we need to be ready for anything.

Zvika asks for new instructions, in light of the report he just received. Ben Shoham, at the junction of the Water and Petroleum Roads, is busy in the APC, on the radio with Erez, trying to get illumination support and ammunition to the 53rd Battalion and organize the defense of the southern front.

Hanan Schwartz, the communications officer, hears Gringold. "Wait," he says to him, "we will get back to you," and he forgets him.

The Artillery War of Hanan Anderman

The clock shows 22:00. They had stood their ground and fired without pause from the outbreak of war. In a few hours they had exhausted quantities of ammunition supposed to last a full day. The standard procedures they were used to – shooting tanks and artillery at long ranges, usually at the rear echelons of the line divisions – were irrelevant and they had been forced to shorten their range. They had reduced the propellant charges in order to support the infantry outposts and the tank emplacements under attack by swarms of Syrian infantry and armor. At that moment, when a pale moon hangs on an edge above Tel Juhader, 2nd Lt. Hanan Anderman, the battery officer of Artillery Battery B, 405th Battalion, is in the command APC, a kilometer west of Khan Juhader, when he thinks he hears tank tracks approaching the battery.

"Let's make sure that our own tanks don't fire on us by mistake," he says and calls through to his deputy battalion commander who is at the nearby battery, a few kilometers to the west.

"Call them on the Mosquito emergency armored corps frequency," Uri Manos, the deputy battalion commander instructs him.

He calls them once, twice and there is no response.

The tank cannons are about to rise out of the area east of the battery and face Anderman, who is outside the carrier, busy unloading ammunition. Yissachar Bruk, the officer of the other battery, who is not doing anything, rushes toward the tanks, with an IDF identification lamp in his hand. "Idiots!" he cries, "They are about to run over us."

A few meters before he reaches the tanks, a flare goes off in the sky. It is bright white. Anderman and Bruk, experienced artillery officers, know that the IDF does not use white flares and an alarm bells goes off in their heads. Syrian forces!

Anderman runs toward the APC and stops a few meters from it, just before it takes a direct hit and he sees body parts flying out in the darkness.

In the light of the flares, the Syrian tanks discover the helpless artillery battery and, within seconds, they turn it into a charnel house. Artillery cannons loaded with ammunition are blown sky high, along with their crews. This swift and horrifying visit of the angel of death has taken the lives of fourteen artillery soldiers.

Brigade Commander's Tank
A few minutes after the logistics convoy had left, several kilometers north of the junction between the Petroleum Road and Water route, Yehuda Porat and his crew join the brigade commander's APC. Porat, still upset and full of adrenalin, tells Ben Shoham about the Syrian tank park they just passed through. Ben Shoham lets out a small sigh and sends Porat back to the tank, to position it with the gun aimed north.

Oded Erez
Slightly after 22:00, Oded Erez sums up the current situation.

The front has been broken. He knows that in the dark, additional Syrian forces continue to flow in without hindrance. Uzi Urieli's attempt to take back the tank emplacements on the Petroleum Road has failed. The reports show that Hushnia has become Syrian territory. His forces are partially surrounded; the brigade commander has notified them that it will not be possible to get the supply convoy to Juhader and they will have to manage with whatever they have. The artillery he is asking for is not coming – and when it does finally come, it is too late, too little and too far.

Avi Ronis and Uri Akavia, two of the three company commanders on the front, have been killed. Outpost 116 is cut off and Yoav Yakir, leader of the 3rd Platoon which is defending the stronghold, is also dead. Reports of additional casualties continue to flow in from all sides.

Ben Shoham Force
The update Ben Shoham has received from Porat confirms Simchoni's report that the Syrian forces are claiming that Hushnia is in their control. Still, no one in the high command has clearly confirmed the presence of enemy forces at Hushnia, so could Porat be wrong? Why aren't there regular updates from the Command?

Since his gut feeling is very bad, Ben Shoham is not taking any risks.

He gets on the radio and instructs Haim Barak, commander of the 82nd Battalion, to move south and take up a position at the Kudna junction. They are to stop the Syrian forces trying to get to Hushnia and to hit the Syrian forces that are already there. Enemy troops are heading their way on the Petroleum Road, fleeing from the pressure applied by the Zvika force.

The Logistics Convoy

At around 22:15 the logistics convoy meets the APC of the 53rd Battalion's aid station.

Giora, the operations officer, agrees with Danny, the doctor, that it was wise to leave the Mashta junction. He tells the medic, "It will be even wiser to leave this position and head to Nafah. The Syrian forces are all around."

By the time the doctor agrees, Giora is already rushing his force toward Nafah. At around 22:30 the two convoys reach the entrance to the Nafah base, awaiting the call from Ben Shoham to rejoin him.

His face pale as one who has just seen the angel of death, Giora bursts into the command bunker and declares, "Everyone stay off the Petroleum Road. It is full of Syrian forces. We need to carry out a brigade attack on Hushnia."

The senior "brass" look at the young officer with amazement. Seeing the 1st Lt. rank on his shoulders, someone says in contempt, "When did you become a great strategist? What do you know about brigade attacks?"

Zvika Force

Zvika continues to lead his force on the Petroleum Road. Hagai Zur is fifty meters behind him.

Track link by track link, Hershko once again takes his steel chariot up to an observation point, quietly, so as not to wake any sleeping Syrians. In observation position, Zvika looks ahead, checking if the area is clear and then moves on.

Three and a half kilometers north of Mashta, near the Zavitan water crossing, as Hershko is carefully driving the tank up to another observation position, a Syrian tank appears from the opposite side, fifteen meters from them, with its weak side exposed to the Sho't Kal tank.

"Fire!" Zvika shouts. Nir Zvi Elimelech, with a shell already in the cannon, fires at Zvika's mark and blows up the Syrian tank. Hershko sees the Tiran explode and moves the tank back.

"Hershko, stop," Zvika instructs the driver, trying to take back control of the tank.

There is no response. He tries again and again and Zvika realizes there is a communication problem. He rotates the turret to 5 o'clock, shouts to Yehuda Akunis to take an antenna rod and hit Hershko on the helmet. The measure works and Hershko stops with one track on the edge of a water crossing bridge, very close to overturning.

Without radio communication, with a gunner who lost the night vision in his periscope, Zvika switches to Hagai's tank, instructing him to switch with him.

"That is the second time today," Hagai thinks to himself, as he transfers his functioning tank to a higher ranking commander. He gets on Zvika's tank, sees that he cannot carry out the necessary repairs, and detaches from the force and heads back to Nafah.

"Straight on the Petroleum Road," Zur instructs Hershko.

Twenty minutes later they arrive at Nafah. The technicians get to work on the tank immediately, to return it to the front as soon as possible. "Things have changed dramatically," Hagai thinks, remembering the hard time he had getting past the guards last time. Someone has finally realized that he and Zvika, out there in the dark on his own, are the only ones who can save them.

North Sector – Fidel Hadash

"What about reinforcements?" Avner Landau, the commander of B Company, asks Yair Nafshi, preparing for another morning of war.

"The 71st Battalion is on its way to your sector," Nafshi answers. "Contact them and join their command."

The 71st Battalion is located somewhere in the Tel Varda area. "Somewhere" is the right description. While contacting them on the radio, Avner senses that Ratess, the battalion commander, is not familiar with the area. He can only hope that someone there, in this unknown unit, will get their act together.

The manner in which the 71st Battalion joined the fight demonstrated the chaos of war. All the elements that add to chaos were there.

Crews assembled at the last minute without training together, most of them not even knowing each other – some of whom had not trained in ages, hardly remembering how to drive a tank, load a shell, correct their misses, or command a tank; there were tanks missing machine guns, without means of observation and no binoculars for the commander.

A herd of unorganized tanks, filled with untrained crews, sets out to stop the Syrian enemy forces. This is a problematic way to start, not for the weak at heart. Sending this force to war all at once, without preparation, without knowing their battalion commander, with code maps that are not up to date and do not allow them to identify themselves, joining an extremely complex battlefield, it is a catastrophe.

With darkness covering the Kramim hills, Mt. Varda and the ramps of Fidel Hadash, between bombing and shelling, with tanks that are not quite cooperating, crews that do not understand how they were assembled and commanders who cannot identify where they are, they are sent to join forces with Avner Landau.

Half an hour passes and the tanks of the 188th Brigade and those of the 71st Battalion join forces in the worst way, with Landau's company being fired at by the 71st Battalion.

"Hold your fire!" Avner shouts on the radio. Ratess holds his fire. He didn't hit them and he does not join them.

North Sector – the Northern 109 Ramp

On the northern 109 ramp, Doron Sadeh Lavan watches in terror as Syrian soldiers sneak toward the tracks of his platoon.

"Fire!" he shouts to the two other commanders. Not having the right angle to fire the machine guns, the three commanders fire their Uzi submachine guns at them.

Maybe it is Doron's mad shouts, or perhaps the knowledge that it is a matter of seconds before the tanks open fire on them with their entire arsenal. We will never know why but the Syrian troops disappeared immediately, without leaving any soldiers behind. The force feels lucky and also understands that they need immediate firing practice with their Uzis.

Before their sense of distress passes, Shmuel's tank gets hit by a shell. The turret goes up in flames. The crew carries out the fire extinguishing drill and puts out the fire. The crews are uneasy, not knowing where the next blow will come from.

South Sector – Juhader

Urieli from the 188th Brigade and Jack Hallel from the 7th Brigade and all the soldiers accompanying them know something bad is happening in the dark. Supposedly, they are conducting a successful battle, with every tank they encounter going up in flames. Yet still, Urieli and his soldiers understand that what they see and destroy on the dark is just a tiny drop in the huge flow, and there is nothing they can do to stop it.

South Sector – 115

In the Battalion Commander's Ramp and around it, shaking in the October cold, Boaz Tamir, Gidi Maklef and Oded Bekman are searching the area. Not far from the ramp, on the big flat area beneath them, is the night parking area of the Syrian 112th Brigade that had completed its mission to bridge and secure the Petroleum Road crossing. The sounds of the soldiers of the Syrian brigade reach the tanks on the ramp.

On the large 115 ramp, the two tanks of the Ronis force are trying to contact the tanks of C Company in the hope that someone will finally give them instructions. But they receive nothing. With a lone tank that is unable to fire and which holds the cold body of Avi Ronis, they are hiding in the trench behind the ramp, helpless and scared.

"If no one is going to help me, I will help myself," Yoram Miromi, the tank commander, decides. He takes the initiative, leaves the ramp and heads toward the deployment base beneath Tel Fares.

At the end of a night drive, crowded together in the tank, with Ronis's body bouncing along with them, the two crews stop at the base. They find Yitzchak Rachamim, the company sergeant who gets on the tank, takes the body of the company commander, places it on a stretcher, and in a short military battlefield "ceremony" he covers it with a blanket.

Oded Erez

Someone reports on the radio that there apparently is a lone Syrian tank moving from Tel Fares heading south. Oded Erez is tense, as is the operations officer beside him.

"Driver, reverse." Shechter drives back. "Driver, forward." The driver does as he is instructed.

Another maneuver and another and Sapir, guiding Shechter, positions the battalion commander's tank behind a low mound, enabling them to have eye contact and fire on the enemy.

"Gunner, do you hear me?"

"I hear you," Itzik Keres answers.

"I am rotating left and putting you on the center of the road," Erez continues. "When the tank appears, you will need to identify it with the moonlight and hit it."

Two minutes pass. They hear tracks from the north and then a dark shadow appears in Kerres's peri-telescope.

"Do you identify it?" Erez asks.

"Yes," Keres answers.

"Fire."

The flash tells Keres that he hit the target, a deadly hit between the turret and the body of the tank. Then he identifies something else in the tank burning fifty meters from him, something that makes him scream.

A few minutes before he died, Avi Ronis responded to the distress calls from the 3rd Platoon, fighting for its life on sector 116 with its last ammunition. He instructed Avi Lavi, the tank commander, who was in a tank with a damaged firing system, to head back to the front and act as a mobile ammunition warehouse for the three tanks desperate for shells.

He was new in the battalion, just coming from the Tirans, still not acquainted with the Golan routes, Avi Lavi got confused and instead of taking the short way to Juhader, he headed north toward Tel Fares.

After a few hours of driving in circles, he approached the Erez crew that thought he was a Syrian tank.

The report that the Sho't Kal tank was on its way to sector 116 was sent only on the company radio. At this point Ronis was no longer alive and there was no one to prevent the fiasco that was developing. Unaware of Ronis's decision, Oded Erez sees a tank approaching and cannot identify it in the dark. He knows that no Israeli tank is supposed to be on the move here at night and opens fire, killing Rami Sulimanov the gunner.

Erez gives the order to drive and they are on the move. No one says a word. The only sound is a small sigh from the battalion commander.

Zvika Force

The (former) commander of the Zeevim G Company from the 74th Battalion quickly introduces himself to his new crew – three soldiers from the 53rd Battalion. He sets the radio to the brigade frequency, moves a few hundred meters from the burning Syrian tank, identifies Hagai heading toward Nafah and takes position northeast of the Petroleum Road.

"Driver, turn right," Zvika instructs the driver, Phillip, whom he does not know. "Driver, move forward slowly."

They reach an observation point and Zvika's eyes open wide. His binoculars and the purple moon still in the western sky give him a view of the Hushnia valley, and it is covered with the round shadows of tanks.

"I identify Tiran anti-collision reflectors," Itzik Arnon, the gunner, notifies Zvika.

"Can you fire on your own, without my help?" Zvika asks him.

"Yes," Arnon says confidently.

"How long have you been a gunner?"

"Two years. The company commander's tank."

"Fire."

Zvika identifies targets for Arnon, Arazi loads and Arnon fires non-stop.

The young Phillip, in the driver's seat, turns out to be a calm and efficient crewman and follows Zvika's orders on changing position in the dark night. They successfully maneuver the tank between the basalt rocks, up and down the ramp, in a very well-coordinated way.

Nafah – Hagai Zur

"The tank is fit and ready," Hagai Zur reports to Yisraeli, the deputy brigade commander.

"Zvika is managing well. Stay here for now," Yisraeli instructs him.

A few minutes pass and the deputy brigade commander issues an organized order. "There is a platoon commander of the 7th Brigade here in the command center, his name is Elon Littwitz. Take him with you, take position on both sides of the Petroleum Road, near the first Booster Ridge (100 meters from the Nafah base). You are responsible to make sure no one gets on the route and heads south, without my authorization. One more thing, Hagai. If a Syrian son of a bitch tries to approach, fuck him." Yisraeli gives the order with his clear Mizrachi accent and disappears with his jeep in the dark, immaculate, clean, with a black beret on his head.

Zvika Force

In the short pause between volleys of fire, Zvika reports to Ben Shoham how huge the force he is facing is. He calls for additional tanks to reinforce him in defending the route.

Arieh Schwartz, commander of the 405th Artillery Battalion, the brigade fire support officer on Ben Shoham's front, gets on the radio and informs Zvika that all the artillery is at his disposal.

Without a compass or a map but familiar with the area like it was his backyard at the Kibbutz, Zvika instructs the artillery officer on the exact location of the enemy forces.

"Copy that," he receives confirmation from Nafah but the artillery is silent and Zvika does not understand why.

Anderman's War

Among the shouts of the injured soldiers and the self-propelled artillery exploding, Anderman finds the evacuation half-track personnel carrier. He throws a terrified soldier out of the driver's seat and thanks God for his natural curiosity that caused him to learn how to drive every vehicle he could find.

The starter grunts, the engine comes to life and twenty soldiers, some of them injured, hold on to the vehicle's steel skin with the last of their strength, fleeing from the valley of death.

Stuttering and choking, the carrier makes its way west toward A Battery located three kilometers northwest of them.

Uri Manos hears the sounds and sets out toward them. What he sees is a group of beaten, terrified soldiers, in shell shock. Anderman tells him what happened and the deputy battalion commander gives them water to drink and asks for everyone to be quiet. They all turn off their engines and radios and listen in the dark. Are the Syrian forces continuing to head toward them? After a few tense moments of silence, without them hearing any hostile activity approaching, Uri Manos splits up the remaining soldiers between his APC and truck. He sends the survivors toward the battalion base at Kazabiya. "The war is over for you."

Zvika Force

Alone in the darkness, in a single tank with four crew members, Zvika Gringold continues to wage the battle for survival for themselves and for the Golan.

Arazi loads the shells and Arnon fires like a madman. All of them, especially Zvika, are amazed at the endless number of sparks of light coming from the Syrian tanks, filling the darkness that is threatening them.

Arazi loads whatever he can get his hands on: armor piercing rounds, shaped charge and squash heads. He keeps a shell between his legs, releases the next shell safety, lifts it with his left hand, opens the breech block with his right, inserts the shell, closes the breech and shouts "loaded" to the gunner. Once again, he releases the safety, with a shell between his legs, a shell in his left hand, he releases the breech and shouts "loaded."

Arnon's eye is glued to the peri-telescope. He identifies a shadow and fires. "That is for Shimon (Akab)," he says every time he pushes the electric trigger. A Syrian tank goes up in flames, lighting up the area in red light, bursting into glowing shards.

"Reverse!" Zvika orders and Phillip obeys. They go up and down and occasionally Zvika tells him to turn off the engine so they can listen for the sound of tracks, to try and work out what the bastards are planning.

While the defense line on the southern Golan has been completely breached, without being aware of it, Zvika is succeeding in delaying the attack on the central Golan and the conquering of Nafah. During those hours on Saturday night, command had sought to push every available tank to the front, to prevent the Purple Line from being breached. If Zvika's force had been reached on the radio, they would have been sent forward, probably to Juhader or sector 111, and the Petroleum Road and the Nafah area would have been breached that night. However, Hanan Schwartz, the 188th Brigade communications officer, had neglected to convey Zvika's request for instructions to Ben Shoham, therefore, Zvika's force was accidentally forgotten.

Zvika's force may not be hitting many tanks, maybe just a handful. They did not have good night vision but they continued to fire continuously, from different positions and this causes the Syrians to believe they were facing a much bigger force, preventing them from surging ahead, toward Nafah.

Once again, it is Zvika guiding the tank with sharp turns right and left, quickly aiming at the next target, causing it to burst into flame and wondering when the reinforcements are finally going to arrive.

As he adjusts his helmet on his head, he suddenly hears a terrified voice on the radio. Shaul Bakal, the Zeevim G Company turret mechanic, calls for help on the brigade frequency. Zvika identifies him, hears the desperation in his voice and asks what his situation is. Bakal reports to Zvika that he and his men found a place to hide at the Mashta junction, beneath the culvert. He asks when they will come to evacuate them.

"I will come to you soon," Zvika ends the conversation with a promise. He believes it is just a matter of time before reinforcements arrive and then they will go make the short trip to the Mashta junction and evacuate the trapped mechanics.

22:45

Nafah

Someone at Nafah finally starts to understand that the problem they are facing is on the southern front, the front that the 188th Brigade and Ben Shoham are in charge of. It is much more serious than they thought it was. Even so, they try to remain optimistic, strangely detached from what is going on at the front.

The Northern Command operations log notes, "There apparently are people at Hushnia, probably infantry soldiers. There is gunfire. Ben Shoham's tanks can hear it."

Brigade Commander Force

The radios in the 188th Brigade command APC increase the confusion and desperation. Bocken sentences of terror and helplessness continue to flow in from all fronts. The Syrian forces are breaking through from all directions, and Oded Erez, who has not received artillery assistance, sounds like he is losing hope. His distress reaches the ears of the 188th Brigade commander and has a strong effect on him, but Ben Shoham has no way of helping him.

The Southern front is swarming with enemy forces. Green flares, marking the movement of Syrian convoys in Israeli territory, are everywhere. Ben Shoham realizes that the way north has also been blocked. Hushnia is now Syrian territory.

South Sector – 111

Deutsch cannot believe what he is seeing. A Syrian Tiran tank is slowly crawling toward them. He wakes up his crew and gets them alert.

Twenty meters from Deutsch's position, at the bend in the road, the Syrian tank shows itself. First the edge of the cannon appears and then the tank body and after a few tense seconds, the turret.

"Fire!" Deutsch shouts and closes his eyes. It is recommended for tank commanders to close their eyes after giving the firing order at night. Otherwise, they will be blinded by the muzzle flash for a while. Nothing happens.

"Fire!" Deutsch shouts. Nothing happens.

"Fire!" the entire crew shouts together, hoping for a miracle from Rosenblau.

Shmulik Rosenblau is not firing because a gunner does not fire without identifying the target and Deutsch forgot to explain that the target is fifteen meters from them. This short distance requires transferring from the tele-periscope (magnifying times ten) to the observation window. That is why Rosenblau does not identify the Syrian tank in his eyepiece.

Finally, Rosenblau takes his eye off the lens, sees the tank and fires. Deutsch forgets to close his eyes, he hears the gunner celebrating but cannot see anything.

Deutsch's tank climbs back up toward the outpost, and the half-blinded commander tries to guide Mantzur the driver toward the area behind the northern ramp. "This is it, we made it," Deutsch tells himself, letting down his level of alertness for a second. Just then he feels the tank land at the bottom of a huge pit, and the right track is thrown off, causing an inner tear that means it cannot be repaired.

At this exact moment, the artillery fire intensifies and everyone on the northern ramp, mainly Deutsch's crew that is neutralized in the pit, close the tank hatches in a complete sense of helplessness and detachment.

Brigade Commander Force

It is almost 23:00. Ben Shoham's tactical command group identifies two vehicles heading up the Water route. Through his binoculars he sees they are Israeli forces – an APC and a truck.

"Where to?" Ben Shoham wonders.

"To Kazabiya," Anderman answers. The young 2nd Lt. leading the convoy updates him on the events of the last hour.

Ben Shoham now understands why he has not received artillery support and he forbids him from continuing north. "There are Syrian tanks on the Petroleum Road," he explains to Anderman, saving his life and the lives of B Battery .

23:00–23:59

The defense doctrine in October 1973 was that, in case of war, the regular forces on the front lines were to hold back the attacking forces and delay them at the forward line of engagement until the reserve forces could be mobilized and arrive at the front.

In all the war scenarios conducted in Israel, prior to October 6, the estimated time it was expected to take to mobilize the combat reserve force was 72 hours. That was the reason that the IDF Intelligence Directorate was required to provide a warning 72 hours earlier. Since the defense doctrine was that there would be a 72-hour intelligence warning, the decision makers knew that once the warning was sounded, 72 hours or more before the war started, the reserve forces would be sent in, in an orderly manner.

As a result of an accumulation of military and diplomatic failures, the reserves mobilization began just *three hours* before the war began. The IDF transportation framework was not designed for a three-hour warning. The Egged bus company did not have enough buses to transport the entire army at the same time. The same was true of the tank movers the IDF had ready.

When the first reserve forces started to arrive at the emergency warehouse units, everyone knew that the chaos was just starting. The warehouse clerks refused to enter a "accelerated battle procedure" and insisted that the soldiers had to sign all the forms.

Ten percent of the tanks in the emergency warehouses turned out to be unfit and in the process of being repaired. Many of the guns were covered in thick grease, as if they were not intended for use during war. Regarding the equipment: the shells were from old or poor quality series, there were missing machine guns, binoculars. Chaos.

At 23:00, without a preventive air strike and after the mobilization time of the reserves was cut to three hours, it was only the regular army that was holding back the enemy forces on the Golan front, just as on the Suez Canal front.

Israel got a lucky break here however. The reserves and the state of Israel "benefited" from the fact that Egypt and Syria chose to start the war on the holiest day of the year for Jews. The majority of civilians were at home or in synagogues and the roads were empty.

That is the reason that at 23:00, 12 hours after the general mobilization was declared, the first reserve forces started arriving on the Golan front, cutting the estimated time to a third of the time it took them in the rapid mobilization drill conducted prior to the war. The fact that the soldiers started arriving after 18 hours brought new hope to the commanders at the Nafah headquarters.

23:00

The reserve forces are coming – The 179th Brigade

At the same time Ben Shoham stops Anderman on the Water route, Lt. Col. (res.) Uzi Mor, commander of the 266th Battalion of the 179th Reserve Brigades, arrives at the gates of Nafah and awaits his orders.

Less than a week before, a different unit on the brigade, the 96th Battalion, had been mobilized in a drill that was very successful.

On October 1, at the end of the drill, Maj. Gen. Hofi asked the Chief of General Staff to keep the reserves mobilized at least until after Yom Kippur. His pleading regarding the situation and his reminder of the indications of war did not convince his superior. "No," Dado declared. In the end, as an act of goodwill to the nagging general from the north, he agreed that the tanks of the 96th Reserve Battalion should remain as they were, armed and equipped.

On Saturday, toward 14:00, four hours after the (almost) full mobilization order was issued, the first soldiers of the 296th Battalion reported to the Filon emergency warehouse unit near Rosh Pina.

Lt. Col. Mor, from Kibbutz Ein Shemer, was hoping to receive the armed and equipped tanks of the 96th Battalion, but that was not going to happen. The 7th Brigade that arrived at the emergency warehouse unit on Friday had already taken the tanks prepared for the reserve soldiers, in addition to the tanks of another battalion and a half, leaving Mor with the tanks in the worst condition, some of which were scheduled to be sent to the repair depots.

As he is wondering what he was going to do now, he notices Amnon Sharon, one of the company commanders of the battalion. "Get organized with crews and tanks and let me know when your company is ready," he says.

Progress is slow. Trucks with ammunition that were supposed to arrive from distant bases are nowhere in sight and the brigade logistics staff fail to understand they are at war. By the early evening, Amnon has managed to put together ten complete crews. The only thing still missing is the ammunition that had not yet arrived.

At 21:00, Col. Ran Sarig, the brigade commander, started to receive urgent messages from Raful. "We need steel immediately. Send any tank that is ready. A platoon of three tanks with half the ammunition? Send it up."

Sarig decides to send the first unit, Amnon Sharon's company, who are in the final stages of preparations, commanded by Uzi Mor, the battalion commander. The ammunition truck finally arrives. Amnon allocates each tank twelve squash-head shells. He reports to Uzi, who reports to Ran, who orders them to move out with whatever they have.

Slightly after 21:00, the sound of ten tanks' tracks of Gison C Company, led by company commander Amnon Sharon and battalion commander Uzi Mor, can be heard loud and clear. They head out of the emergency warehouse unit, on their way to the Bnot Yaakov Bridge and Nafah, crushing the asphalt road.

Right from the start, the tanks justify their "bad reputation" and three get stuck and were left behind. With just seven tanks, each with twelve shells, they continue toward Nafah and arrive at the gate awaiting orders.

Raful instructs Giora Goldberg, the operations officer, to join Uzi Mor and brief him on how to get to the Petroleum Road in order to join the Zvika Force.

The two officers, acquainted from previous reserve duty, meet at the Nafah gate. Goldberg sees a nervous and troubled battalion commander, with seven tanks that have not even boresighted their optics, very low on ammunition and fuel, and with crew members some of whom are still wearing their Shabbat clothes.

Uzi Mor also had another reason to be concerned. In the final preparations before leaving, he inserted bullets into the commander's 0.3 Browning machine gun that responded with spontaneous fire. As an experienced tank crew member, Uzi knew that this is what happens when the gun is not properly prepared. To him this is an indication of what is going to happen.

Giora returns to the command bunker at Nafah and reports to Raful. "This is not a battalion. What we have at the gate of Nafah is seven steel wrecks. Sending them on the Petroleum Road toward Hushnia is a suicide mission."

Zvi Bar, commander of the 820th Regional Brigade, who had worshipped Raful since they served together in the paratroopers, will not accept disrespect of his commander. "Giora, are you disobeying an order from Raful?"

Standing up to his brigade commander and the division commander was a bit too much even for Giora. He returns to the base gate and explain to Uzi where Zvika is located and where the brigade commander is. He tries to hide his bad gut feeling and stresses to him that between Zvika and Ben Shoham there is a Syrian force. "Be careful Uzi," he says. "In the hills right beyond the current position of the Zvika Force, you may find yourself engaged in battle with the Syrians."

A few minutes after 23:00, seven Sho't Kal tanks set out from the east of the Petroleum Road, heading toward the Booster Ridge at the south of the Nafah fence. With their lights on, they pass between the two blocking tanks, the Zur force, who have no chance to stop them.

Hagai Zur calls Yisraeli, he reports that the force passed by him, as if they were on a night parade. He notifies him that he does not know their radio frequency and was unable to stop them.

Yisraeli tells him everything is okay and that they are our forces that forgot to announce their movement. Then he switches to Mor's frequency and instructs him to switch to combat alert mode. "Drive on the route without lights and with your weapons loaded."

Amnon Sharon, a veteran of the Six-Day War and the War of Attrition, with endless battle stories of Arabs that do not fight at night and that are cowards, is not aware of what Giora told his battalion commander. His tank leads the convoy and he is leaning forward on the turret, trying hard to see in the dark, praying that the tank doesn't throw its tracks.

Anderman's War

Stunned by the information he has received from Ben Shoham, Anderman understands that the war is becoming more complicated. He takes the soldiers off the truck, crowds them all into the APC, updates Manos, the deputy battalion commander, with the report received from the 188th Brigade commander and asks him what he should do.

"Withdraw on your own. Do not try to join me. It is full of Syrians here," Manos answers.

While Anderman and the survivors of B Battery are heading toward the Kazabiya base and meet Ben Shoham on the way, Uri Manos and Yehuda Sharoni, the communications NCO, begin their independent withdrawal.

They head southeast, on an APC, in search of the missing soldiers of B Battery. After just two minutes, Manos comes to his senses. "What am I doing? Where is this bravery going to lead me? Who is going to join me in the night? Except for shells from Tiran tanks waiting for additional victims?" Realistic and frustrated, Manos turns around and heads back to the battery.

Brigade Commander's Force

With three officers beside him – intelligence officer Zurich, communications officer Schwartz and reconnaissance officer Ben Yosef – Col. Itzik Ben Shoham, commander of the 188th Brigade, is as alone as he has ever been.

How helpful can the advice of the two officers who are not from the armored corps be? What more can they tell him that he does not already know? Their sources of information are the same as his – a number of communication radios, sending out pessimistic reports that are making the dark night even darker.

Just five hours earlier he had left the commotion of the bunker at Nafah, the bright fluorescent lights, the humming of the air conditioners, the officers working hard, the young soldiers serving black coffee, the comraderie, the ability to share the burden with his senior colleagues. Now he is alone and it is freezing in the summit, colder than he imagined possible.

Ben Shoham knows that the outposts' defense line has been broken, part of the southern Golan is under Syrian control and the Petroleum

Road to Hushnia and Nafah in the north and Juhader in the south is blocked by the Syrian forces. He understands that the APC and the tank, "The Brigade Commander Force," are surrounded, making it impossible to join other units. He knows that as the night progresses, the chances of him getting out of this besieged position diminish. Soon it will become his personal survival battle against the enemy forces hiding in the terrifying darkness, with the remaining light fading as the moon sets in the west.

Ben Shoham also knows that this is exactly when a commander's strength is tested. His soldiers await his orders, hoping for words of encouragement from him, for a magic touch that will change the situation on the shattered front. They are not interested in his personal war.

Ben Shoham hears the sounds, tries to show optimism to the commanders on the battlefield. They are scattered as he never thought they could be, and he knows this is not the war he was educated to fight, not the war he wrote his article about.

In late 1970 an article appeared in the *Maarchot* magazine, written by Lt. Col. Yitzchak. Its title was "Tanks in Battle in Small and Independent Frameworks." Yes, the author was Itzik Ben Shoham and he wrote that tanks can operate independently in small units but only when they have been transferred to the command of an infantry or mechanized infantry brigade.

He wrote, "The biggest question every soldier in armored officer's course has is, as a tank platoon commander, will I be operating independently on the battlefield? Will I take action alone with my platoon?"

His answer to the rhetorical question in the article was:

> *We can say with a great degree of certainty that a company of tanks, in the framework of its organic battalion, will not be sent on independent missions, much less a platoon. We will not see independent action in combat in units smaller than a battalion. Furthermore, the battalion is able to operate independently, but even so, it will usually operate in the framework of a brigade or a division, as one of the forces carrying out the general mission.*

"Ok," Ben Shoham, turns to Dror Sofer, the commander of the carrier. "Let's change our position."

Manos' War

Uri Manos, the deputy artillery battalion commander, came to understood how bad things really were at about the same time as Ben Shoham and Anderman. As far as he was concerned, his main task at this point was to get his men out of there and keep them alive. What will happen after that? We would see.

Manos instructs Yossi Koren, commander of Battery A, to gather all the soldiers and get into their self-propelled guns, trucks and APCs. He takes up position at the head of the convoy of vehicles in the command APC and starts heading west to redeploy to a new position on the "Waterfalls Route," far from the Syrian threat. Manos was well acquainted with the Golan; he had been posted there several times before and was familiar with the various routes on the Golan. Last time he was here, he brought his wife along on a hike to see the flowers blooming along a beautiful path from the Water route to the Waterfalls Route.

He is back on that route again, leading his soldiers who trust him to bring them to safety. The thirty-two year old deputy battalion commander is older than the "tiger bunch" of officers who had been discharged from the military and rejoined during the War of Attrition. Wearing a tight bright tank top, he leads the force in the armored personnel carrier that has all its lights off, to keep them from the eyes of the Syrian gunners.

Right before reaching the JNF (Waterfalls) route, with the shadow of the Kubet Kara (Kipat Nesharim) hill already in sight, Manos looks back and is amazed to see the APC, with the entire convoy following, turning the wrong way, toward the cliffs of the Bazelet/Daliot stream. He runs over as fast as he can and finds the driver in the leading carrier has fallen asleep. They stop, wake themselves up and switch drivers. Fifteen minutes later they are deployed beneath the Bezek Hill. The Syrians will definitely not get this far.

Zvika Force plus 266 battali on

Between 23:00 and 00:00 seven Sho't Kal tanks of the 266th Battalion move on the Petroleum Road, led by company commander Amnon Sharon. "Where the hell are they?" Amnon wonders. It is completely dark and he calls Zvika on the radio asking him to turn on the light in the rear of the tank.

Zvika turns on the light. Near the culvert of the Zavitan stream,

Amnon is shocked to identify a lone tank positioned west of the Petroleum Road, behind the two fences around the pipe.

Sharon's company and Uzi Mor, the battalion commander, continue south on the Petroleum Road, with Zvika to the west of them.

Nafah

The picture of the developing situation finally reaches the command bunker at Nafah. Simchoni is running the war, with the general guidance of Haka. He is calm and in control but this does not hide his grave concern regarding the fate of the southern front.

The Command operations log entry for 23:32 reads, "According to the general, there apparently is an infantry force at Hushnia." Seven minutes pass and at 23:39, the magnitude of the problem becomes clear. "A logistics convoy of Ben Shoham's force driving on the Petroleum Road identified Syrian tanks."

At 23:40, the entry was, "Someone in Ben Shoham's force claims that there are Syrian tanks and artillery at Hushnia."

Zvika Force plus 266 battalion

Amnon Sharon leads the tanks of the 266th Battalion. As far as he knows, there are no enemy forces around. He does not know or see otherwise. In the last two hours, Zvika hit a number of tanks but some of them burned and the crews managed to put out the fires and others were destroyed without lighting up the sky.

Zvika was not asked to give them an explanation of the situation. As far as he is concerned, a new commander had arrived who is higher ranking than him and he is certain that someone has updated him on the situation. Otherwise, he would have come to Zvika's tank to hear it from him.

There are eight tanks moving on the Petroleum Road, heading toward the Mashta junction near Hushnia. After two kilometers, half a kilometer from the Yehudia stream culvert, Amnon Sharon, who is leading the force, identifies a ball of fire heading toward him. As he is thinking what they should do, the "ball" explodes right in front of their tank.

"Cannon, combat range!" he shouts, turning the cannon toward something in the dark.

"Firing!" the gunner shouts, and misses, and the firing system stops working.

What would have happened if the firing system would have remained intact? Not much. They were lacking night vision, which meant that the gunners could not pinpoint the attackers and hit them. "We thought it was going to be a combat day – a few shells and we would head back home. We thought that the tanks of the 188th Brigade surely destroyed enemy tanks and we could boresight on the fires they lit."

Another minute passes and a Syrian shell penetrates the company commander's tank, without causing any damage. As he is thanking his lucky stars, another shell rocks the tank with an enormous bang.

Fire bursts out throughout the tank and then the endless screams begin. The loader jumps out and is shot in the leg. The gunner, with terrible burns, is pulled out by Amnon. The company commander applies his physical strength until he is wounded in his hands by Syrian bullets. Now it is the driver's turn. Amnon helps him out and instructs him to run toward Nafah.

Uzi Mor, the battalion commander, sees the two tanks in front of him bursting into flame and tries to maneuver somehow between the rocks alongside the route. He knows he is in serious danger, and he asks Raful for reinforcements and especially for illumination that will cancel the advantage the Syrian tanks have over them.

The response from the command center is "negative," to both requests, and David Yisraeli, the deputy brigade commander, unaware of the actual situation on the battlefield instructs Uzi, "Continue moving forward and carry out what I instructed you to do (join Ben Shoham)."

As he is wondering how he is supposed to move forward when the two leading tanks in front of him are going up in flames and blocking the route, his turn comes. Uzi Mor is blown out of the tank, he lands on the rocky ground in an aching, bleeding mess.

He is a tough kibbutznik from Ein Shemer and he crawls on what is left of his body away from the tank. He finds a place he feels he can hide and collapses, assessing the damage he has suffered. With one hand cut off and bleeding, almost blind, full of shrapnel in his face and stomach, he feels it is time to let go. Right before he dives into unconsciousness, he suddenly hears the voices of his angels. Asher and Zohar, his crew, find him.

At first, they are horrified to see the blind and crippled battalion commander, but they pull themselves together and support him; in the most excruciating pain, Uzi instructs them, "We need to return to Nafah."

"Where is Nafah?" they ask.

With what remains of his eyesight, he sees the tank silhouette and identifies its rear, "That is the direction."

At the front of the convoy, Amnon Sharon is trying to rescue soldiers from burning tanks. The fire forces him to run into the darkness where he finds an injured platoon commander and a number of additional soldiers.

"Michael," Sharon says to the injured officer. "I am staying here. I will try to find additional soldiers, I will see who can be evacuated and I will take them with me later. In the meantime, run toward Nafah, get reinforcements and be careful not to fire at us when you return."

Sharon is still optimistic. He has seen too many movies and decides that the right thing to do is to replace his destroyed Uzi with the commander's machine gun from the tank. As he is climbing on the tank, a huge blast throws him to the ground and the tank explodes in his face. Sharon drags himself to a pile of rocks nearby and loses consciousness.

"This is probably what they call hell," the bleeding Uzi Mor thinks, while five of his seven tanks burn. Syrian flares light up the sky, exposing the catastrophic site, enabling the Tiran shells, the Sagger missiles and machine guns to hit the tanks and the soldiers of the 266th Battalion. Some of them are injured, others in shell shock, and from just a few hundred meters away, the Syrian fire brings an end to their desperate attempts to flee.

In the back of the line of tanks that were hit, hidden from the enemy fire, the last tank in line is still functioning. Within a few minutes, it becomes the evacuation vehicle. All of the evacuees of C Company and the battalion commander Mor are crowded together inside the tank and on top of it.

As the remains of Uzi Mor's force try to flee from the ambush the 51st Syrian Brigade had set for them on the Petroleum Road, Zvika heads back at full speed, trying to avoid the Syrian forces. As he is withdrawing, one of the tanks in the reserve company accidentally identifies his vehicle as a Tiran tank and fires a shell at him.

Itzik Arnon sees the tank aiming at them and he knows that this is the end. "Hold on tight," he shouts in the internal radio. He sees the ball of fire heading toward them and it feels like the world is falling apart around him and there are sounds of fire in the tank.

With his head above the turret, Zvika takes a powerful blow and his face is burning. Arnon the gunner, fleeing from the flames, crawls out of the tank. Arazi the loader is at the bottom of the tank, the fire is everywhere, catching his coverall. He knows it is now or never and somehow finds the strength to climb up out of the tank.

Two flames, Arazi and Arnon, run from the tank. Zvika also manages to jump off the tank. As he limps away from the burning lump of steel, he realizes that Berkovitch is trapped in the driver's seat. "We have to get him out," he thinks and start heading back to the tank when it suddenly explodes in a terrible ball of fire, turning the driver's compartment into a vast flame.

Zvika joins Arnon and Arazi and the three of them run, falling over, away from the tank, toward the bushes. Suddenly the tank explodes again and they are thrown down to the ground unconscious.

They quickly recover and, confused and helpless, they run toward the Syrian force, until Zvika comes to his senses, directs the crew, and they change their direction and run toward the shadow of a reserve's Sho't Kal, shouting, "Don't fire, we are Israeli!"

In the deputy company commander's tank, the reserve soldiers take their fingers off the triggers and let Zvika get on one of the two tanks that were not hit. Arazi and Arnon get on the other tank that is full of injured soldiers, joining the suffering and moaning soldiers and others that will never see the sun rise again. The tank has trouble finding its way in the dark. With their skin burning, Arnon and Arazi are afraid that this tank they will not get them anywhere. They decide to get off and start running toward Nafah.

The darkness on the Golan is disrupted with lightning and thunder. Arazi and Arnon do not feel the pain, just the paralyzing fear of the unknown, awaiting them behind every rock. However, no one is watching them in the darkness and fear. They continue to run, one kilometer after another, running maybe six or seven kilometers until they reach the fence of the base. As they run, the cold air soothes their burned skin.

A kilometer north of the Mashta junction there are injured and dead soldiers left in the field. Amnon Sharon, the company commander, is unconscious and Zvika Gringold is in the only functioning tank. He is getting used to this. Once again, he is in the tank, commanding the third crew since he left Nafah three hours ago. He makes a short acquaintance with the reserves crewmen he has become commander of. The driver is Arieh Alush, the loader is Yair Levi and Asher Azulai is the gunner. Zvika knows the war is not over for him yet. Injured, burned and in pain under the shadow of death, Gringold reports to Ben Shoham on the latest incidents.

"20 of Tofi, this is the Zvika Force, five of Mor's vehicles have been hit."

"Disengage," Ben Shoham instructs him. "Move back on the Petroleum Road and take a controlling position." After a moment of silence, the brigade commander adds a request. "Don't let any Syrian tank get by you. It is your job to prevent them from heading toward Nafah, until additional forces arrive."

Alone in the dark, Zvika moves five kilometers to the north and takes position to stop the enemy forces near the Eucalyptus grove at Ein Al Kora (2.5 kilometers south of the Nafah base). He knows he is the last line of defense and he is hoping that the Syrian 51st Brigade will not head his way during the night and will settle for their positions at Hushnia.

North Sector – 107

Toward midnight, Shmulik Yachin returns to ramp 107. Gunfire from the infantry outpost ignites an ammunition truck that explodes in an impressive show of light and sound. In the light from the flames and the explosions, Yachin identifies a convoy towing anti-aircraft guns, heading toward the Roman Bridge.

It is like shooting ducks, Yachin thinks, while destroying the guns, as well as a brave Syrian fire truck trying to put out the flames.

Elimelich enjoys watching Yachin and Damir hitting the enemy targets and is sorry when the show ends. As he is wondering how this night will develop, a report comes in from the nearby UN observation post.

"3 of Rekem, take notice," the commander of outpost 107 notifies Yachin. "At the UN building, the same place from where the company you destroyed ascended from this afternoon, there are two Israelis trapped. There apparently also is an injured Syrian soldier with them. Can you evacuate them?"

Yachin does not hesitate. "I am on my way."

He organizes his platoon, curses the darkness again, hopes for the best and heads toward the UN post. At the post he finds a liaison officer and a communication soldier and two UN officers who refuse to hand over the injured Syrian soldier to him. After exchanging a few non-diplomatic clarifications, the Syrian tank driver, one of the few remaining from the company destroyed, is taken onto Vodak's tank.

According to the tradition of calming the enemy with a water canteen, Vodak ensures the prisoner that everything will be okay. Bonamo, Vodak's driver, looks back at the prisoner. "Why are we wasting our time in the middle of a war with prisoners," he complains, making it clear to everyone in the tank what he thinks they should do with the Syrian prisoner.

"Don't hurt him!" Vodak says firmly. He transfers him to outpost 107, moves through the artillery chasing him with terrifying precision and returns "home" to his ramp, where Yachin and Naides are waiting for him.

South Sector – 111

A few minutes before midnight, in his position near the outpost, Aldag hears the continuous sound of Syrian tank tracks heading west into Israeli territory.

They are not trying to conquer the base anymore, he thinks. Why should they waste energy on such unimportant matters, when the road to Hushnia is wide open to them, with the majority of the tanks of their brigade already positioned on the ruins of the Circassian village?

This is the situation, close to midnight. Most of the tanks of the 51st Syrian Brigade are positioned at the Hushnia complex. Walid Hamdon, the brigade commander, is proud of what his forces have achieved. He takes up position behind the leading battalion, identifies the houses of the conquered Hushnia and reconstructs the great moments.

He recalls the message he received that afternoon at the assembly area, hearing the voice of Hassan Turkmany, commander of the 9th Division, with whom he practiced attacking several times. He calmly gave him the command, "Move out, and may Allah be with you."

With great pride he recalls how the brigade moved out in silence in two huge rows. They smoothly moved into company formation, before reaching the anti-tank ditch, just as they had planned and trained for endless times. He thinks of the tanks of the 33rd Brigade that bravely secured the crossing points over the anti-tank ditch and the commander of the 33rd Brigade who recommended, as they planned, to stay away from the Shaf A-Sindiyan infantry outpost and take the wide area south of it.

Then they split into platoons and reached their attack lines, and waited for the thick darkness, their best ally. They moved in the night without lights, coming all this way with hardly any resistance.

Hamdon reports small Israeli forces fighting his advance battalion and receives a report that they were destroyed. He does not believe that anyone will stop him, just as was planned in the order he received from Turkmany and transferred to his soldiers, according to which in six hours, before the reserve forces of the enemy could arrive on the Golan, the first of his tanks will be deployed on the Jordan River crossings

Shortly before midnight, outpost 111 has become an enclave in conquered Syrian territory.

Yuval Shachar, the intelligence officer, and Avi Grinfeld, the medic, join the action. Shachar goes back to being an infantry officer, helping the outpost commander to direct fire from the trenches and sharing the responsibility for defending the hill. Grinfeld is working nonstop in the bunker. He tells himself to disconnect from the sights, work automatically, just as he was taught at the medic's course and in the days of combat.

Without any assistance from another medic, Grinfeld gets a group of healthy soldiers, led by the calm Henry Vidal, to help him with the IVs and personal dressings. He tries to smile at everyone, calming and encouraging them. He strengthens supports, reties bandages and keeps himself from bursting into tears when Zvi Mansbach, with an amputated knee, with his pulse disappearing and his stomach hard as a rock, asks for a Coke as he fades away.

It is Grinfeld and a number of injured tank and infantry soldiers, or crewmen without tanks getting organized for a long night in the bunker, with so many unanswered questions in the air.

Open Questions

At this point, a handful of young men are trying desperately – with their last strength – to stop the seemingly endless Syrian tsunami of forces, with Syrian tanks parked unmolested at Hushnia, soon to threaten the bunker at Nafah. With the first reserves soldiers slaughtered on the Petroleum Road and the rest of the reserve forces still far from the Golan, it is time to ask the harsh and unresolved questions.

Regarding the Northern Command, the night of October 6–7 can be split into two phases:

From darkness to midnight – the phase in which the Command estimated that the battle in the southern Golan was on the front lines.

From midnight on – the phase in which the Command estimated there was a deep Syrian breach of the southern front toward the Kinneret, as the main effort.

In retrospect, we can say that the estimates of the Command were wrong twice.

First, the Syrians broke through the front line long before midnight. Wide areas of the Golan were conquered by the Syrian forces even before 22:00.

Second, the concern the Command expressed, that the Syrian force was concentrating its main effort on heading toward the Kinneret, was also wrong. The movement toward the Kinneret was only secondary; the main Syrian effort was in the central Golan, the spearhead sent out toward Nafah.

This double mistake of the Northern Command joins a series of even more significant mistakes. The strange thing is that they took place under the command of Yitzchak Hofi, Haka, the Northern Command General. During his term, the emergency warehouse units were moved to the front lines, endless access roads to the Golan were prepared, the ramps were improved, inventories filled, procedures renewed, there were clear indications of war and the mines were laid out. That, of all people, he was the one to make these mistakes and mislead many others with him was more than ironic.

When the clock showed midnight, the Golan was soaked with the blood of tens of soldiers who were killed and hundreds injured. They thought they were fighting in another routine combat day and that they would be going home in the evening. What happened there that confused the leaders and sent the young men to their deaths?

The intelligence failure was huge and responsible for terrible difficulties that were cast on the soldiers of the 188th Brigade as they were heading to the ramps, but this should not diminish or cover up the shameful failure of the Northern Command, directly responsible for a series of inconceivable and unresolved mistakes.

Why wasn't it openly called "war?"

Can anyone explain how it is possible that none of the soldiers of the 188th Brigade, not a single one all through the Golan, knew they were going to war?

Ephraim Yosef the gunner, Yitzchak Nagarkar the loader, Aharon Kapoon the driver, Bekman the platoon commander, Landau the company commander, Yair Nafshi and Oded Erez, the battalion commanders, and all the other soldiers with them, none of them were prepared for war. They were ready for a combat day, at the most a small attack, as they had experienced or heard about before.

How can we explain that in the crucial orders given at 10:00, facing the senior commanders convened at the Nafah headquarters, Haka did not stand before them, as their general, and declare: "We are going to war gentlemen, war?"

But Hagai Mann, the intelligence officer of the Northern Command at the time, sits in my office thirty-five years later, looks me in the eye and says, "From 5:30 on, the only word on Haka's lips was war. Those who did not want to hear it did not hear it."

"I have no explanation why most of the commanders were prepared for a combat day," Haka would say later to the Agranat inquiry committee. "I cannot say with confidence that every soldier knew there was going to be war, but the brigade commanders received the order personally."

Is that so?

Wouldn't it be natural for the field commanders to shout "war" with all their might, had they heard in their orders that there was going to be war? How is it possible that three brigade commanders receive their orders, in which Haka says clearly that he announced there was a war, yet do not notify their subordinates of what they just heard? Wouldn't they have said, "Battalion commanders, it is final, war is right around the corner?"

> *At 11:30 I received an order from the Operations Officer of the Line brigade (820th Regional Brigade) to prepare for artillery shelling at 13:00... I was sitting at Tel Abu Nida (Avital) reading the newspaper... I think that at 15:00 or 16:00 I heard on the radio that the Egyptians crossed the Suez Canal. I immediately said, guys, there is a war here. Before anyone told me, I knew there was a war.*

> (Lt. Col. Zeev Unger, commander of the Golani 13th Battalion,
> in charge of the outposts on the northern sector,
> in his testimony before the Agranat committee)

> *...Today we are expecting something... increase the anti-aircraft alert...I was not told war.*

> (Lt. Col. Oded Erez, commander of 53rd battalion, in his
> testimony before Col. Nevo, Agranat sub-committee)

> *...I told everyone "Capital," the code for taking position and the start of a combat day. Who knew there was a war? How was I supposed to know?*

> (Lt. Col. Yair Nafshi, commander of the 74th Battalion, in his
> testimony before Col. Nevo, Agranat sub-committee)

> *The last time I was updated was at the Nafah command center, on Friday. I was told that, in light of the massive increasing of the forces on the Syrian side, we were expecting a "big" combat day, in which the Syrians will probably try to conquer one of the outposts. There was no talk of full-scale war.*

> (Lieutenant Col. Shraga Ben Zvi, commander of the 55th
> Artillery Battalion, in an interview with me)

What about the battalion commanders of the 7th Brigade? In testimonies two of them gave to the Agranat committee, it appears that

Yanush did use the term "war." Loud and clear. Did Yanush hear Haka say "war?"

Looking back after many years, Yanush still recalls the events that preceded the war and is confident and clear about the question of "was the word 'war' used or not?"

From the moment the air force planes shot down the MiGs and the 7th Brigade companies started to move to the Golan, it was clear to me that this time it was heading toward war. That was why I sent the brigade tactical command group to the Golan when the alert started, although formally the companies belonged to Ben Shoham.

As the days passed and it came closer to Yom Kippur, I knew I was right. My motto, all throughout the alert period, in briefings and in my orders, was "We are heading toward war." On Friday, when I was told to send the entire brigade on flights and deploy them in silence in the assembly areas, when I received updated intelligence information showing that the entire Syrian army was near the border and that the missiles were moved forward, when the "lock" order was given all through the IDF, when Defense Readiness Condition C was declared for the first time since the Six-Day War... Do me a favor; what does all this indicate, I asked myself, if not war?

On Friday I was 99.99 percent sure that there was going to be a war the next day, and I briefed the headquarters and the battalion commanders accordingly on Saturday morning, before the orders received at Nafah, that we are going to war.

Later on, when I came to receive the orders at Nafah, Haka was not clear and decisive and his message was ambivalent. It was not clear from him that we were going to war. At the end of the orders at Nafah and regardless of what was said there, the final sliver of doubt that this was war disappeared...not that I needed such proof. When we left Nafah, Raful stopped me and said – probably because he received the order to recruit his reserve brigades – "Yanush, there is going to be a war. Is your brigade ready?" "Yes sir," I answered. "The brigade has been ready for war for a week already.

His soldiers testified that Yanush predicted, "war next week," every week beginning on the seventh day of the Six-Day War. Yanush constantly prophesied war, because he never believed the calming messages from the General Staff. He felt that the generals from the generation that had beaten the enemy in the Six-Day War suffered from arrogance. As a veteran of the War of Attrition, Yanush had watched the Egyptian army renew itself, improve and intensify, and he was always saying it was just a matter of time before the Arabs would try to destroy us again. There is no way they would sit quietly after the way we beat them in the Six-Day War. They still suffered the disgrace of losing their "motherland," a sacred value to them.

On Saturday, Yanush was sure this was the real thing. His combat instinct told him that although he had "cried wolf" for years, this time there really was a wolf. When, on Saturday morning, he declared "war today," he was not doing so as a result of anything he heard at the Nafah headquarters. There, between 10:30 and 11:00 he did not hear the word "war."

How was it that Ben Shoham did not "feel" the war approaching them? Why didn't he shout the warning to his battalion commanders, like Yanush did?

Ben Shoham may have "felt" it, but as an officer educated in the "straight line" school of soldiering, he did not let his personal whims control his actions. An order was an order, an instruction was an instruction. He never tried to take shortcuts or bypass orders he did not like. Ben Shoham always did what he was ordered to and did not do what he was not ordered to. He was a soldier in uniform. He might have been a colonel and a brigade commander but he was still a soldier, making sure to stick to the orders he received from the Northern Command General. Since the orders did not say war, neither did Ben Shoham.

Why didn't they say "war" at the command center at Nafah?

Of course there is the possibility that Haka, the man who never lost his cool, a relaxed Palmach fighter with nerves of steel, did not *shout* "war" but said it quietly, so quietly that none of the brigade commanders got the message.

One thing that significantly supports this explanation – the misleading subdued tone – has to do with the assessment of the Intelligence Branch that there would be no war. This assessment was present in the General Staff and continued to be present on Saturday, even after the warning from Babylon was received.

Haka came to the General Staff meeting early in the morning and met Zeira, who did not appear to be concerned about the warning from the Mossad. He continued to stick with his position that Egypt and Syria had no reason to go to war. If the national assessor keeps repeating, including on Saturday morning, that there is no reason for Egypt and Syria to go to war, it may make more sense to keep a low profile and only say "war" to the brigade commanders in a subdued tone.

If they knew there was going to be war, why didn't the Northern Command prepare properly?

Did they not say "war," or did they say it but quietly, or did they say it loudly and the three brigade commanders just did not listen? Whatever the explanation, the question still remains: Why didn't the Northern Command take the necessary precautions, knowing there was going to be a war?

Why wasn't everything on the Golan set up and prepared from 5:30 on Saturday morning? What was the Northern Command General waiting for, after being notified on the phone before sunrise on Saturday that this time the Syrian forces were going all the way? He knew they were on the border, right on the doorstep of the Zionist homeland, waiting for the great attack to the west.

Why didn't the General take immediate operative action to prepare for war?

What happened at the Northern Command following the early hours on Saturday? Very little, considering "war" was coming. There was an order to add three to five soldiers to each of the infantry outposts. Another order given to the regional brigade was to start preparing the civilians on the Golan for evacuation. Mines were laid at the Quneitra gap (beginning the night before). That was it. Quite a lot, even enough, if this was going to be a combat day, artillery fire, or an attempt to conquer a base or a town. It was totally insufficient if they were preparing for war.

If the General had shouted war, as he was told, and instructed his forces, "Change of plans! What we are facing is not a combat day, it is war. **Prepare immediately for holding the line of defense**" – if he had

318

done this, it is reasonable to assume that the forces would have prepared in a more appropriate, professional and knowledgeable manner.

The General did not have to invent anything from scratch. On Saturday morning when he was notified of the war, he knew that in the command vault there was a defense plan called "Gir" (Limestone) that could have offered a better response for the entire front. On Saturday the Northern Command had a force very close to the size needed for the Gir plan. Yet Haka did not act according to the new situation and the plan he had. He did not allocate forces, define missions and launch tactical command groups. The Northern Command continued to act as if this was a combat day, maybe bigger, but still a combat day.

The Northern Command General had the authority to evaluate the Gir plan and decide it was not the right plan for that time. But we still need to ask: What caused the General, who had signed the plan just a few months earlier, prepared exactly for the scenario developing, to suddenly decide that the Gir plan was not good for him?

Even if we assume that he was convinced that the Gir plan was irrelevant, why did he not take other significant measures on the ground?

The Northern Command General heard from the Chief of General Staff that they were going to war. He knew of his efforts to mobilize the entire reserve force and carry out a preventive strike. He knew that the first reserve soldiers would not arrive till night; he was well aware of the ratio of the enemy forces to his forces. Nonetheless, he still did not instruct the brigade commanders to prepare differently? How can we explain this?

An hour after the orders given at Nafah, Haka was called back to the General Staff. Now it was clear to him, according to the agreement between him and the Chief of General Staff, that the preemptive strike had not been approved by the Prime Minister and they were heading toward a ground war. Yet, even then he did not change the preparations.

How is it possible that the Northern Command General traveled to Hakiryah in Tel Aviv, leaving the northern front to defend itself and the Galilee and the entire country, with the initial ratio of the forces of 6:1?

Even if we set aside the command strategy and operational orders and proper deployment of the forces, there is no doubt that if an anonymous messenger came to the forward tank depot of the 188th Brigade on Saturday morning and notified the battalion and company commanders of the upcoming war, the soldiers would have been spared at least some of the chaos they experienced on the ramps.

The battalion commanders would have issued an order to immediately distribute the night vision equipment. Also, the medical, ammunition and supplies units would have prepared for a long battle, taken supplies and deployed for war.

In addition to improving the physical situation of the forces, there is also great importance to the psychological aspect of knowing what to expect. The knowledge that they were heading for war, and not a combat day, would have eliminated the surprise and strengthened the mental state and preparedness of the forces.

The 188th Brigade soldiers arrived to the ramps lacking basic knowledge regarding the enemy's intentions. The most basic rules of the game were hidden from them. This surprise had a cost, and a very severe one.

So how can it be?

On October 7, the day after the war broke out, the *Maariv* newspaper had a large headline, "The IDF Knew the Time of the Attack but Diplomatic Consideration Determined Not to Launch a Preventive Strike."

The article stated:

> *Following discussion and evaluation, the top officials decided, in agreement with the Defense Minister and the military officials, to prefer the diplomatic considerations over the military considerations and not to be the first to open fire. The diplomatic interest was given precedence, casting extreme military difficulties on us, in order for it to be clear who initiated and who decided to renew the war. Since the Arab radio stations had been reporting in the last few days that Israel was planning to invade Syria, reserves were just starting to be mobilized in the last few hours, in order to make it impossible for the Arabs to claim they opened fire to prevent Israeli attack.*

The article in *Maariv* reflects only part of the truth, that which was convenient to sell to the naïve public in the 1970s. Not a word was written about the military, led by Chief of General Staff David Elazar, insisting that there is a need for a preemptive air strike and mobilization of the reserves. There was no mention of the "intelligence conception" that continued to mislead most people.

Furthermore, what did the article say about the implications of this decision for the regular army? "The diplomatic interest was given precedence, casting extreme military difficulties on us."

"On us" – they took the difficulties on themselves? "Military difficulties," that is what they called what happened? This was doubly wrong. First of all, the decision made it difficult for the soldiers, not them. Second, if you were to ask the soldiers of Avi Ronis and Uri Akavia, the outstanding company commanders of the 188th Brigade, who were no longer living when this article was written, they would agree that they had, indeed, encountered "military difficulties" on the ramps. However, a more accurate description would have been "hell itself."

The late Zeev Schiff, the *Haaretz* military correspondent and analyst for almost fifty years, wrote the following in one of his articles on the Yom Kippur War:

> *...amazing things have been written about the negative symbiosis between the military and political leaders, in which they decided to hide the fact that there was a real chance of war. The writer and journalist Hanoch Bar Tov showed this in his articles and Dado's biography. Part of the cabinet met with a number of generals. Prime Minister Golda Meir conducted the meeting and they decided to hide from the Americans and the rest of the government that there is a real probability that Egypt will launch a war. The concern was that this danger would cause the Americans to apply pressure on Israel to reach an agreement requiring serious concessions. The military commanders, including the Chief of General Staff and the heads of intelligence, witnessed the decision not to tell the other ministers all the important details, misleading them. This is just one of the strange occurrences prior to the war, indicating the nature of the government at that time.*

Zeev Schiff and Hanoch Bar Tov took it a step further and determined that the leaders knew there was going to be a war – but not only did they fail to act, but for different reasons they hid this information from the majority of the Israeli government ministers and the American administration.

Now to my own addition. I have gone through the *Maariv* articles since October 1973 and Zeev Schiff's articles and other sources, and I did not find an explanation for a much more troubling question: Why didn't the 188th Brigade soldiers know?

They did not notify the Americans. They did not notify the ministers. They decided not to carry out a preemptive strike, not to mobilize the reserve forces and to cause "military difficulties" for the field soldiers and commanders. But why didn't anyone notify the soldiers on the front lines, at least the northern front, that a war is about to break out at 18:00?

Or, to ask the same question from a wider angle, how is it possible that the senior government officials knew, while the front line soldiers and commanders did not?

How is it possible that for ten hours, from the time the warning came of "war at 18:00," from the Mossad's most important source, a warning that led to continuous pressure from Chief of General Staff Elazar, with the entire country, the air force and reserve divisions preparing for war, they "forgot" to update the army on the Golan and on the Canal?

I am not a man who believes in conspiracies. All the soldiers I interviewed for this book can confirm this. Yet still, since I do not have a moral, clear answer to the questions raised here, I allow myself to continue what Zeev Schiff implied regarding the improper conduct of the government and ask out loud:

- Is it possible that someone up at the top consciously decided to lower the temperature of the war warnings to the regular army?
- If so, was this due to the concern that such a warning would lead to problematic events in the field. For example, "Let's reorganize the forces in a better manner to stop the enemy."
- Could such changes, on the ground, undermine the intention of the enemy armies to attack Israel?
- Was the possible cancellation of the military confrontation what caused the Israeli leaders to worry that their plan for the final blow to the enemy armies was jeopardized?

- Was it the vision of "the big Israeli kingdom," reaching the outskirts of Cairo and Damascus and granting forty years of peace, that led the leaders to prevent the information from the military on the front lines?
- Was there anyone who instructed the senior commanders, the Command Generals – Haka for example – not to shout "war" too loud, not to cause unnecessary waves? Were they aware that they would be sacrificing the soldiers of the 188th Brigade and others?

Will we ever know?

Sunday, October 7 – From Midnight to First Light

During the next five hours, without any advance warning, history was leading decision makers toward what would be one of the greatest shocks Israel had known.

Their smugness and self-satisfaction – perceiving the Israeli army as powerful and invariably victorious – did not serve them well when the sun rose over the Golan the following morning at 05:35.

The defenders of the Golan, boys in khaki uniforms, were once again going to pay for the negligence of their leaders. Those leaders who were unprepared and had not acknowledged the extent of the anger in Syria and Egypt against Israel for "stealing" their land. Those leaders who did not comprehend the Arab determination to rebuild their forces and saw the Arab soldier as an object of ridicule, not as the equal enemy he was.

00:00

Brigade Commander's Force

A few minutes past midnight, and the situation perceived in the 188th Brigade tactical command group ACP is horrifying. The Syrian forces were on Tel Saki, Hushnia, near base 116 and had just slaughtered an artillery battery near Juhader.

First Lt. Sefi Ben Yosef, the brigade reconnaissance officer, looks at Ben Shoham, his admired commander, and sees him holding his head in his hands. Two minutes pass and Ben Shoham regains composure and loses the temporary signs of depression. He knows that if he wants to continue running this battle, he will need to keep the command group alive and the only option they have is to move, as fast as they can, heading west toward the large step, to the cliffs where streams rush toward the Kinneret. "Take us to the Waterfalls Route," he commands Ben Yosef.

Anderman's War

With Ben Shoham's sharp message etched into his mind, 2nd Lt. Hanan Anderman realizes that the horror he witnessed at the massacre of B Battery may be just the first of additional lethal confrontations in store for him. He calmly departs from the 188th Brigade commander and heads south.

"We are going," Anderman tells his soldiers and sees the fear on their faces.

As Hanan Anderman is gathering what remains of his inner strength, in order to continue their escape, Dror Sofer, the carrier commander, suddenly realizes that Shlomo may have been one of Anderman's soldiers left behind dead. Is it possible that Shlomo, always content, wise, amusing, the best friend he ever had, is lying there not far from Juhader, his body frozen in his final position of death?

Then he is back to the carrier, immersed in the sea of radio nets and, from time to time, in his mind's eye he sees the smiling face of Shlomo Teichman, his classmate at the educational institute in Kibbutz Gan Shmuel, his friend that went to the artillery corps when he went to the armor. Shlomo, who only a few hours ago had surprised him with an emotional meeting while passing through Nafah. "I have to continue, Dror," looking at Dror with his smiling baby face, not waiting for an answer, adding "they are waiting for me at the battery, we'll meet by six o'clock after the war," and he turned his back and disappeared.

A short distance after turning around on the Water route, Anderman finds a path leading west. He is still not sure this is the right way. He jumps out of the halftrack carrier, hesitates and decides this is the path they will take.

The moon is no longer in the sky and it is completely dark. Anderman's eyes are trying to pick out the route and they continue further west, then turn north and he identifies that they are on the Nachal Geshor route that will lead them safely "home." While he is enjoying the satisfaction of finding the main route, he suddenly identifies a Syrian force of tanks and armored personnel carriers right in front of them.

"Jump out of the vehicles," he shouts.

They manage to run fifty meters when machine gunfire opens at them. Moshe Zimmerman, the outstanding athlete, is fatally injured (during the long night he died, the 15th casualty of B Battery).

South Sector – Forward Tank Depot 116

Sometime after midnight, at Forward Tank Depot 116, between Juhader and Tel Saki, Mordechai Ukavi, the medic, regains consciousness and is overwhelmed with joy. The parking area is full of tanks and he is going to see which battalion they are from, maybe they are from his company.

The area is in ruins, the ground is full of pits created by shells, and suddenly a tall soldier from one of the tanks appears in front of him, wearing a strange coverall. *"Mumchan fi sigra mach?"* the figure asks in the dark. Ukavi's blood freezes and he bends down, pretending to tie his shoe. He takes his Uzi in his hands and aims it at the tall Syrian soldier. He runs back to his friends shouting. Now it is Ukavi's turn to run but tens of Syrian soldiers block his path, grab him, passing him from hand to hand, beating him repeatedly. The Syrian soldiers kick him repeatedly, and when he is about to pass out, suddenly the torture stops. Why did it stop, the suffering Ukavi wonders? He prays to his God, asks for his forgiveness for leaving Him during his military service, begging Him to save his life.

00:24

Nafah

At 00:24, the command group at Nafah finally understands the situation.

"Fifty Syrian tanks are entering 116. We do not have any tanks there," someone writes in the Command operations log. Now, at Nafah, they finally understand what the soldiers on the battlefield have known since 21:00. This report, however, refers to sector 116, and therefore they need to first put out the flame started there. Uri Simchoni speaks to Yanush and for the third time since the war began, he instructs him to transfer a battalion to the command of Ben Shoham.

At 00:26, Simchoni notifies Ben Shoham that he will soon be

receiving a battalion from Yanush's force that will be under his command, in order to take care of sector 116.

At 00:27, the Northern Command General decides to do everything in his power to prevent the southern front from falling. Within a few minutes, he speaks to the Chief of General Staff and asks for support from the air force because "there we have no more forces on the ground and we cannot stop [the enemy]."

Two minutes pass and the Head of Operations section in the general staff notifies the command group at Nafah that it won't be possible to receive air support.

No air force? So all we can do is send in whatever forces we have and all we have is Yanush.

Haka puts down the phone and contacts Yanush, ordering him, in continuation of the order he received from Simchoni three minutes earlier, to immediately transfer the force to Ben Shoham's front. Yanush listens patiently to the General, explains that he is still in bad shape and cannot transfer forces to Ben Shoham.

The same thing that happened before happens again. The Command wants Yanush to send a force to Ben Shoham. Yanush convinces them he can't, just as he did before. Things are not bad on Yanush's front, certainly not as bad as on the southern front, but still the General postpones carrying out the order. By the end of the night no one will remember the order that was rejected and the Command abandons the southern front. They will have to manage with whatever they have. It is the same story all over again.

Brigade Commander's Force

Dror Sofer, the armored personnel carrier commander, does not know where they are going. "Drive here," he drives here. "Drive there," he drives there. They stop occasionally; turn off the engine and listen, trying to identify who is out there in the dark. Dror looks at the brigade commander in the carrier and his heart breaks. Just yesterday Ben Shoham had a glorious brigade. When the war started, he was appointed commander of the entire Golan front. Look at him now.

The brigade tanks are scattered all over the front, some with him, some with Yanush. The ones with him are crushed and the artillery is after them, and Oded Erez the battalion commander sounds so defeated.

Dror, just a tank commander from the Golan C Company, suddenly close to his "God," the brigade commander himself, has been with Ben Shoham for over six hours. He hears the words of encouragement he says to Erez, identifies his endless effort to support his forces and wonders, who will support my brigade commander?

00:43
Nafah
Now it is Raful's turn, the man who has ice flowing in his veins instead of blood, to show that he understands how serious the situation is. He instructs Menachem Aviram (Mann), his deputy, to send tank platoons to the Arik Bridge, to block the Syrian forces from heading into the Galilee.

00:45
The terrible news that Hushnia has fallen finally reaches the Northern Command. In the Command operations log it is written that "in the Hushnia area there are around twenty enemy tanks."

00:47
"Ben Shoham is taking on the force at Hushnia with a battalion," this was what was registered in the operations log. Ben Shoham? Leading a battalion to Hushnia? It seems that the situation is still unclear to the command group at Nafah and the fog of war is still blinding the commanders.

01:00
Yoram Yair (Ya-Ya), the commander of the Nahal Battalion, reports to the Nafah headquarters, "The entire 116 area is 'polluted' with Syrian tanks."

The Reserves are coming – 679/The Yotzer Force
Shortly before 01:00, at the Yiftach/Korazim war reserve storage base,

Nitzan Yotzer, the energetic deputy company commander from the 679th Brigade commanded by Col. Ori Or, has just finished loading two thirds of the shells onto four of his company tanks.

He lifts his eyes from the tank and spots the brigade commander gesturing to him to approach him. "The Yehudiya-Katzabiya-Hushnia route has been breached," Ori Or the new brigade commander says, looking Nitzan in the eyes. "Take the four tanks and head up the route as fast as you can, to block any Syrian attempt to head toward the Kinneret. As you are moving, contact the 188th Brigade – they are not answering – and see how you can join their efforts to block the enemy."

Nitzan still does not understand the extent of the catastrophe and he tries to go to battle the way he was taught. "Commander," he turns to Ori Or, "just let me complete filling the tank with ammunition."

Or looks at the young officer and realizes that he still doesn't understand they are in a state of emergency, "The Syrians don't know how much ammunition you have. There is no time. Move out."

Brigade Commander's force

At around 01:00, after driving by night through a rocky black area, hitting the basalt rocks and being thrown around wildly, an APC and a tank reach the Waterfalls Route and take position north of Tel Bezek.

Ben Shoham hears Erez again, reporting with a broken voice that there are endless convoys heading west and that his forces do not have control of the front. Without any artillery available, the commander of the 188th Brigade tries to get him air support. He knows that in such situations there is an agreement between the air force and ground forces. Even if there are not continuous waves of attack, at least one air strike, even if it does not destroy the Syrian force, will at least lift their spirits. The aerial support officer, Moty Hod, has a very limited number of planes, however, and they are ineffective at night. Also, the main effort of the air force at that time was destroying targets in Sinai.

Nafah

At around 01:00 there is consensus at Nafah regarding the catastrophe on the southern front. The fact that the Syrian forces have broken through the defense line poses a threat to Israel, also west of the Jordan River. The weak spot is the Hushnia-Mashta-Katzabiya area. The tanks of the Syrian 51st Brigade – or maybe these are the tanks of the 46th Brigade – are heading west from the Mashta junction. It is just a matter of time before they "release their brakes" and slide all the way down to the Kinneret.

Haka applies pressure to Raful, who in turn pressures his deputy, who pressures the brigade commanders, who pressure the battalion commanders, who pressure the company commanders to speed up the preparation of their forces. "Send up even a tank platoon, just get going already," Raful implores them.

01:21

As the situation deteriorates, Moty Hod, the commander of the aerial support group of the Northern Command, contacts the Air Force command and asks that with first daylight, the air force allocates a significant force to the southern Golan front.

01:30

Assessing the huge change in balance developing in front of him as he listens to the reports on the radios, Haka packs up his things and gets up heavily, with the rest of the command staff. This is not a combat day, this is war. In war, the command headquarters is supposed to be in Tzfat.

He goes over to Raful, shakes his hand, gives him a courageous look and says calmly, "Raful, I am going to Mt. Kana'an. I wish you all the best."

Raful, not a man who needs a long process to take control, pulls the map over to him without any expression and takes over the command of the Golan front.

South Sector – Barak

For Barak and Geva, it is business as usual. It is completely silent. There are no Syrian forces approaching from the west or the east. Ben Shoham's plan to push the Syrians east, where Zvika's force would be the hammer and Barak's the anvil, does not materialize.

It is peaceful at the junction and Barak decides to check what the company's status is. "Half a tank," the tank commanders report. "What about ammunition?" Two platoons have almost nothing and the third has half. Barak updates Ben Shoham. There are no Syrian tanks. There is no ammunition. He requests approval to head north, to resupply the tanks. Ben Shoham approves and instructs him to come to the foot of Tel Yosifun, where he will send the supplies convoy.

02:00
The Reserves are coming – 679/The Yotzer Force
On his way to block the Syrian forces, at the gate of the Naftali war reserve storage base, Nitzan Yotzer loses a quarter of his force. One of the four tanks in the convoy is malfunctioning and must be left behind. With three tanks, led by the jeep of the reconnaissance company, deputy company commander Yotzer proceeds to the road leading up to the Golan. He parts from the unit and starts climbing up toward the unknown.

At around 2:00, a short distance after the famous Kacha cattle farm in the middle of the way to the Waterfalls Route, Nitzan – a fighter of the heroic unit 101 – sees a large fire. As he gets closer to the light, he is horrified to see that the source of the fire is a convoy of Israeli trucks. He sees what is going on but it does not quite sink in, and he continues to move into the area of light, like a calf led to the slaughterhouse. He moves forward, when suddenly a number of shells are fired at him from the right.

Yotzer flees back into the darkness and tries to return fire toward the flashes on the right, but without night vision and having failed to boresight his weapons, it is useless. The three tanks take position behind a hill, hoping they are hidden from the enemy, and pray the night will soon be replaced by day.

02:25
South Sector – Training base 9
Artillery battery C of Training Base 9, positioned at the foot of Tel Fares, receives the order to "temporarily hold fire." The battery, made up of soldiers in artillery courses and their instructors, is under the direction

of the battalion commander Lt. Col. Ben Ami Cohen. He is positioned at the top of Tel Fares, with the tactical command group. Until midnight the battery had fired continuously at the points where the Syrian forces were breaking through and also assisted the outposts that were under attack.

Toward midnight, Shmil Golan, the deputy battalion commander who was on his way to the battery with the supplies convoy, had notified them that he did not know when he will be able to join them. At around 02:00, the battery fires its last shells. Without an open line of supplies, receiving information that Syrian tanks have penetrated and are west of them, they hear the tracks close to them and the battery reports its situation. The battery is given the order to stop firing. They know they need to withdraw, as soon as possible.

02:46

Northern Command

As a result of the Syrian penetration in the southern front, the Northern Command issues an order to immediately evacuate all the remaining civilians from the Golan.

On May 31, 1973, a plan had been drawn up by the Northern Command to evacuate the women and children from the Golan. In order to prevent arguing and confrontation, the civilians were not notified. Who thought there would actually ever be a need to evacuate civilians from the Golan?

The internal document of the Northern Command specified the order of action after the decision to evacuate the civilians was made. However, no one bothered to think it through, to plan and determine what the role of the civilian settlements would be during war. Would they stay? Be evacuated? Everyone? Take part in the defense? Be supported by soldiers?

There was no orderly plan, yet still the matter of the settlements on the Golan concerned military and government officials. In a number of government and General Staff meetings, in the state of alert prior to the war, there was great concern regarding the possibility of a Syrian attack on the Golan and its implications to the safety of the civilians. There was no operational decision or instructions to the Northern Command. It was just registered that there was concern.

On the eve of Yom Kippur, in response to the inquiry of Prime Minister Golda Meir, regarding the readiness of the settlements on the Golan, the Chief of Staff said, "They are ready. We will not send them to the shelters. They are all at home and there is no need for special preparations."

On Saturday morning Dayan suggested immediately evacuating the children from the Golan. "There are just thirty children on the Golan," he said. "We will suggest that the settlements send the children on a trip. Any women who wish to join, will join." The Prime Minister approved Dayan's suggestion and determined that it should be an order, not a suggestion.

On Saturday morning, when Haka returned to the Nafah headquarters from the General Staff meeting, he gave the order to start evacuating women and children from the Golan. The order was not received well. The Golan settlements, unaware of the clouds of war approaching them, refused to part from their women and children. "This is our home. You do not abandon your home."

Due to this resistance, Haka himself, with the little time he had before he was to return to the General Staff in Tel Aviv, had to function as the national spokesman, standing before the civilians of the community of Marom Golan and trying to convince them to agree to the evacuation. "Alright," they said to him, a few minutes before he left for Tel Aviv. "We understand but still, we don't like it."

Just before he left, Haka decided that the role of civilian liaison was perfect for Zvi Bar, the commander of the 820th Regional Brigade, and he sent him to deal with the civilians.

Bar had his work cut out for him. He traveled from settlement to settlement, initiated community assemblies, and implored them to stop their "rebellion" and to cooperate with the army. "We will not leave," "We will not be evacuated," they shouted at him, singing Palmach songs and booing.

The result was that a few hours after the war broke out, there were still women and children in the Golan settlements.

By 4:00, riding in Peugeot and Susita pick-up trucks with their lights on to prevent "friendly fire," all of the civilians were evacuated from the Golan, including Kibbutz Ramat Magshimim, as the enemy forces were closing in on it. They left behind homes, a vision, Zionism and astonishment.

03:00 – 04:00

As they were getting ready at the headquarters at Mt. Kana'an, Haka repeated his request from the General Staff for immediate air support with daylight, intended to cover the reserve forces arriving at the Golan.

The construction work on the new command base on Mt. Kana'an was in process and the war started when it was still in the middle of construction, surprising the contractors in Tzfat.

Since Nafah was not safe and Nazareth inefficient, the Northern Command headquarters had no choice but to borrow the cinema complex in the police recreation center and turn it into the headquarters overnight.

When the commanders arrived at their designated headquarters, they found a standard cinema hall, with its crowded rows of seats, a purple curtain and a big, stained screen that had seen better days.

Haka was given one of the booths, and there on a hard bed and two plastic chairs, he is ready to receive guests and is given continuous updates from his men in the cinema hall.

A large map of the Golan is spread out on a stand. Yossi Nissim, the Command communications officer, completes the installation of the radio equipment. Never-ending clouds of cigarette smoke rise up high to the ceiling, breaking into thin lines in the dim light. Simchoni, Mann, Kayam, Bar-David and others, the Northern Command headquarters, are sitting on the cinema benches and feel like they are in the horror film of their lives.

South Sector – 114

Toward 3:00, dozing off in his tank, Avi Lahman suddenly hears the rumble of unknown tracks. A few hours have passed since he was sent back to his original position, near outpost 114, and his frustration keeps increasing. Over twelve hours have passed since the war began and the three tanks of his platoon are still almost full of ammunition. Lahman knows that the few shells they fired when they were in sector 113, were fired to distant targets and were ineffective. The reality frustrates him – twelve hours of war and he cannot mark his gun barrel. Is it the fate of his platoon to return "from this thing" empty handed?

Then he hears the tracks behind him and his ears determine that it is the sound of Syrian Tirans. Lahman turns his platoon around and they aim their cannons west.

Seven hours after Yoav Yakir, 3rd platoon leader, was killed in face-to-face battles with tens of Syrian tanks in outpost 116, ten hours after the death of Avi Ronis, the company commander at sector 115, twelve hours after Brinberg, the 2nd platoon sergeant, was fatally injured on the Petroleum Road, 1st platoon Venus Company joins the real fighting, for the first time since the war started.

Lahman positions his three tanks parallel to the road that leads to the outpost and they all shut off their engines and listen in the dark for the enemy approaching. As he is wondering where the enemy will come from, two Tirans appear from around the bend and stop five meters from the platoon. They flash their lights, trying to communicate with their "Syrian brothers."

"Fire!" Lahman shouts and dives into the tank. The Sho't Kal tank that is located a bit higher than the Tiran, fires and misses.

"Load whatever you have," Lahman screams. "I can't see the shells," Shitrit the loader complains. Finally, he sees and loads a shell and Lahman lowers the cannon and they fire. Screams in Arabic come from the burning tank next to them.

The second Tiran turns right, directly in front of the cannon of Shimon Cohen, the platoon sergeant.

"Fire!" he shouts. Berger the gunner cannot see a thing but fires anyway, and lights up another torch in the dark night.

Southern/Central Sector – Tiger

As the Barak force completes its move and takes position at the foot of the Yosifun hills, waiting for the supplies convoy, it is another company of the 82nd Battalion that blocks the persistent Syrian effort to expand their control in the Golan.

Shortly after 02:00, a tank commander from Chessner's company, in his damaged tank beneath outpost 111, identifies movement of an armored Syrian force coming from Tel Kudna. Through the thick darkness, he sees the force head north.

Chessner receives the report and passes the hot potato to Yanush, who instructs Zamir, his brigade reserve company, originally from the 82nd Battalion, to head to the boundary area between the 7th and the 188th Brigades, report to Ben Shoham and block the armored force.

Toward 03:00, Zamir (Tiger on the radio) positions himself in an ambush position, at the Reshet-Katakumba junction, south of 109 outpost and north of 110. The outcome is clear. Like cows taken to the slaughterhouse, the Syrian convoy move forward, in a column , on the main road of the Golan, as if they never heard there was a war going on and that they are in Israeli territory.

The ambush of the Zamir company destroyed around 20 armored vehicles. The spearhead force of the 43rd armored brigade takes its last breaths in a spectacular yet vicious sound and lights show.

Was it the ambush of the Tiger force that prevented the Syrian forces from moving through Ein Ziwan, or the Shifon and Yosifun hills, toward Nafah? That may be. In any case, the blow that the spearhead force of the Syrian 43rd armored brigade suffered stops the Syrians and causes the rest of the brigade to withdraw back beyond the purple line.

North Sector – 104
In the middle of the night, sometime at around 03:00, Yoni Meidovnik, commander of infantry outpost 104, hears voices in Arabic and asks for flares.

"The only flare you will receive is the sun in the morning," someone answers. Beyond Manfucha there is the sound of tracks and engines of Syrian Tiran tanks. Shir-On, commander of the 104th Tank Platoon, also hears the sounds and believes they are heading south to find another path for entering the Golan, and he reports it to Nafshi.

As Shir-On is wondering who will help him and Yoni Meidovnik, night turns into day. White Syrian flares fill the black October sky. When the light fades, Aviv receives a message, "Syrian commando forces are headed your way." All night the soldiers of H Company, armored corps soldiers who know nothing about the complex world of the infantry, wait with their hearts pounding and Uzi submachine guns in their hands. They wait for the Syrian commando soldiers to appear in the dark and attack them.

04:00 – 05:00
Northern Command
At 03:56, the General in charge of Northern Command reports to the Chief of General Staff, "...the situation is not good. There is a flow of tanks toward Ben Shoham. The order to evacuate civilians was given...a

large number of tanks have been damaged. We request massive air support. Without assistance, our situation will be even worse."

03:57: The Chief of Staff, in full agreement with the Northern Command General, instructs him to let go. This is the first time since they formulated the defense conception for the Golan Heights, "defend the Purple Line at all cost," that this changes.

The Northern Command log states, "Evacuate bases where there is danger of being besieged. Try to stabilize a line, even at the cost of concessions."

Who would have imagined this happening?

04:04: Raful is unaware of the agreement between the Chief of General Staff and the Northern Command General and presses Ben Shoham to continue firing at the Syrians. Engage at all cost.

Haka hears this order from his headquarters at Mt. Kana'an and restrains him. "There is no need to press and exhaust tanks in pointless night battles," he says to Raful, and adds, "The orientation now is to suspend, not press." Then he refers to the bases, "They should leave, even on foot."

South Sector – Training Base 9

Shortly after 4:00, the Training Base 9 battery below Tel Fares receives the order to withdraw toward the Hatam route (the Water route). They head out on the route (Zivon), in secured operational formation, heading toward the nearby helicopter landing pad.

At 4:30 the APC of the battery, commanded by 2nd Lt. Shaul Shpitz, leading the convoy, passes by the Tel Farej helicopter landing pad. A tank company, with the distinctive flattened turrets of the Tiran tanks, is deployed before them in their overnight combat parking position.

"We are inside a Syrian force," Shpitz half-whispers, half-shouts on the radio. He and the first self-propelled cannon barely manage to pass through it but their luck ends there. The Syrian force comes to life. One of the companies of the Syrian 46th Armored Brigade, the same brigade that two hours earlier had destroyed the artillery battery of Anderman, who is still running between the basalt rocks on the Golan, starts firing in all directions. The three remaining self-propelled guns are hit. Fifteen soldiers are killed, eighteen injured. Those still alive flee on foot toward Tel Fares.

The Northern Command

At 04:14, at the Northern Command there is no longer hope that the enemy penetration in the southern Golan can be stopped with the organic forces of the Command. Haka calls Chief of General Staff Dado and notifies him. "I am afraid it will be impossible to stop them with the forces we have on the Golan." He then presses him to allocate the 146th Division, commanded by Gen. Musa Peled, to him.

The 146th is a General Staff Division, the final armored force that has not been involved in the war. The implications of transferring the division north are severe and grave. Transferring the division from the Ofer base near Jerusalem to the north, will leave the Sinai front facing an Egyptian force that is stronger and more advanced than the Syrians, without any reserve force. Furthermore, if King Hussein, who before anything else is a brother to his Arab neighbors, decides to ride the wave of success and join the war, there will not be any armored force between him and Judea and Samaria. In addition, the decision makers at the General Staff know that there is no way to get the tanks to the front on tank carrier trucks. That means that an entire division would have to drive on their tracks from Jerusalem all the way to the Golan.

This is about the time that the Command also received notice that the Syrian 1st Armored Division was moving south and the 3rd Armored Division was moving west toward the border. Knowing that the southern front in the Golan has fallen, the understanding is that there is a need to create a second line of defense on the Jordan River.

Col. Zvi Bar, Commander of 820th Brigade, is given an order to immediately leave the Nafah headquarters and prepare for defense of the Jordan bridges. A few minutes later Col. Bar and some of his staff officers head toward Mishmar Hayarden and begin planning the defense of the bridges. Among other things, they start preparing to blow them up!

Zvi Bar, a brigade commander proud of the great post-Six-Day War Israel, suddenly feels that they are heading toward a holocaust.

04:30: As the first daylight approaches, things are deteriorating. The Command does not rule out the possibility of the Golan falling and starts preparing accordingly. The Command log reads,, "Outposts 114, 115 and 116 are besieged, they cannot be evacuated. Remove all documents from the outposts. Verify that all the settlements on the Golan were evacuated. Burn any classified material."

At the same time, the Chief of General Staff speaks to Gen. Benny Peled, air force commander, asking him what he can give for the effort on the Golan.

Peled answers, "Almost a full squadron of Skyhawks."

04:40: After taking a short nap, the Defense Minister decides to get to the headquarters on Mt. Kana'an and see the situation for himself. Is the country really about to lose the Golan?

The Reserves are coming – 679/The Brigade Commander Force

At 04:30, with the Galilee still in the dark, twenty-five tanks of the 679th brigade move out of the Yiftach war reserves storage base. "Hurry, hurry," Raful has been pressing Ori Or, the brigade commander, all night. Or is highly disciplined and he does it fast, very fast.

Fifteen hours after the brigade was mobilized, he had already sent out Nitzan Yotzer and now three-and-a-half hours later, he places himself at the front of the "brigade," gets on the main road in the Galilee and crosses Rosh Pina. In the distance, not characteristic of the usual Galilee atmosphere, there are muffled sounds of shells falling. Ori Or looks at the convoy and knows that the quiet is a momentary illusion. The Golan and Ben Shoham are crying for help.

South Sector – Juhader

It is dawn. Jack Hallel and Issy Sitkov, commanders in the 82nd Battalion, are sent to reinforce the Battalion Commander ramp. Jack is uncomfortable about this mission, and his soldiers notice it. He is unfamiliar with the area; he has had enough battles and suffering on the Petroleum Road. The night is just slipping away and two Sho't Kal tanks without night vision are an easy target for anyone waiting for the first light. Deputy company commander Jack Hallel is in distress and more than anything wants to live.

A few minutes later, Jack and Issy arrive at the ramp safely. Jack remains with Tamir in position. Bekman, Issy and Maklef continue up north to the larger ramp, the one that the tanks of Ronis force were at, just a few hours earlier.

South Sector – Tel Saki

A short while before the first morning light, intense and precise artillery fire begins falling on Tel Saki. All the soldiers listed for combat run to the tanks and the rest run to the "bunker," a 2.5 x 2.5 meter concrete cubicle. Unlike real bunkers that are underground, this one is sitting on the hill and includes three bunkbeds and two corridors – north and south.

Inside the bunker, the crews of the 74th Battalion who are without tanks take cover. Moty Aviam and his crew, Yakir's crew, Nati Levi's crew (not including Nati himself, who was sitting just a moment ago on Pesach's tank talking to him and dived into the tank and is now in it as the fifth crew member).

The bunker is dark as death. The soldiers stare into the dark in silence. Moty Aviam is lost in thought. "Do Mom and Dad know we are at war?" A number of figures enter the empty darkness, presenting themselves as part of the 50th Battalion: Menachem, Leizi, Roni, Shaia and Shlomo. Aviam cannot see them and wonders what is going to happen to them.

04:45: "We are moving down to the main road," Danny Pesach, deputy commander of the 82nd battalion, orders on the radio. Nir Atir leads, Waxman follows, Pesach and Goldman are last. Four Sho't Kal tanks complete their descent to the rocky foot of the hill and take position silently on the sides of the path leading to Tel Saki. Asher Goldman is positioned 30 meters west of the road and the three others are a short distance behind him, on the eastern side of the road.

04:55: "I identify red matches (infantry troops) 200 meters to the right at the junction" (Tipa-Pinkas), Atir whispers on the radio, when the first light breaks.

"Roger," Danny Pesach answers. "Take aim on the target. Open fire on my command, out."

Nir aims and then looks through his binoculars and sees Syrian infantry soldiers moving low toward them.

"Deputy Commander, this is 3B," he notifies Pesach, "matches 150 meters from us, closing in."

"Roger, wait. Open fire on my command."

As he completes his sentence, a heavy rain of RPG rockets falls on the four tanks.

Danny Pesach and Yair Waxman move out to the other side of the rocky spur while firing. Nir Atir and Asher Goldman are hit and remain in their position.

"Crew, bazooka, fire," Nir shouts in his tank. Ami Moshe, the gunner, fires independently, Danny Dather, the driver, carries out the fire extinguishing drill and Nagarker with Atir are exposed in the turret, firing their Uzi and commander's machine guns. While carrying out the drill and firing at those shooting at them, Atir's tank manages to disengage and crosses to the other side, joining Waxman and Pesach.

After a minute of reorganization, Danny Pesach discovers what it means to be unacquainted with the area and its rocks. His tank overturns, with its tracks in the air and its cannon aiming at the sky.

Atir carries out damage control in his tank and finds that he is immobilized since his oil filter has been hit. Discovering this damage does not prevent him and Waxman from continuing their second battle. They are used to fighting. Together they exchange fire to the north, at the infantry trying to reach them from the other side of the spur. Waxman is horrified to discover that he now has to continue fighting with just his machine guns, due to an electrical malfunction. The squash-head shells he prepared for facing the infantry and its carriers, remain locked in their cell.

On the northern side of the spur, Asher Goldman's tank remains alone and is in trouble. While moving back, one of their tracks opened and as a result of the fire, their internal radio is not functioning. Inside the tank there is chaos, with everyone shouting hysterically. Hilik Finkel tries to let himself out of the driver's seat but is stuck. His compartment is closed off.

Asher jumps over to equipment cell 1, takes out a hammer and chisel and calmly hits the lock until it opens, and Hilik, terrified, sees the most beautiful sight of his life, the face of his platoon commander, full of soot, with his blue eyes shining, even in the dark. There is no time for elaborate ceremonies of gratitude, and Asher gives him his strong farmer's hand and pulls him out of the driver's seat.

Around the tank, twenty to thirty meters off, there are a massive number of Syrian infantry soldiers heading straight toward them to finish off the remains of platoon 1, D Company, 82nd Battalion.

Now it is every man for himself. Platoon commander Asher Goldman and Itzik Namdar the loader run for their lives toward the deputy battalion commander's tank, on the other side of the road. Without a commander, four abandoned and scared tank crew members are alone – Ruby, Hilik, Koby and David.

They flee from the tank and find a place to hide in a ditch a few meters off the road. Artillery shells fall near them, injuring Koby, David and Ruby. Miraculously, Hilik is not hurt.

A quick evaluation: Ruby's injury is not serious, David's is a bit more so and Koby looks bad. His stomach is open wide, his intestines streaming out and his hand is limp in a strange way.

What should they do? There are Syrian soldiers all around them. Will they get the chance to join the two tanks fifty to sixty meters away, on the valley south of the spur?

Danny Pesach gets on Nir Atir's tank and orders him to switch with him. Nir gives him the list of defects in the tank. Pesach changes his mind and runs to the other tank, Waxman's tank.

Waxman's tank, with its original crew, plus the soldiers of 82nd battalion – Danny Pesach, the battalion's DCO, Asher Goldman the platoon commander and Itzik Namder the loader – is taken over without explanations. Pesach gives the order and they disengage from the 74th. They head south, on the main road, leaving behind the remains of Venus Company.

05:00 – 06:00

The reserves are coming – 179 / Brigade Commander's force

Toward 05:15, two companies of the 69th Battalion, commanded by Yisrael Levine and accompanied by Ran Sarig, commander of 179th Brigade, complete the exhausting ascent from the Arik Bridge to the east. On the way, they pass Nitzan Yotzer's three tanks without noticing them. He identifies them to his right. The companies continue eastward and close to Kazabiya they are surprised by a volley of fire from the east that destroys three tanks and injures Levine, the battalion commander.

The Syrian force hitting them is apparently the same one that Yotzer encountered three hours earlier. The advance force of the Syrian 46th Brigade had decided not to continue toward the Kinneret and during the night had positioned themselves for an ambush back to the east where they "met" the tanks of the 179th Brigade.

Ran Sarig assumes command and pulls everyone in a northbound, deep flanking maneuver, toward Tel Tzabach. Within minutes the picture is changed. Sarig, a brigade commander fighting on a tank, is pleased with his gunners' performance and notice that, slowly and thoroughly, they tilt the scales against the Syrian tanks that are exploding under the Sho't Kals' guns and painting the eastern sunrise skies with fire and smoke.

* * *

Sarig, commander of the 179th Quick Intervention Brigade, had been unable to hide his frustration on Saturday night. At the war reserve storage base at Filon there were only enough tanks left to equip one battalion. The tanks of the other two battalions had been "stolen" by the 82nd and 71st Battalions. The 266th Battalion, the first ones to report at Filon, had received the remaining tanks.

The tank crews of the other two battalions: Yisrael Levine's 96th and Yossi Amir's 278th, were forced to go to the Naftali war reserve storage base, near the Golani junction, where they had to confront orderly master sergeants who were not happy about the disruption of their sleep and determined to keep them out of the stores. "We have not received any order."

Lt. Col. (Reserve) Yossi Amir, usually an obedient kibbutz member from Mizra, did not hesitate. On his order, the forklifts were confiscated, the doors of the storehouse were forced open and the huge ammunition pallets, packed and tied together making it impossible to move them by hand, were taken directly to the tank hangars area.

Slightly before 03:00, Levine's 96th Battalion had completed its preparations and set out on its tracks, all the way from the Golani junction to the Golan.

Before leaving, Raful briefed Ran Sarig, the brigade commander. "Lead the two battalions on two routes: Yehudiya-Kazabiya and Kursi-El Al. On the way you will encounter Syrians and fight them. Remember, from the junction of the Petroleum Road and Mashta to the south, there are no Hebrew speakers...."

The reserves are coming – 266/179

At 05:00, seven tanks of B Company, the 266th Reserve Battalion from the 179th Brigade, report to the gate of the Nafah base. Ijo Ribenbach, company commander, is told to proceed quickly on the Petroleum Road and join Zvika Gringold, the lone tank waiting at Ein Al Kore. At 05:30 they join Zvika, deploy on the line of the Ein Kore springs and Zvika, exhausted from the night, identifies continuous movement of Syrian tanks in front and to the east of him. He asks Ben Shoham to send a higher ranking commander to lead the battle that is about to develop.

"Deputy Tofi (deputy commander of the 188th Brigade) will be joining you shortly," Ben Shoam notifies him.

The General Staff, Tel Aviv

05:35: The Chief of General Staff and his deputy enter the air force control room at Hakiryah in Tel Aviv. Dado notifies them of the conversation he has had with Maj. Gen. Hofi and asks the air force commander if it is possible to carry out the Tagar plan (attacking the missile bases on the Canal) as proposed that morning and the Dugman plan (attacking the missile bases in Syria) in the afternoon. Benny Peled answers that it is not possible.

South Sector – Tel Saki

05:40: The sun, that has just sent its first rays over the eastern hills, finds two tank commanders from Venus (F) Company of the 74th Battalion on the southern slopes of the Tel Saki hill: 2nd Lt. Nati Levi (on the damaged tank of Pesach, with the crew of the deputy battalion commander) and first sergeant Nir Atir. They are still as strong as lions.

The two tanks are immobile and beat up but still have a functioning firing system and most importantly a combat spirit. They continue to fire and hit their targets, not giving up.

Sunday, October 7 – From Daylight Until 09:00

On Sunday morning, in slightly over three hours, the Defense Minister, the Chief of General Staff, the General Staff, the Air Force, the Northern Command and all those around them, would all be facing a reality they never dreamed of in their worst nightmares.

South Sector – 115

2nd Lt. Oded Bekman, positioned on the tank ramp at the top of outpost 115, is not aware of the considerations of the commanders at the supreme command HQ, or of their paralyzing anxiety. An endless line of Syrian T62 tanks, moving forward on the Nava-Rafid route, presents the real situation to him and it is bad. Wearing his sweaty armor coverall that is full of soot, Bekman knows that this may be his last sunrise on the Golan, maybe his last sunrise ever.

So as the sun rises, the massive Syrian force in sight poses a serious threat to the Israeli control of the Southern Golan.

The crewmen tell themselves that, if we do not hang on, the Syrians will continue to advance. Nir Atir, fighting for his life in his immobile tank below Tel Saki, is thinking mainly of Efrat from Kibbutz Dganya on the Kinneret and the tragedy she may suddenly face, her and all of the Israeli people.

Brigade Commander's Force

The brigade command group crew peek over the top of their APC and see the entire horizon full of dust, heading toward them. The carrier and tank turn and speed toward the only route that leads to the Kinneret.

A few minutes later, Manos, the deputy commander of the artillery battalion, identifies two steel vehicles heading toward him. "That is Ben Shoham," he tells himself and calls him on the radio. The tracks stop, there is a short and joyful meeting, and the commander of the 188th Brigade implores Manos to take his forces and move down to the Kinneret, before it is too late.

After giving him his recommendation, he continues his drive in a cloud of dust and is the first to take up position on the route heading to the Kinneret, near Mazraat Quneitra.

South Sector – 115

From their position near outpost 115, Bekman, Maklef and Sitkov try to identify enemy forces on the wide plain east of them. First it is the haze and then it is the sun blinding them, not enabling them to identify anything.

"Ok, we are going to fire," Bekman gets fed up. He narrows his eyes and starts the day firing away at the mass of Syrian tanks below.

Maklef is on the lookout for missiles, Sitkov is correcting their hits and Bekman fires. "The important thing is to show presence," Bekman thinks, unsure of whether he is hitting live tanks or tanks that were already destroyed the night before. "The sons of bitches need to know there are still tanks facing them out here. We don't want them thinking we ran away."

Ignoring the strange Dan Quixote figure on the hill, the Syrians open the day with accurate shelling that falls between the tank ramps.

Jack Hallel, deputy company commander in the 82nd Battalion, who did not like this war from the start, stretches in the first rays of sun, smiling in relief that the night is over, when an artillery shell hits the tank, killing him on the spot.

South Sector – Juhader

"Those guys from the 82nd Battalion are doing a good job," Uzi Urieli the company commander thinks. He sees Oren, Etinger and Siminovsky beside him and is very pleased with the way they performed that night. There are good crewmen in other brigades too, he acknowledges, recalling how professionally they operated, despite their lack of combat experience. They kept hitting the targets, while being careful and remaining calm.

He completes his morning thoughts and raises his eyes to find that the entire area around them, just a few hundred meters away, is flooded with Syrian armored vehicles and infantry soldiers.

A minute passes and Urieli is hit by a shell fired from a Tiran to his south. Luckily it does not penetrate the Sho't Kal's steel. Additional Syrian tanks appear from the Petroleum Road in the east and Uzi realizes that what worked at night is not going to work for the four tanks exposed in daylight.

"Commander, this is Glufa," he calls to Oded Erez the battalion commander.

"This is commander, continue," Erez answers tensely.

Urieli describes the situation and asks him what he suggests they do.

There is silence on the line and then, "This is commander, wait. Over and out."

Oded Erez

After receiving the report from Uzi Urieli, Oded Erez does the inventory. Of the thirty-two tanks of the 188th Brigade he was responsible for yesterday, when the war began, he now has less than half. The three companies of the 82nd Battalion of the 7th Brigade also joined him but most of them are unable to fight. One (Geva's Operational A company) is somewhere near Tel Yosifun, far from his reach. The second (Chessner's Training B company) is licking its wounds on hill 111, under the command of Haim Barak, CO of the 82nd. The third (Danny Levine's training D company) was mostly destroyed, between 116 and Tel Saki.

Erez adds the tanks of the two platoons of the 82nd that joined him on the Petroleum Road, minus the tanks of Tel Saki, surrounded in their front by enemy tanks. He reaches a total of fifteen.

Can fifteen tanks, spread out over a ten-kilometer battle sector, facing an endless flow of Syrian tanks heading toward the Purple Line, carry out their mission to block the enemy? From the reports he has received all through the night, he understands that it is hopeless. The territory from Hushnia to Nafah is under Syrian control. The first Syrian forces have reached the Waterfalls Route. Additional forces are heading toward Ramat Magshimim and the settlements on the southern Golan, and there is nothing to stop them. The advantage the enemy has in terms of numbers is unimaginable and he and the remaining forces with him are almost completely surrounded.

Uri Simchoni receives a report on the situation and approves Oded Erez's withdrawal toward the Kinneret. Then Ben Shoham receives another report from Erez. In a hoarse, defeated voice, unable to hide the deep frustration he feels, Erez describes the situation, making the atmosphere in the command carrier even worse.

Ben Shoham passes the ball to Simchoni who is at the "Palace" on Mt. Kana'an and it is sent right back to Erez.

"What is the situation over there?" Simchoni asks.

"The area is full of Syrians. What do we do?"

The question of what to do is a thorn in the side of the command. In addition to the tanks, there also are besieged soldiers on the outposts in the southern Golan, and what are they to do with Tel Fares, an intelligence base controlling the entire area. The threat that the base, along with the soldiers in it, should be taken by the enemy is very troubling, driving Simchoni mad.

"Concentrate all forces at Tel Fares," the Command Operations Officer instructs him. "You will receive further orders later on."

Still hoping that the great powerful IDF will appear suddenly and join his forces, Erez instructs anyone who can leave their position to join him on Tel Fares.

South Sector – 111

In the first rays of light, Chaim Aldag identifies about thirty tanks coming from the Kudna area, three to four kilometers from his position. They are heading to the low area south of 111 (Ka-Al-Sahal).

He reports this to Chessner and fires what he has left at them – a phosphorus shell that causes a big fire in a field of thorns. The convoy stops, applies its smoke screen and searches for the source of this nuisance. Two minutes pass, the Syrian force understands that there is no serious obstacle in its way and displays indifference as it continues in its movement west. Exhausted and extremely frustrated, Aldag fires another phosphorus shell. The enemy stops, applies smoke screen and after a few seconds continues moving into Israeli territory.

Aldag sees them progressing but he is too far away and has just one phosphorous shell and there is nothing he can do.

South Sector – Tel Saki

Small rays of light enter the tiny concrete room called "the bunker," crowded with a number of tank crews and Nahal paratroopers.

Menachem Ansbacher, commander of the Nahal pioneer platoon and his four soldiers have no intention of giving in. He positions two of them on the wrecked BTR armored personnel carrier, with a 0.5 heavy machine gun, and the other two in a 7.62 mm MAG position.

Moty Aviam hears Menachem shouting "don't fire until they get close." Then he hears the order to open fire, the bark of the machine guns, the cries of joy after hitting them, and Menachem who calms them down and tells them to save their ammunition.

Deputy Brigade Commander's Force

David Yisraeli, the relentless deputy brigade commander, has managed to set mechanics and tank crew members to work on the tanks throughout the night. "Nafah is at risk," he continues to motivate them. "We need every tank we can get." At 06:00 he has six tanks fit to return to combat.

Drained and exhausted, as an armored corps officer who believes in setting an example, Yisraeli switches to "combat" mode and leads the tanks out of Nafah. He deploys the tanks west of the Petroleum Road and heads south toward the Zvika force.

South Sector – Tel Saki

Shortly after 06:00, Menachem Ansbacher enters the bunker and asks for a volunteer to go to the tank of the 82nd that had been hit and get ammunition for the machine gun. Moty Aviam volunteers and gets Fachima the gunner and Riv the loader to join him. Wearing their tank helmets, with their Uzis on their chests, the three soldiers emerge from the bunker and immediately are caught in an exchange of fire. The four soldiers of 50th Battalion are shooting in order to block the attempts of Syrian soldiers to climb up the hill from the west.

Aviam locates the damaged tank thirty meters from the bunker, and he and the two crew members run toward it, trying to stay low. Suddenly, fifteen meters from him, he sees one of the Israeli tank crew rising up and aiming his Uzi at them.

"Noooo!" Aviam shouts with all his might. It is too late. Three bullets hit him and knock him down. Shaya the Nahal infantry soldier comes running, sees the Israeli armored soldier in pain and shouts, "Why didn't you say it was you?"

Screaming in pain, Aviam is surprised that his suffering is not over. Without any warning, he gets a slap in his face. Menachem Ansbacher, the big platoon commander, with a knitted kippa beneath his helmet, slaps his face powerfully trying to prevent Aviam from falling apart at the worst time for them.

With the sign of a palm on his face, bleeding and in pain, Aviam drags himself back into the bunker. Bandages are taken out and applied on his crushed arm and injured knee. He places his finger in the front of the helmet and discovers a bullet hole right above the rubber lining around it. He touches his forehead and cannot believe his luck. A 9 mm bullet penetrated his helmet, right in the middle of his forehead and fell in the space between the helmet and his skin.

The Air Force

05:52: The first formation of Skyhawk warplanes strikes Syrian tanks in the area of the Petroleum Road. The Syrians' anti-aircraft missile system pinpoints them and a sea of fire flies at the Israeli planes. The Skyhawks release their loads at random targets and try to avoid the missiles coming their way. Two succeed, the third is hit and its pilot is killed.

05:59: Another trio of Skyhawks is called in from the 110th Squadron at Ramat David to attack the tanks of the 7th Syrian Infantry Brigade, positioned at the Ahmadia junction near Quneitra. The pilots are unable to identify targets in the low morning sun and they are sent to where the main trouble was at night, the southern Golan front.

06:10: Before the planes get the chance to fire, two of them are hit. The third plane manages to release a string of Napalm bombs on the Petroleum Road and is also hit.

A preventive strike on the missiles would have enabled the air force to provide close support to the forces on the ground, just as they did in the Six-Day War. However, the government does not authorize the air force commander to launch a preventive attack strike on the enemy planes and missile batteries so Israel would not be seen as the aggressor.

On Saturday and Sunday, the IDF General Staff will see the armored forces on the southern Golan collapse and without any alternative, despite the lack of any preemptive strike, they will send the air force in, knowing that the area is full of ground to air missile batteries.

Formation after formation, the soldiers see the planes diving toward the enemy. A few seconds later, on their way back, there is a plane missing in every formation, sometimes even two. The air force, just like the armored corps, was far from its success in the Six-Day War, shattering yet another myth of the young soldiers on the ground.

Yair Nafshi

The first rays of sunshine awaken Yair Nafshi from his short sleep. He returns to scanning the radio frequencies, updating and receiving updates from each of his company commanders – Zvika and Avner from the 53rd battalion and Eyal, "his" last original company commander from the 74th.

Aware of the outsize influence his presence on the communication net has, he is careful to speak calmly and to the point. Dani Avny the operation officer is impressed with his coolness, equanimity and clarity of mind. He notes that the pressure of the events doesn't change his usual way of speaking and he expresses himself as if there is no war.

North sector – 104

As the first light appears in the sky, Shir-On's platoon, reinforced by Eyal the company commander and Yoni Efrat, take up position on 104. "Let's screw them," Eyal encourages his guys. Just as they take position, they receive an urgent call from Yoni Midovnik, commander of the outpost, identifying hundreds of Syrian soldiers climbing the stronghold fences.

"As soon as they stick their nose out, we will fuck them," Eyal reassures him. From this point on the tanks fire at everything moving on the hills around them. With their engines roaring and their tracks rattling, the Sho't Kal tanks take up position against anyone raising their heads. They hit several of them but the Syrian soldiers seem to never end and the Sagger missiles keep flying at them.

Then it happens, for the first time since the war started, 2nd Platoon experiences the horrors of war. An RPG hits Yossi Weisbrott's tank and amputates the leg of Eitan Frish the gunner.

Eyal is notified and he instructs the technical team's carrier to evacuate Frish to Mas'adeh. Then he continues to run the battle. "Don't worry," he calms Midovnik again. The commander of the base from the Golani brigade keeps calling him to make sure he is defending them. "I am with you."

North Sector – 107
After a day and a night of intense action, the morning presents Shmulik Yachin, commander of the 3rd Platoon of H Company on ramp 107, with a relaxed and long-range exchange of fire. This is more like a harmless children's game. The sun blinds them, making it hard for the gunners to perform, and they are now sorry they left their "anti-glare filters" in the camp area.

In those joyous days before the war, the 74th Battalion established a "boar fund." Every time a boar was killed by one of the soldiers, they were expected to take it to Tiberias, where the large animal was sold to the local butcher. The money they received was added to the battalion fund, and one of the things they bought was special anti-glare filters, which Nissim, the deputy battalion commander bought at the Optics store in Tiberias. The lenses were installed on the gunner's peri-telescopes, preventing the sun from blinding them, keeping the gunners focused on the enemy tanks.

But now when they need them, they don't have them.

Northern Command – Command Center
06:05: Moshe Dayan walks off the helicopter pad on Mt. Kana'an. With a heavy tread, he enters the improvised command center. His body language signals great distress. He takes a seat by the General and looks over the map of the Golan. A fan that has seen better days, attempts unsuccessfully to blow away the cigarette smoke and clear the air for the minister to breathe.

They were shouting the truth, he thinks to himself. The fighting on the southern Golan has stopped and the IDF has lost there. There is no way to stop them. His one penetrating eye is lifeless.

While Dayan receives an update, the armored brigades of the Syrian Divisions are renewing their attacks. Their mission is to conquer the entire Golan by 06:00 and then to redeploy on the Jordan River in order to block any counterattacks by IDF reserve armor divisions and to be prepared to capitalize on their success.

In the northern Golan the enemy is still far from success but at this time the Syrian 78th Armored Brigade and 121st Mechanized Brigade, with a battalion from the Rafat Assad force (making a total of five tank battalions in all), begin attacking along the Purple Line, at the Quneitra gap and the Bukata route.

In the southern Golan, the attacks on the Purple Line have ended. The six battalions of the Syrian 51st and 46th Armored Brigades, with a tank battalion of the 132nd Brigade, have crossed the border and are deep inside Israeli territory, creating a conquered enclave near Nafah in the northeast, near Katzabiya in the west and Ramat Magshimim in the southwest. They are trying to expand this bubble toward the Jordan River, just as their mission for that day calls for. They are not far from achieving this goal.

Utilizing their success in breaking through the southern Golan, the Syrian General Staff send in an additional 326 tanks! These are the "second operative level" and they have one objective – to follow the brigades that broke through the lines and destroy and crush the remaining IDF forces in the Nafah-Ramat Magshimim area. More importantly, they are to ride the wave of success and head toward the Jordan River and from there to the Galilee.

Dayan was in real distress. Just eighteen hours earlier, he had asked Dado, in an amused and cynical tone, what they would do with all the reserves they mobilized for no reason. Now he knows that delaying the mobilization of the reserves was a historical error, and he knows that the direct responsibility for this is his. It is not the responsibility of Zeira, or Golda, or Dado; it is his alone.

06:35: On the verge of losing control, Dayan turns to Haka and whispers in his ear, "We need to consider the option of abandoning the Golan." Haka does not respond and Dayan moves aside and calls Benny Peled, the air force commander, to make sure that the air force is on its way to the Golan.

06:42: "Benny," Dayan says with his voice shaking, "our existence is at risk. If you do not concentrate the entire power of the air force on stopping the Syrian forces on the Golan, Syrian tanks will soon be in Israel without anything to stop them."

The swing in Dayan's mood has significant emotional basis in his past experiences. In the War of Independence, twenty-five years earlier, Syrian tanks had descended from the Golan, conquering the kibbutzim of Mas'adeh and Shaar Hagolan and heading from Zemach to the fences of Kibbutz Deganya Aleph. On May 18, three days after the declaration of the state, Dayan was sent, under a direct order from Prime Minister David Ben Gurion, to the Jordan Valley. His mission was to organize the defense of the area and prevent the continuation of the Syrian penetration "at all cost." On May 20, the Syrian forces attacked Deganya, accompanied by rows of tanks and infantry soldiers, with a barrage of artillery fire. After a desperate battle, the few defenders of Deganya managed to hold back the Syrian forces, at the cost of the lives of many young Jews on the basalt rocks of the Jordan Valley. This was a serious trauma that Dayan carried with him. Now, after twenty-five years of gaining strength and six years of feeling like an "empire," once again it is Deganya and "at all cost," as if nothing had changed.

Benny Peled was horrified. Dayan, the IDF Judah the Maccabee, sounded defeated, devastated, close to hysteria.

"Maybe just let me complete Operation Tagar and then I will send the air force to the north immediately?" Peled tried.

"Do as I told you," is the response, and Peled hears the terrible distress again.

"Yes, yes, alright... How far have they gotten, sir? Ok."

The Reserves Are Coming – 179/The Lenchner Force

At midnight, A Company of the 266th Reserve Battalion, commanded by Sasi Keren, had completed equipping the tanks at the Filon base. Baruch Lenchner, deputy battalion commander, placed himself at the front of the force and headed east. At 03:00 they had arrived at Nafah, met an officer from the brigade or the division, and were given the order to get on the Pele route and wait for further orders.

They got on the Pele route, arrived at the Sindiyana area and, without further orders and night vision, decided the right thing for them to do was to take position somewhere, make strong coffee, prepare for sleeping and wait for the morning. Who knows? Maybe it will be over by then.

At 06:30 nothing was over and someone ordered Lenchner to rush to stop the Syrian tanks near Hushnia.

"Hurry, hurry," he ordered the eight tanks that chose random rocks to boresight their weapons and the optics, since they did not have the chance to do so before.

"We are moving out. Move out," Lenchner ordered the tanks and began moving on the Pele route, toward Hushnia.

South Sector – Tel Fares

06:30: Beneath Tel Fares, Yoni Davidson, Moty Amir and Dan Tiroler meet Oded Erez. He signals to Moty to get out of the tank and come to him for a briefing. "Move your tank up quickly," he instructs him. "A Syrian tank has started climbing up the hill. We need to get there before he gets to the base."

Moty starts climbing up, while the other two tanks take position to cover him. At the quarry, half way up the hill, he identifies the Tiran tank and he sees that it was a false alarm, since the tank is heading northeast toward the main road and is not a threat to any base.

"Fire," Moty orders Avi Genger the gunner. He is dying for some action, after the dry night in his area. The first shell misses and so do the second and third. In the fourth attempt, a fire is lit 2,000 meters from him, indicating to the friends of the Tiran that dared to make this attempt, that there are tanks waiting for them on Tel Fares.

After destroying the tank, Moty moves up to an observation point and cannot believe his eyes. The routes and roads that he memorized so well are packed with hundreds of Syrian vehicles. Where is our acclaimed air force that hit convoys in the Six-Day War?

Deputy Brigade Commander's force

06:30: Lt. Col. David Yisraeli, deputy commander of the 188th Brigade, joins Gringold's eight tanks, and Zvika sighs in relief. After the massacre of the tanks of the 266th Battalion, exhausted by his injury, he repeated his request from the brigade commander to send back-up with a more senior ranking officer. Back-up arrived and now there is an officer – Lt. Col. Yisraeli and the six tanks he has with him.

David Yisraeli switches them to the reserve force frequency and starts carrying out drills: the right way to talk on the radio, raising a flag when necessary, the Yisraeli crash course.

After the "training" is over, Yisraeli deploys everyone on both sides of the Petroleum Road, takes position in front and starts movement toward Hushnia. "We are going to take back the territory that Zvika left last night," he announces on the radio enthusiastically.

They move two kilometers without any interaction with the Syrian enemy and then 1,500–2,000 meters ahead they see the tanks of Walid Hamdon's 51st Brigade. For a moment, time freezes. In dark green, camouflaged, there are around 100 Tiran tanks of the 51st Brigade, searching for their new prey. Facing them, most of them fresh and yet to experience the horrors of this war, fourteen cream-colored Sho't Kal tanks spread out along a line a kilometer wide in battle positions. Zvika Gringold, who survived the battles of the previous night, is full of terror and his heart races. He is not scared for himself. He is concerned he will not be able to carry out his mission. Will he succeed in preventing this mass of Syrian forces from reaching Nafah, as Ben Shoham asked him to do?

Standing tall in his tank, with a black beret on his shoulder, speaking in his Iraqi accented Hebrew, Yisraeli gives out the targets, issues commands, guides and warns, giving them a sense of confidence that he is in charge of the situation. The fourteen tanks perform professionally, firing and switching positions, just like a regular combat day, not like this is the last defense line before Nafah. The reserves and regular army soldiers hit the enemy tanks, surprisingly easily, blocking any attempt to advance toward them, astonishingly managing to avoid being hit by the Tirans.

Air Force Command Center, Hakiryah, Tel Aviv

One Skyhawk squadron, sent to stop the progress of the Syrian forces on the southern Golan, turns out not to be enough. In a process they are unaware of, Benny Peled, a calm commander and pilot, and David Elazar, the acclaimed Chief of General Staff, seem to lose their discretion facing the fear of Dayan.

06:45: Following the heated conversation with the Defense Minister, Benny Peled orders additional planes to be sent to the Golan to attack the Syrian forces on the Petroleum Road. "Guys, on the Rafid route there are a lot of Syrian tanks. There are none of our tanks facing them. If we do not stop them, they will reach the Jordan Valley and Bteicha. Start sending flights there. Send everything to the Rafid route!"

A few minutes pass and following another consultation between the

Chief of General Staff and the air force commander, an order is sent from the air force commander to the squadrons, "Activate Dugman 5 Bet, zero hour 11:30. Abort Tagar second flight."

On June 13, 1973, the air force had presented its five war plans to the Defense Minister, the Chief of Staff and the General Staff. Tagar was the plan to attack the missiles in Egypt. Dugman was the attack on Syrian missiles.

Benny Peled had asked for his turn to speak. "If we are not given the choice of when to carry out the plans, there is serious doubt whether we will succeed."

A tense silence spread in the room, and then it was Dayan, his eye studying Peled, who said, "Dear Benny, do you really think that if we have the slightest concern that we are about to be attacked, the air force will not receive the order to strike first?"

South sector – 115

07:00: "Glufa, what do you see?" Urieli's radio comes to life.

"There are vehicles as far as we can see," he reports what he heard from "his man" Bekman, on ramp 115.

This is like a war film, Bekman tells himself, with napalm bombs falling on the Petroleum Road to the south of him and the horizon full of enemy armored vehicles appearing beyond clouds of dust and black smoke.

While he looks on in disbelief, he spots an ambulance with a Red Crescent driving confidently on the main road between the Rafid junction and Ramat Magshimim. Bekman cannot believe how peacefully the ambulance driver moves on the Israeli Golan road without any concern, as if he is in Syrian territory.

The Air Force

07:00: Following the order from the air force commander to send everything they have to the Rafid route on the Golan, there are increasing strikes of Skyhawks in the area between sector 111 to Ramat Magshimim in an attempt to stop the 326 tanks of the "second operative level." They are made up of 231 1st Division tanks and 95 tanks of the 47th Independent Brigade, "The Speeding Tiger." This force was racing in full and fresh force towards the Purple Line, with hardly any tanks there to bother them, certainly not to stop them. The only force that can do anything to stop them is the air force.

Nafah

At 7:05 a report arrives at the Nafah command center from the commander of the 50th Battalion. The report states that there is a platoon trapped at Tel Saki and "there are a lot of casualties." At the headquarters they are devastated.

South Sector – Tel Fares

07:15: Someone in the air force apparently thought there were no Israeli tanks left on the Purple Line, Moty Amir thinks to himself, as a silver a Skyhawk fires a rocket at him, shaking the ground and his tank and sending crushed basalt rocks flying all over.

Moty sticks his head out of the tank, sees the two planes disappear in the west and he starts obsessively listing all the elements of the Syrian force he sees below him in Israeli territory.

Nafah

At 7:30 the evacuation order arrives at Nafah. "The Syrian forces are approaching the base. Every man for himself. We will meet at the Bnot Yaakov Bridge."

"What am I supposed to do with this order?" Dr. Englehard wonders, as he watches the base empty. He had arrived at Nafah just a few hours earlier, joining 1st Lt. Dr. Yaakov Mamet, the 188th Brigade's doctor. In the aid station bunker, the brigade and 53rd Battalion medics are busy treating the injured soldiers remaining there. At some point, he joins the operational command center and sees Raful and his men concerned with the endless reports of the southern front collapsing. He receives an order from Oded Erez to stay where he is and not to try to join him, and he cannot help thinking about his men who left in the evacuation carrier heading to outpost 111 and have not yet returned.

"Danny, we are leaving," Mamet shakes him. Dr. Englehard doesn't move.

"Come on Danny, we don't have time. The Syrians are almost here." The brigade doctor continues, not understanding what has gotten into the young doctor.

"I have an evacuation carrier at 111. I am waiting for it to return."

Mamet looks at him in disbelief but sees his determination and knows there is no point in talking. "Alright, take care of yourself," he says and disappears with the vehicles, abandoning the base.

In the medical halftrack, at the gate of Nafah, Englehard and his crew of medics are the last ones there "to turn off the lights."

The Reserves Are Coming – 679/The Brigade Commander's Force

Shortly after 7:30, a kilometer from Nafah, Ori Or, commander of the 679th Brigade, identifies Raful, his division commander, standing on the side of the road, leaning on his jeep, short stubble already on his face.

In the manner of the men of the valley, Raful expresses his joy in a short groan and immediately instructs Or to move out and take control of the Quneitra gap.

"That is strange," Or thinks. "The information I received was that the central and southern Golan are in danger. I understand the Syrian forces penetrated into the Southern Golan," Or tries to understand the strange order.

"It is okay," Raful answers him. "The southern front is stable, under the command of Ben Shoham. It has been reinforced by a tank battalion of the 7th Brigade. Everything is okay over there."

With the gut feeling that Raful does not quite know the situation on the southern front but an obedient soldier before anything else, Or instructs the operations officer with him to get the tanks on the move and take position on the hills south of Quneitra. They are to move to the hills of Rehaniya, Arsania and Ein Zivan. They are unaware that they are acting as a second line of defense to the five tanks of the Zvika Rak force, commander of A Company 53rd Battalion of the 188th Brigade, ahead of them on the 109 ramps.

They take up position, still overwhelmed by the fast mobilization, detaching themselves from the forgotten civilian life they were just living on Saturday, trying to figure out what is going on and where the enemy is.

Ori Or updates Yanush that he has joined the front and the 7th Brigade commander is enthusiastic and ready to fight. He proposes they launch an immediate counterattack to the east, while he and his forces, located on the controlling hills north of them, act as a covering force for their attack.

Or, who has just been appointed brigade commander, politely rejects the offer. "The timing is not right. We are very unclear on the state of the enemy on the front. Let me get organized first."

Brigade Commander's Force

07:30: Ben Shoham completes his drive down the eastern Kinneret road and meets Danny Pesach, deputy commander of the 82nd Battalion, hears a bit about the occurrences at Tel Saki and has him join the carrier. He hurries his men to keep moving, since there is a war to manage and they need to get to Nafah.

As they are heading toward Nafah, he turns to Zurich, the intelligence officer, and tells him, "What we need to do now is block the enemy until the reserves arrive. To hold on. It will be hard but when the guys come, we will have done our part."

"How could this have happened to us?" Dror Sofer wonders in the carrier commander's cupola, as the engines of the tank and the carrier pull them up to the Yarden base, riding on the Golan roads, in clear violation of the regular brigade commands. How did this happen? He wonders, reliving the sounds of the night, the distress, the anxiety and the last scene in this absurdity – tens of scared, defeated Israel soldiers, fleeing toward the Kinneret.

South Sector – Tel Saki

After leaving Tel Saki, the "Waxman tank," commanded by deputy battalion commander Danny Pesach, arrived at the roadblock of the 50th Battalion, positioned north of Ramat Magshimim. Beside the roadblock there are three BTR armored personnel carriers preparing to evacuate the soldiers trapped at Tel Saki.

"Don't go," Pesach says to them. "The entire area is full of Syrians. It is hell over there."

But they still go.

It is 7:30, hiding behind the western side of the road, the four tank crew members from the 82nd Battalion feel the terror increasing amongst the basalt rocks, and Rubi Reikmanes is praying that this nightmare he is in is a mistake. It is not.

Two Israeli BTR armored personnel carriers appear from the south. They do not see the Syrian force waiting for them or the flags and calls on the radio from the two damaged tanks of the 74th Battalion near the rocky hill, and they fall right into the deadly trap.

Within seconds the two armored personnel carriers are destroyed and the angel of death is on the paratroopers, their bodies piling up beneath the hill.

North Sector – Tel Abu Nida

07:30: Zeev Unger (Oren), commanding officer of the Golani 13th Battalion, positioned on Abu Nida hill (Mt. Avital), receives the order to retreat along with all the outposts on the northern front. "Before retreating, do not forget to destroy all the equipment and if possible, try to salvage what you can."

"What do you mean retreat?" Unger says angrily to Zvi Bar, the commander of the 820th Brigade, his direct commander.

"The order is from the government," the brigade commander answers. "We are getting out of here (Nafah) and you also need to retreat. That is it."

Unger pulls the maps off the walls, starts packing, sees two buses and sends one to the base at Quneitra to start collecting the tens of soldiers there. "Wait a minute, what am I doing?" He asks himself.

A Golani soldier is always a Golani soldier. A stubborn and courageous commander, he is still angry at this unreasonable order. He stops the evacuation preparations and goes over the head of Zvi Bar, calling the Command directly. "Have you lost your mind?" he says to them. "There is no reason to leave. We are fine. None of the outposts have fallen. We are standing strong, the morale is high, and we feel great."

Someone at the Command hears him and says, "Ok, we will check."

At around 8:00, they got back to him. "Ok, stay. The order is canceled."

South Sector – 111

At around 07:00 Chessner realizes there is not much point in staying on ramp 111. Everywhere he looks, the horizon is full of Syrian tanks. He and his men have had no assistance from the air force, no artillery support, and when he looks behind him, he knows there is not a single Israeli tank there.

He contacts Haim Barak, his battalion commander, and asks to leave the outpost and head north.

07:30: Chessner receives approval, divides the injured and dead soldiers from the outpost among the tanks and Yuval Shachar's evacuation carrier, that takes position at the front of a convoy of eight tanks, and leads it on the path heading west, the same path he fled on last night. Right before they reach the main road, 150 meters north of them, they spot three Tirans, terrified by the Israeli force and fleeing west toward Hushnia.

Yuval lets out all his anger from last night, firing continuously from the 0.5 machine gun. He hits one of the commanders who is exposed in his tank. Then he moves north and gives Chessner the lead.

A few meters further on, a blind Syrian soldier searches on the side of the road for his way home. The exhausted convoy of tanks, mourning their dead friends and losing their innocence, manages to find what is left of their humanity and they hold their fire.

08:00

The Reserves Are Coming – 179/The Lenchner Force

After leaving behind a quarter of the force – one tank had fallen into a pit and another had discovered its gun sight was not functioning – the six tanks remaining in the Lenchner force, continue to move forward on the Pele route. At 8:00, they find themselves near the ruins of the Circassian village of Ramtania. Before they get the chance to enjoy the beauty of the remains of the church or appreciate the heroic attempt of Jews from Tzfat to establish a Jewish agricultural settlement here in the late nineteenth century, they are fired on by the tanks of the Syrian 51st Armored Brigade.

"Fire!" six reserves soldiers shout in their tanks. Without zeroing their weapons and in inferior position, they withdraw, leaving behind the tank of the deputy battalion commander that has been hit. They try to hold off the Tirans and not be devoured by them.

Northern Command – Command Center

The Chief of the General staff approves the order to place Musa Peled's 146th Division under the command of The Northern Command. Everyone in the IDF understands the meaning of this and they pray that the Jordanian front stays quiet, and that on the Egyptian front they will manage with whatever they have.

South Sector – Juhader

Uzi Urieli collects all the injured soldiers, divides them between the four tanks that are fit to drive, crushing the fence of the parking area he himself as platoon commander built in calmer days, and heads north.

After driving a few hundred meters, the Juhader base explodes behind them. The most intense artillery shelling since the war began turns it to dust. "There is a God," says the secular Urieli, for a moment forgetting Horen, Barenboim, Akeb and Jack who were with him in officer's training course.

Uzi sends the three tanks with him to Tel Fares on the main road (Tipa route), remaining where he is, alone with his cannon facing east, securing the movement of his soldiers.

South Sector – Tel Saki

In the ditch opposite Tel Saki, Rubi Reikmanes decides it is time to call for help. He waits for the gunfire to stop and runs across the road. Fifteen meters to his left, two Syrian soldiers rise up. He cocks his Uzi and pulls the trigger. Nothing happens. The gun is stuck and Rubi's heart seems to stop beating.

He is tall with long legs, a champion runner, and he knows this is the most important medal of his life. With tracers following him, he runs for his life and reaches Nir Atir's tank. He sees Itzik Nagarker calmly putting out a fire like there is no war going on and reports the situation of the injured soldiers on the other side of the road to Atir.

Nagarker finishes putting out the fire and asks Atir to let him cross the road and help the injured soldiers. Atir refuses, "Absolutely not. There are Syrian infantry soldiers behind every rock. You saw what happened to the BTRs. Besides, I need you here to keep fighting."

Reikmanes has no intention of running past the two Syrian soldiers surely waiting for him again or to join the damaged tank. He hesitates for another second and runs all the way up the hill, to the bunker at the top.

The Brigade Commander's Force

On the way to Nafah, the radio in the command center starts working again and Ben Shoham receives pieces of updated information about the fierce battles that took place during the night on the Petroleum Road. Things are very bad. The Syrians are continuing to move north toward Nafah.

Ben Shoham calls Haim Barak, commander of the 82nd Battalion, who reports to him, and is positioned beneath Tel Yosifun. "Move to Sindiyana, join the deputy commander of the 266th Battalion who is on the Pele route and move south with him in the general direction of Hushnia. Engage with the enemy and destroy it."

Ben Shoham's order is part of an ad-hoc brigade plan, according to which the Syrian force will be crushed from both sides. The deputy brigade commander's force is to block them on the Petroleum Road (Mahaze) while pressing the Syrians eastward, toward the Barak force that is on the Pele route.

South Sector – 111

On the Reshet route, moving north. Chessner is leading, Aldag is behind him. Suddenly a T62 tank appears out of nowhere, with his hatches closed, driving like a madman. Aldag reacts first, fires his last round and misses. Having no idea that the tanks behind him are out of ammunition, the Syrian tank flees into the trees and disappears.

From his position at the front of the convoy, Yuval Shachar sees the Syrian tank, knowing that other tanks will be following, and he decides not to push it. "Avi, make room for me," he says to Grinfeld, beneath him inside the tank. "There is no room Yuval , believe me. There is not room for a pin," comes Grinfeld's answer, crowded between twenty moaning injured soldiers.

Convoy 111 continues north. Yuval prays for someone to watch over him, just as Chessner turns a bend on the road and is surprised by a Syrian tank appearing in front of him. There is no time to fire. "Turn toward the Syrian," Chessner shouts to the driver and he turns and goes for a collision. The Syrian tank driver sees the crazy tank heading toward him, panics and falls in the ditch on the side of the road. Now it is Aldag's turn to take action.

"Give me grenades," he shouts to Efrati the loader. He pulls to a halt next to the Syrian tank and tries to throw them into the turret. He is disappointed to see them fall on the top of the tank.

The Syrian tank crew jump out of the tank and run into the culvert. Aldag is furious with the Syrians, who are conquering his Golan and killing his friends, and he throws another grenade. This time he is on target and they hear a huge explosion with inhuman screams from inside the culvert.

South Sector – The Barak Force

A few minutes past 08:00, the eleven tanks of the Barak force begin movement toward Sindiyana.

"10 of Naka, this is 20 of Tofi," they suddenly hear the voice of Ben Shoham on the radio.

"This is 10 of Naka, over," Haim Barak commander of the 82nd Battalion responds.

Ben Shoham updates him on the reserve force of the 266th Battalion in the area he is heading to and he asks him to join forces with them. A few minutes after Barak passes Sindiyana, he identifies the Lenchner force retreating west of him, near the Petroleum Road.

"What happened there?" he asks Lenchner, seeing the deputy battalion commander's tank in flames.

"The battalion got into battle without boresighting the optics to the cannon," Lenchner responds, sounding upset and frustrated.

"How come you didn't do boresighting?" Barak asks amazed.

"Raful nagged, asked, pressed. We had no choice. Each tank started its engine and we were off."

As they continue withdrawing toward Nafah, the tanks of the 82nd Battalion continue their movement on the Pele route, conducting secure movement procedures.

Then the first round of Sagger missiles hits them from a controlling elevated position. They avoid them and still do not identify enemy tanks. After staying where they are for over an hour, without any Syrian approaching them, Barak decides it is time to move toward the enemy.

The eleven tanks of the 82nd Battalion move forward to take up better positions at Ein Varda. There in front of them, two kilometers away, the valley is full of T62 tanks, the ones with the best cannon on the front.

Encouraged by the success of his forces on the southern Golan front, the Syrian General Staff have decided to maximize their success and in the late night hours they ordered Taufik Gini, commander of the 1st Division, that had been waiting in the Kiswa area near Damascus, to move south and to start crossing the Purple Line.

The leading tank brigade of the Division, the veteran 91st Brigade, commanded by Shafik Faid with its 95 T62 tanks, were sent to lead the Division.

From the early morning hours of Sunday, the division sped forward, crossing in the wide opening created by the tanks of the 51st and 46th Brigades, and by 09:00 the first tanks were in Hushnia, ready to hit anyone daring to rise up in the taken territory.

Shafik Faid, the brigade commander, received reports that the Israeli armored forces along the southern Golan front had collapsed, and to him the eleven tanks of the Barak force were nothing but a slight delay on their way to achieving their intermediate goal of conquering Nafah.

08:45

South Sector –Tel Saki

A third BTR armored personnel carrier of the Syrian 50th Battalion, the third Danny Pesach has seen near Ramat Magshimim, appears near Tel Saki. Nagarker stands in the tank and indicates for it to continue moving, so it does not stop and fall into their ambush. The BTR keeps moving but then suddenly slows down, as if it is searching for the enemy or the soldiers it is there to evacuate, and then there is a deafening explosion and black smoke fills the area and Nagarker closes his eyes.

Nafah

On the verge of losing all faith and right before he abandons the Nafah base, Danny Englehard rubs his eyes in disbelief. A cloud of dust rises from the direction of Tel Yosifun and a single APC appears, heading his way. A few minutes later, the evacuation carrier of the 53rd Battalion, with Yuval Shachar in the commander's cupola and Avi Grinfeld treating the injured soldiers, stops next to the halftrack of the aid station.

Dr. Englehard, a believing Jew, looks at "his crew" with admiration, noting how Grinfeld the medic looks like a solid rock among the sea of injured soldiers. He hugs them, asks a few questions and takes command, instructing everyone to move west, toward Beit Hameches, before the joy of being together becomes their last, since the Syrian forces are on their way to Nafah.

Sunday, October 7 – From 09:00 to 13:00

On Sunday, the Syrian forces had secured an unimaginable advantage. The Israeli forces were dramatically outnumbered and were desperately short of ammunition. The Syrian armored brigades were free to come and go on the routes of the Southern Golan without any interference.

The situation as perceived at the Northern Command headquarters was desperate. The last remnants of the 188th Brigade's tanks were no longer able to keep their finger in the dam and the enemy forces came flowing in, reaching the Hushnia-Nafah area and the routes leading down to the Kinneret. Bases were being evacuated, confidential material burned and shredded, the Nafah headquarters was cleared in a panic and things were very bad.

And then, when everything seemed to be lost and unamendable, a ray of hope shone at the end of the tunnel and the catastrophe was avoided.

There is no doubt that the Golan had many saviors. First and foremost it was the brave warriors of the few tank platoons of the 188th Brigade and the 82nd Battalion that continued to fight with determination and sacrifice, despite the impossible circumstances they faced. This disrupted the schedule of the Syrian General Staff in what was supposed to be a quick conquering of the Southern Golan. Instead their forces suffered severe losses which diminished their enthusiasm.

The air force was another element of this success. In a joint effort with the remaining personnel of the 188th Brigade, they managed to slow the Syrian forces on their way to the Kinneret, giving the Israeli reserves time to prepare for the battle. However, from 10:00 the air force was no longer active in stopping the enemy forces, just as the 188th Brigade no longer was. The air force received an order to "stop bombings."

From 10:00, the battle was handed over to the grey heroes in jeans and t-shirts, civilians who had left their fields, offices, families, homes, and – on the holiest day to the Jews – to rush to the battlefield without any notice. They raced to join their units, where in impossible conditions – lacking ammunition, in unfit tanks, missing optic equipment and without boresighting – they were sent to war.

09:00

The reserves are coming – 278/179

After waiting for almost an hour and a half, like a drawn string waiting to release its arrow, at 09:00, over three kilometers from them, south of Ramat Magshimim, the flat turret enemy tanks appear.

This time the force waiting in ambush is the 278th Battalion from the 179th Reserve Brigade, commanded by Yossi Amir and deputy brigade commander Gideon Zimbel, who had arrived at 07:30 after climbing up the Kursi-Givat Yoav-El Al route, on the main road, with cannons facing north.

Yossi Amir identifies the Tirans, and gives the order to open fire and light more and more fires in the distance, changing the plans of the Syrian brigades – the 132nd Mechanized and 47th Armored Brigades – regarding their progress toward the Kinneret.

After the efforts of the 188th Brigade and the air force, there is no doubt that it was the armored reserve brigades that saved the Golan from the Syrians in the end. The first to report was the 179th Quick-Response Brigade, commanded by Col. Ran Sarig.

Later on, additional reserve forces arrived but early Sunday morning, the force that put the first smiles on the faces of the commanders on the Golan was the 179th Brigade. If they would have arrived an hour or two later, the entire war outcome may have been very different.

Nafah

Less than two hours after fleeing, they are already back. Someone announces that the situation in the Nafah front is not as bad as they thought it was, and Raful and his staff turn around and return to the headquarters at Nafah, still intact, and things appears to be getting back on track.

Ben Shoham

Shortly after 09:00, a tank and an armored personnel carrier arrive at Nafah.

"I do not have a brigade," Ben Shoham says to Schwartz, the communications officer. "I am about to get in my tank and join the deputy brigade commander on the Petroleum Road, Come with me."

Schwartz places his hand on the tank to spring into it, when suddenly a jeep appears. Out comes the blond Benny Katzin, the operations officer (S3) and Shmulik Ben Moshe, the adjutancy officer.

"What brings you here?" Ben Shoham shouts to Shmulik.

"War," Ben Moshe replies. Ben Shoham knows that it is not the adjutancy officer's job to be on the front lines wave an admonishing finger at him, but leaves him alone.

"You were with the brigade commander all night," Katzin says to Schwartz. "Now you should go down, the brigade commander needs a combat soldier with him" and Katzin joins him.

Maj. Benny Katzin, a tank company commander and currently the operations officer of the 188th Brigade, according to protocol, is supposed to be with the brigade commander's tank. Schwartz realizes he is not going to get there and he decides to leave a professional radio operator in the tank. After consulting with Ben Shoham, he instructs Yossi Gavrieli, the radio operator of the brigade commander's APC, to replace Gofelman in the loader's compartment. "There has to be a communications man in the tank to help the brigade commander." Loading shells? Omisei can teach him how to do it, while they are on the move.

"When is the last time you fired a cannon?" Ben Shoham asks Yehuda Porat, the tank commander that accompanied him all night. "A year ago," Porat answers. Ben Shoham keeps Omisei in the gunner's seat and tells Porat to vacate his position in the tank.

As he is changing position, Porat notices Ben Shoham – tall, strong, with an Uzi on his chest – climbing into the tank with a boy's quickness, and he has the feeling that this brigade commander is going to fight for his home.

South Sector – 115

Bekman and Maklef are still in their positions when they hear the call from the commander of outpost 115. "2 of Glufa, this is Sidan, come evacuate me."

"No way," Bekman responds angrily, ignoring the tanks of the 1st Division that continue their movement all throughout the horizon. "We are holding the line. We are strong. I am not evacuating you."

Less than ten minutes pass and he receives the order to evacuate them. He arrives at the outpost with Maklef and Sitkov and before they even stop, the Nahal infantry soldiers rush toward them.

South Sector – Tel Saki

Shortly after 9:00, the Syrian forces are again more accurate in their fire, and this time it is the platoon commander, Menachem, who is shot in the knee and falls. He orders Roni Herzenstein to take the 0.5 machine gun position on the BTR and goes down to the bunker to bandage his wound. Roni does not even have time to warm up with the machine gun before a precise deadly Syrian bullet hits and kills him. Lazie and Shaya, the two soldiers remaining outside, leave their MAG position and take Roni out of the carrier and drag him to the bunker. Menachem orders Lazie to take up position at the machine gun and continue what he and Roni were trying to do – stop the Syrians at all cost.

09:15: Near the main road, there are two tanks of the 188th Brigade that have been hit and are unable to move. They continue their efforts to try to stop the Syrian enemy that is all around. Nagarker, the energetic loader, is not troubled by them. He is troubled that they abandoned an injured soldier on the other side of the road. He jumps out of the tank and before his commander Atir can stop him, he runs across the main road and finds Koby Ariel, lying on his back with his intestines spilling out and his arm hanging by its skin. Nagarker collects the intestines, shoves them back inside his stomach and somehow bandages the mess.

Ben Shoham Force

A few minutes past 09:00, Ben Shoham goes to war.

"22 this is 20. Every tank that arrives, every commander, needs to be received, told to tune into Tofi frequency and sent in. Over," Ben Shoham commands Zurich and Schwartz who remain in his APC at Nafah, at the start of the Petroleum Road.

During the night and the early morning, a number of damaged tanks have arrived from the front, trying to believe that they had made it and that the worst is behind them.

It was Lerer, the brigade's tireless ordnance officer who crushed their dreams. He and his men worked all night repairing tanks, preparing them to be sent back to the front. After that, Shmulik Ben Moshe, the adjutancy officer appointed them to the repaired tanks. For some of them, this was unbearable. Thirty-five years later, Shmulik Ben Moshe tells me:

> *"I am not a commander, I am a logistics officer. To hear the soldiers saying things to me like, 'You are not fighting, it is easy for you to send us back to the tanks, back to the battlefield and get us back in body-bags,' this was like a knife in my heart. I understood their distress and fear but I knew that Ben Shoham and Yisraeli needed them."*

Filled with the sense of being on a national mission, and with intense frustration, Shmulik reappointed these exhausted and burned soldiers and sent them back to Zurich and Schwartz and from there back to the war.

09:30

South Sector – Tel Saki

On the main road, heading toward Ramat Magshimim, Nir Atir suddenly identifies a Syrian Tiran tank, with its hatches closed, its cannon facing south and a red flag flying above it. "That must be the Syrian battalion commander," Atir decides. He instructs Ami Moshe, the natural born gunner, to put his finger on the trigger and then he realizes that Nagarker the loader is across the road.

Atir is an experienced war horse and he gets Dathar the driver into the loader's seat and tests his new skill. Just as he is about to give the order to open fire, he notices that the tank with the red flag is not alone. There is a column of ten tanks behind it.

"Hold your fire!" he shouts, and Ami the gunner takes his finger off the electric trigger just in time.

As if they are aware of Atir's intention to attack, the Syrians take aim at the two 188th Brigade tanks but decide that they are no longer functional and, instead of firing, they head south, just as the hearts of Nati and Nir start slowing down and they continue breathing.

One hundred fifty meters from them, across the road, Nagarker from the 74th Battalion and two soldiers from the 82nd Battalion, are carrying Koby with his stomach ripped open. They start to realize that the worst is yet to come.

For a second, Nagarker has the thought that maybe he is wrong and these are the reserve forces arriving. Maybe he should stand up and signal to them not to fire at him by accident, but at the last second he sees the green color and the flat shadow of the tanks, he hears the tracks and sees the Gorianov gun on the tank. He pushes their three heads down in the ground. He does not want to look death in the eye. In a fetal position, shaking uncontrollably, he wishes farewell to all his family members, just like he heard in the stories about these situations, and he waits for the first gunshots to hit him.

The sound of the tracks tells him that the first tank has passed. There are others following, another and another, he is not counting. He is just huddled together with the other two Israelis and shaking. Finally it ends, the tracks move off in the distance. We are okay he thinks and continues to shake, wondering where the next terror will come from and how much longer he has to live.

Two minutes later, Levi and Atir are glad to have Nagarker back. He just returned from the land of the dead and in his energetic style he says, "Come on Nir, let's destroy this damned company."

South Sector – 115

At around 09:30, while the fifteen soldiers of base 115 are exposed on the three tanks, holding on for dear life, Bekman receives another order.

"Go to outpost 116 ," Erez instructs him. "Take the soldiers from there as well."

Has he lost his mind? Bekman wonders. It is almost five kilometers to outpost 116. It is all conquered territory, full of Syrian forces. The man does not know what he is talking about. Without hesitation, he presses the button on the mouthpiece of the radio, causing interference, forgetting the order.

Urieli, the company commander, hears the order from the battalion commander, he speaks on the radio and declares that he is opposed to Bekman going to the base. "It is a suicide mission," he claims. Erez accepts what he says.

Urieli knows that the tanks from Juhader joined the battalion commander and he hears that sector 115 is also being evacuated, and now he abandons his position on the Shivron route, cuts through the fields to the Zivon route beneath Tel Fares, on his way to join the forces there.

Ben Shoham Force

At 09:30 the commander of the 188th Brigade joins his deputy at the Petroleum Road.

They update each other, and Yossi Gavrieli jumps into the deputy's tank, repairing a radio that is not working and returns to the brigade commander's tank, ready for any task. There is real action in the tanks, he thinks with pleasure.

Omeisi the gunner brings him back down to earth and starts teaching him what he needs to know in order to function as the tank loader. As a communications technician, Gavrieli is well acquainted with the inside of the tank, but now he is required to do something different, and Nissim Omeisi briefs him on the different kinds of shells.

Omeisi lowers the cannon, leaves the gunner's position, crawls next to the cannon, pointing out the different types of shells to Gavrieli. They decide to identify them by their shape. "The pointy one is an armor piercing, a pipe is a shaped charge and the round one is a squash head." After agreeing on the names, they need to practice. Two minutes pass and Gavrieli, from a moshav in the north, is introduced to the hidden secrets of the shells. He learns how to insert them correctly on the floor of the tank and notifies Omeisi that he has it under control and that he is ready to fight.

Fifteen Sho't Kal tanks spot the Syrian tanks on the hills west of the Mashta junction; they fire at them and stop the 51st brigade of the Syrian 9th Division. This is the same brigade that had been the first to penetrate the southern Golan, taken up position at Hushnia, climbed upwards to the north, destroyed the tanks of the 266th Reserve Battalion and forced Zvika back.

"Now is the time to crush them," 2nd Lt. Hagai Zur thinks to himself.

He had joined Zvika early that morning with the deputy brigade commander's force. "Now is our chance to get rid of the sense of helplessness we had in the night between Saturday and Sunday."

South Sector – Tel Fares

By 09:30, all of the tanks under the command of Oded Erez assemble at Tel Fares. Almost all of the tanks. In the Tel Saki front, unable to move their tank, Levi the platoon commander and Atir the sergeant keep on fighting.

Back to Tel Fares. Davidson, Amir, Tiroler and Tamir take up position below the hill, near the deployment camp. They find a safe observation position with their cannons facing south and slightly east. The other eleven tanks climb up the hill and take position in a circle around the quarry, halfway up the hill, carefully watching all sides.

An occasional tank from the Syrian 46th Armored Brigade, located deep in the southern Golan, fires at the defenders of the deployment camp, checking to see whether the hill can be conquered.

In impressive professional tankmanship, four Sho't Kal tanks use their cannons and machine guns to halt the attack of several Syrian infantry companies, accompanied by a few tank platoons.

10:00

The Air Force

At 10:00 the air force ceases its ground strikes on the Golan and begins preparing the front for operation Dugman 5.

Dayan's vetoing of the preventive attack led the air force (and the entire IDF) into the war unprepared. On Saturday night, the air force commander and the Chief of General Staff agreed that with the first light, eighty Skyhawks would head to Egypt to carry out preparatory strike for destroying anti-aircraft missiles, bridges and artillery, then they were to hit eight forward airfields, to prevent the Egyptian air force from disturbing "the jewel in the crown" – Operation Tagar – the attack on the missile bases in Egypt.

Finally, working according to an orderly plan, the air force start to register results. When it seems that the difficulties on the Egyptian front are about to end and all the pilots had left to do was complete their mission, Benny Peled comes up with a change of plans. The pilots are unable to enjoy the fruits of their success, with eighty Skyhawk and Phantom planes destroying tens of cannons and four airfields.

Canceling the Tagar operation was not necessary. The small area of the Golan did not enable the air force to demonstrate its full strength. Furthermore, in the early morning hours, Moty Hod had sent a squadron of Skyhawks from the Ramat David base resulting in the ruins of Syrian tanks piling up along the routes leading to the Kinneret. In addition, the first reserve units were joining the action, climbing the routes to the Golan. So why would he go and cancel Tagar?

Lt. Col. Yiftach Spector, commander of a Phantom squadron at the Hazor base, described it well in his book *A Dream in Blue and Black*.

> *To Syria?! What is going on there, in the north? To rush to hit the missiles? Have the generals thought this through? You don't send planes to strike missile systems without planning. Missiles are a terrible enemy... the air force spent years developing methods for combating missiles – secret, complex and sophisticated. The squadrons were trained to know every detail, to work together as a machine, with perfect coordination between hundreds of planes... It takes such a "Swiss watch" to deal with an array of ground to air missiles... how could the Command send its people to grab maps and run to the planes, arriving and flying out... with no briefing, no preparations, completely disregarding the hundreds of details related to carrying out a successful operation? Has the Command lost its mind?*

The necessary preparations were not carried out. Dayan's panic severely compromised the discretion of the Chief of General Staff, and the air force commander, and Haka, who is not acquainted with the Tagar operation, canceled "because of him," was unable to make them see that they could have left planes in the south as well.

The Tagar operation was stopped in the middle and therefore failed. The fate of operation Dugman 5 that started at 11:30 and ended an hour and a half later is known. Of the thirty-one batteries attacked, only one was destroyed and another damaged. Six planes were shot down. The Golan would be declared a hot missile protected area.

Ben Shoham Force

In Ben Shoham's tank there is a clear division of authority. The commander of the 188th Brigade is the tank commander; Benny Katzin is his right hand. He occasionally helps guide driver Ben Shoef and occasionally points out an enemy tank whose turret rises above the horizon.

At around 10:00 it seemed like things were getting back on track. The supplies convoy took up position a few hundred meters behind the line of the fifteen Sho't Kal tanks, stopping the Syrians on the Petroleum Road. The tanks that are depleted, are sent to refill fuel and ammunition.

Pele Route – Barak Force

At 10:00 Haim Barak shouts to his gunner, "Fire! Fire!" not the precise order required by protocol but necessary due to the lack of time. Anywhere they look, there is movement of endless armored ants painted dark green, who swarm, heading toward him.

Then he is hit by one of the swarm's cannons. The tank suffers a huge blow, Barak is thrown out of the tank and lands beside the tank with an injury in his stomach. Together with him, the operations officer Yochanan Zorea also is thrown out of the tank but in his case, his upper body flew outside while his lower half fell into the tank.

The family of reserve Gen. Meir Zorea was already bereaved. On the first day of the Six-Day War, their oldest son, Yonatan, a pilot, had been hit by anti-aircraft fire on the Golan on his way to strike targets near Damascus.

Not far from where the Syrian shell hit Yochanan's tank, another brother, Giora, was serving as the commander of the Sayeret Matkal elite unit operating against Syrian commando forces on the Golan.

North Sector – 105

While the situation on the southern Golan front was very bad, the forces of the Syrian 7th Division continue to attempt to break through on the northern front as well.

Wave after wave of attacks continues on the tanks of the 7th Brigade and the 188th Brigade in the area. Landau is on the Bukata route, Yachin does not move from his position at 107 and Kaimo, the energetic deputy company commander, together with Nissim the deputy battalion commander, blocks the poor attempts of the Syrian forces to climb ridge 105. The failure of the Tiran tanks led to additional attempts, this time of Syrian infantry companies, to get rid of the stubborn Israeli tanks.

Repeated attacks by Syrian infantry soldiers are blocked on the fences of 105 and Kaimo, in charge of the area, is sent from time to time to block the determined attempts to penetrate. He sends squash-head shells at them.

The third time he arrives at the base, the Syrians prepare a surprise. In a planned ambush waiting for him, a round of Sagger missiles is fired at him, just barely missing his head. "Call me only if there are tanks attacking the base," Kaimo decides. "Deal with infantry yourselves."

North Sector – Northern Ramp 109

Following repeated attacks by Syrian commando forces on his platoon, Doron Sadeh Lavan decides to improve their position by moving to somewhere there they will have a wider view.

He leaves the northern ramp, leading his platoon, forgetting he is in the middle of an intense war, and before they take up position on one of the hills nearby, the three platoon tanks are ambushed and hit.

His firing system is hit but his engine is still working and he withdraws and calls A Company to help them. Sadeh Lavan's cry for help is received at the southern ramp on outpost 109. Deputy company commander Yisraeli takes Eiland with him and they rush to his assistance.

Suddenly, 400–500 meters from them, Zeevik Tuashi, the gunner of the deputy company commander's tank identifies a Syrian tank aiming at them. Before he can react, the Tiran's cannon flashes and a steel shell flies just centimeters over the tank.

Yisraeli sees the trouble they are in and shouts, "Fire!" Nothing happens.

"What is going on, Goldshaft?" he shouts at the loader.

"It is stuck in the cannon," Goldshaft answers with his usual indifference.

"Get it out!" Yisraeli shouts, twisting in horror on the commander's stool.

"I can't," Goldshaft answers at his regular pace.

Tuashi looks desperately at the loader and sees another problem, in addition to the danger their tank is in. The cable linking his helmet to the intercom is wrapped around his neck, about to choke him.

While Tuashi and Goldshaft try frantically to release the shell stuck in the breach and the cable so Goldshaft can breathe, Yisraeli knows they are about to be hit.

"Move!" Yisraeli shouts to Yaakov Moshe the driver and he moves the tank back to a fold in the ground. Tuashi slides over from the gunner's seat to the loader, grabs a huge special metal tool, sticks it between the breach and the shell, and pulls it out.

In the tank next to them, Eiland notices that something bad is going on in Yisraeli's tank. Efraim Yosef the gunner is called to fire at the Tiran and hits it with one shot, lifting the threat from the deputy commander. At that exact second, Tuashi returns to his seat, looks through his peri-telescope and right before he fires, he sees the Syrian tank hit. Thank you, Eiland.

Government Meeting – Hakiryah, Tel Aviv

At 10:00, as Eiland is saving Yisraeli in sector 109, a government meeting takes places at Hakiryah in Tel Aviv. In the absence of the Defense Minister, who is at the Southern Command headquarters, the Chief of General Staff takes over and gives them a dry and general description of the collapse on the Golan, "The war is very difficult... the battles are bitter and harsh... we are blocking the enemy."

Then he gives them a bit of hope. "We are preparing a mass of planes to hit the Syrian missile bases starting at 11:30... the reserve forces are helping the regular forces recover... hundreds of Syrian tanks are in flames... we have managed to stabilize the lines."

Toward the end of the meeting, Dado returns to the bad news. He notifies them that the Syrians are holding significant territory on the Golan. There are settlements that are under Syrian control, for example Ramat Magshimim. The ministers are shocked and the Minister of Housing, Zeev Sherf asks the Chief of Staff, "Do we have an estimate of the number of enemy soldiers and tanks in our territory?"

Dado does not hesitate, "There is no way of estimating."

Sherf insists, "Do they have hundreds or thousands?"

Dado sees he has no choice and he drops the bomb. "My rough

estimate is that there could be 10,000 Syrians on the Golan. There may be 300–400 tanks."

Hushnia sector – The Technical Crews

As Minister Zeev Sherf fights for his right to know how many Syrians are in Israeli territory on the Golan, one of the biggest tragedies of the Yom Kippur War takes place in the Hushnia front.

The Syrian soldiers who are moving through the Hushnia area like it is their own, find the soldiers of the technical crews of Golan C Company of the 53rd Battalion and the Zeevim G Company of the 74th Battalion. They leave the seventeen soldiers of the 188th Brigade no choice and they are taken prisoners. Immediately upon capture they are all tied up and slaughtered.

What was going through the mind of David Nurian,[30] the Golan Company sergeant, who had just joined the technical APC? What was Shaul Bakal[31] telling himself, the turret mechanic of the Zeevim Company, holding on to the promise Zvika Gringold gave him to join them, as the Syrian soldiers surrounded the culvert where he and his friends were hiding? How can we express in words what happened there?

South Sector – Tel Saki

Unlike the government ministers, the soldiers on Tel Saki don't need any updates regarding the situation on the ground. On the western side of the Golan road, the drama of blood and fire, the screaming and moaning of the injured and dying soldiers and the unbearable smell of burnt flesh continues. Alongside the tank crews on Tel Saki are the remaining soldiers of the paratroopers from the 50th Battalion, terrified and shell-shocked.

Beneath Tel Saki, on the eastern side of the road, there are two immobilized Sho't Kal tanks, sitting ducks for the Syrian soldiers operating the anti-tank RPGs who come ever closer to them.

---

30. The technical crew of Golan Company of the 53rd battalion consisted of: David Nurian (company sergeant), Menachem Mishali, Yitzchak Levinger, Zvi Yarkoni (Grinoiza), Gil Cohen, David Bnaya, Zion Swisa, Yoel Shalit, Avner Yaacov (medic) and Yoel Sharabi (carrier driver).
31. The technical crew of the Zeevim Company consisted of: Shlomo Zippori, Shaul Bakal, Daniel Zaguri, Avraham (Herzl) Biton, Rafael Hen/Ben Hamo (medic), Meir Mizrachi (APC driver), Moshe Hodrian (tank crew member).

The order "Do not move from the border line" came directly from Defense Minister Moshe Dayan and was passed to Chief of General Staff Dado, Northern Command CO Haka, the division commander Raful, the brigade, battalion and company commanders. It eventually reaches the commander of the 2nd Platoon , 2nd Lt. Nati Levi, and the 3rd Platoon sergeant, Nir Atir, who are stuck beneath Tel Saki.

They are not in contact with anyone but still they know this is a war they have to win, and even though they are not so sure this is possible, an order is an order and they need to fight "to their last drop of blood." So they just stand there and fire, refusing to give up. They are exhausted, scared and out of heavy ammunition. They are watching the ammunition for their machine guns running out. But they are still determined to fight, trying to prevent the Syrian infantry from climbing up to the hill.

11:00

North Sector – Fidel Hadash

As they approach the afternoon, the aim of the Syrian forces become more accurate. An armor piercing shell slides off the tank of Rani Friedrich, 1st platoon leader in Avner Landau's company, and shakes the steel chariot.

Before they have the chance to realize they have been hit, an artillery shell lands on sergeant Arieh Feigenbaum's tank, lightly injuring gunner Eli Cohen and ruining the engine. Friedrich calls Feigenbaum on the radio and there is no response. He hurries over to the sergeant's tank to see what his situation is.

The crews of both tanks jump out for a moment, stretch their limbs and Friedrich's driver sees this as his only chance to save his own life. He grabs Eli Cohen's hand, the driver of Feigenbaum's tank, and tells him he can no longer function because of an injury in his back and forces him to take his place, and he runs blindly towards the horizon and disappears.

Just a few months earlier, this same driver was chosen to be sent to the President's Residence as the battalion outstanding soldier, and now he flees. It turns out you cannot predict how a person will function in battle from the way he does in training.

War is a terrifying ordeal and is essentially in conflict with the basic human urge to survive. There are people who, during war, are fighting to survive before anything else. Not for their friends, not out of concern for what others will say, not for their homeland, not for Zionist ideals. This basic urge to live overcomes all other values that are supposed to cause a young man to stand up and block or engage the enemy and persist until ordered to stop.

In the sergeant's tank, routine prevails. Arieh Feigenbaum still hasn't quite acknowledged that this is war, not a combat day. He ignores the artillery shell that just damaged the tank and contacts Asaf Sella. He asks the deputy company commander to help him get through the damage report form he will have to fill out for losing the camouflage net that burned.

Another two minutes pass and a shard of a mortar shell that lands on the tank of the commander of 2nd platoon, Moshe Efrati, ends the time granted to B Company by the god of luck. Efrati is hit by the shard in his chest and the company mourns its first casualty.

Before noon, the Syrian artillery officers mark B Company as their target. Endless shells fall on them, sending basalt rocks flying and shrapnel everywhere. The Syrian artillery shells are joined by Sagger missiles and occasional rockets and bombs from the enemy's MiG planes. At one point, the company succeeds in creating a "company fire box" and a MiG 19 is hit and falls not far from them.

Slightly behind them, in a natural position that affords no vision, Avshalom Levi observes and corrects the firing and Asaf Sella and Yigal Rubenstein fire.

"Deputy," Avshalom calls Asaf, "you are standing too high in the tank, that is not a good idea."

At around 11:00, he is proven right. An artillery shell falls on the tank and crushes his hand.

One of the characteristics of war, certainly in the armored corps, is the game of "musical chairs." Crew members are killed or injured and others replace them, since the tank has to have four crew members.

Most of the tanks that were hit, some with soldiers killed and injured, were driven back by the crew members to the repair workshops. There, they waited for them to be ready to return to battle. There were those that went from tank to tank, unstoppable. Others, very few, found the detachment from the battlefield as a remedy to their distress and remained there in the protected bases, finding ways to avoid returning to the front.

A month before the war, Sergeant Yoel Emanuel was serving at an armored corps base in the south, training reserve soldiers on the Tiran tanks that Israel had captured in the Six-Day War. As a result of the car accident of the A Company commanders of the 53rd Battalion, he was sent to the Golan as a reserve tank commander in B Company. Before Saturday, Landau notified him that he is positioning him in the technical crew APC. Yoel was infuriated, "That is not what I became a tank crew member for." Impressed by his determination, the company commander decided to reassign him as a loader in tank 3. When Sella is injured, Yoel Emanuel leaves his position as the loader of Avshalom's tank and decides, on his own, to join the tank of the deputy commander, where he takes command.

Taking his place as loader in Avshalom's tank is the original loader of this crew, Moshe Abutbul, who leaves the technical crew APC that had just arrived to evacuate Asaf to safety.

North Sector – 107

Before noon, Muli Dgani, the 1st platoon commander to have been injured, surprises everyone and arrives at the Booster Ridge, leading Yaakov Veidenfeld (Videy), the battalion commander's stand-in tank commander.

With a bandage on his head, Dgani finds Nafshi. They greet each other and are sent to sector 107. Half an hour later, the two reinforcement tanks join the Yachin force, increasing the number of tanks under his command to eight. Shmulik Yachin, who had refused 1st Lt. rank by Ben Moshe, the brigade adjutancy officer and who Nafshi, the battalion's commander had appointed platoon commander, now becomes a *de facto* company commander.

South Sector – Tel Saki

At 11:30 they finish the last machine gun ammunition they had. Shia and Lazer leave their positions, enter the bunker and report to Menachem, who contacts an artillery battery and requests "fire on our forces."

At 11:30, after fighting consecutively for almost twenty-one hours, unprecedented on the entire Golan front, 2nd Lt. Nati Levi and sergeant Nir Atir, commanders in the Venus Company, of 74 battalion, 188th Brigade, have no choice but to give in to the balance of power. Unable to move, without any ammunition left, sitting ducks, easy targets for the anti-tank teams, the two tank commanders positioned farthest south on the Golan, know that it is time to give in. It is just a matter of time before a Syrian infantry soldier hits them.

Carrying grenades and ammunition for their Uzis, Levi and Atir end the brave war they fought beneath the hill and abandon the two tanks. They run as fast as they can to the top of the hill.

This is the sixth time since the start of the war that 2nd Lt. Nati Levi has had to abandon his tank. It is hard to grasp the emotional strength required from a young platoon commander to continue fighting after everything he went through so far – commanding the tank platoon that was the first in line, alone, facing the endless stream of Syrian tanks on the Petroleum Road, and losing his veteran sergeant who was fatally injured in the first hour of battles. Right after this, Levi's tank took first one direct hit and then another, causing serious damage that forced them to withdraw to Juhader. Then the tank of the injured sergeant was repaired and they returned to battle, among the remains of the blood and flesh.

Then he returned to the Petroleum Road on his second tank, joined the forces and discovered that "our" ramps were conquered by the Syrian forces. There was the order to move to sector 116, encounters with Syrian tanks at close range and a third tank he took due to communications problems. He continued on his fourth tank after blowing up a mine outside outpost 116. The crews crowded together in the tank and they continued fighting until they were hit and the tank fell into the anti-tank ditch. He then fled on foot through a dark canal, surrounded by Syrian soldiers, escaping to the tank of the commander of platoon 3, his fifth tank, with his colleague who is now lying dead on the tank. This tank got stuck with its track opened, forcing him to hitch a ride to the top of Tel Saki where he took his sixth tank, the tank of the deputy commander of the 82nd Battalion, where he had fought as a commander until Sunday afternoon.

Time and again, taking one hit after another, suffering malfunctions and encounters with the persistent angel of death. He had so many chances to find his way out of this hell but he did not take them.

Maybe it was his father's genes, Amichai, the veteran colonel from the paratroopers; or perhaps the sense that as a commander he needs to set an example, even in the impossible circumstances of that Yom Kippur.

Still, no one ever imagined continuous fighting on six different tanks, in less than twenty-four hours.

11:40: Nati Levi, Nir Atir and most of their crews enter the bunker. One of the soldiers, Albert Cohen, the loader of the Pesach crew, under the command of Nati Levi, notifies his friends that he would rather flee on foot than be fortified at Tel Saki (he managed to join a reserve force, fight with them and was killed later on in the battles).

Pele Route – Barak Force

At 11:30, A Company of the 82nd Battalion, commanded by Eli Geva, remained alone in the battle in the Hushnia-Ramtaniya-Sindiyana area. Behind the company, on the Dalhamia hills, Chessner's force of eight tanks have taken up position, observing the battle from a distance. The T62 tanks of the Syrian 91st Brigade enjoys an unfair balance of power, applying constant pressure on the ten tanks of the Geva force. The Syrian divisional commander, Shafik Faid, sends an additional battalion to attack Geva from the east.

Fighting for his life and the lives of his company, with hardly any ammunition left, Eli Geva attempts to control the fire between the tanks, holding back the enemy in the north and finally reaching the conclusion that the right thing to do is to disengage and withdraw as quickly as possible.

Geva calls David Yisraeli on the radio but there is no response. He tries the division frequency. No response. He calls to Yanush, "his" brigade commander and described the situation.

"What should I do?" Geva asks him.

"Come back to the brigade to me and bring Chessner with you," Yanush answers.

How is it that two companies abandoned the battlefield? On other sectors, different forces with hardly any ammunition, facing unreasonable balances of power, insisted on remaining in position even when some of their soldiers were hit and they managed to block the Syrian forces.

Receiving the distress call from Geva, it would have been right to first understand the ramifications of pulling out two companies from the battlefield before telling him to "come back to the brigade to me and bring Chessner with you." Was A Company of the 82nd Battalion the only force in trouble while all the other tank crews on the Golan were relaxing in the warm autumn sun? What happened to the Command? Had communication between the 7th Brigade and the Northern Command/the division collapsed? Why didn't Yanush check with Haka/Simchoni/Raful on the situation at Geva's sector before making this decision?

Without having the full picture of the battle and without the approval of the commanders above him in charge of the Golan front, Yanush pulled twenty tanks from their positions where they were playing a crucial role in blocking the enemy on the Hushnia-Yosifun-Nafah triangle. Doing so left a huge void for the tanks of the Syrian 91st Armored Brigade to run into. The lack of a trained, regular force to stop the Syrians coming from the east significantly increased the danger of Nafah falling.

Toward noon, Geva and Chessner's companies leave the battle sector of Hushnia-Yosifun. Without anything to stop them, the tanks of the Syrian 91st Brigade continue north and west, taking control of the Pele route, heading toward the fences of the Nafah base.

The Ben Shoham Force

Shortly before noon, the deputy brigade commander's tank takes a direct hit to his track wheel. Yisraeli transfers to a nearby tank of the 179th Brigade, replacing 1st Lt. Yoav Barkai. Yisraeli instructs him to move to the loader's seat. On entering the tank Yisraeli greets the driver Benny Baranes and Moshe Eliyahu the gunner.

Before completing his acquaintance in the new tank, 1,500 meters from them, his commander and friend, Yitzchak Ben Shoham, commander of the 188th Brigade, now acting as a tank commander, defending Nafah, identifies a T54 tank aiming at Yisraeli. He places Omeisi the gunner on the target.

"Loaded!" Gavrieli shouts.

"Fire!" Ben Shoham orders.

"Long," Benny Katzin reports, and Omeisi in the chaos and smoke in the tank corrects himself and hits the target on his second shot.

Ben Shoham pats the gunner on his helmet. "Champagne" he says on the internal radio

"It is Nissim Omeisi," Benny Katzin point out and Ben Shoham adds, "Nissim, you showed them what a professional gunner can do."

Yossi Gavrieli does not join in the festivities. Omeisi didn't tell him that the shell case comes out of the cannon after being fired when it is burning hot and therefore, he is supposed to use gloves if he wants to remove it. "Ouch!" Gavrieli shouts and his hands burn. Aware of his mistake, Omeisi tells Gavrieli about the gloves and he promises him his hands will be okay.

At that moment Uri Simchoni, the Command Operations Officer, calls them:

"20 of Tofi, what is the situation over there?"

"First champagne," Ben Shoham replies.

"I hear you, I am glad," is Simchoni's response. He has the entire Golan under his responsibility and he would love to have some champagne himself.

A few minutes pass and Ben Shoham continues to give Omeisi champagne. They are ecstatic and feeling great. "Guys, this is going well. I hit ten tanks and I am pushing them back. Get more tanks and send them to me," the 188th Brigade commander says.

12:00

Tel Saki

At 12:00, twenty-five soldiers and commanders[32] crowd into the bunker on Tel Saki, without knowing what their fate will be. The group is made up of fifteen armored corps soldiers of the 74th Battalion, three from the 82nd Battalion and seven infantry soldiers from the 50th Battalion who had been defending the bunker until this point.

Inside the crowded bunker, the young men hear the first shell fall not far from them, and Menachem realizes this is the artillery he

---

32. From the 74th Armored Battalion: Nati Levi, Nir Atir, Moty Aviam, Rafi Cohen, Zion Edri, Michael Zibola, Ami Moshe, Nagarker Yitzchak, Dany Dather, Menachem Shmueli, Andrei Sakal, Brom, Shalom Fachima, David Riv and Michael Swisa.
From the 82nd Armored Battalion: Rubi Reikmanes, Bentzy Kotler, Benny Miller.
From the Nahal 50th Battalion: Menachem Ansbacher, Shlomo Avital, Laizey Agasi, Shaya Levi, the driver Moshe Levi. Also two additional soldiers that had fled from the burning BTRs and joined them in the bunker: Baruch Ochanik, Amiram Bartan.

requested. He calls the battery and corrects their aim based on where he hears the shells fall. Another shell falls on the hill with a huge bang and lifts the spirits of the soldiers. "Continue," the soldiers mumble in the dark between the concrete walls, with their fingers crossed for the artillery soldiers. One more shell falls and it stops. Why did they stop?

At Tel Saki the soldiers don't know that two of the artillery batteries have been destroyed and that a third has withdrawn. They do not know that most of the Southern Golan is now under Syrian control.

Danny Pesach Force

From noon, Maj. Danny Pesach is also on the western side of the Petroleum Road.

This is the same Pesach, deputy commander of the 82nd Battalion from Tel Saki, who had a long and difficult journey with his tank, toward the Bteicha, joining the brigade commander's APC. The same Pesach who, finding himself at 09:00 at Nafah, organized a new task force. He put together the armored force he is now leading with the last tanks of the 679th Brigade – four old Sho't Meteor tanks. They had climbed up from the Bnot Yaakov Bridge moaning, shaking and showing signs of discomfort all the way towards Nafah and Pesach.

As they head to their positions, they cause panic at Nafah. "T55 tanks in the base," Barzani reports, and immediately corrects himself. "Correction, those are our tanks."

Ben Shoham force

At around 12:30, Raful decides it is time to check on Ben Shoham on the Petroleum Road. "20, this is 40, what is your status?"

Unaware of the situation on the ground, Ben Shoham sounds sure of himself, "Fifteen tanks in excellent positions, conducting fire."

Itzik Ben Shoham is pleased. He admires professional gunnery and the guys with him are doing a great job. Fifteen Sho't Kal tanks are blocking the attempts of the Syrian 51st Brigade to move toward Nafah.

Since Ben Shoham is also the commander of the 188th Brigade, he assumes that the Barak force, on the Pele route east of him, are blocking the enemy's 91st Brigade, and together with the tanks of the 679th Brigade, near his front, there is no reason they will not succeed in blocking the Syrians, who will surely soon start withdrawing. Then, finally, our forces will be on the attack, as always.

Ben Shoham is unaware of two important facts. First, the Barak force is no longer on the front and the eastern side is wide open. From 12:00, the commanders of the Syrian 51st Brigade have understood that there is no point in hitting their heads on the unwavering wall facing them on the Petroleum Road. Rather, the Syrian brigade commander sends T55 tanks in a deep flanking maneuver to the west, where Ben Shoham's force cannot see them. Hidden Syrian forces gather in Ben Shoham's future and he is blind to their presence.

13:00

Northern Command headquarters, Mt. Kana'an

12:45: The Southern Golan is still full of Syrian forces but the Galilee now seems to be out of the reach of Syrian hands, and there is a huge sigh of relief at the General Staff and the Northern Command. There is no more talk of the destruction of the Third Temple.[33]

That is when the Northern Command CO, encouraged by the inflow of reserve forces, decides to redistribute the forces in the Golan, for the third time since the war started.

Until the war began, the defense of the Golan had been divided between the two battalions of the 188th Brigade. The 74th Battalion – commanded by Yair Nafshi – on the northern front, and the 53rd Battalion – commanded by Oded Erez – on the southern front. The line was drawn at Tel Hazeka (base 110). The entire front was under the command of Yitzchak Ben Shoham, the commander of the 188th Brigade. The 7th Brigade – commanded by Yanush Ben Gal – was kept as a reserve force.

From 15:00 on Saturday, all of the units of the 7th Brigade had taken up position in the sectors they had been assigned to, together with the tanks of the 188th Brigade. The 82nd Battalion had been sent to the southern Golan front. The 77th, 71st and 75th Battalions had been sent

---

33. The Temple in Jerusalem was, when it stood, the center of Jewish national life. So much so that the destruction of the First Temple (in 586 BCE) and the Second Temple (in 70 CE) are synonymous with the destruction of Jewish national life and sovereignty. Hence the phrase "Destruction of the Third Temple" implies the collapse of the reborn Jewish state of Israel and expresses a national apocalypse.

to the northern Golan front. At around that time, the Golan fronts were divided between the two brigade commanders, Yanush Ben Gal of the 7th Brigade was the commander of the northern front and Itzik Ben Shoham of the 188th Brigade, was responsible for the southern Golan front. The division was approved, *de facto,* by the Command CO, after he arrived at the command headquarters at around 18:00 on Saturday.

From midnight until 13:00 on Sunday, two reserve brigades had arrived on the battle fronts on the Golan. The 679th Brigade – commanded by Ori Or – joined Yanush Ben Gal's force in the north, and the 179th Brigade – commanded by Ran Sarig – joined Ben Shoham in the south. (In practice, the 179th Brigade was commanded by Raful from the Nafah headquarters and Uri Simchoni from the "Palace" on Mt. Kana'an, since the 188th Brigade tactical command group was on the move outside the front.)

Shortly before 13:00, the third distribution of fronts is made, by the Divisions. From Nafah to the north under the command of Raful – 36th Division CO, and from Nafah to the south was under the command of Gen. Dan Laner – commander of the 210th Division.

Raful was in command of the organic battalions of the 7th Brigade (the 75th, 77th and 82nd), in addition to the 71st and 74th Battalions. These were all under the command of Yanush Ben Gal and the 679th Brigade was commanded by Ori Or.

Gen. Dan Laner – commander of the southern front – received a mishmash of different units under his command: the 96th Battalion of the 179th Brigade fighting in the Waterfalls Route area under the command of Giora Birman, the brigade operations officer. He had taken over after the brigade commander and battalion commander had been injured. He also received the 4th Brigade – commanded by Yaakov Hadar (Pepper) – made up of two mechanized infantry battalions; a battalion of Sherman tanks that still had not arrived, plus the Sho't Kal tanks of the 39th Reserve Battalion of the 188th Brigade – also yet to join the battle; the 9th Brigade of Motke Ben Porat (consisting of two mechanized infantry battalions) and the 377th Battalion of Sherman tanks that was not ready to join the action yet. All these were in addition to the Sho't Kals of the 278th battalion of the 179th brigade, which had been in battle on the Kursi–Givat Yoav–El Al sector since that morning. These forces were in addition to the Ben Shoham force

– the remains of the 188th Brigade on the southern Golan front – plus the remains of the 266th Battalion of the 179th Brigade, fighting on the Petroleum Road.

Danny Pesach Force

12:45: As the Northern Command decided on the divisional deployment of the forces, the four tanks of the Pesach force encounter two companies of Syrian tanks of the 51st Brigade south of Nafah, in a western flanking movement. Pesach notifies Ben Shoham and in desperation he reports that he cannot stop them.

"Hang in there," Ben Shoham encourages him, wondering how to deal with this new trouble approaching them from behind.

12:55: Ben Shoham calls Pesach again, hoping for the best. He tries again and again and there is silence. Ben Shoham starts to understand the meaning of this.

A few minutes before 13:00, the four tanks of the 679th Brigade are hit. They had not boresighted their peri-telescopes to their guns and could not fight back against the fifteen tanks facing them. Maj. Danny Pesach, a new deputy commander in the 82nd Battalion – who wanted to repay the Syrians for what they did on Tel Saki – and Maj. Moshe Vax (Taxi) – a company commander in the 679th Brigade, who had hardly had time to change out of his festive Shabbat clothes – were, along with other members of their crews, lying dead in their tanks.

The Battle over Nafah

At 13:00 it is clear to the Northern Command that the main Syrian effort in the Southern Golan front is not focused on the three routes descending to the Kinneret. The generals on Mt. Kana'an realize that the main enemy force is heading northwest, toward the valleys on the foothills of Shifon and Yosifun hills, toward Nafah.

At 13:00, the optimistic mood in the Northern Command undergoes a sharp change. Their optimism had been based on the arrival of reserve forces. These had already taken control of the routes ascending from the Kinneret, while others continued to arrive. This optimism is brutally crushed by three Syrian brigades, hundreds of squat turret tanks heading to destroy the Nafah base and then to continue to the Bnot Yaakov Bridge and from there to the "Finger" of the Galilee.

Nafah

At 13:00 on Sunday, Danny Agmon, the intelligence officer of Division 36 (G2) decides it is time to leave the cramped underground war room for a few minutes and get some air outside. As he is stretching his body, his intelligence officer sensors observe first-hand information. Tank shells are being fired directly on the Nafah base!

He climbs up on a mound of dirt and is amazed to see a Syrian tank moving on the road near the base.

He hardly has a chance to absorb this new information, when additional tanks start to descend from the hills around them with their cannons aimed at the headquarters bunker.

His breath is taken away; he hardly can move his legs and he flees for his life. "Raful!" he shouts in the ear of his commander. "The Syrians are here. We are a minute before midnight!"

Wearing his famous Australian felt hat, armed with unconquerable courage, Brigadier General Eitan hears the tank shells outside, feels the bunker shake and sees the fluorescent lights blinking. He turns around to the intelligence officer and knows everyone there is waiting to hear what he has to say.

"We are too late. There is nothing we can do," Raful says as he turns his wide back, with his poker face, and he adds with his characteristic nonchalance, "Don't we have an anti-tank team outside?"

No one tells him they don't, because everyone knows that Raful understands that they don't. A small smile is on the face of the division commander who has seen it all before. "Even if they come in here, I have my Galil rifle..."

Ben Shoham Force

A few minutes past 13:00, Raful speaks on Ben Shoham's brigade frequency and in his dry tone, he instructs the brigade commander to return to Nafah since the Syrians are on the fences.

Once again Ben Shoham's world collapses around him.

He is devastated by a series of events. The encounter he had during the night with a Syrian tank that clarified to him that the Southern Golan had been conquered by the Syrian forces. The terrible feeling of failure for not succeeding in the defense of his front. His inability to help Oded Erez who has been crying for help all night. The withdrawal to the Kinneret. These are all still burning in his flesh.

In the last three hours he had recovered a little, feeling that the balance was starting to change in his favor, and now suddenly he has to return and defend Nafah.

Just like in the Hebrew children's song, there are Syrian tanks "in front of him, on his sides and behind him." The ones behind him are heading toward Nafah and there is nothing to stop them.

The Reserves Are Coming – 679
It is a few minutes past 13:00 and Ori Or is going crazy. The twenty-five tanks he has with him are not doing anything, and behind him, in the west and the south, he hears the explosions. What is going on there at Nafah, the commander of the 679th Brigade wonders?

"20 of Shemer, this is 92 on your frequency," the Northern Command CO calls him, as if he is reading his mind.

"This is 20 of Shemer, continue," Or answers, sensing that finally something is about to change.

"Has Raful asked you to return to Nafah?" he asks.

"Negative," Or replies.

"The Syrian forces are close to Nafah, move there immediately," Haka orders in a very serious tone.

As they are preparing, dividing up tasks and forces , Raful speaks on the radio and in his nonchalant tone reports that the situation at Nafah is serious. "I have already received the order from Haka," Or answers. "We will be moving out in a few minutes."

The Ben Shoham Force
Filled with adrenalin from the update from Raful, Ben Shoham instructs Yisraeli, the deputy commander, to stay where he is with three tanks and to continue blocking the enemy from the south, while the rest of the force will join him and head toward Nafah.

"Three tanks are staying here with me," Yisraeli shouts on the radio, informing them who the three will be. "The rest of you, turn around and move out quickly after Tofi commander. The 'cages' (home base) we came from this morning are under attack."

This report shocks Zvika Gringold. Just like Ben Shoham and Yisraeli, at that time he too was under the impression that the worst was over and that they were about to head out with the reserve forces that were surely to continue arriving, to crush the Syrian force that dared to come this far. Now he hears this update and the tense voice of the deputy commander.

He takes position to the right of Ben Shoham. Together they spread out to the east of the beaten up road and head north, occasionally stopping to take up position on the roller coaster that is the Petroleum Road.

Zvika looks behind him and he sees the rest of the convoy lagging behind lazily, not keen for another battle. The source of the straggling is clear. For an unknown reason, Ben Shoham had not switched to the company frequency, the one all the tanks were using, since Yisraeli – the deputy brigade commander – had arrived. As a result, every tank is acting independently. Since in war there are some that are braver than others, those less courageous are taking advantage of the silence on the radio to move at their own pace, comfortably lagging behind, in no hurry to get to the new front that is opening up.

13:15: Ben Shoham identifies Syrian tanks four kilometers northeast of his position. They are bridge-laying tanks and APCs heading toward Nafah. He reports this to Simchoni and asks for air support to deal with the threat.

"Wait," Simchoni replies, "you will have an answer shortly."

13:25: Ben Shoham gets closer to the enemy and his identification becomes unquestionable – tens of Syrian tanks are in firing positions right in front of the Nafah base.

"There are many vehicles around the headquarters," he reports to Raful.

"Could they be ours?" Raful asks him, ignoring the report from Agmon in the characteristic Raful manner, making sure Ben Shoham does not fire on our own forces.

"Negative, they are firing at you," Ben Shoham responds.

"Then hit them from behind," Raful declares.

A few more minutes pass, Ben Shoham and Zvika fire from long range. The Syrian tanks do not identify the source of fire but are also not affected by the few hits. Ben Shoham realizes he needs Yisraeli beside him and he orders him to join.

Ben Shoham never imagined that Syrian tanks would reach the fence of the "great base." He and his men never thought they would be firing toward their home. Everything they assumed and took for granted was no longer relevant; everything they thought they knew about the IDF and its power, had been blown up in their faces. There assumptions had been demolished by the tens of Syrian tanks – the T62s of the 91st Brigade to the east of Nafah and the T55s of the 51st Brigade to the west, along with the PT76 APCs – right outside their home, ready to attack.

Nafah – Leaving

13:30: After receiving the report from Ben Shoham, Raful knows that Agmon was right. He gets up, still with ice in his veins, and he says quietly, "It is starting to get unpleasant here. We are leaving."

The commanders are forced to skulk away from the Tiran tanks outside the eastern fences of the base. They steal away to the western side, crossing what used to be an impressive divisional base, now with nothing left but buildings in flames, vehicles piled on each other, trucks and carriers blown to pieces, crushed trees and ditches all around them. The worst sight however was the flag pole with a tattered blue and white flag, symbolizing their situation and – perhaps – that of the entire nation.

Nafah – Still staying

While Raful and the division headquarters are leaving Nafah and heading toward Tel Shiban below the Wasset junction, Lt. Col. Finya Kuperman, deputy commander of the regional brigade, with a number of officers and soldiers, remain in the base. For them, Nafah is home, regardless of what Raful says. They are staying and fighting if necessary, like their military forbears in the War of Independence, to their last bazooka shell.

For almost half an hour, tens of Syrian tanks remain gathered outside the base, without attempting to enter the headquarters.

Apparently, the Syrian commanders did not consider conquering the Nafah base an important objective. They settled for controlling it with fire, and their plan is to flank it from the north and south, toward the Bnot Yaakov Bridge.

Yet still, they are so close and it is tempting. Why not check what the situation in the most important base on the Golan is? Occasional tank platoons are sent to reconnoiter. Are there any Zionist soldiers still alive in there?

Giora Goldberg, the operations officer, takes up position on a low mound near the bathroom outside the bunker, together with Ami Segal his assistant and Nimrod Harel, the assistant intelligence officer. Giora appoints Nimrod to be the MAG machine gun team while he and Ami become the bazooka team. Pini, the deputy brigade commander, takes position right behind them, making sure everyone is in a good position and ready to correct their fire.

"Fire," Giora tells Ami, as he fires twice and misses. "Shit, I fired on the wrong scale," he explains to Finya, who shouts at him that that is no way to fire, instructing Giora to replace him. Giora places the scale in the right place, balances the bazooka, holds his breath and hits the target. The crew of a T62 tank that got too close jumps out of the tank and is shot by a frustrated and angry assistant intelligence officer, who like everyone else, does not understand how the Syrians got this far.

At 13:50, before the full picture of the battle on the Petroleum Road becomes clear, the last soldiers defending Nafah are also ordered to leave.

Leaving behind radios and maps on the walls, the soldiers of the 820th Brigade headquarters crew get into the two APCs and a number of other vehicles and frantically flee toward the Bnot Yaakov Bridge.

Right before they leave, Giora Goldberg remembers the flags his father captured in the Six-Day War and he decides to do something. He parks the carrier outside the entrance to the office, grabs the flags and the brigade standards and quickly joins the rest of the convoy.

Deputy Brigade Commander's Force

13:48: Yisraeli updates Ben Shoham that he is on his way to join him, and he turns and maneuvers near the Petroleum Road. To the west of him, the three other tanks are deployed and next to him is the big Lt. Shay Nachshon. He is someone you can always count on. Initially, he was supposed to stay with the maps at Aleika.

On May 27, Lt. Col. David Yisraeli had been appointed deputy commander of the 188th Brigade, after serving as the commander of the 77th Battalion for two years. He had taken a special liking to Shay

Nachshon, the tall platoon commander from the 77th Battalion. Something in the clumsy manner of the young officer from Neve Magen, with his good spirits and loyalty, had him marked as having promise.

In May 1973, 1st Lt. Shay Nachson, a deputy company commander at the time, had parted from David Yisraeli as he left for the Golan. It was a short parting. The company commander and his deputy were both involved in a jeep accident. This angered Yanush, the brigade commander, and he sent the first to prison and Nachson out of the brigade.

A few days before the war broke out, Nachshon had arrived at the headquarters at Aleika. Yisraeli was surprised and glad to see him. "What are you doing here?" he asked and immediately appointed him to replace Shraga Ibler, the operations officer who was about to get married on Sunday, October 7, and to return after his honeymoon to serve as a company commander.

On Yom Kippur eve, the future operations officer, Shay Nachshon, was on leave at home in Jerusalem, like many others in the brigade. On Saturday he was called back. His father volunteered to drive him to the Golan.

He reported to operations, experiencing the start of the attack on the Golan and together with Ibler he witnessed the horrors during the night, as they volunteered to serve as a "repair/fix unit," receiving what remained of the crushed company of Amnon Sharon, after the ambush on the Petroleum Road.

In the first morning light, Nachshon started nagging Yisraeli, "Deputy commander, what about a tank for me?" Yisraeli looked at him with his piercing black eyes and smiled. "Don't worry Shay, I need someone like you with me." An hour later he took him with him to war.

The Reserves Are Coming – 679/Secondary Force
13:55: Hanan Schwartz, the brigade communications officer, stops three tanks of the 679th Reserve Brigade at the entrance to the Petroleum Road and sends them urgently to the route crossing into the base, to pass through the regional repair center, crush the southern fence and leave.

"The Syrians are on the fence in the east. Move south, be ready to engage. I am transferring you to the 188th Brigade frequency," he instructs them.

They move forward, with their cannons facing east. Hanan Anderson, the platoon commander, is in front, Getman in the middle, Rami Ben Zeev, the deputy company commander, is in the back. They identify Syrian tanks approaching the fences in the east, open fire on them and continue the efforts of Giora, Ami and Nimrod to stop them.

They take up position near the regional repair center, at the exit from the base. In front of them, this time from the southwest, a company of T55 tanks emerge.

"Fire!" the three tank commanders shout, not aware of the fact that these are the west flanking tanks of the 51st Syrian brigade.

Ben Shoham Force

In his binoculars, Ben Shoham identifies fifteen T62 tanks approaching the Nafah fence.

"Where are the planes?" he asks Simchoni. "They need to hit the tanks around the base!"

A minute passes and finally there are Skyhawks in the sky, but the joy he feels is immediately replaced by fear when a half-ton bomb falls right next to his tank, shaking it like it was a toy. Annoyed, Ben Shoham contacts the air support officer at Nafah and asks for an explanation for this.

Another minute passes and the officer gives him the explanation, "From the air, all the tanks look the same. Mark your tanks with tactical signs."

He is right, but under such pressure, even an organized brigade commander like Ben Shoham doesn't have the time to find the tactical marking panels and deal with tying them on.

There is no reason to explain to Nissim Omeisi, in the gunner's seat, why there is no time to tie on the tactical panels. His peri-telescope is full of enemy Tiran tanks.

"Fire, Nissim. Fire!" Ben Shoham tells him and Nissim aims on his own and fires.

In the loader' compartment, operations officer Benny Katzin suddenly sees a Tiran waiting behind the hill, hidden by bushes and he directs Omeisi to aim at the tank. A huge flash comes from the tank when they hit it and Ben Shoham exclaims in the commander's cupola, "Nissim, I love you."

13:52: Yisraeli informs Ben Shoham that he is near him and raises a blue and white flag for identification. "Eye contact," Ben Shoham declares happily and adds, "move all the tanks on your right forward."

13:58: Ben Shoham decides it is time to move forward and he needs more tanks with him. "I do not see tanks joining me in a right flank," he complains to Yisraeli.

"The tanks on the left also have good targets and we are lighting them up," he explains.

"Don't leave me alone," the brigade commander implores, "I am improving my position."

14:00

1st Lt. Yoav Barkai, a reserve soldier from Ein Harod, almost the same age as Yisraeli, turns to the deputy brigade commander next to him and he wonders how they are supposed to attack Nafah with the two shells they have in the tank.

"We do not have time to replenish ammunition," Yisraeli answers. "The brigade commander needs us urgently," and he urges Benny Naranes the driver to cover the distance, hoping that their two shells and a speeding tank will do the job.

14:02: Ben Shoham slides down the hill, closing the distance to Nafah to 1,500 meters and seeing the tanks on the fences. "Let's storm them," he calls to Yisraeli on the radio. "They are attacking the base, come on!" he shouts.

14:04, "I think they are fleeing. Let's go!" the brigade commander encourages himself and anyone listening.

14:11: Ben Shoham discovers that the rocky landscape is making it difficult to pass through, and he instructs Ben Shoef the driver to turn left to the Petroleum Road. He looks around and sees he is on his own. Where is Zvika? Where is Yisraeli? Where is everyone? He calls Yisraeli on the radio, "21, please, I am in front by myself. Send in tanks on the left and right." There is no response.

At that exact moment the deputy brigade commander is moving forward and reporting there are tanks and APCs 300 meters in front of them. He is firing his machine gun and saving the shell for the last minute. That minute comes. A T62 of the Syrian 91st Brigade, the leading armored brigade of the Syrian army, targets the tank of the deputy brigade commander that is speeding toward the Kadariya creek while firing in all directions and sends a deadly armor piercing shell that easily penetrates the Sho't Kal's steel.

Inside the tank there is chaos and flames but the crew is still breathing. Moshe Eliyahu, the gunner is still keeping their last shell as he was ordered, and he suddenly hears the machine gun fire tapping on the tank and David Yisraeli shouts in pain and jumps out of his compartment.

Eliyahu looks up and sees Yoav Barkai trying to jump out of the loader's seat. It is too late, the machine gunfire hits him and he collapses dead on the tank.

Eliyahu jumps out of the tank, hiding behind it, and sees Yisraeli lying on his back motionless. He shouts to him, "What should I do? What should I do?" but David Yisraeli does not answer.

One hundred meters to his right, Shay Nachshon sees the tank of the deputy brigade commander hit and the cloud of white smoke coming from it. While he is wondering what is going on there, a burst of bullets hits the machine gun in front of him and one bullet pierces his right arm.

With a bandage on his right arm and limited movement of his left (still in pain as a result of the jeep accident he was in), Shay knows he needs to get out of that cursed valley. He directs the driver west and then north, in the spirit of the order to stop the enemy at Nafah.

As he is leaving the valley, he looks back and he sees Yisraeli's tank emitting smoke from the turret and remembers him telling him that morning, "I need someone like you near me" and there is nothing he can do.

14:13: The commander of the 188th Brigade is fighting for his life. He is in the only tank approaching the Petroleum Road and he is calling Yisraeli again, begging him this time, "21, this is 20, I do not know what our tanks are waiting for. Send them forward, give them the order." Yisraeli does not answer.

14:16, "21, this is 20. Answer me." Ben Shoham continues to look for his deputy, wanting to line up with him before attacking the enemy at Nafah.

14:19, "21, this is 20. Answer me." Maybe he already knew by now.

14:23: Without a deputy brigade commander, without any tanks at his side, the commander of the 188th Brigade tries to spread the spirit he still has to his invisible forces. "Everyone turn to the right, attack on our base. Out." He hopes someone hears him. But, without having the company frequency, Ben Shoham finds himself alone in a fight. This in contrast to everything he believed in and wrote about: "We are saying that in general, we will not see independent action during battle of units smaller than a battalion..."

Exposed in the tank, the commander of the 188th Brigade rushes forward toward Nafah, the main IDF base on the Golan, operating against the manner he recommended in the article he wrote, but life – or death that is all around – forces him to fight as a lone tank that is being fired at. He is going to fight with whatever he has available.

"21, this is 20, answer me," he tries again, hoping it is the radio that is not functioning. Standing tall in the turret, he moves on, on his own, firing his machine gun at Syrian crew members jumping out of the tanks that were hit.

Not far from him the Nafah camp is in flames. Just yesterday he left the base as the proud commander of a brigade of tanks, and now he is alone, as if there is no IDF in the world. His young men, his soldiers, have been scattered along the lines, and he knows he will never see many of them again. Now it is his turn to play his part.

14:27: In the commander's cupola of his tank, fighting alone for his homeland and his values, Ben Shoham does not forget he is also a brigade commander and updates Simchoni, who is far away on the top of a calm hill in Tzfat. "82, I am engaging tanks that are attacking the Nafah base. It seems that they are fleeing."

14:30: Ben Shoham joins the Petroleum Road, on his way to cross the Kadariya creek, unaware of the body of his deputy lying 200 meters west of him, bleeding into the basalt rocks.

A few hundred meters east of him, a Syrian tank sends up smoke and Ben Shoham searches for better prey. Suddenly, in an evil act of magic, the machine gun in the smoking Syrian tank comes to life.

In the gunner's seat Omeisi hears a short cry of pain, and the long body of Ben Shoham falls above him motionless.

On the other side of the tank, Yossi Gavrieli senses a strange silence and he finds Benny Katzin falling and sitting on the loader's seat.

"What is going on, Benny?" Yossi asks.

Benny does not respond, his eyes roll up and Yossi realizes he is talking to an operations officer who has just died. Then he climbs up and sees Ben Shoham, his hand motionless and his head shattered by a bullet. He too is dead.

14:33: Raful, who left Nafah an hour ago, now in a temporary head-quarters near Aleika, takes the radio. "Ben Shoham, do you read me?" There is no answer.

"If you hear me, key the microphone twice." There is silence.

14:34: Yossi Gavrieli suddenly realizes that someone is calling the brigade commander on the radio repeatedly. He takes the microphone that is full of blood and answers in a broken voice, "The brigade commander has been killed, the brigade commander has been killed."

One thousand meters. That was the distance Yitzchak Ben Shoham had left to get back home. All he needed to do was cross the Kadariya creek, ascend, descend, the Booster Ridge and the fence of the Nafah base. Just 1,000 meters.

Like the best of the knights, he had stormed forward on Nafah, falling defending everything he believed in. Now he is lying shattered in the tank, like the lowest ranking private, and there is no one to help him.

A few seconds pass from the time the brigade commander and the operations officer were killed and tank 20C becomes a sitting duck, target practice for the Syrian machine gunners. The gunfire shatters the periscope in the driver's seat and Ben Shoef understands it is time to move quickly, before the shell comes and finishes them off. He swerves left wildly, does not see a huge pile of rocks and lands on it.

"A ditch! Look what happened," Omeisi shouts to Gavrieli who climbs out of the tank, sees them in the air and shouts to Ben Shoef "reverse." The driver hears him say "forward," tries to move forward and to the right and the tank overturns on its side.

Gavrieli jumps out of the tank and lies down near the rocks. Omeisi tries to get out but the body of the brigade commander is blocking his exit. He shouts to Ben Shoef to help him but he is stunned by the fall and does not hear him. He somehow manages to rotate the turret, climbs into the driver's compartment and together they climb out to the endless war outside.

14:35: A single Sho't Kal tank bursts into Nafah, after passing the training area from the west and entering the repair center, finding its way for the first time inside the base.

Shay Nachshon maneuvers his tank between the ruins of the base and identifies four Tiran tanks 200 meters from him.

"Fire!" Nachshon shouts four times, destroying the immediate threat on what remains of the Nafah base.

14:35: Zvika Gringold is alone again, just like he was at night. He does not understand what has happened to the brigade commander and his deputy and where everyone is. He just continues firing at the tanks outside Nafah and he is now trying to improve his position, and he encounters the Kadariya creek that is not easy to cross. He guides his driver west, toward the Petroleum Road, and when his tracks hit the pavement he is horrified to see the brigade commander's tank on its side.

There is no reason to stop here, he thinks, and he flanks the Petroleum Road from the west, distancing himself from the tanks east of him, crossing the training area and speeding into the repair center. He is the second tank returning to defend their home.

Inside Nafah, his fortress and home, he hears the driver of his tank having trouble breathing and he instructs him to stop.

"What happened to you?" Zvika asks. There is no reply. One of the crew members is sent out to open the driver's compartment but it is locked and cannot be opened. The gunner rotates the turret to 5:00 o'clock, enabling access to the driver from inside the tank and in a joint effort they manage to pull him out. He is in tears having trouble breathing. He has not been physically injured but is in severe shell shock that will not let him deal with the situation any longer, and he flees.

A number of soldiers approach Zvika. He identifies Shmulik Ben Moshe among them, the brigade adjutancy officer. He asks him to get him a new driver.

As he goes to find a driver for him, Simchoni gets on the radio and asks Zvika if he knows what happened to the brigade commander who is not responding.

"I don't know," he answers, "but his tank is on its side. He may have been killed."

"Go get him," Simchoni instructs him.

Without a driver to drive the tank, Gringold finds Shay Nachshon, who just completed firing, and he passes him the hot potato. Shay sets out and near the Booster Ridge outside the fence he identifies an officer he knows. "Where are you going?" the officer asks him.

"To the Petroleum Road, to find out what happened to the brigade commander and his deputy," Shay answers.

The officer he has been friends with since before the war, looks at him gravely and says, "There is no need. They are both dead. Go to Aleika; we will all get organized there to continue fighting."

South Sector Tel Saki

At 14:00, the road below Tel Saki is under Syrian control, and columns of tanks and APCs of the enemy's 132nd and the 47th Brigades come and go as if it was their own backyard. A little higher, at the top of the hill, intense shelling enables the Syrian soldiers to come closer, running from rock to rock, heading toward the bunker at the top of the hill.

Inside the small and dark concrete structure that for some reason is called "the bunker," it is unbearably crowded. 2nd Lt. Menachem Ansbacher tries to encourage twenty-four exhausted, injured, scared young men. He is almost the same age as them, and he too is injured and is doing the best he can.

The minutes pass and he takes out a bible, reads a psalm and the soldiers answer "amen." In an attempt to give them hope, he says in the dark to whoever is able to hear him, "You will see that we will get through this and we will have a party at my parents' house in Jerusalem."

Shortly after 14:00 they hear the sounds of the Syrian soldiers outside the bunker, and Menachem Ansbacher, a rationalist, speaks on the radio and notifies someone at the Northern Command, "The Syrians are attacking us, tell our families we loved them, we will never see them again."

In the spur of the moment, he decides that if he is to die, he will die fighting, and he prepares to launch a counterattack. Shalom Fachima, Moty Aviam's gunner, gets up and announces that he is joining him. Before they set their foot outside the bunker, a grenade is thrown toward them, ending the life of Fachima and the planned attack. Injured a second time, with the dead Fachima next to him and Kalashnikov bullets flying through the bunker, Ansbacher aborts his plan to attack.

The sound of the argument of the Syrian soldiers of whether they are dead or not reaches them, and two minutes later a number of grenades are rolled in, followed by a huge explosion and then silence.

"You are shouting," someone says to Moty Aviam, temporarily deaf as a result of the explosion. Then his hearing returns and what he hears is heart-breaking cries. In the occasional light inside the bunker, he sees that three paratroopers are seriously injured, and he does not understand how anyone is still alive in the crowded Tel Saki bunker.

The soldiers in the bunker pile upon each other and suddenly Menachem says, with quiet authority, "Whoever is not injured and can go outside, should go and tell the Syrians we surrender."

Once again it is Yitzchak Nagarker, Atir's loader, who volunteers. He makes his way carefully, his eyes darting around. He is wearing his turquoise tank coverall and he walks out, staying close to the BTR. Suddenly two Syrian soldiers are facing him with another few covering them. The Syrian closest to him, indicates with his hand to him to move, aiming his gun at him. Nagarker sees that the finger of the Syrian soldier is moving on the trigger and bullets hit the BTR and a bullet or several bullets or shards hit him in the leg. The other Syrian does the same and fires near Nagarker's legs and indicates for him to move toward the entrance to the bunker.

"How many are inside?" the Syrian indicates, spreading his palm and rotating it with the universal question mark at the end of this.

"Three," Nagarker indicates, instinctively thinking of Nir Atir, Danny Dather and Ami Moshe, his crew.

At the same time, Meir Brukental, one of the remaining soldiers of the 590th Battalion, is located in a hidden post, just yards southwest of the bunker. He sees an Israeli soldier in a turquoise coverall (Nagarker) lying on the ground and Syrian soldiers kicking him repeatedly. Then they pick him up and shout "Tirat, Tirat" (pilot, pilot) and carry him to the Syrian BTR outside the bunker.

Inside the bunker, the soldiers hear the gunfire outside and they understand that the Syrians have no intention of taking prisoners. The injured Menachem looks around and all he sees is hopeless eyes. At the southern corridor are the bodies of Roni from the paratroopers and Yoav the tank platoon commander. At the northern corridor there is the still-warm body of Fachima, the gunner. Ansbacher gives the order, "Take out grenades. The second the Syrians come in, throw the grenades at them." They hold the grenades, pull out the pins and wait for the Syrians.

For an unknown amount of time they sit there, bent over or lying on top of each other in the darkness, terrified, and again it is Menachem, seriously injured but still functioning, who decides that he no longer hears voices outside and maybe the Syrians left. He instructs everyone with a grenade without a pin in it to find the pin and push it back in. They find them, reinsert them, and wait.

The horrible moaning of Michael Swisa, his driver who is in pain, wakes up Moty Aviam who slips in and out of consciousness. "My eye. My eye. I can't see." Aviam, also in terrible pain, pats Swisa, "It will be okay. Don't worry Michael, in the end it will be okay."

Then Aviam focuses on his own pain and it is his arm that is tearing him up and his back that is burning and now his bladder is about to explode. "What do we do now?" he asks in the dark and someone suggests, "Piss in the coverall." He gladly does as he is told and he lets go, as Swisa next to him continues to moan.

Sunday, October 7 – Afternoon to Dark

Shortly after 14:30 the general feeling at the headquarters on Mt. Kana'an was of a catastrophe in process. The remains of the improvised force of the 188th Brigade and a number of reserve companies, the only force available to stop the enemy in the central and southern Golan, has been dispersed in all directions. They continued to receive reports of the last nail in the coffin of the Nafah base, perhaps of the entire Golan Heights. The chain of command of the 188th Brigade – the brigade commander, his deputy, the operations officer – has been wiped out.

At the Mt. Kana'an headquarters they felt the blow of the tragic fall of the "Golan Commander," the commander of the 188th Brigade, but they knew they had no time for self-pity. Time was running out on the Golan and they had to find a solution immediately.

The fall of Nafah had two immediate implications. The first was that the entire northern Golan front – the front where they had been successful in stopping the Syrian tanks without much effort – was now under siege. They knew that if Nafah fell, then the forces of Eiland, Yachin, Kaimo, Shir-On, Nafshi, Kahalani and Yanush would also fall, since they too would be besieged like the forces of the 188th Brigade in the southern Golan. Furthermore, conquering Nafah would enable the enemy forces to easily descend to the Bnot Yaakov Bridge, Kibbutz Gadot and from there to the entire Galilee.

Farther west, on the routes to the Kinneret, the Syrian advance was blocked by the reserve forces – but here in the central Golan, where things had seemed so safe just a few hours ago, events were deteriorating to the point of no return.

What will happen if the Syrians continue west? Who is there to stop them when all the "reserve" forces are spread throughout the Golan, busy blocking the Syrian enemy?

Lacking answers, with a sense of deep despair taking over the headquarters, Haka and Simchoni were praying for a miracle. Would it somehow be possible for the remains of the 679th Reserve Brigade commanded by Ori Or to manage to stop the enemy?

The Northern Front – 104

The drama at Nafah continued to develop. At the same time, to the north, at the Shechita hill – the hill farthest north on the Golan, Israeli tanks are continuing to fight Syrian forces. Here, the crew of Eyal Shaham – the commander of H company of the 74th Battalion of the 188th Brigade – know that once again they will have to get the job done on their own.

David Golan, the gunner, identifies targets independently, firing and correcting his misses, while Ami Turgeman the loader and Moshe Nili the driver work together with him as an efficient machine. After fighting together on combat days, as the company commander's crew, their experience gives them an obvious advantage.

At 14:00, Eyal is busy running the battle, when an efficient Syrian fire observer starts to show his capabilities and orchestrate heavy artillery bombardment, which starts falling on outpost 104 and the Shechita hill overlooking it from the north.

Eyal knows that artillery shells cannot harm crews that are closed inside their tanks, and he calls to Koby Greenbaum who is right next to him. "It does not seem serious," he estimates, "but even so, close the tank hatches and wait for it to pass."

Greenbaum closes the commander hatch, the crew observes from its periscopes and Koby himself maintains eye contact with the company commander's tank as the shelling continues and intensifies.

Eyal Shaham does not close his hatch. He is sure the shelling is not serious and he knows that his job as the company commander takes precedence over the risk, and it is important to locate the artillery batteries. Even if the tank shakes occasionally, it will soon be over.

Exposed in his tank, Eyal Shaham continues to direct the IDF artillery toward the enemy batteries. Koby Greenbaum realizes that the

Syrian artillery is taking their tanks very seriously. "Commander, get your head in the tank!" he shouts to Shaham in a tone that only veteran sergeants can use with their commanders.

He does not have the chance to receive a response, and Yoni Midovnik, the base commander, also calls Shaham.

"What can I do for you?" Eyal asks just as the radio is cut off.

A few meters from Eyal's tank, Koby Greenbaum hears a metallic sound different from the regular sound of a shell falling. He rotates the tank to where he thinks the shell fell and sees that the commander's hatch is gone.

In the company commander's tank there is silence.

Moshe Nili, Eyal's driver, suddenly feels a massive thrust. Maybe it is Turgeman who fired without calling it? He looks behind him over his shoulder and hears Ami Turgeman breathing his last breaths. Nili ignores the sounds of death and mechanically carries out the fire extinguishing drill. He turns off the engine and activates the fire extinguishing system. Somehow, he manages to climb out of his seat, despite the cannon that is lowered over him. He gets on the turret and looks inside. Eyal's body is shattered. Golan is leaning on the cannon, he looks whole but his eyes show death.

Nili slides back into the driver's seat, starts the engine and moves back. Without anyone directing him, the tank falls into a pit. He gets out of the tank stunned and helpless.

The commander of the 2nd platoon, Aviv Shir-On, on the hill near them, asks what is going on.

"Rekem commander has taken a direct hit," Koby Greenbaum reports to Shir-On. "I do not know the situation there. I am going to check." Koby drives over to the damaged tank and he sees Nili the driver leaning on the tank. "What happened?" he asks. Nili does not respond. Koby gets on the tank, looks inside the tank, sees the mess of bodies and gets off the tank immediately.

"What is the situation, 2B?" Shir-On asks on the radio.

"I am taking this tank to the camp area. There is not much to do," Greenbaum answers shortly, trying to keep it business as usual.

Nili gets back into the driver's seat, and Koby sits on top of the damaged tank and signals to him to move back and down, meaning west, off the cursed hill. His entire crew has been killed and Nili tries to control his emotions. He almost slips off the cliff. Almost hits a building. But in the end, he manages to get the tank, Koby and the bodies of his three friends to the company camp area at Mas'ade.

Nili jumps out of the driver's seat, Koby jumps off the tank, and they stand there embarrassed while Moshe Keren, the battalion ordnance officer, the responsible and practical adult, gets on the tank, removes the bodies of their friends and covers them with blankets.

Between Nafah and Aleika

While at the "Palace" at Tzfat they are hoping for a miracle (the 679th Brigade) to come and save Nafah, the remains of the forces that fought on the Petroleum Road reach the main road. They are beat up, defeated, without a chain of command to lift their spirits. One by one they turn west, continuing their withdrawal toward Aleika. They are told by unfamiliar officers from the brigade that the remaining forces are getting organized to stabilize the last line of defense on their way to the Jordan River and the Galilee.

Among the soldiers heading to Aleika is Zvika Gringold. He finally received a new driver in his tank and he crushes the main road with his tracks. He is shocked at the sight of the entire army retreating; this is a sight they were used to seeing in previous wars but then it was always the enemy retreating. This time however, it is us, the proud IDF, fleeing on foot and in vehicles, crammed together, hanging outside the vehicles, terrified, injured and lacking combat spirit.

Exhausted, his burned face painful and blistering, Zvika arrives at Aleika, stays close to the brigade command carrier, falls out of the tank into the hands of Zurich the intelligence officer, and he says, "I can't take any more."

The Reserves Are Coming – 679/ Nafah sector

As Zvika ends his heroic fighting, collapsing into Zurich's arms, the army gathering at Aleika is in a state of crisis, and at the "Palace" at Tzfat they have a sense of a real emergency. This is when the angels of the 679th Reserve Brigade appear at the Quneitra gap.

Since that morning, different tank forces had taken part in the battles at Nafah: the 188th Brigade, 7th Brigade and 179th Reserve Brigade. The troops of these brigades have been killed, injured, had their vehicles damaged or been forced to withdraw, and now all that remains are the tanks of the 679th Brigade. The only force on the front, trying to keep its finger in the dam.

In an armored battle that starts when the morale of the Israeli forces is at its lowest, two reduced tank battalions of the 679th Brigade manage to stop the Syrian 91st brigade. The Syrian force is equipped with the best arsenal the Syrian army has – T62 tanks with the best cannons on the front.

The 289th Battalion, commanded by Raful Shefer, moves quickly west on the main road between Ein Zivan and Nafah (the Yabasha route), encountering Syrian tanks that had already broken through to the north of the road and taken position between Tel Shifon and Dalawe (Ortal). On making contact they conduct face-to-face battles at close range.

The 57th Battalion, commanded by Moshe Harel, with the brigade headquarters, heads toward Tel Yosifun (the Raziel route) in a deep flanking maneuver from the south. It is there, on the southern slopes, that they identify the tanks of the Syrian 91st Brigade. They start to hit them from the side, one by one, while the enemy has no idea where this assault is suddenly coming from.

An hour earlier, after completing their preparations and arming at the Yiftach base, the twenty-two tanks of the 93rd Battalion, the third battalion of the 679th Brigade, arrived at Nafah under the direct command of Raful, the divisional commander. They had been sent on the Pele route toward Hushnia in order to help Ben Shoham (while he still was alive). The battalion commander Ran Gotfried, who had not been notified that there were Syrian tanks so close to Nafah, had crossed the Kfar Giladi quarry near Nafah and headed toward the main road, still in a column formation. Accurate tank shelling hit two of his tanks. Gotfried was shocked. Could these be booty tanks taken by the IDF that had not been notified that we are arriving? Then it sinks in. Located in very bad open positions, he starts to return fire, stopping the Syrian forces closest to Nafah and paying a heavy price. In three hours of fighting, he loses most of the battalion tanks.

15:00

Shortly after 15:00, while the forces of Ori Or are blocking the Syrians, Haim Dannon the deputy commander of the 57th Battalion arrives slightly west of Nafah.

In the afternoon hours on Sunday, Haim Dannon was the only combat officer at the war reserve storage base of the 679th Brigade, and his mission was "to turn off the lights" and to take the last tanks to the front lines.

Three Sho't Meteor tanks under his command headed toward Nafah, and near the Upper Beit Hameches they met an open jeep. In it was Man Aviram, Raful's deputy.

"Hurry, the Syrians are already at Nafah," he tells him.

Dannon led the tanks, as fast as their old engines and tracks would allow, toward Nafah. On the way he encountered endless convoys of vehicles retreating toward the Jordan River. From one of the APCs, a petrified infantry company commander shouts to him, "The Syrians are at Nafah. They are killing us."

He approaches Nafah from the west, arriving at the outskirts of the base with three tanks. He stays close to the base fence, toward the training areas. Half an hour later, he takes up an observation position, identifies ten T55 tanks 800 meters from him, and opens fire. Some of them are destroyed, others retreat. He takes the chance to improve his position and heads south. He finds himself in the Kadariya stream and he decides to head east, toward the Petroleum Road.

At the entrance to the Petroleum Road, he sees a Sho't Kal tank near the fence, with the 20C tactical sign on it, lying on its side. Standing there like a statue is a crew member with a yellow flag in his hand.

Dannon gets off the tank and finds Nissim Omeisi, in complete shock. He keeps saying, "The brigade commander and the operations officer have been killed. Then the tank overturned. The brigade commander and the operations officer have been killed. Then the tank overturned."

Dov Zolden and Etzion Ashkenazi – A Night of Agony

While the tanks of the 679th Brigade fight the Syrian Tirans, not far from there the personal survival struggle of two soldiers from A Company, 53rd battalion, continues.

During the night between Saturday and Sunday, two good friends met at the deployment base in Quneitra. Dov Zolden was the gunner of handsome Nimrod Kochavi, who had been killed by a shard of shrapnel to his brain. Etzion Ashkenazi was the driver of the fire support tank. He had come to the base with the damaged company commander's tank, carrying the body of Zuaretz the loader.

At around noon on Sunday, Hatuka – the communications sergeant – arrived at the bunker at Quneitra driving an APC, and someone gave the order for all the fit tank crew members to get in it and go to Nafah, where they will be reassigned to tanks and return to battle.

"Is the path OK?" Zoldan asks, after having endured a short but painful first experience.

"Fine," the communications sergeant answers. "This is the main road to Nafah." After being reassured, they lay an injured company commander from the 71st Battalion on a stretcher in the APC and set out.

There is silence In the vehicle. They are all lost in their own thoughts, swaying from side to side in quiet acceptance. They are hoping their driver will bring them safely to Nafah and there they will see what will happen.

Two kilometers from Nafah, a Syrian tank spots them and fires a shell, cutting off the fingers of one of the soldiers who stuck his hand out at the worst time. Now they all disrupt the silence with shouts, when a deadly shell hits the back of the carrier.

Hearing the cries in the passenger compartment, feeling the carrier shake, the driver speeds off, stops at a spot that offers concealment, brakes abruptly, jumps out and runs toward Nafah. He is not the only one. Anyone who is physically capable runs or limps after him.

Three soldiers remain in the carrier. The injured company commander on the stretcher, Zoldan who has been hit between the hip and thigh, his leg dangling on a muscle and in terrible pain, and Ashkenazi, with his knee torn open and a tear under his armpit.

Despite the serious injury, perhaps due to the shock, Ashkenazi still does not feel pain and he tells himself he has to evacuate Zoldan, who has a more serious injury than him. As he is dragging outside the carrier, he feels a hand on his leg.

"Don't leave me here," the injured company commander demands.

"We won't leave you," Ashkenazi promises. "Just let me evacuate my friend and I will be back for you."

As he is dragging Zoldan on the ground, filling it with blood, he hears the familiar sound of an engine. He looks over his shoulder and is amazed to see the carrier driving away and leaving them alone. It is heading toward Nafah, driven by the injured company commander, who apparently was not going to settle for his promise.

In the distance, Ashkenazi sees two abandoned tanks on top of the hill.

"I will be right back," he promises Zoldan. "I will run up there, start one of them and come back to pull you up, and together we will escape to Nafah."

Two burnt Sho't Meteor tanks of the 679th Brigade await him on the hill. He bends down into the tank and is overwhelmed by the smell of dead bodies that hits him.

Sticking to the escape plan, Ashkenazi forces himself to overcome his reaction, passes over a dead driver and tries to start the tank from outside. There is no response. He gives in and returns limping to Zolden, who is in the same position he had left him in on the ground, in pain.

With his last ounces of strength, he grabs Zoldan's coverall and tries to drag him. A loud and heartbreaking objection comes from the mouth of the injured soldier.

"I am not leaving you here!" Ashkenazi says, as he starts to feel the pain in his own body and can hardly stand on his foot.

"Go save yourself," Zoldan says. "Then come back for me."

"I am not leaving you," Ashkenazi determines.

Behind the veil of pain, Zoldan whispers to him, "Etzion, get out of here. Together we have no chance of getting out alive, at least save yourself."

Ashkenazi still hesitates.

"Run, run," Zoldan says to him. "The Syrian tanks are getting close. Run."

He places Zoldan in the ditch on the side of the road, rises up with tears in his eyes. "I am going, but know that I did not leave you. I will be back, hold on for now."

They both burst into heartbroken tears and finally Ashkenazi detaches himself and leaves, leaning on his healthy leg, heading west. He turns back his head repeatedly, refusing to believe he left his good friend behind.

As he is on his way, a Sho't Meteor tank appears and Ashkenazi waves at the commander, shouting that he has an injured friend in a ditch behind them. "Stop, let's take him." The tank commander ignores him and continues to exchange fire with an invisible enemy, until his own vehicle is hit. The tank crew jumps out of the tank and together with Etzion, they all drag themselves toward the eucalyptus trees.

In the grove, they find some of the soldiers who escaped from the APC. Ashkenazi asks for their help in evacuating Zoldan. No one volunteers.

Without any choice, Ashkenazi moves on, passing the fence of Nafah, with Syrian tanks firing at it, and he continues toward Aleika. Near the loading area, by the gate of the base, he finds artillery soldiers getting organized. He gives them the location of Zoldan and asks for their help in evacuating him.

The artillery soldiers get in their APC, encounter the deadly tank battles around Nafah and flee toward Aleika, without getting to Zoldan.

After a while, Ashkenazi is evacuated to the battalion medical evacuation center near Beit Hameches, and he begs them to evacuate his friend. "We will take care of it," he is told. "For now, we will evacuate you." Ashkenazi refuses. "I want to see that you managed to evacuate him."

A rescue force moves out and returns in less than half an hour reporting that there is no way to get near the area. There are Syrian forces all around Nafah.

All this time Zoldan is in the ditch. When there is a relatively quiet moment, he takes out his military ID card and writes to his parents – "I was killed on Sunday, October 7, not far from Nafah."

After a while, he hears tank tracks and soldiers jumping out of tanks and speaking in Arabic, and in a basic survival instinct he smears blood and dirt on his face, the only two materials around him – and he is hit in the face with a stream of hot urine. A few minutes pass and the enemy soldiers finish the break they took, get back in their tanks and head in the same direction Ashkenazi went, to Nafah.

Darkness falls, his thirst is driving him mad, Zoldan uproots weeds and wets his mouth and throat. Night comes and it is completely dark. He is bleeding and his strength is running out. He looks up at the sky full of stars and whispers, "God, if you exist and can hear me up there, get me out of this hell and I will be yours forever." A minute later an IDF armored personnel carrier passes by Zoldan who screams for help with all his might. They do not hear him. Another minute passes and another carrier arrives. Zolden throws rocks at them. The alert soldiers hear the knocking on the metal and they stop and look around the darkness. They find a figure lying on the side of the road and they head toward it, with their guns pointed at him. They recognize him – it is IDF soldier Dov Zoldan – and they carry him to the carrier, as his consciousness slips away.

North Sector – 107

On Sunday afternoon, with two new tanks full of ammunition beside him, Yachin decides it is time to send the other tanks to resupply at Beit Hahazit in Quneitra.

Vodak and Naides are sent back to the base and pass the graffiti written by Sergeant Naides in the tank camp area, "When it is our turn to die, we will die, so don't tell us how to live."

This matter of life and death was something Sergeant Yossi Naides was concerned with very much. "Look at you," his fellow commanders would tease him, when he appeared smiling, smeared with grease, soot and oil.

"It is better to be alive and dirty than dead and clean," he would reply cheerfully. "Also," he would add, when the atmosphere was too serious, "no dumb bastard ever won a war by going out and dying for his country" – he quoted George Patton, the American armored corps general who rode all the way to Berlin over the bodies of the Germans –"he won it by making some other dumb bastard die for his country."

Back at the 107 ramps the darkness falls on the eight tanks of Shmulik Yachin while they continue exchanging fire with enemy tanks at long ranges. It seems calm and Yachin is the only one who disrupts the pastoral atmosphere. He starts losing his voice and insists on grunting on the radio. "Shut up," Muli Dgani says to him. "The army will manage without you for a while" and Shmulik remains quiet.

The reserves are coming – 4th Brigade / Maale Gamla Route

Shortly before 13:00, the Arik Bridge rings with the continuous rumble of tracks on the northern Kinneret. The first Sherman tanks of the 95th Battalion of the 4th Brigade, commanded by Col. Yaakov

Hadar (Pepper), cross the finishing line, after starting their long and exhausting drive at 06:30, all the way from the Kurdani war reserve storage base near Acco.

Pepper does not let his men enjoy their accomplishment. "The real task is yet to come." He urges them to head to the conquered route of Maale Gamla, the route ascending from the Beit Zaida valley in the Kinneret to the ancient Gamla. (At that time there still was no road and the Maale Gamla and Kanaf settlements had yet to be established.)

At 13:30, while the Sherman tanks slowly made their way up the Maale Gamla route, the first tanks of the 39th Reserve Battalion commanded by Lt. Col. Yoav Vaspi arrived.

The 39th Battalion was the organic reserve unit of the 188th Brigade. As a result of the short notice given to the IDF reserve forces, all of the tanks of the organic battalion had been assigned to the forces of the 7th Brigade. The battalion crews had been sent to the Naftali base near the Golani junction and found themselves with tanks stripped of all their equipment, just like the tanks of the 179th Brigade who had come before them. "Shells and peri-telescopes, that is what matters," Yoav Vaspi instructed Haimke Porat, his deputy. "We will move out with whatever we have, even without bullets for the machine guns."

In the late morning hours of Sunday, nine tanks leave the Naftali base, led by Yoav Vaspi.

Vaspi joins Pepper the brigade commander and is notified that, from this point on, he is under his command. Together, they identify in the distance, outside their firing range, the clouds of dust that a Syrian company of tanks is raising, as they start to descend toward the Kinneret. Vaspi is sent to block them and the Shermans, the World War 2 veterans, gladly make the way for him.

The Syrian tank battalion they encounter reached its current location by mistake. IDF intelligence had received information that the Syrian 47th Armored Brigade was heading toward the Southern Golan, to Ramat Magshimim and El Al. The first battalion, commanded by the deputy brigade command battalions, made a mistake in navigation and headed west instead of south and ended up on the Maala Gamla route. For Yoav Vaspi and Pepper, the fact that these Syrian tanks were there was a complete surprise.

Vaspi was in front, followed by Yosef Sarig, the company commander, and company commander Avraham Sela was last. As they are moving toward engagement, Sela identifies the Syrian tanks and opens fire. "You are firing at me," Vaspi shouts on the radio, feeling the shells flying over his tanks.

"It is not at you, it is above you," Sela reports, updating the battalion commander about the enemy force; he continues firing, destroys three Syrian tanks and joins the battalion battle positions south of the conquered route.

Until the sun sets, the nine tanks of the 39th Battalion conduct "as in the training manuals" tank battles. They start out with nine tanks in their force and end with nine tanks. They do not suffer any damage or injuries, and remain clean and in perfect condition.

On the other side, there is severe damage – any Tiran that dares to appear is destroyed. The majority of the Syrian forward battalion returns its souls to Allah and the rest retreat.

As it starts to get dark, the nine tanks of the 39th Battalion improve their positions by moving to the same positions that the Syrian tanks had occupied. Here they prepare for the night parking (at the location where the base of the 75th Battalion base is located today).

Vaspi organizes everyone in spearhead battle positions, ready for the enemy, should they dare come back. Avraham Sela and Yoav Vaspi take up position in the front, the rest of the tanks in the rear and to the sides. Pepper, with the brigade command group and a battalion of Sherman tanks, take up position farther back, maintaining eye contact with the force in the front.

South Sector – Tel Fares

The report of the deaths of Ben Shoham and Yisraeli shock the headquarters on Mt. Kana'an but in the "enclave" at Tel Fares the remaining forces remain in battle positions and they do not know that their commander has fallen. They are too busy with their own effort to stay alive.

In the early afternoon, on the northern side of the hill, with eleven tanks secured in a circle, Oded Bekman hears someone from the Northern Command asking them how they are doing.

"There are a lot of Syrian forces," Bekman answers, as he identifies a huge cloud of dust indicating the route of the 58th Mechanized Brigade of the Syrian 1st Division toward Hushnia. Everywhere he looks there is a wall of dust, hiding the horizon.

Below the hill, Tamir, Davidson, Amir and Tiroler continue what they had started in the morning, this time relentlessly hitting the tanks of the Syrian 58th Brigade. The enemy force continues to attack them and get hit, just as their comrades from the 46th Brigade had done that morning. The Sho't Kal tanks light up more and more Tiran tanks, bringing their opponents' motivation to a low point.

Slightly above them, in a calm atmosphere, battalion commander Erez and the eleven tanks with him, observe the Syrian attempts failing, due to the tanks guarding the deployment base.

To Bekman's surprise, the people around him display moods ranging from accepting to not caring. Till yesterday they had been the spearhead of the self-confidence of the IDF and now here they are – burned out, exhausted, with low spirits, confused, besieged and not knowing what will happen. Maybe because of this, they are in a state of indifference. It is as if they have come to terms with the situation they are in; with shocking clarity, the soldiers believe that from here they will either be taken prisoners or die. In a surreal pause that occurred on the hill, they each make different vows to keep if there somehow is a miracle and they make it out of this alive.

Suddenly, the artillery fire stops and so do the attempts of the Syrian mechanized brigade to conquer the hill, and fifteen minutes of a divine pause covers the area in a veil of silence.

Empowered by the sudden tranquility that fell on them, as the son of a Beitar family, Bekman gives a speech about their own personal Masada and he suggests that his crew fights till their last drop of blood. There should not be any talk of being taken prisoners, he says. They all nod their exhausted and sooty agreement. Bekman is relieved, he leans on the tank and writes a farewell letter to his parents and his best friend and titles it "Last Will."

At 16:00, the air fills with the terrifying humming of four enemy helicopters. Commando forces! One of them, hovering right in front of Bekman's tank, starts to slowly descend, as if he is examining how serious the intentions of the platoon commander are. Bekman bends over his machine gun, after just inserting fresh ammunition, and fires at the window of the helicopter through which he can clearly see the pilot with a white helmet and the images of soldiers. The helicopter jumps through the air, loses altitude, dives toward the east and crashes on the rocks of the Purple Line.

Bekman is not alone. All the forces on the Tel Fares sector are raising their guns to the sky and firing. Another helicopter crashes and on the radio there are many soldiers taking credit. Then a third helicopter arrives, sees the danger, keeps his distance and manages to land on the south side below the hill. Commando soldiers jump out and deploy in the area, unaware of the extent of anger and hatred in the hearts of the four Sho't Kal tank crews waiting for them at the deployment base.

Moty Amir lets out his anger by firing a machine gun at the Syrian helicopter which starts to go up in flames in a vicious light and sounds show. Before he has the time to absorb the spectacle, Syrian commandos move forward with admirable determination right in front of the machine guns of the four. A few minutes pass and the basalt ground fills with fresh Syrian blood, and the cries of injured soldiers fill the air as they join the panicked shouts of the survivors of the withdrawal.

Erez, the battalion commander, continues to receive reports from the battlefield. He understands that one helicopter did manage to land the commando troops, and he reports to operations officer Simchoni about the disposition of the helicopters. Two had been shot down and one had mysteriously disappeared. Horrified by Syrian commandos landing on the Hermon, Simchoni orders the immediate shelling of the mountain, and now there is a mixture of Syrian and Israeli shells hitting Tel Fares and the remaining force of the 188th Brigade on the Southern Golan front.

Aware of the enemy helicopters landing, the artillery fire and the Hermon falling, the IDF soldiers on the hill – paratroopers, artillery, intelligence, anti-aircraft – start heading down the hill. They meet Oded Erez and his tanks at the Tuf quarry and notify anyone who wants to hear, "Syrian infantry forces are attacking us from the northeast and the force that was brought in by the helicopters is also about to attack the hill."

Erez sends two tanks to check. Uzi Urieli and Oded Bekman climb the steep hill to the base, placing grenades beside them, preparing ammunition for the machine guns, waiting for the ambush with their hearts beating fast. Bekman is leading, with an Uzi aimed at the cliff to his right where enemy soldiers may appear. At the entrance to the base, they have their first "encounter" – a Dodge 400 IDF truck, is blocking their path. Without hesitating, they drive over it and wind into the base. Enemy soldiers! In the middle of the volcanic hill a number of figures are bent down and running. Bekman opens fire and then identifies them as IDF soldiers, fleeing from the bunkers. He continues with Urieli and makes sure the Syrian forces have not arrived yet. He confirms that he did not hit any of the soldiers and lets out a sigh of relief and clears his conscience.

South Sector – Tel Fares

Toward sunset, Oded Erez receives the approval from Uri Simchoni to evacuate the hill and retreat west toward the Kinneret. Now he is notified that the brigade chain of command is no longer alive. He keeps the information to himself, now is not the time to spread the news and he starts preparing the urgent task, continuing the battle for the lives of his soldiers.

Erez knows he needs to lead everyone home to the Kinneret and to survive a long drive west, through a territory full of enemy forces. He decides they will wait for the dark.

North Sector – 104

As it starts to get dark, Koby Greenbaum, arrives at sector 104 and Aviv Shir-On positions his platoon in night combat parking. Just as they get into position, one of the operations NCOs arrives with trucks carrying fuel and ammunition and Aviv asks him how the drive was. "I took a long detour, through Kiryat Shemona," the operations sergeant answers.

"Are you serious?" Aviv asks. "What has gotten in to you? Why not come straight from the battalion?"

"What battalion?" the operations sergeant answers. "Don't you know that there are Syrian tanks at Nafah?."

The Reserves are coming – 679/Nafah sector

"They are breaking, thinking of retreating," the intelligence reports state, regarding the Syrian forces, supporting the new situation in the Hushnia-Tel Yusifun-Nafah triangle.

By sunset on Sunday, with endless sacrifice and determination, the tanks of the 679th Brigade, together with a few tanks of the 266th

Battalion of the 179th Brigade had managed to stop the momentum of the Syrian tanks.

Without being aware of how crucial this point is, the tanks of the 679th Brigade brought about the crucial change in the huge battle over Nafah, sticking a bleeding yet stable finger in the eye of Walid Hamdon, commander of the Syrian 51st Tank Brigade. From the start of the afternoon, Hamdon had been sending continuous reports to Hasan Turkmany, commander of the 9th Division, according to which the Nafah base was in his hands, that the tanks of the Syrian 91st Brigade were progressing east and it was all going according to plan. "We will soon be on the crossings of the Jordan River," he predicted. This however, did not come to pass.

Sunday, October 7 – From Night to Morning on Monday, October 8

On Sunday night the pendulum of the mood in the Northern Command stops on "relatively calm." The decision makers at the headquarters at Mt. Kana'an understand that the desperate efforts of the 188th Brigade, assisted by the tanks of the 82nd Battalion of the 7th Brigade, have slowed the Syrian blitz on the Southern Golan and given the reserve brigades time to get organized.

On Sunday, all of the reserves sent to the Golan had just one mission, to block the enemy.

Reserve Gen. Dan Laner, who fought in World War 2 in the German department of the Palmach and then in every subsequent war Israel had fought, was called in to rescue the Southern Golan and change the situation.

On Saturday, Laner left his kibbutz in the Galilee, Neot Mordechai, arriving at the Golan with the feeling that he was fighting to save his home.

Calm, older than Dado and Hofi, with all of the forces on the Southern Golan under his command, his impact was immediate. Together with the commanders of the reserve brigades: Col. Ran Sarig, commander of the 179th Brigade, Col. Yaakov Hadar (Pepper), commander of the 4th Mechanized Brigade, and Col. Motke Ben Porat, commander of the 9th Mechanized Brigade, he succeeded in his mission to block the Syrian forces trying to head to the Kinneret on the three main routes they had.

On the Nafah front, the main cause of distress of the commanders at Tzfat, things seemed to be calming down. There are intelligence reports that the Syrian 76th Armored Brigade had received an order from Shafik Faid, commander of the 1st Division, to remain in its position in Syrian territory and monitor developments.

In the first hours of Sunday night, starting from 18:00, for the first time since the battles at Nafah started, the tanks of the enemy 91st Brigade show signs of breaking and begin to withdraw. Raful's Division – mainly the tanks of the 679th Brigade commanded by Col. Ori Or – block the Syrian attack on Nafah and the route leading to the Bnot Yaakov Bridge, pushing them back in defense at the Hushnia-Ramtaniyot area.

In the northern Golan nothing has changed. The tanks of the 188th and 7th Brigades stand firm in their positions and, with the exception of infiltration attempts on the Hermonit hill, facing the tanks of the 7th Brigade, no enemy forces cross the Purple Line.

18:00

South Sector – Tel Fares

At 18:00, Oded Erez instructs everyone on Tel Fares to prepare for immediate withdrawal. He is unaware that, in less than two hours, Northern Command will order a counterattack.

Erez, the new battalion commander with just two months of experience on the Golan, and Yossi Sapir, the new operations officer, there for just three months, were not very familiar with the Golan landscape.

Uzi Urieli, the commander of C Company, breathed and lived the landscape and therefore he was naturally at the lead of the long convoy. Beside him in the loader's seat is Yossi Sapir the operations officer. The second tank is that of Oded Bekman, and the rest of the tanks follow.

"A ghost convoy,"[34] Bekman thinks. He looks at the stream of unfamiliar people; the soldiers from outposts 114, 115 and Tel Fares, with the deputy battalion commander Menachem Zatorsky; the remains of the artillery battery with battalion commander Ami Cohen; unknown intelligence soldiers and many others. They are all crowded together on the armored convoy, holding on to every possible handle. He sees the dead and hears the cries of the wounded.

---

34. These are the tanks in the "ghost convoy":
The tanks of the 188th Brigade: Oded Erez, Uzi Urieli, (Boaz Tamir, with eye injuries, as a fifth crew member), Oded Bekman, Yoni Davidson, Moty Amir, Dan Tiroler, Avi Lahman, Harman Shmuel, Shimon Cohen, Yoram Miromi.
The tanks of the 7th brigade: Gigi Oren (with Gabi Refaeli the deputy company commander), Shmulik Etinger, Isi Sitkov, Gidi Maklef and Rafi Siminovsky.

After driving for two minutes, Yossi Shechter, the driver of battalion commander Erez, discovers that the track of his tank has split under the impact of the basalt rocks.

2nd Lt. Gigi Oren sees a short soldier in a wind breaker climbing onto his tank, and the soldier asks if he has a radio. What an annoying question, Gigi thinks, and he barks to the soldier to sit down and shut up. I overreacted, Oren thinks, as he sees the short soldier get off the tank and try on another tank.

Sergeant Shmulik Etinger now sees the short soldier getting onto his tank, and without any hesitation, before he even introduces himself, the soldier says, "Sergeant, jump off the tank, I am the commander now." Etinger, usually a calm person, shouts at the mysterious figure, "Get out of my face and get off the tank now."

The mysterious soldier gets off and jumps on the tank of Issy Sitkov from Rechovot, who finally sees that it is Oded Erez, CO of the 53rd Battalion. He lets him enter the tank and take command.

Uzi orders the convoy to aim their cannons at the route slope and they head west. In the command center at Tzfat, Simchoni follows the progress of the convoy tensely. After Erez notifies him they are on the move, he briefs him on the best route to take, the one with the lowest chance of encountering the Syrians on the way.

In the leading tank, Uzi Urieli does not hear the conversation between Simchoni and Erez and he has no interest in advice. He knows the southern Golan like the back of his hand. So far, this has been paying off.

In the darkness, with the light of the half-moon above them, an armored convoy makes its way on the Zivon route toward its junction with the Petroleum Road. This is the same route that fourteen hours earlier had led to the disaster destroying the artillery battery of Training Base 9. How can it be that we are retreating from the Golan? Urieli is horrified in his tank. He knows that if this is the order, there must be no other way and he prays that the Syrians don't bark suddenly and more importantly do not bite.

From a distance in time and location, Lt. Col. (res.) Zvi Ofer, researcher of the battles of the 188th Brigade for the IDF History Department, who examined every angle of this event, offers a definitive evaluation:

There was no need to evacuate the hill. What was relevant in the morning hours of Sunday was different by noon and evening, with the start of the retreat, with the IDF forces gaining power from hour to hour. The 39th Battalion attacked at Gamla, a battalion from the 179th Brigade attacked at El Al, toward Ramat Magshimim. Another battalion was near Katzabiya and Ori Or's partial 679th Brigade was fighting at Sindiyana.

According to the war doctrine, this was not the right decision and it caused grave damage. The troops that stopped the Syrian forces in the early afternoon hours launched a counterattack in the southern front and it was important to have control of this strategic hill. Possessing it would delay the arrival of additional forces and act as the eyes of the Northern Command and make it possible to join the counterattack efforts.

There was no justification for leaving the hill. There were fifteen tanks there, 100 soldiers. The Syrian forces already realized they had no chance of conquering the hill, after all their attempts were easily shattered by the defense force. Fifteen tanks is a lot. It is about half the amount of tanks that Ori Or's "brigade" had at the time.

Furthermore, at Tel Fares there were fuel containers that could have been used to fuel the tanks (that were not at a crucial shortage of fuel yet) and at this point in the night, there still were enough shells, since the six tanks of the Lahman platoon and the Davidson force fired very few and they could have controlled the ammunition.

Years after his testimony before the Agranat Commission, in an interview to *Ma'ariv*, Uri Simchoni, operations officer of the Northern Command, also agreed, "I think it would have been wise to concentrate the force there and hold on to the hill until the reserves arrived."

19:00

Northern Command – Mt. Kana'an

With the first stars appearing in the Golan sky, former Chief of General Staff Haim Bar Lev arrives at the headquarters on Mt. Kana'an.

During the three hours that morning, in which Moshe Dayan was at the headquarters in Tzfat, he had received the impression that the Northern Command CO was not running the war properly. He then contacted Gen. Elazar and asked him to get Gen. (ret.) Bar Lev to come to the command and replace Haka.

Dado sees the intense pressure on Dayan, is concerned that something has disrupted his perception but he does not want to confront his superior, the Defense Minister, the most acclaimed security authority in the country. With the wisdom of a calm commander, he finds a way to present the replacement of the commander at the Mt. Kana'an headquarters as something minor. He takes the advice of the Defense Minister and brings Bar Lev to the Northern Command to assist Haka, making sure it is not a formal change in command, concerned that it might harm the morale of the staff of the Northern command.

Starting at 19:00, when he arrived at Mt. Kana'an, Bar Lev, "the ice man," succeeded in spreading a more relaxed atmosphere and, more importantly, putting things into the proportion they had lacked in the last few hours.

A few hours after Dado recommended bringing Bar Lev to help Haka, before he got there, Brigadier General Musa Peled, commander of the 146th Division, arrived at "the Palace" in Tzfat with three of his staff members. He was very troubled with what he found there.

"There was chaos in the Northern Command headquarters," he said. "There was terrible noise coming from everywhere. Different radios were roaring all at once and the staff officers of the command were in serious distress." His intelligence officer described what happened then. "Musa was looking for the Commanding Officer, in order to receive an update and orders. He was directed to one of the rooms. The room was dark and Haka was lying on the bed. He seemed to be very, very tired and that is an understatement."

According to Peled, Maj. Gen. Hofi ordered him to establish a second line of defense across the Jordan River.

"What for?" Peled asked the general. "The Syrian forces are being blocked all through the front. I think we should use the fresh force of my division to attack in the Southern Golan."

Haka hesitated and decided that in the meantime they would wait and not decide. Peled left the room and hoped someone would finally step up and give the order to launch a counterattack.

This person did step up.

20:30

Three things had happened. The IDF had succeeded in blocking the Syrian forces on all fronts. Brigadier Gen. Musa Peled, commander of general staff 146th Reserve Division that drove on its tracks all the way to the Golan, was there to apply relentless pressure to the invaders. Bar Lev had supplied calm and level-headed leadership. Due to these factors, at 20:30 on Sunday evening, the crucial decision was made at the HQ on Mt. Kana'an.

"What is the condition of our forces?" Bar Lev asks Musa Peled.

"One battalion will reach the Arik Bridge in the middle of the night. By morning I will have 160 tanks," Peled answers and fills with hope.

"Musa, tomorrow is your big day," Bar Lev's grey steel eyes pierce the moustache of the shining Peled. All those present knew what this meant – Bar Lev was suggesting to Peled that he send his division on a counterattack. No one spoke against Bar Lev's authority and Haka accepted the proposal.

In his characteristic gentlemanly style, Bar Lev lets Haka issue the order to do what he had proposed. Tomorrow, Monday, October 8, starting at 08:00, the stage of merely blocking the forces that had penetrated Israeli territory would end. Three divisions: the 36th in the central and northern Golan, under the command of Brigadier Gen. Rafael Eitan; the 201st Division, under the command of reserve Gen. Dan Laner; and the 146th Division, commanded by Brigadier Gen. Musa Peled, will launch simultaneous counterattacks against the Syrian forces that had penetrated their fronts. The objective will be to force them back behind the Purple Line. The main effort of this attack will be supplied by Musa Peled's fresh division, moving from south to north, cutting off the main route the Syrian forces are using. The other two divisions will carry out a secondary effort, in their own respective sectors.

Looking back, many years later, Haka admitted that he was not at his best that night but he denied the rumors that he collapsed.

> *Of course I did not look good in this situation. I was tired, I hadn't slept, I was not shaved and my mood was not good. In this position, I felt much worse than when I was under fire myself, in tens of battles in the War of Independence, in paratrooper operations at the Mitla Pass and elsewhere. The responsibility for the fate of others was much harder. There is still a long way to go however, between this difficulty and collapsing.*

Aleika

While Bar Lev and Haka prepared the counterattack on the Southern Golan front and the Syrian forces withdrew to the Hushnia-Ramtaniya area, someone forgot to notify the remaining forces near the loading area, east of the fences of the Aleika base, of the change in the balance of powers.

Mann Aviram, Raful's deputy, goes tank to tank, Sho't Kal and Sho't Meteor, with a serious face befitting a national emergency. He instructs everyone, including Shay Nachshon, with his paralyzed and aching arm, to prepare to defend the main road against Syrian forces that will head toward the Bnot Yaakov Bridge during the night. He updates the commanders that there are preparations for blowing up the bridge if necessary.

Armored corps soldiers, with soldiers from the artillery, the Golani infantry brigade and many others, all of them somehow ending up here, prepare for the unknown in an improvised defense complex on the outskirts of Aleika. Their bodies ache, their spirits are low and their eyelids keep closing involuntarily.

The Government

On Sunday evening a shocking report is placed on the Chief of Staff's desk: In the course of the first two days of battles, 250 tanks and tens of planes have been destroyed on the two fronts with Syria and Egypt. Dado knows that if the war continues in this manner, the reserve equipment will run out. He transfers the report to Dayan who passes the hot potato to Golda who instructs Abba Eban, the Foreign Minister, to issue an urgent request to the US for the immediate supply of arms and ammunition.

According to foreign sources, the afternoon hours brought the government to adopt one of the most fateful decisions since Israel's independence. The feeling of existential threat pushed the ministers of the Defense Cabinet to order the arming of nuclear Jericho missiles and loading them with strategic targets data. They were then to wait for a launch order if the fronts were to collapse.

North Sector – Booster

A supply convoy with fuel and ammunition arrives at the Booster Ridge tank camp during the night, providing the battalion commander's tank and Yachin's company's eight tanks with some much-needed breathing room.

After unloading, a tall figure approaches Danny Avni, the operations officer. Danny wonders, "What does this guy want from me now?" and then he recognizes his beloved cousin Arik Toren, a soldier in the 7th Brigade reconnaissance company, who had come to the parking area with the supply vehicles.

As they are enjoying their reunion, Yair Nafshi instructs his operations officer to take the tank and lead the fuel truck to sector 105. Arik asks to join the tank but Avni refuses, despite his joy in meeting him. "Then you would have to go searching for your unit." Arik gives in and they decide to meet in two days.

Danny leaves with the tank, making sure to keep his head inside, he looks back out of the periscopes and admires the courage of the fuel truck driver driving a primed bomb on wheels.

The unsung heroes, at least on the northern Golan front, were the unknown soldiers of the logistics headquarters of the 74th Battalion. These soldiers continued delivering convoys of supplies of fuel, food and ammunition throughout the war, to the forces on the front lines. They did so while driving what were, in effect, bombs waiting to be detonated.

In addition to the courage required of Jackson, Ovadia Yisraeli (the deputy brigade commander's brother), Shpitzer and their soldiers, the endless training that they underwent made their actions automatic. This made their actions disciplined and efficient, enabling them to operate without thinking.

A few more minutes of this tense drive and Shpitzer identifies infrared lights directed at them. Right before Avni gives the order to open fire, they realize these are the tanks of the 71st Battalion who somehow joined the front and are not quite focused.

North Sector – 107

During the night, the injury of 2nd Lt. Muli Dgani started to bother him. He leaves the ramp on his way to infantry outpost 107, where there is a medic and medication that can ease his pain.

Following a short treatment, his wounds properly dressed, he heads back to the ramp and finds himself under Syrian fire from an unknown direction. Who is firing there at night? He arrives at where Yachin is positioned, with his bandages full of blood and surprise him with a canteen of hot tea.

All around them it is a dark night and the sound of near and distant engines, and the "cat eyes" of Syrian tanks glimmer all around. What a pretty sight, Yachin thinks, what a shame it is ruined by the threat of the Syrian commandos crawling toward us in the night.

There is no sign of the mighty IDF. The State of Israel is sleeping beyond the hills and the problem at this stage, Yachin thinks, is to resist the urge to fall asleep that may end with an encounter with the devil's executioners.

Suddenly Yachin has an idea. He instructs everyone to turn up their radios in the tanks and he asks "the entertainment crew" to start their show. Muli Dgani, with Yossi Naides and Yoni Vodak, two soul mates and the regular entertainment crew in Yachin's platoon, fill hours repeating the skits of the Gashash,[35] adding cracks about "the White Horse," the legendary disciplinarian master sergeant of the armored

---

35. HaGashash HaHiver (The Pale Tracker), also known as the Gashashim, were an extremely popular Israeli comedy trio of unparalleled cultural influence. Their comedy skits were known to all, to the extent that whole routines could be quoted verbatim by most Israelis in the 1960s and '70s.

corps school, the fear of all the soldiers. The exhausted soldiers of Elimelech also tune in to the radio, at outpost 107, and they all join the surreal party.

The Ghost convoy
Two kilometers before the Zivon-Mahaze junction (leading from Tel Fares to the Petroleum Road), Uzi Urieli, with the assistance of the half-moon in the sky, identifies two trucks, two APCs and two tanks, parked north of the Petroleum Road. He has no doubt they are not Israeli forces.

Urieli gets out of the tank, finds Erez and updates him. "Do not fire," Erez instructs him and he notifies the commanders. "There is a Syrian force parked in front of us. We cannot bypass it, we will pass by quietly."

It is hard to understand what kind of quiet Urieli had in mind, when referring to a convoy of tanks but no one had a problem with the order since the soldiers hanging outside the vehicles made it very difficult to fight anyway. The convoy of tanks moves forward "quietly," nearly touching the Syrian vehicles while passing them. Urieli passes and then Bekman, the others pass one after another, until it is the turn of Sergeant Rafi Siminovsky. When he is passing, a Syrian tank commander suddenly identifies the Israeli tank, aims his cannon, fires and hits the tank suspension, leaving the crew stunned but alive. A moment passes and the Syrian tank is hit by a number of shells from close range and is blown away, followed by the tank next to it.

Were these two tanks part of the Syrian force that attacked the artillery battery retreating from Tel Fares the night before? Were they tanks that were part of the attack below base 115? Gigi Oren is busy with much more practical matters. Where did these metal shards come from, filling his entire body? This is not the time to ask for help and he pushes the others forward.

"Full speed," Oren shouts to his driver, firing at the remaining Syrians and continuing south-west, through a field of burning thorns and clouds of dust and smoke.

In Issy Sitkov's tank things are out of control. Oded Erez, in the loader' compartment, is trying to command the tank and the entire force and the driver, through his periscopes, sees fire in front of them. He panics, swerves right, is given a number of confusing orders from both

Sitkov and Erez at the same time and responds accordingly, landing the tank on a ditch with its two tracks spinning in the air.

Erez gives the order to abandon the tank and they all flee. Somehow they manage to stop the last tanks in the convoy and continue forward. Thirteen armored vehicles. Our lucky number? Sitkov wonders.

The Syrians do not know what had hit them. Where did the Israelis come from? Flares are fired in the air and the Israeli convoy, led by Urieli, chooses a route that is harder to detect and to pass through. They are now off the path, on the Mesil Najil, northern canyon of the Basalt stream.

When they arrive on the Petroleum Road, Urieli estimates that there may be additional Syrian forces at the intersection of the Waterfalls and Maale Gamla routes and he leaves the path.

Bekman, second in the convoy, looks back and sees the armored force passing through a large veil of fire and the smell of burned rubber of the tank wheels is in the air. White strips of cloth of machine gun bullets are hanging out of the tank, hundreds of bullet shells glitter among the equipment cases, and the survivors of the Southern Golan front hold on with all their might. Their faces are like masks and far in the distance behind them, above the flames, is the dark silhouette of Tel Fares.

23:00

South Sector – Tel Saki

While the convoy of the soldiers evacuated from the Southern Golan continues its descent to the Kinneret, the drama continues in the Tel Saki bunker.

An hour before midnight, Nir Atir decides to take action. Together with another three soldiers, they crawl out of the bunker, praying that the Syrians are not waiting for them in the dark. They are not. There is the damaged tank and Nir quickly sneaks into the turret, trying to find food and water.

Right before leaving the tank, he has an idea. He puts the radio on the infantry battalion's frequency and begs, "Everyone is injured or dying. If you do not come immediately, we are done."

A moment later, he hears the voice of Ya-Ya (Yoram Yair), commander of the 50th Battalion. "Hold on. Give the guys water, cheer them up, and tell them we will be there soon. I have tanks here. We are all on our way to you."

The four soldiers return to the bunker with the good news but discover the jerrycan they brought is leaking. Avital the medic pours water into the cap and decides there is only enough for half a cap each.

Two hours later, Atir sneaks back to the tank, this time with the injured Nati Levi, the platoon commander. They go through the tank and are disappointed to find that there is no more food and water. At least help is on its way, Atir and Levi encourage each other. They contact Ya-Ya again who is sorry to let them down. "Sorry, the force will only arrive in the morning. Hang in there."

$$* * *$$

While twenty-four soldiers of the armored corps and infantry lie injured, in pain and desperation in the "bunker" on Tel Saki and as the sixteen soldiers of outpost 116 continue to fight, they are the last regular soldiers on the Southern Golan front, Mordechai Okavi the medic gets back his life.

In the Syrian forward tank depot he is being held in, one of the tanks suddenly explodes. He grasps the opportunity and, in the commotion, runs for his life. He tells himself that the safest option is to join his company and he heads toward Juhader in the dark.

The parking areas appear before him, with a large fire burning in the middle. Like a thief in the night, he sneaks between the destroyed buildings, identifies the shadows of Syrian tanks, sees the Syrians singing and dancing in celebration and a sense of helplessness threatens to paralyze him.

North Sector – 109
Late Sunday night, Yisraeli, Eiland and Hashenberg leave the ramp and head toward the deployment base at Quneitra to refill on fuel and ammunition.

At the junction of the main road with the route they are on (Peleg-Reshet), Oded Yisraeli identifies a Syrian tank heading toward them, from south to north.

"Fire," Yisraeli orders and a huge flame rises in front of them. He orders Eiland and Hashenberg to stay where they are and secure the south side, in case the Syrian tank they hit is just one of another wave of Syrian tanks.

In the daunting dark night, with the half-moon hidden in the west, Oded Yisraeli continues to head toward the base, fighting off a sense of terror in the face of the unknown. He continues moving forward with the force of his survival instinct. He tells himself that the main war is yet to come and it will take place mainly on the front opposite 109, not on the road to Quneitra. But he still is dying to get there already.

When Yisraeli arrives at the deployment base at Quneitra, there is no one there to take over, encourage and support him. Not even a logistics sergeant or officer. He sees people all over taking care of themselves on their own. He sees damaged tanks, destroyed buildings and soldiers in shell shock and a medical center that is crowded with injured soldiers.

"What shell series should I load?" Goldshaft asks Yisraeli, when they decide to take ammunition from the damaged tanks.

"Transfer whatever you can. Who knows what we will need," Yisraeli answers. He gets off the tank and disappears in the ruins.

"What a shitty officer," Tuashi complains. "We are loading shells and he takes off."

A few minutes later, Yisraeli returns with two boxes of soda drinks and chocolate wafers in his hands.

"Where did you get that?" Tuashi asks him.

"From the Shekem[36] canteen," he answers.

"Who is it for?"

"For the guys."

"What guys? Bring it to the tank!"

When Oded heads back out of the base, he meets a fat and scared maintenance officer at the gate.

"Where are you going?" he asks them.

"To ramp 109 ," Oded answers.

"Are you crazy? You shouldn't go there; the Syrians are on their way to Haifa!"

---

36. The military canteen that sells various "treats" for soldiers. Based on the British NAFI.

In the meantime, hidden in the dark, blind to the two steel shadows awaiting them, the remains of the Syrian tank crew try to flee.

"Someone is passing by us," Harashti, Hashenberg's loader whispers. There is machine gun fire, the sounds of falling and in the faint moonlight there are two bodies lying on the side of the road. David Eiland, the well-educated and polite son of Esther, looks at them indifferently.

They all come together at ramp 109 and Yisraeli takes out the goodies he brought and gives four bottles to each tank and two wafers to each soldier. Tuashi is a bit surprised. Kibbutz members do not splurge and suddenly Yisraeli is giving out things like he is a millionaire. It is amazing what war can do to a man.

"How much did this cost you?" he asks politely, thinking he perhaps should collect money from the guys and pay him back.

"It didn't cost anything. A shell hit the canteen. So I took this for the guys."

Now everyone shouts together, "Then why didn't you take more?"

The Ghost Convoy

Sometime before midnight, Uzi Urieli arrived at the sandstone path leading to Maale Gamla (the Picardo route), continuing with it to the west.

After driving three kilometers, with the help of the faint light of the moon in the western sky, he identifies two Tiran tanks south of the path, in a grove near Rasam Abu Rajam. They appear to be abandoned, their cannons aimed at the sky.

"The air force did a good job," Urieli thinks and he reports it to his battalion commander. He is amazed to see that the Syrian forces reached this point, and who knows where else he will encounter them. He is suddenly not so sure that the tanks are Tirans.

The convoy continues west, passing the destroyed tanks that turn out to be Tirans and part of the enemy forces. Everyone feels relaxed, and just when they rise round a bend, less than 600 meters away, Sapir and Urieli identify a large tank force, but they are sure "they are ours." That is what they tell each other. Then they realize there is also the possibility that the force in front of them does not know they are also their own and that is why Urieli shouts, "Pearlman, stop. Drive back."

A short while before this, Yoav Veaspi, commander of the 39th Battalion, and Yair Gutman, the operations officer with him in the tank, heard the creaking of tracks on the route and they reported, or didn't, called on the armored corps emergency radio channel, or did not, received approval to fire, or did not. They do what every tank crew does at night, with enemy forces around him, when a tank appears opposite them. At the front of the spearhead of forces two orders to open fire are given in the tanks of Avraham Sela, the company commander and Yoav Vaspi, the battalion commander.

Yossi Sapir, a sweet boy, the operations officer of the 53rd Battalion, Bekman's instructor in the armored corps officer course, is hit by the jetstream of gas from the shaped charge shell fired at them and he is killed on the spot.

"Pearlman, reverse," Uzi cries on the internal radio, full of holes from the shards. He notifies the convoy, "we have been hit, it is friendly fire, do not fire." Only then does he let himself lose consciousness.

Boaz Tamir, deputy commander of Golan, C Company, cannot see anything. He is sitting between the legs of Yossi Sapir when suddenly a body falls on him. He overcomes the shock, places Yossi's warm body on the floor of the tank, reports on the radio that the commander has been hit, tells Bekman to take command in the lead and "Don't shoot, the tanks facing us are our own forces."

Bekman is nearly run over by Urieli's tank when moving back and he realizes that he is now responsible for getting them out of this catastrophe. He keeps shouting on the radio repeatedly, "4 of Dallas, this is Glufa, calling on your frequency," but there is no response.

Once again, he adds a green flare to the cry but there still is no answer. He tells himself not to give up and carries out the protocol again, this time adding tracer bullets fired in the black sky, darkened by the death of Yossi Sapir. Nothing happens.

What do we do with Uzi? Oded Bekman asks himself. The 2nd platoon leader in the Golan Company knows that Uzi Urieli, the admired company commander, is injured and in desperate need of medical treatment. What about the tanks opposite us in the dark? Will they continue to fire at us, acting in the damned uncertainty of night, on their way to the Kinneret?

"4 of Dallas, this is Glufa, the force in front of you," Bekman tries again. He transfers to his practical mode, losing the shaking in his voice. "I am turning on my lights and driving in front of you." He moves forward, keeping himself down low in the tank and driving in front of the dark shadows of the tanks, praying that Uzi was right and these are Israeli tanks.

A moment passes and he notices a ray of light going on and off and the front lights of a Sho't Kal tank are turned on.

"Stop," he shouts to Bertian the driver, cursing the soldiers opposite them in his heart, and he continues, "4, we have casualties, send your 17 (doctor)." He immediately turns back, nearing Urieli's tank and jumps off the tank to check on his commander.

A few minutes later a military ambulance arrives. The doctor takes one look at Sapir. There is no chance. Then he loads up the commander of the Golan Company who is in terrible pain and he rushes toward the Bteicha. Urieli wakes up, sees Dr. Englehard, the battalion doctor. "I am examining you," he tells him. "Shrapnel..." he mumbles, "torn eardrum," he whispers, "half a finger missing." "Give him morphine," he instructs the medic Rami Wahaba.

At the moment of the engagement, all the infantry soldiers had abandoned the tanks and run to the Daliyot stream canyon and they were wise to do so. What were they supposed to do on the tanks? Defend them? As sitting ducks for the enemy? Continue to be in the way of the tank operators? Why didn't Menachem Zatorsky, the infantry deputy battalion commander, notify Oded Erez?

Suddenly the commander of the 53rd Battalion found himself missing between fifty and sixty infantry soldiers, that had disappeared without a trace. If he hadn't made the effort to send the message on the radio to anyone listening that our own infantry soldiers were descending from the Golan on the Daliyot stream canyon, someone might have mistaken them in the dark for enemy soldiers and their journey would have ended differently.

The convoy continues on its way. Bekman leads and Simchoni contacts Boaz Tamir, who gives him an update on the incident, but the drama is not over. Yehuda Ardman has just completed his basic training and was immediately sent to the 188th Brigade to be the driver of Moty Amir's tank. "Driver, left!" Amir shouts to him anxiously, at one of the bends of the route.

Ardman doesn't respond. According to the drill, everyone jumps inside the tank, holding on to any handle they can grab as the tank overturns and comes to a stop on its side. They are all intact, bruised but okay. In a convoy with soldiers that are injured or dead, no one takes notice of bruises. Amir collects the equipment and the maps and the entire crew returns to the dirt path. An APC approaches them and they signal with a flashlight. The refugees of Tel Fares are picked up by the refugees of the artillery battery of Training Base 9, also from Tel Fares. They leave the overturned tank behind and speed toward the Kinneret.

Oded Bekman leads the rest of the way from Maale Gamla to the Bteicha with a combination of indifference and apathy. The retreat from the Golan almost passed successfully, remembering Sapir the operations officer lying dead on the ground.

With the first morning light of Monday, they arrive at Bteicha, joining the chaos and a 175 mm artillery battery firing toward the east. Who is going to help, Bekman wonders, we are all here.

Some fresh morning air, a cigarette he took from somewhere, and Bekman orders the convoy to continue moving toward the Yarden base.

"Syrian commando is on its way to attack the Yarden base," an unfamiliar voice says on the radio. Exhausted, apathetic, the survivors of the Southern Golan front are not affected by this message. They decide that the Syrian soldier that appeared on the road, with his arms raised in front of the cannon, is the commando.

The Yarden base is packed with a mixture of soldiers and vehicles, they are all beaten, desperate, exhausted, behaving like the losing side. Then they fall anywhere they can and sleep, to get away from it all.

All through the night, until early Monday morning, Ukavi the medic was walking through the Golan. Not north, not south, not east, not west. Somewhere out there. Then when the Syrians are gone and he is no longer sure it was not just a dream, a BTR armored personnel carrier appears out of nowhere and his lights shine on the terrified medic. He just barely manages to sneak beneath the fence of a mined area, praying to his God to save him. He sees Syrian soldiers jumping out of the carrier and they too crawl beneath the fence with the warning signs and are after him. He watches as his bond with God is renewed when one after another the Syrians soldiers are blown up by the mines.

At some point, in times that got erased and mixed up and became a large, smeared collage, Ukavi hears Hebrew and comes out of the dark, rejoicing. After the IDF soldiers open fire on him, maybe it was the regular soldiers or the reserves, almost completing what the Syrians failed to do, they give him crackers and more and more water that he drinks and drinks, like a camel. He does not remember what happened after this.

Monday, October 8 to the Morning of Tuesday, October 9

Monday morning on the Golan saw the start of the major change in the war. One hundred sixty-nine fresh tanks of the 146th Division were poised to pounce, as part of the planned massive counterattack on the Southern Golan. The force included 110 Sho't Meteor tanks of the 205th Armored Brigade, commanded by Col. Yossi Peled and fifty Sherman tanks of the 670th Armored Brigade, commanded by Col. Gideon Gordon and the commander of the Divisional reconnaissance battalion, Lt. Col. Zvi Dahab.

They were not alone. Acting on the order from the general the night before, the remaining reserve forces on the Golan prepared to act as the secondary effort in the counterattack, turning it into a three-divisional attack.

What was happening in the Northern Golan at this time?

The 7th Brigade – including the 74th Battalion of the 188th Brigade which was under its command – as well as the regular forces of the 36th Division, were not expected to push back Syrian forces that penetrated, for the simple reason that there were no Syrian forces on the Northern Golan. Not yet.

So as the entire reserve force on the Golan prepares for the counterattack, the forces on the Northern Golan front wake to a calm spring morning routine.

Morning
North Sector – 104/105
By Monday morning, the attempts of Syrian tanks to hit Israeli tanks in the northern front have died down. The attempts to break through

continues with infantry companies that repeatedly try to reach the hilltops near outpost 104. Attempts that are brought to an end by the machine guns of the tanks of H Company.

Further south, in sector 105, Yossi Nissim and Avner Landau are enjoying the warm sun on the hills and the Fidel Hadash route, facing south toward the Quneitra gap.

Syrian artillery shells continues to fall occasionally, bringing down its lashes of death, creating holes in the basalt ground, disrupting the serenity, a reminder that there still is a war going on. "The Syrians have been stopped," deputy company commander Kaimo tells himself in his position, unaffected by shells and anti-tank missiles flying by him, feeling that they have gotten through the worst part of it.

North Sector – 107

The tanks of the Yachin force, on both sides of infantry outpost 107, also greet the morning with the sensation that the worst is over. A stoic tranquility came over the tanks and they take the time to attend to their tanks, including cleaning the tank guns by passing a long rod with an oiled cloth through it and pulling it out from the other side. In the middle of this pulling game, there are sudden shouts on the radio. Two Syrian tanks appear on the border road behind.

Haim Damir's platoon, positioned on the southern ramp at sector 107, hear the unmistakable roar of the engines and the tracks of Tiran tanks. A moment passes and then they see the two tanks heading north on the border route, with their cannons up in the sky, approaching the junction at the entrance to outpost 107.

"Do not fire," Damir orders, and the three tanks aim west, to the border route that is 400 meters behind them, and they wait tensely.

"Fire!" Damir shouts when the two Tirans appear in front of the cannons, and the rest of the tanks of Yachin's force join in the festivities. The first Tiran explodes opposite the southern ramp, and the other tank flees, is hit and stops in front of the northern ramp.

"Get in the tank! Prepare to fire," Yachin's crew, positioned on the northern ramp, jumps inside and the tank turns back toward the border route.

"Did you take the cleaning rod out?" Yachin asks the crew, as he dances on his seat. It turns out that they forgot. He stops the tank, jumps out and pulls the rod stuck in the cannon out.

"Drive to the Tiran," Yachin orders Aharon Kapun the driver.

They drive up to the Syrian tank that was hit. "Closer?" Kapun asks. "Closer," Yachin answers.

When they are right next to the tank, Yachin climbs on to the Syrian tank, throws a grenade inside the turret and sees the escaped crew running away.

"Should I take prisoners?" he asks his battalion commander.

"If you have extra bandages," Nafshi answers, affected by his three company commanders being killed.

South Sector – Tel Saki

Unlike sector 105, the bunker on Tel Saki is dark and there is no autumn sun bathing the soldiers in its warmth. Here, the Syrians decide in the early morning hours, that it is time to put an end to this. They repeatedly gather outside the bunker and throw grenades inside. These are blocked by the pile of bodies of Yakir, Herzestein and Fachima.

Suddenly there are shouts. "I want water," Shaya shouts going deaf after a grenade blew up by his ear.

"Shut up," Ansbacher whispers to him. "Don't shout, we don't want the Syrians to hear us."

Shaya does not hear Ansbacher and continues, "Water, water."

Ansbacher is also seriously injured himself. He finds Lazie in the bunker and tells him, "Shut him up, do whatever it takes."

Lazie is an obedient soldier, he gets close to Shaya, looks him in the eyes and retreats with fear. Unaware that his life was just saved, he responds with ungrateful shouts, "Water, water." No one knows what to do until Avital the medic has the brilliant idea of writing on a cigarette box. "Shaya, shut up. You are deaf. The Syrians can hear you."

Shaya stares at the cigarette box stuck in his face curiously. It is lit with a match that is dimming and he somehow gets the message and remains silent.

They are all frozen in fear, tormented with their injuries, with just one thing on their mind – how to get out of this nightmare. All of them, including Shaya who remains silent and thankfully did not have to be choked, have no idea how they will get through this.

Rambam Hospital, Haifa

It is an early morning hour. Etzion Ashkenazi awakens after undergoing surgery during the night and beyond the veil of the anesthetics, he hears a nurse knocking on his door and asking, "Does anyone know where Dov Zolden is lying?"

Without thinking, he answers immediately, "Here, here." He is still overwhelmed by the guilt he feels for abandoning his friend and he keeps the memory of their parting with him. He apologizes to the back of the nurse for being confused and sees her by the bed of an unidentified figure covered in bandages and tubes.

Still in a daze, he stares at the injured figure two beds from him and he suddenly has a spark of hope. "Excuse me nurse, why were you asking for Dov Zolden?"

"I needed to change his IV," the nurse answers without any emotion. "It is ok, I found him, I am changing it now."

North Sector – 107

It is not until morning that Muli Dgani receives notice of the death of 2nd Lt. Yoav Yakir, his friend who was like a brother to him, killed on the southern Golan front. He is numb and does not respond. His face hardens, his eyes wide open, all the scenes in his head from last night disappear all at once and he turns to Yachin and tells him, "Any task you need a volunteer for, send me."

Yachin does not answer. All he does is hope with all his heart that this will end soon. He has had enough of these volunteer tasks. He wants to hug Muli but young officers, twenty-one years old, in the middle of war do not have the luxury of such sudden bursts of emotion.

As he is wondering how Muli Dgani is going to be, Elimelech, commander of outpost 107, calls out on the radio. "A company of T62 tanks is leaving Han Ureinbe heading on the road toward me."

At noon on Monday, President Assad personally sent one of his Presidential National Guard battalions to sector 107, with 40 T62 tanks. This was part of one of the most elite units of the Syrian army. They are told not to return until they have achieved victory.

Yachin takes up position and starts exchanging fire with tanks over four kilometers away. There are no hits, ammunition is wasted and the company of T62 tanks, sparkling new and clean, continues to move opposite them without any problem.

"Can we get the air support?" Yachin asks his battalion commander.

"No."

"What about artillery?" he tries again.

"They are busy someplace else," Nafshi replies, hearing the disappointment in his voice. He gives Yachin an alternative plan for action. "Go down to beneath the ramp, so you are not seen. Let them come closer. When they are in combat range, I will let you know on the radio and then you move up and hit them."

The Yachin force moves down to waiting positions, letting the T62 company, with a false sense of confidence, move west.

When the Tirans are 900 meters away, Nafshi shouts, "Move up now." Yachin's predators move into firing positions. They fire at them like they are sitting ducks.

During the exchange of fire between Yachin's eight tanks and the Syrian Rifat force, Haim Damir lets his tank stay in firing position a moment too long. Boom! A Syrian gunner identifies their tank, fires a precise shell that hits cell 8 in the turret, damaging the aiming system. The Sho't Kal has taken a serious hit but luckily no one is hurt.

Vidy identifies the Tiran that hit Damir and in his rage he sends the Syrian crew to the world of silence. Damir jumps out of his damaged tank and he joins Levital's.

Avishai Levital takes Damir's damaged tank to Beit Hahazit for repairs. The crew recognize their platoon and company member, Andrei Strul, or Bundy, as his family calls him. He is a new immigrant from Romania and an outstanding gunner who was on Yom Kippur leave. He just arrived and is keen on joining the fighting. "When do we return to the ramps?" he urges them but he does not get the chance. A stray bullet hits him in the neck on the stairs of Beit Hahazit. Strul collapses by Shtizky and Blinder, from his platoon, and dies at their feet.

North Sector – 109

While Nimrod Kochavi, who was fatally injured, is fighting for his life at the Rambam Hospital in Haifa, his fellow company members are also struggling to stay alive. "We need to do whatever we can not to get hit by the artillery shells," Zvika Rak, commander of A Company, thinks to himself. He is leading the five tanks between the northern and southern ramps in sector 109.

Zvika looks around him, and sees the tanks of A Company at their finest. They are firing, hitting, operating well under pressure and he says to himself, "We are going to win."

Yair Nafshi

Since Saturday at 15:00, Yair Nafshi has been maneuvering his tank, without the ability to raise the cannon, between the Booster Ridge and the ramp beneath it. Enough is enough. Nearly forty-eight hours after the war started, the commander of the 74th Battalion allows himself to commandeer a functioning tank.

2nd Lt. Yossi Zamri is ordered to immediately leave sector 109 and head to the Booster Ridge position, where he transfers the ammunition from the battalion commander's tank to his. If he is going to act as a body guard, he might as well have some muscle.

North sector – 109

Like every good thing in life, the peace in sector 109 also comes to an end.

1st Lt. Udi Ben Gera, deputy company commander of the Golani Mesayaat, joined the base on Saturday as part of reinforcements. He sees that Syrian tanks are close to the fences.

Udi goes to the 20mm gun post and decides to stop them. "We are Golani baby. We do not give up because of a few tanks." He removes the camouflage net from the gun. That is enough for a Syrian gunner to identify him and fire a deadly shell at him.

On the ramp south of outpost 109, the four tanks of A Company hear the broken voice of someone from the stronghold. "Tanks are firing at us. Our people are getting killed."

David Eiland and Shuki Hashenberg are sent to the northern ramp. They take out their binoculars and identify the tank that killed Udi Ben Gera on a hill 1,200 meters away.

Zion Awad, Hashenberg's gunner fires. It is long, then short and the third AP round flashes brightly as it penetrates and destroys the Tiran turret.

"That is it," Eiland says on the company radio. "We restored the balance with this fuck."

It is quiet in sector 109 again and Eiland allows his crew to carry out the "urination procedure." Efraim the gunner passes an empty 0.3 bullet box to Yehuda Shani the driver. He sticks his hand through to the turret, takes the box and releases the pressure he was holding in him for so long. He returns it to Burko, the loader who bends over to reach him, returning the yellow liquid to Efraim, who passes it to Eiland who throws it out of the tank.

After a few more quiet minutes, Yehuda Shani asks to come out of the tank, this time for "heavier" needs. Someone on the Syrian side is merciful, is considerate of his "needs" and waits until he is done and has re-zipped his coverall, before continuing the massive shelling of the ramp. Yehuda dives back into the driver's seat and hits an unidentified figure who whimpers in pain. Right before he dived back in, 1st Lt. Asher Diamant, the forward observer had entered the driver's seat. "It is time to stretch out in the spacious driver's seat and leave the cramped turret," he whispered to Eiland with pleasure.

There goes his nap and the artillery officer and Yehuda Shani somehow cram into the driver's seat together and in the commander's seat, Eiland cannot hold back the laughter that overcomes him.

South Sector – Tel Saki

Monday afternoon. The soldiers besieged in the tiny concrete room on Tel Saki are injured, bleeding, driven mad by thirst, losing focus and clarity, after forty dark and hopeless hours. They are unaware of the counterattack of the 146th Division from the Southern Golan toward Ramat Magshimim and Tel Fares.

Reinforced by the two reserve mechanized brigades of Pepper (4th) and Ben Porat (9th), the huge division commanded by Musa Peled heads northeast and north-northeast, giving the generals on Mt. Kana'an a reason to smile. For every tank of the 188th Brigade that left the front the night before, the division has now sent twenty tanks, shattering the Syrian hold on the southern Golan.

At the head of the division spearhead, the reconnaissance battalion is in the lead, and commanding the first tank is 1st Lt. Hilik Weinstein. He had completed his army service in the 188th Brigade just ten months earlier and is devastated by the death of Avi Ronis, his class-mate from Haifa.

These two friends, Avi Ronis – who everyone in Haifa knew as Avi Greenwald, the handsomest boy in the class – and Hilik were in the same class. After school they went their separate ways, with Ronis joining a kibbutz. They later met as officers in the 188th Brigade. Hilik was discharged and Ronis continued to climb the ranks in the army.

After a sleepless night, driving on their tracks all the way from Je-rusalem, the 146th Division stopped on the way at the Zemach gas station and the tanks took over the fueling stations, leaving behind a stunned gas station worker and a written promise to pay after the war.

Then they continued to Ein Gev, and the Kibbutz members stood outside cheering and shouting, "Show them!" Then they started the ascent to the Golan, crawling up the hill, speeding on the flat areas and meeting a lone tank, with a confused commander, trying to under-stand who is this tank commander facing them. "I am from Venus (F) Company," Avi Lavi said to them. "The Golan has been conquered by the Syrians and everyone is dead, including Avi Ronis."

Now it is the entire Division, with Hilik at the lead, conducting a mobile fight against the remains of the Syrian armored forces on the Southern Golan. "Don't stop, continue moving," the commanders urge them and they continue north, when suddenly Hilik sees two aban-doned Sho't Kal tanks near the trail up to Tel Saki.

"There is hope," he tells his crew that left the Ofer base without ma-chine guns and their personal rifles. "Go to the damaged tanks and get the machine guns and ammunition."

After collecting a big pile of ammunition, they notify him that there is no one in the tanks.

Hilik looks up to the top of the hill and sees the concrete block sitting there and something bothers him. Could the tank crews have found shelter up there?

"I am going up there," he shouts and runs up the hill. He carefully approaches the opening of the bunker and shouts, "Are there any ar-mored corps soldiers here?"

First Sergeant Nir Atir limps out of the bunker. His coverall is full of blood, his face black, in his hand he is pressing on a grenade, he is blinded by the light and quietly he says, "Yes."

A few minutes later, the medical crew is on its way to the top of the hill and the injured soldiers are treated one after another, getting back their lives. The medics examine their injuries, bandage, give them IVs, sew, inject morphine and call for heli-vac.

"Get them," Menachem Ansbacher demands of the reserve officer who helps him out of the bunker. He breaks down and weeps bitterly, "Make them pay for what they did to us…"

"It will be alright, Menachem," the officer pats his head.

Northern Command – Mt. Kana'an

In the afternoon hours Maj. Gen. Bar Lev feels that he is no longer needed on the northern front. Things on the ground and in the headquarters are stabilizing and are under control. Maj. Gen. Hofi is at his best and now is the time to step down. "Goodbye and good luck with the rest of the battle," he says out loud in the cinema hall on Mt. Kana'an, and he heads toward the helicopter on his way to the southern front. There the Southern Command – led by Gorodish – is a suffering an organizational disaster that requires his immediate assistance.

The Reserves Crush the Enemy

The reserve forces on the Golan have impressive success, and the counterattack is developing to the satisfaction of the decision makers at the "Palace" in Tzfat.

By the afternoon, most of the armored forces of the Syrian 132nd Brigade and the tank battalion of their 47th Brigade have been destroyed and the Druze deputy brigade commander is taken prisoner. At the end of a quick and intense tank battle, the reserve forces take control of the Petroleum Road–Juhader junction.

North of there, the Syrian 46th, 47th and 51st brigades are forced east, with the pressure applied by the reserve forces focusing on the Arik Bridge–Yehudiya route and the Maale Gamla route.

Near Nafah the reserve tanks stop a counterattack of the Syrian 1st Division – the 91st brigade and the tank battalion of the 58th brigade – pushing them back away from Nafah, to the Ramtaniyot and Hushnia area.

The "Ghost Convoy"

Route- 7.10.73 19:00- 8.10.73 10:00

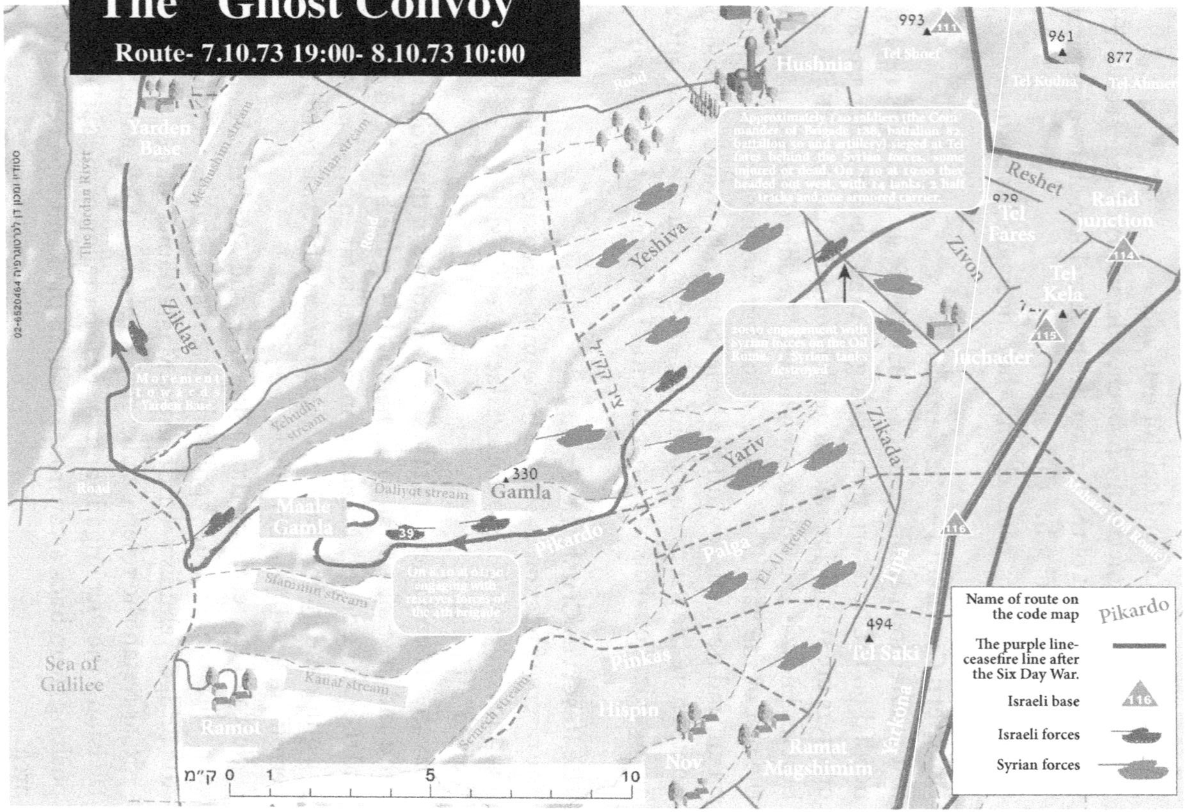

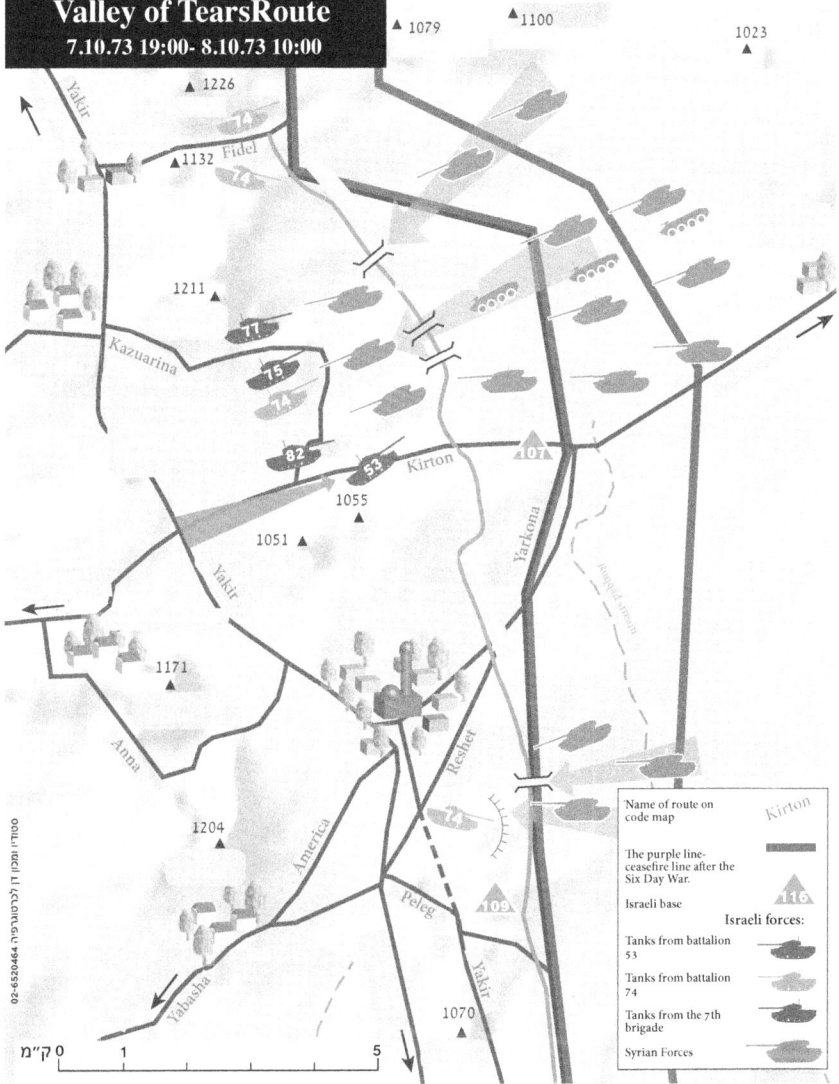

The Decisive Battle at the
Valley of TearsRoute
7.10.73 19:00- 8.10.73 10:00

▲1079   ▲1100   1023
                        ▲

▲1226

▲1132 Fidel

1211 ▲

Kazuarina

1055 ▲

1051 ▲

Kirton

Yarkona

1171 ▲

Anna

1204 ▲

America

Reshet

Peleg

Yabasha

Yakir

1070 ▲

Name of route on
code map

The purple line-
ceasefire line after the
Six Day War.

Israeli base

Israeli forces:

Tanks from battalion
53

Tanks from battalion
74

Tanks from the 7th
brigade

Syrian Forces

ק"מ 0   1   5

451

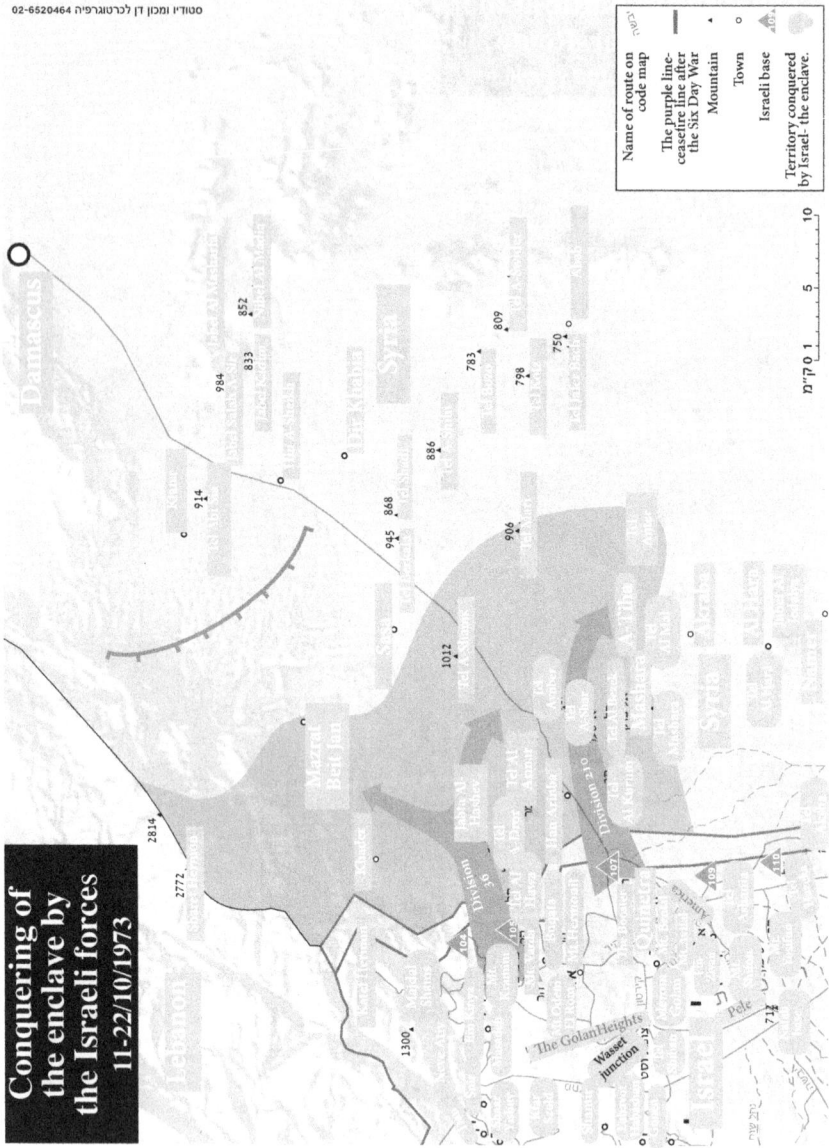

Conquering of the enclave by the Israeli forces 11-22/10/1973

452

The Return to Nafah

The leadership of the Northern Command are successfully leading the counterattack from Mt. Kana'an, and the commanders of Raful's 36th Division – responsible for the northern Golan at this stage – are located at Tel Shiban near the Wasset junction. At the same time, the commanders of the 820th Brigade decide that "you do not leave your home." The situation on the Golan is improving and that is enough to convince deputy brigade commander Finia Kuperman and operations officer Giora Goldberg to get in a jeep and head toward Nafah.

They enter the gate of what remains of the empty base, they find the radios still crackling. They recharge the batteries, turn the devices on and notify everyone that "They can come back." They feel a small but significant victory in taking back control of Nafah.

Yarden War Reserve Storage Base – Returning to Life

While Yossi Peled's reconnaissance unit rescues the soldiers besieged at Tel Saki, the soldiers of the "ghost convoy" wake up at the tank hangars area at the Yarden base, after a few hours of sleep, the first in thirty-six hours of war.

There is an old aluminum pot with a dark bitter liquid – topped with scum – cooking in it. In the IDF they call it coffee but for the soldiers it is a divine nectar that hits their raw stomachs and is a clear proof to them that they are still alive.

As they wander around the base, reorganizing themselves, wondering what is going to happen, they find Shmulik Askarov.

Shortly after their arrival at the Yarden base, Shmulik Askarov, deputy commander of the 53rd Battalion, with a huge bandage around his neck, had also turned up. Just the day before, he was "moderately injured, with his life in danger" (shrapnel in an artery in his neck) and this morning he already walked out of the hospital in Tzfat. On his way to the Yarden base he gathers up stray armored soldiers, and at the Yarden base he found the remaining soldiers of the 188th Brigade from the Southern Golan front.

Askarov sits down next to Oded Erez, who has his head in his hands, and he tries to cheer him up, unsuccessfully. He then leaves the battalion commander mourning the lives he lost and the shattering of all he believed in and he gets up to move the living – the crewmen that are staring at them.

"Come on guys," he tries to connect with them. "We have no choice, we need to repair tanks and return to the war."

Yarden Base – Burial Ceremonies

On Monday afternoon, Shraga Ibler, the brigade operations officer, was sent to the Yarden base to organize an armored crew to evacuate the bodies of the brigade commanders.

Eighteen hours earlier, on Sunday evening, Shmulik Ben Moshe, the brigade adjutant, had come to Ori Or, the commander of the 679th Brigade, in command of the Nafah sector following the death of the commanders of the 188th Brigade, and demanded to go to the Petroleum Road and evacuate the bodies of his commanders.

"Are you crazy?" Or reprimanded him. "There is a war there. Wait for tomorrow. Let's see what develops."

On Monday afternoon, he repeats his request to Or, who knows that the area is no longer under the immediate threat of Syrian tanks. "Alright Shmulik, you can go in."

Shraga approaches the tank crews at the Yarden base, who are trying to overcome the shock of leaving the Golan and withdrawing from Tel Fares. Sitting separately, he sees Oded Bekman, who appears to be physically and mentally fit. Oded immediately volunteers for the task. Ibler drives in the jeep, Bekman follows in a tank and they set out toward Nafah. On the way they pass a lost tank, a reserve soldier left from Ori Or's force. Ibler stops the jeep and instructs him to join them.

That is the way it is in war, Bekman tells himself. Forces are shattered and the remnants move around until they find a new force to join.

At Nafah, Shmulik Ben Moshe, the brigade adjutancy officer, joins Ibler's jeep, adding a truck with Maj. Yitzchak Telem the brigade ordnance officer, 1st Lt. Dr. Yaakov Mamet the brigade doctor and the chaplain, 1st Lt. Shnior Kramer. The convoy set out, crossing the training area west of the Petroleum Road. The two tanks lead, occasionally taking up observation positions, searching for enemy forces.

At the slopes of the Kadariya canyon, on the dirt road parallel to the Petroleum Road, Bekman identifies it. The 20C tactical sign is still on the tank, turned on its side, leaning on huge rocks. It is Ben Shoham's tank.

A few hundred meters from there, Bekman stops by another damaged tank, with the 21C tactical sign. He gets out of the tank and sees a body, with a gun in its belt, lying on its side near the damaged tank. Bekman approaches and turns it over. The face of deputy brigade commander David Yisraeli looks up at him, frozen and peaceful.

Bekman knew Yisraeli from the days he commanded the 77th Training Battalion, where he taught them discipline and tankmanship and became the terror of the young soldiers. The second time he met him was at the platoon camp area, near outpost 116.

Yisraeli had just been appointed deputy brigade commander and Bekman had prepared himself for his strict inspection. Yisraeli examined the tanks without comments. The condition of the soldiers' rooms and bathrooms were praised. The visit was about to be a great success, when Yisraeli entered the kitchen. The cooking and storage areas passed his inspection but then instead of turning around and leaving, he went out to the waste area. Suddenly the storm began, "Is that the way to cut a pepper?" Yisraeli shouted in his characteristic manner. He pulled out the edge of a pepper cut that morning. The cook opened his mouth in order to answer him and so did Bekman, but Yisraeli was too quick for them. "Why are you throwing away half a pepper that is the army's property?"

The soldiers were well aware of the importance the deputy brigade commander placed on not wasting anything, and that is why they would throw the leftover bread over the fence, for the animals to eat, far from the examining eye of the deputy brigade commander. But the edge of a pepper? No one imagined this being a problem. This started a discussion on the right way to cut a pepper and what part of it is not fit to eat. Brilliantly using professional logistics terms, analyzing the process of salad cutting and explaining how it is equivalent to the spare parts and ammunition the army needs, Yisraeli explained the connection between the pepper and winning the war. At the same time he also confined the cook to the base.

Now Yisraeli, who they feared and admired, will no longer be confining cooks. His body is on the ground, like a wax dummy, looking at Bekman with frozen eyes.

"What did he die from," Binyamin Herzl asks.

"From the war," Bekman explains.

What a world, Bekman thinks to himself. Just forty-eight hours ago, a level-headed brigade commander and his energetic deputy were commanding the proudest armored corps brigade in the IDF, and now they are lying dead in the battlefield. Can we, the survivors of this brigade, rise up after this?

North Sector – 109

Shortly after noon, a Syrian MiG dives on the northern ramp of 109 and scares even the most experienced armored corps soldiers. As the plane rises for another round, the soldiers take action and anyone with anything that fires, shoots into the sky. Someone above is protecting them apparently, and they manage to hit the plane which then crashes.

In the middle of the sky, a parachute sways in the wind with the pilot. The four tanks on ramp 109 watch him through their binoculars and see him land 100 meters into Syrian territory.

"Go get him," Zvika instructs Eiland.

Eiland speeds ahead on the Peleg route, crosses the border into an area full of mines, not knowing that he is carrying out the first crossing of Israeli forces into Syrian territory in the Yom Kippur War. He sees the pilot rise up behind a mound, he raises his hands in the air, with a pistol in his left hand.

Eiland, left handed himself, shouts to him in Hebrew, "Drop your gun and get on the tank." Facing a cannon aiming at him and fifty tons of steel, the Syrian pilot, who looks like a model out of a magazine, has no choice. He puts down his gun, takes off his helmet and gets on the tank. "A lefty with common sense," Eiland comments.

Since Eiland was educated to be loving to others and hospitable, he seats the pilot/model in Burko the loader's seat and to make sure the pilot does not reject the hospitality of tank 2A, he seats Burko above him, with a cocked Uzi in his hand.

North Sector – 107

In the afternoon, after destroying significant parts of the Syrian army in their sector and emptying the ammunition supplies in their tanks, Vidy, Yachin and Naides go to resupply the tank at Beit Hahazit.

As they are busy with preparations and maintenance, Eli Shemesh, the energetic intelligence officer of the 74th Battalion, suddenly appears. "Don't tell anyone," he says quietly to Yachin, "but the brigade commander, the deputy brigade commander and the operations officer are gone. Your company commander was also killed. Except for your company, there is nothing left of the brigade." He climbs back into his APC, heading west and disappears, into the undeciphered void of the war.

Alone with his world collapsing around him, Yachin sits down on the stone stairs of the Hahazit building and stares into space. To the outsider, these are four officers who died in battle, but for a twenty-one-year-old platoon commander, they are his father and mother and his big brothers, who had been watching him every moment and guiding him every step of the way.

As he is collapsing on the stairs, with his head in his hands, the rumor of the commanders that were killed spreads among the soldiers. "Get in the tank!" Naides fondly scolded his platoon commander. "Now is not the time," he implores him. "After the war, we will deal with it."

North Sector – 109

After transferring the Syrian pilot that they had taken prisoner to the infantry outpost, Eiland and Hashenberg return to the southern ramp, alongside Rak and Yisraeli. The sun is on their backs, their observation spot is excellent and Eiland identifies a battery of anti-aircraft missiles taking up position four to five kilometers from their ramp.

"Asher," Eiland calls the fire observer with him. "Look at those sons of bitches. Look how close they dare to come to us."

Asher takes action. A few minutes pass and the IDF artillery hits the Syrian SAM battery, sending its remains into the October sky, accompanied by the cheers of the tanks on the southern ramp.

Eiland decides now is the perfect time to deal with the stench of the last two days. In front of the amazed crew, one from a moshav, another from a Kibbutz and the third from the disadvantaged south, he takes out his hidden perfume, opens his coverall, and sprays the air with the smell of Paris. "If you don't bathe, you will die of the stench..." he smiles his perfect prince smile and continues to spray his armpits.

Yair Nafshi

Still positioned at the Booster, not receiving any intelligence, not understanding why his intelligence officer, or those of the 7th or the 188th Brigade, are not giving him any information, Nafshi discovers he is on his own. He realizes that things have been reversed and it is him sending information to the brigade and the higher commanders.

Deputy battalion commander Nissim takes advantage of the break in the war and tries to show that it is still business as usual. "10, this is 11, do you want the results of the ordnance inspection?"

"And what score did the Philistines (53rd Battalion) get?" Nafshi asks, not forgetting that in war, as in life, you first need your "esprit de corps."

Night

North Sector – 107

It is night. The shrieks of Tiran tracks heading east, back into Syrian territory, is in the air. The enemy have suffered a severe blow trying to climb up the Hermonit mountain, in the face of the tanks of the 7th Brigade.

Yachin estimates that some of them will attempt to return to Syria through the Kirton route and he positions an ambush on the road, toward the border route, with the tank's cannons facing west, back toward Israeli territory.

Suddenly out of nowhere, a Syrian BTR armored personnel carrier appears on the road. Yachin kicks Maman the gunner who has fallen asleep. He pulls the trigger and the shell flies into the sky and the brave BTR passes them, and now it is the turn of Naides to rotate the cannon east. Barely awake, the gunner Yossi Friedman pulls the trigger and sends a shell into the dirt mound of outpost 107.

It seems that the BTR is going to survive but it is not over until it is over. In the dark, the Syrian driver does not notice the mines placed on the road. The night is shattered by a huge explosion and the endless cries of the enemy soldiers who also wanted to live.

North Sector – Fidel Hadash

Night, Avner Landau gathers the vehicles with him to a combat parking area on the large ramp on the border route. The anti-tank ditch is thirty meters behind them. He positions sergeants Hoss and Goren to secure the flank, 200 meters from the rest of the force.

It is completely dark on the ramp of B Company, while most of the commanders, just as in the rest of the 188th Brigade, are not equipped with night vision equipment. On Saturday they had set out on a routine combat day that was supposed to end by sunset. So who needed night vision equipment?

The few who did leave the night vision equipment in the tank – a passive "Shfanfan" SLS device for the commander and a "Karnaf" IR device for the driver – did not feel much safer. The outdated equipment they had did not do much to overcome the thick darkness around them.

Without night vision, Rani Friedrich exhausts his eyes, trying to identify who is sneaking up on him in the dark. He begs the company commander repeatedly for illumination flares. Avner makes the request but nothing happens.

Without any light, completely blind, they cannot wait for the night to end. The warning of a possible commando attack keeps them alert. Although they were "promised" commando attacks on the previous two nights as well but they didn't materialize. Why is this night different?

At 02:00 the commanders of B Company are fighting the sleep that threatens to overtake them when Landau suddenly hears a whisper coming from inside his helmet. Yigal Rubinstein, Avshalom's sergeant, reports that he hears voices speaking in Arabic coming from the anti-tank ditch.

Avner does not hesitate and opens fire. All the other tanks, well drilled in the open fire procedure in a tank combat parking, imitate the company commander, and they each fire in their designated sectors.

While the tanks continue to fire, the commanders move up and down and to the sides, trying desperately to make out where the enemy is. They do not see anything. Now they are all firing at the anti-tank ditch but Rani Friedrich knows they are wasting their ammunition. The deep folds of the ditch act as perfect cover for the Syrian forces.

Two minutes pass, maybe three, and brave Syrian commando soldiers, equipped with anti-tank rocket launchers, run toward them. Friedrich wonders, as he fires continuously with the commander's machine gun at the shadows moving in the dark, who had come up with the ridiculous legend about the Syrian soldiers that run back to Damascus as soon as you fire at them?

Five or ten minutes after the gunfire starts, Landau decides to move back, which means retreating, to disengage from the closed area where they are sitting targets for the anti-tank teams that continuously try to destroy their tanks.

"Move to a different parking, follow me," Landau commands on the radio.

Landau cuts through the fields, heading northwest to Mt. Varda. As he is moving back, he notices two tanks missing, those of Hoss and Goren. He calls them on the radio, repeatedly but there is no answer.

While Yigal Rubinstein hears whispering in Arabic from the anti-tank ditch, Shmuel Sinfrada, Efra Goren's loader, ends his guard duty shift, wakes Efra up and goes back down into his compartment.

"I am leaving the loaders hatches open," Sinfrada announces, "so some air gets in."

"Out of the question," Efra responds. "It is better to keep it closed."

Sinfrada stretches out in the loader's seat and just as he is falling asleep, he hears Efra shout "Crew, bazooka. Fire!" and the tank shakes with two horrible blasts. When Sinfrada regains consciousness he hears Landau shouting on the radio, "2A, answer me, 2A." Then he hears him instructing Zeev Hoss, "Hurry over to 2A. There is smoke coming from it, they have probably been hit."

Sinfrada realizes that 2A is their tank, he looks up and knows something bad has happened to Efra. He tries to move Efra's head and his hands are in a mixture of blood and tissue.

"Can anyone hear me?" he shouts. There is no answer. Now he struggles with the loader's hatches that refuses to open, trying to release the smoke that is threatening to suffocate them in the tank. Nothing happens. Just as his strength is about to run out, the hatches open and Sinfrada fills his lungs with the fresh air outside the tank.

As he is enjoying being alive, he hears shouts in Arabic, accompanied by bullets whistling past him, forcing him to dive back into the tank. Inside the dark tank he sees Nissim Sasbon the gunner, frozen on his peri-telescope.

"What is going on Nissim?" he asks. There is no response. From the driver's compartment he hears Yehoshua Zeller call him, "Shmulik, come help me. I can't open the hatches, maybe the cannon is on top of them."

Sinfrada has found someone to share his distress with. "Efra is dead," he shouts to Zeller. "Nissim is not answering me."

He decides to check on the gunner again. "Nissim, wake up, wake up." Nissim does not respond.

Sinfrada does not give up. He thinks he sees Sasbon's chest moving up and down. He gets closer to him, looks him in the eyes and without any explanation he slaps him on his face with all his might. It helps. Nissim snaps out of the shock he was in and together with Sinfrada they leave the tank. After jumping out of the tank, Sinfrada sees that Zeller was right and the cannon is blocking the driver's exit. He returns to the turret, pushes Efra's body aside, turns the turret, enabling Zeller to join them.

Hoss's tank is 100 meters away. "Run over there," Sinfrada whispers. "I will stay here and cover you."

As Zeller and Sasbon are running, Sinfrada sees the sergeant's tank take a direct hit and Hoss's crew jumps out, just as Zeller and Sasbon get there.

Now it is his turn. The shadows of the commandos are on the mound near him. He realizes there is just one way to survive and he runs the fastest 100 meter run of his life, throwing grenades and dodging bullets fired at him.

Out of breath, he collapses in the arms of his friends and together they leave the tank and hide behind the terrace. "Where is Efra?" Zeev Hoss shouts and Sinfrada does not answer.

Landau reports the commando attack to Meshulam Ratess, the sectors' commander, as well as the two tanks left behind and the switching of parking areas.

In the practical tone of commanders, Ratess instructs him, "Go back and evacuate them."

"I am not evacuating them now. There is an anti-tank unit at close range all over. Any attempt to evacuate them will end in casualties. I am waiting for the first daylight and then I will evacuate them."

There is a moment of silence and then Ratess answers, "If you are not evacuating, I will send a force from my battalion."

"Don't send anyone" Landau begs him. "Whoever you send will be hit by the anti-tank teams"

At 03:00 Landau identifies the flashing of tank lights heading east from Bukata on the Fidel Hadash route. Has he lost his mind? He is concerned in his mind, understanding that Ratess decided to send an evacuation force.

When the tanks of the 71st Battalion, led by deputy battalion commander Gideon Willer, arrive at the anti-tank ditch, there are a series of explosions and fires light up in the dark.

From his position overlooking the scene, Ratess sees the catastrophe developing but he still does not grasp the situation. He orders Landau, "Rush over there."

"Ratess," Landau answers quietly, "you saw what happened. There is no point in heading their way now. If I go there, more tanks will be hit. I am asking you again, let's wait until the first light and then I will go."

Ratess does not answer. His answer is sending another tank toward the three that were hit. After covering a short distance, driving forward on the Fidel Hadash route, the tank is hit by an RPG that blows off its bazooka shields. It just barely manages to withdraw.

It is almost dawn. Overcome with worry for the crews that were disconnected during the night, Landau continues to call them on the radio. Suddenly Zeev Hoss answers him.

"Where are you?" Avner asks him, with a deep sense of relief.

"I am in the Bukata gas station. With me are the crews of Efra and the technical crew," Hoss replies in a strange monotonous tone.

"What about Efra?" Landau asks.

"Not here," Hoss replies.

"What do you mean not there?" Landau loses his temper with Hoss. There is chaos but the good order Landau is used to dictates that a soldier and his tank cannot just disappear.

"Efra remained in the tank," Hoss answers. "He is dead."

There are times when a loader can be a hero. That is exactly what happened during those moments behind the terrace, when Sinfrada took command.

In the argument that erupted – whether to try to join the other tanks of the company or to escape on foot toward Bukata – Sinfrada determined that the only way to survive was to move west to Bukata, since in the pressure the tanks were under, there was no way they would identify them among the Syrian commando soldiers. They would be shot by their own friends.

This convinced everyone and they set out with Sinfrada leading. He located a shallow water canal along the road and he instructed all of them to crawl through it. They moved forward in this manner until they reached a bridge with a big water pipe beneath it that transfers rain water to the wadi. They entered it and hid.

After what seemed like an eternity, they heard the sound of an engine and a vehicle stopped above them. Then someone asked in Hebrew if there was anyone there.

"Yes, yes!" they all answered together.

At dawn, after "bazooka night" – the name they had just given to this event – Landau examined the situation. Everything seemed quiet, except for occasional random artillery fire. The Syrian commando had been satisfied and disappeared. Now is the time to see if there is anyone alive left behind.

"We are going on evacuation," he announces to Friedrich and Levi, the platoon commanders, leaving Yigal Rubinstein to cover them from a distance. Three tanks descend toward the anti-tank ditch and Landau, concerned for unwanted visitors, positions Friedrich and Levi to cover him, and he continues alone toward the tanks of Efra and Hoss.

He climbs on to the tank of Efra Goren and confirms Hoss's report. Efra is dead. He pulls himself together and continues to the three tanks of the 71st Battalion. What he sees is hell.

The tanks are full of an unidentifiable mass of body parts, blood and tissue. It is hard to believe that until a few hours ago, these were young men, still alive.

Landau continues to the driver's hatches and bangs on them. With the last remains of his sanity he shouts, "Is there anyone here?"

When he is about to leave, he hears moaning from the driver's seat in the third tank.

"Is there anyone in there?" he asks again, not trusting his ears.

"Yes," a shaking voice answers from inside.

He enters the tank, moves aside body parts, turns the turret and pulls the driver out. He is black from smoke and yellow with fear.

"What is your name?" he asks, trying to regain his authority as company commander.

"Shai Kantor," the driver responds, his voice lifeless and his eyes without a spark.

"Everything will be alright now, Shai."

Back with his force, after the traumatic encounter with Willer's force that cost its life, Landau looks behind him. Syrian MiGs strike the abandoned tanks over and over again. The soldiers of B Company sit and watch the burned remains of the tanks of the 71st Battalion taking repeated hits by the planes and they thank their lucky stars that the Syrians chose those targets instead of them.

First light
Yair Nafshi
Toward the end of the night, right before dawn on Tuesday, the situation on the Booster Ridge is terrifying. The reports of the Syrian commando attack on the tanks of B Company has the other tanks wide awake, and Nafshi and Zamri are not calm. There are Syrian infantry soldiers all around them.

As the sun rises, Nafshi decides to put an end to the threat of the infantry on his position. He calls Yachin on the radio and asks him to send a tank to the Kirton route (107 – the Manzura/Brown junction), to identify the infantry threat and destroy it.

Shmulik refuses. "I am not going to send just one tank," he tells Nafshi, who agrees for him to send two tanks toward him.

Muli Dgani[37] volunteers for the task and Yossi Naides[38] joins him. They start moving forward on the route and identify two enemy APCs. They destroy them and report this to Yachin. Shmulik is very troubled by the presence of the infantry on the route. "Let them come back safely already," he mumbles to himself.

Zamri and Nafshi take up position to cover them on the Booster Ridge route, waiting for the two tanks to clear the Kirton route. But then, when Dgani and Naides are opposite their ramp, 1,000 meters north, something goes wrong.

There is a sound of an explosion on the Kirton route and then a black cloud of smoke rises from Dgani's tank. From their position at the Booster, Nafshi and Zamri follow the occurrences with their binoculars. They see Yossi Naides, the company clown from Ein Shemer, stop his tank and fire in all directions. Naides continues on the route

---

37. The crew in Dgani's tank consists of: commander Muli Dgani, gunner Dani Barzilai, loader Daniel Herzl (later he transferred to the Naides crew), driver Yaacov Hazan.
38. The crew in Naides's tank consists of: commander Yossi Naides, gunner Yossi Friedman, loader Avi Bot, driver Aharon (Homian) Magen.

when he suddenly sees Daniel Herzl, Dgani's loader, running pell-mell toward him. He climbs on the tank and shouts, "They are all dead."

Naides reports to Yachin on the platoon frequency, "Only one is alive."

Naides makes room for Herzl in the tank and he urges Homian to continue heading toward the tank that was hit. Maybe someone is still alive. Another anti-tank team, well camouflaged, identifies the exposed tank and fires a volley of RPG rockets, which hit the front fuel tank, ending the shortly lived luck of Daniel Herzl the loader. The tank of first Sergeant Yossi Naides is blown into a thousand pieces of steel, with the five crew members in it.

Two weeks before the war, right after he completed his basic training as a tank driver, Aharon (Homian) Magen had arrived at the tank camp 107. "You are Yossi Naides's driver," he is told. Born in Teheran, he came to Israel by himself and has no family in the country. He did not connect with the loud group of soldiers. The only thing they knew about him in his platoon was that he had been approved leave to visit his parents in Teheran (this was the period before, Khomeini and the Ayatollahs, when Israel had good relations with Iran) after the holidays.

On Saturday there was a war and Homian, as always, did not speak in the tank. He did not say a word, from the beginning of the war to its end. A new driver had no reason to be heard in a place where your experience and veteran status were what determined how much you wanted to stand out. Uncharacteristically, he left this world with a huge bang, accompanied by fire and smoke, before anyone in his crew got to know him.

From his position at 107, Yachin hears the deafening explosion but he does not know what has happened.

On the Booster Ridge, Nafshi, Avni and Zamri hear the same explosion, even louder. Unlike Yachin, they see the blinding flash that comes from Naides's tank. The tank is simply blown into the sky, in a sea of steel shards and burning fire.

"Go see what is going on over there," Nafshi instructs Yachin. Yachin starts moving and Nafshi pulls himself together and realizes he does not want to lose his platoon/company commander's life as well. The anti-tank teams may be waiting for them. "Stop. Go back. There is nothing for you to do there."

Emek Habacha — The Valley of Tears

Tuesday, October 9

The Quneitra gap spreads from the Hermonit mountain (Tel A-Sicha) in the north and the Bnei Rasan hill (Tel Asnia) in the south, with the city of Quneitra located in its southern part.

In the scenarios examined by the Northern Command, prior to the Yom Kippur War, the Quneitra gap was perceived to be of great military and strategic importance. The assessment was that should the Syrians succeed in breaking through the gap, this would lead to a large-scale catastrophe, the largest on the Golan front.

First of all, the city of Quneitra — abandoned and ruined since the Six-Day War but still the historic capital of the Golan, a political symbol for both sides — could fall into Syrian hands. Second, controlling Quneitra or the area would give the Syrians another bonus — access to the main route of the Golan and its current capital, Nafah. From that town it is not far to the Bnot Yaakov Bridge. There, on the banks of the Jordan River, without the obstacle of the Kinneret to delay them, the Syrian forces could easily reach their destination, the kibbutzim of the Upper Galilee.

In order to face this threat and prevent it from materializing, the enemy's ability to cross had to be limited. An anti-tank ditch was dug across the gap, dense mine fields were laid near the border and infantry outposts were manned at all times — 109 in the south, 107 in the center and 105 in the north.

When the war started, the tanks of the 74th Battalion took up their positions, ready to face the immediate threat of an attack from Quneitra. In positions on the ramps, on both sides of outpost 107, the Yachin force identified the movement of the Syrian tank battalion of the 85th Brigade, trying to break through on the America (main road from Damascus)–Kirton route. They crushed their repeated attempts, firing with the cannons of their Sho't Kal tanks. In sector 109, Zvika Rak and the tanks of A Company had blocked the attempts of the tank battalion of the Syrian 52nd Infantry Brigade to break through. The tanks of B Company, commanded by Avner Landau, had taken up position on the Fidel Hadash route, north of the gap, blocking attempts to cross the anti-tank ditch.

This was not enough. On the northern side of the Quneitra gap, beneath and to the east of the Hermonit mountain, there was a wide flat area. This plain reached as far as the Purple Line and the Manzura junction (Yakir – Kirton routes) in the south and the Bukata-border road in the north (Fidel Hadash route). There were no Israeli tanks deployed in this area. Something went wrong in the regional defense perception, between Yachin, positioned at the south of the gap, and Landau in the north.

Suddenly, the grooved plain east of the Hermonit mountain, between outposts 107 and 105, became the preferred point where the Syrian forces planned to break through, correctly identifying it as the weak spot in the Quneitra defense.

Was it the intelligence that the Syrian army had collected prior to the war, regarding the deployment of the Israeli tank platoons, that led them to choose the spot for breaking through beneath the Hermonit? This is very likely. Starting Saturday evening, the attempts of the Syrian 85th Brigade (the few tanks that were not destroyed by the 74th Battalion) concentrated their effort on the weak spot, north of Yachin force located on the 107 ramps, slightly south of Avner Landau's company beneath outpost 105, on the Fidel Hadash route.

On Saturday afternoon, well aware of the locations of the Israeli forces, the Northern Command operations officer (J3), Lt. Col. Uri Simchoni, sent most of the 7th Brigade tanks to this weak spot. The perfect solution? Not quite.

The layout of the landscape in the gap, forced the tanks of the 7th Brigade to take up positions farther back from the Purple Line and the anti-tank ditch, in the fire controlling areas of the Hermonit Mountain. As a result, a few kilometers of the plain lacked any Israeli tanks. Instead of presence, they controlled it from a distance. This area started at the anti-tank ditch in the east and ended three kilometers from there, at the positions of the 7th Brigade tanks in the west.

Even at this distance from the Purple Line, beneath the Hermonit, the tanks of the 7th Brigade had succeeded in blocking the repeated Syrian attacks on Saturday night. On Sunday morning the situation had changed. The commander of Syrian 7th Division, Omar Abrash, had been notified that, during the night, bridges and crossings had been placed on the anti-tank ditch. He then sent in the second wave of tanks: ninety-five tanks of the 78th Armored Brigade, in addition to the forty-one tanks of the 121st Mechanized Brigade. They had been tasked with the mission of conquering the Quneitra gap.

Despite this massive number of tanks, the IDF Sho't Kal tanks continued to block the attempts of the 7th Division, also on Sunday and Monday, causing them significant damage.

During the daylight hours, it was mainly the tanks of Nafshi's force, the 74th Battalion, who hit any Syrian vehicle daring to enter their range.

When the night came, without any night vision equipment, the tanks of the 74th Battalion could not defend the Purple Line, and the Syrian forces, aware of the deployment of the Israeli forces, crossed the anti-tank ditch "behind the shoulder" of the 74th Battalion, in the undefended area they had located there. They snuck in like thieves in the night, heading west in an area clear of Israeli tanks, fighting fierce battles in the night with the tanks of the 7th Brigade waiting for them beneath the Hermonit Mountain.

Then Tuesday morning came.

Yachin Force – 74th Battalion

In what had become his routine in the last two days, at 07:00, Shmulik Yachin raised his binoculars facing east... what the hell?!

An endless cloud of dust covers the horizon and beneath it an equally endless line of Tiran tanks, led by bridge-laying tanks. It looked like the Syrian army was starting the war all over again.

On outpost 107, the infantry commander, 2nd Lt. Elimelech Avraham (Miley), orders the soldiers to start counting the Syrian tanks moving in front of them. The observer reaches the count of 100 and the flow continues.

How come this day is different? Yachin wonders, as he identifies additional forces, leaving clouds of dust behind them. They are moving parallel to the main force, to the north of it, in the area leading directly to the anti-tank ditch and the area beneath the Hermonit Mountain. He sees and hears the veil of fire rolling in front of them.

After another moment of amazement, he rubs his hands together in enjoyment and returns to his routine of the last few days – pinpointed hits. He is not alone. On the two ramps there are the four tanks of Videy, Vodak, Damir and Farkash, and in a calm and professional manner, they start to crush the "southern effort" of the force facing them.

Landau Force – 74th Battalion.
At the same time Yachin is opening fire, the four remaining functioning tanks of B Company – Landau the company commander, Friedrich and Levi the platoon leaders, and Rubinstein the sergeant – are positioned slightly south of the Fidel Hadash route. They fire at the distant targets in the southeast, attempting to disrupt the efforts of the Syrian northern battalion.

As they are firing, Levi's tank has an electrical malfunction and they disengage and drive toward the technical crew positioned at the Bukata gas station.

Nissim Force – 74th Battalion, deputy commander
From his position near outpost 105, Yossi Nissim, the deputy battalion commander, identifies an endless cloud of dust coming from Han Urineva. He moves forward, with Kaimo, Gitai and Frost, and the four of them try their skill in hitting targets from a long distance. To their disappointment they are not successful. Without any other instructions, the deputy commander remains in his position, ready to face whatever comes.

The 7th Brigade
At the same time, with the sun blinding his force, turning the morning into an impenetrable blanket of white drops, Lt. Col. Yossi Eldar, commander of the 75th Battalion, learns what the meaning of a rolling fire screen is.

An endless wall of smoke, layered with shards of steel and basalt, rises on the front. Beneath his feet the ground is shaking and the commanders of the nineteen tanks under his command are exhausted from this endless fight.

Tuesday, October 9, is the day when the Syrian army starts to withdraw from the territory it conquered in the southern and central Golan. Three IDF armored divisions fight three divisions of the Syrian army. Inch by inch, at a heavy cost, they push the forces of Hafez Assad back toward the Purple Line.

At the headquarters on Mt. Kana'an it appears that the forces are finally managing to put the lid on the boiling Syrian lava and things are getting back on track. At last, we are getting back to being on the winning side. That is when the focus is transferred, for the first time since the war began, to the Quneitra gap, between the center and north of the Golan.

Seeing their forces withdrawing from the southern Golan, the Syrian General Staff decide to launch a double-headed counterattack: 150 tanks, the remains of the 91st and the 51st Armored Brigades, together with the fresh T62 tanks of the 76th Tank Brigade that had crossed the border the previous day. All are now attacking with fury the central heights toward Nafah, trying to push back the tired defenders – about sixty tanks from the 679th Reserve Brigade under the command of Ori Or.

(The further battles of the 679th Brigade will not be described. Sufficient to say that by the end of fierce armored fights, the 679th had crushed what remains of the pride and fighting spirit of the Syrian armored facing them.)

Twenty kilometers north, in the northern Quneitra gap – a more attractive area due to its topography and the small number of Israeli forces defending it – the second arrowhead is heading with a clear intention. "We are here to take your assets. We are going to push you westward, we'll take control of the main road and we'll roll happily, though a little bit late, with victors' élan, all the way westward toward Nafah and the Jordan River."

The Syrians concentrate 380 artillery pieces that fire continuously on the outposts, the tank ramps and serve mainly as a rolling screen of fire for the main force.

One hundred fifty tanks move forward on three main routes. One hundred of these are T62 tanks of the 81st Brigade, 3rd Division, with fresh crew members who have yet to experience the trauma of battle. Their tanks are still sparkling clean, their crews full of motivation to fight and change the outcome of the war. In addition, there are another fifty tanks of "experienced" soldiers, the remains of the 7th Division and the Rafat Assad force. Accompanying them are two anti-tank companies with Sagger missiles and convoys of trucks and armored personnel carriers, with hundreds of infantry soldiers given the task of cleansing the area.

Facing this Syrian force there are fifty Sho't Kal tanks, with exhausted crews that have lost many of their friends in battle, many in very low spirits, some on the verge of shell shock. None of them grasp the extent of the power of the Syrian tiger speeding toward them.

07:00

Sector 109 – 74th Battalion

On the southern ramp of outpost 109 the four tank crews of A Company awaken and are ready for another combat day.

Toward 07:00, Zvika the company commander and Yisraeli his deputy head toward the Quneitra base, on their way to quickly refuel and replenish ammunition and then return. They leave the defense of the area to Eiland and Hashenberg.

Less than half an hour later, outpost 109 and the two tanks defending it come under heavy artillery fire. The shells turn the upper part of the base into what looks like the cratered face of the moon. Even a finger stuck outside the bunker is immediately hit.

On their way, Yisraeli identifies three Sho't Meteor tanks firing at targets already destroyed by A Company. He stops by them, he pulls Tuashi out of the gunner's compartment and sends him to see what is going on there. Reserve soldiers, some still in civilian clothes, stare at the soldier with the face full of soot, who is criticizing them for wasting ammunition. "How is it possible that you came here without bore-sighting your optical sights?" he barks at them. With their furious eyes on his back, he leaves them and returns to the tank.

Yachin and Nafshi – 74th Battalion

As Yachin continues to hit the targets in front of him, Yair Nafshi calls him on the radio and instructs him to leave his position and come with his force quickly to the Booster Ridge position.

"If we leave, the outpost will be conquered," Shmulik begs on behalf of Elimelech Avraham, the commander of infantry outpost 107, aware of the size of the Syrian force still on the route.

"Get over here immediately," Nafshi says sharply. He has counted over ten tanks that the Yachin force destroyed, and seeing the rest of the Syrian battalion stop, he knows that there are more important things to take care of.

Gathering all the emotional strength he has left in him, Yachin notifies Elimelech of the order he received, afraid that he just pulled the rug from under him.

Elimelech reports to his direct commander, Lt. Col. Zeev Unger, the commander of the Golani 13th Battalion, positioned on Mt. Avital, that the tanks are leaving.

The Yachin force arrives at the Booster Ridge shortly before 08:00 and immediately receives the order from Nafshi to take command of the force, while he heads west to receive orders at Beit Hahazit at a meeting with Pzira.

Early that morning Nafshi was notified that a company of Sherman M51 tanks, Pzira, part of the Command armored battalion, would arrive and replace him. He tried to contact them on the radio but there was no response. Then he remembered they use the old GRC radios and that is why they are not answering. The emergency armored corps frequency is supposed to reach GRC, so he calls them on that, over and over. Someone apparently was not doing their job. He decides to join them and guide them to the Booster.

While Nafshi is heading west, Yachin takes position at the Booster Ridge pump. They move two to three kilometers to the west of the ramps and the continuous tension of avoiding the aim of the Tiran tanks slowly slips away. Videy, always efficient, takes this chance to repair the track of the battalion commander's tank that is stuck there.

Then Yachin recalls the tanks of the southern Syrian force that had remained intact opposite the ramps of 107. Who will face them in battle? What will happen when they overcome the stop he panicked them into making and start heading toward Elimelech?

At outpost 107, Elimelech "pulls himself together," fighting his own private war.

He contacts the battalion again and demands artillery fire support. "The Syrians are moving in front of me in two columns and are right on the original targets." A couple of minutes pass and the answer is not surprising, "There is no artillery, no air support, you will have to manage."

"Manage?" That is what Elimelech has been doing since the war started but he does not understand what he is supposed to do with these tanks that are not attacking the stronghold but are passing a few hundred meters north of him.

In the days before the war, Syrian intelligence units had infiltrated Israeli territory, mapped the area and examined the options for breaking through on the designated routes.

The land mines laid out on Friday across the Quneitra gap had disrupted the Syrian intelligence assessment and were a serious setback to the planed Syrian blitz. Here also, across the Kirton route, the tanks leading the force were surprised to find tight rows of mines.

The commanders of the squat turreted Syrian tanks decided that they are better off staying away from local trouble and instead to focus on the main effort, concentrating on the area beneath Mt. Hermonit.

Elimelech decides to contribute his part to the war effort and fires machine guns at the external fuel tanks of the Tirans. Nothing happens. After a few minutes with no results, it is time to fire bazookas. Within minutes, five tanks go up in flames. There are cries of joy and celebrations at outpost 107, and the only ones not affected are the Syrians. The bazookas fire but the convoy continues forward. The Tiran tanks continue to flow toward the plain north of outpost 107.

As he is wondering how Elimelech is doing Yachin looks to the north, and before him he sees a panorama of war. North of where he is standing, beneath Mt. Hermonit, an endless stream of Syrian tanks is on the move. It does not seem like they have any intention of stopping.

The tanks of the 7th Brigade are located somewhere out there, opposite the Syrian movement, but how many of them could be left by now? How can they possibly stop this wave of evildoers, on the wide plain in front of them? Now he realizes why Nafshi's order to leave everything and come here was so urgent. For the first time since the war started, he is not sure who is going to win.

While he is lost in questions and worries, strange looking tanks start climbing up the Booster Ridge from the west. Just as he is about to give the order to fire on these tanks that flanked him, he identifies them to be IDF M51 Sherman tanks, taking positions on the rear slopes. Yachin, the commander of the sector until Nafshi returns, drives up to them and is amazed at the surreal picture he sees. Reserve soldiers are, apparently, of a different nature. The veteran Sherman crews are just pouring the water for their morning coffee, acting as if there is no war going on.

A few minutes later, Nafshi returns from receiving orders and locates the Pzira company commander. He positions the tall tanks inside the Booster Ridge complex, instructing their commander to guard the Quneitra gap and make sure no one passes to the west. "We are going to make order down there. We will return to you later," he tells them and departs from the reserve soldiers and their coffee.

08:00

The 7th Brigade

At 08:15, after consulting with Yanush, the commander of the 7th Brigade, Yoss Eldar, moves his tank force a few hundred meters to the west, to positions on the rear slope that are hidden from the Syrian artillery forward observers. Here he escapes from the terror of the doomsday shelling that will not end.

Ofer Glusman, a platoon commander in the "patched up" 71st Battalion, gets detached from his force and joins M company commanded by Amnon Lavi of the 77th Battalion. Together with Noah Timianker, Amnon and Nir Keren Zvi, he does his best to survive the days and nights at the Quneitra gap.

By the fourth day of fighting, Glusman feels immune. He knows he cannot be hit. After full batteries of artillery firing at him wherever he goes, tens of Syrian tanks trying to hit him, the best Syrian gunners shooting at him, all having failed, he knows he is invincible.

But now, on his way back from the ramp through a wall of fire, smoke, shrapnel, and dirt, with his commander's hatch stuck open at a 90 degrees angle, Glusman is sitting on his seat, sticking his head as far into the tank as he can.

Then the world is turned upside down and Sharabi the driver is shouting from his compartment, "Glusman, what is that? What is that?" Glusman is no longer sure about how invincible he is. With his head inside the tank, he ignores the question and his deep bass voice is loud and clear, "Sharabi, full speed, do you hear me? Full speed. If you take your foot off the gas pedal, we are dead."

Sector 109 – 74th Battalion

Yossi Wolf, the reserve platoon commander had become the commander of outpost 109 after Ehud Ben Gera had been killed. Toward 08:30 he hears the eerie silence throughout his sector being suddenly broken by the sound of tracks moving around the stronghold. He immediately requests the assistance of the tanks. "Finally!" Eiland thinks to himself.

Eiland and Hashenberg leave their position on the southern ramp and rush toward the outpost.

Oded Yisraeli completes the resupply of ammunition and he parts from Zvika, the company commander. It is just then that he hears the distress call from the stronghold. The crew jumps into the tank and rushes toward outpost 109. As they are crossing the road, between two basalt hills, Yisraeli stops Yaakov Moshe the driver and says calmly, "Something buzzed by my ear." Then he changes his tone and shouts to Tuashi, "Turn around! Turn around!."

Tuashi understands that he means for him to turn the turret around and if that is what Yisraeli, the master of order and discipline tells him to do, they are in trouble. He turns the turret around and now he has a problem. Since the tank is high, they are in a "micro-switch" situation and he rises the cannon up so it does not hit the tank body and they cannot lower it.

Yaakov hears Yisraeli and then he hears Tuashi's wail – unable to lower the cannon! – and he takes action. He switches to neutral, pulls the steering wheel to one side and, presses down on the gas and without pressing the brakes, he turns the tank around. The Syrian tank appears in front of them and Tuashi fires and smashes it in a great ball of fire.

Before they get the chance to celebrate, Yisraeli shouts, "There are another seven tanks here."

"I can't see anything" Tuashi shouts from the gunner's position.

"One second Zeevik," he replies. "I will put you on target."

Tuashi has his eye glued to the periscope and he keeps lowering the cannon, searching. Suddenly he feels two knees in his back and he shouts, "Oded, watch where you are kicking."

A strange sound comes from the commander's seat, "I am not

kicking. I took a serious hit." Tuashi turns and looks back at Yisraeli who has his hand on his coat.

Tuashi moves his hand and sees a hole there. He removes the coat and sees that it penetrated his chest and Oded begins to fade.

"Deputy has been hit! Deputy has been hit!" Tuashi shouts on the radio, lowering the cannon so the breech block rises and he slides through. Together with Goldshaft the loader, they place Oded on the empty shells basket and look at him helplessly.

In the middle of the chaos inside the tank, there is a moment of self-examination. In the days before October 6, Yisraeli would check the crew every morning. From top to bottom. He would especially enjoy checking their pockets for the things they were supposed to have: a prisoner card, a range card, radio instructions, and a personal bandage.

Tuashi puts his hand in Yisraeli's pocket and he does not have a bandage. "You are good at checking others!" Tuashi says to his silent commander.

He uses his own bandage on Yisraeli but Yisraeli continues to bleed and Goldshaft takes out his bandage and somehow they cover the hole that is overflowing.

"Commander As, this is deputy's gunner" Tuashi reports to Zvika Rak the company commander. "Deputy has been hit. I am taking him to the medical aid station."

Tuashi doesn't know the way very well, so Yaakov the driver takes control and he rushes them forward, slipping a bit more than necessary, climbing on a rock and dangling the tracks in the air.

Tuashi shouts orders to Yaakov the driver from the commander's seat and he shouts back to him, "You take care of Oded, I will get us out of here," and that is what he does. They don't know the way exactly but they suddenly see the mosque of Quneitra and they drive straight toward it.

Yisraeli continues to lose blood and is in and out of consciousness. Goldshaft holds on to his head, so it does not get hit. Finally, they arrive at the medical center and they carry out the drill for evacuating an injured soldier from the tank. They never practiced dragging a bleeding "rag," that was bouncy and energetic just minutes earlier. Yisraeli is placed on a stretcher and taken to the medical bunker, with Tuashi at his side. A doctor looks at the injured officer, touches here and there, takes out a huge syringe and sticks it in Oded's chest. Tuashi shouts at him, "What are you doing to my commander?" and the doctor shouts back, "Get out of here right now."

After a short while he returns to the bunker to check on his admired commander and he finds Yisraeli lying there resting. The bandage on his chest goes up and down slowly and he opens his eyes occasionally.

"How do you feel, Oded?" Tuashi asks him, and he shakes his head.

"Do you need anything?"

Yisraeli grunts, "Zeevik, get me some chocolate."

Tuashi runs out like a madman, finds a chocolate covered wafer and when he returns, he finds Yisraeli unconscious again.

After being treated at the aid station bunker, Yisraeli was transferred to the Rambam Hospital in Haifa. There he laid next to Yitzchak Sarig (commander of the 2nd platoon, A Company), one of the commanders injured in the accident before the war.

"Zachki!" Oded would whisper to him at night.

"What?" his answer would come through the heavy dosage of medication he was taking.

"Don't believe anyone!" Yisraeli would continue quietly.

"What?" Zachki would continue to ask vaguely.

"Don't believe them. They are all dead..." Yisraeli's whisper filled the room with desperation.

As Eiland and Hashenberg are on their way to help outpost 109, they hear the call on the company frequency, "Deputy has been hit, deputy has been hit." "Those sons of bitches keep hitting us," Eiland tells himself, as they are turning toward the stronghold. Five hundred meters north of them they find every tank crew's dream: seven brand new T62 tanks, without camouflage colors, their squat turrets shining in the sun, with their weak side turned to them.

"Driver, stop!" Asher Diamond, the artillery forward observer, clears the loader's area and bends behind the commander's cupola. Eiland rotates the turret and aims at one of the tanks. "Fire!"

Efraim fires and hits the first tank and then the second and the third. Zion Awad, Hashenberg's gunner, hits another three. "There is one left," Asher shouts to Eiland, pointing at a tank appearing through a cloud of smoke. Efraim fires and another Syrian crew is sent on to the next life.

"Take that, you bunch of fucks," Eiland says, counting the seven fires they just lit.

7th Brigade

Sensing the growing pressure of the tanks on the front lines, Yanush orders all the tanks acting as the brigade reserv e force – the eight tanks of the 77th Battalion, commanded by Avigdor Kahalani – to move immediately to reinforce the gap.

Meshulam Ratess, commander of the 71st Battalion, with his forces in the northern Hermonit area on the Fidel Hadash route, trying to evacuate the bodies of the crews ambushed by the anti-tank teams during the night, also receives a direct order from Yanush. They too are to move south immediately to help block the main Syrian effort opposite Wadi Shabrak.

In the past two days the Syrian forces concentrated their attacks on a topographic "funnel." It is formed from the grooved plain, a valley, two kilometers wide, extending from the southern slopes of Mt. Hermonit, to Tel Jit, near the Kirton route. One of the places where the Syrians tried to ascend, in the dark of the previous nights, was the Shabrak wadi north of this funnel.

9:00

Landau – 74th Battalion

Between 08:30 and 09:00, the Syrian forces rolled into the flat area beneath the Hermonit while the three tanks of B Company were firing at them from short range. Avner Landau receives an order on the radio. He is instructed to take the company and move immediately to the Elrom area. "The Syrian forces are on their way there," Ratess implores him.

Landau resists, "We are in great firing positions, no one can get by us. Is this necessary?"

A few minutes later, Ratess is impatient and he repeats the order, "Move to Elrom immediately, the Syrians are already there."

Landau leaves his position, with its wonderful control over the northern movement of the Syrian 81st Armored Brigade, and he sets out on his new mission.

The 7th Brigade

A few minutes after taking up position, the commander of the 75th Battalion discovers that they are running out of ammunition. He reports this to Yanush who approves for him to thin the line and send tanks to refuel and resupply with ammunition.

Just a few moments earlier, Avigdor Kahalani had left the night combat parking area, a kilometer west of the Kirton-Yakir route (Manzura junction) and here he is leading an eight tanks force (Emmy Falant company), heading straight on the Kirton route. Shortly before Tel Jit he cuts north toward the positions controlling the Wadi Shabrak gap.

After crossing the anti-tank ditch, the Syrians had continued in two battle columns. The northern force headed on the regular route of the previous days, through Wadi Shabrak. The southern force headed toward Tel Jit.

The Syrians did not wait for the game of musical chairs between the two battalion commanders of the 7th Brigade to end. They have not heard about Yoss, or Kahalani and they continue moving forward.

Hidden in the heavy smoke, they progress towards the southwest, toward the southern slopes of the Hermonit, guiding themselves through Wadi Shabrak – the weak spot in the rocky topography of the valley – above its draining basin, opposite the junction of the Tarzan and Kazorina routes (a spot they identified in advance as a convenient route for passing).

The Syrian Tirans move through the creek, hidden from the Israeli forces, aiming at the commanding positions above them, the very positions that Kahalani's force are trying to reach before them.

Around 09:00, with his tank hidden behind a large mound of rocks, Kahalani identifies four T-62 tanks appearing just a few meters from him. He destroys all four and continues toward the commanding position above Wadi Shabrak.

Once he is in position, he identifies to his right, south of him, the Falant company he left behind. From what he hears on the radio communication he understands that Kauli his deputy, Lavi the company commander and Baruchin the operations officer and the other tanks with them are scattered all over and are all doing their best. He is not sure this will be enough, however.

Landau – 74th Battalion

The three tanks of the Landau company speed through, cutting diagonally toward the Elrom road, when they hear Ratess changing their mission. "Abort my previous order – move quickly to the southern slopes of the Hermonit."

Landau arrives at the Elrom junction and meets the tanks of the 71st battalion, preparing to move east. He orders the tanks accompanying him to join the convoy. In his enthusiasm toward the new mission he does not notice that Friedrich and Rubinstein are not with him.

Rani Friedrich and Yigal Rubinstein do not hear Landau's order on the radio and somehow, they lose him in the Elrom area. They look around and see no enemy forces. Nothing. They stop and call Landau on the radio but there is no reply.

There were no Syrian tanks at Elrom but who was there?

In addition to the concentrated armored fists that the 7th Syrian division sends to the Quneitra gap, in the northern side of the area, since the late night hours, a Syrian commando battalion had also in been in action. This commando battalion was very well equipped and trained and moved without any disturbance, ambushing Israeli forces. Since Tuesday morning, two of the battalion companies had been positioned in the fields of Bukata, opposite Kibbutz Elrom.

Sector 109 – 74th Battalion

While Landau's tanks join the forces of the 71st Battalion, Eiland and Hashenberg descend to the northern ramp, awaiting their next task. A few minutes later, Zvika the company commander joins them.

Opposite them, 1,200 meters away, they identify movement of ten light and heavy vehicles. They target them, demonstrate professional gunning at its best and destroy them all.

The 7th Brigade

At the head of his force, Meshulam Ratess, commander of 71st Battalion, urges his tanks on, "Hurry, hurry, the Syrians are already on the Hermonit."

Nine tanks and another one – Avner Landau commander of B Company, 53rd battalion – are moving on the Kazorina route, maintaining visual contact with Kahalani's tanks to their right. They take up position in the most advanced firing positions, near the junction of the Kazorina-Tarzan routes. They are unaware of how close they are to the enemy tanks.

Avner looks around, he and Ratess are the only ones in firing positions. What is keeping all the others? Down below, to the south, he identifies the 77th Battalion tanks exchanging fire with the enemy. The time for observation is up, and with Ratess at his side, they fight for their lives. It is an armored fencing match. Syrian tanks continue to rise from the top of the Shabark creek and Ratess and Landau destroy three of them, in face-to-face combat at a distance of just fifty meters.

Shortly before 09:30, Landau improves his position toward the edge of the hill, now having better control over the wadi. He turns to see if Ratess came with him and he sees black smoke coming from the battalion commander's tank.

Ratess' tank had taken a direct hit and there is silence. An armor-piercing projectile slides on the cannon, flies up, beheads the veteran commander who was about to be appointed brigade commander, spreading shrapnel that injures Benny Baratz, the operations officer, and leaves the crew in shock.

Landau indicates with his flags for all the tanks of the 71st Battalion to come to him. No one moves. He tries again, there is no response. Now is not the time to be a hero, Landau tells himself. He leaves his position, passes by the tank of the battalion commander who is dead in the tank, he takes two of the crew members into his tank and retreats. He does not succeed in contacting the other tanks of the battalion.

He continues moving and transfers to the Shoter frequency (of the 77th Battalion) and announces that he is joining them. Avigdor Kahalani, who is in the midst of a desperate battle against the Syrian force, hears that there is trouble with his other forces that retreated to a rear slope. He confirms and together they retreat southwest, to the slope where some of the tanks of the 7th Brigade are hiding.

At 09:30, Kahalani reports from his new position, "I was forced to move back," and in order to maintain hope for Yanush and maybe for himself as well, he adds, "when three or four tanks rise up, they get hit. I cannot identify the size of the force. I am at a flat plain, every time they rise, we hit them."

Danny Ashkenazi's private war

At 09:30, after Kahalani and Ratess's tanks withdraw from Wadi Shab-rak and Nafshi's tanks are yet to arrive, a lone tank takes up position at the northernmost point in the area. The commander of this tank is 1st Lt. Danny Ashkenazi, the operations officer of the Chief Armored Corps Officer.

Until Saturday, Ashkenazi had been serving at the training base at Kastina. Like many of the officers at the base, he too was given an emergency appointment – operations officer of the Chief Armored Corps Officer.

On Saturday afternoon, when all hell broke loose from both north and south, he was at the "Pit," in Hakiryah headquarters in Tel Aviv, with Motke Zippori, the Chief Armored Corps Officer.

Surrounded by armored veterans who had come to give advice on how to conduct the war, Ashkenazi felt his patience running out and his frustration mounting. On Sunday morning he decided that he had had enough. He told Zippori that he has no intention of missing the war to sit in Tel Aviv at Hakiryah, when all the soldiers who trained with him were fighting on the front lines.

He received the approval of Zippori and went to Julis, where two re-serve officers joined him and they took a jeep and drove directly to the front lines on the Golan.

"It is too dangerous to drive a jeep to the Golan," they were told when arriving at Kibbutz Gadot. They left the jeep at the Kibbutz and caught a ride to Nafah, arriving just when Raful left.

Hanging from the APC fleeing from the Syrian tanks on the fences of the divisional base, they arrived at Aleika with Raful. They introduced themselves to Raful and without any delay were sent to join the forces of the 7th Brigade.

Near the Wasset junction they parted. As Ashkenazi started to get organized at the improvised repair center, Jacky Hizkiya, the deputy commander of the 7th Brigade, appeared next to him and handed him a frequency card. He pointed to a damaged tank of the 188th Brigade and explained to him that that is his tank. "We will add another one later," he added.

Inside the tank Ashkenazi met the crew of Udi Friedman of B Company, 53rd Battalion (Shlomo Yitzchaki the gunner, Morris Vaknin the loader and Yossi Shemesh the driver) who had been hit on Saturday. As a result Udi Friedman had lost an eye and the tank its ability to rotate its turret.

"Hi, I am Danny," he tried to connect with the burned-out soldiers who shook their shoulders at him slightly and said, "We will only return to our own brigade."

On Monday afternoon Jacky Hizkiya sent Ashkenazi to prepare another tank to return to battle. When he entered the commander's cupola, he found the beheaded body of Amir Bashari, who he commanded in tank commander's course.

"I am not getting back in that tank," he informed Hizkiya.

During the night, Sergeant Yoel Emanuel arrived at the brigade repair workshop. He was a tank commander from the Avner Landau company. In the afternoon, an artillery shell hit his tank drive system and since then he had been "crawling" toward the repair center.

At 03:00, Ashkenazi was awoken by loud pounding on the tank.

"Prepare the tanks to move out. We repaired another one for you," Hizkiya instructed him.

"Where to?"

"To Yoss Eldar's battalion."

They left and at 05:00 arrived at the Manzura junction and met Yoss. Then the Ashkenazi force continued with the tanks of the 75th Battalion, in order to replace other tanks that had been in position all night.

They hardly had a chance to take up their posts when they came under withering artillery fire. The tanks of the Yoss force withdrew and for some reason Ashkenazi stayed where he was with a number of unfamiliar tanks. A few minutes passed and contact with Yoel Emanuel was cut off. There was no sign of him. Ashkenazi decided to leave the shelled ramp and move north. He passed a Sho't Kal tank that had been hit. He continued north, without any Israeli tanks around him, accompanied by an unclear silence on the radio. He eventually took up position on a hidden ramp above Wadi Shabrak and waited.

Positioned on a forward slope, giving him the advantage of being able to lower the cannon maximally, hidden behind a row of huge basalt rocks, screened behind the fall bushes, Ashkenazi feels this is the position that will make him one of the warriors. And he is right.

Completely unaware of the presence of the predator at the top of the hill, a number of Syrian Tiran tanks appear. From a range of 100–200 meters, Yitzchaki the gunner opens fire on the sitting ducks.

After destroying five tanks, four more manage to pass them and begin moving on the road beneath the Hermonit. Now Ashkenazi has a problem. This route passes just ten meters from him. If they see him, it is his end. Morris Vaknin shouts "loaded" and Yitzchaki fires at the green shapes filling his peri-telescope, destroying three of the four. From the driver's seat, Yossi Shemesh sees the last tank, twenty meters from their position. Ashkenazi shouts, "Yitzchaki fire!" but Vaknin announces that they are out of shells.

"Load whatever we have," Ashkenazi shouts and a smoke shell is fired and hits the Tiran, forcing the crew to jump out.

In the position above Wadi Shabrak, Ashkenazi decides he is not going to let any of the crew members of the Tirans sneak up and attack them. He fires continuously from the commander's machine gun, a deadly outburst that leaves none of the Syrian soldiers alive.

He fires his machine gun until he runs out of ammunition, he bends into the tank to get more when the tank is hit and shakes wildly.

"Driver, reverse. Now!" Ashkenazi shouts, with shrapnel filling his body, knowing it is now or never. No. Boom, another shell hits the tank. The engine coughs and chokes and dies, a 750 horsepower refusing to continue.

The gunner was not injured, the loader is full of shrapnel, and the commander is desperate for air. They half run, half limp to a draining channel on the side of the road. "Where is Yossi?" Ashkenazi asks.

Inside the driver's compartment, full of smoke, Yossi Shemesh cries in terror, "Get me out of here!" He sees death approaching and his life flashing before him, when suddenly the hatches open and the light of life fills his compartment. "How did you forget me?" he shouts at Yitzchaki's black face. He is not angry but happier than ever. Together they run, helping each other, as far from the front as their legs will take them.

Yair Nafshi – 74th Battalion

As some of the 7th Brigade tanks retreat, Nafshi gathers his men and briefs them. "We are heading toward the Hermonit. The 7th Brigade has a problem there."

Seven tanks of the 188th Brigade are moving swiftly forward and

Nafshi feels that he is on a mission to rescue the 7th Brigade, the 36th Division, perhaps even the entire country.

09:45: Nafshi's force arrives at the route leading to Ein Hawara and continues eastward. At Ein Hawara they identify a company of Sho't Kal tanks. The tank closest to them is marked "10C."

Second in line, behind Nafshi, Yachin looks at the tanks to his left. He does not understand what is going on and why they are standing there. He hears Kahalani on the radio calling them to move forward. None of the tanks move. Nafshi does not understand this either. Why are they just standing there? Kahalani takes out two flags and indicates for them to follow him. Still no one moves.

"Look at the Syrian forces fighting like lions," Kahalani says on the radio. "I don't understand what is happening to us. Move forward with me," he tries to revive their spirits. Someone fires near the tracks of the paralyzed force, in an attempt to awaken them but still no one moves.

Nafshi has no time for useless thoughts. They refuse to move but there is a war and the Syrians have to be stopped. With Kahalani or without him. He orders the tanks of the 188th Brigade to turn right and they start to move slightly up the hill, regrouping at the watershed line, in natural positions near a rocky spur. He starts exchanging fire with Syrian tanks that have already conquered the ramp he wanted to reach. Lior Zalel, the gunner, does a great job hitting the enemy tanks.

By the time they reach the rocky mound and exchange fire, only three of the seven tanks that started out remain.

Shortly after arriving, 1st Lt. Yossi Zamri discovered he was on his own, disconnected from the force and that is when his tank is hit by a shell and he is forced to evacuate to Beit Hahazit.

2nd Lt. Haim Damir only manages to fire one shell, hitting the tank facing him, when he discovers he too has been hit, with a Syrian shell stuck between the tank body and the turret. Damir instructs the gunner to lower the cannon and in response he hears him shouting, "I can't lower or rotate..." He gives in to the pressure from his crew and the simple logic that it is impossible to continue with a tank in this state and withdraws, heading towards Beit Hahazit.

Yoni Vodak and Yaakov Veidenfeld (Videy) get lost. After leaving the road, they had turned too far south, taking up position at Tel Jit and fighting from there.

In the improvised positions they take, in the area they are well acquainted with from their previous activity on the Golan, Nafshi finds additional tanks next to him. Maybe they are the 7th Brigade, maybe reserves. While Yachin is wondering who they are, one of them is hit and an injured reserve soldier jumps out and runs toward him asking where the evacuation spot it. Just then a Syrian tank appears and Yachin improves his position and leaves the shouting soldier behind.

Then Yachin sees additional tanks that are burning around him. He has no idea who they are. He cannot speak to them on the radio because he does not know their frequency. Two hundred meters from him, there are Syrian tanks firing at him and he has to fire faster if he wants to survive.

Shalom Maman, his gunner, proves that the war has turned him into a well-cut diamond. He does not miss any target and he keeps his crew alive, at least for now.

As they are standing there, they hear the scream of a Skyhawk jet approaching. "The air force is here," Yachin cheers on the radio and the Skyhawk let loose his bombs and hits right next to them. Again they are shaken and chunks of dirt fly at them and there are shouts on the radio to the air force to get their act together.

Once again it is the Syrians help them to forget the mistakes of the air force, when a precisely aimed shell hits the spare track link in the front of Nafshi's tank and shakes the crew.

Nafshi switches to Yachin's tank, takes his place as commander and has Yachin move to the loader's position. After settling in, he instructs Danny Avni, the operations officer who has remained in the tank that was hit, to lead the tank to the repairs center so it can be sent back to battle.

Someone above is protecting Moty Avadish, the driver behind the spare track link in Nafshi's tank, but he is unable to drive – the hit has ruined the steering system. While Avni the operations officer is wondering what to do, Moty manages to use pliers on the steering column to steer the tank.

As Moty Avadish drives the damaged tank toward Beit Hahazit, the Syrians push forward. All the tanks on the rocky mound slowly move back, to rear slope positions, where their hearts pound as they await the Syrian tanks.

The enemy finally arrives, unaware of the hunters waiting for them as they climb up to take fire positions at the top of the hill. A blend of diesel engine smoke and black basalt dust rises to the sky, indicating to Nafshi's two gunners where they are coming from. Their antennas appear and then the turrets and then it is a matter of who fires first.

The two gunners aim and without waiting for order, they fire and hit the Syrian tanks. All along, Nafshi thinks of the mantra he heard from Yosefi, his instructor in the officer's school, "I know that you are acquainted with defense on a forward slope and on a controlling position but you need to know that there also is defense on a back slope. Yes, you heard me, a back slope." He was right.

10:00

7th Brigade

At 10:30 Meir Zamir, located on the southern side of the Tel Jit hill, announces that he is nearly out of ammunition. On the other side of the radio is the nasal voice of Yanush, "Tiger, hang in there another fifteen minutes. Reinforcements are on their way."

Ten minutes pass and Zamir calls again, "The enemy is around me, I am barely hanging on."

The Syrian pressure in the southern Quneitra gap, on Tel Jit sector, was just as intense as the pressure on the Wadi Shabrak in the north sector. The Syrians may have planned it in advance, or they may have improvised based on the reports they received of their heavy casualties at Wadi Shabrak. Either way, Meir Zamir's eight tanks were doing a great job in defending the area, but even the highest quality must yield to superior numbers.

When Yanush hears Zamir, he tells himself that this is it, the defense line is collapsing, and it is just a matter of time until the Syrians reach the Quneitra-Masada road. It may be best to withdraw the forces and take position on the hills behind the road, before they are surrounded.

He contacts Raful and describes how serious the situation is. Raful implores him to wait a few more minutes, since he already updated him earlier. "There is a fresh force of tanks heading your way." Yanush sighs and knows he has no choice but to trust his forces and to try to get lucky and manage to hang on for a few more minutes. "When it rains it rains on both sides."

Yair Nafshi – 74th Battalion

Shortly after 10:30 there are no more Syrian forces on the ridge. Nafshi takes his two tanks and they start heading east slowly, on their way back to the "rocky positions." They reach their destination and continue to ride their success. They continue toward the front ramp that had been held by the tanks of the 7th Brigade that morning. "There have not been Israeli tanks here for a while," Nafshi thinks. "We did it, we have a positive momentum on the ground."

Just then he hears the call on the radio, "This is 20 of Tofi," and Nafshi does not understand. This war is certainly chaotic but could Yitzchak Ben Shoham really be here after being declared dead two days ago?

* * *

Just yesterday, at 19:00, Lt. Col. Ben Hanan, commander of the 53rd Battalion, 188th Brigade until two months earlier, had landed at Ben Gurion airport in Tel Aviv. On Saturday afternoon, when the front was shaking and the Syrian tanks were heading west, Ben Hanan was still on his honeymoon, enjoying the eastern atmosphere in Kathmandu, Nepal. On Sunday he heard about the war and he immediately started looking for a way to get back to Israel. After a long and tiring flight, the man who had been the 7th Brigade operations officer in the Six-Day War, the soldier who jumped into the Suez Canal with a Kalashnikov, whose face became the symbol of the great victory, was now at Ben Gurion airport, returning to a confused, troubled and scared country.

His father, Michael Ben Hanan, the famous morning exercise broadcaster of the '60s, picked him up. After exchanging a few words of affection, he got into the car waiting for him, parted from his wife Nati, took his beloved photography bag and set out on his way.

At 21:00, he arrived at the "Pit" in Hakiryah in Tel Aviv and he saw the red arrow on the map of the Golan marking the progress of the

Syrian forces, deep in Israeli territory. "Is that real, what I am seeing?" Ben Hanan asked in shock, as Talik whispered to him, "The brigade is in terminal condition." A few minutes later he was on his way to the Northern Command headquarters on Mt. Kana'an in Tzfat.

On the winding ascend from Tiberias to Rosh Pina, he saw three unidentified figures, walking on the side of the road. He offered them a ride. The three soldiers, exhausted, black with soot, with dried blood on their coveralls, got in the car, and he discovered they are part of "his" battalion. They were on their way on foot from the front lines to Rosh Pina. "There are many soldiers dead and the Syrians are everywhere and it is hell," they told him. When he dropped them off, he realized that the red arrow on the map at Hakiryah base was real.

At midnight, between Monday and Tuesday, he arrived and even Ben Hanan, an admired and acclaimed officer who was used to being honored and praised, was surprised by the festive welcome he received at the headquarters. Haka turned to him with a serious look on his face and explained the cause for the joy of his arrival. "The situation on the Golan is very bad. The 188th Brigade is shattered. The brigade commander, deputy brigade commander and operations officer are gone. A deputy battalion commander was seriously injured, three company commanders are dead, and a fourth is injured. From this point you will act as the commander of the 188th Brigade. There is a force of tanks from the remnants of the 53rd Battalion at the Yarden base. Get over there and organize the force. You will receive orders by tomorrow morning."

Back at Rosh Pina he could not find the three soldiers. He continued alone in his vehicle on the road toward Beit Hameches, while the roar of cannons continued.

At 1:30, Yossi Ben Hanan entered the Yarden base and in the dim light he saw a jeep with his deputy battalion commander Shmulik Askarov leaning on it, with a huge bandage on his neck. He had been told he was seriously injured.

He gave him a huge hug and Askarov, who had trouble speaking because of the injury, whispered the details of the force he managed to put together in the base so far.

"How are you doing?" Ben Hanan asked him.

"It is just a scratch," Askarov answered.

The size of the bandage and Askarov's voice indicated otherwise. Ben Hanan instructed him, "Shmulik, help me complete the preparations and then go straight back to the hospital."

They examined the tanks together and met Oded Erez, who was mentally crushed. Ben Hanan, often brutal and arrogant but very professional and perceptive, knew it was up to him now. This was one of those moments that history granted to extraordinary soldiers, those who were not scarred by the traumas of the efforts up to this point. Now is the time.

02:00, Tuesday. Some of the soldiers from the Ghost convoy had still not gotten any rest and Askarov gladly handed over the command to his former commander. Ben Hanan rushed everyone back to the war. He did a wonderful job, continuing what Askarov started, establishing a new force in place of the defeated Erez force.

All the tank crews, along with Shmulik the adjutancy officer, Schwartz the communications officer, Zurich the intelligence officer and Ibler the operations officer, gathered in the large shed. They all gave their reports and Yossi gave a Zionist speech stressing the importance of this moment and task.

At 03:00, Raful instructed Ben Hanan to join the commander of the 679th Brigade, Col. Ori Or, in the morning near Hushnia. All attempts to contact Or failed and Raful, notified of this, instructed Ben Hanan to wait for orders.

He waited and in the meantime, he passed among the tanks, spoke to the crews, many of whom had been his soldiers just two months earlier. He placed his hand on their shoulders, encouraged them, trying to lift their spirits, awakening their motivation and promising them they were going to make the Syrians pay.

Gradually, like a miracle, like the legendary phoenix, one by one they rose, returned to life. Bent shoulders straightened, the spark returned to their eyes, the fire of battle and the desire to get revenge was lit inside them.

At 09:00, Raful was speaking on the radio again, "Head toward Nafah, where you will receive your orders on where to go." Backed by the Northern Command CO's appointment as the new brigade commander, he answered, "This is 20 of Tofi, over and out."

"It was not just Haka who said what he said. We appointed him our brigade commander," Shmulik Ben Moshe, the brigade adjutancy officer tells me thirty-five years later. From the moment Ben Shoham was killed, he was busy rebuilding the brigade. "Ben Hanan was a senior battalion commander and to the remaining officers in the headquarters – Zurich the intelligence officer, Schwartz the communications officer, Ibler the operations officer and me – he was the right brigade commander to appoint. Oded Erez, who helped reorganize the forces, was appointed deputy brigade commander."

On Tuesday morning, Lt. Col. Yossi Ben Hanan, former commander of the 53rd Battalion, was now the new commander of the 188th Brigade. He led a force of eleven tanks, with full crews, many of them commanded by officers.

Shortly after 0:00, the eleven tanks left the Yarden base, with the flame of combat burning inside them, most of them were survivors of the battles on the Southern Golan.[39] They sped forward, their tracks crushing the Golan roads, arriving at Nafah before 10:00. Raful gave the order, "Continue north and join Yanush."

Half an hour later, they arrived at the Wasset junction and Yossi instructed all the tanks to boresight their cannons on the nearby Tel Shiban. On their way east, they passed mechanics repairing tanks that had been hit and the endless movement of damaged tanks accompanied them all through their journey.

Waving to the Bental and Avital hills, right before reaching the sharp bend of the seasonal lake, Yanush spoke on the radio and said, "Yossi, the armored personnel carriers on your left are my tactical command group, come over here quickly."

Ben Hanan arrived at the Quneitra gap to join the forces of Yanush, his close friend from the Six-Day War and the War of Attrition.

Yossi Ben Hanan is like a twin to Yanush, born a bit later than him. They served together in the Canal, they rented an apartment together, lived the wild life during their free nights and kept each other's secrets. They were both always ready to go to battle and to give their lives for their country. Here they were together again, big brother and little brother. Theirs is a friendship of blood. They give each other a strong

---

39. These are the names of the commanders of the Ben Hanan force: Yossi Ben Hanan, Shmulik Askarov, Oded Bekman, Adir Stern, Avi Lachman, Shimon Cohen, Rafi Rubin, Hagai Zur, Yoni Davidson, Moty Amir and Dan Tiroler.

hug but that is all, they do not have time for more, since the Syrians are about to break through the defense line.

"The situation is very bad," Yanush looks Ben Hanan in the eye, checking to see if he got the message. "Go to Daharat Ibrahim and block the gap between the Booster Ridge and the anti-tank ditch."

Ben Hanan speaks on the battalion frequency, "We will move forward at full speed. Syrian tanks are advancing and there none of our forces are on the ground to stop them. Whoever gets to the positions first will win the battle."

* * *

Near Tel Jit, Ben Hanan tries to understand where exactly the tanks of the 7th Brigade are located. Zamir explains that they are on the right and left.

"Don't direct me with right and left!" Ben Hanan cuts him off. He is back to being the tough commander from before his honeymoon. "Talk to me in north and south."

As he is trying to decide how to deploy his force on the Kirton route, fifty meters from them a Syrian bulldozer appears. "Fire!" a squash head shell reduces the bulldozer to a fireball, and Ben Hanan knows it is time to deploy his force.

Part of the force takes position south of the road, others on the north, some west of Tel Jit and others to the east. They all take controlling positions, with the wide plain of the Quneitra gap spread out before them. There in the valley they see what looks like the end of the world. Tens of green Tiran tanks, frozen in all kinds of unnatural positions of death. Some have smoke or flames rising from them and others are calm, with the silence of death.

A better look shows that there still are a number of tanks that were not hit and they all hurry to fire at them, repaying them for the trouble they caused the 7th Brigade. They join their brothers in the Valley of Tears.

"Yossi, watch out, on your right," Askarov warns his commander who is next to him.

Ben Hanan looks to his right and sees a Syrian tank with its cannon aimed right at him. A shell hits the Sho't Kal tank, fails to penetrate but injures Ben Hanan, who falls into the tank.

His loader, Menachem Markus, bandages him and gets him his spare glasses, replacing the ones that were smashed. A moment later, injured in his left arm, blood smeared on his face, Ben Hanan is back in the commander's cupola and he reports to Yanush. "I have been injured but everything is alright. I am continuing the battle."

Suddenly Ben Hanan sees two Syrian soldiers running and firing at him. With great difficulty he cocks the commander's machine gun, fires and hits one of them. As he is wondering where the other soldier is, he notices the deputy battalion commander's tank reversing strangely, without anyone in the commander's cupola.

"Deputy has been hit, deputy has been hit," he hears shouts on the radio. He is notified that his deputy, who refused to stay at the Yarden base, took a bullet in his head, seeming to be more dead than alive. He gives the order to evacuate him and is filled with sadness, as the cost of this damned war suddenly dawns on him.

At the same time, north of the road, the remaining soldiers on the southern Golan find themselves in a luxury war.

Oded Bekman thinks that someone exaggerated in describing the battle awaiting them. He is in control of the valley, just like Moty Amir, Avi Lahman and the others from the brigade and Adir Stern, who has been with him since he left the Yarden base. He is watching for missiles and correcting his misses. Below them they see a valley full of burned tanks. The few that survived retreat toward the open bridges on the anti-tank ditch, stopped by the shells of the gunners of the 188th Brigade.

After three days of battle, the number of tanks of the 7th Brigade that remained functioning is thirty-five. That is when Ben Hanan arrived with eleven fresh tanks, full of ammunition. They were extremely important, real relief.

Just how big was the role that Ben Hanan's force had in changing things in the Southern Golan front? That depends on who you ask. Part of the soldiers who fought in the battles on Tel Jit, honestly and modestly say that there was not much left to do. "We mainly fired at burned ruins. Zamir (Tiger) announced that he was out of ammunition and withdrew but when we arrived the Syrians were also withdrawing."

Others take more credit. "Yes, when we arrived the Syrians were withdrawing but they withdrew because we arrived. They saw the force rising against them and they knew they had no chance. There were occasional Syrian tank commanders who thought of doing something and the shells we hit them with helped them decide."

Hagai Zur suddenly sees suspicious figures approaching the tank. Right before opening fire, he discovers that they are tank crew members from the 7th Brigade who left tanks that had been hit.

He holds his fire and Eli Geva, a company commander in the 82nd Battalion, climbs on the tank and orders him to switch with him.

"I am not getting off the tank," Zur barks at him, deciding enough is enough. He is not leaving the tank for any senior commander again.

All together

With two tanks of the 188th Brigade positioned on the ramp, suddenly a third tank appears next to them, with the 10C sign on it. Yachin looks at the loader's compartment and sees Gidi Peled, his childhood friend and the operations officer of the 77th Battalion. They ignore the war and both jump out of the tanks and hug each other, getting a strong aroma of home in their tanks.

Positioned on the front ramps, with a clear advantage over the Syrian tanks beneath them, the tanks from all the battalions and brigades fire at the enemy tanks in motion below, like firing at fish in a barrel. A few minutes earlier, the tanks of the 77th Battalion had finally responded to the call of Kahalani, the perfect battalion commander, moving forward behind the tanks of the 74th Battalion, in order to retake the ramps.

The crowded enemy tanks below remind Yachin, a fan of nature films, of a herd of scared antelopes surrounded by a pack of lions, or of pesticide sprayed on ants.

Whatever the analogy – antelopes, ants, fish – it is the mother of all retreats of the forces of the Syrian 7th Division, as its green Tiran tanks continue to be blown up by the gunners above them.

How did the balance of power change so dramatically? What exactly made the difference? Was it the additional tanks that joined on Tel Jit? Was it Nafshi and Yachin's determination? Ben Hanan's battle cries? Danny Ashkenazi's madness?

One thing is certain, Yachin tells himself. The situation changed due to the courage and strong spirits of the soldiers who had been there and are there now. All of them, Yoss, Zamir and Kahalani.

"Hold your fire. Don't hit all of them," Nafshi instructs the three tanks with him. "We need them undamaged."

Shortly after taking position on the long ramp, they are joined by Yoni Vodak. He updates Nafshi that in the exchange of fire on Tel Jit, Yaakov Veidenfeld, the efficient, hardworking, pleasant commander from Kibbutz Ayelet Hashachar, had been killed. As always in war, the feeling of joy over defeating the Syrians, blends with a feeling of deep sadness and frustration.

As they are saving their ammunition, the artillery of the Northern Command begins to bring down its wrath on the retreating Syrians. Again the ground in the east shakes and smoke and basalt shards fly through the air, but for the first time since the war began, it is happening in Syrian territory.

In the battle at the Valley of Tears, the power of the artillery corps was significant – for the first time in the war on the Golan Heights.

When the war had started, Maj. Arieh Mizrachi, commander of the 405th Artillery Battalion, was appointed as the artillery assistance commander of the 7th Brigade. Mizrachi was well aware of the battle situation at the Valley of Tears and used all the firepower he had, twenty-one batteries – ten batteries more than there were on the Golan front when the war started. Mizrachi obtained these numbers by simply taking a "bite" out of every artillery battalion heading to the Golan.

Starting at 10:45, aware of the change in the situation at the Valley of Tears, Mizrachi starts to bring down artillery on the more distant enemy forces as well, the ones retreating and already back in Syrian territory.

11:00

Ben Hanan force
Shortly before 11:00, as the tanks of Tiger (Meir Zamir) company start to withdraw and leave the Tel Jit front, Yossi Ben Hanan arrives.

Infantry outpost 107
As a mixture of Sho't Kal tanks reconquer the ramps and stabilize their control of the northern Quneitra gap, there is a stubborn Syrian tank that was detached from the main force. The tank remained close to the

Irish Bridge over the Ruqad stream (the Ahmadia Bridge) and kept trying to hit outpost 107.

Through the periscope of the observation point in the bunker, Elimelech sees the damage outside, as the Tiran hits the external posts and destroys the platoon weapons.

They are hoping for something or someone to come and put an end to this, when finally an artillery shell falls near the Tiran, making it clear to him that it would be wise for him to flee and that is exactly what he does.

This is also when Elimelech's soldiers see the first Syrian tank crews, in their grey coveralls, abandoning their vehicles and running in chaos and panic back east, into Syrian territory.

Elimelech sends the report to the battalion, and fifteen minutes later he receives a direct call from the operations division at Hakiryah in Tel Aviv and he confirms what he saw.

Northernmost Sector – 74th Battalion

While the occurrences in the Valley of Tears shake the young soldiers to their core, the northern sector of the Golan is detached from the events. As far as they are concerned, Tuesday is just like the day before. The Syrians continue their attempts to break through the lines with infantry soldiers, especially at the northern outpost near Shechita. Facing them are Shir-On's tanks that stop them with machine guns and cannon shells. In addition, there are occasional strikes by two MiG 17s. As they prepare for a second round of strikes, they encounter a "box of fire" created by the tanks and the soldiers of outpost 104. One of the MiGs crashes in front of the tanks and the other one disappears.

12:00

Ben Hanan Force

Sometime after 12:30, on Tuesday, October 9, very concerned for the safety of his deputy Askarov, Ben Hanan announces on the radio, "Prepare for attack!" He divides his forces and determines who will stay behind to cover them and who will join him in the attack.

Bekman's heart "dives to his underwear." "What is wrong with that crazy Ben Hanan? Does he have to bring scalps from the valley? What is the point of attacking now?"

As Bekman is praying for a miracle, Ben Hanan asks Yanush for authorization.

"Negative," Yanush replies, taking the position of the responsible big brother, "Wait."

When Bekman hears there is no authorization for an attack and he knows they will not be reaching the enemy tanks, he realizes that the war on Tel Jit is over. He stops by a burned Syrian APC, takes a Gorianov machine gun off it and decides to create a memorial for Nati Levi, his friend from the Nave Magen neighborhood, trapped at Tel Saki and surely no longer alive.13:00

Sector 109 – 74th Battalion

Toward 13:00, Zvika Rak, commander of A Company, is asked to join Nafshi at the Booster. He is sad to leave Zamri (who just got back), Eiland, Hashenberg and the three reserve tanks that joined them in the morning. He transfers command to the reserve force deputy company commander.

Before the roar of the engine of the company commander fades in the distance, Eiland identifies a Syrian command tank beneath the ramp, fleeing for its life, with a huge red flag flying above it. Unable to lower the cannon enough, the Syrian tank battalion commander is lucky to pass by alive.

From the early afternoon hours, it is completely silent in sector 109.

Ilan Sahar, the intelligence officer of the 7th Brigade during the war, and now a researcher of the Yom Kippur battles on the Golan, writes,

> *During all the efforts to block the enemy, from Saturday noon, we were unaware of seven passageways and two tank-laid bridges that the Syrian 52nd Infantry Brigade deployed north of outpost 109.... We were unaware of the efforts and the battles that took place in the three days of attempts to block the Syrians, with A Company blocking them, almost alone....*

Since Tuesday was one of the days in which the enemy was blocked, it is not surprising that the arrival, with dawn, of the Syrian 43rd Armored

Brigade, with seventy tanks and APCs of infantry soldiers, right in front of outpost 109, went unnoticed by the brigade intelligence.

The 43rd Brigade was the force that had ambushed the Tiger force on Sunday before dawn. They had been hit hard and this had caused the entire brigade to retreat, abandoning its planned attack on Quneitra and returning to regroup in Syrian territory.

Now they are back again, reinforced with new T62 tanks, a significant addition to the original T55 tanks, preparing to penetrate the area around outpost 109 again.

"The Syrian maneuver at 109," Ilan Sahar continues, "was a second effort of the Syrian General Staff to conquer the Quneitra gap."

The headquarters of the 7th Brigade and of the other brigades, was unaware of this effort, and the tanks of the 188th Brigade – originally Eiland and Hashenberg and later joined by Zvika Rak, Yossi Zamri and three reserve tanks – stood in their positions, and without causing any drama on the radio, carried out the task of blocking the Syrian effort.

What would have happened if the enemy had managed to get through? Sahar determines that "the entire defense of the gap could have been overturned. The forces at the Valley of Tears would have been surrounded, and the path to the Galilee and the Kinneret would have been wide open, without any reserve tanks there to stop them."

Yair Nafshi – 74th Battalion CO

At 13:00, Yair Nafshi has his mission changed. "Move toward Elrom immediately." Two tanks head toward the main road, turn right toward the north, and continue toward Bukata, followed by medical and ordnance crews.

As they are climbing up the final bend before the Elrom junction, an armored personnel carrier appears with a pile of injured and dead soldiers. A scared officer warns them, "Don't go in there, it is full of Syrian commandos. We are the last ones, there is no one left to evacuate." They continue a bit farther and arrive at the ambush area. The officer was right, there is nothing left to do there. The ones left behind are all dead, including Arik Toren, Danny Avni's beloved cousin.

It seems that the same Syrian commando force that was in the Fidel Hadash-Bukata area, which had caused terrible damage during the night – hitting five tanks and killing and injuring so many soldiers near the border route – had decided to attack the infantry soldiers this time.

In a planned anti-tank ambush in the fields of Bukata, they hit, during the morning, the 12th Battalion force of Golani in its APCs, killing and injuring many, including Lt. Col. Yaakov Shachar, the battalion commander. The 7th Brigade reconnaissance company had arrived at the Bukata fields in the afternoon in APCs to evacuate the soldiers to the aid station at the Manzura junction. They were also tasked with stopping the Syrians from carrying out their plan of cutting off the 7th Brigade from its logistical support and reinforcements. Two companies of Syrian commandos, well concealed behind rocks, trees and the remains of old bunkers, succeeded in disrupting the IDF plan in just half an hour of battle. They managed to take the 7th Brigade reconnaissance company out of the order of battle the IDF had on the Golan front. Twenty-four of its soldiers were killed, including company commander Uri Kar-Shani and his deputy Itzik Mevorach.

The heroic fighting of the IDF troops did manage to delay the Syrian commando force, causing it damage and enabling a reserve tank force to arrive later on and clear the area of enemy forces.

It is in the aftermath of all this that Nafshi and his men turn back and head toward Yanush to receive new orders.

"Outpost 107 is not answering," Nafshi updates when he returns. "It may have fallen into enemy hands. We will go to the Ta'asuka base at Quneitra and escort a convoy of Golani APCs and soldiers to the outpost."

They head toward the base, passing through the ruins of the city of Quneitra. Yachin, still the loader in Nafshi's tank, identifies Syrian commandos on the side of the road. Yachin fires his Uzi and Nafshi fires the commander's machine gun at them, and the commandos flee. Yachin looks around and examines the damage. He registers a historic achievement. He is the first soldier in the 188th Brigade to cut off his antenna with his own firing.

They continue to pass through the remains and the cinema hall that has seen better days. Then there is a big bang and another one. The tank is shaken. The bazooka defense shields prevent them from being killed.

Finally they reach the Ta'asuka base. Nafshi jumps out of the tank, goes down into the bunker and meets Ilan Biran, the deputy commander of the 13th Battalion, who shouts to him, "You are alive? You are alive? I was told on the radio that you had been killed!"

Nafshi notifies his deputy Yossi Nissim on the radio that it is not time to switch commanders of the 74th Battalion yet, and he is still alive and well.

As they prepare to leave, an open truck enters the base, in the back of it there is a stretcher with a medic holding an IV attached to the bleeding and unconscious Yoni Vodak, Yachin's soldier.

An hour earlier, Yoni Vodak had arrived at Hahazit base to repair his tank. On their way to the repair center they were hit by a shell that filled the driver's compartment with thick smoke and the smell of burnt sulfur. David Bonamo, the driver, grabbed the tube of the gas mask and put it in his mouth and breathed through it. They somehow managed to get the gunner out and Bonamo managed to crawl out of the damaged tank. They all stood outside the tank to examine the damage. After finding the "standard" damage – a torn equipment compartment, slashed wheels – they found an armor piercing penetrator stuck between the hull and the turret. The crew decided that statistics were on their side and from now on nothing bad could happen to them.

At Hahazit base they prepared a new tank for themselves, one of the damaged tanks of the 7th Brigade. Someone joked that it is bad luck to get into a tank of the 7th Brigade. While they were joking, 2nd Lt. Doron Sadeh Lavan joined them and they heard the report on the radio, "Peleg commander has been ambushed at Quneitra."

They jumped into the tanks, started the engines, connected to the radio and rushed to rescue the battalion commander. In Quneitra, they took a slightly different route and cut through a fallow field behind the abandoned cinema.

RPG rockets fired at them killed Yoni Vodak. The funny, amusing, gifted performer, who survived the horrors of Saturday, Sunday, Monday and Tuesday, had found his death on his way to help someone in need.

Once again, the sky fell on Yachin. In the last eight hours he has lost his platoon sergeants Vodak and Naides, Muli Dgani, the injured platoon leader who returned to battle, and Veidi that he became so fond of. Something has gone seriously wrong here, he tells himself, mourning the loss.

"Yachin," Nafshi's voice reaches him through the veil of agony, bringing him back to reality. "I know this is hard for you but we have no choice. Pull yourself together, we must continue."

Dragging himself back to the tank, Yachin takes the loader's position, with Nafshi at his side, a packed convoy of APCs with supplies behind them. Yachin prays that they find soldiers to feed at outpost 107.

After being beaten at Quneitra, Nafshi bypasses the city from the east. He then leads the convoy northwest, to Hahazit base, and they are welcomed with the wide smile of Danny Avni, the operations officer, waiting for them with a repaired tank ready to go.

"Stay in the tank," Nafshi instructs Yachin. "I am getting back into my tank."

On his way to his tank, Nafshi sees Moty Avadish, the driver, sitting on the ground.

"Come on Moty, we are leaving," Nafshi lays a hand gently on his shoulder.

"Leave me alone," Moty answers, traumatized by their last hit and exhausted from driving to Hahazit base.

"Come on Moty, it will be alright," Nafshi tries to cheer him up.

"Leave me alone," Moty insists.

"Alright Moty, we will manage without you," Nafshi changes his tactics. "Stay here." Then he adds nonchalantly, "Is your Uzi functioning? Do you have enough ammunition? Great. There are Syrian commandos in the area. Be prepared, they will be here soon."

Suddenly, Moty Avadish is back to himself again and jumps into the tank. They set out at the head of the convoy.

In the afternoon, Yair Nafshi leads the convoy of vehicles toward outpost 107. He sends the tanks to deploy on the south and north ramps. He takes two APCs and enters through the gate of the base, finding Elimelech welcoming them joyfully.

Yachin enters the base, embraces Elimelech, and they are both happy that they were concerned for no reason and that all is well. What happened was that the Syrian tank that kept pestering them destroyed the base position, disrupting the radio communication and leaving the base cut off, which was a cause of great concern.

Late at night, Yachin is on duty standing in the commanders cupola at the Booster Ridge position, looking into the darkness, and his heart is hard. There are stars shining above them and the lights of Syrian vehicles below, where the bodies of his friends and soldiers are laying. Suddenly, he feels a pat on his shoulder. "I was not asleep," he is about to answer the person who is about to reprimand him for putting the country and the tank platoon at risk.

Who is that? He tries to make out in the night. A soldier black with soot bends down to him and whispers in the darkness in a broken voice, "I am Hazan, Dgani's driver."

Yaakov Hazan had a lot of luck. When Muli Dgani's tank had been hit in the anti-tank RPG ambush, he had miraculously survived. He crawled out of the tank, saw Syrian soldiers in front of him, lay on the ground, pretending to be dead. They kicked him and spit at him and he did not move. Eventually, they left him there.

During the day, two Skyhawks rocketed the Syrian commandos hiding near him and he still remained alive. When it got dark, he got up, dragged himself to the Booster, which he was familiar with after training there so many times. As he walked toward it, what concerned him the most was that he would be killed by his own forces. That almost happened, but Yachin, who was supposed to fire at any figure in the darkness, fell asleep holding the machine gun.

Valley of Tears Epilogue

On Tuesday, as the soldiers heroically blocked the enemy on the Quneitra gap, there was another heroic effort, almost of the same magnitude, ten kilometers from there.

The 679th Reserve Brigade blocked a series of attacks by the remaining forces of the 1st Syrian Division, reinforced with additional units. The Israeli force managed to stand firm on the Sindiyana front, causing the Syrians severe losses and crushing their ability to continue to attack.

In the southern Golan, the attack by the reserve forces ended with them pushing the Syrians back behind the Purple Line. There were just two remaining small Syrian enclaves that refused to surrender, at areas 110 and 111.

During Tuesday night , with almost all of the Golan back in Israeli hands, tens of fires lit the darkness of the Valley of Tears, telling the story of the bravery of the regular soldiers. They were there in the morning and the afternoon, and prevented the final catastrophe, perhaps the most severe, that the Syrian General Staff had prepared for Israel.

Inside his tank, overwhelmed by the arrival of Hazan, Yachin is having a hard time controlling his emotions. He keeps thinking of his brothers in arms who were killed, trying to find someone or somewhere to direct his rage, to let out the sadness, but he does not find his resolve.

A Moment before the Breakthrough

At dawn on Wednesday, October 10, the eve of the holiday of Sukkot, the armored divisions began their final operation of shattering the remaining enemy forces on the Golan.

Wednesday, October 10 – Early Morning
07:00
At 07:50, Haka sends a telegram to Dado, "I am happy to inform you that after four consecutive difficult Days of Battle, the Northern Command, with massive assistance from the air force, has managed to break the Syrian army. We have control of the ceasefire line."

The sense of euphoria spreading in Hakiryah and at the Palace in Tzfat was darkened with the shadow of failure.

The commanders of the 146th Division, blinded by their success, decided to continue, to cross the Purple Line, to "Pursue, overtake and divide the spoil,"[40] or as the command had put it, "To ride the success and conquer the Syrian outposts in the Um Lukas–Tel Kudna–Tel Zabach area."

However, reality has a way of changing very quickly. In what was a completely unnecessary attack, with forces divided into companies, the old Sherman and Sho't Meteor tanks encountered mine fields and fortified defense systems, with the fresh anti-tank artillery of the Syrian front line brigade awaiting them.

The slap in the face that the fresh forces of the 146th Division received ended in a humiliating withdrawal and an evacuation battle that took many more lives.

---

40. Exodus 15:9.

Hundreds of reserve soldiers, who thought that the descriptions of the horrors of this war were exaggerated, learned a bloody lesson on the fickle nature of this damned war.

The drama developing opposite the Um Lukas complex did not trouble the regular and reserve forces on the Tel Yosifun sector.

It was Wednesday morning and the company tank combat parking areas awoke to the pleasant sun in the east, coloring the large basalt rocks in shades of a bright, calm, beautiful and exciting new morning.

In the midst of this general sense of optimism and beauty, after Haka declared, "We have control of the ceasefire line," once again the situation changes and the air is filled with the cries of soldiers injured and killed. The many different forces, commanded by Ori Or, the commander of the 679th Brigade, are suddenly attacked from all sides by effective and brave Syrian commando units, using the basalt rocks as cover as they fire RPGs at the targets in front of them.

In the Chessner force, the company commander from sector 111, also under the command of the 679th Brigade, Eitan Kopstein, always Berkovitz's gunner, sees Gabi Refaeli, the tall deputy company commander from the 82nd Battalion, blown out of his tank and injured, finding cover among the rocks.

"Me and Kopstein are going to see what is going on there," Berkovitz says to Chess, who is positioned in their commanders cupola after his tank had been hit.

"Go on your own," Chess orders him. "Kopstein is staying in the tank."

Calm as he always is, first sergeant Danny Berkovitz heads toward Refaeli, bending over him. He is mistakenly identified as a commando soldier, and a squash head shell is fired at him from one of the reserve tanks, hitting him and slicing him in two.

"No, no!" Kopstein shouts in the tank, refusing to believe that the best company commander in the 53rd Battalion, maybe in the whole world, the one he always relied on, who he was willing to follow anywhere, was just cut in two, in front of his horrified eyes.

"Hold your fire!" Ori Or shouts on the radio, making it clear to everyone that they have to choose their targets more carefully. They head east and continue to fire, with the assistance of the artillery, finally joining them. If the artillery shells had fallen earlier, things may have been different. At the end of the day, with dozens of dead bodies in speckled uniforms scattered between the rocks and the remains of the infantry and commando soldiers pushed back beyond the Purple Line, it is Kopstein again in the tank, who cannot believe that Danny Berkovitz will never smile at him again.

12:00

On Wednesday afternoon, the last remains of the Syrian forces in sectors 110 and 111 are destroyed and pushed back. Now Hofi's telegram from the morning is more accurate. For the first time in four days, IDF forces are positioned all along the Purple Line.

The Generals know that this is not the time to end the war. The Syrians are retreating and now is the time to cause them as much damage as possible. The Syrians have to understand, once and for all, that they need to bury any future intentions of having a confrontation with the IDF. Every young officer knows that the only way to get them to understand this is the hard way, with the IDF shells falling on the outskirts of Damascus.

"How far should we go?" Haka wonders, during the meeting at the Northern Command.

"As close as possible to Damascus," Dayan responds. "Damascus is more important than the Bar Lev line."

The order is given the same day. Tomorrow, the IDF forces are to enter Syria. On Thursday, October 11, at 11:00, the Northern Command will use the success of the forces on the ground to attack on two main routes. The northern route, through outpost 104, will be taken by the 36th Division, commanded by Refael Eitan. The central route, through outpost 107, will be taken by the 210th Division, commanded by Dan Laner.

Mourning its soldiers, crushed and shattered from the day's outcome, the 146th Division is instructed to remain in its position, to act as a blocking force on the front.

On the Booster Ridge, Yanush, the commander of the northern effort force, gathers all of his commanders, notifying them that the attack into Syria will be carried out on two routes. The attack on the northern route will be led by Kahalani, with the original forces of the 7th Brigade. The southern route, perceived to have the "higher status," leads directly to the Halas bases and to Damascus. It is to be led by Yossi Ben Hanan. He is to bring the tanks of the 188th Brigade, the brigade that four days earlier had been taken off the order of battle on the Golan.

"In order to express our appreciation and admiration of the soldiers and commanders of the 188th Brigade that were killed, I appoint Yossi Ben Hanan and Yair Nafshi to lead the southern route," Yanush announces in his high voice, feeling the emotion among the soldiers and he adds in pathos, "Tomorrow let's get revenge for the 188th Brigade."

On Wednesday, based on the Ben Hanan force, the 53rd Battalion is revived. The remains of Avner Landau's company arrive at the reorganization spot, beneath the Booster, in addition to the tanks of the Yarden base and others that heard of the miracle of the revival of the 188th Brigade.

Not far from there, Yair Nafshi gathers the 105th Platoon, the 107th Platoon commanded by Yachin and a few tanks of the original 53rd Battalion, commanded by Zvika Rak. Kaimo, who had been deputy to Eyal Shaham before he was killed, is now the commander of H Company.

"Get ready for a formation," Nafshi instructs him.

"Are these all the tanks?" Kaimo asks in shock, counting eight.

"What you see is all that remains," Nafshi answers, as a hidden tear streams down his face.

Notes from the Breakthrough

Thursday, October 11 – Morning

On Thursday morning, the beginning of the Sukkot holiday, thousands of soldiers awaken along the Purple Line on the Golan and they know that today is the day. They are determined, believe they are doing what needs to be done, and are ready to send a steel-clad fireball at Syria. They are also still confused.

After they managed to avoid being smitten by the angel of death, they are exhausted, in pain, with their coveralls turned to rags and their faces covered with stubble, dirt and soot. They know it is important to continue. To hit, crush, grind and shatter, just as their commanders taught them, but they still feel deep distress.

Yossi Ben Hanan stops his force near the main Golan road (the Yakir route). There are three reduced companies commanded by Maj. Avner Landau from 53rd Battalion, Maj. Ehud Dafna, currently a reserve officer who had been the commander of A Company of the 53rd Battalion in the past and 1st Lt. Shraga Ibler, the brigade operations officer.

Yossi knows that now is the time, and he gives them a speech on Zionism and motivation. "It is working," Moty Amir, one of the survivors of the Zeevim (G) Company thinks, as he looks around him. Bent shoulders start to rise up, the question marks disappear and they are surrounded with a silent aura of strength, as the first smiles appear on the dark faces.

Near outpost 105, Nafshi gathers his soldiers and says loudly, "We are going to show the Syrians." He looks around at the young men in their stained coveralls, with their lifeless eyes and he adds, "If the Syrians reject the ceasefire, we will destroy 200 of their tanks, we will stand on their heads and finish off Damascus."

Shmulik Yachin looks around, he sees Haim Damir near him, just like on the 107 ramps, all that are missing are Muli, Videy, Vodak and Naides. He meets Damir's eye and identifies the same determination he is feeling – we cannot stop now. We have to continue, even if it is just for the sake of the soldiers killed at sector 107. They jump into the tanks and join the convoy as it crosses the border.

On Thursday at 11:00, the first IDF forces cross the Purple Line. Yossi Ben Hanan, with the survivors of the 188th Brigade from the Southern Golan front, lead the forces on the plain south of outpost 105. The Syrian 7th Division came this way just five days earlier and now it was time to reverse it.

Two beat up Sherman tanks lead the convoy, along with a bulldozer tank and a Morag (flail) tank for blowing up mines. The pace of progress is too slow for Avner Landau and he leaves them behind. As he rushes forward, he triggers a mine.

Ben Hanan takes the lead, pulling the entire battalion behind him through the basalt rocks, as they arrive at the route of the Syrian bases, and very soon they are on the outskirts of the Jubata Al-Hashav Druze village.

Hagai Zur, the commander from the 53rd Battalion (who refused to give up his tank, even if God himself, or the next closest thing – the battalion commander – asked for it), sees three crew members approaching them on foot.

"What happened guys?"

"Our tank was hit," they answer, losing the spark in their eyes, pointing to the nearby Tel Dahur hill.

"Where is the fourth crew member?" Hagai wonders.

"He is dead, we left him behind," they lower their eyes.

Something doesn't add up in Hagai's head, as they tell him their story near the Jubata Al-Hashav village and the Tel Dahur quarry. He takes Rami Wahaba, the medic, with him in his tank, they climb up, are twenty meters from the tank, when suddenly the damaged tank slides down the hill, straight toward the Syrian forces. Just like in the Western films, Hagai positions the Sho't Kal tank right next to the other one, he jumps onto the damaged tank and there is no one in the turret. He realizes that he just found the soldier who was killed, the same soldier who is driving the tank.

"Stop!" Hagai shouts to the "dead" soldier.

"How?" comes a shout from the driver's compartment.

Zur instructs him how to take his foot off the gas pedal and finally the tank stops. He jumps into the driver's seat and he sees a bleeding skull. The blow the loader suffered to his head has peeled his scalp and is forcing him to drive the tank with his eyes closed.

With the help of Rami the medic, they take the loader who came back to life, into the turret, Hagai sits in the driver's seat and, reversing in a wild zigzag, he flees from the shells flying at them.

On the outskirts of Jubata Al Hashav light fire is fired at the brigade, hitting and killing Captain Elhanan Korach, the fire support officer. Ben Hanan does not stop and speeds ahead, on the path that bypasses the fire from the north. He passes by the village of Taranjiya and he stops by Tel Ahmer that is blocking the route.

Ben Hanan does not hesitate. He does not believe in any delays and certainly not in withdrawal. He sets out to attack the hill full of infantry soldiers and anti-tank teams.

Shraga Ibler leads the attack, Ben Hanan is right behind him. Dafna and Landau are covering them. Back on the hill, the angel of death decides it is time to take someone else. He approaches the tank of the operations officer. A deadly RPG rocket penetrates the driver's compartment and crushes the entire tank crew: Marko Avigdor the driver, David Shaharbani the loader who survived the horror at 111, Eli Rahamim the gunner who survived the attacks on Juhader and the Petroleum Road, and even Shraga the commander, who was supposed to get married that same day.

On Friday, before the war started, Shraga Ibler and Hani Ziv went to buy clothes for the wedding that was to take place on Sunday October 7, at Tivon, below Mt. Carmel.

On Saturday Ibler was called to the Golan. He parted from his fiancé with a long kiss beneath the loquat tree in his parent's garden. At 22:00 he called and said, "Call off the wedding. A war has broken out."

On Monday Ibler called his fiancé, "I wanted so much to get married," he said and she tried to encourage him and told him to take care of himself. Then there were a few more sentences in a tired and hoarse voice. He hardly said anything, she didn't ask. There was a long silence.

A month earlier, when they decided to get married, Shraga Ibler –

the funny guy who wrote all the skits for the parties, wrote the wedding invitation, "Dear friend, what I feared most is occurring. The evil one has grabbed my hand, forced a ring on me and is placing me beneath the wedding canopy... In order to ease my suffering, please have mercy and grace me with your presence to console me in Tivon on Thursday, October 11."

On Thursday, October 11, the groom was sent to lead the attacking force. In his final moments, did he think of his wedding in store for him? Did he remember his bride awaiting his return? Did he think of the wedding dress, the veil and his suit, hanging in the closet in his room?

As the small Tel Ahmer hill is taken, the Syrians are pushed east and lose control of the route heading toward the Halas bases (Amrat Al Fawer). Ehud Dafna is leading the force and they rush forward, as the path seems to be clear. But not quite. Out of nowhere, a shell hits them, killing the tank commander, Yigal Rubinstein, leaving Avshalom Levi, his platoon commander, stunned and in agony.

The tank commander from Rosh Pina in the Galilee, was everything that a soldier or a commander could ask for in training. During the war, he became even better. Just two days earlier, it was Yigal who identified the Syrian force behind them, warning everyone and saving their lives. Why is there no justice in the world? Avshalom is suffering, and the picture of the calm leader and friend that Yigal Rubinstein was, will not leave his head.

In the late afternoon, as evening approached, the 53rd Battalion arrives at the Hales bases, takes up position for the night. They are proud of their progress and loose themselves in thoughts of the friends they have lost.

Ben Hanan does not let his men wallow in self-pity. He gathers the officers, spreads out a large map on one of the tanks, and gives them orders according to protocol – and Hagai Zur thinks that this is refreshing after all the improvisation they have gotten used to.

Further behind Ben Hanan's force, the tactical command group of the 36th Division are moving forward, led by Raful, in the lead APC. Near Jubata Al Hashav, a MiG 17 strikes at them. They all fire back continuously, some crouch down, others lay on the ground near the

APCs. Only Raful, the ice man from the Jezreel Valley, remains standing tall, near the headquarters table, provoking the Syrian plane. As if he is saying, "Don't you see your time is up? We are the ones calling the shots now."

Nafshi's 74th Battalion was positioned to provide cover and back-up for the attack of the 53rd Battalion. Zvika Rak, the veteran company commander, Kaimo the new company commander and Yachin the platoon leader, who acted as a company commander during the war, see the magnificent forces of the IDF crossing the border, and an unfamiliar feeling overcomes them.

After unbearable days, after barely managing to stop an enemy dramatically outnumbering them, after hearing of the catastrophe on the Southern Golan front, they cannot believe the change developing in front of them. The IDF is back to what it is supposed to be, back on the attack, the soldiers with their heads high in the tanks, sending forth its powerful fists of steel. An hour passes, and another, and the heavy sense of frustration they had been feeling for so long is replaced with a feeling of victory.

After the spearhead of the force of the 53rd Battalion takes position at the Hales bases, the 74th Battalion moves forward, passing on the route paved for them, taking position for the night in Taranjiya

* * *

A few hours before the attack into Syria, Yair Nafshi arrived at sector 104, took the crew of Sergeant Greenbaum from Aviv Shir-On's force and ordered the platoon commander from Ashkelon to remain with his three tanks on the ramps of 104 and secure the flank of the 36th Division.

From his position on the ramps, Aviv watches the tanks of the 7th Brigade cutting through the northern route, and he curses the moment that Nafshi left him there, so far from the action, while Greenbaum and the others are in the limelight. As he is thinking these thoughts, Yossi Nissim, the deputy battalion commander, appears at his side and instructs him to leave his position and join him with his platoon and they head east, trying to catch up with the Golani and the 7th Brigade.

In the central attack force, the reserve brigades encounter the enemy in fortified defense positions at the Han Urineva front. They come under attack and lose a large number of vehicles and soldiers.

At Han Urineva the 188th Brigade lost another soldier. When the war broke out, 1st Lt. Netanel Aharon (Tani) had been at Kibbutz Beerot Yitzchak in central Israel, far from Venus (F) Company , of the 74th Battalion, where he served as the deputy company commander. He rushed to the Golan, joined a reserve tank unit, got separated from the rest of the force, took a direct hit, survived and wended his way – on foot – between the tanks of the Syrian 51st Brigade. He headed toward the Upper Beit Hameches, rejoined a reserve tank unit, continued fighting with that unit and on October 11, he set out with them on the attack. On the outskirts of Han Urineva, he was hit by anti-tank fire and died instantly.

A few hours earlier, a forest of antennas and command vehicles had sprung up on the Booster Ridge. The generals came to observe the battles from there. 2nd Lt. Oded Bekman left the positions he was responsible for in sector 107 under the responsibility of three of his fellow commanders. As a representative of the 188th Brigade, very keen on entering the battle, he ascended to the Booster Ridge to see if he could change his boring mission.

A few minutes later they received a task and a frequency, in the same manner that forces had been sent on missions since the war started. "Go to Han Urineva, turn right, tune in to this frequency and join the force there."

In the evening, with the IDF forces deep in Syrian territory, four tanks of the 188th Brigade settle into night positions on the outskirts of Han Urineva. They discover that they are part of the attack efforts of the 179th Reserve Brigade, commanded by Ran Sarig.

Friday, October 12 – Morning

Friday, October 12, promises to be a beautiful day, with the smell of autumn, the birds chirping and the final victory within reach. Early Friday morning, the soldiers of the 188th Brigade feel that the angel of death's time is up and it is now time for living. They are blind to the dark clouds above Tel Shams, waiting for them to be led to the altar for sacrifice.

Assault on Tel Shams

In the early morning hours, Avner Landau's company leads the 53rd Battalion in an attack on Tel Shams. The seven tanks move forward on the main road (the America route), knowing that conquering the hill will open the way for them to the Sasa bases and from there they will have an "express" path to Damascus, just as is written in bright white paint on Ben Hanan's tank.

They are surprised when they are suddenly fired at from all sides. Avner Landau, in the leading tank, is hit by a shell near the driver's compartment, and despite the big explosion, they are all alright. They still feel no one can stop them. The fire intensifies and they are forced to take cover. Soon they realize they have no choice but to retreat to the Misgad-America junction, finding it hard to believe that the enemy is still so strong.

Ben Hanan does not give up, and he decides to use deceit to reach the hill blocking their victory ride to Damascus.

Carefully examining the aerial photos, together with Sahar the intelligence officer of the 7th Brigade and Zurich the intelligence officer of the 188th Brigade, they find a hidden way through. It is their very own "Burma road," just like in the effort to reach besieged Jerusalem in the War of Independence. The path passes between the basalt rocks, enabling them to strike the hill from the north, from the side no one is expecting them from.

Yossi takes the Landau company with him again, adds Adir Stern, who he appoints his "partner," and they are off. After a difficult drive through the rocks, they reach a relatively flat area, from which they see the northern slopes of the large hill. Ben Hanan leaves two tanks under the command of Avshalom Levi to cover them and with the other six tanks he heads south-east and takes up new positions, 1,500 meters from the hill.

After they succeed in destroying all the targets they can see on the hill, Ben Hanan feels confident that it is time for them to score. He asks Yanush for approval to attack, receives it, orchestrates the six tanks in a straight line and rushes forward to set things straight. Five minutes later, when they are already at the top third of the hill, about to cross the finishing line and destroy the remaining enemy forces, Sagger missiles are fired at them from an unknown enemy post located northwest of them.

In less than two minutes, the gates to hell open wide and the angel of death catches up on what he missed out on until now. Four of the six tanks are destroyed.

The missile that hits Avner Landau passes between him and the loader, killing Meir Cohen the gunner. Amnon Gideon, a deputy logistics company commander before the war and a tank crew member during the war, stops by Landau who escapes from the tank, with blood streaming from his waist. He brings him into his tank, makes the obvious conclusion, turns the tank around and gets out of there as fast as he can.

Ranny Friedrich, the last in the line, is away from the fire and moves forward and takes cover, waiting for it to pass. He takes Menachem Marcus who was injured, Ben Hanan's loader and he too flees from the reach of the angel of death.

The four damaged tanks remain at the top of the hill.

Hagai Zur, with burns from head to toe, is catching up on the war he thought he missed. Suffering terribly, he leaves the tank with his crew, looks around through burned eyebrows, and cannot find Yehuda Akunis the loader. He returns to the tank and with arms full of shrapnel, he pulls him out with an injury in his back. After getting ten meters away, he sees the tank take another missile and explode.

Twenty meters to his right, Adir Stern's tank is in flames, and Hagai continues, dragging himself to the next tank, marked 2OC, that of Ben Hanan. This one is also in flames but small flames. He knows it is risky and the tank may blow up in his face but he climbs on the tank, looks inside and sees the gunner, Henry (Aharon) Vidal, the operations NCO, beheaded.

He jumps off the tank, not noticing Ben Hanan who is bleeding and Zvika Rosenzweig the driver with him, hidden in a ditch, twenty meters from the tank.

Keep moving, Hagai tells himself, as he continues to examine the damage to the Ben Hanan force. He continues toward the damaged tank of Avner Landau. Eli Cohen, the tank driver, refuses to open his hatches until he identifies the voice of Hagai shouting, "Open up." He opens and Hagai sits down on the tank and shouts to him to move out of there immediately. They withdraw west, cross the road and continue until they meet the rest of the battalion.

The tank of Adir Stern, with the bodies of Stern and Edi Avrahamov the gunner and the tank of Ben Hanan, with the words "Damascus Express" written on it, remain on the hill.

In a small ditch, twenty meters from there, the battalion commander who had been appointed brigade commander, is fighting for his life, with a serious injury in his leg and Zvika Rosenzweig, his driver, treating him, giving him water and encouraging him.

Ben Hanan switches between the frequencies of despair and unconsciousness and Rosenzweig continues to be resourceful and brings a radio from the tank and sends an update on their situation. Then he directs the artillery fire, protecting them from any intention of Syrian soldiers to attack them and end their lives, keeping his commander alive.

As his existence is slipping away, Ben Hanan reaches the most crucial moment of his life. For the first time since he started out in the military boarding high-school fifteen years earlier, he sets aside his ego and is generous and compassionate toward himself. At that moment, he does not care what people think of him, since it is his life that is coming to an end. He shouts and begs on the radio, with everyone hearing, "Yanush, brother, come save me."

Just as the impressive life of Ben Hanan is about to end on the battlefield, something happens that changes the outcome.

An armored force of the Sayeret Matkal elite unit, commanded by deputy commander Yoni Netanyahu, reaches the tank and finds Ben Hanan and Rosenzweig. They drive through the night and stop out of the range of the death on the hill. As Lt. Col. Yossi Ben Hanan is about to pass on to the next world, he hears the most beautiful sound of his life – the whistling of the helicopter landing next to them that evacuates him to the Rambam Hospital in Haifa.

At the same time that Ben Hanan's unit was carrying out the failed attempt to conquer Tel Shams, the tanks of the 74th Battalion were serving as a covering and back-up force. When hell breaks loose on Tel Shams and Yossi Ben Hanan lays seriously injured by his tank, it is Yachin's turn.

Syrian missile carriers, in fortified positions on Tel Shams identify the movement of the back-up force and open fire at them. As he comes out of the cover of the trees that suddenly appeared between the basalt rocks, he rises up to a better observation position. Then he sees the black cloud heading his way and he knows he is doomed.

There is a terrible explosion and the tank is hit. Shalom Maman the gunner suffers a serious stomach injury, Rahamim Cohen the loader is also wounded. Haim Lavon the forward observer and Yachin commanding the tank are lightly injured and are thrown clear of the vehicle. Yachin drags himself next to the tank and lies down near a flowing stream of water that appears miraculously. He quenches his thirst, looks at his shredded feet and knows the war is over for him. He wonders how all this is going to end.

Friday Afternoon

On Friday afternoon, the tank force of Yossi Nissim arrives at Mazrat Beit Jan. He finds tanks of the 7th Brigade and Golani infantry in a state of chaos. He starts blocking the counterattacks of the Syrian tanks and commandos.

On the central front, the four representatives of the 188th Brigade demonstrate just how good they are in combat. They manage to rescue a pilot, evacuate two reserve force tanks that have been hit, with their injured and dead crews, taking a long drive on a frontal slope. In the process, they also "conquer" Tel Anter that is left without enemy forces.

Friday Night

On Friday night, after Ben Hanan is evacuated, Yair Nafshi is appointed commander of the forces on the front. The first decision he makes is to carry out an orderly night attack, the third attempt to conquer Tel Shams.

Ehud Dafna, the last company commander remaining from the 53rd Battalion and the Ben Hanan force, became the commander of the tanks in the planned attack. He returns to Kfar Hales where his company is positioned and he updates the commanders of the details of the attack. The plan is for a battalion of reserve paratroopers to be flown in helicopters to the hill. They are to conquer it in an attack on foot, while the tanks pass through the Small Laja to assist the infantry force and if necessary, ascend the hill and complete the mission.

Moty Amir feels that they are heading on a suicide mission. To hell with this hill, he says to himself, as he looks at Davidson, Tiroler and the other commanders in the dark and sees that they share his concern.

Dafna leads, Amir follows, the Sayeret Matkal soldiers sit on the tanks, guiding them through the black basalt paths, in the dark. To the east of them, Amir sees the tracer bullets and he knows that the paratroopers have already engaged. They continue north, the lights of the Sasa village are bright before them, and suddenly a convoy of enemy tanks appears in the dark. The Tirans are about to cross the route they are on.

Dafna deploys the force in an ambush, brings the Sayeret Matkal soldiers into the tanks and opens fire at close range. Some of the enemy tanks are destroyed, others flee.

Saturday, October 13

It is Saturday, October 13, a week since the war broke out. It is the holiday of Sukkot and in Moscow they are threatening Israel. Since yesterday they understand that the Syrian front is falling. Not only did they fail to conquer the Golan, now Damascus is in danger.

"The Soviet Union cannot remain indifferent to the criminal acts of the Israeli military," is the statement in the Soviet media. In order to demonstrate that this is not just an empty threat, the Russian army prepares two airborne divisions. The commanders of one of them fly to Damascus and join one of the Syrian divisions.

In the few days prior to this, there had been an airlift from the Soviet Union to its two allies in the Middle East. The Kremlin was trying desperately to resupply the military equipment shortage the Egyptian and Syrian armies have.

On Saturday, Moscow issue a call to the Arab countries to join the war against Israel. Kuwait and Libya take action and declare that they are preparing armored brigades to assist the Egyptian army. On the Syrian front, the Iraqi 12th Armored Brigade, in combat with Dan Laner's division and 2nd Lt. Bekman, is to be reinforced by eighty Centurion tanks of the Jordanian 40th Brigade.

Assistance and Neglect

Until Saturday, the Americans had been following a line of quiet diplomacy with the Soviet Union. Seeing the real involvement of the Russians, the White House decided to respond with a huge airlift, supplying Israel with planes, weapons and equipment.

Before the first planes took off, the European NATO alliance reveals its true face. Their concern about being prevented from using Arab oil – entirely justified – and being affected by other financial aspects if they assisted Israel, led them to choose their own interests over that of the senior member of NATO.

What about helping the people that just thirty years earlier had lost 6 million of their number, in the biggest madness in history, mainly on European soil? This formed no part of their considerations. The European countries had a long history of hatred toward Jews and this was just another opportunity to demonstrate it. Spain and Britain announced that they would not fuel US planes on their way to Israel. West Germany prohibited Americans from loading weapons on Israeli ships harbored in German ports. Britain went even further and announced a unilateral arms embargo on Israel and delayed a shipment of medicine donated by British Jews to the injured Israelis.

Morning

Saturday morning, October 13. Moty Amir is wondering whether "thirteen" is a good or bad number for Jews. He thinks of all the superstitions connected to this number. Every combat soldier knows that superstitions are a source of power for soldiers. As he continues to consider the hidden world of numbers, Ehud Dafna orders him to move south on the main route (America) with Dan Tiroler, to make sure that the paratroopers on the hill are not surprised from the south.

Amir completes the drive, encountering Syrian infantry soldiers fleeing, reaches the America-Yair junction and joins Yair Nafshi and the rest of the battalion. He reports that everything is fine and he returns north. Near Tel Shams he meets the rest of the company tanks, in natural positions in the landscape on the northern side of the hill.

Directly above them in the east, the sun rises, blinding the tanks of the Dafna Company and enabling a battalion of Syrian tanks and APCs to come within 1,500 meters of them.

"Get inside," Koby Greenbaum, the senior tank commander from H Company, who has become a loader in the company commander's tank, shouts to Ehud Dafna, seeing he is acting too boldly.

Before he gets a response, one of the Tirans decides to hit their tank. The first shell misses and is too long, the second is too short and Koby knows it is now or never. "Let's get out of here," he screams to Dafna.

"He is closing in on us." Ehud Dafna, the sensitive boy from the kibbutz in the valley, forgets about himself and his home and family. He does not hear Koby shouting; all he knows is that they have to stand there and not let them pass. Koby was right, just like the previous time with Eyal, the previous company commander. The shell hits them and Ehud Dafna, the last company commander of the Ben Hanan force, collapses lifeless into the tank.

This is "Udi Hamudi," for whom the famous song "Lama Udi Hamudi" ("Why, Udi Sweetheart") was written, when he turned three. It was written by his grandfather, Moshe Dafna, the poet and educator. The song is about Udi Hamudi, who will not be able to ask, "Why is the sun always the first to go to sleep at night?" Moty Amir decides that thirteen is definitely a very bad number.

When Maj. Ehud Dafna is killed and collapses into the tank and while the Foreign and Defense Ministries around the world are in a frenzy, the Iraqis, together with the Syrians, launch a counterattack on Dan Laner's front. The attack is blocked and the four remaining tanks of the 188th Brigade – Bekman, Lahman, Rubin and Cohen – make an impressive contribution to doing so.

On this cursed Saturday, it is finally time for the bored force on ramp 109 to join in the battles.

In the days before, Eiland had complained continuously, "Zvika screwed us over. Why are we left behind to secure the southern side?" They used the time to perfect the aroma of their coffee, spent days and nights playing trivia games, asking questions like, "How many soldiers do you think were killed in the southern front and who of the soldiers we know are still alive?" They also found the time to collect the remains of the equipment of the Syrian pilot that he left behind, including a life raft. If they are still alive at the end of the war, they will surely get a day off on Lake Kinneret.

The rattling of the tank caused the plug of the boat to open and a yellow cloud rose above it, covering the terrified crew with yellow air that they feared was a chemical attack. They survived and later discovered that it was a substance to keep away sharks from the Soviet pilots, who were supposed to fight the American pilots in the oceans.

On Saturday night, they joined Ori Or's reserve brigade, raising the pride of the 188th Brigade on the attack on the central front.

THE LAST DAYS

Sunday, October 14

On Sunday, October 14, at dawn, the tanks of the 188th Brigade take up position and pray for clouds to appear and block the sun that is blinding them in the east. Using the sun as their cover, the Syrian commando force fired a volley of RPG rockets at the tanks and immediately following this, Syrian Tiran tanks sped forward, coming as close as 100 meters from them.

Yoni Davidson, who is running the "company" battle, is hit. Moty Amir's tank is also hit and the equipment compartment starts to burn. The fire extinguishing drill lowers the flames and Amir looks around him, locates the remains of the Dafna company – his sergeant Tiroler and another tank – and takes command. He is relieved when reinforcements arrive in the afternoon, commanded by Kaimo and the tank commanders Frost, Winter and Zinberg.

Kaimo, who in the last few days was in battle with the 7th Brigade, has returned to his battalion. He was given command of the sector and used it to destroy five tanks and the logistical force with them, shattering the counterattack.

Monday, October 15

On the next day, Monday October 15, the Tel Shams ritual repeated itself.

At the same time, things are calm in the conquered southern enclave. All of the forces stay where they are and lick their wounds. The IDF uses the ceasefire to stabilize the conquered lines, push artillery forward and send additional tanks that had been repaired in the maintenance centers on the Golan back to the front.

The Syrian army is crushed, in a state of panic, with its back to the wall. They gather their remaining forces and begin planning the counterattack, supported by the Iraqi and Jordanian forces that have just arrived.

Shmulik Ben Moshe, the brigade adjutancy officer, does not have experience as a combat soldier but he is one in his heart. He hears the sounds from the front, knows that the soldiers of the 188th Brigade are scattered all over, and decides that reinstating the 188th Brigade into the IDF order of battle on the Golan is something that needs to be done. It will stand as a memorial for the commanders and soldiers that have been killed.

Together with the injured soldiers that are starting to be released from the hospitals, he carries out a Sisyphean task. He sends Gringold, Atir and Boaz Tamir to tow tanks from the battlefields and verify that the mechanics are repairing them.

He uses any method that works – sweet talking, threatening, pleading, using guilt and conscience – demanding that once the official ceasefire is announced, all of the brigade commanders release the officers of the 188th Brigade that have joined their forces.

"Well done Shmulik," the remaining soldiers tell him. "We are with you every step of the way, but first of all, get us a ceasefire."

Tuesday, October 16

On Tuesday, October 16, an alliance of forces from Syria, Iraq and Jordan, launch a counterattack against the forces of Dan Laner. After a few hours of a failed attack, they are shattered by the division's cannons, abandon tens of damaged vehicles and retreat in panic.

On that same day, Tuesday, October 16, the routine on the front is shattered, also for the 188th Brigade.

Zvika Rak, the last of the six company commanders of the proud 188th Brigade from before the war, is still active in the commander's cupola. He holds binoculars in his hands and looks out at the front, when the screech of an artillery shell erupts and lands on the tank, cutting off one of his arms and leaving the other hanging by a thread.

The tank crew reverses in panic, stops by the medical APC and Yehuda Azulai (Golan), the medical sergeant runs toward him, finds super-human power and manages to lift the large body of the company commander out of the tank; he presses his fist on an open, bleeding artery.

The doctor arrives and tries to sew up the open wound, transferring him to the aid station. They all wait for the helicopter to arrive, and they are quite certain that Zvika is dead and they even cover him with a blanket. The diagnosis is clinical death.

Dr. David Cohen, a reserve soldier who is a nose, ear and throat specialist, passes by the stretcher and sees a leg move beneath the blanket. A medical team is called to the body and starts giving him fluids. Dr. Cohen continues to press his armpit with his fist until the helicopter arrives.

At the hospital in Tzfat, Dr. Danny Reis, who had just completed an operation in the next room, is called in. In an innovative surgery that had never been performed before, he shortens what is left of Zvika's left arm by seven centimeters and saves his life.

Far in the north of the enclave, in Mazrat Beit Jan, on Tuesday, October 16, the angel of death finds Itzik Ben Shushan, the company sergeant from Elifelet and takes his soul. Ben Shushan had been fighting as part of the 7th Brigade, far from A Company of the 53rd Battalion and the 188th Brigade, where he had been an outstanding tank commander and become a sergeant. He even had the chance at the beginning of the war, on Saturday, to bring the soldiers combat meals and challah for Shabbat, until the angel of death got hold of him.

On Wednesday and Thursday, October 17-18, there was another quiet period on the front. Almost quiet.

Wednesday, October 17

On Wednesday, the short life of Danny Weinstein, a tank driver from the Venus Company of the 74th Battalion ended. He had fought bravely as part of the 3rd Platoon in sector 116 and he had continued on to the Yarden base. In the chaos that developed, in which every able-bodied soldier joined a tank crew, he ended up being part of the 7th Brigade force, in the northern enclave.

On the night between October 18 and 19, and all through the next day, the Arab alliance attempted another attack in Dan Laner's front.

Once again, the enemy's attacks were blocked by the Sho't and Sherman tanks as well as the seven soldiers of the 188th Brigade.

Saturday, October 20

Starting Saturday, October 20, there is a tense silence along the front lines, and the exhausted soldiers know by now that this is the line and these are the hills and the enemy, and very soon the ceasefire will be announced and it will all finally end. But what about the Hermon base?

On Saturday, October 20, Yossi Nissim, the deputy commander of the 74th Battalion, receives an order to come to the gathering point beneath the Hermon. The six tanks he is commanding join the Golani forces, in a final attempt to cancel the disgrace of having the "country's eyes" on the Hermon conquered by the enemy.

Sunday, October 21

On Sunday, the 21st, the six tanks begin climbing up the winding and steep road, as part of the Golani task force, on their way to take back the Hermon base. 2nd Lt. Aviv Shir-On, commander of the 2nd platoon, H Company, 74th Battalion, sees the impossible landscape, with a wall on one side of the road and a cliff on the other. He realizes how difficult it will be to move back if necessary, or to bypass a tank that is hit, or even to rotate the turret.

The Syrians are well aware of what Shir-On is concerned about, and therefore, they positioned commandos at the bends of the road. With the light of the half-moon in the sky on the first day after the Simchat Torah holiday, they hear the screech of the tracks approaching. They identify the armored force through their binoculars, aim their anti-tank rockets and open fire.

Monday, October 22

In the first morning light on Monday, October 22, a "battle" develops, with the tanks at a clear disadvantage. The engineering APC in the front is hit by an RPG rocket. The Sherman tank behind it takes in the dead and injured soldiers, knocks it over the cliff and takes the lead and is immediately also hit by an RPG. Aviv Shir-On pushes the Sherman over the cliff and takes the lead. A moment passes and a bullet scratches his helmet. He understands that he is facing snipers with night vision and jumps down into the tank, closes the hatch and discovers that the bullets are following him into the periscopes.

The same thing happens again. Nissim, the deputy battalion commander is injured in his stomach and is evacuated, and Aviv the platoon commander is hit by a shard that cuts off his finger. He declares on the radio that he will continue but is forced to evacuate himself after losing too much blood.

Two additional tank commanders are injured and Avi Ben Atia, a reserve tank commander, Shir-On's friend from Ashkelon, is hit in the final minutes of the war and dies in the turret.

Two of the six tanks try to continue forward. In the tank of Nissim, the deputy battalion commander who had been evacuated, Natan Nagar the gunner is in the commander's cupola firing his machine gun in fury. He refuses to lose and to absorb the cost paid by his comrades. Yossi Weisbart is in the tank behind him, the last of the tank commanders, who was sent to help the 51st Golani Battalion to conquer the Hermon. A Syrian sniper puts Weisbart in his telescopic sights and fires a precise bullet that hits him between the eyes, making him the last soldier killed in the 188th Brigade breakthrough battle.

Yossi Weisbart, from the Shir-On's platoon, the outstanding swimmer, the beloved youth movement counselor, the young lover of music and art, who painted beautiful decorations at tank camp 104, colors his last painting on the rocks of the Hermon base, with his blood.

On Monday, October 22, at 10:00, the Hermon returned to the control of the IDF. The ceasefire between Israel and Syria is declared on that same day. Two days later the ceasefire is announced with Egypt. The Yom Kippur War is over.

THE END

Two days before the ceasefire, Danny Vardi, who had been the commander of 53rd Battalion before Ben Hanan, is appointed commander of the "phoenix" 188th Brigade. He only gets to serve in this position for forty-eight hours. The patrol jeep he is traveling in to mark the ceasefire line drives over a landmine. The reconnaissance company commander is killed, and the brigade commander and the battalion commander (Oded Erez) are seriously injured.

Once again, fate intervenes in the chain of command of the 188th Brigade. They thought they were back on their feet but things change again. Now it is Amos Katz who replaces Vardi, Moshe Verbin replaces Oded Erez and once again it appears that nothing will stop the 188th Brigade on its journey to stay alive and in the national collective memory.

In the coming days and weeks the winter also becomes part of the picture, bringing snow – a lot of snow. Now in addition to the winter routine, there is another matter that becomes part of the routine. More and more artillery shells fall on the soldiers, continuing to take their pound of flesh. Yona Brick, a tank driver from the Ze'evim Company, is killed by the shelling in December, and two days later it is Michael Cohen, a gunner who had joined the company.

From 2,200 meters up on Mt. Hermon – the highest point in Israel – "the eyes of the country" fill with tears as they watch the remaining soldiers of the 188th Brigade scattered throughout the Syrian enclave. They are still wondering how this happened. In the midst of the great national pride, this hit them. They start to pick up the pieces, checking who was injured and who was killed. On their way to the tanks buried in the snow, they sing loud and clear, with all their hearts. "May it be tomorrow already... the men shouted that it is over."

Back in Israel the sounds of protest are rising. The public demands explanations.

In early November, 1973, in response to the rising protests against him, Defense Minister Moshe Dayan conducts a briefing with the committee of editors of the national newspapers. The message he tried to convey was that it was all just a technical mistake. "Our assessment was that if this and that happens, we have 300 tanks in the Canal and 180 on the Golan and that is enough. What happened was that it was not enough."

Different "analysts" were quoted as saying that "from a military aspect, the war that started under the worst possible circumstances for Israel and the best circumstances for Egypt and Syria, ended in the victory of the IDF forces."

The Israeli people mourned the 2,350 soldiers that had been killed. They listened, saw and read the explanations but did not accept them.

Reserve Captain Moty Ashkenazi, the commander of the Budapest stronghold in the northern Canal in the war, ignited the public unrest with a forty-eight-hour hunger strike outside the office of the Prime Minister. He called for the resignation of the Prime Minister and the Defense Minister. As a result of the continuous public pressure, on November 21, 1973, a national committee of inquiry was established, led by Supreme Court President Shimon Agranat.

In April 1974, the first interim report of the committee was submitted. Moshe Dayan summoned Moty Ashkenazi to his office and told him he was wrong. "The committee did not find me guilty of the failure," he said, looking Ashkenazi in the eye. He read from the report, "As long as he (Dayan) accepts his advisors' opinions, he (Dayan) is not personally responsible."

Following the report, Chief of Staff David Elazar resigned. Eli Zeira (head of Military Intelligence) and Shmuel Gonen (chief of Southern Command) were both released from service.

In May 1974, Golda Meir also resigned, followed by the entire government. In an interview she gave the press, Meir admitted that a significant part of her reasons for resigning had to do with the public pressure.

Eight months on from the ceasefire agreement, on May 30, 1974, a separation of forces agreement is signed between Israel and Syria.

Three weeks before the signing of this agreement, on May 9, the fate of Meir Tal, the twenty-two year old tank commander and company sergeant in the 74th Battalion, is determined. A deadly artillery shell that fell on the headquarters of the 74th Battalion at the Hales camps explodes into thousands of tiny shards. One of them finds its way to the opening in the bullet-proof vest Meir is wearing and at once gives him the title he never wanted – the last soldier of the 188th Brigade killed in the Yom Kippur War.

Now it really is over.

A convoy of chariots of fire head out of the enclave, back to their old home, the ramps of the Purple Line of the border. At the end of the convoy is Oded Bekman, just appointed deputy commander of C Company. He feels as if the keys to hell are in his hands and he treats it properly, crushing and destroying anything in his way. Revenge.

Arriving at its permanent base, which has been renovated, the 188th Brigade presents its new chain of command. Moshe Verbin is commander of the 53rd Battalion. Haim Barak is commander of the 74th Battalion (the commander of 82nd battalion that returned from an injury). Uzi Urieli had just returned from the hospital and as compensation was appointed commander of C Company, replacing Boaz Tamir. Joining him as company commanders are Yossi Zamri and Amnon Gideon in 53rd Battalion. Shmulik Yachin, Danny Avni, Moty Amir and Oded Yisraeli are in 74th Battalion. Before they get the chance to grasp the transition from the sacred battalion, they learn of yet another battalion being annexed – the 71st. Ran Gotfreund, one of the battalion commanders from Ori Or's reserves brigade, is appointed its commander.

The 188th Brigade, with its three battalions, stands proud and strong, ready for the glorious military future awaiting it. But who knows? Maybe there will not be any more wars?

On December 12, 1973, before the committee was established, before the forces were separated, before the responsible leaders resigned, before Bekman fired at everything in his way, the Northern Command Intelligence issued a report of the casualties the Syrians suffered in the war. While the Syrians lost 3,000 soldiers, 1,000 civilians, 1,150 tanks, 400 armored personnel carriers and 400 artillery cannons, the Israeli side lost much less: 772 IDF soldiers were killed and 250 tanks damaged. Among the casualties, there were 79 soldiers of the 188th Brigade.

"You only lost 79 soldiers? You were lucky. Others did much worse."

Optimistic as young people are, appearing to be mentally well, the soldiers of the 188th Brigade hang on to these encouraging words. They look ahead to the future that the generals in their air-conditioned offices promise them will be better, and they return to the routine of training and maintaining the tanks. The armored corps will keep moving.

Bekman and Eiland, Atir and Shir-On, Kaimo and Yachin, are sure that soon this will all be behind them. War is just like in training – difficult, then it ends and then you move on. They are close to completing their service and becoming civilians, in what will surely enable them to bury the sounds and the sights that are in their heads.

But the sights and sounds cannot be buried.

Many years since the day on which Yoni Vodak was killed at Quneitra, Shmulik Yachin would be back there in his dreams, driving among burned Syrian tanks that suddenly awaken and follow him in a terrifying silence. As he is expecting the shell to hit him, he wakes up startled. Every single night, for years.

Many years later, David Eiland took a painting course at the Avni Institute. You cannot kill the soul of an artist, even if it is injured. In one of the classes, he learned of an artistic concept that uses child-like techniques and motifs to convey harsh messages of the self-aware adult.

"Please practice this type of painting," the teacher instructed them.

On a black background, bright and optimistic, Eiland painted a train with a teddy bear in the first car, a red heart in the second and an Israeli flag flying proudly in the third. The title was "Here Comes the Train."

He signed the painting, "David, class B 2." Two days later he added another painting. On a murky grey background, he painted the teddy bear with its arms ripped off, one of its eyes missing. The title of the painting was, "The Train Returns." He signed it, "2nd Lt. David Eiland, A Company, 53rd Battalion, 188th Brigade."

Thirty-six years after the war, they built houses, families, had children, grandchildren, did business, found love and fulfilled dreams. But the war remained with them, always in the background. A persistent shadow, black and heavy that refused to detach itself.

Thirty-six years after losing their innocence and their faith in their righteous path, they still cannot find peace for their souls.

For some the nights are the most difficult. Others are restless and cannot keep a regular job. There also are those who trouble the people around them with outbursts of anger and rage, and there are the cynics who do not trust anyone from the establishment. Some cannot fall in love because love is a connection and they are terrified of the thought of what will happen if the connection unravels and burns their souls again. The scar in their hearts that has closed cannot deal with the thought of another blow, like the one they suffered so many years ago when the country betrayed them.

For all of them there is Yom Kippur. Every year, thirty-six of them.

"Dad," their young children would ask them. "Why do you always cry on Yom Kippur?" David Eiland, Nir Atir, Moty Amir, Aviv Shir-On and all of the fathers that somehow managed to live and tell their story would cover their children in their beds and answer, "It is because of something very far back, my child, from many years ago."

All the children would ask, "Dad, why are you still sad over something from so many years ago?"

Special Thanks

This book could not have materialized without the devotion and commitment of a special group of people that decided that the time had come to tell the story.

It was not easy, but neither is fighting a war.

A small number of commanders from the Yom Kippur War acted as the practical and moral backbone of the project of writing this book. They were there every step of the way. Pioneers, establishing action committees, appointing representatives for each company, working hard to raise funds, relentlessly convincing the unconvinced, supporting those who had second thoughts, holding everyone above water, with the belief that this day would come eventually.

Special thanks go to:
Moty Aviam
Uzi Uriel
David Eiland
Oded Bekman
Yossi Gvili
Ofer Glusman
Efraim Yosef
Avshalom Levi
Rafi Nagler
Dror Sofer
Moty Amir
Nir Atir
Rani Friedrich
Avraham Kayam (Kaimo)
Yitzchak Sarig

On Monday, July 13, 2009, in the early hours of the morning, Moty Amir, just fifty-six years old, passed to another world. The last living officer remaining of G company, 74th Battalion. A few days before, Tzachki Sarig had met with him. "Moty the Iceman," the one that never gave in to pressure, the wonderful friend, the best professional, the one who never raised his voice, wept silently in his bed.

"I probably won't be able to see the book published," he whispered to Tzachki. He was right.

If there is heaven above, may Moty find a suitable place in it, in the name of all the good things he left in the loving and very painful memories of us all.

Appendix

Military Terms

*(Related mainly to 1973 and to the Sho't Kal
tank used by 188th Brigade)*

Weapons and Ammunition

Sho't Kal: An upgraded British Centurion tank. One of the two types of tanks of the regular army in the war (the other is the Patton/Magach tank that only fought on the Egyptian front). The Sho't Kal had a 105mm gun and power pack from the M-48 tank.

Sho't Meteor: The original British Centurion tank with 105mm gun and the original Rolls-Royce Meteor engine. Used by some of the reserve forces during the war.

Sherman: The oldest tank that took part in the war. A tank that was used in World War 2. The model used in the Yom Kippur War had undergone extensive upgrades.

Armored Personnel Carrier (APC): An armored combat vehicle, designed and equipped to transport a combat infantry squad.

M-113, Zelda: An APC manufactured in the US and used by the IDF in the war.

FN MAG: Platoon machine gun. Used on the IDF APCs.

Commander's machine gun/anti-aircraft machine gun: A Browning 0.3"machine gun, positioned on the tank near the commander, enabling him to fire at planes flying low and deal with immediate threats of enemy infantry.

Parallel Machine Gun: A machine gun identical to the commander's gun, operated by the gunner and located parallel to the cannon. Firing it requires aiming the cannon on the target. The firing is electronic and is carried out by the gunner. The ammunition is loaded by the loader.

0.5/Heavy Machine Gun: A heavy machine gun, with bullets with a bigger caliber than the parallel/commander machine guns (0.5"), with a longer range (1,000 meters), used by infantry bases and APCs.

Armor Piercing Round (AP): Kinetic energy penetrator projectile. Used mainly to destroy tanks.

Shaped Charge (HEAT): A dual purpose shell, for fighting against tanks as well as soft shell targets.

High Explosive Squash Head (HESH): A dual purpose shell, used mainly for fighting soft shell targets.

Phosphorus Shell: A shell intended for use against soft shell targets and for marking.

Tiran (T54, T55, T62): Tanks manufactured by the Soviet Union. The tanks used by the Syrian forces in the war.

SU-100/Tank Destroyer: A hull-only tank manufactured by the Soviet Union. Used in combat mainly as a fixed position anti-tank weapon. They saw limited use by the Syrians in the war.

BTR: An armored personnel carrier manufactured by the Soviet Union and used by the Syrian army.

Bridge Laying Tank: A type of tank used by the Syrian army, with a hydraulic bridge that can be used to cross problematic areas, for example anti-tank ditch.

Sagger Missiles (AT3): NATO designation for a first generation Soviet anti-tank guided missile used by the Syrians. It is operated by a crew of soldiers, on foot or in a vehicle. It is wire guided and has an effective range between 500 and 3,000 meters.

RPG: Rocket propelled grenade. A Soviet manufactured shoulder fired anti-tank rocket used by the Syrian army. Effective range of up to 300 meters.

Gorianov: A Soviet manufactured heavy machine gun in the Union used on the Syrian tanks. Equivalent to the 0.5 heavy machine gun in Israeli use.

The Structure of the Tank and Its Contents

Tank hull: the lower part of the tank, containing the engine, the transmission (the gears), fuel tanks and the majority of the equipment and ammunition compartments. The driver sits in the front of this part.

Turret: The upper part of the tank, where most of the combat activity takes place. In the Sho't Kal turret, the commander is positioned on the right with the gunner beneath him. the loader's compartment is to the left of the cannon. Most of the weapons systems are in the turret, as well as the optics and communication systems. An electro-mechanical system enables the crew to rotate the turret 360 degrees around the body. The tank turret is the most protracted area.

Continuous Track: A system of vehicle propulsion that connects to the tank body on both sides. Its large surface area on the ground improves the tank's ability to pass through sandy or muddy grounds.

Wheels: The tank track wheels, on which the continuous track rotates.

Rack: A part of the track that absorbs shocks.

Supporting Wheel: A system of small wheels that is used to maintain the track at the right pressure.

Movement Wheel: A single large wheel on each side of the tank, at the end of the transmission, converting the engines power to movement of the tracks.

Tracks: A chain of connected links on which the tank moves.

Hatches: A general name for the doors closing the openings for the crew members. The crewmen have different size hatches that they open or close according to the situation in combat. The driver has his hatches closed at all times during combat, while the hatches of the commander and the loader are opened at the commander's discretion, depending on artillery fired and other factors.

Periscopes: The observation windows of the crew. The periscopes enable the crew to see when their hatches are closed.

Cat Eyes: Tiny lights located on the tank wings and activated when moving at night. These lights help the crew to identify other tanks, reducing the risk of a collision.

24 Volt Switch: The master electricity switch in the tank. If the switch is not turned on, none of the electric systems in the tank can be operated (most of the tank systems – communication, firing, lighting, starting the engine – are electronic).

Bazooka Plates (Shields): Thin, removable steel shields, covering parts of the suspension and providing added protection to the hull. They were given this name due to their original purpose – to protect the tank hull from being hit by anti-tank fire.

Turret Basket: An open compartment on the back of the turret where the camouflage net is usually stored.

Equipment Compartment: Compartments scattered throughout the tank body and on the sides of the turret, for storing the equipment required for tank maintenance.

Ammunition Belly: The total ammunition in the tank. In a Sho't Kal tank there are 72 105mm shells and 26 boxes of 0.3 bullets for the machine guns.

Machine Gun Bullet Boxes: A box containing a chain of bullets (230) for the tank machine guns.

Ready Shells: 13 shells in the tank turret, closest to the cannon, available to the loader. 9 of them are on the foldable upper/lower floor.

Lower Floor: a surface on which the majority of the tank shells are stored. To get them out, the upper floor needs to be folded and repositioned.

Firing Generator/Emergency Generator/Commander's Firing Generator: A firing mechanism similar to a vehicle dynamo. A quick turn of the handle creates a current that enables the shell to be fired when the electric trigger is not operating, or when the gunner is injured or does not identify the target.

Peri-telescope: An aiming and observation device used by the gunner, has a wide window for observation and 10x magnified vision with NATO crosshairs for aiming and correcting fire.

Karnaf: Infra-red night vision device used by the driver.

Shfanfan: Night vision device used by the tank commander.

8x30 Binoculars: Binoculars used by the tank commanders, with an 8x enlargement and 30mm objective lenses.

Rotation: An electro-mechanical system for rotating the turret, regardless of the direction the tank is driving.

Gyro: a mechanism that enables the gunner to maintain the cannon on the identified target, without being affected by sudden sideways movement of the tank.

Tank Crew Members Training/Commander's Terms

Armored Corps Basic Training (Boot Camp): A three month training course in the basics of infantry combat, without any focus on tanks.

Professional Training: A training period following basic training. This two and a half month period was the first training the soldiers received in using tanks. The training was carried out in classrooms and on the tanks of the armored corps school. At the beginning of the course, the soldiers were divided in two tracks, gunnery and driving. At the end of the course, some of the gunners were converted to be loaders.

Crew, Platoon and Company Training: The armored corps tank basic training which take place after the professional training. This training took three months, in which each soldier trained as part of a crew according to his position in the tank. At the end of the training period, the soldiers received their tank crew member pins.

Tank Commander's Course: A three month training course for soldiers who had completed the Crew, Platoon and Company training course or veteran soldiers from the battalions who had been chosen to become tank commanders.

Bahad 1 (Instruction school number 1): The IDF officer's course, where the armored corps cadets trained for three months, in order to become platoon commanders. The training was carried out together with cadets from all field corps of the IDF, giving the armored corps officers the strong basis in infantry warfare required from every officer.

Armored Corps Officer's Course: A three and a half months training course, in which the cadets that completed the Bahad 1 officer's training learned everything needed to command a tank platoon. At the end of the course they were commissioned with the rank of 2nd Lt. and were appointed platoon leaders in the battalions and training bases.

Loader: Tank crew member tasked with loading shells and bullets for the parallel machine gun for the gunner and responsible for operating the communication system.

Gunner: Fires the gun shells and the parallel machine gun.

Tank Platoon: In the IDF, usually three tanks.

Tank Company: In the IDF, usually 11 tanks (three platoons plus the company commander and deputy commander's tanks).

Tank Battalion: In the IDF, usually 36 tanks (three companies plus the battalion commander, deputy commander and forward artillery observer's tanks).

Positions and Gunnery

Waiting Position: The position the tank descends to after firing the ready shells, to refill shells from the floor. This position is not exposed to the enemy.

Observation Position: One position lower than firing position. Most of the tank is not exposed and just the commander, standing tall in the turret can observe the area in front of him. He identifies targets and directs the gunner to them and then continues to ascend to the firing position.

Do Not Identify/No Lowering: The cannon has greater ability to elevate rather than being depressed. Sometimes when conducting fire on targets at a lower elevation the gunner doesn't have a line of sight to the target.

Firing Position: A natural or man-made position that enables the gunner to fire at the targets while providing protection for the tank from the cannon down.

Tank Hull Up Position: A firing position where even the hull is exposed. Entering this type of position is a result of limited landscape conditions making it impossible for the gunner to lower the cannon. E.g., firing on a lower target when the tank is positioned on a steep hill.

Ramp: A man-made mound of earth specially built as a firing position for combat. The ramp takes into consideration all of the elements of the tank. It defends it from three sides and enables it to lower the cannon, without exposing it in the firing position.

On Target: The gunner's verbal confirmation to the commander that the target has been identified and the aim at.

Fire: The command from the commander to fire, after the gunner has reported "On target."

Cannon Combat Range: A firing drill for all types of shells, for ranges of up to 1,000 meters. Quick, efficient, with a high percentage of hits with the first shell fired.

Crew Bazooka Fire: An emergency drill in the tank when encountering an anti-tank team at close range (usually used against an RPG, the Syrian equivalent to the Israeli bazooka). The cannon is turned toward the enemy and the cannon and machine guns open fire.

Self-Correction: An action carried out by the gunner when no correction is ordered by the tank commander. This action saves time and shells in the effort to hit the target.

Boresighting: An action required daily to synchronize the gunner's line of sight aim and the center axis of the gun.

Communications

VRC Helmet: Tank crewmen do not wear steel helmets. Their helmets are made of reinforced fiberglass, with the communications system built inside it.

Chords: The wires connecting the helmet to the communication system.

Internal Communication (Intercom): A system enabling communication inside the tank. The communication is through the crew's helmets and is independent of the external system.

External Communication: A communications system operated through the crew's helmets, enabling them, by pushing a lever forward, to communicate outside the tank.

Antennas: At least one in every tank, sometimes two (depending on the number of radios). The antennas rise above the tank up to 2 meters high, expanding the range of reception.

Radio Names: Code-names given to forces and commanders. Examples: Tofi – the frequency of the 188th Brigade. Peleg – the frequency of the 74th Battalion.

92: The code for the head of Northern Command.

82: Northern Command Operations officer.

40: Divisional commander.

20: Brigade commander.

21: Deputy brigade commander.

10: Battalion commander.

11: Deputy battalion commander.

The standard protocol is to call every commander by his radio code-name. For example, 10 of Peleg = commander of Peleg = Commander of the 74th Battalion, Yair Nafshi.

Frequencies: Each radio network code-name is assigned its own frequency. In addition, Mosquito is the emergency safety frequency of the armored corps. Every platoon should have one tank listening in to this network in order to prevent friendly fire casualties.

Tofi: The frequency of the 188th Brigade during the Yom Kippur War.

Rear Telephone: A telephone handset connecting to the internal radio, located in a compartment on the back of the tank. This telephone enables communication between infantry soldiers positioned behind the tank and the tank crew.

General

Capital: the code in the 188th Brigade, prior to the war, for a combat day.

Fire On Our Forces/Overhead Fire: A request for the air force or the artillery to fire at IDF forces. When a force is besieged such fire causes damage to the attackers.

Friendly fire: Mistaken firing between forces of the same side.

Medical Center/Aid Station: The place set up for evacuating the soldiers injured or killed in battle to.

Regional Brigade: The brigade that is responsible for a certain front, in regular days, when there is no war.

War Reserve Storage Base: A military facility where all the equipment required for the reserve forces to join the battles is located.

Tactical Command Insignia

Tactical Insignia: White painted insignia on the tanks and canvas strips on the turret, marking the tanks for the soldiers to know what force they belong to. 20C (Gimel), is the brigade commander tank. 21C, is the deputy brigade commander's tank. 10C, is the battalion commander. 11C, the deputy battalion commander. C (Gimel) is the company commander tank and D (Dalet) the deputy company commander. 1/2/3 are the platoon commander tanks. 1A (Aleph)/2A/3A are the platoon "cubs" tanks and 1B (Bet), 2B and 3B are the platoon sergeant's tanks.

Air to Ground Tactical Insignia: Bright orange canvas sheets spread on tank turrets to indicate to the planes that the tank is part of the Israeli forces.

Infantry Outpost: A base located on the Purple Line or close to it, housing 10–20 infantry soldiers. Their main role is to act as an observation force and defend the base.

Explosion Layer: A huge pile of basalt rocks shielding IDF bases from artillery shelling, preventing the base from collapsing.

Explosion Vest: a protective vest worn by the soldiers.

Tank Camp: A tank "base" close to the infantry outpost (a few hundred meters to a few kilometers).

20x120 binoculars: Long range, tripod mounted, binoculars with 120mm objective lenses supplying 20 x magnification.

Artillery

Battery: In the IDF, usually four cannon.

Self-Propelled Gun Commander: Equivalent to a tank commander, usually a sergeant or first sergeant.

Battery Officer: The first position for an artillery officer after completing officer's course. Equivalent to a tank platoon commander.

Artillery Position Officer: Equivalent to a tank deputy company commander.

Artillery Battery Commander: Equivalent to a tank company commander.

Brigade Artillery Commander: Usually an artillery battalion commander, with this being his emergency position in war.

Forward Observer: In the Yom Kippur War there was supposed to be one in each tank company. This is usually the youngest officer in the battery. He is a "spare" officer, helping out with whatever is needed.

Artillery Fire Support Officer (Battalion Level): In routine times acts as a battery commander. During war he is mounted on his own tank.

Sho't Kal v. Tiran

Facing the 188th Brigade's Sho't Kal tanks, the Syrian army had the older T54 and T55 tanks and the new T62 tank. Hundreds of the older tanks were taken as booty by the IDF in the Six-Day War, became part of the armored corps and were called Tirans.

The Christy suspension of the Tiran tanks (to make things simpler, until the end of this comparison, the term Tiran will refer to the T62 tank as well) gave them better maneuverability and limited risk of throwing/opening tracks.

With an engine with the same power as the Sho't Kal tank and weighing 10 tons less, the Tiran was faster.

The stabilization of the cannon in the Tiran tanks was about the same as in the Sho't Kal. The rotation system of the Sho't Kal however, had a tendency to malfunction and that of the Tiran was more reliable.

The Tirans had a parallel and anti-aircraft machine gun of 12.7 mm, more advanced than the Browning 0.3 of the Sho't Kal. There was another thing that the Tirans had that the Sho't Kal tanks did not. This was a system that had already been trialed in the Six-Day War in Sinai, which diverted fuel toward the ignition, creating a cloud of smoke hiding the tank.

The T62 tanks had two additional advantages over the Sho't Kal tanks – a fire extinguishing system and automatic loading. There are different opinions about automatic loading. Every time the T62 had to load, it was required to raise the cannon, temporarily putting it at risk and sending a clear indication to the Israeli tanks.

The Tiran had one big advantage over the Sho't Kal, an advantage that had not materialized in the Six-Day War but waited for the next war. This advantage was the infrared aiming system for the gunner. This system that enabled firing in the dark, installed in all the Tiran tanks, from the first T54s onwards.

The Sho't Kal had its own advantages. The tanks of the 188th Brigade definitely had the best steel protection. In addition, the bazooka shields and the compartment boxes installed on the turret increased the crew's chances of survival. The Sho't Kal was able to take blows that would have shattered the Russian tanks.

The distance that the tanks could drive was about the same but the Sho't Kal carried a significantly greater amount of ammunition. Furthermore, the Tiran tanks did not have the ready shells on the floor of the turret. In the Tiran tanks, after every firing, they had to rotate the cannon, in order to enable the loader to take out the next shell.

The small size and low height of the Tirans should have made them harder to hit but their ridiculous depression angle (4 degrees in a Tiran, compared to 10 in the Sho't Kal) forced them to stand in more exposed positions.

As far as ergonomics and being user friendly, the Sho't Kal was no doubt much more comfortable. The Sho't Kal was not a spacious limousine but compared to the Tiran it was much more comfortable. So, in comparison to the crowded Russian tanks, in the Sho't Kal, even a large soldier like Reuven Goldshaft, a loader in A Company of the 53rd Battalion, managed to find a comfortable position in the tank. If he had to fight inside a Tiran, he may not have been able to do so for very long. If he was in a Tiran, he also would have discovered that he had to load the shells with his left hand, even though he is right handed.

It was very easy to spot the Tiran drivers among the soldiers in training. Anyone no higher than 160 centimeters was thrown into the driver's seat. The driver's compartment was an impossible sized box that required a small body and acrobatics. The drivers of the Russian tanks were mutations of small and powerful wrestlers. They needed to be extremely strong to operate the manual gear, unlike the automatic gear in the Sho't Kal.

Not only the loader and the driver suffered from the size of the Tiran. The commander and the gunner were also crowded into the tiny box, feeling every bump and bounce, due to the hard Cristy suspension of the Tiran. The Vickers suspension in the Sho't Kal enabled larger vertical movement of the tank wheels, reducing the shock felt by the crew members.

In the Tirans (with the exception of the T62 tanks), the position of the gas evacuator (in the front part of the cannon, compared to the back in the Sho't Kal), led to a reduced clearing of the gas after firing. This led some of the crew members to suffer from nausea every time they fired and the sensitive ones even reported being close to losing consciousness. In addition, there was the "firing effect." Every time the Tiran fired, it jumped up with a great leap that would stun the crew for a moment.

The Sho't Kal tank had even more advantages. For example, the "wait-a-minute-opening." This was a unique feature of the Centurion tanks. An opening in the turret enabled the crew to dispose of shell cases quickly and efficiently, even when the crew was fighting with closed hatches, due to artillery shelling. The Tirans did not enjoy this opening and had the spent cases pile up inside the tank.

We cannot forget to mention one thing the Centurion did not have installed – exterior fuel tanks. These tanks were installed on the Tiran tanks, in what was near madness, significantly increasing its chances to go up in flames, with any explosive touching the tank.

Finally, in the cannon performance there is a tie. The performance of the "Sharir" 105 mm gun was much better than that of the 100 mm of the T55 and T54 tanks (with improved ammunition). However The 115 mm cannon of the T62 tanks was better and was considered to be the best in the world in the 1970s, with excellent ammunition and amazing muzzle velocity.

List of Brigade Soldiers in the Combat Deployment

Command of the 53rd Battalion

Commander	Gunner	Loader	Driver	Location at 13:55	First firing position
Oded Erez, battalion commander + Yossi Sapir operations officer	Itzik Keres	Rachamim Simchi	Yossi Shechter	West Hushnia	115
Shmulik Askarov, deputy battalion commander	Itzik Hemo	Zalman Yehezkel	Zvika Rosenzweig	Hushnia	111

A Company, 53rd Battalion

Commander	Gunner	Loader	Driver	Location at 13:55	First firing position
Zvika Rak, company commander	Eli Sharoni	Yitzchak Zuaretz	Haim Safra	Quneitra, Hahazit building.	Booster Ridge
Oded Yisraeli, deputy company commander	Zeev Tuashi	Reuven Goldshaft	Yaakov Moshe	Quneitra, Hahazit building	Booster Ridge
Haim Damir, platoon 1 commander + Haim Lavon, front observation officer	Shimon Shtizky	Ami (Amran) Moshe	Moty Avdish	Quneitra, Hahazit building.	Booster Ridge
Avishai Levital, commander	Unknown	Unknown	Shay Blinder	Quneitra, Hahazit building.	Booster Ridge with Nafshi
Moshe Farkash, sergeant	Eli Mizrachi	Shmuel Solomon	Ben-Zion (Bentzy) Shimon	Quneitra, Hahazit building	Booster Ridge with Nafshi
Yossi Zimri, platoon 2 commander	Amnon Tiram	Rachamim Shviro	Ofer Nevo	Quneitra, Hahazit building	Booster Ridge
2nd Lt. David Eiland	Efraim Yosef	Moshe Baram (Burko)	Yehuda Shanai	Quneitra Hahazit building	Booster Ridge
Nimrod Kochavi, commander of platoon 3	Dov Zoldan	unknown	Gidi Hertz	Quneitra, Hahazit Building	Booster Ridge
Shuki Hashenberg, commander	Zion Awad	Emanuel Harashti	Yigal Eden	Quneitra, Hahazit building	Booster Ridge
Artillery officer tank + Asher Diamond	Unknown	Unknown	Ezion Ashkenazi	Quneitra, Hahazit building	Booster Ridge

B Company, 53rd Battalion

Commander	Gunner	Loader	Driver	Location at 13:55	First firing position
Avner Landau, company commander	Natan Cohen	Benny Mauda	Herzl Cohen	Wasset	Fidel Hadash, near the border
Asaf Sela, deputy company commander + front observation officer Gidi Lefbar	Unknown	Unknown	Unknown	Wasset	105
Rani Friedrich, platoon 1 commander	Meir Cohen	Avraham Azulai	Amnon Frishta	Wasset	Fidel Hadash, near the border
Udi Friedman, commander	Shlomo Yitchaki	Yossi Shemesh	Moris Vaknin	Wasset	Fidel Hadash, near the border
Arie Feigenbaum, sergeant	Shuki Yisraeli	Yitzchak Berliner	Eli Cohen	Wasset	Fidel Hadash, near the border
Moshe Efrati, platoon 2 commander	Moshe Bikobizky	Asher Gabai	Yehoshua Zeller	Wasset	Fidel Hadash, near the border
Zeev Hoss, commander	Yaakov Eliasaf	Shmuel Abuaf	Arieh Azuvi	Wasset	Fidel Hadash, near the border
Efra Goren, sergeant	Nisim Sasbon	David Gitler	Shmuel Sinfrada	Wasset	Fidel Hadash, near the border
Avshalom Levi, platoon 3 commander	Arieh Kagan	Yoel Emanuel	Zvi Eizman	Wasset	105
Commander-unknown	Paul Cohen	Hanania Amar	Yisrael Regev	Wasset	105
Yigal Rubinstein, sergeant	Shalom Mantzur	Yehoshua Don	Yehuda Avraham	Wasset	105

C Company, 53rd Battalion

Commander	Gunner	Loader	Driver	Location at 13:55	First firing position
Uzi Urieli, company commander	Itzik Arnon	Mordechai Arazi	Yossi Abramovitz	Hushnia west	Botmia near 115
Boaz Tamir, deputy company commander	Doron Farkash	Morris Hazut	Philip Berkovitz	Hushnia west	The Oil Route firing position
Hagai Zur, platoon 1 commander	Daniel Partush	Herzl Binyamin	Herzl Bertian	Hushnia west	Botmia near 115
Yehuda Akunis, sergeant	Gigi Daniel	Zion El	Avraham Shaval	Hushnia west	Botmia near 115
Oded Bekman, platoon 2 commander	Eli Rachamim	Mark Eilenberg	Shmuel Walman	Hushnia west	115
Koby Birnboim, commander + forward observation officer, Yaron Shapira	Yishai Daniel	Shimon Akeb	Hezi Kalner	Hushnia west	The Oil Route firing position
Ilan Orenstein, sergeant	Yosef Zuridiker	Shmuel Solomon	Ron Pearlman	Hushnia west	115
Zeev Hochstein, platoon 3 commander	Yossi Eliyahu	David Shaharbani	Marko Avigdor	With the Askarov force at Hushnia	Tel Abas near 111
2nd Lt. Chaim Aldag, commander	Pini Ben Yisrael	Yirmiyahu Efrati	Haim Nizri	With the Askarov force at Hushnia	Tel Abas 111
Dany Berkovitz, sergeant	Eitan Kopstein	Shmulik Isaac	Ezra Yitzchak	With the Askarov force at Hushnia	Tel Abas 111
Shabtai Horen + forward observation officer, Yigal Sapir	Nir Zvi Elimelech	Zvi Yahalomi	Arman Shnier	With the Askarov force at Hushnia	The Oil Route
Yehuda Porat/ brigade commander tank	Nissim Omeisi	Yaakov Fogelman	Menachem Ben Shoef	Hushnia west	------

Command of the 74ᵗʰ Battalion

Commander	Gunner	Loader	Driver	Location at 13:55	First firing position
Lt. Col. Yair Nafshi, battalion commander + 1st Lt. Danny Avni, Operations Officer	Yaakov Veidenfeld (Veidi)/ Itzik Atias	Yossi Merder	Avigdor Shpitzer	Hahazit building Quneitra	Booster
Maj. Yossi Nissim, Deputy Battalion commander	Muli Dgani crew	Muli Dgani crew	Muli Dgani crew	Aleika	105 (after Muli Dgani's injury)

F Company, 74ᵗʰ Battalion

Commander	Gunner	Loader	Driver	Location at 13:55	First firing position
Avi Ronis, company commander	Ptachya Azari	Yisrael Hershko	Gideon Aharoni	Juhader	115
Avi Lahman, platoon 1 commander	Yair Stern	Avraham Shitreet	Aharon Maswari	Tank parking 114	114
Shmuel Herman, commander	Eliyahu Hayun	Haim Zozovsky	Shmuel Rimbrot/ Reshef	Tank parking 114	114
Shimon Cohen, sergeant	Eliyahu Berger	Nissim Shitreet	Yitzchak Leibovitz	Tank parking 114	114
Nati Levi, platoon 2 commander	Michael Zibola	Zion Edri	Rafi Cohen	Juhader	Petroleum Road
Moty Aviam, commander	Shalom Fachima	David Riv	Michael Swisa	Juhader	Petroleum Road
Asher Brinberg, sergeant	Eliyahu Hemo	Avi Shachar	Alex Perlstein	Juhader	Petroleum Road
Yoak Yakir, platoon 3 commander	Menachem Shmueli	Andrei Sakal	Brom	Tank parking 116	Opposite Zeida
Yair Waxman, commander	David Levi	Moshe Berkovitz	Danny Weinstein	Tank parking 116	Opposite Zeida
Nir Atir, sergeant	Ami Moshe	Yitzchak Nagarker	Danny Dather	Juhader	Opposite Zeida
Avi Lavi	Rami Sulimanov	Unknown	Unknown	Juhader	115
Yoram Miromi	Unknown	Unknown	Emanuel Gueta	Juhader	112

G Company, 74th Battalion

Commander	Gunner	Loader	Driver	Location at 13:55	First firing position
Uri Akavia, company commander	Asher Peretz	Asher Kahalani	Avi Pozlantz	Hushnia	111
Yoni Davidson, deputy company commander	Shor Layuba	Shmuel Mayorchik	Bezalel Ovadia	Hushnia	113
Danny Overlander, platoon 1 commander	Yehuda Krasenty	Yehuda Raz	Meir Ben Ritan	Hushnia	111
Yair Deutsch, commander + front observation officer Ariel Kovlantz	Shmuel Rosenblau	Yitzchak Ripstein	Roni Manzur	Hushnia	111
Zvi Mizrachi, sergeant	Zvi Mansbach	Danny Mechani	Zion Sharabi	Hushnia	111
Doron Sadeh Lavan, platoon 2 commander	Herzl Daniel	David Nahon	Nahum Yondof	Ta'asuka base Quneitra	109
Shraga Shmuel, commander	Danny Barzilai	Shlomo Goldstein	Ilan Duek	Ta'asuka base Quneitra	109
Ave Brener, sergeant	Haviv Imrio	Eli Wahaba	Yona Brik	Ta'asuka base Quneitra	109
Moty Amir, platoon 3 commander	Avi Gengar	David Gross	Yehuda Erdman	Hushnia	113
Dan Tiroler, sergeant	Nissim Harir	Avraham Ben Hamo	Moshe Versano	Hushnia	113

H Company, 74th Battalion

Commander	Gunner	Loader	Driver	Location at 13:55	First firing position
Eyal Shaham, company commander	David Golan	Ami Turgeman	Moshe NIli	Mas'ade	Shechita 104
Avraham Kaimovitz (Kaimo), deputy company commander	Yehuda Markovitz	Shmuel Shtiglitz	David Sabo	Mas'ade	Manfucha
Muli Dgani, platoon 1 commander	Natan Nagar	Itzik Atias	Yossi Abekasis	Tank parking 105	105
Giti Zinberg. Commander	Nissim Benuzio	Paul Aharon	Avi Vizenfeld	Tank parking 105	105
Avraham Frost, sergeant	Avraham Berger	Moshe Weinberger	Shmuel Nissim	Tank parking 105	105
Aviv Shir-On, platoon 2 commander	Eli Kopulevitz	Yossi Gershino	Uri Yona	Tank parking 104	104
Yossi Weisbrot, commander	Eitan Frish	Naftali Rabbi	David Hollander	Tank parking 104	104
Koby Greenbaum, sergeant	Mordechai Atias	David Amsalem	Shlomo Yifrach	Tank parking 104	Shechita 104
Shmulik Yachin, platoon 3 commander	Shalom Maman	Rachamim Cohen	Aharon Kapon	Tank parking 107	107
Yoni Woodeck, commander	Moshe Ben Haim	Amnon Nissim	David Bonamo	Tank parking 107	107
Yossi Naides, sergeant	Yossi Friedman	Avraham Bot	Homain Magen	Tank parking 107	107
Yoni Efrat, artillery officer tank (without artillery officer)	Zeev Boimel	Gregory Bix	Ezra Anzrot	Mas'ade	Shechita 104

List of 188th brigade soldiers killed in the Yom Kippur War

Name of fallen soldier	Battalion	Date killed
Captain Netanel Aharon	74th	11.10.73
1st Lt. Danny Overlander	74th	6.10.73
1st Lt. Moshe Efrati (Kakun)	74th	7.10.73
Corporal Avraham Bot	74th	9.10.73
Sergeant Avraham Biton (Herzl)	74th	7.10.73
Master Sergeant Shaul Bakal	74th	7.10.73
Sergeant Daniel Barzilai	74th	9.10.73
Sergeant Major Asher Brinberg	74th	15.10.73
Sergeant Yona Brik	74th	2.12.73
Corporal David Golan	74th	8.10.73
1st Lt. Shmuel Dgani (Muli)	74th	9.10.73
Corporal Herzl Daniel	74th	9.10.73
Maj. Ehud Dafna	74th	15.10.73
First Sergeant Yoni Woodek	74th	9.10.73
Sergeant Major Yaakov Veidenfeld (Veidi)	74th	9.10.73
First Sergeant Yossi Weisbrot	74th	22.10.73
Corporal Zion Weitzman	74th	6.10.73
Sergeant Daniel Weinstein	74th	17.10.73
Sergeant Daniel Zaguri	74th	7.10.73
Corporal Moshe Hodrian	74th	7.10.73
Sergeant Refael Hen (Ben Hamo)	74th	7.10.73
First Sergeant Meir Tal (Bishkol)	74th	9.5.74
Sergeant Shimon Yosef	74th	7.10.73
1st Lt. Yoav Yakir	74th	6.10.73
Corporal Michael Cohen	74th	4.12.73
Corporal Yehuda Kresenty	74th	6.10.73
Corporal Aharon Magen (Homian)	74th	9.10.73
Corporal Meir Mizrachi	74th	7.10.73
Sergeant Major Zvi Mizrachi	74th	6.10.73
Sergeant Zvi Mansbach	74th	6.10.73
Sergeant Major Yossi Naides	74th	9.10.73

Name of fallen soldier	Battalion	Date killed
Sergeant Rachamim Sulimanov	74th	7.10.73
Captain Uri Akavia	74th	6.10.73
Corporal Shalom Fachima	74th	7.10.73
Sergeant Yossi Friedman	74th	9.10.73
First Sergeant Shlomo Zippori	74th	7.10.73
Captain Avi Ronis (Greenwald)	74th	6.10.73
Corporal Yehuda Raz (Katan)	74th	6.10.73
Maj. Eyal Shaham	74th	7.10.73
First Sergeant Amram Turgeman (Ami)	74th	7.10.73
Corporal Mordechai Avigdor (Marko)	53rd	11.10.73
Sergeant Edward Avrahamov (Edi)	53rd	12.10.73
First Sergeant Shimon Akeb	53rd	6.10.73
Sergeant Yaakov Birnboim	53rd	6.10.73
Sergeant Major Shushan Ben Yitzchak	53rd	16.10.73
Corporal David Bnaya	53rd	7.10.73
Sergeant Major Danny Berkovitz	53rd	10.10.73
Sergeant Philip Berkovitz	53rd	7.10.73
Sergeant Major Efra Goren	53rd	9.10.73
First Sergeant Shabtai Horen	53rd	6.10.73
Sergeant Major Aharon Vidal (Henry)	53rd	12.10.73
First Sergeant Yitzchak Zuaretz	53rd	6.10.73
First Sergeant Nachshon Hermoni	53rd	6.10.73
Sergeant Avner Yaakov	53rd	7.10.73
Sergeant Zvi Yarkoni (Grinoiza)	53rd	7.10.73
First Sergeant Gil Cohen	53rd	7.10.73
Sergeant Meir Cohen	53rd	12.10.73
1st Lt. Nimrod Kochavi	53rd	17.10.73
Sergeant Menachem Mishali	53rd	7.10.73
Sergeant Yitzchak Levinger	53rd	7.10.73
Sergeant David Nurian	53rd	7.10.73
First Sergeant Zion Swisa (armored)	53rd	16.10.73
First Sergeant Zion Swisa (munition)	53rd	7.10.73

First Sergeant Haim Stroll (Andrei)	53rd	7.10.73
Captain Yossi Sapir	53rd	8.10.73
First Sergeant Yigal Rubinstein	53rd	11.10.73
Sergeant Eliyahu Rachamim	53rd	11.10.73
Corporal David Shaharbani	53rd	11.10.73
Sergeant Major Adir Stern	53rd	12.10.73
Sergeant Yoel Shalit	53rd	7.10.73
Sergeant Yoel Sharabi	53rd	7.10.73
Captain Shraga Ibler	Brigade headquarters	11.10.73
Col. Yitzchak Ben Shoham	Brigade headquarters	7.10.73
Sergeant David Hermalin	Brigade headquarters	10.10.73
Lt. Col. David Yisraeli	Brigade headquarters	7.10.73
Corporal Yuval Cohen	Brigade headquarters	21.2.74
First Sergeant Azar Cohen (Eliazar)	Brigade headquarters	13.10.74
Maj. Binyamin Katzin	Brigade headquarters	7.10.73
Captain Zeev Shtender	Brigade headquarters	17.10.73